MASONIC WORLD GUIDE

To Jan,
for her eternal patience

Masonic World Guide

K.W. Henderson

Ian Allan Group

LONDON

LEWIS MASONIC

© 1984
Kent W. Henderson
Published by
LEWIS MASONIC
Terminal House, Shepperton, Middlesex
who are members of the Ian Allan Group

First published in the United Kingdom in 1984

ISBN 0 85318 139 X

British Library Cataloguing in publication data:
Henderson, Kent W.
    Masonic world guide.
    1. Freemasonry—Lodges—Directories
    I. Title
    366'.1'025   HS381

Printed and bound in Great Britain by
Butler & Tanner Ltd, Frome and London

 Sole distributors for the United States of America
MACOY PUBLISHING & MASONIC SUPPLY CO INC
3011 Dumbarton Road, Richmond, Virginia 23228 USA

Sole distribution in Australia
KENT HENDERSON, P.O. Box 301, Belmont Geelong
Victoria, Australia 3216

CONTENTS

Foreword

Brother Kent Henderson's book is a well-conceived and well-executed project for a number of different reasons. First of all, this is an age when people in general, and freemasons amongst them, are becoming very mobile. We cross borders quite casually, and have far more opportunity than our fathers to pay our Masonic respects in strange and far-away jurisdictions. And yet, how many of our less-experienced brethren are disinclined to visit while abroad for fear of making embarrassing errors, or committing solecisms? A vade-mecum of this nature is likely to become more and more indispensable for the novice visitor, as well as for the travel-scarred veteran, who merely needs to refresh his memory from time to time!

Of very specific value is Chapter Four (Section I), which provides a needed, and very clearly expressed, warning to the potential visiting brother about the dangers of irregular masonry. Brother Henderson's explanation of the problem is lucid and accurate, reflecting the particular care he has exercised, and the interest he feels, in this often complex aspect of the Order. That care and interest is reflected elsewhere in the work, and in this area he is to be congratulated for exposing the minefields without frightening the sailor onto the shore.

The Guide itself fits neatly in a vacant niche in the masonic student's library. It is a novel piece of work, and one that is unique in my experience, in its subject and scope, and is the more valuable as a result.

This work is no mere compilation, but a genuine work of masonic scholarship. Its author's credentials are impeccable, and include membership or associate membership of research lodges in Victoria in his native Australia, in New York, in France, in New Zealand, in Ireland, and in England. His membership of the Mark and Royal Arch, the Ark Mariners, the Cryptic Degrees, the Allied Degrees and the Secret Monitor, the Knights Templar and the Scottish Rite, are an indication of the breadth of his interests, and this is reflected in one aspect at least of this work, which is a form of bonus to the reader—the book is not only informative, it is genuinely readable, and will give considerable enjoyment even to the brother whose visiting is vicarious, and who travels only in his carpet slippers and fireside armchair.

The guide, finally, is well ordered and easy to use. It deserves success. I have no doubt that it will achieve success, both as a reference work and as a masonic travelogue. It will, I hope, impress the new brother with a sense of the richness and diversity of the world-wide structure of our Order, wherein so much is different and yet the same, where our dissimilarities are our strengths, where fascination exists and awaits discovery at so many different levels. Those whose wandering feet have pressed 'from Kohat to Singapore' will gain from it many a moment of nostalgia, while those who do not give it a place on their shelves will be the poorer. I wish the guide a widespread readership, and its author a notable masonic career.

J. David F. McKee, MA
Foxrock
Dublin, Ireland
January 1984
Past Master, Lodge 11 & Lodge 500 IC.
Past Acting Master, Grand Master's Lodge IC.
Senior Warden, Lodge of Research No CC., Ireland.
Assistant Grand Director of Ceremonies Grand Lodge of Ireland.

Preface

My first idea of producing a book for travelling freemasons arose five years ago, as a result of visiting lodges in Austria and Switzerland, where the ritual employed was somewhat removed from my masonic experience at that time. I was subsequently struck by the variety of masonic customs existing in the masonic world, and more particularly, by the problems and difficulties a visiting freemason can experience when attending a strange lodge. It also came to my attention that a great number of masons, largely through ignorance, fail to even attempt to visit when they travel outside the domain of their own jurisdiction.

The present work is an endeavour, and I hope a reasonable one, to assist in overcoming these problems. I have particularly sought to compile a practical reference book. It is my hope that in using this guide, visitors will be in a position to attend the meetings of unknown lodges with considerably more motivation and ease than may have been the case in the past.

It needs to be stressed at the outset that this book is, indeed, a 'guide' and not a 'gospel'. For the visitor to treat the information herein supplied in the latter sense would be folly.

In addition to its primary purpose of providing information for the travelling mason, this guide is structured as a preliminary reference for those masons wishing to understand or study the development of the worldwide Craft. One would, therefore, hope that this book will hold something of interest for the mason who is not inclined to leave his own masonic doorstep.

Quite naturally, a book of the nature of this current work will require a few minor alterations as the result of future masonic developments. Undoubtedly some small inaccuracies exist in the current text, although I have made every effort to avoid them. Therefore, I would envisage producing revised editions at appropriate intervals, given some personal restraints. Should any brother possess any constructive information or knowledge which he considers would be useful in revising this edition, then I would be most pleased to receive his correspondence. While I will endeavour to reply to any letters I might receive, the pressures of life may prevent me from so doing in every case. Therefore, I beg to thank in advance those who may care to put pen to paper.*

In the interim, I will conclude here by expressing my hope that brethren reading this Guide will find it instructive, useful, and an aid to the furtherance of their masonic experience and enjoyment.

January 1984   Kent Henderson
                                                                        Victoria
                                                                       Australia
* *The Publishers will be pleased to forward correspondence to the Author.*

Acknowledgements

It is not possible to produce anything worthwhile without the help and co-operation of others. One can state without hesitation that nowhere is such help and co-operation more readily found than within the body of freemasonry. I am greatly indebted to those many brethren with whom I have exchanged hundreds of letters over the past four years, and without whose ready counsel, advice, and assistance, this book would not have been possible.

I refer, among many others unfortunately too numerous to mention individually, to John Hall, Beau Grinter, James McConchie, Warren L. Smith, Dr E.F.E. Kellar, William P. Russell (California), John Sullivan, Brian Tolliday, Jim Smith, George Hookman (South Africa), D.E.G. Vieler (South Africa), R. Baptie (Zambie), Frank Howland (Zimbabwe), Bryce McColl (NSW), Ralph Castle (Queensland), Phil Page (South Australia), Bert Lewis (Librarian Victoria), S.H. Peattie, Sir James Stubbs, KCVO, Cyril Batham, George Draffen of Newington, MBE, Frederick Smythe, H.H. Solf, the Grand Secretaries of the various Grand Lodges who have so readily co-operated, and in particular, Don Plaisted, PJGW, Grand Secretary of the United Grand Lodge of Victoria, whose ready acts of liaison on my behalf I deeply appreciated.

In particular, I shall remain eternally indebted to Donald S. Robinson (Massachusetts) for his continuous encouragement and valued advice over many years; to Jacques Peron, my Junior Warden, for his translations from the French; to J. David F. McKee (Ireland), for his unfailing support and wise counsel; to Frank Oldfield, PJGW (Victoria), for his ready helping hand; to Sid Martin, PGLec (South Australia), my Masonic Mentor, for his sound advice and copious correspondence; and to Arch Moses, PSGW, Grand Librarian Emeritus (Victoria), for his help and boundless patience. To all these brethren, and many others, I extend my sincere gratitude.

Section 1

A Traveller's Digest

Some Notes to Begin

Aims and Objectives
The aim of this guide is to assist in placing the masonic visitor in a strange lodge with the least difficulty and the greatest comfort. Probably the foremost factor which dissuades some travelling freemasons from visiting is ignorance—the what, when, where, how, and why.

WHAT?
The 'What' is regular freemasonry and regular lodges. For the purposes of this guide, the Grand Lodges recognised as regular by the Grand Lodges of England, Ireland, and/or Scotland are used. Only the addresses pertinent to the Grand Lodges and their constituent Craft lodges that fall within these parameters are detailed. Virtually every country and area in the world is mentioned, to enable the visitor to readily determine where regular masonry exists, and where it does not exist. The whole question of regularity and recognition is dealt with in the pages following.

WHEN?
Meeting times of various lodges are provided as appropriate. Often, within one area, lodges meet at varying times, and therefore the parameter of meeting times is provided. In addition, there is some variance between lodges around the world as to the frequency of meeting. In many jurisdictions, lodges recess for a part of the year, often during the applicable summer months (June, July and August in the Northern Hemisphere, and December, January and February in the Southern Hemisphere). Information is appropriately provided in this area.

WHERE?
The 'Where' is constantly provided throughout this guide. If regular masonry exists in an area of the world, then the relevant addresses of the appropriate Masonic Halls and Temples will usually be provided. The address of every regular Grand Lodge is also detailed. Often such an address will be that of the applicable Grand Lodge office. These Grand Lodge addresses tend to be permanent. However, a very small number of Grand Lodges have no Grand Lodge office as such, but rather they list their address as the place of residence of their Grand Secretary for the time being. Obviously, Grand Secretaries tend to change, and consequently so does the Grand Lodge address. Where this occurrence prevails, specific mention is made.

HOW?
This aspect, in all its forms, is constantly explained throughout the guide. The procedures of visiting around the masonic world do vary quite a bit in detail, but nevertheless there are a number of constants that commonly prevail across the Masonic spectrum. Again, full details are provided.

WHY?
Without doubt, visiting is one of the greatest privileges of masonic membership. Yet, there are many masons who travel, but never visit another lodge. The reasons for this are no doubt many, but certainly the what, when, where, how and why figure prominently. With the use of this guide, hesitations should be greatly van-

quished. There is no other organisation in the world whereupon a man may walk
into a room full of complete personal strangers, yet be immediately welcomed and
honoured as a friend and brother. This is an experience of which every freemason
with the opportunity should not fail to avail himself.

The Layout of the Guide
Except where otherwise indicated, the body of this guide is laid out alphabetically
for easy reference. The main sections are grouped by continents. Where masonry
exists in some strength, or where a regular Grand Lodge exists, discussion will
usually be found compartmented. In these sections, the monologue is headed with
addresses and useful statistics, followed by a brief history. Thereafter ensues details
of usages and customs. At the end of the Guide are found several appendices, the
most important of which is that setting out the fraternal recognitions of the various
regular Grand Lodges.

The Thrust of the Text
The thrust of the text is towards English-speaking masonry. English is the language
which the vast majority of regular lodges employ. A far fuller discussion of
English-speaking jurisdictions is undertaken, although not at the expense of creating
undue brevity when detailing non-English-speaking Masonry. It must also be noted
that this guide is tailored for the Craft Freemason. Therefore, with few exceptions,
little discussion is centred on the so called 'Higher Degrees' associated with freemasonry.

The Matter of Content
Quite obviously, the content of this guide is selected purposefully. Nonetheless,
certain types of material have been consciously omitted. The emphasis has been to
provide information which will not date, or which will not date rapidly. For this
reason, no attempt has been made to include such information as the names and
addresses of various lodge Masters or Secretaries. Of course, these details are apt to
regular change. Conversely, it is quite usual for lodges to retain the same meeting
place, and days of meeting, for long periods of time. Therefore, such information is
usefully included. Occasionally perhaps, the visitor will come across a defunct lodge
or a case where two lodges have consolidated into one. However, over the breadth
of lodges these occurrences are not particularly common. In short, the information
included is that which is the most unlikely to change in the short or medium term,
and therefore it should be of maximum use to the visitor. Nonetheless, the visitor
should, if at all possible, endeavour to check the meeting details of any individual
lodge he proposes to visit prior to attempting to do so. As will be consistently
mentioned in this guide this can, and should, be done at the appropriate Grand
Lodge office.

The Matter of Semantics
There are a number of oft used words to be found in the text which can usefully be
subjected to comparative derivation here. The first group are the words jurisdiction,
constitution, and obedience. In masonic terms, these three words are largely inter-
changeable. A jurisdiction is the geographical territory over which a regular Grand
Lodge has masonic authority. A constitution technically consists of the documented

laws under which a Grand Lodge and its constituent lodges operate. A Grand Lodge that does not possess chartered lodges outside its geographical territory is usually referred to as a Jurisdiction. This word is commonly used especially by the North American Grand Lodges. Thus, one refers to the 'New York Jurisdiction' or the 'Jurisdiction of the Grand Lodge of New York', and so forth. The word constitution is largely applied to describe a Grand Lodge which possesses a number of lodges physically located outside its masonic territory, in addition to those within it. Thus, one refers to the English Constitution (EC), the Irish Constitution (IC), and the Scottish Constitution (SC), and so on. Most Grand Lodges directly derived from British Grand Lodges subsequent to the English Union of 1813 describe themselves in this manner as well (for example—the Australian Grand Lodges). The word obedience is generally a European masonic term. Thus, an Austrian lodge, for example, would describe itself as belonging to the 'Obedience' of the Grand Lodge of Austria. Generally, these three words as just derived in terms of masonry will be used in those contexts within the text.

The second group of words to require explanation are 'Warrant', and 'Charter'. These two words mean exactly the same thing. A warrant or a charter is the formal written document granted by a Grand Lodge to constitute a constituent lodge under it. In broad terms, the Americans largely refer to a charter, while the English call it a warrant.

A Question of Dates

All statistical information provided in the body of the guide is current as of 1983, on the latest figures available. Therefore for the most part, for example, quoted Grand Lodge memberships are 1983 figures, unless otherwise indicated. In addition, all information provided is based on masonic usages and customs prevalent in the jurisdictions detailed as of 1983. While some minor changes in this area may occur subsequent to the circulation of this guide it is not expected these, where they occur, will effect the content herein provided to any notable extent.

The Basic Assumption

The basic assumption of the entire text of this guide is that the visitor will have no previous experience or knowledge of masonic practices outside his own jurisdiction. Of course, for many visitors this will not be the case. Nonetheless, such an assumption is obviously necessary.

The History and Limitations of Masonic Travel

The habit of freemasons to travel and to visit other lodges, or even affiliate with them, is one of the oldest and most widely practised customs of the Craft. In operative times, well before the emergence of the Speculative Craft as we now know it, masons were itinerant workers who were forced to travel to renew their employment as each building project was completed. This fluid nature of the Operative Craft led to the formation of trade societies, known as lodges, to protect the professional integrity of their occupation, and to enhance the moral and social practices of their members. It is surmised, not without some evidence, that the modes of recognition were originated in the operative period as a means of identifying the genuinely skilled mason who came to visit a lodge in search of work.

It is therefore reasonable to deduce that the tendancy of masons to visit other lodges is very old custom indeed. Many of the oldest extant masonic manuscripts contain charges associated with visiting, and the reception of visitors.

Visiting as a Right
As has just been outlined, the right to visit and sit in every regular lodge is one of the oldest masonic customs. This custom hinged on the theory that all lodges are only divisions of the 'Universal Brotherhood'. Indeed, in some areas of old, visitors could even vote at lodge meetings.

However, the growth and spread of the Craft saw many variations in forms and procedures develop, and the evolution of the Grand Lodge system as we know it today. In turn, this necessitated that the concept of visiting as a right undergo changes. The movement towards qualification of the right to visit appears to have begun in the early eighteenth century. There are records of lodges in this period setting out limitations to visiting, in terms of the number of visits a non-member mason could make to a lodge in a twelve month period; and limiting the types of meeting a visitor could attend. Certainly, by the end of the eighteenth century, visiting had ceased to be a right, but rather a privilege.

Visiting as a Privilege
The situation today is that visiting is a privilege—indeed, it is one of the greatest privileges of masonic membership. It must be immediately stated that a mason has no absolute, prescriptive right to visit a lodge wherein he is not a member. However, with that fact clearly stated, it must be observed that visiting as a privilege is most definitely encouraged and welcomed in every regular jurisdiction. A regular freemason in good standing will always encounter masonic hospitality and brotherhood in his travels.

The Limitations on Visiting today
There are four basic limitations on visiting in the masonic world today. The first two, as listed below with explanations, are common to every regular jurisdiction; while the last two are less prevalent. They are:
1. *The Recognition of Regularity:* This is a limitation on visiting whereby the only

visitors a lodge may receive are those who are members of another lodge whose Grand Lodge is recognised by its own. This whole question is detailed at length in a later chapter.

2. *The Master's Prerogative:* It is, by custom and often by Grand Lodge statute, the prerogative of the Master of a lodge to refuse to admit any visitor if he is not satisfied that he is a regular mason of good standing; or he feels that such a proposed visitor will disturb the harmony of his lodge. The former power is only occasionally used as a matter of necessity; the latter very rarely. Nevertheless, the prerogative power of the Master of a lodge is wide.

3. *Business Meetings:* Under some forms of masonic practices, business meetings are held separately to meetings held for degree conferment, and where this is the case, visitors are often excluded from the former, but never the latter. Similarly, in some jurisdictions where ordinary lodge business and degree conferments are held in the space of a single meeting, visitors are sometimes not admitted until after the lodge has completed the business part of its activities.

4. *Visiting by Invitation:* In some jurisdictions, notably England, it is largely usual for visitors to receive an invitation from a lodge member. In other areas, while such a restriction does not exist with respect to ordinary meetings, it does apply to Installation Meetings. These practices are not adhered to without reasons, and they will be examined when we come to discuss those jurisdictions concerned later in this guide.

The Procedures of Visiting

There are ten steps, or procedures, involved in successful masonic visiting—most of which are sequential. They move from obtaining the appropriate documentation, to the actual sitting of a visitor in a strange lodge. These steps must be followed before a visitor can be admitted into a lodge wherein he is not known, and their whole purpose is to establish the bone fides of a true and lawful brother.

Step One: Advise your own Lodge Secretary

The first step is to inform your own lodge secretary of your desire to visit outside your own jurisdiction, and to provide him with details of your travels. He will liase with your Grand Lodge office to procure all the necessary documents, and obtain advice.

Step Two: The Procuration of Masonic Documentation

To establish himself as a true and lawful brother to the satisfaction of his hosts, the visiting mason must first produce the appropriate documents which will attest to his regularity as a freemason. The following documents *should* be carried by a mason seeking admittance into any regular lodge wherein he is not personally known:

A Grand Lodge Certificate, or Diploma: Every Grand Lodge issues this, or similarly named, documentation. It is a credential provided to the Master Mason to prove in writing that he is a regular mason. It invariably contains the dates appropriate to his admission into the Craft, the signature of his Grand Secretary, the Grand Lodge Seal, and his signature.

A Receipt of Dues: It is not enough for a visiting mason to produce his Grand Lodge Certificate when seeking admission to a strange lodge. While his Certificate provides proof that the person named on it is a freemason, it does not prove that he is a current financial member of a regular lodge. To be a mason in good standing is the usual masonic terminology describing a financial member. Some jurisdictions provide their financial members with a receipt of dues as a right, while others provide it only on request.

The Dues Card: The Dues Card is a form of receipt of dues provided by lodges under a number of jurisdictions, notably in North America. This is considered in these jurisdictions as the most important masonic 'Passport'. Indeed, in the United States, lodges have little interest in sighting a Grand Lodge Certificate, but no visitor will enter their Temples without first producing a Dues Card or satisfactory equivalent. In lieu of a Dues Card or other direct form of receipt of dues, a recent lodge summons (notice of meeting), or letter of introduction may suffice.

In addition to the largely compulsory documents just detailed, it is *recommended* that a visitor also carry, and if necessary present, the following additional documents:

A Letter of Introduction: Many Grand Lodges provide a letter of introduction to intending visitors through their Grand Lodge office. Such letters carry the Grand

Secretary's recommendation, and all the masonic details of its bearer. It can usually be used as a substitute for a 'receipt of dues' if personally carried. Some Grand Secretaries will forward a visitor's 'letter of introduction direct to Grand Lodge under which he proposes to visit, thus giving its Grand Secretary pre-warning of the visitor's imminent presence.

A Passport: All foreign travellers carry a passport, and while it is rarely called upon for masonic purposes, it has the effect of attesting to its bearer's actual identity.

There are other masonic documents issued by some Grand Lodges. Many provide a Past Master's Certificate to appropriately qualified masons. Past Masters are advised to carry this document, or similar documentation, especially if they wish to witness an Installation Ceremony in full, in those jurisdictions wherein only Installed Masters may witness certain parts of it.

Visitors who are not yet Master Masons (ie they are Entered Apprentices, or Fellow Crafts) will not yet have received, nor be entitled to receive, their Grand Lodge Certificate. However, they can usually obtain appropriate documentation from their Grand Secretary's office prior to departure from their own jurisdiction. It is as well to mention that masons in this category may not be able to visit in some jurisdictions. English-speaking and Continental freemasonry, in particular, usually restrict visiting between themselves to holders of the Master Mason Degree. Jurisdictions working a Webb-form ritual have a similar restriction. Even in those jurisdictions where such a mason may be permitted to visit, limitations often apply. Such a mason is strongly advised to consult with his own Grand Lodge office prior to departure. It may even be possible for him to receive the degrees that he is yet to obtain by courtesy in another jurisdiction. The matter of courtesy degrees is dealt with later in this section.

Step Three: *Check for Regularity*

It is essential that each mason check that regular freemasonry exists in the area he proposes to visit. A chapter explaining regularity and its importance follows shortly. At the rear of this guide is to be found a list of Grand Lodge recognitions. Given the parameters explained at that point, these lists may be used to determine whether or not the jurisdiction that is proposed to be visited is recognised by your own Grand Lodge. A mason's own Grand Lodge office will assist further in this regard.

Step Four: *Visit its Grand Lodge Office First*

The recommended form of making contact, and of advising a particular Grand Lodge of your presence in its jurisdiction, is in person. Most Grand Lodges are based in the capital city, or principal city, of a country or area. As such a city usually doubles as the main point of entry into the area, a visit to the local Grand Lodge office is generally quite practicable. On visiting a Grand Lodge office, a visiting mason can always be assured of full assistance. Indeed, should a visiting mason be in need of advice or assistance of any nature, not necessarily masonic, he can always find it amongst his brethren in the Craft, no matter in which country he may find himself.

Step Five: *Direct Lodge Visiting*

As a second preference, to be used if for some reason a visit to the appropriate Grand Lodge office proves impossible, a visitor can use the information contained in this guide to directly attend a lodge meeting. However, due to the restrictions of space it has not been possible to list the details of lodges in every jurisdiction. In addition, it is appreciated that several Grand Lodges have warranted lodges without their geographical jurisdiction, so that a visit to the appropriate Grand Lodge office is not possible. This particularly applies to lodges in Africa and Asia under the British Grand Lodges. Meeting details for most of the lodges in these areas are included in this Guide, as a consequence.

Step Six: A Letter to a Grand Lodge

As a last alternative to make contact, a mason proposing to travel masonically can write a letter to the Grand Jurisdiction he is to visit, seeking advice. However, this method should only be used as a last resort if the appropriate Grand Lodge office cannot be personally visited, or if no details concerning constituent lodges are available. If this approach is to be undertaken, such a letter *Must* be sent via your own Grand Lodge office. Such a letter should be addressed to the Grand Secretary of the Grand Lodge concerned; and should contain your name and address and full masonic details, together with your places of residence in its jurisdiction and the dates applicable to your itinerary.

Any such letter must be directed via your own Grand Lodge office for several reasons. Firstly, and most importantly, correspondence directed through a mason's own Grand Lodge office assures the Grand Lodge being asked for advice that the enquiring brother is indeed a regular mason deserving of receiving the desired assistance. Secondly, by directing a letter through your own Grand Lodge office, your Grand Secretary can enclose an accompanying letter of support, which in turn will ensure a useful and speedy reply. It needs to be added that if a mason sends a letter direct to any foreign jurisdiction, he is unlikely to receive a response. Thirdly, it must be appreciated that Grand Lodges get enough mail as it is, and letters from hundreds of inquiring visitors will not alleviate this situation. Clearly then, this whole matter is one of masonic protocol, and protocol must be followed. Any letter that is to be sent must be arranged well before your planned departure, to ensure a reply is received in time for your visit.

Step Seven: Know your own Ritual

As will soon be appreciated, it is necessary for visitors to undergo a masonic examination prior to entering a strange lodge. It is, therefore, most desirable for masonic travellers to be full conversant with their home ritual, and in particular, with the examination procedures used by lodges under their home Grand Lodge. This knowledge will be of great assistance to the visitor. While rituals and examination procedures do vary around the world, the modes of recognition and basic ritual content are not dissimilar. Therefore, a mason with adequate knowledge of the practices in his own jurisdiction will experience no trouble elsewhere.

Step Eight: Arrive early

Having completed all the above procedures as appropriate, you are now in a position to visit. It is essential that you arrive at your chosen lodge meeting *at least* half an hour prior to its commencement. This will enable you to complete the remaining procedures as detailed below. A tardy, or late, arrival might well prevent you from visiting.

Step Nine: *Strict Trial and Due Examination*

Having arrived at the lodge you wish to visit, your first task is to advise its Tyler of your presence; and present to him your masonic credentials as already detailed. However, in all regular masonic jurisdictions, it is necessary that in addition to presenting these documents, an unknown mason seeking to visit a lodge undergo a personal examination. A travelling mason must be prepared for this eventuality.

In masonic terminology, this process is called 'Strict Trial and Due Examination'. Both amount to the same thing. Either means the ascertainment that a stranger is a freemason, or he is not. The nature of freemasonry does not allow documentary evidence alone to be the final testament as to whether a man is a freemason. It is possible, although unlikely, that a person seeking admission may be carrying false, or stolen documents. There have been rare occurrences in the past of unqualified persons, or imposters, seeking admission to lodge meetings.

An imposter may be a person who has never been a mason, one who is under suspension or expulsion from a lodge or one whose Grand Lodge is not recognised as regular. A mason who cannot prove that he is in good standing may also be prevented from visiting.

The procedures of masonic examination and recognition vary throughout the world, and these differences are based on ritual divergences. However, these procedures are all designed to achieve the same ends, and provided a mason is well acquainted with the practices of the Craft in his own jurisdiction, he will experience little difficulty elsewhere. As we shall discover in a later chapter; while the forms of masonic rituals around the world vary somewhat, the content is reasonably similar.

In most jurisdictions, masonic examination is carried out by an examining committee; appointed by the Master of the lodge, either formally or on an ad hoc basis as the need arises. This committee can consist of the Master himself and his two Wardens, two or three Past Masters, or a small number of senior lodge members. In some areas, the examination is carried out by the lodge Tyler.

In most jurisdictions the examination, while thorough, is informally presented. It is usual for the examiners to select features of masonic knowledge at random, even to the point of requiring information out of sequence from each of the three degrees. This practice tends to uncover the 'Parrot Mason', or fraud with a good memory. Some committees even ask quite broad questions such as; 'tell us all you know about how you were raised to the degree of a Master Mason', although this is rare. In some jurisdictions, notably Ireland and those of the United States, visitors are required to repeat the Tyler's Oath. The wording of this Oath is contained under the heading of the United States. As a final comment, it can be readily said that provided the man under examination is indeed a true and lawful brother, he will be discovered and acknowledged as such. The reverse, of course, is also true.

Step Ten: *Avouchment and Vouching*

In masonic terminology, 'Avouchment' is the lawful information which a mason provides to the lodge he seeks to visit, and the actual procedures which allow hin to sit therein. 'Vouching technically means a mason being able to state that he has 'sat in open Lodge' with another. Therefore, if a mason visits a lodge wherein he knows one or more of its members and has sat in open lodge with them, they will vouch for him, and he will not need to pass a 'Strict Trial and Due Examination. Whereupon he is unknown, after he has presented his credentials and has been examined, the Examining Committee or one of its members will vouch for him.

The avouchment procedures inside lodges vary widely between jurisdictions, but are all designed to evince to the lodge membership that the visitor is masonically entitled to be present. In some jurisdictions, the visitor will enter after the lodge is opened. In others, he will be present from the beginning, and all visitors will be asked to rise to be vouched for by a member present prior to the lodge opening. Unknown masons will have already passed an examination. In Ireland and the United States jurisdictions, this is accompanied by what is known as 'purging the Lodge'. This practice will be detailed in its proper place later in this book. All these procedures pose no problems for the true and lawful brother, and they will certainly be of interest to the mason who has not experienced them before.

In other jurisdictions, notably of direct English descent, visitors will be vouched for inside the lodge while the visitor himself remains outside, to be admitted after he has been cleared. Many lodges using this form of vouching often accompany it with a card system, whereupon the visitor (having been properly examined) records his name, lodge and masonic rank on a card, which is then passed inside the lodge and read out. Upon the name of each visitor being read, the member vouching for the named visitor will stand and signify his assent to the Master.

All these forms of avouchment will be more fully explained later in this guide, as they apply to the jurisdictions wherein they are used.

Courtesy Degrees

Most regular Grand Lodges of the world, upon a written request from a recognised sister Grand Lodge, will confer 'courtesy degrees' upon a mason from that sister jurisdiction. Courtesy degrees is the term used to describe the conferment of degrees upon a mason from another jurisdiction in a lodge under a host jurisdiction. In many cases, only the second and third degrees can be conferred, but some jurisdictions, notably in the United States, will confer any or all of the three Craft degrees by courtesy.

A mason travelling to another country or area, and who has not taken all the three Craft degrees, may wish to have a degree, or degrees, conferred upon him in another jurisdiction. This course of action may well suit a mason who has been transferred to another locality in the course of his employment. For courtesy work to be carried out, a mason will need to be in the host jurisdiction for at least several months. A quick tourist visit rarely affords enough time for courtesy work to be effected.

A mason wishing to receive a degree by courtesy *must* follow a standard procedure. The steps to be undertaken are as follows:

1. On a brother's behalf, his lodge secretary will write to his Grand Lodge office informing his Grand Secretary of the brother's desire in the matter. The letter will set out all the relevant details including the country to be visited by the brother, his residence therein, his current masonic rank, and the dates of his residency.
2. Assuming that:
   (i) a regular Grand Lodge exists in the country to be visited by the brother, and
   (ii) this jurisdiction will normally conduct courtesy work, and

(iii) his Grand Secretary is satisfied that the brother's circumstances and reasons warrant the conferment of a courtesy degree, and

(iv) the ritual forms used by the proposed host jurisdiction are somewhat comparable with local practices,

then the brother's Grand Secretary will communicate with the Grand Secretary in the jurisdiction concerned, requesting that he act on behalf of the brother.

3. Invariably, such a request will be met, and the host jurisdiction will prevail upon one of its constituent lodges close to the place of temporary residence of the brother, to confer upon him the appropriate degree, or degrees.

4. The brother's Grand Secretary will then be informed of the arrangements made by the hosting jurisdiction, and he will see that this information is passed back to the brother. Generally, the brother will be contacted by the hosting jurisdiction, or hosting lodge, and informed of the final arrangements. This will occur after he has taken up residency within its area.

Courtesy degrees, when conferred, have the full force of the conferment of degrees in the normal way. Upon receiving the Master Mason degree, a brother's home Grand Lodge will issue him his Master Mason's Certificate.

The Limitations of Courtesy Conferments

Several limitations apply to the conferment of courtesy degrees. Firstly, Grand Lodges require that a brother receive degrees in his own language. Therefore, unless a particular mason is suitably bilingual, it is most unlikely that an English-speaking jurisdiction would permit one of its members to receive a courtesy degree in a non-English-speaking Lodge. For example, the United Grand Lodge of England is unlikely to permit one of its members to receive a degree, by courtesy, in, say, Sweden.

Secondly, as we have already mentioned, the type of ritual used by the proposed host jurisdiction is taken into account. Should the ritual concerned be somewhat removed from the brother's home ritual, then courtesy work may not be permitted. However, as a general rule, it can be stated that English-speaking jurisdictions will permit courtesy conferments between themselves.

The fees for the conferment of courtesy degrees, where they occur, are usually collected from the mason concerned by his home Grand Lodge, but in a minority of cases the candidate will be called upon to pay a fee to the lodge doing the work. If this matter arises, the brother concerned will be informed accordingly by his home Grand Lodge. A brother visiting a lodge for the purposes of receiving a courtesy degree will not, of course, have yet received his Grand Lodge Certificate. His own Grand Lodge will provide him with other appropriate travel documents, and he will be alerted to any masonic examination procedures that he may encounter.

Useful Masonic Literature

There is a range of masonic literature available that will be of use to the travelling freemason. Most Grand Lodges publish a list of lodges in some form. The English, Irish and Scottish Grand Lodges annually produce a *Year Book* containing, amongst other information, the meeting details of all their constituent lodges, including all those located in foreign countries. The *Tashenbuch*, published every year by the

United Grand Lodges of Germany, and the *Annuairre* of the French National Grand Lodge (GLNF) perform similar functions.

Many of the American Grand Lodges also publish a list of lodges, variously called a *Roster*, *Directory*, and a variety of other names. However, some of the smaller US Grand Bodies simply produce their lodge meeting details towards the rear of their annual *Grand Lodge Proceedings*.

A number of jurisdictions regularly publish a magazine/periodical for general distribution to their memberships. Most are produced bi-monthly or quarterly. They contain a wealth of information concerning the jurisdictions that publish them, and they will be of interest to the travelling mason. Most are available on twelve month subscriptions. Travellers desiring to purchase such a subscription can make enquiries at their own Grand Lodge office, and arrangements will be made with the jurisdiction concerned on the brother's behalf. In addition, most Grand Lodge libraries around the world subscribe to a range of foreign masonic periodicals, and these are readily available for consultation by the intending visitor.

Regularity and Recognition

This is the most complicated area associated with masonic travel, and one which must be dealt with at some length. The basic fact is that not every Grand Lodge recognises every other Grand Lodge as being 'regular'. If a mason's own Grand Lodge does not recognise a particular Grand Lodge elsewhere, then that mason *CANNOT IN ANY CIRCUMSTANCES* visit a constituent lodge under it, or associate masonically with any of its members.

All the Grand Lodges discussed in this guide, and for which addresses are given, are recognised as regular by either, or all, of the Grand Lodges of England, Ireland, and Scotland. A small number of other Grand Lodges are briefly discussed, but their addresses are not given, as they are not recognised by the three Grand Lodges just named.

The Grand Lodge recognitions of England, Ireland and Scotland have been chosen as the basis of information provided by this guide as English, Irish and Scottish freemasonry is the most widely dispersed over the world; and because their recognition is widely respected and sought. However, it needs to be stressed that Grand Lodges recognised as regular by the three British Grand Lodges may themselves recognise other Grand Lodges NOT enjoying fraternal relations with the English, Irish and Scottish Grand Lodges. All the recognitions of all the Grand Lodges that are recognised by the three British Grand Lodges are fully listed in an appendix located at the rear of this guide.

What is meant by Recognition?
When one Grand Lodge recognises another it acknowledges its masonic regularity, authority, and territorial integrity. Such recognition, to be effectual, must be mutual. When it is achieved, Grand Lodges are said to be in 'amity', 'mutual intercourse', or 'fraternal relations'. The processes whereby one Grand Lodge recognises another are often involved, and sometimes are preceded by a settlement of prior differences. The most usual method of assessing the regularity of an unrecognised Grand Lodge petitioning for recognition involves the seeking out of the opinions of Grand Lodges already recognised. In effect, fraternal relations involves something quite similar to diplomatic relations between countries.

Why is Recognition a Problem?
The problem of whether, or not, to recognise has perennially beset every Grand Lodge throughout Masonic history, and will continue to do so. It is entirely within the province of each Grand Lodge to decide which other Grand Lodges it will recognise as regular, and which it will not. Each Grand Lodge has its own set of criteria upon which it bases its decisions in this regard. Amongst the regular Grand Lodges, and certainly amongst those regular Grand Lodges discussed in this book, the criteria used is largely the same, as shall shortly be discovered.

As has already been premised, when two Grand Lodges recognise each other, masons from each jurisdiction can visit lodges under the other, and associate masonically with its members. If a particular Grand Lodge does not recognise another,

then as far as each is concerned the other does not exist, and there is no communication of any kind between them. Indeed, it is *A MOST SERIOUS MASONIC
OFFENCE* for any mason to visit a non-recognised Lodge, or to be associated
masonically with a member of any unrecognised Grand Body.

The great problem caused as a result of recognitions occurs in countries wherein
there are lodges under more than one constitution. Where there are lodges under
two or more allegiances in one area, and these allegiances do not recognise the same
Grand Lodges elsewhere, real problems occur. Consider the anonymous case of
Grand Lodges A, B and C, all of which have warranted Lodges in the same city.
Grand Lodge A and B recognise each other, but only Grand Lodge A recognises
Grand Lodge C. The members of the lodges under Grand Lodge B and Grand
Lodge C cannot therefore, visit each other. However, if members of Grand Lodge
B attempt to visit lodges of Grand Lodge A, they might well find members of Grand
Lodge C also visiting at the same time. The members of both Grand Lodge B and
C must withdraw from their visit to A, as they cannot be masonically associated
with each other. This situation is not uncommon in the masonic world. Freemasonry
in Japan provides a vivid example of the manifestation of this problem, and readers
are directed to that section of this guide.

Recognition and Masonic History

In seeking to understand the whole question of recognition and regularity, a brief
look at masonic history proves enlightening. The reasons for the current situation
stem from the historical development of the masonic fraternity as a worldwide
institution, and from the nature of freemasonry itself as it spread and changed over
the years.

The Grand Lodges of the various nations and states are completely autono-
mous bodies, and they are bound by no common laws and regulations; except the
'Ancient Landmarks and established usages and customs of the Order'. The question
of Landmarks is looked at in the next chapter.

Variations in procedures occurred even before the first extant masonic records,
and as early as the seventeenth century there were considerable differences in the
practices of English and Scottish masonry. For instance, by the seventeenth century,
most English freemasonry had become symbolic, whereas Scottish masonry remained basically operative into the eighteenth century. With the rapid spread of the
Craft from the British Isles to all parts of the world; this brought about variations
in procedures and customs. These changes to the body of freemasonry increased
with time, and this multiplication of innovation increasingly made the subject of
recognitions more complex.

The first major occurrence which saw freemasonry diverge into two directions,
came about with the division of the English fraternity into two competing Grand
Lodges, known as the 'Antients' and the 'Moderns'. Masons of the 'Antient' school
of thought accused those who practised 'Modern' freemasonry of making unacceptable innovation in the practices of the Craft. While this division was healed by the
union of English freemasonry in 1813, it nevertheless resulted in lasting innovations
in masonic practices in many parts of the world.

In Europe, and subsequently in Latin settled parts of the world such as Central
and South America, great innovations occurred in masonry as it had come from the
British Isles. The French, in particular, adapted the Craft to include a profusion of

degrees and rites of a colourful nature. The sum total of this dispersion and innovation in the Craft meant that it became increasingly difficult for Grand Lodges to
determine the regularity of others, and therefore decide whether or not to grant
recognition.

What is meant by regular?

Every Grand Lodge considers itself to be regular. This is a self-justified precondition
for existence. However, this belief in itself which every Grand Body possesses does
not necessarily extend to others. Each Grand Lodge has a set of written criteria or
principles upon which it will entertain recognition. These principles are similar for
all regular Grand Lodges. The following are the 'Basic Principles for Grand Lodge
Recognition' adopted by the United Grand Lodge of England. Those of the Irish
and Scottish Grand Lodges closely resemble those of England.

1. Regularity of Origin; ie: each Grand Lodge shall have been established lawfully
   by a duly recognised Grand Lodge or by three or more regularly constituted
   Lodges.
2. That a belief in the GAOTU and His revealed will shall be an essential qualification for membership.
3. That all Initiates shall take their obligation on or in full view of the open Volume
   of the Sacred Law, by which is meant the revelation from above which is binding
   on the conscience of the particular individual who is being initiated.
4. That the membership of the Grand Lodge and individual lodges shall be composed exclusively of men; and that each Grand Lodge shall have no masonic
   intercourse of any kind with mixed lodges or bodies which admit women to
   membership.
5. That the Grand Lodge shall have sovereign jurisdiction over the lodges under its
   control; ie that it shall be a responsible, independent, self-governing organisation,
   with sole and undisputed authority over the Craft or Symbolic Degrees (Entered
   Apprentice, Fellow Craft, and Master Mason) within its jurisdiction; and shall
   not in any way be subject to, or divide such authority with, a Supreme Council
   or other Power claiming any control or supervision over those degrees.
6. That the three Great Lights of Freemasonry (namely, the Volume of the Sacred
   Law, the Square, and the Compasses) shall always be exhibited when the Grand
   Lodge or its subordinate lodges are at work, the chief of these being the Volume
   of the Sacred Law.
7. That the discussion of religion and politics within the lodge shall be strictly
   prohibited.
8. That the principles of the Antient Landmarks, customs, and usages of the Craft
   shall be strictly observed.

How the Recognition Principles work in Practice

It is on principles of recognition that Grand Lodges determine regularity. Those
Grand Lodges which follow these principles will almost certainly be recognised as
regular, and those that do not will not be recognised. It will be noticed that these
principles, while quite specific, do not mention the actual forms used in masonic
government, nor do they narrow the ritualistic practices that may be adhered to.
These points are looked at in subsequent chapters.

In order for masonic travellers to gain further understanding in the matters pertaining to regularity and recognition, a review of selected cases will prove useful. In 1877, the Grand Orient of France changed its Constitution to delete from it all reference to the Supreme Being, and authorised the removal of the Sacred Volume from its Lodges. This is obviously a clear irregularity, and the United Grand Lodge of England, followed by nearly every other Grand Lodge, withdrew recognition from it. The Grand Orient had for many years been developing into an agnostic society, and this was the final outcome of that development.

In 1971, the Grand Lodge Alpina of Switzerland was briefly de-recognised by the United Grand Lodge of England for allowing irregular masons, mainly members of the Grand Orient of France, to attend meetings of its lodges. The Swiss body moved to correct this situation, and happily fraternal relations were restored in 1972.

The Grand Orient of Italy was not recognised for many years because it allowed its lodges to be used to some extent by members to further political and religious views. It was not recognised by England until as recently as 1972.

In Egypt, the National Grand Lodge, founded in 1786, was at one time widely recognised as regular. However, by the 1950s it had become controlled by a 'superior body' controlling 'higher' degrees. It was subsequently blacklisted by regular Grand Lodges.

In addition to basic recognition principles, Grand Lodges look carefully at the descent of any Grand Lodge petitioning for recognition, and also at the question of territorial integrity, although the latter is strongly alluded to in the British recognition principles.

Grand Lodge Descent

Often the descent of Grand Lodges is obscure, and this is particularly the case in Central and South America. Provided that Grand Lodges can show that they are descended from regular lodges under some recognised Grand Lodge which was itself regular at the time of their original warranting, and that they themselves follow the principles of Grand Lodge Recognition; then they are likely to be recognised.

Where regular descent cannot be established a Grand Lodge may, with examination of the current position, still be deemed as regular. However, this can take several years from first application to decision. There are many Grand Lodges that like to observe over some time that the Grand Lodge under consideration has a consistent record of regularity. The United Grand Lodge of England, in particular, has been known to be quite tardy in the matter of a new recognition, probably for this reason. Indeed as we shall see shortly, the English position is often crucial to wider recognition.

Grand Lodge descent is looked at closely—mainly as a reassurance of regularity, as the two following examples illustrate. The Grand Loge Nationale Francaise (National Grand Lodge of France) was basically formed under British influence. Its membership consisted of masons wishing to be regular, and who adhered to the principles of Grand Lodge recognition. It was widely recognised as regular.

In 1970, the Grand Lodge of Turkey was recognised by England, and subsequently by most other Grand Lodges. It was earlier suspected of drawing its masonic inspiration from the Grand Orient of France, but it was eventually established that originally the National Grand Lodge of Egypt was its principal sponsor. It was also established that Turkish masonry came from Egypt in those days when the Egyptian and English Grand Lodges were in accord. As Turkey could not be held responsible for the later sins of its original sponsor, it was recognised as regular.

Territorial Integrity

Grand Lodges are very territorial creatures. Each Grand Lodge claims a geographical area as its masonic territory, and every Grand Lodge holding fraternal relations with it recognises this territory. It is a strictly adhered to convention amongst regular Grand Lodges that no Grand Lodge may erect subordinate Lodges in the territory of another. Where lodges under one jurisdiction continue to work in a territory which has gained a new regular Grand Lodge, a concordant is usually arrived at whereby only the new sovereign Grand Lodge can warrant any new lodge in the future. Grand Lodge territory, therefore, is masonically inviolable. There are a few Grand Lodges that have 'rival' irregular Grand Bodies operating within their masonic territory. It needs to be added that in those territories not claimed as the jurisdiction of a regular Grand Lodge, any regular Grand Body can erect subordinate lodges. Consequently, there are many lodges located outside the juristictional territory of any regular Grand Lodge, notably in Africa, Asia, and the Carribean. The vast majority of these lodges hold warrants from either England, Ireland or Scotland.

The English Lead

As has already been mentioned, the recognitions of the United Grand Lodge of England remain the most influential in the masonic world. Many Grand Lodges follow the 'English Lead', and look to London for advise in the matter of any new recognition. Nonetheless, English recognition does not provide for complete consistency. However, when England withdraws or grants recognition, many other Grand Lodges follow suit.

The reasons for this are probably a combination of the facts that England is the oldest, largest, most experienced, and most respected Grand Jurisdiction in the masonic world. Many Grand Lodges are directly descended from it, and all are indirectly its masonic offspring. Therefore, these directly descended Grand Lodges often tend to value English advice, and look towards London in these matters.

The North American Grand Lodges, particularly those of the United States, on the other hand tend to form largely independent assessments in the matter of recognitions. There exists in the United States a committee on fraternal relations, erected and maintained jointly by all the regular North American Grand Lodges. While each American Grand Lodge is naturally entirely independent in its decisions concerning recognitions, this committee is most influential.

The Omission Factor

It is pertinent to be aware that there are some cases wherein two Grand Lodges have not recognised each other simply because neither has actually got around to it. Grand Lodges do not always go out of their way to secure recognition, but rather wait until some Grand Body applies for it, then to examine the case in question.

Where there are two Grand Lodges which adopt this approach to the matter, it is not totally uncommon to find that neither recognise each other. Doubtlessly, when one finds a need or desire, the matter would be quickly effected. An important point to note in this area is that of Grand Lodge seniority. Masonic convention has it that it is up to the 'junior' Grand Lodge to petition the 'senior' for recognition. Thus, the United Grand Lodge of England, being the most senior jurisdiction, never petitions anybody. A list of Grand Lodges in order of seniority is located in appendix at the rear of this Guide. If one examines the recognitions of various Grand Lodges, an inconsistancy can sometimes be found whereupon there would appear to be absolutely no reason whatsoever for non-recognition. In most cases, the 'Omission Factor' applies.

Recognitions and the Travelling Freemason

As the masonic visitor will now understand having read this chapter, there are strict 'Rules of Visitation' in terms of Grand Lodge recognitions which must be adhered to. They can be collated as follows:

1. A mason can only visit constituent lodges under a jurisdiction recognised as regular by his *own* Grand Lodge.
2. If a mason happens to belong to two different lodges under two different constitutions, then he can only visit lodges in a third jurisdiction which is recognised by *both* Grand Lodges under which he is a member.
3. When a mason visits a lodge under a jurisdiction recognised by his own Grand Lodge, he may find a person present who is a member of a third jurisdiction recognised by that Grand Lodge, but *not recognised* by his own. Under these circumstances, the said mason must withdraw immediately from that lodge meeting. At no time can a mason be masonically associated with a member of a constitution not recognised as regular by his own Grand Lodge. Such an occurrence is, mercifully, rare. However, it can occur. A mason who finds himself in such a situation should withdraw with all due tact and courtesy, and should later inform his hosts as to the reasons for his actions.

Masonic Government

There are two main types of masonic government—the Grand Lodge and the Grand Orient. Both systems have their similarities, and their differences. It is useful for the travelling mason to be aware of these differing structures, as he is likely to meet both.

The Grand Lodge

This is by far the most common form of masonic government. It is a superintending, or pinnacle, governing body; and it possesses certain distinguishing characteristics. The four main features of a Grand Lodge are:

it consists of free and equal representation of its constituent lodges,

it is independent, sovereign and self-governing, and is formed and maintained by the freemasons of its jurisdiction,

it assumes, through written constitutions, all legislative power over its constituent lodges, and many administrative and judicial powers,

it is controlled by a Grand Master elected by its membership, and Grand Lodge Officers, all of which are responsible to it.

There are a number of other characteristics of a Grand Lodge, but for the purposes of comparison with the Grand Orient system, the four listed will suffice.

The Limitations of Grand Lodge Power

The individual and independent powers of Grand Lodges are limited only by those conventions accepted throughout the regular masonic world. Indeed, it is these conventions which make a Grand Lodge regular. Each regular Grand Lodge, in effect, acts as the 'policeman' of every other Grand Lodge. Whereupon a Grand Lodge strays from these conventions, it is likely to be ostracised by other Grand Masonic bodies. These conventions consist largely of the so called Ancient Landmarks of the Order. These 'Landmarks' are a set of masonic mores which effectively bind the actions of every regular jurisdiction to a fairly large extent. There is considerable scholarly debate as to what is, and what is not, a Landmark. However, all regular Grand Lodges at least tacitly accept some form of list of Landmarks. A great deal of masonic literature is available on this subject, and the interested visitor can readily consult this at any masonic library. For the purposes of explanation here, it is enough to say that these 'established usages and customs of the Order' unite the worldwide masonic fraternity, and it is these that the visitor will observe as constants no matter where he visits.

The Landmarks of the Order include such things as: the division of the Craft into three degrees, the necessity of masons to congregate in lodges, the modes of recognition, the legend of the Third Degree, the right of every mason to be represented in the assemblies of the Craft, that candidates profess a faith in a Supreme Being, the government of the Fraternity by a Grand Master, the equality of masons, the secrecy of the fraternity, the indispensibility of the Volume of the Sacred Law in lodges, and several others. It is not within the power of any Grand Lodge to alter these Landmarks, and regular freemasonry requires a strict adherence to them.

Nevertheless, it must be clearly understood that provided the Landmarks are adhered to, individual Grand Lodges are in a position to entirely govern their own affairs.

Type of Grand Lodges

The term Grand Lodge in itself is but a convenient title for central masonic government. The structures of Grand Lodges, while similar, are certainly not the same. The nature of each Grand Lodge depends to a large extent on where it gained its masonic descent and inspiration. Grand Lodges whose descent derives directly from the United Grand Lodge of England tend to be appointive in nature, while those that are American derived tend to be elective. Many European Grand Lodges, particularly those whose inspiration was originally French, tend to be appointive under various forms of the Grand Orient system.

Appointive Grand Lodges

In these Grand Lodges, its members consist of all Past Masters of all constituent lodges, incumbent Masters and Wardens, and all present and past Grand Lodge Officers (who must usually be Past Masters in any case). Membership of these Grand Lodges therefore tends to be very large. The Grand Master is elected by the Grand Lodge membership, and the Grand Master himself (subject to certain conventions) appoints most Grand Lodge officers. In many jurisdictions using this system (and Englnd is a well known example), while the Grand Master is elected, in practice there is invariably only one candidate for the position, with the nominee determined by senior Grand Lodge officers. In England and Ireland, the Grand Master is usually a Prince of Royal Blood, or a Peer of the Realm, and unopposed re-election of the Grand Master is the common pattern. Therefore, the Appointive System offers the 'ordinary mason' little participation in the selection of his highest leaders. On the other hand, through a very large Grand Lodge membership, it does allow a wide participation in the legislative government of the Craft. Grand Lodges of direct English descent, such as in India, New Zealand, Australia, and some in Canada, for the most part follow the Appointive System.

Elective Grand Lodges

In these Grand Lodges, its members are drawn from the equal representation of its constituent Lodges. Usual practice is for each lodge to elect from among its Past Masters a small number of masons (usually two or three) to represent it in the Grand Lodge. In some jurisdictions, the Master and his two Wardens are the statutory choices. In turn, the members of the Grand Lodge elect the Grand Master and senior Grand Lodge officers (generally the Grand Master, Deputy Grand Master, the two Grand Wardens, the Grand Secretary, and Grand Treasurer). In some Elective Grand Lodges, most or all Grand Officers are elected in this manner. However, by convention, the highest Grand Lodge offices are usually progressive. A Junior Grand Warden, for example, could reasonably expect to be elected Senior Grand Warden in the next year, and so on. Grand Masters under this system often hold office for only one year, and Grand Lodge Officers generally cease to hold Grand Rank once their their term has expired. The Elective System is most prevalent in the United States, and under American inspired Grand Lodges such as Japan, Finland, and the Philippines.

Grand Lodges—Governmental Variations
There are several variations to both the Appointive and Elective Grand Lodge
Systems. Some could be described as Partly-Elective or Partly-Appointive. In some
Elective Grand Lodges there are several Grand Officers that are appointed, and in
some Appointive Grand Lodges there are officers who are elected. There is even the
occasional example of an English-derived Grand Lodge which is elective, but otherwise follows usual English-form masonic government.

The Grand Orient
This form of masonic government possesses many inherent differences to Grand
Lodge-type structures. A Grand Orient can in many ways be termed as a 'subsitute'
for a Grand Lodge. It is of French origin, and is in effect, a masonic oligarchy. The
term means Grand East—the east being only part of the lodge. This terminology is
most definitive, as a Grant Orient is usually comprised of a Grand Master and a
council. The Grand Master is always appointed by the council, and the council has
the sole power to appoint any member to it, with the result that it is entirely a
self-perpetuating body. The net result of this Grand system is that it excludes the
effective voice of far more than it includes. The ordinary mason, therefore, has no
say whatsoever in masonic government under a Grand Orient. This system, not
surprisingly, has historically faced many challenges from within and without. In
terms of regular masonry, those jurisdictions using a Grand Orient system have seen
it modified to make it more democratic and representative.

Grand Orients and Supreme Councils
The prevalent feature of many Grand Orients is that they have often come to be
controlled by a Scottish Rite Supreme Council. This type of masonic body is also
a masonic oligarchy, even in Britain and America, although this is not a point of
issue here. Of course, as was explained in the last chapter, such an occurrence is
regarded by regular Grand Lodges as being a gross irregularity. However, there are
some Grand Orients wherein this Supreme Council control has not occurred. Some
Grand Orients (controlling the three Craft degrees) also control the Scottish Rite
within their jurisdiction; while some are independent of any Supreme Council control and maintain their sovereign integrity. These two latter occurrences do not in
themselves make a Grand Orient irregular. It must be understood that the Principles
of Recognition of regular Grand Lodges do not differentiate between the Grand
Orient and Grand Orient forms of masonic government. Indeed, provided the Landmarks are adhered to by a Grand Orient, it is not unusual for it to be widely
recognised. In practice, there are many Grand Orients that do not strictly adhere to
the Landmarks—often the requirement that candidates profess a belief in a Supreme
Being. The Grand Orient of France is the largest numerically of the Grand Orients
in the world, and it has long since been irregular for this very reason.

    It must be pointed out that to some extent, a name is one thing, and the type of
government another. Most of the Grand Lodges of Europe describe themselves as
Grand Lodges, but in fact use a modified Grand Orient form of government. Only
two regular Grand Craft bodies use the actual term Grand Orient in their title (Italy
and Brazil).

The Modified Grand Orient

As has already been mentioned, the Grand Orient structure has rarely endeared itself to its mass membership. The historical result of these pressures has seen modifications to the system in many areas. This has had the result of the Grand Council being indirectly (sometimes directly) elected by the wider membership of its jurisdiction. An example of one form of modified Grand Orient is explained later in this guide under the heading of 'Greece'. Of course, there are others. The modified Grand Orient system does compare more strongly with the Grand Lodge system. However, Grand Orients still usually have more influence over their composition than does a Grand Lodge, in terms of personnel. Under a traditional Grand Orient, Masters are usually elected for life until they die or retire; and there are some modified Grand Orients that still endorse this procedure. Often the range of candidates available for election to the Master's chair in any of its constituent lodges is governed by Grand Orient statute. It is therefore necessary for such a candidate to have Grand Orient patronage.

How Grand Lodges form

A brief look at the origins of the various masonic jurisdictions, in a broad sense, will provide a greater insight into the relations that exist between the Grand Lodges of the world. It is these relationships, initially expressed in fraternal recognitions, that are crucial to an understanding of the worldwide masonic fraternity. For any freemason, particularly one who visits outside his own jurisdiction, such an historical examination will be of value. Grand Lodges either form or evolve in one of the following ways.

1. EVOLUTION FROM OBSCURITY

With most of the oldest Grand Lodges, it is impossible to determine origin except through conjecture—there being no extant records or reliable information available. Of course, the Grand Lodges of England, Ireland, and Scotland fall into this category. In the cases of England and Scotland, records exist of the formation of their respective Grand Lodges, but it is only speculation as to the actual origins of freemasonry in Britain other than to say it evolved from operative sources. There are more recent Grand Lodges for which records are virtually non-existent, especially in South America and Europe. Some of these appear to have evolved from a combination of operative sources and influences from other Grand Lodges (such as French and German masonry), while for others their inspiration is so diverse as to make the tracing of origin impossible.

2. SCHISM

Not a small number of Grand Lodges have been formed through breaking away from some other Grand Body. Sometimes reunion is effected, while in other cases the daughter body has eventually superseded the original body, the 'mother' Grand Lodge in many such cases later sinking into irregularity. Schisms can be internal or external. An internal schism, the most common form, occurs when a body of lodges break away from the parent body and form a new Grand Lodge in the same jurisdictional area. This form of schism immediately involves territorial disputation regardless of other causes or effects, and as such it is usually hard to heal. The masonic histories of Denmark and Germany afford examples of healed internal schisms, whereas those of France and Brazil attest to continued masonic division.

External schism is a rare occurrence. It happens when a group of lodges under a particular Grand Lodge, but geographically without its territorial jurisdiction, break away without permission or agreement to form a new Grand Body. This form of action is uncommon simply because secession can usually be achieved regularly, unless some fundamental differences in principles or procedures have occurred between the two areas. The division of one country into two or more separate countries has seen this form of schism occur. Examples are to be found in the masonic histories of various Central American countries, whereupon one country has in the past split into one or more new countries.

In terms of masonic recognition, the general rule is that if the parent body remains regular, a daughter schismatic body will find recognition difficult to obtain without the parent's consent. Only if the parent body was, or subsequently becomes, irregular will the daughter body be in a position to claim recognition.

3. A CONVENTION OF LODGES

This method of Grand Lodge construction is the most common, and occurs when a group of regular warranted lodges (not less than three) in a new area, meet in convention to form a Grand Lodge with the blessings of their parent jurisdictions. Upon this having been harmoniously effected, the new Grand Body generally attracts wide recognition. A very recent example is the formation of the Grand Lodge of Alaska. There have been occurrences in the past whereby bad communications or a lack of general understanding have resulted in a new Grand Body being formed without the immediate blessings of its former Masonic authorities. While initially forming an external schism, these rare occurrences are usually rectified. The formations of the Grand Lodges of Japan and New Zealand are examples of this occurrence.

4. A WARRANTED DISTRICT SPONSORED

In this case, a group of lodges under one Grand Lodge which is geographically removed from its parent, gain permission to form a local Grand Lodge-type organisation, while still retaining their original allegiance. These forms of local masonic government are called 'Provincial' or 'District' Grand Lodges, and they provide local masonry with a fair measure of autonomy. These intermediate governmental structures have been progressively set up by the Grand Lodges of England, Ireland and Scotland. This has occurred as the result of local desire, bad communications in years gone by, and because the vastness of these Grand Lodges have made them a practical necessity.

In a number of cases, the local Grand Lodges eventually felt the desire for complete masonic autonomy, whereupon a new sovereign Grand Lodge was formed. The usual progression of events in the past has been that when a British colony became politically independent, its masonic offspring therein followed the same course. Nevertheless, there are still many countries, notably in Asia and Africa, where District or Provincial Grand Lodges have chosen to remain under allegience to England, Ireland or Scotland, as appropriate.

5. WARRANTED DISTRICTS SPONSORED

This category of Grand Lodge formation is an extension of the one above, and indeed, is far more common. It occurs when lodges under Districts or Provinces of more than one Grand Lodge unite to erect one new Grand Lodge. Most Australian Grand Lodges were formed in this way. It has been, and still is, quite common for

foreign lands to possess lodges warranted from England, Ireland and Scotland; and
these lodges have in the past united to form one new Grand Lodge. Sometimes this
is only achieved with some difficulty, as the accommodation of rituals and procedures has to be first achieved.

6. A GENERAL ASSEMBLY OF MASONS
This method of forming a Grand Lodge is not common, and examples are restricted
to North America. It involves masons meeting together as individual members of
the Craft, not as lodges or lodge delegations, and thereupon establishing a new
Grand Lodge. This procedure was sometimes found to be expedient in North America, as the Craft in this area spread so rapidly that it was not uncommon for any
new area of settlement to possess lodges warranted from a variety of sources.
Wherein this was the case, it was sometimes found that this method was the easiest,
rather than involving many different Grand Lodges as sponsors.

7. A CHARTER FROM A MOTHER GRAND LODGE
This method is most rare. It occurs when a Grand Lodge actually charters a daughter Grand Lodge, rather than the lodges in a new area agreeing at convention, or
in a General Assembly of masons, to form a new Grand Lodge. The direct chartering of the Grand Lodge of Tennessee by the Grand Lodge of North Carolina
forms the most celebrated example of this method.

8. GRAND LODGE UNION
In this method, two or more previously independent Grand Lodges within the one
territorial jurisdiction unite to form a single Grand Lodge. In some countries, a
number of Grand Lodges have evolved, or have been established through schism.
It is not particularly rare, where this situation exists, for two or more Grand Lodges
to unite to form one new Grand Lodge. Sometimes, such a union will, in effect, heal
an internal schism. In any case, such a union, particularly if it unites all masonry
within one country, generally is conducive to wide fraternal recognition. The formation of the United Lodges of Germany, originally by two Grand Lodges (and
later joined by three others), forms an interesting example of this method.

9. LODGE SPLITTING
This last method of Grand Lodge erection has found occasional usage, notably in
South America, and sometimes in Europe. It occurs when one lodge splits itself into
three new Lodges, and these three then form the Grand Lodge. Often, this is not
achieved regularly. A convention (arguably a 'Landmark') of the Craft is that a new
Grand Lodge must be formed by at least three lodges. Herein lies the reason for
lodge splitting as a means of Grand Lodge formation.

The Grand Representative System
The Grand Representative system is an old masonic custom whereby each regular
Grand Lodge appoints a member of another Grand Lodge to represent it at the
meetings of the latter. Such a representative is commonly said to be 'near the latter'.
For example, the United Grand Lodge of England will appoint a member of the
Grand Lodge of Scotland to represent it near the Grand Lodge of Scotland. Scot-
land will pursue the reverse course. Thus, each Grand Lodge will have a represen-
tative near the other. Of all the Grand Lodges recognised by the Grand Lodges of
England, Ireland and Scotland, only four (Iowa, Pennsylvania, New Mexico, and

Wyoming) do not exchange representatives. Upon two Grand Lodges entering into fraternal relations, it is usual for them to exchange representatives. Each Grand Lodge will normally recommend one of its members, for appointment, to the other. It is, therefore, quite common for any given regular Grand Lodge to possess in excess of one hundred Grand Representatives in its jurisdiction representing the Grand Lodges with which it maintains fraternal relations.

Originally, it appears that these representatives were to be something akin to Ambassadors. However, the system has long since operated on an honourary basis, with business correspondence between Grand Lodges being dealt with by the respective Grand Secretaries. Nonetheless, it is fairly usual for representatives to receive a copy of the annual Grand Lodge Proceedings of the Grand Lodge they represent, and to be kept abreast of its masonic activities. Many Grand Representatives regularly correspond with their opposite number on a private basis. A visitor will often find it useful to talk with the Grand Representative near his own Grand Lodge of the jurisdiction he proposes to visit, prior to his departure. The visitor will readily gain the name and address of the appropriate Grand Representative at his own Grand Lodge Office.

The Matter of Affiliation

It is far from uncommon for freemasons to seek membership in more than one lodge. However, the laws of the various regular Grand Lodges are certainly not uniform in this area. When a mason wishes to affiliate with a second lodge in his own jurisdiction, this is usually referred to as dual membership. When he seeks to join a third or fourth lodge, this is termed as plural membership. In some jurisdictions, the transfer of membership is permitted within it. The whole question of affiliation presents matters which must be carefully outlined.

The Demit (Dimit), or Clearance Certificate

When a member of a lodge withdraws from membership, masonic law and custom decrees that he receive a Demit, or Clearance Certificate, subject to certain preconditions. 'Demit' is the masonic terminology largely used in North America, while many other areas refer to it as a 'Clearance Certificate'. Both designations mean the same thing, and testify that the holder—

 (1) is a regular 'unaffiliated' freemason,
 (2) has resigned from the lodge named in the Demit,
 (3) is clear of all dues and fees payable to that lodge,
 (4) has not been suspended or expelled from freemasonty as of the date of issue.

The holder of a Demit is thus an unaffiliated mason, and a member of no regular lodge. In most jurisdictions, Demits are issued automatically as a right upon the lawful cessation of membership, while in a few they are only issued on request. By old custom, it is the duty of every mason to belong to a lodge and contribute to its work and financial support. Consequently, it is the usual rule that where a mason fails to join a new lodge within twelve months of being demited, he loses all his masonic privileges, including the right to visit. However, in some jurisdictions masonic privileges cease immediately the Demit is issued; while in others the unaffiliated mason retains the privilege to visit once in any twelve months. In all jurisdictions, it is only by the presentation of a Demit, or similar documentary evidence, that an unaffiliated mason may again seek membership of a regular lodge.

The Unaffiliated Mason

The Demited, or unaffiliated, freemason is in a position to join another lodge. Nevertheless, his Demit alone, while an essential prerequisite, is insufficient for the purpose. No matter which lodge he seeks to join, or where, he must be first accepted as an affiliate by its members. This usually requires a ballot of members, and often an inquiry into the person concerned. It is generally more simple rejoining a lodge in one's own original jurisdiction, than in affiliating with a lodge in another. In the latter case, it is usual that the lodge considering such an application will first refer the matter to its Grand Lodge. In some cases, the Grand Secretary will then seek the advice of the mason's original jurisdiction prior to approving the affiliation. The actual mechanics of affiliation varies between jurisdictions, but it is universally provided that a mason affiliating from one Grand Lodge be required to sign or affirm loyalty to his new Grand Lodge and its laws.

Dual and Plural Membership
The practices of regular Grand Lodges with regard to dual and plural membership are quite diverse, particularly in America. These practices can be placed in
categories.
(1) *Single Membership Grand Lodges.* These Grand Lodges provide that its members
can belong to only one lodge within its jurisdiction. In order to join a second
lodge, the member must resign from the first. In some jurisdictions, this is made
difficult by the imposition of residential requirements, whereupon a mason must
belong to a lodge located in proximity to his residential address. Some American
Grand Lodges, and some European Grand Bodies, require single membership.
(2) *Dual Membership Grand Lodges.* These Grand Lodges provide that members
may belong to two lodges, but no more. In some, dual membership is restricted
to the membership of two lodges within the jurisdiction, but more commonly a
dual membership Grand Lodge will permit its members to belong to only one
lodge in its own jurisdiction, and one other lodge in some other recognised
jurisdiction.
(3) *Plural Membership Grand Lodges.* These Grand Lodges permit their members
to belong to more than two lodges if they wish—in other words, as many as
they like. Quite obviously, if a Grand Lodge permits plural membership, it also
permits dual membership. However, some jurisdictions do place some restrictions on pluralism. In some single or dual membership only is permitted within
its jurisdiction, while plural membership is allowed outside it.
Of course, before a mason can achieve dual or plural membership outside his own
jurisdiction, both Grand Lodges concerned must permit the relevant practice. An
important point to note in the area of membership by affiliation is that each mason
will be bound by the laws of the jurisdiction in which he resides, as well as that of
which he was a member. Of course, where a Grand Lodge does not permit plural,
or dual, membership the affiliating mason will need to resign his original membership to effect his new affiliation. Any mason considering dual or plural membership
should seek the advice of his own Grand Lodge prior to any action. Whether, or
not, individual Grand Lodges permit dual and plural membership in one or other
of its forms, is listed near the beginning of the part of this Guide dealing with each.
It is possible to loosely group Grand Lodge practices in this matter in geographical areas. In Europe, most jurisdictions do not permit plural membership, but many
do allow dualism outside its obedience. The three British Grand Lodges, together
with those of Australasia, all permit plural membership. In Central and South
America, dual membership is far more common than plural Membership. In
Canada, most favour plural membership, while in the United States all systems are
in use—there being no great majority amongst its fifty Grand Lodges in any affiliation systems relative to dual and plural membership.

The Transfer of Membership
This practice is rare in the masonic world. A small number of jurisdictions, notably
in the United States, permit members who have moved their residence within the
jurisdiction to transfer their membership from one lodge to another without demit.
This does not mean that the receiving lodge has no vote in the reception of its new
member. This procedure has arisen as the result of an American practice whereby
in some jurisdictions individual lodges have masonic custody of candidates and

affiliates located within their immediate vicinity. Therefore, a person seeking to join
the Craft in such a jurisdiction is virtually 'zoned' to a certain lodge, or small choice
of lodges. It is under such circumstances that transfer of membership has been
approved.

Life Membership
There are various forms of 'life membership' systems used in the masonic world.
Some jurisdictions have adopted provisions in their Constitutions to accommodate
this practice. In some, the status is granted for appropriately long service to the
Craft. A mason gaining 'life membership' is no longer required to pay any dues,
although he is still deemed as a 'financial member'. By definition, therefore, a life
member has no need of a demit. In some jurisdictions, the term 'honorary member'
is substituted, although in these the voting rights of the member are sometimes
removed as a result. In the United States, life membership is often purchased by the
member. This is achieved by him paying a substantial sum in advance. A more
accurate description would probably be an advance payment of dues for life. Actually, the term 'life membership' is something of a misnomer. A member's tenure
in the Craft can be concluded through suspension or expulsion. In order to affiliate
elsewhere, a life or honorary member will usually be given a certificate or card
attesting to his status. It should be noted that only a few Grand Lodges use a life
membership system, and those that do have found problems associated with it.

Research Lodges
Research Lodges fall into a special category as far as affiliation is concerned. The
vast majority of Grand Lodges that do not permit dual or plural membership
exempt Research Lodges from these restrictions. Many Research Lodges, in addition to possessing normal members, also have what is often known as corresponding
or associate members. These members are not full members as such, and do not
possess voting rights. However, they do pay a fee, which enables them to attend as
a member rather than as a visitor, and to receive all the normal correspondence and
literature that the Research Lodge may produce. Corresponding membership allows
for masons not resident near the lodge to still be involved in its activities.

Religion, Race, Politics, and the Masonic Visitor

A discussion of religion, politics and race in terms of freemasonry represents a complex topic, and it is an area that has already been touched upon, in part, under the heading of Regularity and Recognition. It is desirable that the masonic visitor has some insight into these matters.

Among the essential characteristics of regular freemasonry are that all members must profess a belief in a Supreme Being, that the Volume of the Sacred Law must always be open in every Grand Lodge and constituent lodge while at work, and that religion and politics cannot be discussed in any lodge. These characteristics have already been examined in terms of regularity and recognition. It is to the historical and current effect these aspects have on the worldwide Craft that discussion will now be centred.

Prior to the masonic union of the Antients and Moderns in 1813, English freemasonry was certainly Christian in character. Candidates were of the Christian Faith, and it was the Bible that was open in lodges. However, the rapid expansion of the Craft to all corners of the globe resulted in many non-Christians seeking admission. It was therefore necessary to modify the 'Christian position' of the Craft to absorb these pressures. It emerged that a man could be made a mason if he possessed a belief in a Supreme Being, and the Bible came to be called the 'Volume of the Sacred Law'. This position seems to have emerged during the eighteenth century. The concept of the Volume of the Sacred Law became officially part of the British masonry in 1929, although it had long been recognised by that time. This altered position allowed men of all the great faiths of the world to join the fraternity. In countries such as India where many faiths are represented, it is far from uncommon to see in lodges many different Volumes of the Sacred Law placed together on the altar. Of course, England is a Christian country, and the vast majority of English masons in England profess the Christian Faith.

All regular jurisdictions came to accept the Supreme Being and the Volume of the Sacred Law as essential characteristics when examining another Grand Lodge with a view to recognition. However, internal 'religious policies' vary somewhat more than this. In the United States, while acknowledging the right of masons to profess which faith they choose, American Webb-form ritual remains quite Christian in character. The development of American ritual precedes that of current English ritual. In most Scandinavian countries, the rituals are most Christian in character, and membership is still restricted to men who profess the Christian Faith. However, in comparatively recent years, the Scandinavians have granted the rights of membership to non-Christian masons who have received the degrees abroad. In terms of the masonic visitor, it is enough to realise that every major creed is recognised in the masonic world, and that in his masonic travels he is likely to encounter them.

The various Volumes of the Sacred Law of which the visitor may note to be open in lodges include: the Pentateuch (Old Testament) of the Jews, the Bible of the Christians (usually the Old and New Testaments), the Koran of the Moslems, the Zend Avesta of the Persians, the Rig Venda (and other Vendas) the Brahmin Hindus, the Bhagavad-Gita of the Hindus, the Tao Te King of the Taoists, and the Tripitaka of the Buddhists.

Politics, like religion, is banned from discussion within every regular masonic lodge. Of course, the political history of many countries has had a great effect on the development, or otherwise, of the worldwide Craft, as even the briefest study of masonic history will quickly reveal. The repression of the Craft by totalitarian regimes has occurred in many places, with varying effects, and these occurrences are discussed elsewhere in this guide under country headings.

One of the main reasons why most irregular Grand Lodges have been branded as such is that they allow their members to use their lodges for political purposes. Indeed, under the irregular Grand Orient of France and those Grand Bodies which take their inspiration from it, religious and political discussion is encouraged in lodges. Such practices are deplored by regular masonry, and the masonic visitor can be assured that these two divisive subjects are never placed before regular lodges.

The racial question, like that of religion, requires some discussion. Race has, most regretably, formed barriers between peoples almost since time began, and the masonic fraternity has not escaped these problems. The racial question arose in freemasonry as soon as it spread out from British shores, and the question of admitting men of non-European origin became a very real one. The three British Grand Lodges have never had a 'discriminatory policy' as such, and of course, such a policy would run against the teachings of the fraternity.

However, as masonry spread to African and Asian shores with the expansion of the British Empire, there was a definite reluctance to admit non-Europeans as members. Apart from anything else, lodges worked in the English language, and the view was held that only English-speaking men could be practically admitted. The passing of time saw many Africans and Asians receive English educations, or learn the English language, and it is from these people that the earliest non-European masons came. However, at least until the nineteenth century, non-European admissions were conferred sparingly. Lodges remained largely Anglo-Saxon, and it is probably unlikely that a British Grand Lodge would have granted a warrant to a lodge largely composed of aliens. Of course, this colonial practice was not just confined to masonry, but applied to virtually all British Colonial Institutions. The vastly changed world that emerged from World War Two saw this situation progressively altered, and these race distinctions have long since disappeared from British-warranted lodges. Mixed lodges, or even completely Asian or African Lodges, are now far from uncommon.

In the United States, with its long history of racial problems, a similar pattern of discrimination held sway and indeed, it has been far more overtly followed than under British masonry. It must be clearly stated that, with few exceptions, regular lodges in the United States do not initiate 'coloured men'. Exceptions in this area are few, but one noted example is mentioned later in this guide under the heading of New Jersey. Again, no regular American Grand Lodge discriminates, by statute, against the membership of non-whites. Nonetheless, each individual lodge is free, under general masonic law, to accept, or refuse to accept, any man. The oft used argument appears to be that the reception of a coloured man would 'disturb the harmony of the Lodge'. It must be understood that this 'feature' of American masonry largely applies to visitors, especially in the southern states. A regular black freemason coming from, say Nigeria, will likely experience considerable difficulty in being admitted as a visitor to most regular lodges in the United States.

It is necessary to add here that there exists in the United States, and elsewhere, a large body of irregular Grand Lodges known as Prince Hall Freemasonry, whose membership is exclusively black. Prince Hall Lodges are to be found in most corners of America. While it is arguable that Prince Hall Freemasonry was regular in origin (and there is evidence to suggest that it is not), the racial situation in America doubtlessly stimulated its separate development. This apparently has suited both 'sides', as Negroes in North America have quite naturally sought to join Prince Hall lodges, rather than seek admission into regular 'white' lodges. There has been a move in some of the more northern American states in recent years, notably in Wisconsin, to reach an accommodation with local bodies of Prince Hall lodges. In Wisconsin, there has even been the suggestion of 're-chartering' various Prince Hall lodges under the regular Grand Lodge of Wisconsin. Nonetheless, it appears that masonic advances in this area will not be rapid. A number of other American Grand Lodges, especially in the southern states, have expressed disapproval of these proposals.

In South Africa, until very recently, non-whites were not permitted to join the fraternity. Regardless of the individual feelings white South Africans may have in this area, the well known apartheid laws of this country made mixed lodges legally untenable. A few years ago the regular Grand Lodge of South Africa 'took over' three lodges then chartered in that country by the irregular Prince Hall Grand Lodge of New York. The South African Government gave its special permission for this event, and also gave its authority for lodges generally to admit non-whites to membership. Of course, any Lodge still has the final say as to whom it will admit, and given the social structure of South Africa it is probably unlikely that non-whites will enter the Craft in that country in great numbers.

In Europe, there has never been any racial problem concerning colour, doubtlessly because Europe remains essentially white. However, prior to the Second World War, Jews were very largely prevented from becoming masons in many parts of Europe. Subsequent to the War, this situation was rectified.

Rites and Rituals

It is not uncommon for a mason who has never visited a lodge outside his own area or jurisdiction to assume that all masonic ceremonies are similar, or the same, to those with which he is familiar. On reflection, this view is not unnatural, particularly with the younger mason. Of course, nothing can be further from the truth. Indeed, the visitor will invariably find that observing other ways of working will be a highlight of masonic travels.

The divergences of the Craft degrees as worked around the world are not few. If one informs an English mason that in the United States lodges largely open and close their proceedings in the Third Degree, stunned silence might well be the initial response. Doubtlessly, many a nescient American mason would share similar feelings if instructed with the English system. However, despite such divergences as these, all Craft ceremonies have much in common, especially in basic content if not in form.

Content and Form

The content of the Craft degrees as worked around the world is fairly similar, regardless of which ritual may be used. Every jurisdiction practises the three degrees of Entered Apprentice, Fellow Craft, and Master Mason. Every regular jurisdiction adheres to the Ancient Landmarks of the Order. Similarly, the legend of the Third Degree, the modes of recognition, and the general teachings of the Order are all constants. It is quite true to say that any masonic visitor, no matter which jurisdiction he belongs to, will (language excepted) readily relate to and basically understand any Craft ceremony he comes to view in his travels. The content may be in a different order of arrangement to that with which he is familiar and there may be a few strange additions or omissions, but he will readily understand what is taking place without any difficulty. In short, the wordings of the rituals around the world may be re-ordered and somewhat different, but the overall context and teachings of each degree ceremony are the same.

It is the form of the Craft ceremonies which can, and often do, vary widely. By form is meant the order of parts of the ceremonies, the movements of officers and candidates, variances in the modes of recognition, in receiving visitors, in opening and closing the lodge, in lodge layout and seating arrangements—the list is quite a long one. In order to appreciate these diversities, a detailed study of ritual history is needed, and such a study is well outside the scope of the intentions of this discourse. Nonetheless, it will be useful for the travelling freemason to have some insight into the major masonic Craft rituals in current usage, and where he is likely to encounter them. However, it is not the intention here to go into great detail. Aside from the obvious restrictions in this area of which every mason will be aware, a thorough detailing is outside the parameters of this guide. The aim here is to comfortably place a visitor inside a 'strange' lodge, not to minutely detail what he will experience once inside.

Rites and Rituals

The terms 'rite' and 'ritual' will be well known to most freemasons. While there is some masonic disagreement as to the exact meaning of each term, basically a rite is a series of progressive degree ceremonies, and a ritual is the wording pertaining to the ceremonies. In common masonic usage, however, the word *Ritual* is used to collectively describe the three Craft degrees, while *rite* is used to describe a system of degrees beyond the Craft, or which includes the Craft degrees. Examples of a rite are the Ancient and Accepted Scottish Rite (a system of 33 Degrees), and the Swedish Rite (a system of 11 Degrees).

Rites and Rituals by Location

There are in excess of one hundred different Craft rituals in use in the regular masonic world, many of which are very similar. In England alone in excess of fifty are in use, but all of these are quite similar in both content and form. In some jurisdictions, the Craft ritual used is standard by Grand Lodge decree, while in others many are permitted and are in use. It is, however, possible to locate Craft rituals geographically to some extent.

England: The most prevalent English ritual is *Emulation*. Others include *Stability*, *Taylor's West End*, *Logic*, *Bristol*, and many others. With the possible exception of the *Bristol* ritual, the differences in the various English workings often devolve on only a few changed words, and only the well versed observer will notice the differences between one English ritual and another. England has never laid down any fixed, or single Grand Lodge approved, ritual for use in its lodges. The emergence of English masonry from operative to speculative precluded such a possibility, although English ritual forms were largely standardised within certain parameters subsequent to the English masonic union of 1813. For the purposes of the discussion following, English-form Craft ritual will be used as the basis for comparison. For those unfamiliar with the English-form, the Master Mason will find that most masonic libraries possess copies of the *Emulation* working.

Scotland: As the student with the inclination to read Scottish masonic history will readily discover, Scottish masonry evolved from operative to speculative in different ways, and at a slower pace, than in England. Scottish ritual has retained a few more operative traits than its English counterpart, as well as several features lost to the English when English ritual was standardised after 1813. As with England, there is no set Scottish ritual, and several versions are in use, all of which are reasonably similar to each other, but more dissimilar to English versions. In several Scottish rituals, the Third Degree tends to be somewhat more dramatic than the English, with the Hiramic Legend being acted out to a much fuller extent.

Ireland: Irish Freemasonry has two distinctive features that set it apart from England and Scotland. Firstly, Irish ritual is officially uniform as laid down by the Grand Lodge of Ireland, and secondly, unlike most other jurisdictions in the world, Irish ritual is not permitted to be printed in any form. On the first impression, one must doubtlessly consider that uniformity of working and the lack of a printed ritual to be incompatible. This problem is overcome by the existence of a body known as the Grand Lodge of Instruction, established by the Grand Lodge to oversee its ritual, to impart instruction, and to encourage and sponsor exemplifications of the Craft degrees. Membership of the Grand Lodge of Instruction is restricted to acknowledged experts in Irish ritual, who have Grand Lodge status. This body authorises Classes of Instruction that are under the control of approved instructors, and not associated with particular lodges. A major variation of ritual is, nonetheless, tacitly permitted to exist in the southern province of Munster, for historical and traditional reasons, and which much resembles the English *Bristol* working. Again, Irish forms differ to some extent from both English and Scottish practices, but the content remains quite similar. Additional details concerning Irish ritual can be found under that heading later in this Guide.

British Commonwealth Countries: Masonry in all British Commonwealth countries largely derives directly from English, Irish, and Scottish practices. Many of these countries still possess a large number of lodges warranted directly from London, Dublin, and Edinburgh, working either English, Irish, or Scottish rituals. Nonetheless, in a number of Commonwealth countries, indigenous Grand Lodges have been formed. India now has a Grand Lodge using English-form ritual (with adaptations). Tasmanian ritual is virtually pure *Emulation*, while most other Australasian rituals are quite similar to it, yet also exhibit a few Irish and Scottish influences. Canada, while having great British influences in the rituals of its nine Grand Lodges, is not without considerable ritualistic influence from the United States, and geographically this is quite understandable. Many Canadian Grand Lodges permit their constituent lodges to work either an English-form ritual, or an American Webb-form ritual. The strength of allegiance between these forms tends to vary between Canadian jurisdictions.

Europe and Scandinavia: This area of the world is probably the most ritually diverse. From the introduction and dispersion of freemasonry in Europe, great innovations have taken place in ritual practices. The European, historically, took some delight in varying Craft ritual into several differing forms. Interested masons can research these occurrences at their leisure, but it is the current situation which must be the subject of outline here. In addition to British and American rituals used in regular masonry in Europe (and these are largely used only in English-speaking lodges), there are five main 'indigenous' ones which must be briefly discussed, as follows:

1. The French Rite: This masonic system was originally formulated under the Grand Orient of France. It was at its outset predominately Christian in character until modified to largely omit its religious traits when the Grand Orient sank into irregularity (see under France). It consists of the three Craft degrees, plus four 'higher' degrees, giving a total of seven. The Grand Orient originally formed the Rite about 1786 (and evidently revised it about 1801) as part of a policy of stabilising its profusion of higher degrees. Several GLNF Lodges have in recent years adopted the French Rite Craft degrees, having first purged them of agnostic irregularities. The French Rite Craft ceremonies are of very great beauty, and it has been said that it is really the Rectified Scottish Rite simplified.

2. The Ancient and Accepted Rite: This degree system is more commonly referred to simply as the 'Scottish Rite', although it has nothing historically or ritualistically to do with Scotland. There is not much difference in the content of this Rite as practised in Europe, and its content in English-speaking countries. The Rite is composed of thirty-three degrees, of which the first three are the Craft degrees. It is of French origin, and it came to English-speaking masonry from France. Not surprisingly, the three Craft degrees of the Rite are French-type. In non-European and Latin countries, the Rite is completely separate from the Craft, and these jurisdictions (such as those of Britain and America) will confer their usual Craft degrees and the mason possessing them may later, if he wishes, petition to join a 'Lodge' under an appropriate Supreme Council to receive the Ancient and Accepted Rite or 'Scottish Rite' degrees (*ie*, the fourth Degree onwards). In many European jurisdictions, and most in Latin America, the Craft Degrees worked are, in fact, the actual French-form Scottish Rite Craft degrees. In form, the Scottish Rite Craft degrees practised are fairly similar between those jurisdictions using them. However, there are somewhat wider variations in use for degrees above the third. The Rite as practised in the British Isles is quite Christian in character, whereas these Christian aspects have been largely removed from European and Latin forms.

3. The Rectified Scottish Rite: This Rite is the third of the major French-derived degree systems currently in usage. It consists of the three French-form Craft degrees, and several higher degrees as an extension. The title of the Rite is largely self-explanatory. It appears to have originated about the late 1770s in an effort to purge the higher degrees of the more objectionable features of the 'Rite of Strict Observance'; a German inspired incursion into European masonry. In the practices of European jurisdictions 'above the Craft', the mason who is unfamiliar with them might have some difficulty in distinguishing between the Rectified Scottish Rite and the French Rite. Beyond the Craft degrees, the Rectified Scottish Rite is very Christian in character, and its central theme is the legend of the Knights Templar.

It is necessary to expand upon the three French-derived Rites by way of comparison in terms of the Craft degrees. The three Craft degrees used in French Rite, the Scottish Rite and the Rectified Scottish Rite are not particularly dissimilar, in the same way as, for example, the various English rituals in current usage are not greatly dissimilar. Of course, the workings of the three Craft degrees in Europe does vary somewhat between jurisdictions, and between rites. The French-type Craft degrees derive from England in the earliest times of speculative masonry, and maintain many operative-style features no longer found in British workings. Typical of the gamut of European Craft ritual are such things as sort ceremonies, the use of a 'Chamber of Preparation' for candidates (and ritual forms associated with it which are quite unknown in English-speaking rituals). the 'Chain of Union', the extensive use of lengthy catechismic lectures, and a very dramatic Third Degree.

4. The Schroeder Ritual: Schroeder was a prominent German mason of the eighteenth century. Along with many other masons of his time, he was concerned with the 'excesses and innovations' through which Continental masonry was passing. He decided to rectify this situation by translating the English ritual of the time into German, whereupon was derived the *Schroeder ritual*. One must remember that here we are talking of eighteenth-century English ritual, not the post-1813 English rituals in use today. The content of the Schroeder-form ritual is thus more comparable to the French-type Craft rituals. Aspects of *Schroeder ritual* are thus more comparable to the French-type Craft rituals. Aspects of *Schroeder ritual* are discussed under the headings of Germany and Austria later in this guide. It needs to be added that *Schroeder ritual* is certainly not the same throughout German-speaking masonry in Europe, but again, it has been altered in largely minor ways in different jurisdictions over the years.

5. The Swedish Rite: The fifth main European system to warrant discussion is the Swedish Rite. It is a system of eleven degrees, of which the first three are the Craft degrees. The Swedish Rite system is explained in some detail under the heading of

Scandinavia later in the guide. In content, the three Swedish Rite Craft degrees do vary somewhat more than those of Britain and Europe generally. For example, the Third Degree legend under the Swedish Rite deals largely with Adoniram, rather than with Hiram Abiff.

The Dispersion of European Ritual

Under the French National Grand Lodge, the Rectified Scottish Rite Craft degrees, the Scottish Rite Craft degrees, the French Rite Craft degrees, and the English *Emulation ritual* are all worked, with the first two predominating. There are also a small number of French chartered lodges using Webb-form American rituals.

In German-speaking lodges in Germany, Austria and Switzerland, *Schroeder*-form ritual is largely used, although one of the German Grand Lodges prescribes the Swedish Rite. All the Scandinavian countries use the Swedish Rite, although in Finland Webb-form ritual is used.

The Netherlands, Belgium, and French-speaking Swiss lodges largely work in either the Scottish Rite or Rectified Scottish Rite Craft degrees, with the former predominating. Greece and Luxembourg use French Rite-derived Craft degrees. Those English-speaking lodges warranted in Europe tend to work in an English ritual, or by various American Webb-form rituals. Again, it needs to be stated that, with the exception of the Swedish Rite, the various European Craft rituals are not dissimilar between themselves.

Central and South America

In this area of the world, the Scottish Rite or Rectified Scottish Rite Craft degrees (largely in Spanish or Portuguese) are the most widely worked. The Scottish Rite degrees from four to thirty-three are available in all jurisdictions under various Supreme Councils. German-speaking lodges in South America work by *Schroeder*, while there still remains a useful number of English-speaking lodges warranted from the three British Constitutions using the expected rituals. The few English-speaking lodges warranted under indigenous Grand Lodges in Central and South America work what they call the 'York Rite'. In fact, in most common usage in these lodges is English-form ritual, with *Emulation* being favoured, although in some a Webb-form ritual is used.

North America

Throughout most of the United states, the Webb-form ritual is used. The term 'Webb-form' must be considered broadly as, like English ritual, there exists minor variations in form between the rituals of the American Grand Lodges. A few eastern American jurisdictions, such as Pennsylvania, never 'adopted' the *Webb Ritual*, but use a ritual which could possibly be described as being closer in character to Scottish or Irish forms. The Canadian situation has already been outlined.

Africa and Asia

The vast majority of lodges locaed in these two continents hold warrants from either London, Dublin or Edinburgh, and work the expected rituals. There are a growing number of French-speaking lodges in Africa working under the French National Grand Lodge, in addition. The Grand Lodge of South Africa works the Dutch (Rectified Scottish Rite-type) ritual (with some adaptions). There also remains a few lodges in Zimbabwe still holding charters from the Netherlands. The Grand Lodges of Japan and Philippines both use a Webb-form ritual.

A Final Comment
From the foregoing discussion, the visitor will now perhaps appreciate that Craft ritual in current usage around the world is not as diverse as he may have imagined. Indeed, in very broad terms, it is possible to say that there are only seven Craft ritual forms that he is likely to encounter, namely—The English-form, the Scottish-form, the French-derived form, the Schroeder-form, the Irish-form, the Webb-form, and the Swedish-form.

Other Masonic Degrees and Rites

We enter here a difficult area to effectively detail for the travelling mason. In each regular jurisdiction the visitor will invariably find a large number of rites and degrees in excess of Craft freemasonry. In some areas many are indeed viewed from elsewhere as being excessive. However, when attempting to document the area of fraternal relations between Grand Lodges and the 'additional' masonic orders of the world, and those between the orders themselves, we reach a most complex situation, which virtually requires a book of its own to effectively detail. As a result, it is not intended to venture far into this area in this guide.

The major rite 'beyond the Craft' practised in the masonic world is the Ancient and Accepted Rite (also called the Scottish Rite, although it has nothing historically or ritualistically to do with Scotland). This rite consist of 33 degrees, of which the first three are the regular Craft degrees. This rite has been briefly looked at already in an earlier chapter, and forms the extent of the discussion that we will undertake concerning it, except as it applies in the United States. The Scottish Rite in the United States will be looked at in its proper place later in the guide.

The two most popular degrees practised outside the Craft in English-speaking masonry are the degree of the Holy Royal Arch and of Mark Master Mason. In the British Isles these two degrees are worked either as an extention of the Craft, or are governed by separate Grand Lodges controlling them. In the United States, they are worked as part of the York Rite, a discussion about which will be undertaken later under that heading.

Other degrees and orders worked under varying forms of masonic government in the masonic world include the Royal and Select Masters, the Ark Mariners, the Order of the Secret Monitor, the Order of Knights Templar, the Red Cross of Constantine, the Holy Royal Arch Knight Templar Priests, the Allied Masonic Degrees, and several others.

Most Grand Lodges recognise, or simply permit their members to belong to, many other degrees, rites and orders within their jurisdiction. However, often some of these orders are not in any way countenanced by other regular jurisdictions. This is certainly an area of 'MASON BEWARE'. A particular order in any foreign jurisdiction may well have the same name, and the outside look similar or the same as an order in a mason's home jurisdiction, but could still be irregular.

A mason who is a member of a particular degree, rite, or order beyond the Craft in his home territory, and who wishes to visit such an order in another part of the world, MUST strictly adhere to the following procedures before attempting to do so.

He must:
1. check with the sovereign body of the order of which he is member to ascertain if it recognises a sister body in the area he proposes to visit.
2. check with his own Grand Lodge office that such a visit will be in order as far as his Craft Grand Lodge is concerned. Generally, if the regular body of which he is a member in his own home area approves, his Craft Grand Secretary will approve also.

3. *in no circumstances* attempt to visit an order beyond the Craft in another part of the world unless he has first checked out that it is regular and permissible for him to visit under it. It is, of course, a serious masonic offence to do otherwise.

Section II

Visiting in Africa

Africa

An Overview
Freemasonry came to Africa in the form of a lodge in 1772, with the erection of Goede Hoop Lodge, No 18, at Cape Town, holding a charter from the Grand East of the Netherlands. However, there had reputedly been masonic activity in West Africa as early as the 1740s. Masonry was not quick to flourish early in its African career. It needs to be remembered that it was not until the nineteenth century that any real development occurred in many areas of the 'Dark Continent'. Indeed, the number of lodges in Africa prior to the First World War were relatively few, and it was not until after that War that the Craft began to stride forward. Since the Second World War, the number of lodges in some African areas has increased at a steady rate.

In looking at the spread of masonry in Africa, a rather fragmatic view must be taken. By far the greatest masonic growth has occurred in the former British colonies of Eastern, Western and Southern Africa. It is not difficult to equate African masonic development in terms of economic advancements, and white population factors. Indeed, one must not lose sight of the fact that freemasonry is largely the creation of white Europeans in general, and Anglo-Saxons in particular. It is hardly surprising, therefore, to find the Craft in Africa most developed in areas of large European population. It is really only in this century that non-whites have joined the Craft in any number. In some countries, such as Nigeria, the Negro race has entered the Craft in increasing numbers, and it is in areas such as this that have seen the greatest impetus in masonic expansion since the Second World War. It is also worthy of note that in many African areas, it is the expatriate Indian population that has provided much of the non-white membership of the African Craft. In most parts of Africa today, the future of the Craft will lie largely with its non-white membership.

The other great colonial powers to carve up Africa were the French, Germans, Italians, Belgians, Dutch, Portuguese, and Spanish. Of these, German and Italian incursions, as the result of the two World Wars, were not extensive or long lived. Spanish possessions were largely confined to the north-west of the Continent, the Belgians to the Congo, and the Portuguese to the relatively small holdings of Angola and Mozambique. The Dutch, originally with suzerainty over parts of Southern Africa, later lost control to the British. It was the French, however, who controlled the great bulk of Africa that was not British. Outside British territory, the Craft met with quite limited success. This was largely the result of the fact that it was not strong in any case in the European home countries. The vast majority of non-British lodges that were formed emanated from the irregular Grand Orients of France, Belgium, and Portugal. A number of irregular French lodges still work in former French possessions in Africa, and in some of these countries irregular Grand Orients have been established under European inspiration. Clearly then, in the past regular freemasonry has largely existed only in 'British' Africa. However, it has been a happy occurrence of recent years that the regular French National Grand Lodge (GLNF) has erected a number of lodges in many areas of the former French African Empire, and this process continues at a steady rate.

Two other factors have had influence on the development of masonry in Africa. The first of these is political. Politics has had a central, and usually unwelcome, position in African masonic history. While Africa remained colonial, it was the attitudes of the various European powers towards the Craft that effected development. Where a colonial power was opposed to masonry at home, masonic progress in its African territories was not assisted. A striking example is the closure of German lodges in South West Africa (Namibia) in the 1930's, as a result of Nazi pressure on German masonry. In post-colonial times, many indigenous African Governments have become authoritarian, or totalitarian. In countries where this has occurred the Craft has generally faced a torrid time. In some countries, such as Uganda, the political situation has forced the Craft to close on an organised basis. In most Moslem countries in northern Africa, the road of the Craft has been blocked by religious opposition, often combined with Government intolerance.

At first view, it might appear strange that, despite the great masonic strength in countries of former British Rule, new independent regular Grand Lodges have not been formed anywhere in Africa, except in South Africa. However, the Grand Lodge of South Africa, as will be later explained, was largely spawned for reasons other than a desire for complete local masonic autonomy. The reasons for this 'lack of independence' appear to be twofold—masonic security, and masonic loyalty.

In terms of security, it has long been perceived that as a 'foreign institution', freemasonry might be less likely to attract the adverse interest of Governments. Indeed, while all regular Grand Lodges strictly avoid, with good reason, anything remotely political, there seem often to be many masons in Government positions in Britain, and elsewhere. Doubtlessly in the past, freemasons as individuals in such positions of influence have assisted in terms of promoting masonic security in places such as Africa. Of course, if local lodges in Africa severed allegiances to the British Grand Lodges, it may be perceived as resulting in a loss of British protection. Nonetheless, in cases of opposition from totalitarian Governments, any 'help from home', would probably be futile anyway. However, in cases of less severe opposition, such may be useful, or even crucial.

Masonic loyalty can readily be cited as the other main reason as to why Africa remains largely devoid of regular independent Grand Lodges. It must be recalled that the main source of masonic membership in Africa has historically been British. Quite naturally, these members had no desire to severe links with their home Grand Lodges. Nevertheless, that is not to say that localised lodges were not interested in some form of autonomy closer to their doorstep. Impetus in this regard has resulted in the erection of District and Provincial Grand Lodges still under the home Constitutions. These bodies do assume a large degree of local autonomy in terms of masonic government, while still working strictly under the rules of the relevant Grand Lodge, and remaining responsible to it. Indeed, from the administrative point of view, Grand Lodges are most happy with this form of intermediatory tier in masonic government, and such is most necessary for such large and geographically spread organisations as the United Grand Lodge of England, and the Grand Lodge of Scotland.

On the other hand, since the Second World War in particular, many non-Europeans have joined the Craft in Africa in increasing numbers, and perhaps in time this might provide the springboard whereupon localised African masonry seeks full masonic independence. Indeed, in very recent times, moves have been made in

Nigeria to form a new sovereign Grand Lodge. While this move apparently did not attract the support that was initially envisaged, it is possible that a Grand Lodge may eventually be established.

The second factor which has had an effect on the development of the Craft in Africa has been the racial question. Up until the Second World War and the subsequent political independence of most African nations, there had been a reluctance in many lodges, but by no means all, to admit non-whites to masonic membership. With the exception of South Africa, such practices have long since departed the masonic scene. Even in South Africa, the masonic racial question has been largely repaired as was noted earlier in this guide, when the whole question of race was broadly discussed.

In having provided an overview of masonry in Africa, it is now possible to proceed to look at individual countries and areas as the travelling freemason will find them. Aside from the contents that will follow, one further practical point needs explanation.

The addresses given as points of contact in some areas might not be of the greatest use as one would normally expect. It is not so much that the masonic meeting places listed will change, as this is unlikely in most cases. The problem is that in a few places they may be hard to physically locate. This is certainly not the result of any intention by lodges to 'hide' their Temples, but simply results from the permutable geography of some African towns. The main example is that of Zambia. In Lusaka, for instance, it would be the skilled mason indeed that found the location of its Masonic Temple without being personally accompanied to the door by a local mason. For this reason, it is advised that on some occasions, it may be wise to write to a local lodge care of its Post Office Box address well before entering its area. By this means, the visitor can be readily contacted when he arrives at his hotel, and thus be immediately placed in good fraternal hands. Of course, it will be noted that visitors have been strenuously advised earlier in this guide against writing directly to foreign Grand Lodges. However, some local African circumstances perhaps allow some exception to this rule. Where this problem may occur, the Post Office Box address of individual lodges are detailed. If there is definitely a location problem in any particular area, this is specifically mentioned. Nonetheless, if writing to an individual lodge, or to a District or Provincial Grand Lodge, visiting masons are still well advised to direct their correspondence through their own Grand Lodge Office.

ALGERIA

A former French colony, Algeria evidently possesses lodges chartered from the irregular French Grand Lodges, the earliest of which was erected by the Grand Orient of France in 1832. No regular lodges work in this Country as yet.

ANGOLA

This former Portuguese colony, as late as the 1960s, had several lodges originally holding warrants from the irregular Grand Orient of Portugal. They were as misguided as their parent body, and in any case it is unlikely that they survived the totalitarian government that has lately come to rule the country.

BOTSWANA

This lightly populated country in southern Africa was once part of the British African colonies. It possesses four lodges currently, two warranted from Scotland, and two by England, all of which are detailed below. The second named Scottish lodge was chartered only in 1982. One of the English Lodges (No 8715) is a constituent of the English District Grand Lodge of Zambia, while the other (No 8781) has recently come under the English Grand Lodge of the Transvaal. This situation would at first appear somewhat strange, but is explained by the fact that these two lodges are located at different ends of the country. The two Scottish lodges report direct to Edinburgh.

Pikwe Lodge No 8715 EC	Meets at the Congregational Church Hall, Selebi Pikwe, Botswana; 3rd Monday, Monthly, except June. Installation: 4th Saturday, June.
Gaborone Lodge No 8781 EC	Meets at the Masonic Hall, Gaborone, Botswana; 1st Friday, Monthly, except December and January. Installation: March.
Lodge Notwani No 1633 SC	Meets at the Masonic Hall, Gaborone, Botswana; 2nd Friday, Monthly, except December.
Lodge Ntshe No 1746 SC	Meets at the J.O.A. Hall, Francistown, Botswana; 3rd Saturday in odd months.

CAMEROUN

Another former French colony, Cameroun has for several years possessed an irregular Grand Orient, composed of lodges originally under the Grand Orient of France.

DAHOMEY

This small West African country, also formerly French territory, has one regular lodge warranted in 1973 by the regular Grande Loge Nationale Francaise. The irregular Grand Orient of France also reportedly has Lodges there. The regular lodge is Africante Lodge, No 160, meeting at Cotonou.

EGYPT

The masonic history of Egypt is most confused, and only the briefest résumé will be undertaken here. Lodges began appearing in Egypt about the early nineteenth century, with the earliest warrants coming from France and Germany. In the 1860s, England, Scotland, and the Grand Orient of Italy all chartered a number of lodges. In the period immediately following the Second World War, England had about a dozen lodges in the country under a District Grand Lodge; while Scotland had three lodges still in operation. The story of the non-British lodges is one of schism and confusion with several Grand Orients rising and falling; and heavy influences from Supreme Councils and other Higher Degrees and Rites. A National Grand Lodge of Egypt was the predominant body, and this had an uneasy relationship with the British Grand Lodges. Its lodges worked variously in Arabic, Greek, French, Italian, Hebrew, and German.

However, the rise of the Nationalist Movement in Egypt and the assumption to power of President Nasser led to freemasonry being proscribed. All British lodges closed, and Egyptian lodges were severely repressed. The remnants of the Craft in Egypt would appear to still work on a clandestine basis, and there remains a Grand Orient of Egypt which is probably the successor of the former National Grand Lodge. Of course, it is irregular, and little would appear to be known about it, other than the fact that it appears to be based in Alexandria.

ETHIOPIA

The irregular Grand Orient of France was active in the early years of this century in Ethiopia, and it appears to have had a lodge in Addis Ababa about 1902. Similarly, the Grand Orient of Italy had a lodge there during the years of Italian occupation. Masonry appears to have long since become extinct in Ethiopia, and its current Communist Government makes any future revival out of the question.

THE GAMBIA

This tiny West African country was once the property of Britain, and so it is not surprising to find two English lodges within its borders, together with one lodge chartered from Scotland. All three lodges are administered by their respective District Grand Lodges based in Sierra Leone. All three lodges meet at the Masonic Hall, Cape Road, Banjul, Gambia.

Banjul Lodge of St John No 6878 EC	1st Monday, Monthly. Installation: June.
Winward Lodge No 7364 EC.	3rd Monday, November to June. Installation: January.
St Mary's Lodge No 1711 SC.	2nd Tuesday, in odd months.

GABON

Yet another former French colony, Gabon possesses irregular lodges holding charters from the Grand Orient of France, and the equally irregular Grand Lodge of France. In very recent years, regular freemasonry has become established in the country, with three lodges having been erected at the Capital City, Libreville, under the Grande Loge Nationale Francaise. Le Dialogue Lodge No 209, was established in 1977; and this was followed by Tolerance Lodge No 252; and La Paix Lodge No 253. An irregular Scottish Rite Supreme Council was founded in Gabon in 1980, under the influence of the French Grand Orient.

GHANA

Ghana, originally called the Gold Coast, is a former British colony in West Africa where the Craft has flourished, particularly in recent years. It possesses large District Grand Lodges of both England and Scotland, and an Irish Provincial Grand Lodge.

The District Grand Lodge of Ghana (Under the United Grand Lodge of England).
  Address: Freemasons' Hall, Liberty Avenue, Accra, Ghana.
  Lodges: 44
The District Grand Lodge of Ghana (Under the Grand Lodge of Scotland).
  Address: Freemasons' Hall, Kwame Nkrumah Avenue, Accra, Ghana.
  Lodges: 28

The Provincial Grand Lodge of Ghana (Under the Grand Lodge of Ireland).
Address: Freemasons' Hall, Liberty Avenue, Accra, Ghana.
Lodges: 15

History

Ghana's first lodge was warranted in 1859, by England. This was Gold Coast Lodge No 773, meeting at Cape Coast. A second lodge, Victoria No 2392, followed in 1891; and was erected at Accra, also with an English warrant. Scotland chartered its first lodge at Cape Coast in 1921. This was Lodge Progressive No 1261. Ireland was relatively slow to move into Ghana and its first lodge, St Patrick Lodge No 793, was not established until 1956.

Rapid development of the Craft in Ghana has occurred in relatively recent years, and this appears to be partly the result of a reasonably wide acceptance of masonry by the non-white community of Ghana, which naturally accounts for the vast majority of its population. Indeed, some lodges are today almost exclusively black in terms of ethnic composition. Prior to the Second World War, only five English lodges existed in the country. Today, of the forty-four English lodges now working in Ghana, twelve have been erected since 1965. The histories of Scottish and Irish masonry in Ghana follows the same healthy pattern. Of the fifteen Irish lodges now working in Ghana, all but one received its charter after 1970. There is every reason to expect that more lodges will be erected in this country in the future.

Notes for Visitors to Ghana

Lodges in Ghana largely follow the ritual and customs of the obedience from which each has obtained its warrant. Dress is a dark suit, although non-Europeans can sometimes be seen attending in the more formal attire associated with their ethnic backgrounds. Meeting times are all in the evening, with some lodges meeting as early as 5.30 pm, while others are tyled as late as 8 pm. Lodge afterproceedings largely follow English, Scottish, or Irish practices as appropriate.

Information which has recently come to hand indicates that the Ghana Government has in the recent past seized virtually all Masonic Temples in the country, and removed paraphernalia. This disturbing news is somewhat offset by ongoing talks between local Craft leaders and the Government. It appears probable that the temples may be returned to their owners early in 1984. Visitors are therefore strongly advised to seek the advice of their own Grand Lodge, prior to entering the country.

List of Lodges

As Ghana currently possesses eighty-seven regular lodges under three Constitutions, it is not possible to list them all here. However, listed below are those working at the capital city, Accra, together with meeting places of other lodges in Ghana. Postal addresses of Lodges, if applicable, are also noted.

ACCRA

English lodges meet either at the Freemasons' Hall, Liberty Avenue, Accra denoted (1) below, or at the William Galloway Memorial Temple, Liberia Road, Accra denoted (2) below.

Victoria Lodge No 2392	Meets (1), Wednesday on or before the full moon, monthly. Inst: 3rd Saturday, December. P.O. Box 36, Accra.
Accra Lodge No 3063	Meets (2), 1st Wednesday, monthly. Inst: January. P.O. Box 76, Accra.
Harmonic Lodge No 4190	Meets (1), 3rd Saturday, July to May, except December. 3rd Thursday, December. Inst: Saturday after 24th June. P.O. Box 261, Accra.
Three Pillars Lodge No 4867	Meets (2), 3rd Friday, October to March. Inst: November. P.O. Box M.262, Accra.
Travellers Lodge No 6758	Meets (2), 2nd Saturday, even months. Inst: February. P.O. Box 4009, Accra.
Amity Lodge No 7140	Meets (1), 2nd Thursday, monthly, except January. Inst: 2nd Saturday, January. P.O. Box 1430, Accra.
Concordia Lodge No 7199	Meets (1), 2nd Monday, even months, except October. Inst: 4th Saturday, October. P.O. Box 3426, Accra.
Osu Lodge No 7627	Meets (1), 4th Saturday, odd months, except July. Inst: January. P.O. Box 3031, Accra.
Tema Lodge No 7718	Meets (1), 4th Thursday, odd months, except July. Inst: 4th Saturday, July. P.O. Box 1471, Accra.
Sir Charles Tachie-Menson Lodge No 8058	Meets (2) 2nd Saturday, odd months. Inst: September. P.O. Box 770, Accra.
Lodge of Perfection No 8559	Meets (2), Last Friday, even months. Inst: February.
Public Service Lodge No 8587	Meets (2), Last Thursday, even months. Inst: August.
Commerce and Industry Lodge No 8666	Meets (2), 2nd Friday, in January and October; and 3rd Friday, in April and July. Inst: July.
Militia Lodge, No 8723	Meets (2), 1st Saturday, in March, June, September, and December.
Hippocrates Lodge No 8794	Meets (2), 1st Saturday, in February, May, August, and November.
Unicorn Lodge No 8840	Meets (2), 2nd Saturday, in February, May, August, and November. Inst: November.
Circle Lodge No 8964	Meets (2), 1st Monday in April and July; and Last Saturday in September. Inst: 1st Saturday, January.

Scottish lodges in Accra meet either at the Freemasons' Hall, Liberty Avenue, Accra denoted (1) below: or at the William Galloway Memorial Temple, Liberia Road, Accra denoted (2) below; or at the Freemasons' Hall, Kwame Nkrumah Avenue, Accra denoted (3) below; or at the St. George's Temple, McCarthy Hill, Accra, denoted (4) below.

Lodge St. Andrew No 1299	Meets (1), Friday on or before the full moon, monthly.

Lodge Unity No 1466	Meets (1), 2nd Saturday, in January, March, July and September; 4th Saturday in May and November.
Lodge Charity No 1473	Meets (3), 1st Friday, monthly.
Lodge Academic No 1550	Meets (3), Last Saturday, in January, April, July, and October.
Lodge Ghana No 1588	Meets (3), 3rd Friday, in odd months.
Lodge Perfect No 1597	Meets (1), 3rd Tuesday, monthly.
Lodge of Research No 1671	Meets (2), 3rd Saturday, in odd months.
Lodge Olympus No 1698	Meets (4), 1st Friday, in May, June, September, December.
Accra Academy Lodge No 1699	Meets (2), 3rd Friday, in odd months.
Lodge Liberty No 1715	Meets (1), 1st Monday or 2nd Wednesday, in odd months.

The three Irish Lodges located in Accra meet at the Freemasons' Hall, Liberty Avenue, Accra.

Anniversary Lodge No 157	Meets on the 2nd Saturday, monthly.
St Patrick Lodge No 793	Meets on the 1st Tuesday, in odd months.
Greater Accra Lodge No 882	Meets on the 3rd Monday, monthly.

Other Main Meeting Places in Ghana
Achimota, Cape Coast, Keta, Kumasi, Sekondi, Sunyani, Tamale, Tarkwa, Winneba.

GUINEA

French Guinea has possessed lodges stemming from the irregular Grand Orient of France since 1916. However, no regular lodges have yet been established in this country.

GUINEA/BISSAU

This small West African country, formerly a Portuguese colony, has in the past had lodges holding charters from the Grand Orient of Portugal. Their current fate appears to be unknown, and in any case, no regular masonry has ever existed in the country.

IVORY COAST

The Ivory Coast, again a former French possession, has a few irregular French lodges. However, in recent years the Grande Loge Nationale Francaise has warranted three regular lodges at Abidjan. These are Nucleus Lodge No 178; Reflexion Lodge No 214; and L'Equerre Lodge No 270. These lodges meet monthly, at the Masonic Temple, Rue des Majorettes, Abidjan.

KENYA

Kenya, a former British colony, is a large East African country that has enjoyed a long history of political stability and prosperity. It is slightly surprising, therefore, to discover that the Craft in Kenya has not developed to the same extent as in some of the other former British possessions in Africa. English Masonry is controlled by a District Grand Lodge, which also looks after lodges in neighbouring Tanzania. Scotland has four lodges in Kenya under a District Superintendent, while Ireland has so far only one lodge, erected at Nairobi.

The District Grand Lodge of East Africa (Under the United Grand Lodge of England).
Address: Freemasons' Hall, Nairobi, Kenya.
(P.O. Box 40828, Nairobi)
Lodges: 20
The District Superintendent of East Africa (Under the Grand Lodge of Scotland)
Address: Freemasons' Hall, Nairobi, Kenya.
Lodges: 4

History
Masonry first came to Kenya in an organised form in 1904, with the erection of Lodge Harmony, No 3084 EC, at Nairobi. Scotland quickly followed with No 1008, in 1906; also at Nairobi. Ireland's first (and only) Lodge was not chartered until 1950.

The development of freemasonry in Kenya has been steady, but not spectacular. Two more English lodges were warranted at Nairobi about the time of the First World War, with the fourth English lodge there not commencing until 1952. However, in this interim period a number of English lodges had been erected in other Kenyan towns.

The development of Scottish masonry has been fairly slow, with its second lodge in Kenya not being chartered until 1949 following the Second World War. Three others have been established since, with the latest forming at Nairobi in 1965. Two new English lodges have been recently established at Nairobi, both in 1978; and this would appear to indicate a strengthening of momentum.

Notes for visiting in Kenya
The state of the Craft in Kenya is that of good health and vitality. As with other African locations, the lodges of Kenya tend to largely observe the customs and rituals of their various home Grand Lodges. Thus, English lodges enjoy a festive board after a meeting, while Scottish Lodges usually observe 'Harmony'. Perhaps the only addition to a Toast List in Kenya is to begin with a toast to 'The President and Republic of Kenya'. Dress for Kenyan lodges is a dark suit, although Safari Suits are sometimes worn. The majority of lodges meet at a time between 6.30 pm and 7.30 pm.

List of Lodges
As the travelling freemason will doubtlessly arrive in Kenya by way of Nairobi, the capital city; listed below are the lodges meeting at Freemasons' Hall, Nairobi.

English Lodges

Lodge Harmony No 3084	Meets 1st Tuesday, monthly. Inst: May. P.O. Box 40118.

Orient Lodge No 3703	Meets 2nd Saturday, monthly. Inst: February. P.O. Box 40152.
Progress Lodge No 3737	Meets 3rd Tuesday, October to July, except December. Inst: January. P.O. Box 40162, Nairobi.
Lodge of Nairobi No 7187	Meets 1st Thursday, monthly, except January. Inst: December. P.O. Box 45583, Nairobi.
Meridian Lodge No 9442	Meets on the Friday before the 4th Saturday, odd months, plus June. Inst: November.
Peace and Prosperity Lodge No 8852	Meets on the 1st Wednesday, in January, February, March, May, July, October and November. Inst: January.
Fidelity Lodge No 8853	Meets 3rd Wednesday, monthly, except April, August and December. Inst: March.

Scottish Lodges

Lodge Scotia No 1008	Meets 2nd Tuesday, monthly, except August and December.
The Lodge of the Highlands No 1439	Meets 3rd Thursday, monthly except July, August, December.
Lodge Osotua No 1528	Meets 1st Friday, monthly, except January and December.
Lodge Unity No 1611	Meets 3rd Friday, monthly, except April, August, December.

Irish Lodge

Hibernia Lodge No 749	Meets 4th Tuesday, monthly, except July, August, December.

LIBERIA

This interesting West African Republic was formed in 1821 by freed American Negro slaves. Its masonry is derived from the irregular Prince Hall Grand Lodges of the United States. Again, no regular freemasonry currently exists in this country.

LIBYA

Libya was once an Italian colony, and the Grand Orient of Italy had three lodges in Tripoli during the Italian occupation. These lodges appear not to have survived Libyan independence.

MADAGASCAR (MALAGASY REPUBLIC)

Madagascar, another former French colony, has irregular lodges owing allegience to either the Grand Orient of France, or the Grand Lodge of France. However, only a few years ago, the regular Grande Loge Nationale Francaise formed Lodge Chaine D'Union Outre-Mer No 278, at Tananarive; thus providing regular masonry with a foothold that should lead to further development.

MALAWI

This elongated East African Republic is another country that formerly formed part of the British African colonies, and as such was the recipient of regular masonry.

Scotland currently reports four lodges in the country, all of which report directly to Edinburgh. A further two lodges hold English warrants, and these are administered by the English District Grand Lodge of Zimbabwe. The details of these six lodges are as follows:

Lodge Blantyre No 956 SC.	Meets Freemasons' Hall, King's Road, Blantyre, Malawi; 2nd Thursday monthly.
Lodge David Livingstone No 1162 SC.	Meets Masonic Temple, Zomba, Malawi; 3rd Thursday monthly, except December.
Lodge Angoni No 1404 SC.	Meets Masonic Temple, Lilongwe; 3rd Friday monthly. P.O. Box 76, Lilongwe, Malawi.
Lodge Viphya No 1571 SC.	Meets Freemasons' Hall, King's Road, Blantyre, Malawi; 1st Friday in odd months except May.
St George Lodge No 7763 EC.	Meets Freemasons' Hall, King's Road, Blantyre, Malawi; 4th Friday February to November; 4th Saturday January. Inst: February.
Nyala Lodge No 8862 EC.	Meets Masonic Temple, Lilongwe, Malawi; 1st Friday in even months, except June. Inst: 1st Saturday June.

MAURITIUS

Mauritius is a former French island located in the Indian Ocean to the west of Madagascar. It contains two lodges, an English one dating from 1877; and a Scottish one dating from 1864. Interestingly both have the same name, and this name augers very well indeed for the reception of any masonic visitor to the island. The details of both lodges are as follows:

The Lodge of Friendship No 1696 EC.	Meets at the Masonic Temple, Phoenix, Mauritius; 2nd Friday March to December. Inst: December.
Lodge Friendship No 439 SC.	Meets at the Masonic Temple, Phoenix, Mauritius; 1st Thursday monthly.

MOZAMBIQUE

Mozambique is a former Portuguese colony which now possesses a totalitarian government, and one would suspect that it would not permit Masonry within its borders. There were several irregular Portuguese-warranted lodges working in the country in the 1960s, but it is most doubtful if they still exist.

MOROCCO

This former French colony has an interesting masonic history. The irregular Grand Orient of France formed five lodges there, beginning in 1891. Subsequently, the Grand Lodge of France and the Grand Orient of Italy erected lodges in the country. In 1902, Lodge Coronation No 934 was established with a Scottish warrant, and England chartered New Friendship Lodge, No 4997, in 1927. Both these lodges started their lives at Tangier, but both soon moved to Gibraltar. New Friendship Lodge subsequently changed its name to Gibraltar Lodge. Moroccan Independence in 1956 would appear to have not been condusive to tranquil masonic development. Nonetheless, the Grand Lodge 'Atlas' of Morocco was erected at Casablanca in

1967. It was formed by three lodges then under the Grand Lodge of Switzerland. It is irregular.

NAMIBIA (SOUTH WEST AFRICA)

South West Africa was originally a colony of Germany, and three German lodges were erected there prior to the First World War. The adverse result for Germany in that war saw it lose its African possessions, and the German lodges also perished. Since the First World War, South West Africa has been under South African Administration, although its control of the territory is disputed by the United Nations.

In 1925, English Masonry came to the area. In that year Damaraland Lodge No 4758 received a warrant to operate at Windhoek. Five more English lodges have been established in the Territory since the Second World War, and together all these English lodges now form the English District Grand Lodge of South West Africa.

Scottish masonry came to South West Africa in 1923, preceding the English by two years. The first Scottish lodge was Lodge Caledonian No 1307, meeting at Keetmanshoop. Six Scottish lodges now work happily in the Territory, of which one (No 1613) works in German, and another (No 1616) in Afrikaans. The Scottish lodges form part of the Scottish District Grand Lodge of the Western Province of the Cape of Good Hope, based at Cape Town, South Africa. In recent years, the Grand Lodge of South Africa has chartered a lodge in South West Africa. This is Makalani Lodge No 114, operating at Grootfontesin. Details of the English and Scottish lodges are as follows:

English Lodges

Damaraland Lodge No 4758	*Meets at Freemasons' Hall, Leutwein Street, Windhoek; 2nd Thursday February to November. Inst: June.*
Etosha Lodge No 7148	Meets at the Masonic Temple, Otjiwarango; 2nd Friday February to November, except May. Inst: 3rd Saturday, May.
Omutena Lodge No 7376	Meets at Freemasons' Hall, Leutwein Street, Windhoek; 3rd Thursday February to November. Inst: April.
Optima Lodge No 7380	Meets at the Masonic Temple, Oranjemund; 3rd Wednesday except February and March. Inst: 3rd Saturday March.
Namutoni Lodge No 7473	Meets at the Community House, Tsumeb; 2nd Wednesday February to November. Inst: August.
Welwetschia Lodge No 8768	Meets at the Masonic Temple, 7th Street, Walvis Bay; 3rd Tuesday except January and December. Inst: April.

Scottish Lodges

Lodge Caledonian No 1307	Meets at the Masonic Temple, Keetmanshoop; 2nd Saturday February to November.
Lodge Fish Hoek No 1390	Meets at the MOTH Hall, Recreation Road, Fish Hoek; 3rd Tuesday monthly.

Lodge Dunedin Star No 1454	Meets at Freemaons' Hall, Leutwin Street, Windhoek; 4th Thursday, February to November.
Lodge Namib No 1489	Meets at the Masonic Temple, 7th Street, Walvis Bay; 1st Tuesday monthly except January.
Lodge Zum Kreuz des Sudens No 1613	Meets at Freemasons' Hall, Leutwein Street, Windhoek; 3rd Tuesday monthly except January and December.
Lodge Benguela No 1616	Meets at Freemasons' Hall, Leutwein Street, Windhoek; 1st Wednesday monthly, except January and December.

It is interesting to note that Lodge Zum Kreuz des Sudens was originally one of the three German lodges warranted by the Grand Lodge of Hamburg. It was re-erected in 1928, and closed in 1933 under Nazi pressure. It was revived under the Scottish Constitution in 1965. It works in German according to the *Schroeder Ritual*, and was the first Scottish lodge to be permitted to do so.

NIGERIA

No other country in Africa possesses more lodges than Nigeria, except South Africa and Ghana. Nigeria's current eighty-five lodges work under district or Provincial Grand Lodges under England, Ireland and Scotland.

The District Grand Lodge of Nigeria (Under the United Grand Lodge of England)
    Address: P.O. Box 227, Lagos, Nigeria.
    Principal Temple: St George's Hall, 28 Broad Street, Lagos.
    Lodges: 27
The Provincial Grand Lodge of Nigeria (Under the Grand Lodge of Ireland)
    Address: P.O. Box 279, Lagos, Nigeria.
    Principal Temple: St. George's Hall, 28 Broad Street, Lagos.
    Lodges: 9
The District Grand Lodge of Nigeria (Under the Grand Lodge of Scotland).
    Address: P.O. Box 372, Lagos, Nigeria.
    Principal Temple: St George's Hall, 28 Broad Street, Lagos.
    Lodges: 49

History
The English Grand Lodge had the pleasure of seeing the first lodge in Nigeria. This was Lagos Lodge No 1171, established at Lagos in 1867. It was followed in 1897 by St John's Lodge No 2668, also English, and also erected at Lagos. Scotland's first lodge, Academic No 1150, commenced operations at Lagos in 1915. McDonald Lodge No 197 was the first Irish Lodge in the country. It was warranted at Calabar in 1896.

While England and Ireland preceded Scotland in establishing lodges in Nigeria, Scottish masonry in the fullness of time would appear to have become the dominant force in the country. Shortly after the Second World War, there were twenty English, nine Scottish and two Irish lodges in Nigeria. However, by the 1980s, Scotland had forty-nine lodges in the country, compared to twenty-seven for England, and nine for Ireland. Indeed, Scotland's main activity has been outside Lagos. There is scarcely a town of any size in Nigeria which does not possess at least one Scottish lodge. Larger centres, such as Ibadan, Ebute Metta, and Port Harcourt have several lodges under the various Constitutions.

The racial question appears to have been a problem in Nigerian lodges between the two World Wars. In the 1930s some lodges refused to admit Negroes to membership, while in others they were freely admitted, with some lodges becoming predominantly black. Happily, these problems have long since passed, and men of many races continue to compose the Craft in Nigeria, which has expanded steadily for many years, and continues to do so.

Notes for Visitors to Nigeria

The customs and working of the Craft in Nigeria closely parellel those already discussed under Ghana, so it is not proposed to embark on extensive repetition here. Dress for lodge meetings is a dark suit, or sometimes a dinner suit, particularly for Installation meetings. Lodges mostly meet in the early evening, at a time between 7 pm and 8 pm. All lodges have some form of after proceedings, and many follow the practice of a formal dinner with Toast List afterwards. While members contribute to the costs of any dinners held, visitors are never expected to follow suit. Nigerian lodges are famous for their hospitality, and visitors can expect a warm reception.

List of Lodges

As Lagos will doubtlessly be the first or main port of call for visitors to Nigeria, lodges meeting at that location are listed below. Postal addresses are provided, as applicable. Visitors desirous of attending meetings elsewhere in Nigeria can readily obtain assistance when in Lagos. All lodges listed meet at St George's Hall, Lagos.

Lagos Lodge No 1171 EC	Meets 1st Thursday odd months. Inst: January. P.O. Box 227, Lagos.
St John's Lodge No 2668 EC	Meets 2nd Tuesday, even months, except June. Inst: June 24th. P.O. Box 227, Lagos.
St George's Lodge No 3065 EC	Meets 1st Friday monthly. Inst: September. P.O. Box 227, Lagos.
Traveller's Lodge No 3726 EC	Meets 3rd Saturday monthly. Inst: June. P.O. Box 227, Lagos.
Nigeria Master's Lodge No 7628 EC	Meets 1st Monday in March, July and November. Inst: March. P.O. Box 227, Lagos.
Excelsior Lodge No 643 IC	Meets 1st Saturday even months.
Harmony Lodge No 847 IC	Meets 2nd Thursday monthly.
Surulere Lodge No 864 IC	Meets 3rd Wednesday monthly.
Tranquility Lodge No 875 IC	Meets 4th Tuesday odd months.
Lodge Academic No 1150 SC	Meets 2nd Saturday even months. P.O. Box 3143, Lagos.
Lodge Scotia No 1166 SC	Meets 3rd Friday in January, April, July and October.
Lodge Faith No 1271 SC	Meets 4th Saturday monthly. P.O. Box 1111, Marina, Lagos.

Lodge Trinity No 1674 SC	Meets 2nd Friday in March, June, September and December.
Lodge Classic No 1678 SC	Meets 2nd Tuesday in March, June and December; and 2nd Saturday, September. P.O. Box 1135, Lagos.
Lodge Eko No 1703 SC	Meets 1st Tuesday in March, June, September and December.
Lodge Lagos Island No 1717 SC	Meets 3rd Saturday in March, June, September and December. P.O. Box 2098, Lagos.

Other Principal Meeting Places in Nigeria

Calabar:	Masonic Hall, Calabar Road, Calabar.
	Hope Temple, Hawkins Road, Calabar.
Ebute Metta	(a suburb of Lagos):
	Masonic Hall, Printer's Lane, Railway Compound, Ebute Metta.
	Forester's Mainland Hall, Surulere, Ebute Metta.
Benin City:	Liberty Masonic Temple, Mission Road, Benin City.
Ibadan:	Oluyoke Masonic Temple, Oke Ado, Ibadan.
	Masonic Temple, Old Barracks, Ibadan.
Kaduna:	Masonic Hall, College Road, Kaduna.
Kano:	Masonic Hall, 29 Airport Road, Kano.
Onitsha:	Masonic Hall, Egerton Road, Onitsha.

REUNION

Reunion is an island located in the Indian Ocean to the west of Madagascar, and is a French possession. It contains a lodge erected by the irregular Grand Orient of France. No regular freemasonry has yet found its way there.

SEYCHELLES

This small island group lies in the Indian Ocean to the north of Madagascar. One English lodge works in the islands, dating from 1977. Its details are as follows:

Seychelles Lodge No 8789	Meets at the Masonic Rooms, Marie Laure Drive, Bel Ombre, Mahe, Seychelles; 2nd Wednesday monthly. Inst: September.

SENEGAL

Another former French colony, Senegal contains lodges erected by the irregular French Grand Lodges. However, the regular Grande Loge Nationale Française has been active there in recent years. It began with warranting Kumen Lodge No 133, in 1968. This was followed by Ansitoe Lodge No 149, established in 1972; and the even more recent Adam Lodge No 244. All three lodges meet at the Masonic Temple, Patte-d'Oie Street, Dakar, Senegal; and meet twice monthly.

SIERRA LEONE

Sierra Leone, as a British colony, was one of the oldest in West Africa, and as such was an early recipient of freemasonry. The first lodge erected in the Colony was the

Freetown Lodge of Good Intent No 721; which was established under English warrant in 1820. Unfortunately, it fell on hard times and was erased in 1862. Today, the Craft in Sierra Leone remains strong and expansive. England boasts a District Grand Lodge, with seven lodges under it (and two more in the Gambia). Scotland also has a District Grand Lodge constituted by twelve lodges in Sierra Leone, and one in the Gambia. One lodge works at Freetown under Irish warrant.

The District Grand Lodge of Sierra Leone and the Gambia (Under the Grand Lodge of England)
    Address: Freetown Masonic Temple, 30 Lightfoot Boston Street, Freetown.
    Lodges: 9
The District Grand Lodge of Sierra Leone and the Gambia (Under the Grand Lodge of Scotland)
    Address: George Ackland Masonic Temple, 24 Lightfoot Boston Street, Freetown.
    Lodges: 13

History
The revival of masonry in Sierra Leone came with the establishment of Freetown Lodge No 1955, EC; erected in 1882. Further English warrants were granted for lodges at Freetown in 1894 (St George Lodge No 2506), and 1899 (Rokell Lodge No 2798). The first Scottish lodge to receive a charter was Sierra Leone Highland Lodge No 997; in 1905. Many more English and Scottish lodges have been established down to the present time, including the country's first (and so far only) Irish lodge (Trinity Lodge No 848), in 1972. The latest addition to the strongly expanding Craft in Sierra Leone was the Lodge Sierra No 1743, erected only in 1982. The stable political situation in Sierra Leone, coupled with the increasing number of non-white masons enjoying membership, would appear to make the future of freemasonry in this country certain.

Notes for Visitors in Sierra Leone
As is usual for expatriate British masonry in Africa, the lodges in Sierra Leone follow the customs and rituals of the Constitution from which each obtained its warrant. English lodges follow their meetings with the traditional festive board. The only notable addition to the usual Toast List is to commence with a Toast to the 'President and Republic of Sierra Leone'. A toast to 'Sister Constitutions' is often also proposed, particularly at Installation Meetings. Dress for meetings is a dark suit, and the majority of lodges commence between 6.30 pm and 7.30 pm. Earlier starting times are often set for Installations. It should be noted that several different faiths are represented in Sierra Leone, and this is naturally reflected in the membership of the lodges. Since 1970, a publication entitled the *Masonic Memento* has been locally published. This small pocketbook sets out the meeting details of all lodges in Sierra Leone and the Gambia in calendar form, and often contains short articles of masonic interest.

List of Lodges
Almost all the lodges located in Sierra Leone meet at its capital city, Freetown, which contains three masonic meeting places. These are: the Freetown Masonic Temple, 30 Lightfoot Boston Street, Freetown denoted (1) below; the George Ack-

land Masonic Temple, 24 Lightfoot Boston Street, Freetown denoted (2) below; and the Rokell Masonic Temple, Rokell Street, Tower Hill, Freetown denoted (3) below. The following are the details for lodges meeting at Freetown:

English Lodges

Freetown Lodge No 1955	Meets (1); 2nd Wednesday monthly. Inst: December.
St George's Lodge No 2506	Meets (2); 1st Tuesday monthly. Inst: April.
Rokell Lodge No 2798	Meets (3); 3rd Thursday monthly. Inst: November.
Loyal Lodge No 3719	Meets (1); 1st Thursday monthly. Inst: May.
Progressive Lodge No 6431	Meets (1); 3rd Friday monthly. Inst: January.
Wilberforce Lodge No 6432	Meets (3); 3rd Tuesday odd months. Inst: March.
Granville Lodge No 7212	Meets (1); 2nd Monday monthly. Inst: October.

Scottish Lodges

Sierra Leone Highland Lodge No 997	Meets (2); 1st Monday monthly.
Lodge Academic No 1138	Meets (2); 2nd Thursday monthly.
Lodge Tranquillity No 1446	Meets (2); 2nd Saturday in February, April, June, August and October.
Lodge Harmony No 1448	Meets (2); 1st Saturday monthly.
Traveller's Lodge No 1455	Meets (2); Last Friday monthly.
Mount Aureol Lodge No 1612	Meets (3); 4th Wednesday September to May.
Lodge Sapiens No 1620	Meets (2); 4th Saturday monthly.
Lodge Leone No 1644	Meets (2); 1st Wednesday in February, April, October and December.
The Earl of Eglinton & Winton Lodge No 1650	Meets (2); 4th Wednesday in March, June, September, October and December.
Lodge Sierra No 1743	Meets (3);

Irish Lodge

Trinity Lodge No 848	Meets (2); 1st Friday odd months. Inst: September.

SOMALIA

This East African country, located at the base of the Horn of Africa, once possessed a lodge established by the irregular Grand Orient of France, but it is presumed to have expired.

SOUTH AFRICA

South Africa contains the most diverse package of regular masonry anywhere in the world, and as such it requires careful examination. This large country possesses one self-governing Grand Lodge, six District Grand Lodges under the English Constitution, four District Grand Lodges under the Scottish Constitution, three Provincial Grand Lodges under the Irish Constitution, and finally a single lodge holding a warrant from the Grand East of the Netherlands. It can be readily seen, therefore, that the discussion below must be somewhat complex. However, the wide variety of regular masonry in South Africa prevents a detailed examination of any one area. Therefore, a generalised commentary must form the approach. The basic details of the government of the Craft in South Africa are as follows:

The United Grand Lodge of England
Founded: 1717

English masonry in South Africa is ranged under six District Grand Lodges, whose details are noted below:

The District Grand Lodge of Natal.
  Address: P.O. Box 386, Pietermaritzburg, Natal. 3205.
  Principal Temple: Masonic Temple, 25 Hunt Road, Durban.
  Lodges: 46

The District Grand Lodge of the Orange Free State.
  Address: P.O. Box 12, Bethlehem 9700, Orange Free State.
  Principal Temple: Masonic Temple, Spitzhop, Bloemfontein.
  Lodges: 15

The District Grand Lodge of South Africa, Central Division.
  Address: P.O. Box 124, Kimberley, Cape Province. 8300.
  Principal Temple: Masonic Temple, Dudoitspan Road, Kimberley.
  Lodges: 14

The District Grand Lodge of South Africa, Eastern Division.
  Address: P.O. Box 203, Port Elizabeth. 6000.
  Principal Temple: Masonic Temple, Landsdowne Place, Port Elizabeth.
  Lodges: 41

The District Grand Lodge of South Africa, Western Division.
  Address: P.O. Box 70, Howard Place. 7450.
  Principal Temple: Masonic Temple, Piers Road, Wynberg, Pinelands (Suburban Capetown).
  Lodges: 35

The District Grand Lodge of the Transvaal.
  Address: P.O. Box 17037, Hillbrow, Transvaal. 2038.
  Principal Temple: Freemasons' Hall, 6 Park Lane, Parktown, Johannesburg.
  Lodges: 119

The Grand Lodge of Ireland
Founded: 1725

Three Provincial Grand Lodges:

The Provincial Grand Lodge of South Africa, Northern.
  Address: P.O. Box 2919, Johannesburg, 2000.
  Principal Temple: Freemason's Hall, 6 Park Lane, Parktown, Johannesburg.
  Lodges: 31

The Provincial Grand Lodge of Southern Cape Province.
  Address: P.O. Box 2059, Cape Town. 8000.
  Principal Temple: Temple de Goede Hoop (Temple of Good Hope), Bouquet Street, Cape Town.
  Lodges: 10

The Provincial Grand Lodge of Natal.
  Address: P.O. Box 574, Durban. 4000.
  Principal Temple: Port Natal Masonic Temple, Berea Road, Durban.
  Lodges: 17

The Grand Lodge of Scotland
Founded: 1736

Four District Grand Lodges:

The District Grand Lodge of the Eastern Province of the Cape of Good Hope.
Address: P.O. Box 1212, East London. 5200.
Principal Temple: Masonic Temple, Landsdowne Place, Port Elizabeth.
Lodges: 14

The District Grand Lodge of Natal.
Address: P.O. Box 1026, Durban. 4000.
Principal Temple: Masonic Temple, 25 Hunt Road, Durban.
Lodges: 25

The District Grand Lodge of the Transvaal, Orange Free State, and Northern Cape.
Address: P.O. Box 5713, Johannesburg. 2000.
Principal Temple: Freemasons' Hall, 6 Park Lane, Parktown, Johannesburg.
Lodges: 100.

The District Grand Lodge of the Western Province of the Cape of Good Hope.
Address: c/o 3 Birkett Road, Rondebosch, Cape Town. 7700.
Principal Temple: Temple de Goede Hoop, Bouquet Street, Cape Town.
Lodges: 15

The Grand Lodge of South Africa
Founded: 1961

Address: Grand Lodge Centre, 67 13th Street, Orange Grove, Johannesburg. 2192.
Postal Address: P.O. Box 46203, Orange Grove, Johannesburg. 2119
Lodges: 128   Permits Dual and Plural Membership. *Membership:* 4,362.
Descent: Netherlands. *Government:* Appointive Grand Lodge.
Courtesy Degrees: All correspondence must be through Grand Lodges.
Minimum Time Lapse between Degrees: One Month. *Ritual:* Netherlandic (with adaptations)
Main Publications: Constitution. Annual Year Book. Annual Proceedings.

Grand East of the Netherlands
Founded: 1756

Grand Inspectorate of South Africa.
Address: P.O. Box 3786, Johannesburg. 2000.
Lodges: 1

History
South Africa is a bilingual country with two official languages, English and Afrikaans. All official documents, street signs, and so on, must be printed in both languages. Not surprisingly the majority of citizens are fluent in both languages. A visitor should be aware that because a question to a stranger is answered in English, that stranger might not necessarily use English as his first language. In South Africa, it is considered common courtesy to reply in the language of the first person; and the Afrikaans-speaking South African will most readily change to English when speaking to visitors. Most visitors to South Africa will be aware of the problems experienced in this country, particularly in terms of the racial question. Visitors are cautioned to remember that there are two sides to every argument. With this point recalled, the visitor to South Africa need not fear giving offence. It is not proposed

to dwell further on these matters here, and doubtlessly each travelling freemason will experience only warmth and hospitality in his sojourn into the realms of South African masonry.

The first lodge formed in Southern Africa was warranted by the Grand Lodge of Holland (now the Grant East of the Netherlands), at Cape Town in 1772. This was Goede Hoop Lodge No 18. The first English lodge was erected in 1811, also at Cape Town. The year 1860 saw the appearance of the first Scottish lodge, again formed at Cape Town; and Irish lodges followed. Each of these four Constitutions continued to warrant lodges, and this process continues. The earlier part of this century saw the English, Irish and Scottish lodges being formed into District or Provincial Grand Lodges; and this provided further impetus for masonic development.

Until 1961, the four Constitutions—English, Irish, Scottish, and Netherlandic— operated in South Africa through their respective Districts and Provinces. At that time a situation arose in which the Grand East of the Netherlands was seen as at risk of losing the recognition of the other three Grand Lodges. These misunderstandings at Grand Lodge level were rapidly cleared up, but in the meantime the possible consequences of such a split were viewed, quite naturally, with deep concern in South Africa, where the closest amity had always existed between the four Constitutions. It was accordingly agreed that the Netherlandic lodges should be allowed to form a new Grand Lodge. However, it needs to be understood that the clear intention was to preserve and protect the fraternal amity of all South African lodges, and not to form a National Grand Lodge, as such. As a result, the Grand Lodge of South Africa was duly formed, but there was no change in the allegiences or operations of the English, Irish and Scottish lodges. All the Netherlandic lodges, with only one exception, joined the new Grand Lodge of South Africa; and the Grand East of the Netherlands undertook not to issue any further warrants in the country.

Today, the constitutional position remains unchanged, with the English, Irish, Scottish and South African bodies free to erect new lodges as they think fit. Any move towards a National Grand Lodge in the sense of uniting all regular lodges under a single Grand Body would require an entirely new approach, and this would appear unlikely in the foreseeable future. In the meantime, all South African masons enjoy the freedom of constitutional choice, under conditions of fraternal amity.

Notes for Visiting in South Africa

1. MEETING TIMES, AND DRESS

The majority of South African lodges meet between 7 pm and 8 pm. Standard dress is a dinner suit, and white gloves are worn by members of South African Constitution lodges. In Scottish and Irish lodges, often only lodge officers wear gloves; while each English lodge decides for itself whether white gloves will be worn. If so, they are worn by all members. A visitor to a lodge in South Africa should therefore be certain to arrive prior to 7 pm, to enable his masonic identity to be established. In all cases, a visitor can expect to be examined by one or more Past Masters. A visitor from outside South Africa should not be dissuaded from visiting if he is not carrying a dinner suit, as he will be welcomed to attend in a lounge suit.

2. LODGE AFTERPROCEEDINGS

All lodges in South Africa, regardless of affiliation, hold some form of 'afterproceedings' following the conclusion of a lodge meeting. For the sake of convenience and clarity, each Constitution can be dealt with separately in this regard.

English Lodges: A festive board follows every English lodge meeting. This may take two forms—Dining or Sem-Dining. At a Dining Festive Board, a full Toast List is proposed, in combination with a 'Sit-Down Dinner'.

Semi-Dining is in effect a 'Stand-Up' supper. Indeed, the two practices are usually termed simply Dining, or Supper. The festive board method employed by English Lodges varies between the two from lodge to lodge. Some use the full dinner method at every meeting, while others conduct a Supper. Still others use a combination. However, most English lodges have a full dinner following an Installation Meeting. An example of a full Toast List is as follows:

1. 'The State President' is the first toast of the evening. In some lodges this may be 'The President and the Republic of South Africa', while in others simply 'Our Country.'
2. 'Our Ancient Craft', or simply 'The Craft'. This toast replaces in most lodges the usual English Toast of 'The Queen and the Craft.'
3. 'The Most Worshipful the Grand Master.'
4. 'The Right Worshipful Pro Grand Master, the Right Worshipful Deputy Grand Master, the Right Worshipful Assistant Grand Master, and Grand Lodge Officers Past and Present.'
5. 'The Right Worshipful District Grand Master.'
6. 'The Deputy District Grand Master, Assistant District Grand Master, and District Grand Lodge Officers, Past and Present.'
7. 'The Heads of Sister Constitutions, their Deputies, and Representatives.'
8. 'The Worshipful Master.'
9. 'Visiting Brethren.'
10. 'Absent Brethren.'
11. 'The Tyler's Toast.'

The above is an example of a full Toast List that a visitor may experience when attending an English lodge in South Africa. However, toasts do vary from masonic district to masonic district, and widely between lodges themselves. Several toasts are optional and may only be given when a recipient is actually present. The toast to Sister Constitutions is often only given on Nights of Installation. The Toast to the Master is only given on such an occasion. Similarly, the toast to Absent Brethren is not used in many lodges. A reply to a toast is only given if the recipient is present. A full Toast List is used at most festive boards which compose of a full dinner. At 'Suppers', the list is usually abbreviated.

Irish Lodges: Irish afterproceedings tend to be quite informal affairs. A supper is served, and toasts are limited, often to 'Our Country', 'The Grand Master and Grand Lodge', and the 'Visitors'. Visitors may be asked to reply to the Visitor's Toast, but prior notice will be given. No charity collection is usually taken. On Nights of Installation, a full dinner will follow the meeting, and a more extensive Toast List will be used, similar to the English Toast List just outlined.

Scottish Lodges: As with the Irish, Scottish lodges tend to have informal suppers associated with their lodge meetings, known under the Scottish Constitution as 'Harmony'. Toasts are kept to a bare minimum. Again, however, Scottish lodges tend to revert to a formal dinner and full Toast List on Nights of Installation, similar to the English pattern.

South African Constitution Lodges: In South African Constitution lodges, a formal Festive Board-type arrangement is usually only held after the working of a First Degree ceremony, but even then a lodge may decide to hold an informal supper. However, if the afterproceedings are to be formal, a dinner will normally be served, and those attending will be allotted seats. The toast list will be brief, but formal, and will include a toast to the candidate. The toast to the visitors often provides guests with the opportunity to present fraternal greetings. A usual custom under S.A.C. lodges is for the Master of the lodge to repair to the door to bid farewell as brethren leave at the end of the night.

Lodge Afterproceedings in general: 'Masonic Fires' generally accompany the proposition of many of the formal toasts that are proposed, regardless of which lodge is attended. Each Constitution has, by and large, 'Fires' peculiar to it, or to a particular degree that a candidate has taken on the night. Visitors unfamiliar with these matters can readily seek guidance from a suitable lodge member.

For the great majority of lodges in South Africa, the costs of formal dinners are not covered by members' lodge dues; although in many, informal suppers may be covered. Under the English Constitution, lodges usually make a charge on members attending the festive board, whether it be a dinner or a supper, and this price is printed on the lodge summons. As a result of South African licensing laws, the cost of any liquor, if served, is included in the charge made upon members. Nevertheless, there are still English lodges that charge higher dues to include dining and refreshment costs.

However, regardless of which method any individual lodge uses to accommodate the costs of dining, a visitor will never be called upon to pay, and an offer to do so may offend. However, if a visitor frequents one lodge on a regular basis, a contribution to costs will be favourably received. In any case, a donation from a visitor to any charity collection a lodge may undertake is always appreciated.

3. NIGHTS OF INSTALLATION

All lodges in South Africa install a new Master annually. However, only English, Irish, and Scottish lodges use the Inner Working as part of the Ceremony. Masters of the South African Constitution are installed in a shorter ceremony, which may be witnessed by all Masons present, regardless of masonic rank. However, Installed Masters under the S.A.C. may attend a Board of Installed Masters at an Installation under the other three Constitutions, and so witness the actual Installation of a new English, Irish or Scottish Master. Irish lodges generally install in January, February or March. Scottish lodges often prefer to install on the Feast Day of a Saint (for example, St Andrew's Day), although many still opt for a convenient and regular time each year. The Installation of an English lodge is fixed to an annual time, with the widest variations of day quite evident.

Visitors are welcome to attend Installation Meetings, but they should if at all possible give plenty of notice of their intention to be present. Indeed, this applies to ordinary meetings, as such notice assists with catering arrangements. Nevertheless, a visitor should not feel prevented from visiting if he cannot provide notice. As has already been mentioned, a formal dinner often accompanies an Installation Meeting in South Africa, but not always. Outside the main cities, in country areas, Installation afterproceedings are sometimes attended by the ladies of members and visitors. Where this practice occurs, toasts are often limited, or are dispensed with altogether except for a toast to 'The Ladies'. Again, there are some lodges which replace more usual afterproceedings with a dinner dance. Visitors are advised to make appropriate inquiries as to which form of afterproceedings is to be used by the lodge whose Installation they intend to visit. It should also be noted that Installation Meetings often commence at an earlier time than normal meetings. Lodges installing on a Saturday usually commence in the afternoon, allowing afterproceedings to commence in the early evening.

4. OF VISITING IN GENERAL

The procedures for visiting lodges in South Africa vary between Constitutions, and between lodges themselves. Scottish lodges generally require all members and visitors to be present in the lodge room prior to opening. Once this had been effected, the Master and his principal officers will then form a procession into the lodge.

The English lodges follow one of two systems. The first is most similar to the Scottish practice, whereby members and visitors repair to the lodge room prior to opening. However, not all English lodges follow the procession procedure. In some lodges, the Master and officers will be present from the start, and will open the lodge as soon as everyone is in readiness. The second alternative practice employed by some English lodges is to open the lodge in the presence of members only. Visitors will not then be admitted until after the lodge has dealt with its ordinary business (minutes, correspondence, accounts, etc.)

Irish lodges largely follow a pattern similar to the Scottish, except that visitors to an Irish lodge can expect to be asked for the password leading to the first degree upon entering. Visitors unfamiliar with this procedure are advised to discuss it with an appropriate lodge officer after they have completed normal avouchment procedures.

South African Constitution lodges normally open with only lodge members present. After the opening, visitors are then admitted according to rank and seniority. Visitors may seek the permission of the lodge's Master to be present for the opening, and such permission will normally be granted, particularly to visitors from outside South Africa who may not have witnessed such an opening before. At the discretion of the Master of the lodge, and depending on the lodge's programme for the evening and the number of visitors, admittances will be handled by one of the two following methods. The first method involves the initial admittance of all visitors below the rank of Installed Master; to be followed by a second admittance of Sitting Masters and Past Masters, who enter in terms of juniority.

The second method consists of three admittances. The first is that of all visitors below the rank of Installed Master who are not accompanying the Master of their lodge. The second consists of all Past Masters not representing their lodge, or not accompanying their Master or his representative. The third admittance is that of deputations from other lodges, whereupon members thereof will accompany the lodge Master, or his representative.

However, there are other variances to these admission procedures, but the above suffice as examples. In determining the order of the entrance of lodges, the Seniority of lodges (by number), and their Constitution (by age) prevails, although South African Constitution lodges are taken last. Lodges enter in order of juniority. Thus, the order of lodge admission is Scottish first, Irish second, English third, and South African last. Upon entering, visitors below the rank of Installed Master will be directed to seats by the Master of Ceremonies, where they remain standing until all visitors are admitted. Both Sitting and Past Masters will be escorted to the East, whereupon they will be welcomed by the Master, and then invited to sit on the Master's right. It may also be noted that in lodges of other Constitutions, regardless of admission methods, Installed Masters will always be invited to sit in the East.

In the course of the closing ceremonies of all lodges in South Africa, except those under the South African Constitution, visitors may be called upon to convey fraternal greetings to the Master, who will respond suitably. The Master, or his representative, will convey greetings in the case of a visiting lodge. Individual visitors from overseas are most welcome to convey greetings from their own lodge and Constitution, should the opportunity arise. In S.A.C. lodges, visitors will be thanked for their attendance during the closing ceremonies, but fraternal greetings will not normally be exchanged, this practice usually being reserved for the lodge afterproceedings. Lastly, it is worthy of note that virtually all lodges in South Africa take up a charity collection in association with meetings. In many this will be done during the closing ceremonies, in others at the afterproceedings, while in some a collection will be taken both inside and outside the lodge. In a few lodges, a charity levy is imposed as part of annual lodge dues, and these lodges as a result may be less regular in this regard. In any case, visitors are well advised to carry a small sum of money with them for this purpose.

Visitors coming to South Africa from overseas are advised to make contact, at least in the first instance, with the appropriate Grand Lodge, District Grand Lodge, or Provincial Grand Lodge, under which they propose to visit. The addresses of the majority of major masonic temples in South Africa have already been noted, and probably the best to attend are those in Johannesburg and Cape Town. Visitors will find that the largest temples are staffed, from whom they will receive full assistance. In the second instance, a visitor can make inquiries at the masonic temple in the town in which he finds himself. Virtually every town in the country possesses a masonic temple, and most have a caretaker. Outside each is usually located a notice board which states where the caretaker or lodge secretary can be contacted.

5. INTERESTING ASPECTS OF MASONRY IN SOUTH AFRICA

There are many temples in South Africa of great interest, and some of the larger ones possess a library and museum. Two in particular merit special mention. The Temple de Goede Hoop in Cape Town is a remarkable structure, and is the birthplace of masonry in Africa. Freemasons' Hall, Johannesburg, is the largest masonic structure in Africa. It is an imposing edifice, housing four temples, the largest of which seats 280 people. It also contains dining rooms, and one of the largest libraries and museums in the Southern Hemisphere. While it is owned by the English Constitution, lodges from all allegiences meet there on an equal footing, and it possesses in excess of one hundred and thirty tenants (including lodges of various additional degrees). Indeed, the pressure of accommodation is so great in some parts of South Africa that some lodges meet in municipal halls, or church halls. It should also be noted that no lodge meets in licensed premises anywhere in South Africa.

A majority of lodges in South Africa hold Ladies' Nights, usually on an annual basis. These occasions are not necessarily associated with lodge meetings, and may take the form of a dinner, dinner dance, or ball. As already mentioned, some lodges invite ladies to the afterproceedings of an Installation meeting.

All lodges in South Africa have Lodges of Instruction, but this term must be immediately explained in context. Lodges of Instruction, as found in England as separate instructional bodies are rare in South Africa. For example, there are only two English Lodges of Instruction in the Transvaal. The more correct term in a practical sense is Lodge of Rehearsal, and all lodges have rehearsals although some lodges, particularly English ones, call their rehearsals Lodges of Instruction.

It is quite common in South Africa for masons to be members of more than one lodge, often under more than one Constitution. Those wishing to affiliate with another lodge must be proposed and seconded by members of the lodge to be joined, and be successfully balloted for in open lodge prior to admission, in addition to presenting the appropriate masonic credentials. If a mason affiliates with a lodge under another Constitution, his signature will normally be required on forms of allegiance to the Constitution he joins.

6. LODGE WORKINGS, REGALIA, AND RITUAL

The workings and rituals of the various Constitutions largely approximate those of their home Grand Lodges, although S.A.C. lodges work a ritual which has been largely adapted from the original Netherlandic version. It is useful to look at each allegiance separately in this regard.

English Lodges: Emulation ritual is the most popular ritual amongst English lodges, although others are in use, all of which are similar.

Irish Lodges: The Grand Lodge of Ireland, while refusing to print an official ritual, does require all its lodges to work a uniform ritual, and this applies to its constituents in South Africa. Details of Irish workings are to be found elsewhere in this guide.

Scottish Lodges: There are several different, but similar, rituals in use under the Scottish Constitution. Scottish Rituals are not overly different from those of the English, with the most divergent features being in the third degree ceremony. Scottish lodges are probably the most thorough in the examination of unknown visitors.

South African Constitution Lodges: S.A.C. ritual is quite removed from those of the other three Constitutions. It is based on the ritual of the Grand East of the Netherlands, which in turn was originally based on old English ritual. The Temple layout is the first thing a visitor will notice. Both Wardens are seated in the west—the Senior Warden in the south-west, and the Junior Warden in the north-west. Members sit in two 'columns' on either side of the Temple—the north column under the control of the Junior Warden, while the south column is controlled by the Senior Warden. The Master sits in the east, with the altar in front of him. The Tracing Board of each Degree (in the old operative form of a floor cloth) is placed in the centre of the lodge. In the First degree, this is surrounded by the rough ashlar, Ionic column, Corinthian column and Doric column; flanking the north-east, south-east, north-west and south-west corners of the Tracing Board, respectively. The three columns are topped by tall candles. In the Second Degree, there are five columns and candles surrounding the Tracing Board, representing the five noble orders of architecture.

Members are seated in columns as follows: Stewards are seated, half in the north column and half in the south column, closest to the Wardens. Fellow Crafts are seated at the head of south column closest to the east, while Apprentices are seated at the head of the north column. The Orator is seated in front of the Past Masters, to the Master's left; while the Preparators (equivalent to English Deacons) sit in front of the two Wardens. The actual degree ceremonies themselves largely approximate continental forms, and will be of intense interest to any visitor unfamiliar with them.

No business of a routine nature is dealt with in open lodge. Minutes, reports, ballots, and the like are conducted at separate meetings of Master Masons. Apprentices and Fellow Crafts have no right to visit or participate in the running of the lodge until they become Master Masons. S.A.C. lodges, as has already been premised, do not use the Installed Master Ceremony in the course of an Installation. However, Installed S.A.C. Masters can partake of this ceremony later as an option.

The Grand Lodge of South Africa has promulgated a uniform ritual for use in its lodges, and while it is basically Netherlandic, several modifications have been made, although these are far from extensive. A major alteration has been to include an obligation in each degree ceremony, whereas in Netherlandic Ritual only an Apprentice is obligated.

It should be generally noted that the Modes of Recognition vary between each of the four Constitutions. However, each is aware of the forms of the others, and they are well recognised. Indeed, it is quite usual for a visitor to a lodge outside his own Constitution to use the signs which he himself has been taught.

Regalia: Again, regalia varies between the Constitutions. However, aside from some differences in colour and style, all aprons worn in South Africa are similar. Some lodges trim their aprons with a specific colour (tartan, in the case of some Scottish lodges). The Grand Lodge of South Africa has abandoned the plain white type aprons used in Europe, and instead has opted for a Master Mason apron-form not dissimilar to the English. Visitors, regardless of masonic origin, are welcome to wear their own regalia at any lodge they attend in South Africa.

7. MASONIC ADMINISTRATION

The Provincial Grand Lodges under the Grand Lodge of Ireland, and the English and Scottish District Grand Lodges, all operate along the lines of administration of their home Grand Lodges, according to their various Grand Lodge constitutions and regulations. Each local Grand Body operates with a Provincial or District Grand Lodge heirarchy. While Irish Provincial Grand Lodge offices, and Scottish District Grand Lodge offices, tend to be elective; those of the English District Grand Lodges are largely appointive. Actual Grand Lodge rank stems directly from the home Grand Lodges themselves. The local Grand Bodies have a fair deal of masonic autonomy, particularly in terms of administration. The names and responsibilities of each Provincial and District Grand Lodge rank corresponds, in a local sense, to those ranks of the home Grand Lodges.

The Grand Lodge of South Africa is basically an Appointive Grand Lodge, although not a few of its forms stem from its Dutch ancestry. Its Grand Lodge officers, in order of seniority, are as follows: The Grand Master, Deputy Grand Master, Assistant Grand Master, Senior Grand Warden, Junior Grand Warden, Grand Orator, Grand Secretary, Grand Treasurer, Grand Master of Ceremonies, Assistant Grand Master of Ceremonies, Grand Almoner, Grand Ambassador, Grand Inspector, Grand Architect, Grand Sword Bearer, Grand Standard Bearer, Grand Director of Music, Grand Inner Guard, Grand Tyler, and Grand Stewards. As can be seen from this list, there is considerable British influence in the offices of this Grand Lodge, and these largely correspond accordingly. The European offices are analogous in a 'Grand sense' to those of ordinary S.A.C. lodges. The Grand Lodge of South Africa meets annually, usually in August, and all its constituent lodges must have a representative present or be liable to be fined! The operations of the Grand Lodge are decentralised through three Provincial Grand Lodges, working in a similar pattern to the English, Irish and Scottish 'local' Grand Lodges. It is possible, by invitation, for visitors to attend a meeting of the Grand Lodge of South Africa.

8. OFFICERS OF CONSTITUENT LODGES

The officers that comprise English, Irish and Scottish Lodges have been detailed elsewhere in this guide, and these apply as appropriate to lodges in South Africa. The officers of S.A.C. lodges are as follows: Worshipful Master, Senior Warden, Junior Warden, Secretary, Treasurer, Deputy Master, Orator, First Preparator, Second Preparator, Architect, Almoner, Master of Ceremonies, Ambassador, Inner Guard, and Stewards. The office of Orator largely corresponds to that of Chaplain in a British-type lodge, and the Preparators to Deacons. The duties of the Ambassador largely involves responsibilities connected with the reception of visitors.

List of Lodges

As of 1983, there were over 600 regular lodges working in South Africa, and it is obviously impractical to list them here. The addresses of all major masonic edifices in South Africa have already been noted above. By and large, except in December and/or January in many cases, lodges in South Africa meet on a monthly basis. This applies to all lodges, regardless of constitution. Visitors seeking to attend a lodge in December or January should be particularly careful to check meeting details prior to their visit. This can be achieved at any main masonic temple. All 'local' Grand Lodges, and the Grand Lodge of South Africa, annually publish their own *Year Book*, or similar directory, containing the full meeting details of their lodges. Visitors may care to purchase appropriately in this regard when in South Africa.

One particular lodge, which might well be of special interest to visitors, is detailed below. This is the only lodge remaining directly under the Grand East of the Netherlands, in South Africa. It dates from 1899.

Eendracht Maakt Macht Lodge No 88	Meets at Freemasons' Hall, 6 Park Street, Parktown, Johannesburg; 2nd and 4th Mondays monthly.

Finally, the language situation as it affects lodges needs to be explained. About sixty to seventy percent of all lodges in South Africa work in the English language. Most of the rest work in Afrikaans, although there are a small number that work in German or Greek. However, it would be a mistake for visitors to assume the language worked by any particular lodge simply on the basis of its warrant. Many S.A.C. lodges work in English, while there are a reasonable number of English, Scottish and Irish lodges that work in Afrikaans. It is therefore advisable for a visitor to assume nothing in this regard, but rather seek to discover the working language of any lodge he plans to visit. A question in this regard will be readily answered at any major temple upon personal inquiry.

ST. HELENA

This small South Atlantic island adjacent to Southern Africa, is a British Possession; and it contains one old English lodge, dating from 1843. Its details are as follows:

St Helena Lodge No 488   Meets at the Masonic Hall, Napoleon Street, Jamestown, St Helena; 2nd Tuesday monthly, except December. Inst: December 27th.

SUDAN

The masonic history of the Sudan closely parallels that of Egypt, and it once had several lodges warranted from Britain. However, none of these lodges has survived.

SWAZILAND

This small African country borders on South Africa. It possesses three English lodges, one Irish lodge, and one Scottish lodge. The English and Scottish lodges are governed by their respective District Grand Lodges of the Transvaal, while the Irish lodge comes under the Provincial Grand Lodge of South Africa, Northern. The details are as follows:

Swaziland Lodge No 7035 EC   Meets at the Masonic Temple, Manzani, Swaziland; 4th Friday monthly, except December. Inst: June.

Amiantos Lodge No 8288 EC   Meets at the Havelock Mine, Bulembu, Swaziland; 1st Saturday monthly. Inst: June.

St George's Lodge No 8322 EC   Meets Masonic Temple, Mbabane, Swaziland; 1st Friday monthly, except January. Inst: June.

Mbabane Lodge No 822 IC   Meets Masonic Temple, Mbabane, Swaziland; 2nd Thursday monthly, except March. Inst: 1st Saturday, March.

Lodge Dwaleni No 1559 SC   Meets Masonic Temple, Mbabane, Swaziland; 2nd Saturday in February, March, May, July, September and November.

TANZANIA

This East African country was formed out of a union of the former English colony of Tanganyika, and the island of Zanzibar located off its coast. Zanzibar has a very long history as an Arab Sultanate, infamous for its slave trade. It became a British Protectorate in 1890, and remained so until 1964, whereupon it became part of Tanzania. England chartered a lodge at Zanzibar in 1903, and a few more were erected prior to the Second World War. Unfortunately, none of these survived. However, lodges erected in mainland Tanganyika were more fortunate. England warranted Haven of Peace Lodge at Dar-es-Salaam in 1921; and this was followed by Tanga Fraternity Lodge erected at Tanga in 1926. Scotland chartered Lodge St Andrew No 1360 at Dar-es-Salaam in 1928; and this remains the only Scottish lodge in Tanzania. Six other English lodges have since been established in the country, the latest receiving its warrant in 1956. Of the nine regular lodges working in Tanzania, four are located at Dar-es-Salaam; two at Tanga; and one each at Arusha,

Moshi, and Mwanza. The details of the lodges meeting at Dar-es-Salaam are listed below:

Haven of Peace Lodge No 4385 EC	Meets Masonic Temple, Main Avenue, Dar-es-Salaam; 2nd Monday March to November. Inst: April.
Dar-es-Salaam Lodge No 5095 EC	Meets Masonic Temple, Main Ave, Dar-es-Salaam; 3rd Monday March to November. Inst: September.
Guiding Star Lodge No 5299 EC.	Meets Masonic Temple, Main Ave, Dar-es-Salaam; 4th Monday March to November' Inst: November.
Lodge St Andrew No 1360 SC.	Meets Masonic Temple, Main Ave, Dar-es-Salaam; 1st Monday April to December.

TOGO

Togo has the distinction of being the only former French colony in continental Africa possessing lodges warranted from Britain. This is probably explained by the fact that Lome, the capital city of Togo, is located very near to the border with Ghana, a former British colony in which masonry has flourished. In addition, the Grande Loge Nationale Française has four regular lodges working in the country. Irregular French Masonry reportedly also exists in Togo. The incursion of regular French lodges has occurred only in very recent years, the latest being erected in 1972. England and Scotland currently have one lodge each working at Lome. The details of each regular lodge are as follows:

The Lodge of Togo No 1677 SC.	Meets at the Masonic Temple, Rue de Seminare, Tokoin, Lome, Togo; 1st Saturday in November, January, March, May, July and September.
Togo Lodge No 8605 EC.	Meets at the Masonic Temple, Rue de Seminare, Tokoin, Lome, Togo; 2nd Saturday odd months. Inst: July.
Franchise-Lome Lodge No 148 GLNF	Meets at the Masonic Temple, Adjololo-Nyekonakpoe, Lome, Togo; 1st Saturday monthly, at 6 pm.
Jephte Lodge No 161 GLNF.	Meets at the Masonic Temple, Adjololo-Nyekonakpoe, Lome, Toga; 2nd Saturday monthly, at 6.30 pm.
Avenir Esperance Lodge No 170 GLNF.	Meets at the Masonic Temple, Adjololo-Nyekonakpoe, Lome, Togo; 3rd Friday monthly, at 7.30 pm.
Perseverance et Sincerite Lodge GLNF.	Meets at the Masonic Temple, Adjololo-Nyekonakpoe, Lome.

TUNISIA

This North African country once possessed several lodges under the irregular Grand Orient of France, and they reportedly were working after the Second World War. It is probable that they did not long survive subsequent Tunisian independence.

UGANDA

Uganda is a former British colonial territory, which contained several English lodges until 1971. In that year a military dictatorship assumed control of the country, and all lodges were subsequently forced to close. Although this dictatorship was overthrown recently, no masonic activity had been resumed in 1984.

ZAIRE

Formerly the Belgian Congo, Zaire at one time possessed a few lodges established by the irregular Grand Orient of Belgium, but whether they are still working remains unclear. No regular masonry currently exists in this country.

ZAMBIA

Zambia is one of the many former British colonial areas in which masonry has become well established. It currently possesses thirty lodges, arranged under three local Grand Bodies.

The District Grand Lodge of Zambia
(Under the United Grand Lodge of England).
　Address: P.O. Box 90088, Luanshya, Zambia.
　Principal Temple: Masonic Temple, Lusaka.
　Lodges: 12 (plus one in Botswana).

The District Grand Lodge of Zambia
(Under the Grand Lodge of Scotland).
　Address: P.O. Box 20510, Kitwe, Zambia.
　Principal Temple: Masonic Temple, Lusaka.
　Lodges: 12

The Provincial Grand Lodge of Zambia
(Under the Grand Lodge of Ireland).
　Address: P.O. Box 29, Lusaka, Zambia.
　Principal Temple: Masonic Temple, Lusaka.
　Lodges: 6

History
The first lodge to be formed in the area which now forms modern Zambia was established on the northern bank of the Zambesi River between Northern and Southern Rhodesia. This was Lodge David Livingstone No 1321 SC, consecrated in 1924. It was followed two years later by the Luangwa Lodge No 4820 EC. The first Irish lodge was Pioneer Lodge No 764, established in 1953.

From the outset, except for English lodges erected before 1930, the formation of any lodge in Zambia relied on the support of masons from sister constitutions as foundation members. This facet of masonry is quite common throughout Africa, and it is usual in Zambia to find individual members belonging to several lodges under different allegiances. As with many African countries, local political independence has provided concerns for the continuance of the Craft. Shortly before independence in 1964, when Northern Rhodesia became the Republic of Zambia, and for about ten years thereafter, there were grave doubts expressed for the continued existence of masonry in Zambia. However, there fears have so far proved groundless.

Lodges in the copper mining area of the country (located in the north and usually referred to as the Copperbelt) are composed predominantly of Europeans, with a small number of Asians; but elsewhere in the country membership tends to be more cosmopolitan.

The 1980s are expected to see a decline in the number of British citizens remaining in the country, as the British Government Support Scheme winds down. This occurrence may well dampen the expansion on the Craft in Zambia. However, in recent years there has been a significant number of Asians of Zambian origin joining the various lodges, and this augurs well for the future. On the other hand, the number of African members remains somewhat disappointing.

Notes for visitors to Zambia

1. MEETING TIMES, AND DRESS

Lodges in Zambia tend to meet at 7 pm, although there are some that meet up to half an hour earlier. Senior lodge members are often present at 6 pm, and visitors are encouraged to follow that example so that the normal examination procedures can be readily undertaken. The large plurality of membership in Zambia will often enable a visitor to be vouched for at other lodge meetings after he had attended his first one. As already mentioned, plural membership, and substantial inter-visiting between lodges is very common in Zambia. Members of Zambian lodges are expected to wear dinner suits to meetings, although this is not mandatory on new members, and the rule in this regard is fast becoming more interpretative. Visitors are welcome to attend in a dark lounge suit, or even a safari suit. There are also members of Scottish origin who wear formal highland dress.

2. LODGE AFTER PROCEEDINGS

Afterproceedings in Zambian lodges, regardless of affiliation, consist of a full evening meal which is generally prepared by members or their wives on lodge premises. No charge is made on visitors for meals taken, although in some lodges the purchase of drinks is the responsibility of the individual. There is usually an opportunity for all members and visitors to contribute to lodge charitable funds through a raffle, and visitors will doubtless be moved to assist in this regard.

As a dinner is the norm of Zambian lodges, a formal Toast List will usually follow the meal. An example of such a Toast List is:

1. The President of Zambia.
2. The Grand Lodge, and its officers.
3. The District Grand Lodge, and its officers.
4. Sister Constitutions.
5. The Candidate.
6. The Visitors.
7. Absent Brethren.
8. The Tyler's Toast.

Of course, the order of presentation may vary between lodges. Some will only be presented as the need arises, while extra toasts may be added on Nights of Installation. Toasts to visitors are usually proposed by a lodge's Junior Warden. Masonic visitors from outside Zambia are not particularly frequent, so a visitor is likely to be called upon to speak. It is usual for the Senior Warden to propose the toast to Absent Brethren, and most lodges honour this toast at a fixed time, usually 10.30 pm. In Irish lodges, the Tyler's Toast is not usually given.

3. OF VISITING IN GENERAL, AND NIGHTS OF INSTALLATION

At ordinary lodge meetings, all members and visitors take their places in the lodge for the opening, unless their lodge is making an official visit. Official visitors are received after the routine business of the lodge has been completed, and a lone visitor may be invited to join an official delegation. At the conclusion of each meeting in many lodges, the Master or a senior member of a visiting lodge may be given the opportunity to tender fraternal greetings on behalf of his lodge. This procedure is particularly likely to be followed at Installation meetings. Where this practice occurs, an individual visitor, especially if he comes from outside Zambia, will be welcome to convey fraternal greetings from his own lodge.

On Nights of Installation, all visitors are received officially. A lone visitor will normally 'attach' himself to either a lodge of his own constitution, or to some other convenient lodge. After all visitors of a lesser rank are admitted, those holding Grand Lodge Rank, or Provincial or District Grand Lodge Rank, will retire to accompany the official representative of the Provincial or District Grand Lodge into the lodge room. This official representative will usually be the Provincial or District Grand Master.

While there is no restriction on visitors to Installation Meetings of any lodge in Zambia, overseas visitors should endeavour to give the lodge whose Installation they propose to visit prior notice of their intention, as this will assist with catering arrangements.

4. INTERESTING ASPECTS OF MASONRY IN ZAMBIA

Lodges in Zambia tend to have a majority of members who are not citizens of the country. This expatriate nature of Zambian lodges is shared by lodges in other African areas, and tends to impose some differences in customs to those elsewhere. Most expatriate members are working in Zambia on two or three-year contracts, and they tend to return to their native lands after their tenure has expired. The effect on Zambian lodges of this mobility in their memberships is not inconsiderable. In particular, it tends to leave some lodges short of experienced members. As a result, the floor work of lodges is often divided between members regardless of rank, and even Entered Apprentices are encouraged to take part.

As another result of membership mobility, the rate of progress can be quite fast, and in some lodges it has been known for a member to move from his initiation to the Master's Chair in four years. Declining membership is also a problem in Zambia, and it is not entirely unknown for the membership of two lodges in the same location to at times be almost identical.

Lusaka lodges, in particular, have a long history of hospitality, and are always ready to receive visitors who have been called to the capital city at short notice. On the other hand, some time might elapse between the visits of 'strange' Masons, and they thus become something of a 'prize' when they do turn up. As a result of the somewhat insular nature of masonry in Zambia, local members are very curious to hear about the Craft elsewhere, and are always delighted to receive a visitor from overseas.

Many social occasions accompany the life of lodges in Zambia. Each holds a ladies' night annually, either at a masonic building or in an hotel. No lodge meetings are usually associated with these nights, which consist of a dinner and dancing, and sometimes a cabaret. Other social events conducted by lodges include barbecues, film nights, golf tournaments, and various sports events.

Zambia possesses no lodges of instruction as such, although all lodges carry out rehearsals. However, the Irish Provincial Grand Lodge encourages degree demonstrations by its constituent lodges at its meetings.

5. LODGE WORKINGS, REGALIA, AND RITUAL

English lodges in Zambia work the *Ellis Robbins* Ritual (with one exception), which is almost identical to the *Emulation* working. Scottish and Irish lodges use the rituals approved by their respective Grand Lodges. Again, the officers of lodges, and lodge layouts, are strictly in accordance with those specified in the rules of each Grand Lodge, as relevant.

List of Lodges

All Craft lodges meeting in Zambia are listed below, which is in turn followed by the addresses of meeting places. The three Constitutions working in Zambia are listed in detail in the local publication: *Masonic Calendar for Zambia.* A brother visiting a lodge in Zambia can acquire a copy of this booklet on request, if he so desires.

Each lodge in Zambia has its own *permanent* Post Office Box address. A brother planning to visit Zambia should choose a lodge meeting applicable to his travelling schedule, and write to its Secretary at its P.O. Box address. The courtesy of informing a lodge of a brother's impending visit, while not necessary, is nevertheless appreciated. Nonetheless, any letter that is sent should be directed via a visitor's own Grand Lodge office.

English Lodges

Luangwa Lodge No 4820	Meets Masonic Temple, Kabwe. 3rd Thursday except April when it meets on the Saturday after 3rd Thursday. Inst: April. Address: P.O. Box 4.
Roan Antelope Lodge No 5278	Meets Masonic Temple, Luanshya. 2nd Tuesday except June when it meets on 3rd Saturday. Inst: June. Address: P.O. Box 112.
Mufulira Lodge No 5326	Meets Masonic Temple, Mufulira. 3rd Tuesday September to July. Inst: 4th Saturday August. Address: P.O. Box 100.
Victoria Falls Lodge No 5327	Meets Masonic Temple, Kabompo Road, Livingstone. 1st Friday, October to August. Inst: September 1st Saturday. Address: P.O. Box 100.
Jubilee Lodge No 5582	Meets Masonic Temple, Kitwe. 4th Monday January to November (December, no meeting). Inst: May. Address: P.O. Box 143.
Itawa Lodge No 7072	Meets Masonic Hall, Ndola. 1st Thursday monthly. Inst: June. Address: P.O. Box 339.

Eagle Lodge No 7232
Meets Masonic Temple, Lusaka. 3rd Thursday monthly except December. Inst: January. Address: P.O. Box 1043.

Tranquillity Lodge No 7287
Meets Masonic Temple, Luanshya. 1st Tuesday December to October. Inst: November, 3rd Saturday. Address: P.O. Box 49

Coronation Lodge No 7329
Meets Masonic Temple, Chingola. 4th Friday monthly except December (no meeting) and February. Inst: 4th Saturday February. Address: P.O. Box 404.

Falcon Lodge No 7510
Meets Masonic Temple, Lusaka. 1st Thursday February to December. Inst: March. Address: P.O. Box 8075, Woodlands.

Konkola Lodge No 7549
Observatory Lecture Hall, Mopani Road, Chililabombwe. 1st Wednesday, October to August. Inst: 1st Saturday September. Address: P.O. Box 1143.

Mwana Lodge No 8706
Meets Masonic Hall, Ndola. 2nd Monday April to February. Inst: March. Address: P.O. Box 1649.

Irish Lodges

Pioneer Lodge No 764
Meets Masonic Hall, Chingola. 7.15 pm. 2nd Tuesday monthly. Inst: August. Address: P.O. Box 9.

Downpatrick Lodge No 785
Meets Masonic Temple, Lusaka. 7 pm. 1st Friday except January. Address: P.O. Box 30308.

Failte Lodge No 805
Meets Masonic Temple, Kitwe. 6.45 pm. 1st Wednesday monthly. Address: P.O. Box 1366.

Shannondale Lodge No 816
Meets Masonic Temple, Ndola. 7.15 pm. 3rd Friday November to September. Inst: Saturday after 3rd Friday October. Address: P.O. Box 816.

Zambia Masters Lodge No 856
Meets Masonic Hall, Ndola. 6.30 pm. 5th Friday in any month where occurring. Inst: 1st Friday after March 17th. Address: P.O. Box 71364.

Cashel Lodge No 863
Meets Masonic Hall, Luanshya. 4th Thursday February to December. Inst: 1st Saturday January.

Scottish Lodges

Lodge David Livingstone No 1321
Meets Masonic Temple, Livingstone. 3rd Friday monthly. Address: P.O. Box 52.

Lodge Lusaka No 1368
Meets Masonic Temple, Lusaka. 2nd Tuesday June to April. Inst: 2nd Saturday, May. Address: P.O. Box 30052

Lodge David Ogilvie No 1371
Masonic Hall, Ndola. 4th Wednesday monthly. Address: P.O. Box 141.

Lodge Broken Hill No 1374
Meets Masonic Hall, Kawbe. 1st Friday monthly. Address: P.O. Box 354.

Lodge Nkana No 1378	Meets Masonic Temple, Kitwe. 2nd Thursday monthly. Address: P.O. Box 1079.
Lodge Chingola No 1394	Meets Masonic Temple, Chingola. 4th Tuesday except December. Address: P.O. Box 385
Lodge of Unity No 1510	Meets Masonic Temple, Lusaka. 1st Wednesday except January. Address: P.O. Box 1303.
Lodge Choma No 1480	The Temple, Chome. 2nd Saturday except November. Address: P.O. Box 70.
Lodge Luanshya St Andrew No 1481	Meets Masonic Hall, Luanshya. 3rd Monday January to November. Address: P.O. Box 177
Lodge Ichitwe No 1493	Meets Masonic Hall, Kitwe. 3rd Wednesday January to November. Address: P.O. Box 1068
Lodge Border Eagle No 1496	Meets Masonic Hall, Mufulira. 2nd Friday monthly. Address: P.O. Box 43.
Lodge Star of the North No 1527	Meets Masonic Temple, Chililabombwe. 3rd Thursday except November. Address: P.O. Box 564.

Synopsis of Meeting Days (check above to ensure months of meeting)

1st Mon.	Nil	3rd Mon.	1481(SC)
1st Tue.	5278(EC), 7287(EC)	3rd Tue.	5326(EC)
1st Wed.	1510(SC), 805(IC), 1510(SC)	3rd Wed.	1493(SC)
1st Thu.	7072(EC), 7510(EC)	3rd Thu.	1527(SC), 4820(EC), 7232(EC)
1st Fri.	785(IC), 1374(SC), 5327(EC)	3rd Fri.	816(IC), 1321(SC)
1st Sat.	Nil	3rd Sat.	Nil
2nd Mon.	8706(EC)	4th Mon.	5582(EC)
2nd Tue.	764(IC), 1368(SC)	4th Tue.	1394(SC)
2nd Wed.	Nil	4th Wed.	1371(SC)
2nd Thu.	1378(SC)	4th Thu.	863(IC)
2nd Fri.	1496(SC)	4th Fri.	7329(EC)
2nd Sat.	1480(SC)	4th Sat.	Nil
		5th Sat.	856(IC)

A Note on Masonic Temple Addresses

Apart from the masonic temples in Kitwe, Chingola and Luanshya, meeting places in Zambia are not particularly easy to find when one searches for them. This is particularly so for the temple in Lusaka. Therefore, it is again stressed that unless a visitor coming from outside Zambia knows a mason residing in the country, he is well advised to write beforehand to one of the lodges care of its post office box address. Similarly, telephone numbers are not much use in terms of this Guide, as Zambian authorities have a happy knack of often issuing new numbers!

ZIMBABWE

The last area of Africa to capture our attention is Zimbabwe, a former British colony which was until recently known as Rhodesia. It possesses a number of lodges under the English, Irish, Scottish, and Netherlandic Constitutions; all of which work in amity.

The District Grand Lodge of Zimbabwe (Under the United Grand Lodge of England)
Address: P.O. Box 1286, Harare, Zimbabwe.
Principal Temple: Masonic Temple, Glenara Avenue, Harare.
Lodges: 31

The Provincial Grand Lodge of Zimbabwe (Under the Grand Lodge of Ireland)
Address: P.O. Box 313, Harare, Zimbabwe.
Principal Temple: Masonic Temple, Glenara Avenue, Harare.
Lodges: 8

The District Grand Lodge of Zimbabwe (Under the Grand Lodge of Scotland).
Address: P.O. Box 313, Harare, Zimbabwe.
Principal Temple: Freemasons' Hall, Gaul Avenue, Harare.
Lodges: 22

The Provincial Grand Lodge of Zimbabwe (Under the Grand East of the Netherlands)
Address: P.O. Box 930, Harare, Zimbabwe.
Principal Temple: Freemasons' Hall, Gaul Avenue, Harare.
Lodges: 7

History

Masonry came to Rhodesia with the first white settlers, and the first warrant granted was for Rhodesia Lodge No 2479, EC; in 1893. With the change of political status of the country in recent years, this lodge has now changed its name to Founders Lodge. This was quickly followed by a second English lodge, Bulawayo Lodge No 2566, established at Bulawayo in 1895. The initial Scottish lodge was also chartered at Bulawayo, in 1897. This was Lodge Alan Wilson No 851. Ireland's first lodge was not erected until 1921. This was St Patrick Lodge No 517, located at Salisbury. The Netherlandic lodges originated from South Africa, and two were working in the country shortly after the Second World War. This number has now grown to seven.

Cecil Rhodes, after whom Rhodesia was named, and who is credited as the founder of the country, was himself a freemason, and was largely responsible for the introduction of the Craft into the area. Various local District and Provincial Grand Lodges for the four operating Constitutions were progressively formed, and the Craft flourished. Sixty-eight regular lodges now work in the country. The political history of Rhodesia is well known. After many years of white minority Government and civil insurgences, black majority rule was established in the country in 1980. In the period of the civil war prior to 1980, many whites emigrated from the country, and this pattern has not slowed since. Of course, this exodus took with it many masons, and continues to do so. The effect of the Craft in Zimbabwe, as Rhodesia was thereafter called, has been to drain lodges of membership and experience. The longer term effects are harder to gauge, and largely depend on how the white population perceives its future in the country. No lodges have as yet been forced to close as a result of declining membership, but if this trend continues that possibility will increase. The new Government appears not to have formed an adversary position towards freemasonry but, again, the future would appear uncertain.

Notes for visitors to Zimbabwe

1. MEETING TIMES, AND DRESS

The majority of lodges in Zimbabwe meet at or about 7.30 pm, while there are some that meet on Saturdays, whereupon the commencement time is often mid-afternoon, ranging from 3 pm to 4 pm. There are also lodges which, while meeting normally on a weeknight, conduct their annual Installation Meeting on a Saturday, and if so meet in the mid-afternoon.

Dress for lodges varies somewhat. Many lodges prefer members to attend in a dark lounge suit (generally black, with white shirt and black tie), while others prefer a black dinner suit. However, visitors are welcome at any lodge in either form of dress, and from outside Zimbabwe they will certainly not be prevented from attending if wearing a dark jacket and tie.

2. LODGE AFTERPROCEEDINGS

Every lodge in Zimbabwe conducts some form of afterproceedings. In the larger centres they are held in a hall connected to the Temple, while in smaller country centres lodges usually dine at a local hotel. All English lodges hold a festive board after a meeting, which generally includes a full meal and Toast List. The majority of lodges under other Constitutions also follow similar practices. All lodges include a dinner in association with an Installation Meeting. In Zimbabwe, the costs associated with afterproceedings rarely form part of members' lodge dues, and so members are levied accordingly at each meeting. It is customary for lodges to state the cost of dining on their summonses or agendas. However, visitors are never called upon to pay when attending a lodge meeting in Zimbabwe. An example of a Toast List used in English lodges in the country is as follows:

1. Zimbabwe and the Craft.
2. The Grand Master.
3. The Pro Grand Master.
4. The Deputy and Assistant Grand Master, and Grand Lodge officers, past and present.
5. The District Grand Master.
6. The Deputy and Assistant District Grand Master, and District Grand Lodge officers, past and present.
7. The Visitors (often proposed by the Junior Warden).
8. The Tyler's Toast.

The Full Toast List above is more likely to be offered at an Installation Meeting, while at normal meetings an abbreviated list may be used. Responses to toasts are only made when the appropriate persons are present. A respondent to the Visitor's Toast will be given forewarning. The lodges of other Constitutions tend to use a shorter Toast List than those common in English lodges. A raffle is often held at lodge afterproceedings.

3. OF VISITING IN GENERAL, AND NIGHTS OF INSTALLATION

Visitors are always made most welcome to lodges in Zimbabwe, and the modes of reception are quite similar to those just outlined in terms of lodges in Zambia. Lodges under the Grand East of the Netherlands tend largely to follow local customs in this regard as well. At Nights of Installation, the reception of visitors is quite formal, and they are admitted in groups according to seniority of rank, lodge and Constitution, with the last admittance being that of the appropriate District or Provincial Grand Master, or his representative. As with any lodge, it is most advisable for visitors to be early. The dress for Installation Meetings is generally a dinner suit.

4. INTERESTING ASPECTS OF MASONRY IN ZIMBABWE

The vast majority of lodges in the country, regardless of affiliation, hold a Ladies' Night annually, and normally no lodge meeting is associated with such functions. Members are usually at liberty to invide non-Masons and their wives to attend. Interestingly, at Ladies' Nights lodge members are not generally addressed by their masonic rank. The Master is referred to as the chairman, and others simply as mister. Only two toasts are given, which are: *1*. Zimbabwe. *2*. Our Ladies and Visitors. The latter toast is often replied to by the Master's Lady, or a visitor.

There are three Lodges of Instruction, as such, on the English model in Zimbabwe. Visitors are welcome to attend and details are readily available from members of any English lodge. Most lodges under the other three Constitutions hold rehearsals of degree workings for the instruction of lodge officers and members.

Zimbabwe possesses one Lodge of Research—Research Lodge No 8309 EC. Until recently it was called the Salisbury Installed Master's Lodge, but it changed its name when Salisbury came to be renamed Harare. It publishes an excellent quarterly periodical (in March, June, September and December) entitled *The Masonic Review*, and it contains much of interest—its contents not restricted just to research papers. Many articles for, and about, the Craft in Zimbabwe are also contained within it. Subscriptions are welcomed, and can be obtained from the Business Manager, *The Masonic Review*, P.O. Box 2792, Harare, at a rate of $5 per annum (1983 rates, in Zimbabwean currency).

List of Lodges

The large number of lodges meeting in Zimbabwe precludes providing a full list here. Of most initial use to visitors will be details of lodges meeting in Harare, the capital city of the country, and these are detailed below. Visitors planning to visit other areas of Zimbabwe can readily obtain pertinent details when in Harare. Where applicable, the Post Office Box address of each lodge is also detailed.

All lodges meeting in Harare meet at either the Masonic Temple, Glenara Avenue, Harare denoted (1) below, telephone: 46284 (Caretaker); or Freemasons' Hall, Gaul Avenue, Harare denoted (2) below, telephone: 81409 (Caretaker).

English Lodges

Founder Lodge No 2479   Meets (1), 2nd Thursday monthly. Inst: June. P.O. Box 271, Harare.

United Services Lodge No 5034   Meets (1), 1st Friday monthly, except December and January. Inst: August. P.O. Box 940, Harare.

Msasa Lodge No 6802   Meets (1), 3rd Friday monthly, except December and January. Inst: May. P.O. Box 1189, Harare.

Lister Lodge No 6842	Meets (1), 3rd Thursday in February, May, July and October. Inst: February. P.O. Box 3636, Harare.
Federation Lodge No 7363	Meets (1), 3rd Saturday monthly, except October, December and January. Inst: March. P.O. Box 8508, Causeway, Harare.
King David Lodge No 7471	Meets (1), 1st Wednesday monthly, except December and January. Inst: September. P.O. Box 3681, Harare.
New Sarum Lodge No 7626	Meets (1), 4th Saturday monthly, except March, April, June, September, December. Inst: 2nd Saturday in April. P.O. Box 1947, Harare.
Mopani Lodge No 7734	Meets (1), 2nd Wednesday monthly, except April, September, December and January. Inst: February. P.O. Box 3376, Harare.
Llewellin Lodge No 7771	Meets (1), 4th Friday odd months. Inst: 4th Friday, June. P.O. Box 8524, Causeway, Harare.
Charter Lodge No 7834	Meets (1), 3rd Friday in March, June, August, October. Inst: August.
Research Lodge No 8309	Meets (1), 4th Tuesday in March, June and September. Inst: 1st Tuesday, December. P.O. Box UA 39, Harare.

Scottish Lodges

Lodge Salisbury Kilwinning No 1097	Meets (2), 4th Tuesday odd months. P.O. Box 1033, Harare.
Lodge Umvuma No 1157	Meets (2), 2nd Friday monthly, except December. P.O. Box 8259, Causeway, Harare.
Lodge Scotia No 1323	Meets (2), 4th Thursday monthly, except December. P.O. Box 731, Harare.
Lodge Farquharson Smith No 1458	Meets (2), 2nd Tuesday monthly. P.O. Box 1061, Harare.
Lodge Hatfield St Andrew No 1512	Meets (2), 3rd Tuesday monthly. P.O. Box 2927, Harare.
Lodge Starr Jameson No 1554	Meets (2), 3rd Thursday monthly, P.O. Box 2853, Harare.
Lodge Acacia No 1582	Meets (2), 3rd Saturday monthly, except December. P.O. Box 1983, Harare.
Lodge Richard Cooper No 1661	Meets (2), 3rd Friday monthly, except December. P.O. Box 8110, Causeway, Harare.

Irish Lodges

St Patrick Lodge No 517	Meets (2), 2nd Monday monthly. P.O. 313, Harare.
Mashonaland Lodge No 621	Meets (2), 4th Friday monthly. P.O. Box 1067, Harare.
Frank A. Lowe Lodge No 813	Meets (2), 1st Friday monthly, except January. P.O. Box 2636, Harare.

Netherlandic Lodges

Lodge Israel No 132	Meets (2), 1st Thursday monthly. P.O. Box 930, Harare.

Lodge Milton Park No 177	Meets (2), 4th Monday monthly. P.O. Box 3137, Harare.
Lodge Nydiri No 229	Meets (2), 1st Monday monthly.
Lodge Salem No 244	Meets (2), 2nd Thursday monthly. P.O. Box 1855, Harare.

Section III

Visiting in Asia

Asia

An Overview

The earliest traces of freemasonry in Asia are found in India, which has had about two hundred and fifty years of masonic history, dating back to at least 1730. Indeed, the oldest English-warranted lodge still existing outside England (Lodge Star of the East No 67) was founded at Calcutta in 1740. The earliest outposts of the British Empire in Asia were quickly the location of lodges. Singapore, Hong Kong and Burma each possess at least one lodge established prior to 1850.

While the Craft has long since been formed in these areas, it is probably India that has seen the greatest masonic development since the Second World War, and the large population of that country would suggest that expansion will continue well into the future. Outside of former British territory, masonic development has not been so nearly marked. The Philippines has a long masonic history, beginning with Spanish lodges and later American lodges. Japan also has its own Grand Lodge, although its membership is as yet comparatively small.

Regrettably, the many success stories of the body of freemasonry is Asia have been somewhat matched by its tragedies—most of which have occurred in recent years. The Craft has been suppressed in Pakistan under pressure from its current military dictatorship. Communist supremacy in China and Indo-China have seen masonic activity vanish from these areas. Masonry in Indonesia has been wiped out by military repression. Nevertheless, outside these countries masonry remains a vibrant force for good, with Asia currently possessing nearly seven hundred regular lodges under various Constitutions.

Since the Second World War, the Craft in Asia has largely become ethnic Asian in composition with caucasian membership, while still substantial in many areas, becoming progressively less. However, as with Africa, there has been no great movement to form new independent Grand Lodges. The Grand Lodges of India, Japan and the Philippines remain the only regular Grand Lodges in Asia at this time. Similarly, as with Africa and largely for the same reasons discussed under that heading, it is unlikely that new Grand Lodges will be a feature of the Craft in Asia in the future.

Probably the greatest feature of Asian masonry is its diversity of membership in terms of ethnic backgrounds. On entering a lodge in India, Singapore or even Hong Kong, the visitor will often notice several different Sacred Volumes open on the altar or the Master's pedestal. These will include the Sacred Writings of every faith represented amongst its membership. One of the great joys of visiting in Asia is being able to sit in lodge with men of many different and diverse backgrounds—an ethnic and racial unity not often found outside the lodge room in the wider community. Unlike Africa, the racial question in masonic terms was not felt in Asia to any great degree, although in its early days in Asia the Craft certainly remained Anglo-Saxon in character.

By and large, the travelling freemason will experience little difficulty in locating the meeting places of lodges in Asia. With the possible exception of India, the vast majority of lodges meet in the large Asian cities, often at one central location. Even in India, its four main cities each have a large, centrally located Masonic Hall. On occasions, a letter might be the best method for initial contact. If this approach is undertaken, the correct procedures as outlined elsewhere in this guide must be followed. Nonetheless, without doubt the best method of making contact is in person, and generally this will be easily manageable in Asia.

AFGHANISTAN

Afghanistan is basically an Islamic country, and is located between Iran, Russia, and Pakistan. It was formerly absorbed as part of Britain's Indian Empire, but it received independence as a Constitutional Monarchy in 1919. During the British occupation, a very short lived lodge was erected at Kabul. This was Seaforth Lodge No 1866 EC. It commenced work in 1880, but expired in the following year. Afghanistan has, in recent years, come under communist control, and so the possibility of masonic development in the future would appear bleak.

BANGLADESH

Bangladesh was originally known as East Pakistan, and formed part of Pakistan upon the partitioning of the Indian sub-continent by the British in 1949. However, it subsequently became an independent nation. The population of the country is largely Moslem, and this may be the major reason for its general lack of masonic development. England and Scotland had a small number of lodges in East Pakistan after the Second World War, but only one has survived. This is Star Lodge No 4444, warranted by England in 1922. It has the unusual distinction of having two meeting places, with the lodge meeting at each alternately. Its details are as follows:

Star Lodge No 4444 EC   Meets at the Masonic Hall, Chittagong, Bangladesh; or the Masonic Hall, Lingla, Sylhet, Bangladesh; 1st Tuesday October to May, except February. Installation: 1st Saturday after 1st Tuesday, February.

BRUNEI

Brunei is a small sultanate under British protection, located in North Borneo. It possesses two lodges, one Scottish (formed in 1958), and one English (formed in 1973). Details are as follows:

Lodge Brunei No 1545 SC   Meets at the Masonic Rooms, Kuala Belait, Brunei; 4th Thursday October to June (except December), December—3rd Thursday.

Berakas Lodge No 8560 EC.   Meets at the Masonic Club, Jalan Berakas, Bandar Seri Berawan, Brunei; 2nd Monday monthly. Installation: April.

BURMA

As with Afghanistan and Pakistan, Burma was once part of the British Empire, until it achieved independence in 1936. The oldest lodge in the country was Lodge Philanthropy No 542, founded in 1847, but it later expired. It was followed by

Star of Burma Lodge No 614, and this remains the oldest extant lodge in Burma. Scottish masonry came to Burma in the form of Lodge Peace and Harmony No 834, formed in 1896. In the 1950s, England had sixteen lodges in Burma, although the total for England is now ten. Scotland currently has three lodges under charter. Both the English and Scottish lodges work under respective District Grand Lodges, as follows:

The District Grand Lodge of Burma (*Under the United Grand Lodge of England*)
Address: Freemasons' Hall, 65 Goodliffe Road, Rangoon, Burma.
Lodges: 10
The District Grand Lodge of Burma (*Under the Grand Lodge of Scotland*)
Address: Freemasons' Hall, 65 Goodliffe Road, Rangoon, Burma.
Lodges: 3

Notes for Visitors to Burma
The membership of Burmese lodges was once largely Anglo-Saxon, but by the nineteenth century a large number of non-whites had been admitted, including Buddhists and Parsees. In the event of political independence, a decline in European membership followed, and today the Craft in Burma is very largely composed of ethnic Chinese, with an ethnic Burmese minority. In many ways, the survival of freemasonry in Burma has been fortunate. Burma as a nation has for many years remained fairly insular, and the Burmese Government has been of a nature which in other places has not viewed freemasonry with great benevolence. However, it would appear that the vast majority of the Burmese who have joined the Craft have been men of some stature in the community, and in the halls of power. As a result, while many other foreign institutions have not endured, the Craft is well understood and respected in Burma, not the least because of some outstanding charitable work. A succession of very able District Grand Masters and District Grand Lodge Officers has also been a telling factor. Nevertheless, the body of Burmese Masonry has not expanded greatly. The last lodge erected in the country received its warrant in 1952. In the last three years, three English lodges have surrendered their warrants. Despite these setbacks, the Craft in Burma appears to remain secure, thanks to its ethnic membership.

The majority of lodges in Burma meet monthly in the early evening, at times between 7 pm and 8 pm. Dress is generally a dark lounge suit. Indeed, the isolation of Burma has enabled Burmese masonry largely to avoid the change and innovation that has crept into masonic workings as a result of large scale constitutional interaction in other areas of Asia and Africa. Therefore, visitors will doubtless notice certain traits of individuality. Lodge afterproceedings generally follow British patterns, and a dinner usually accompanies Installation Meetings. Burma does not receive many masonic visitors, but those who do arrive can expect the warmest fraternal welcome and assistance. Visitors are advised, in the first instance, to make themselves known at the Freemasons' Hall in Rangoon.

List of Lodges
All Scottish and most English lodges meet in Rangoon, the capital city. Listed below are all lodges currently working in the capital; all meeting at Freemasons' Hall, Rangoon:

Star of Burma Lodge No 614	Meets 2nd Wednesday monthly. Installation: December.
Lodge Victoria in Burma No 832	Meets 2nd Friday monthly. Installation: January.
Greenlaw Lodge No 1095	Meets 1st Monday monthly. Installation: November.
Pegu Lodge No 3330	Meets last Wednesday except April, July, October and December. Installation: January.
Meiktila Lake Lodge No 3426	Meets 2nd Saturday monthly. Installation: January.
Rangoon University Lodge No 4603	Meets 2nd Monday monthly, except April and May. Installation: February.
Light in Burma Lodge No 5081	Meets last Friday monthly. Installation: March.
Temperance Lodge No 7191	Meets 3rd Monday monthly. Installation: January.
Lodge Peace & Harmony No 834 SC	Meets 1st Tuesday monthly.
Lodge Hanthawaddy No 1053 SC	Meets 2nd Tuesday monthly.
Lodge Ady No 1377 SC	Meets 3rd Tuesday monthly.

CHINA (AND TAIWAN)

In terms of the parameters of this guide, regular freemasonry does not exist in China or Taiwan, at the present time. However, this has not always been the case. The first lodge erected in China was established by England in 1767. This was Amity Lodge No 407, at Canton, but it was no longer working by 1813. Shortly after the Second World War, ten lodges holding warrants from England or Scotland were working in mainland China, all of which were established either in the seaport of Shanghai, or the major inland cities of Tientsin, Hangkow, and Foochow. The Craft in Hong Kong will be examined under its own heading.

The Grand Lodge of Massachusetts also maintained five lodges in China at this time, with three in Shanghai, and one each at Peking and Tientsin. Ireland had also warranted one lodge, in Shanghai. Finally, China possessed six lodges chartered by the Grand Lodge of the Philippines, making a total of twenty-two regular lodges.

On 15 January 1949, the Philippines lodges, with a membership total of about six hundred, formed the Grand Lodge of China. Scarcely had it been established when the Communists came to power, which made further masonic activity impossible. All the English, Scottish and Massachusetts lodges were either erased; or moved from China to be re-erected elsewhere. Many of those that did manage to survive moved to Hong Kong. One of the Massachusetts lodges, Sinim, moved to Tokyo.

When the remnants of the anti-Communist forces fled to Taiwan after the Communist takeover of the mainland, the Grand Lodge of China followed, where it still works today. In 1983, it reported six lodges, and a total membership of 863. It works a version of the American Webb Ritual, in either English, or Chinese. The Grand Lodge of China is recognised as regular by all the United States and Canadian Grand Lodges, and by many in Europe. However, it is not recognised by the Grand Lodges of England, Ireland and Scotland. Therefore, in terms of this guide, the Grand Lodge of China's details cannot be included.

HONG KONG

Hong Kong is a British Crown Colony, abutting China. It is one of the largest commercial centres in Asia, and remains a popular tourist destination. Freemasonry has long held a place in the life of the colony. English and Scottish lodges range under relevant District Grand Lodges, while the two Irish lodges are governed directly from Dublin.

The District Grand Lodge of Hong Kong and the Far East (Under the United Grand Lodge of England)
Address: Zetland Hall, 1 Kennedy Road, Hong Kong.
Lodges: 12 (plus one in Japan).
The District Grand Lodge of the Far East (Under the Grand Lodge of Scotland).
Address: Zetland Hall, 1 Kennedy Road, Hong Kong.
Lodges: 5 in Hong Kong (Korea: 3; Japan: 2).

History
The oldest warranted lodge working in Hong Kong is Royal Sussex Lodge No 501. It was originally established by England at Canton on mainland China in 1844. Subsequently it moved to Shanghai, and later to Hong Kong. Indeed, several lodges formerly working in China moved to Hong Kong when conditions on the mainland became impossible. Scotland's oldest lodge is Lodge Cosmopolitan No 428, erected in 1864. Lodge Erin No 463, established in 1919, is Ireland's premier lodge in the colony. All Hong Kong lodges meet at Zetland Hall, which is possibly the largest masonic structure in the Far East. It contains two temples, administration areas, a library, and a museum.

The Craft in Hong Kong has developed steadily over the years, although no new lodges have been erected in the colony since 1946. Aside from a substantial British content, the membership of lodges in Hong Kong also consists of a not insubstantial number of ethnic Chinese.

Notes for visiting in Hong Kong

1. MEETING TIMES, AND DRESS
Most lodges in Hong Kong meet at 6.30 pm, so a visitor should be in attendance by at least 6 pm, to enable the necessary avouchment procedures to take place. Dress for ordinary meetings is a dark lounge suit, white shirt and dark or black tie. Dinner suits are usually worn to nights of Installation, although a visitor will nonetheless still be made most welcome if wearing a dark lounge suit.

2. LODGE AFTER PROCEEDINGS
All lodges in Hong Kong, regardless of affiliation, hold a form of afterproceedings at the conclusion of a lodge meeting. This is almost invariably a dinner, which visitors are most welcome to attend. Usually, visitors will not be expected to pay for dinner, as most lodges have a levy which covers the costs of visitors' meals. However, the costs of alcoholic refreshments are paid for by each individual as his needs demand. English festive boards often involve an extensive Toast List, while those toasts presented at the afterproceedings of Scottish and Irish lodges are often abbreviated. All lodges hold an extensive formal dinner after an Installation, and a full toast list is the norm. At ordinary meetings, the proceedings will normally

conclude between 10 pm and 11 pm. A toast to the visitors is always proposed, generally by the lodge's Junior Warden, and visitors will be given an opportunity to respond, although prior notice will be given. An overseas visitor has a far greater chance of 'winning' the visitors' response than a local visitor.

3. OF VISITING IN GENERAL

The large majority of lodges in Hong Kong meet between September and May, recessing in the cooler winter months. During July and August in particular, Zetland Hall is virtually closed. It is advisable to visit Zetland Hall prior to attending a meeting, to enable some notice to be given of an impending visit, if at all possible. Alternatively, the Hall Custodian can be phoned on 5448970, or 5220643, and he will readily provide full assistance.

On arrival at a lodge meeting, a visitor will normally ask for the Junior Warden, who will arrange for the necessary procedures to be undertaken, usually by a Past Master. Visitors should bring their own regalia, if possible. It is normal for members and visitors to assemble in the small dining room at Zetland Hall prior to a lodge meeting. The bar will be open, although most members generally restrict themselves to soft drinks prior to meeting. Usually, regardless of Constitution, visitors will enter the lodge Temple with members prior to the opening. At the end of each meeting, visitors will be able to convey fraternal greetings to the Master and the lodge, although depending on the type of lodge this happens in slightly different ways.

Zetland Hall is located centrally on Hong Kong Island, and is easily found. It is reached on foot or by taxi from the Admiralty Metro Station, the Star Ferry, or from the business centre. It is architecturally a very interesting building, and visitors are especially directed to its library and museum, where they will discover much of interest.

Each lodge holds an annual Installation Meeting, which tends to be longer and more formal than an ordinary meeting. As the catering for the dinner following usually involves fairly large numbers, it is always greatly appreciated if a visitor can give notice of his intention to be present.

4. MASONIC GOVERNMENT

The English and Scottish lodges are both governed by District Grand Lodges. These comprise a District Grand Master, District Grand Lodge officers, and the Masters and Past Masters of lodges. They meet at regular intervals, generally with a dinner following. These bodies control the Craft locally, and enjoy a reasonable amount of independence from the Home Grand Lodges. It may be possible for visitors to attend a District Grand Lodge meeting if so desired, but enquiries in this regard should be made well in advance at Zetland Hall.

List of Lodges

All the nineteen regular lodges working in Hong Kong meet at Zetland Hall, 1 Kennedy Road; as follows:

Royal Sussex Lodge No 501 EC   Meets 4th Wednesday monthly, except August and December. Installation: October.

Zetland Lodge No 525 EC   Meets 1st Tuesday monthly. Inst: December.

Victoria Lodge of Hong Kong No 1026 EC	Meets 2nd Friday October to June. Inst: March.
Perseverance Lodge of Hong Kong No 1165 EC	Meets 3rd Thursday September to May. Inst: December.
United Service Lodge No 1341 EC	Meets 2nd Monday September to May. Inst: December.
Corinthian Lodge of Amoy No 1806 EC	Meets 3rd Monday September to May. Inst: February.
Foochow Lodge No 1912 EC	Meets 3rd Friday September to May. Inst: April.
Star of Southern China Lodge No 2013 EC	Meets 1st Monday September to May. Inst: November.
University of Hong Kong Lodge No 3666 EC	Meets 4th Monday September to May. Inst: February.
Swatow Lodge No 3705 EC	Meets 1st Thursday September to May. Inst: February.
Cathay Lodge No 4373 EC	Meets 1st Friday monthly, except August and September. Inst: April.
Paul Chater Lodge of Installed Masters No 5391 EC	Meets 4th Friday in April, May and August. Inst: 4th Tuesday, January.
Lodge Erin No 463 IC	Meets 3rd Wednesday monthly, except July and August.
Shamrock Lodge No 712 IC	Meets 2nd Wednesday monthly, except July and August.
Lodge Cosmopolitan No 428 SC	Meets 3rd Thursday in June, July and August.
St Andrew-in-the-Far-East No 493 SC	Meets 3rd Thursday monthly, except June, July, August and December.
Lodge St John No 618 SC	Meets 2nd Tuesday monthly, except June, July and August.
Naval and Military Lodge No 848 SC	Meets 1st Wednesday monthly, except June, July and August.
Eastern Scotia Lodge No 923 SC	Meets 3rd Tuesday monthly, except June, July and August.

INDIA

India is a central Asian country with a very large and diverse population, and it possesses more regular lodges than any other eastern location. Aside from lodges forming various English, Irish and Scottish Districts and other Provinces, India also has a regular Grand Lodge, dating from 1961.

The District Grand Lodge of Bengal (Under the United Grand Lodge of England)
   Address: P.O. Box 9047, Calcutta, India.   Phone: 249134.
   Principal Temple: Freemasons' Hall, 19 Park St, Calcutta, 16, India.
   Lodges: 24

The District Grand Lodge of Bombay (Under the United Grand Lodge of England)
   Address: Freemasons' Hall, Ravelin St, Fort, Bombay 1, India.   Phone: 262889.
   Lodges: 23

The District Grand Lodge of Madras (Under the United Grand Lodge of England)
Address: Freemasons' Hall, 87 Commander-in-Chief Road, Madras 600 105,
India.   Phone: 86769.
Lodges: 18

The District Grand Lodge of Northern India (Under the United Grand Lodge of
England)
Address: Freemasons' Hall, Janpath, New Delhi, 110001, India.   Phone: 320508.
Lodges: 5

The District Grand Lodge of Eastern India (Under the Grand Lodge of Scotland)
Address: Freemasons' Hall, 19 Park St, Calcutta, 16, India.
Lodges: 5

The District Grand Lodge of Western India (Under the Grand Lodge of Scotland)
Address: Freemasons' Hall, Ravelin St, Fort, Bombay 1, India.
Lodges: 24

The Provincial Grand Lodge of Ireland in India (Under the Grand Lodge of Ireland)
Address: Freemasons' Hall, Ravelin St, Fort, Bombay 1, India.
Lodges: 10.

The Grand Lodge of India
Founded: 1961

Address: P.O. Box 681, New Delhi, 110001 India.
Principal Temple: Freemasons' Hall, Janpath, New Delhi.   Phone: 311956.
Lodges: 250   Permits Dual and Plural Membership   *Membership:* 13,647.
Descent: English, Scottish & Irish.   *Government:* Appointive Grand Lodge.
Courtesy Degrees: All correspondence must be through Grand Lodges.
Minimum Time Lapse between Degrees: One Month.   *Ritual:*   English-form.
Main Publications: Constitution.   Proceedings.   Periodical: G L Newsletter.

History

Freemasonry has long been established on the Indian sub-continent. The British
Raj formed probably the earliest part of the British Colonial Empire, and its
masonic history is closely bound with that of the Armed Forces and the British East
India Company—the latter at one time holding commercial concessions over most
of India. Masonry came to India barely after the creation of the Premier Grand
Lodge in 1717. The first English lodge was erected in India in 1730, but it failed to
survive. However, this was followed by Lodge Star in the East No 67, which still
works happily at Calcutta. The second oldest surviving lodge in India works at
Madras. This is the Lodge of Perfect Unanimity No 150, erected by England in
1786. The oldest lodge still under Scottish warrant is Lodge Perseverance No 338,
established at Bombay in 1847. The senior Irish lodge is St Patrick's Lodge No 319
working at Bombay, and erected in 1911.

During the era of the British Raj, India had a large number of military lodges,
meeting wherever the regiment to which each was attached was based. Indeed, it
can be readily stated that the early development of the Craft in India was achieved
largely through the efforts of masons serving in the Armed Forces. Some difficulties
were experienced in India as a result of the Antient-Moderns feud in England, but
the English masonic union restored harmony. The growth of the Craft in India
created the need for local administration, and the home Grand Lodges erected

District Grand Lodges as a result. In 1847, Scotland formed the Grand Lodge of All Scottish Freemasonry in India, which was actually a very large District Grand Lodge governing Scottish lodges between Aden in the west, and Burma in the east. The independence of Burma, and later Pakistan, saw lodges in these areas re-form under their own District Grand Lodges.

Ethnic Indians began to enter the Craft in some numbers in the early nineteenth century. In 1844, a Scottish lodge (Rising Star No 342) was erected at Bombay for the purpose of admitting non-Europeans. Freemasonry subsequently became very popular amongst most of the ethnic groups in India, particularly the Parsees, the Hindus and the Sikhs. The Moslems, while certainly providing their share of members, would appear to have been the most cautious in espousing masonry. In the Bombay area, the Parsees probably account for the majority of masons, while the Hindus appear to have the numbers around New Delhi. In the Calcutta area, the British presence is still well felt. By the second half of this century, the Craft in India was certainly dominated numerically by non-Europeans, and there arose a movement to create an indigenous Grand Lodge. The Grand Lodge of India was established in 1961, with 145 lodges ranging under its banner—all of which surrendered English, Irish or Scottish warrants to join. However, almost an equal number chose to remain under their old allegiance. The lodges that did join the new Grand Lodge were often largely composed of non-Europeans, while those remaining under the home Grand Lodges were less so, although several other factors were involved in the decisions of individual lodges in this regard. The new Grand Lodge was erected in complete harmony with the home Grand Lodges. Indeed, harmony has always existed between all Constitutions in India, and between all masons regardless of ethnic background. Upon the foundation of the new Grand Lodge, the English, Irish and Scottish Grand Lodges henceforth ceased to warrant any new lodges in India. The Grand Lodge of India inherited the administrative and organisational forms of the home Grand Lodges, with those of England being the most influential. Indeed, while Grand Lodges in other parts of the world have been having problems with falling memberships, the reverse has been true in India. Since its formation, the Grand Lodge of India has added about one hundred new lodges to its roll.

Today, masonry continues to thrive in India, and the visitor can expect to experience a great diversity of lodges, within the bounds of the regular Craft. He can also be assured of a warm fraternal welcome throughout the breadth of the approximately four hundred and sixty regular lodges operating in India.

Notes for Visitors to India

1. MEETING TIMES, AND DRESS
Lodges in India, regardless of Constitution, for the most part meet in the early evening, generally at a time between 6.30 pm and 7.30 pm. Therefore, visitors should endeavour to be attendance at their chosen lodge meeting by at least 6 pm, to enable the usual avouchment formalities to be dealt with. Dress for lodges in India is varied, and it depends somewhat on each member's ethnic background. A dark lounge suit is the norm, although national dress is not uncommon, as it applies to the various Indian sects. Similarly, a mason serving in the Armed Forces is welcome to attend in military uniform. Dinner suits are used normally by a small number of lodges in India, but by many more on Nights of Installation. For the visitor from

outside India, a dark lounge suit is appreciated although, if inconvenient, a jacket and tie will suffice.

2. LODGE AFTERPROCEEDINGS

The lodge afterproceedings of English, Irish and Scottish lodges largely follow the practices widely associated with each type elsewhere. English lodges use the festive board of formal dinners with toast lists. Scottish and Irish lodges also tend to follow the practice of following a meeting with a dinner, but toast lists are often abbreviated. Indian lodges tend to opt for formal festive boards, largely along English lines. The vast majority of lodges, regardless of warrant, conclude an Installation Meeting with an expansive and formal festive board. The Toast List employed by English, Irish and Scottish lodges in India is basically the same as outlined elsewhere in this Guide, except that the first toast in India is usually 'The Indian Republic'. An example of a full Toast List under an Indian lodge is as follows:

1. The Indian Republic.
2. The Craft.
3. The Most Worshipful the Grand Master.
4. The Deputy Grand Master, and the Assistant Grand Masters, and G.L. Officers.
5. The Regional Grand Master.
6. The Deputy Regional Grand Master, the Assistant Regional Grand Master, and Regional Grand Lodge Officers.
7. The Master and Officers of the Lodge.
8. The Outgoing Master, and his Officers.
9. The Visitors.
10. Absent Brethren.
11. The Tyler's Toast.

The above forms an example of a Toast List a visitor may experience at an Installation meeting of an Indian lodge. At a normal meeting, the list is likely to be shorter. Responses are only made if an appropriate respondent is present. If a visitor is to be asked to reply to the toast to the visitors, he will be forewarned. It is often the case that members will be charged for their meal taken at the festive board or lodge afterproceedings at a lodge meeting in India, regardless of its affiliation. Visitors, unless they regularly frequent the same lodge, will never be expected to contribute.

3. OF VISITING IN GENERAL

Visiting a lodge in India is a relatively easy affair. Each major Indian city, and one assumes it is to these that the vast majority of visitors will gravitate, has a Masonic Temple or Freemasons' Hall, and these buildings are not difficult to locate. In the main cities, such as New Delhi, Calcutta, Madras and Bombay, as well as in others, their Masonic Temple is staffed by masons during normal working hours. These staff members will be only too happy to assist a visitor. Advice concerning individual English, Scottish and Irish lodge visiting corresponds with that already fully outlined elsewhere in this guide. Indian lodges largely follow English practices in admitting visitors.

4. MASONIC GOVERNMENT

The formation of the Grand Lodge of India meant the reorganisation of British masonry, to take into account the many lodges no longer on British rolls. England formed, or carried on, with four District Grand Lodges, while Scotland now has two. Ireland had a Provincial Grand Lodge of Western India governing five lodges in Bombay, while its four lodges at Calcutta and one lodge at New Delhi were governed directly from Dublin. However, in 1983, these ten lodges united into the new Provincial Grand Lodge of Ireland in India.

The Grand Lodge of India is an appointive Grand Lodge, very much on the English model, and the titles of its offices correspond largely with those of England. Its membership, as with England, consists of all past and present Grand Lodge Officers, and all Masters, Past Masters and Wardens of its constituent lodges. Interestingly, the Indian Grand Lodge has adopted a form not unlike that of old European Grand Orients. The Grand Master is not elected by the membership of the Grand Lodge. Instead, the position is determined by an Electoral College consisting of the most Senior Grand Lodge Officers. In addition, the Board of General Purposes of the Grand Lodge is non-elective, but consists of members appointed equally by the four Regional Grand Lodges. As just mentioned, the Grand Lodge of India has formed four Regional Grand Lodges as intermediate administrative organs, viz: the Regional Grand Lodges of Northern, Western, Southern and Eastern India. Each has its own Regional Grand Master and Regional Grand Lodge Officers, and each works along similar lines to an English or Scottish District Grand Lodge.

List of Lodges
It is not practical to list the lodges meeting in India in these pages, not through lack of information, but simply through lack of space. The addresses of the four main masonic edifices in India have already been detailed, and a visitor attending any of these will readily gain information concerning any lodge meeting in India.

INDO-CHINA (Cambodia, Laos, and Vietnam)

Indo-China consists of the countries of Vietnam, Laos, and Cambodia; all of which were formerly French possessions. In years gone by, the irregular Grand Orient of France was active in the area. It erected lodges at Saigon (1868), Haiphong (1892), and Phomn Penh in Cambodia (1906). All these lodges appear to have expired when the French left the region. The Grand Lodge of the Philippines evidently had a lodge at Saigon in South Vietnam servicing American masons during the Vietnam War. As all of Indo-China is now firmly in Communist hands, freemasonry is extinct in this region.

INDONESIA

Regular freemasonry no longer exists in Indonesia, having been suppressed by the Indonesian Military Government in the 1960s. England had established at lodge in Sumatra as early as 1765, but it later expired. By the 1950s, the Grand East of the Netherlands had four lodges in Sumatra, and nineteen in Java. All these lodges were subsequently forced to close. There is scant information concerning an irregular Grand Lodge operating in Indonesia, but if it does exist the politics of the country would indicate an 'underground' operation. It is certainly not recognised outside Indonesia by any other regular masonic body.

JAPAN

Japan has a fairly short masonic history, having taken its masonic inspiration largely from the Philippines and the United States. Aside from its own regular Grand Lodge, Japan possesses lodges warranted from England, Scotland, Massachusetts, and the Philippines.

The Grand Lodge of Japan:
Founded: 1957
Address: Tokyo Masonic Centre, 1–3 Shibakoen, 4-Chome, Minato-ku, Tokyo 105. *Phone:* 4334981
Lodges: 18   Permits Dual and Plural Membership   *Membership:* 3879
Courtesy Degrees: Conferred on request. Correspondence must be through Grand Lodges.
Minimum Time Lapse between Degrees: None—candidates may advance when proficient.
Main Publications: Constitutions. Annual Proceedings. Periodical Magazine: *Masonic Shimbun.*

History

The first lodges in Japan were chartered from England. Five lodges were erected between 1866 and 1883, but only one—Rising Sun Lodge No 1401, survived the Second World War. It was founded in 1872, and works at Kobe. Scotland was slightly more fortunate with its offspring. The Grand Lodge of Scotland chartered three lodges in the 1870s, two of which survived past the War. They are Lodge Hiogo and Osaka No 498, at Kobe; and Lodge Star-in-the-East No 640, at Yokohama.

Subsequent to the Second World War, Japan found itself occupied by American Forces, amongst whom were many masons. In order to accommodate the desire of these masons to meet as such, the Grand Lodge of the Philippines erected several lodges in Japan from 1950 onwards. The Philippines would appear to have been the logical warranting authority in view of its geographical proximity to Japan, and the fact that its lodges worked a form of the American *Webb* Ritual. By 1952, the Philippines lodges in Japan had over 900 members.

In 1947, the Grand Lodge of Connecticut chartered a lodge at Tokyo, but it did not survive. However, Japan does possess one lodge warranted from Massachusetts, and meeting at Tokyo. This is the Sinim Lodge, which was originally erected in mainland China some eighty years ago. The Communist takeover in China saw it first move to Hong Kong, and then onto its present home.

By 1957, the Philippines-warranted lodges felt strong enough to form their own Grand Lodge, and fifteen lodges then working under that obedience came together for the purpose. Three Philippines lodges decided to remain with their old Grand Lodge in Manila. At this time, the new Grand Lodge reported a membership of 10,500. However, as time elapsed the American military presence in Japan declined, and the Japanese Grand Lodge suffered falling numbers as a result. It needs to be borne in mind that the majority of members under the Grand Lodge are not Japanese nationals. Currently, only about one-tenth of its membership consists of ethnic Japanese, but this number is increasing. The membership of the Grand Lodge has stabilised in recent years at about 4,000, and in 1983 it reported eighteen lodges.

The last few years have seen a very large multi-storey Masonic Centre erected in Tokyo. Tokyo also possesses a Masonic Hospital, and the Grand Lodge involves itself in some quite outstanding charity work.

Notes for Visiting in Japan

1. THE RECOGNITION PROBLEM IN JAPAN

Japan represents something of a problem for the masonic visitor, as a result of Grand Lodge recognitions. While matters relative to recognitions have been dealt with earlier in this guide, it is still necessary to detail the Japanese situation. All lodges in Japan hold warrants from either the Grand Lodges of Japan, Scotland, England, Massachusetts, or the Philippines. The problem is that while Scotland, Massachusetts and the Philippines recognise the Japanese Grand Lodge, the United Grand Lodge of England does not. Of course, Scotland, Massachusetts, the Philippines, and England all recognise each other.

One can immediately appreciate that this situation causes problems in the body of masonry in Japan. Fortunately, perhaps, England has only one lodge in Japan located at Kobe, and this city does not currently possess a Japanese-warranted lodge. However, Kobe does have a Scottish lodge. While England does not recognise the Grand Lodge of Japan, English and Japanese masons cannot visit each other's lodges, or be masonically associated. This situation obviously causes certain limitations on intervisitations between some lodges. Whatever the reasons for this situation may be, no presumptions will be undertaken here. In terms of the effect on the masonic visitor, it can be stated that with the exception of England, Ireland, Iceland, Paraguay, and the Grand Orient of Brazil, all regular Grand Lodges detailed in this guide maintain fraternal relations with the Grand Lodge of Japan, enabling intervisitation.

2. OF VISITING IN GENERAL

Dress for Japanese lodges is a dark lounge suit, although some members can be found attending in a jacket and tie. Visitors are welcome to bring and wear their own regalia. Lodges open between 6.30 pm and 7.30 pm for the most part, with the majority commencing at 7 pm. An informal light supper follows each meeting, and visitors may be called upon to speak. A charity collection is often taken. Inside the lodge, visitors can extend fraternal greetings during the closing ceremonies. Visitors should note that all official masonic functions are 'dry'—no alcohol is permitted. This also extends to the Sinim Lodge (Massachusetts), but not to lodges under England or Scotland. The English lodge at Kobe follows the English practice of festive boards, while the Scottish lodges adhere to the Harmony practices of Scotland. While visitors can readily visit any Japanese lodge, it is an appreciated courtesy to call at the Masonic Centre in Tokyo, if possible.

3. LODGE WORKINGS AND RITUALS

Japanese lodges work a form of the *Webb* Ritual, with small variations inherited from the Philippines, which in turn derived their ritual from California. Thus, the content and form of Japanese ritual is largely similar to general American practices. Its central features include the opening and closing of lodge meetings in the third degree, strict proficiency examinations for candidates, and a very full and dramatic

Third Degree ceremony. A fuller discussion of aspects of Webb ritual forms is contained elsewhere in this guide under the heading of the United States.

Most Japanese lodges work in the English language, with ethnic Japanese masons being bilingual. However, in order to attract wider membership, the Grand Lodge of Japan is well advanced in translating its ritual into Japanese. However, many of the 'Old English Forms' have made this a difficult task, and therefore a slow process.

List of Lodges

As Japan is a popular tourist destination, and as only a relatively small number of regular lodges currently work in the country, details of each are provided below:

The Grand Lodge of Japan

Far East Lodge No 1	Meets at the Masonic Temple, 3 Bluff, Yamate-cho, Naka-ku, *Yokohama*; 1st Wednesday monthly, at 7.30 pm.
Tokyo Masonic Lodge No 2	Meets at the Tokyo Masonic Centre, *Tokyo*; 1st Thursday monthly, at 7 pm.
Square and Compasses Lodge No 3	Meets at the Masonic Temple, 1-2-1 Naka, 3-chome, *Kunitachi*-shi; 1st Friday monthly, at 7 pm.
Kunitachi Lodge No 4	Meets at the Masonic Temple, 1-2-1 Naka, 3-chome, *Kunitachi*-shi; 1st Tuesday monthly, at 7 pm.
Kyoto Masonic Lodge No 5	Meets at the Masonic Building, i66 Ebiscu-cho, 3-chome, Sanjyo, Shirakawabashi, Higashiyama-ku, *Kyoto* 605; 1st Tuesday monthly, at 7.30 pm.
Torii Masonic Lodge No 6	Meets at 1-11-6 Futako-cho, Kasugai-shi, Aichi-Ken, *Nagoya*; 1st Monday monthly, at 7 pm.
Honshu Lodge No 8	Meets at the Masonic Temple, 1-2-1 Naka, 3-chome, *Kunitachi*-shi; 1st Monday monthly, at 7 pm.
Nippon Lodge No 9	Meets at the Community Building, *Sasebo*; 1st Wednesday monthly, at 1 pm.
Aomori Lodge No 10	Meets at the Masonic Building, Shimokubo Aaz, Misawa Oaza, *Misawa*; 1st Tuesday monthly, at 6.30 pm.
Tokyo Vuai Lodge No 11	Meets at the Tokyo Masonic Centre; 1st Monday monthly, at 7 pm.
Sagamihara Lodge No 13	Meets at Building No 733, North Camp Zama (US Military Base), *Zama*; 1st Tuesday monthly, at 7.30 pm.
Kokusai Lodge No 15	Meets at the Masonic Temple, P-171, American Village, Hamuramachi, Nishitama-gun, *Tokyo*; 1st Thursday monthly, at 7 pm.
Kintai Lodge No 16	Meets at the Marine Corps Air Station, *Iwakuni*; 1st Wednesday monthly, at 7 pm.
Hokkaido Lodge No 17	Meets at 75 Suehiro-cho, Eniwa-shi, *Chitose*, 1st Tuesday monthly, at 7 pm.
Harmony Lodge No 18	Meets at the Tokyo Masonic Centre, *Tokyo*; 2nd Wednesday monthly, at 7.15 pm.

Teikoku Lodge No 19	Meets at the Kishaba Masonic Temple, 306 Banck, Aza Kishaba, Kita-Nakagusuka-Son, Okinawa; 4th Monday monthly, at 7 pm.
Yokosuka Lodge No 20	Meets at Building B-53, Yokosuka Military Base, *Yokosura*; 1st Tuesday monthly, at 6.30 pm.
Wakkanai Centennial Lodge No 21	Meets at 15–130 Higashi, 1-chome, Kita 19-Jyo, Higashi-ku, *Sapporo*; 1st Tuesday monthly, at 7 pm.

United Grand Lodge of England

Rising Sun Lodge No 1401	Meets at the Kobe Club, 125 Kitano-cho, 4-chome, Ikutaku, *Kobe*; 3rd Thursday October to May, except January. Inst: 3rd Saturday, January.

Grand Lodge of Scotland

Lodge Hiogo and Osaka No 498	Meets at the Kobe Club, 125 Kitano-cho, 4-chome, Ikutaka, *Kobe*; 1st Thursday monthly, except June, July and December.
Lodge Star-in-the-East No 640	Meets at 3 Yamatecho, Nakaku, *Yokohama*; 2nd Tuesday monthly, except July and August. P.O. Box 97, Yokohama 231-91, Japan.

Grand Lodge of Massachusetts

Sinim Lodge	Meets at the Tokyo Masonic Centre, *Tokyo*; 3rd Tuesday monthly.

Grand Lodge of the Philippines

Okinawa Lodge No 118	Meets at the Kishaba Masonic Temple, Aza Kishaba, Kitanakaguka-son, *Okinawa*; 2nd Tuesday monthly, at 7.30 pm.
Loo Choo-Coral Lodge No 142	Meets at the Kishaba Masonic Temple, *Okinawa*; 2nd Friday monthly.
Rising Sun Lodge No 151	Meets at North Camp Zama (US Military Base), *Zama*; 1st Thursday monthly, at 7 pm.

KOREA (NORTH)

It would appear that North Korea has never possessed a masonic lodge. In view of the fact that this country is communist controlled, it would seem fairly certain that none will be erected in the future.

KOREA (SOUTH)

South Korea possesses three lodges holding warrants from Scotland, and two erected under the Grand Lodge of the Philippines. The first of the Scottish lodges, Lodge Han Yang No 1048, was established in 1910 by British, Canadian and American miners and merchants. It was never large in membership, and the Second World War saw it suspend activities. It revived after that War, only to face the same fate during the Korean War. However, the large influx of American troops during, and after, this War gave the lodge new impetus. Two more Scottish lodges have been erected in recent years. The Grand Lodge of the Philippines has warranted

MacArthur Lodge No 183 at Seoul; and Morning Calm Lodge No 189. Both these lodges were established in the 1970s.

The membership of all five regular lodges in Korea is composed largely of American servicemen. The Scottish lodges are administratively attached to the Scottish District Grand Lodge of the Far East, based at Hong Kong, while the Philippines lodges are governed directly from Manila. The full details of all five lodges are listed below, including the permanent postal address of the two oldest Scottish lodges. If a visitor knows his arrangements and itinerary for travel to Korea well in advance, a letter addressed to either post office box would be useful. This will provide notice of the visit, and assist in smooth lodge visitation. However, it is most advisable to forward such a letter through the visitor's own Grand Lodge Office. Nevertheless, if prior notice is not possible, the details below will assist.

Scottish Lodges

Lodge Han Yong No 1048 Meets at the Seoul Club, Samilro Building, *Seoul*; 1st and 3rd Wednesdays monthly, except June, July and August. Postal Address: C.P.O. Box 661, Seoul, South Korea.

Lodge Pusan Korea No 1675 Meets at Building 454, Haileah Compound (US Military Base), *Pusan*; 1st and 3rd Saturday monthly, except July and August. Postal address: The Secretary, Pusan Korea Masonic Lodge, US Army Garrison, Pusan—P.O. Box 308, APO SF 96259, South Korea.

Lodge Harry S Truman No 1727 Meets 1st and 3rd Saturday monthly, at the Chapel Annexe, *Osan Airbase*, Korea.

Philippines Lodges

MacArthur Lodge No 183 Meets at the Seoul Club, Samilro Building, *Seoul*; 3rd Friday monthly, at 5.30 pm.

Morning Calm Lodge No 189 Meets at the Masonic Temple, Camp Walker (US Military Base), *Taegu*, 1st Thursday monthly, at 7.30 pm.

MALAYSIA

Malaysia is a South East Asian country consisting of the former British colonies of Malaya (now East Malaysia), and North Borneo (Sarawak and Sabah, now West Malaysia). Malaysia does not include the Sultanate of Brunei, located in Northern Borneo—a largely independent protectorate of Britain. English masonry in this area is controlled by the District Grand Lodge of the Eastern Archipelago, while the Scottish lodges range under the curiously named District Grand Lodge of the Middle East. Ireland possesses only one lodge in Malaysia, and this is governed directly from Dublin.

The District Grand Lodge of the Eastern Archipeleago (Under the United Grand Lodge of England)

Address: Freemasons' Hall, Coleman Street, Singapore. 0617.

Principal Temple in Malaysia: Masonic Hall, Jalan Pekeliling, Kuala Lumpur, Malaysia.

Lodges: 18 in Malaysia (8 in Singapore, one in Brunei).

The District Grand Lodge of the Middle East (Under the Grand Lodge of Scotland)
Address: Masonic Temple, Jalan Pekeliling Street, Kuala Lumpur, Malaysia.
Lodges: 7 in Malaysia (2 in Singapore, one in Bangkok).

History

It is somewhat difficult to separate the masonic histories of Malaysia and Singapore, but in terms of the format of this guide, an attempt will be made. The first lodge in the country (then known as Malaya) was established at Penang in 1809. This was an English lodge warranted by the Antients, but it subsequently expired. Singapore received a permanent lodge in 1845, but it was not until 1875 that Malaya received a lodge that was to survive. This was the English lodge, Royal Prince of Wales No 1555, which still works happily at Penang. Scotland's earliest surviving lodge also works at Penang. This is Lodge Scotia No 1003, warranted in 1906. In the 1980s, the capital city of Malaysia, Kuala Lumpur, possesses the most lodges. Ireland has currently only one lodge in the country. This is Lodge Emerald in the East No 830, established at Kuala Lumpur in 1967.

In recent years, the Malaysian Government has taken an interest in the Craft within its boundaries. The Government's Societies Act requires that masonic lodges regularly disclose their membership and certain other details to the Registrar of Societies. However, this statute does not appear to have been directed against freemasonry in particular, although the Craft has in the past been discussed in the Malaysian Parliament. Nevertheless, good relations between Craft authorities and the Government have been maintained, and there appears to be no reason to suspect that this relationship will not be continued in the future.

Notes for visiting in Malaysia

Probably the first thing a visitor will notice when visiting a lodge in Malaysia is its ethnic makeup. While the Craft in South East Asia was once dominated by Anglo-Saxons, this is certainly not the case today. Today, Malaysian citizens constitute the majority of members. However, it is the Chinese and Indians who have joined the Craft in some numbers, not ethnic Malays, although there are certainly Malays who are members.

The majority of lodges in Malaysia meet in the early evening, generally between 6.30 pm and 7.30 pm. Dress is a dark lounge suit, and visitors are welcome to bring and wear their own regalia. Lodge workings and afterproceedings follow respective English, Irish and Scottish practices outlined elsewhere in this guide. All lodges generally follow an Installation Meeting with a formal dinner.

List of Lodges

Visitors should, at least in the first instance, make themselves known at the Masonic Hall in Kuala Lumpur, where they will receive every assistance. However, as lodges are somewhat geographically spread, a full list is contained below:

KUALA LUMPUR:
Lodges meeting at the Masonic Hall, Jalan Pekeliling Street, Kuala Lumpur.

Read Lodge No 2337 EC	Meets 3rd Friday monthly, except October. Inst: Saturday nearest to 21st October.

Klang Lodge No 3369 EC	Meets 2nd Wednesday monthly, except October. Inst: 2nd Saturday, October.
Makepeace Lodge No 3674 EC	Meets 2nd Friday monthly, except April. Inst: 2nd Saturday, April.
Baldwyn Lowick Lodge No 7004 EC	Meets 1st Thursday montly, except March. Inst: 1st Saturday, March.
Sentosa Lodge No 7661 EC	Meets 3rd Tuesday monthly, except August. Inst: 3rd Saturday, August.
Edward Holiday Lodge No 7997 EC	Meets 1st Friday monthly, except March. Inst: 2nd Saturday, March.
Lodge Emerald in the East No 830 IC	Meets 3rd Wednesday monthly, except July. Inst: 3rd Saturday, July.
Lodge Tullibardine-in-the-East No 1118 SC	Meets 4th Friday monthly, except June. Inst: 3rd Saturday, June.
Lodge Kilwinning in the East No 1606 SC	Meets 1st Wednesday monthly, except November. Inst: 1st Saturday, November.

PENANG

Lodges in Penang meet at the Masonic Temple, Western Road, Penang.

Royal Prince of Wales Lodge No 1555 EC	Meets 1st Wednesday monthly, except December. Inst: 1st Saturday, December.
Lodge Scotia No 1003 SC	Meets 4th Thursday monthly, except May and December. Inst: 3rd Saturday, May.

IPOH

Lodges in Ipoh meet at the Masonic Temple, Tiger Lane, Ipoh.

Kinta Lodge No 3212 EC	Meets 3rd Thursday monthly. Inst: July.
Napier Lodge No 3418 EC	Meets 2nd Saturday monthly. Inst: September.
Lodge Angus No 1529 SC	Meets 3rd Wednesday monthly. Inst: June.

OTHER LODGES AND MEETING PLACES

English Lodges

Johore Royal Lodge No 3946	Meets Freemasons' Hall, Jalan Scudai, *Johore Bahru*, Johore, East Malaysia; 3rd Wednesday monthly. Inst: October.
Elliot Lodge No 3557	Meets at the Masonic Hall, Koon Cheng Road, *Malacca*, East Malaysia; 2nd Saturday monthly. Inst: December.
Johore Utara Lodge No 5342	Meets at the Masonic Rooms, *Muar Johore*, East Malaysia; 3rd Saturday monthly. Inst: February.
Negi Sembilan Lodge No 3552	Meets at the Masonic Hall, *Seremban*, Negri Sembilan, East Malaysia; 1st Saturday monthly. Inst: January.
Lodge Kedah No 3830	Meets at Freemasons' Hall, *Sungei Patani*, Kedah, East Malaysia; 2nd Friday monthly, except August. Inst: 2nd Saturday, August.
Perak Jubilee Lodge No 2225	Meets at the Masonic Hall, *Tiaping*, Kedah, East Malaysia; 2nd Wednesday monthly, except December. Inst: 3rd Saturday, December.

Beaufort Lodge No 7989	Meets at the Woodford Estate House, *Beaufort*, Sabah, West Malaysia; Last Saturday in February, May, August and November. Inst: November.
Lodge Kinabalu No 7047	Meets at the Masonic Hall, *Kota Kinabalu*, Sabah, West Malaysia; 2nd Thursday monthly. Inst: January.
Elopura Lodge No 7545	Meets at Elopura Hall, Siburga Road, *Sandakan*, Sabah, West Malaysia; 3rd Wednesday monthly. Inst: January.

Scottish Lodges

Lodge Sarawak No 1452	Meets at the Masonic Hall, Batu Lintang Road, *Kuching*, Sarawak, West Malaysia; Last Tuesday, monthly (3rd Tuesday in December), except January. Inst: 3rd Saturday January.
Lodge Royal Pahang No 1589	Meets at the Masonic Temple, *Kuantan*, Pahang, East Malaysia; 2nd Saturday monthly. Inst: March.

NEPAL

Nepal is located in the Himalayas, to the north of India. This ancient Kingdom was devoid of freemasonry until 1967, whereupon an English lodge was erected at Kathmandu, the capital city. It remains the only lodge in the country, and is governed through the English District Grand Lodge of Bengal. Its details are as follows:

Kathmandu of Nepal Lodge No 8194	Meets at the Hotel Shanker, Kingsway, Kathmandu, Nepal; 1st Monday monthly. Inst: December.

PAKISTAN

Until recently, the British Grand Lodges had quite a number of lodges located in Pakistan, under appropriate District Grand Lodges. However, in the last few years Government pressure has forced most to close, and the future for the few still working does not look promising. The Scottish District Grand Lodge was closed in 1980, and the eleven Scottish lodges working in the country previously were erased from the Scottish Roll of lodges. The English District Grand Lodge still appears on the English Roll as of 1983, but only two of is fourteen lodges are shown as working.

The District Grand Lodge of Pakistan (Under the United Grand Lodge of England) *Principal Temple:* Freemasons' Hall, Strachan Road, Karachi. *Lodges:* 14.

History

Until 1947, when the Indian sub-continent was partitioned, the modern history of Pakistan was largely that of India. The establishment of the British Raj brought the area now occupied by Pakistan into the British Empire. The first lodge established was erected at Lahore in 1858. This was the Lodge of Hope and Perseverance No 782 EC. Doubtless, the significance of the name of this lodge has not been lost to masons in Pakistan in the light of recent events. This lodge was followed by two more early lodges established at Hyderabad (1861), and Karachi (1863). Scotland's first lodge, still remaining on its roll until 1980, was Lodge Hope No 337, established in 1847, and was thus the premier regular lodge in the country.

The Craft has worked smoothly in Pakistan until recent years, whereupon a military dictatorship assumed power in the country. Indeed, successive Pakistani Governments appear not to have viewed the Craft generally with great favour. In addition, Pakistani nationals of the Moslem faith who make up the bulk of the population, have not formed a significant part of lodge memberships. The coming of military Government to Pakistan has seen official opposition to the Craft in recent years. As of 1983, only two English lodges were reported to be still working in the country.

Notes for Visitors to Pakistan
The current unhappy situation of the Craft in Pakistan makes its future most uncertain, and it would appear likely that no masonic activity will soon be possible. While the two remaining lodges still reported to be working are listed below with details, visitors are most strongly advised to seek information from their own Grand Lodge Office prior to attempting to visit in Pakistan.

Lodge Light in the Himalayas No 1448 EC	Meets at Freemasons' Hall, Karachi, 1st Wednsday in January, March, April and May. Inst: April.
Quetta Lodge No 2333 EC	Meets Tams Boq Building, Sanobar Colony, Tarbela Dam, District Hazara, Pakistan; 3rd Thursday September to May. Inst: April.

PHILIPPINES

The Philippines has had a long, although not always happy, masonic history. It possesses a large regular Grand Lodge, dating from 1917.

The Grand Lodge of the Philippines
Founded: 1917

Address: Plaridel Masonic Temple, 1440 San Marcelino Street, Manila.

Lodges: 211   Permits Dual Membership.

Membership: 15,037.

Descent: California.   *Government:*   Elective Grand Lodge.

Courtesy Degrees: Permitted. Correspondence should be through Grand Lodges.

Minimum Time Lapse between Degrees: One month.   *Ritual:* Webb (with variations).

Main Publications: Annual Grand Lodge Proceedings. Constitution. Periodical: *The Cabletow*, published bi-monthly.

History
Freemasonry appears to have come to the Philippines about the 1760s, with merchants and mariners. While no records seem to exist of early lodges, there must have been some activity as in 1812 the Spanish Government banned freemasonry, ordered the expulsion of masons from the Islands, and the confiscation of their property. In context, it needs to be appreciated that the Philippines was then a Spanish possession with Roman Catholicism dominant. This ban appears to have been rigorously enforced, at least until the 1850s.

The first recorded lodge erected in the Philippines was established with a Portuguese charter in 1856, followed by a German lodge. In the 1880s, the Grand Orient of Spain warranted four lodges, and these lodges started to admit Philippine nationals, among the first of whom was Jose Rizal, regarded as the Father of the Philippines. The Craft continued under repression until the Spanish–American War of 1888, which saw the end of Spanish rule. Finally, freemasonry was in a position to develop peacefully.

A number of American lodges were soon erected, mostly with Californian warrants. By 1901, the irregular French Grand Orient had three lodges working in the country. Scotland erected lodge Perla del Oriente No 1034 in 1907; and Lodge Cebu No 1106 in 1912. The former still works happily in Manila, while the latter subsequently expired.

By 1917, the Craft in the Philippines was strong enough to form a sovereign Grand Lodge, and the Grand Lodge of Philippines was born. Its principal sponsors were three Californian lodges, which were later joined by several lodges then under the Spanish Grand Orient, and one lodge chartered from Portugal. The Grand Lodge has developed steadily since, although in its early days it did suffer two minor schisms which remain unhealed. As a result two irregular bodies, namely the Gran Logia del Archipelago Filipino, and the Grande Orient Filipino still work in the country.

Notes for Visiting in the Philippines
All constituent lodges of the Grand Lodge of the Philippines work a form of the American Webb Ritual, closely aligned to Californian forms. Consequently, lodges open in the third degree, and conduct normal lodge business at separate meetings. Somewhat consequential to its parentage in the masonic sense, the 'higher' degrees are popular in the Philippines, particularly the Scottish Rite. The majority of Philippines lodges meet at a time between 6 pm and 7.30 pm, and meetings are followed by a light supper, or in some cases preceded by one. Refreshments served at such suppers may not be alcoholic. Toasts in the English sense are not known, although there may be a few short addresses, and visitors recognised. Dress used by Philippines masons is almost invariably the Barong, which is a national-type dress. It consists of a particularly fine cotton shirt, worn with open neck, and dark trousers. These Barongs often feature coloured embroidery. Visitors are welcome to wear a lounge suit, or jacket and tie, but they might feel slightly out of place in such attire. Therefore, an open-neck shirt and dark pants are advised. Visitors can bring and use their own regalia, although this will be supplied to those without it.

Administratively, the Philippines lodges are divided into forty districts, each under a District Deputy Grand Master. All Grand Lodge Offices are elective, and the Grand Lodge meets annually, in April.

List of Lodges
The Grand Lodges of the Philippines currently has over two hundred lodges under warrant, but space prevents the provision of details for all of them. However, a visitor to the Philippines will doubtlessly enter via Manila, its capital city. Therefore, lodges meeting at that location are listed below.
(1) denotes lodges meeting at the Scottish Rite Temple, 1828 Taft Avenue, Manila, and

(2) denotes lodges meeting at the Plaridel Masonic Temple, 1440 San Marcelino Street, Manila.

Manila-Mount Lebanon Lodge No 1	Meets (1); 1st Tuesday monthly at 7 pm.
St John's Corregidor Lodge, No 2	Meets (1); 2nd Thursday monthly at 7 pm.
Bagumbayan Lodge No 4	Meets (1); 2nd Wednesday monthly at 6 pm.
Island Luz Minerva Lodge No 5	Meets (2); 4th Saturday monthly at 3 pm.
Biak-Na-Bato Lodge No 7	Meets (2); 2nd Tuesday monthly at 8 pm.
Cosmos Lodge No 8	Meets (1); 1st Friday monthly at 6 pm.
Nilad Lodge No 12	Meets (2); 1st Saturday monthly at 4 pm.
Walana Lodge No 13	Meets (2); 4th Saturday monthly at 2 pm.
Dalisday Lodge No 14	Meets (2); 1st Tuesday monthly at 6 pm.
Sinukuan Lodge No 16	Meets (2); 2nd Friday monthly at 6 pm.
Araw Lodge No 18	Meets (2); 2nd Saturday monthly at 2 pm.
Dapitan Lodge No 21	Meets (2); 3rd Monday monthly at 6 pm.
Jose Rizal Lodge No 22	Meets (2); 1st Wednesday monthly at 6 pm.
Batong Buhay Lodge No 27	Meets (2); 2nd Saturday monthly at 6 pm.
Zapote Lodge No 29	Meets (2); 3rd Tuesday monthly at 7 pm.
Luzon Lodge No 52	Meets (2); 1st Thursday monthly at 5 pm.
Labong Lodge No 59	Meets (2); 1st Saturday monthly at 3 pm.
Kasilawan Lodge No 77	Meets (2); 1st Tuesday monthly at 6 pm.
Taga-ilog Lodge No 79	Meets (2); 4th Saturday monthly at 6 pm.
F.D. Roosevelt Memorial Lodge No 81	Meets (2); 3rd Saturday monthly at 4 pm.
High Twelve Lodge No 82	Meets (2); 2nd Saturday monthly at 2.30 pm.
Hiram Lodge No 88	Meets (2); 1st Friday monthly at 5.30 pm.
Mencius Lodge No 93	Meets (1); 1st Wednesday monthly at 7.30 pm.
Service Lodge No 95	Meets (1); 2nd Friday monthly at 6.30 pm.
Noli Me Tangere Lodge No 148	Meets (2); 1st Saturday monthly at 5 pm.
King Solomon Lodge No 150	Meets (2); 2nd Monday monthly at 6 pm.
Manuel Roxas Lodge No 152	Meets (2); 2nd Monday monthly at 6 pm.
Saigon Lodge No 188	Meets (2); 1st Wednesday monthly at 7 pm.
Jacobo Zobel Lodge No 202	Meets (2); 3rd Thursday monthly at 7 pm.
Lodge Perla del Oriente No 1034 SC	Meets (1); 3rd Saturday monthly.

Visitors to the Philippines are advised, in the first instance, to make themselves known at the Grand Secretary's Office in Manila, if possible. If wishing to visit elsewhere in the Philippines, the visitor can obtain all details and assistance there. Alternatively, a full directory of lodges is published annually in the Grand Lodge's periodical, the *Cabletow*, usually in the May–June Edition.

SRI LANKA (CEYLON)

The island of Ceylon (renamed Sri Lanka in 1972), is aptly known as the Pearl of the Orient. It lies in the Indian Ocean to the south-east of India. Sri Lanka has a long masonic history, the Craft having existed on the island for over two hundred years. Currently, an English District Grand Lodge operates in the country, and an

Irish Inspectorate. Scotland possesses only one lodge in Sri Lanka, located at Colombo.

The District Grand Lodge of Sri Lanka (Under the United Grand Lodge of England)
  Address: Victoria Masonic Temple, Galle Face, Colombo 3, Sri Lanka.
  Lodges: 9
The Grand Inspectorate of Sri Lanka (Under the Grand Lodge of Ireland)
  Address: Victoria Masonic Temple, Galle Face, Colombo 3, Sri Lanka.
  Lodges: 3.

History

The island of Ceylon became a British possession in 1796, the Dutch having been ejected. However, in the last 26 years of their occupation, three Dutch lodges were erected in the colony. These lodges continued after the British annexation of the island, although the subsequent French occupation of Holland itself brought these lodges under the Grand Orient of France. By the 1830s, all three lodges would appear to have had a large content of English members, and in 1838, one of them was re-warranted by England as the St John's Lodge of Colombo No 454. It remains the oldest lodge surviving in Sri Lanka today—the other two former Dutch lodges having become extinct.

As with many other parts of the British Empire, military lodges played an important part in the development of freemasonry in Ceylon. Between 1800 and 1863, nine military lodges worked in the colony under various British charters, and these lodges largely spawned the permanent lodges to be established in the country. The years 1861 and 1868 saw two separate Irish lodges receive warrants, largely under the influence of Irish military lodges then in the colony. A second English lodge was formed in 1886. Scottish masonry came to the island in the form of Lodge Bonnie Doon No 611. It was erected in 1878, and remains the only lodge of the Scottish Constitution to be established in Ceylon. There was not complete harmony between the various lodges in the early days of masonic development, although this had disappeared by the twentieth century.

Today, the thirteen lodges in Sri Lanka work in complete amity, and many native-born Ceylonese hold membership. However, numbers are somewhat restricted by religious and income groupings. The low income of many Ceylonese restricts membership to the more affluent who can afford the dues. Similarly, some locally practised religions are not consistent with masonic membership. Nevertheless, lodges in Sri Lanka contain members who are Hindus, Mohammedans, Sikhs, Parsees, Zorastrians and, of course, Christians. The future of freemasonry in Sri Lanka looks fairly secure, although the Government appears to have taken some interest in masonic activities at various times.

Notes for Visitors in Sri Lanka

1. MEETING TIMES, AND DRESS

The meetings of lodges in Sri Lanka usually start at 6 pm, or 6.30 pm. Visitors are advised to be early. It is probably fair to say that most masons in Sri Lanka visiting between lodges will be known by at least one member, and will be readily vouched for. Of course, at least for the first visit, an overseas visitor is unlikely to be known, and must be present early enough for the usual formalities to be undertaken.

The dress worn at all ordinary meetings is a dark lounge suit, with white shirt and black tie. At Installation meetings, it is usual for dinner suits to be worn, although this is not mandatory, and overseas visitors are certainly welcome in a dark lounge suit.

2. LODGE AFTERPROCEEDINGS, AND NIGHTS OF INSTALLATION

The afterproceedings of all lodges in Sri Lanka are usually short, as no evening meal is served. In its place, savouries, sandwiches, cheese and biscuits, are on the tables, and afterwards members travel home for their evening meal. Refreshments, including alcoholic drinks, are available on the lodge account, up until the Tyler's Toast. The toasts themselves are kept short, but do include one to the visitors.

The Installation meeting of every lodge is followed by a banquet and formal festive board, accompanied by a full toast list. Banquets are usually held at one of the large hotels, or in Colombo often at the Victoria Masonic Temple. The cost of the banquet is met by the lodge out of members' dues. A visitor from overseas will be welcomed as a guest of the lodge, and will not be required to pay. However, visitors should provide notice of their impending attendance, if at all possible. The Toast List at Installation meetings is the same for all three Constitutions, and is as follows:

1. His Excellency, the President of Sri Lanka.
2. Her Majesty the Queen.
3. The Grand Master.
4. The Pro Grand Master, and officers of Grand Lodge, Past and Present.
5. The District Grand Master (or Grand Inspector in Irish lodges).
6. The Deputy District Grand Master, and District Grand Lodge Officers, Past and Present.
7. The Worshipful Master, and his officers.
8. The Installing Master (invariably the Immediate Past Master of the Lodge).
9. The Visitors.
10. Absent Brethren
11. The Tyler's Toast.

Replies are given if the recipient of a toast is present. Overseas visitors can normally be expected to ask to reply to the Visitors' Toast. At ordinary meetings, as applicable, a toast to a candidate will be given. Once the formalities are completed, many members choose to remain for a while and engage in conversation. The Victoria Masonic Temple has its own private bar facilities, which remains open for one hour after the Tyler's Toast, or from 10 pm, whichever is the later. Lodges located at Kandy and Kurunegala also possess private bars with their masonic halls, while the country lodges usually meet in special halls belonging to a country club, to which most lodge members belong.

3. OF VISITING IN GENERAL

A visitor arriving in Sri Lanka should first endeavour to visit the Victoria Masonic Temple in Colombo. This will normally be possible as Colombo is the main point of entry into the country. The 'VMT', as it is locally called, is the headquarters of freemasonry in Sri Lanka; and the temple secretary resides on the premises. He is a senior Past Master, and remains ready to offer every assistance to a visitor. In the lobby of this temple is a notice board, which shows all masonic meetings to be held in the succeeding two months, together with full details.

On arrival at a lodge meeting, a visitor is usually met and welcomed by the Junior Warden, who will see to his place in the lodge. Overseas masonic visitors are not particularly common in Sri Lanka, and such a visitor can expect to be invited to attend as many lodge meetings as fit into his schedule. The VMT is very centrally located in Colombo, and overseas visitors are invariably offered transport from their place of residence. A visitor wishing to travel to a country lodge meeting should make some arrangements regarding transport. As a result of the high cost of petrol in Sri Lanka, members generally join together and travel by coach. The distances involved are about sixty to seventy-five miles, and coaches are organised to leave the VMT about 1 pm on the meeting day, and return the same night. Seats can be reserved with the VMT secretary.

4. LODGE WORKINGS, REGALIA AND RITUAL

Visitors should carry their own regalia with them, although this can be loaned if necessary. The ritual of all English lodges is *Emulation*, while the Irish and Scottish lodges use their Grand Lodge approved rituals. In lodges under all three Constitutions, all ordinary members and visitors will be inside the lodge room prior to the opening. When all is in readiness, the Master and his principal officers will enter in procession, whereupon the lodge will be opened. During the closing ceremonies of each lodge, fraternal greetings are exchanged between the Master and visitors. Overseas visitors are welcome to do likewise, stating the name and constitution of their lodge.

List of Lodges

The following are the details of all regular lodges working in Sri Lanka. All lodges in Colombo meet at the Victoria Masonic Temple, Galle Face, Colombo 3, while lodges in Kandy meet at the Masonic Temple, in central Kandy. Other meeting places are as indicated.

COLOMBO

St George Lodge No 2170 EC	Meets last Thursday June to February, except December, then 3rd Tuesday. Inst: January.
Duke of Connaught Lodge No 2940 EC	Meets 3rd Thursday odd months. Inst: January.
Orion Lodge No 5130 EC	Meets 3rd Wednesday June to February. Inst: June.
Robert Coleridge Scott Lodge No 7784 EC	Meets 1st Tuesday even months, except August. Inst: 2nd Saturday, August.
Sphinx Lodge No 107 IC	Meets 4th Monday monthly, except December.
Leinster Lodge No 115 IC	Meets 3rd Friday monthly, except December.
Lodge Bonnie Doon No 611 SC	Meets 1st Saturday monthly.

KANDY

St John's Lodge of Colombo No 454 EC	Meets 3rd Saturday in January, March, April, July, September, October and November. Inst: Saturday nearest June 24th.
Nuwara Eliya Lodge, No 2991 EC	Meets 1st Saturday even months. Inst: February.

OTHER PLACES

The Grant Lodge No 2862 EC	Meets at the New Oriental Hotel, *Galle*; last Saturday in odd months. Inst: May.
Kurunegala Lodge No 3629 EC	Meets at the Masonic Temple, *Kurunegala*; 2nd Saturday in odd months. Inst: March.
Adam's Peak Lodge No 2656 EC	Meets at the Masonic Temple, Talawakelle Club, *Talawakelle*; 4th Friday even months. Inst: October.
Dimbula Lodge No 298 IC	Meets at the Talawakelle Club, *Talawakelle*; 4th Tuesday odd months.

SINGAPORE

Singapore Island sits off the southern tip of Eastern Malaysia. It is a former British colony, and remains the main commercial centre of South East Asia, and a popular tourist destination. Singapore currently possesses eight lodges forming part of an English District Grand Lodge, and two lodges forming part of a Scottish District. One Irish lodge also works in the country.

The District Grand Lodge of the Eastern Archipelago (Under the United Grand Lodge of England).
   Address: Freemasons' Hall, Coleman Street, Singapore.
   Lodges: 8 in Singapore (Malaysia: 20).
The District Grand Lodge of the Middle East (Under the Grand Lodge of Scotland).
   Address: Read Masonic Temple, Kuala Lumpur, Malaysia.
   Lodges: 2 in Singapore (8 in S E Asia).

History

Singapore was long a British colony until it received independence as a separate nation after the Second World War. Freemasonry has, equally, had an extensive history on the island. The oldest surviving lodge is Zetland in the East Lodge No 508, English warranted in 1845. Of the two Scottish lodges now working in Singapore, the oldest is Lodge Aisla No 1172; established in 1918. Ireland was relatively late in entering the scene, with only one lodge currently working in the country, dating from 1954. Lodges in Singapore now have a very high proportion of Chinese members. All lodges in the country work in complete harmony and meet at the same address.

Notes for Visiting in Singapore

All lodges meeting in Singapore commence at or about 6 pm to 7 pm. Dress is a dark lounge suit, although dinner suits are often worn by members to Installation meetings. The customs of masonry in Singapore are largely similar to those already discussed in terms of Malaysia and Hong Kong, and therefore it is largely unnecessary to repeat those points here.

In the first instance, visitors should make their way to Freemasons' Hall, Coleman Street, where all lodges in Singapore meet, regardless of Constitution. This imposing edifice is staffed, and visitors will receive full fraternal assistance. It also contains an outstanding library and museum which are sure to be of interest to the visitor.

List of Lodges
All lodges working in Singapore are detailed below, and all meet at Freemasons' Hall, Coleman Street.

Zetland in the East Lodge No 508 EC	Meets 2nd Friday monthly. Inst: December.
The Lodge of St George No 1152 EC	Meets 4th Friday monthly. Inst: April.
Lodge St Michael No 2933 EC	Meets on the 29th day of January, April, July and September. Inst: September.
Eastern Gate Lodge No 2970 EC	Meets 3rd Thursday monthly. Inst: July.
Lodge Singapore No 7178 EC	Meets 1st Monday monthly. Inst: February.
Stamford Raffles Lodge No 7444 EC	Meets 1st Wednesday monthly. Inst: September.
Horsburgh Lodge No 7533 EC	Meets 2nd Thursday monthly. Inst: January.
Centenary Lodge No 7629 EC	Meets 4th Wednesday monthly. Inst: October.
Lodge St Patrick No 765 IC	Meets 2nd Wednesday monthly. Inst: March.
Lodge Ailsa No 1172 SC	Meets 4th Thursday monthly. Inst: March.
Lodge St Andrew No 1437 SC	Meets 3rd Monday monthly except June, July and August. Inst: November.

THAILAND

Thailand possesses only one extant lodge. This is Lodge St John No 1072, warranted at Bangkok by Scotland in 1910. As the only lodge working in the country, it has quite a large membership—235 in 1981—which is considerable in terms of a British lodge. Quite naturally, it is also very active, and recently it reported thirty-five office bearers! While the majority of its members are expatriates, a number of native Thais also belong to it. It is governed by the Scottish District Grand Lodge of the Middle East based at Kuala Lumpur, Malaysia; and its details are as follows:

Lodge St John No 1072	Meets at No 11 Soi Prompong (Soi 39), Sukumvit Road, Bangkok, on the last Wednesday monthly except July. Inst: January.

Section IV

Visiting in The British Isles

The British Isles

An Overview
The British Isles possesses three regular Grand Lodges—those of England, Ireland, and Scotland. These three are, in the order just given, the oldest Grand Lodges in the world, and certainly the most respected. Naturally, the premier (United) Grand Lodge of England holds pride of place in this regard.

All three Grand Lodges have been most active in the past in warranting lodges outside their immediate geographical jurisdictions, and still are. Indeed, these three Grand Lodges have, either directly or indirectly, been the sources of all other Grand Lodges in the world. In this sense, all freemasonry is descended from the British Isles, and England in particular. An English lodge is still to be found on every continent, and most possess many. Of course, the spread of English, Irish and Scottish masonry was largely the result of British colonialism, and in particular the vast expansion of the British Empire in the nineteenth century. While this Empire has now vanished, many of the lodges have remained, as will be noted elsewhere in this guide.

The matter of jurisdiction in this respect is an interesting one. Of course, it is universally accepted amongst the regular Grand Lodges that one's geographical jurisdiction is masonically inviolable. Therefore, for example, no other foreign Grand Lodge would ever attempt to erect a lodge in, say, England. However, it is generally equally accepted that where a country or area has no regular Grand Lodge, this is 'open territory' at least until a new regular Grand Lodge is formed therein. Technically, most of Asia and Africa falls into the category of 'open territory'. Nevertheless, for the historical reasons just mentioned, it is rare to find any of these open territories possessing other than English, Irish or Scottish lodges—although there are some, mainly in French-speaking Africa. These overseas British lodges are dealt with elsewhere in this guide under appropriate headings. In broad terms, therefore, the following texts concerning England, Ireland and Scotland apply to English, Irish and Scottish masonry in the British Isles itself. Nonetheless, quite obviously English, Irish and Scottish masonry tends to be very similar whether it be located in the British Isles, or in foreign parts. In some cases, a few minor differences have arisen in overseas lodge practices—the relative remoteness of various lodges from home providing explanations in this area.

All the three British Grand Lodges organise themselves with intermediate administrative structures, although this cannot be seen as a devolution of masonic power. All possess what are termed 'Provincial' or 'District' Grand Lodges. For England and Scotland, lodges inside their geographical jurisdictions are placed in 'Provinces', whilst those overseas are placed in 'Districts'. For Ireland, the term 'Province' is used regardless of whether or not the administrative unit is inside or outside Ireland. A Provincial Grand Lodge, or a District Grand Lodge has fairly wide administrative powers within its own area. All the three British Constitutions are administratively divided in this way. Most lodges are, therefore, placed into a Province or District. The exceptions to this are London lodges in the case of England, and lodges which are geographically removed. Generally, a Province or District requires several lodges, at least, before one can be formed. Overseas areas with some lodges, but not quite enough to form a full District, are often placed under a District Superintendent until masonic growth has become sufficient for a District Grand Lodge to be established. Overseas lodges without near neighbouring lodges under the same constitution, are generally governed directly by the applicable Grand Lodge.

A Provincial, or a District, Grand Lodge functions in an analogous way to its actual Grand Lodge. A Provincial or District Grand Master and Grand Officers are appointed (or elected, as applicable) and these bodies meet, generally on an annual basis. A Provincial, or District, Grand Master has a fair range of masonic powers within this own province. It is not difficult to appreciate that the relative vastness of the three British Grand Lodges has made these intermediate tiers of masonic government most necessary, and the system works well. Nonetheless, it must be noted that the applicable Grand Lodge in each case is completely sovereign, and Provinces and Districts can in no way be seen as Grand Lodges in their own right.

The last point to be made in terms of a 'British Overview' is that of the titles of lodges. Lodges under England, for the most part, place the word 'Lodge' last in their name, whereas the Scottish usually place it first. For example, assume that a lodge is called 'Friendship'. Under England, it would likely be styled 'Friendship Lodge', whereas under Scotland it would probably be called 'Lodge Friendship'. A minority of Irish lodges (mostly in Northern Ireland) carry no name, but are known only by number. Where this occurs the word 'Lodge' is always placed first (for example: Lodge No 500). For named Irish lodges, some use the Scottish system, while others prefer the usual English practice—there being no great allegiance in either direction.

ENGLAND

England possesses the oldest, largest, and most respected masonic jurisdiction in the world. It is also the most widely diffused, and probably the most diverse. It is therefore essential that English freemasonry be examined at length.

The United Grand Lodge of Antient, Free and Accepted Masons of England.
Founded: 1717.
Address: Freemasons' Hall, Great Queen Street, London, WC2B 5AZ. Telephone: 01-831 9811
Lodges: Circa 8, 170. Permits Dual and Plural Membership. *Membership:* Circa 600,000.
Descent: Early Operative. *Government:* Appointive Grand Lodge.
Courtesy Degrees: Permitted. All correspondence must be through Grand Lodges.
Minimum Time Lapse between Degrees: Twenty-eight Days. *Ritual:* Various English.
Main Publications: Constitutions. *Masonic* Year Book. Masonic Year Book Historical Supplement (1969). Grand Lodge Proceedings.

History
The Premier Grand Lodge possesses the longest masonic history of any jurisdiction, and space here prevents no more than the briefest outline. It was formed in 1717 by four Old Lodges then meeting at various London taverns, with Anthony Sayer as

first Grand Master. The earliest years of the English Grand Lodge era proved far from harmonious, and the eighteenth century saw six Grand Lodges emerging at various times to claim jurisdiction over England or part of it; in some cases as a result of schism.

However, only two of these Grand Lodges persisted with any substantial following. These were the Premier Grand Lodge of England (usually referred to as the Moderns Grand Lodge, or Moderns), and the Antients or Atholl Grand Lodge (usually referred to as the Antients). From its very beginnings, the Moderns Grand Lodge was not particulary well organised or efficient, and according to its opponents, it introduced unacceptable changes in ritual and customs. Certainly, it would appear that some members were less than satisfied with its administration of the Craft.

By 1751, the Antients Grand Lodge was fully formed. It was established originally by Irish brethren unhappy with the Premier Grand Lodge, and subsequently many masons came to range under it. Both these Grand Lodges developed and expanded membership over succeeding years, and this occurred quite independently of each other. Both Grand Lodges were rivals, often bitter rivals, and each considered the other to be irregular. Generally, the Moderns tended to attract more 'upper class' members, while the Antients appeared to have a far broader membership base. In terms of organisation, the Antients, unlike the Moderns, widely practised the Royal Arch Degree; and to some extent the 'Chair Degree of Installed Master'. A fair number of differences in practices developed between the two Grand Lodges. However, except at an official level, ordinary masons were not overly interested in this rivalry, and the bulk of membership on both sides either ignored these divergences or paid little heed to them.

In most places, the rapid expansion of the Craft and the passing of time saw these old discords largely disappear. Newer members on both sides had no understanding of the issues involved, and even less interest in them. The pressure for union increased, and the chance of such an occurrence was greatly enhanced upon the election of the Duke of Sussex as Grand Master of the Moderns, and his brother the Duke of Kent as Grand Master of the Antients. Joint Committees of the two Grand Lodges met and overcame remaining problems, and the union was happily effected on 13 May 1813. The title *United* Grand Lodge of England was adopted, and the Duke of Sussex became its first Grand Master.

The United Grand Lodge subsequently has developed into the largest in the world today, having lodges warranted on every continent. English masonry has directly, or indirectly, been the source of all regular Grand Lodges elsewhere on the globe. The Grand Temple, at Freemasons' Hall, London, is probably the most magnificent in the world. Some of the great institutions associated with the United Grand Lodge include several Masonic Benevolent Institutions, Masonic Homes for the Elderly, and the Royal Masonic Hospital.

The 250th anniversary of the Grand Lodge was celebrated on 27 June 1967, with an especial Grand Lodge Communication held in the Royal Albert Hall, London. HRH the Duke of Kent was installed as Grand Master on that occasion—an office he still holds today.

Notes for Visitors to England

1. MEETING TIMES' AND DRESS

As already indicated, the English Constitution is fairly diverse in terms of its practices, and the meeting times of lodges prove no exception. As with many English customs, it is nearly impossible to generalise, except in the broadest terms. The majority of lodges in London meet about 5 pm, and dine after the lodge is closed. A few London lodges meet in the afternoon, dining about 6 pm. In many English provincial centres, lodges will often meet between 6.30 pm and 7.30 pm. In view of these variations, visitors will need to have some knowledge of the particular lodge, or lodges, they seek to visit.

Prior to World War Two, a dinner suit was the common form of dress when attending a lodge meeting, but this became impractical during the war. Subsequently, a dark lounge suit has become the norm. Many members wear a black suit, white shirt, and long black tie. White gloves are also commonly worn. However, there are still a few lodges that prescribe a dinner suit for their members. Nevertheless, a visitor will always be welcome in a dark suit. In addition, there are lodges that require members to dress in a dinner suit for Installation meetings, while a dark suit is approved for normal meetings. Again, visitors are welcome to wear a dark lounge suit to such meetings. It is even quite usual to wear a dark lounge suit when attending meetings of Grand Lodge, or a Provincial Grand Lodge.

2. LODGE AFTERPROCEEDINGS—THE FESTIVE BOARD

Unlike meeting times, the practices associated with English festive boards are similar throughout England and Wales. The festive board in English lodges always includes a dinner. The vast majority of English masonic premises are licensed to serve alcohol. Upon retiring from the lodge room, members and visitors will commonly gather at the bar, where Stewards will serve pre-dinner drinks. The costs for drinks are borne by those receiving them. After a short time, those present will be called to dinner. During the meal, no further drinks will usually be served, so it is advisable to take a full glass when repairing to the dining table. The meal is usually served by lodge stewards, and is quite substantial. It generally consists of a soup, a main course, a sweet, coffee, and cheese and biscuits. At Installation meetings, and at Christmas meetings, some lodges employ waitresses to attend the meal. The serving of the meal commences as soon as all present are seated. The proceedings that then follow are invariably under the control of the lodge's Director of Ceremonies. Up until recent years, during the serving and partaking of the meal, the practice of 'Taking Wine' was observed. It came to the attention of the Grand Lodge that 'Taking Wine' was occasioning some excessive practices in some lodges. As a consequence, the Board of General Purposes of the Grand Lodge ruled in 1956 in the following terms: 'The practice by the Master of "taking wine" at dinner becomes detrimental to congenial conversation unless kept to a minimum, and should be confined to brethren in their masonic status. The Board wishes to emphasise that masonry can be brought into disrepute unless the Master ensures that afterproceedings are conducted with decorum. Challenging and cross-toasting should not be permitted.'

While the Grand Lodge did not expressly ban the practice of taking wine, it is discouraged by it. Nonetheless, it persists in many areas, although the practice is diminishing. As it may be encountered by visitors, details concerning it are herein-after set out.

The procedures for taking wine are largely unique to English masonry. They precede the proposition of formal toasts which begin after the meal is finished. Taking wine consists of the Master and the recipients of the toast rising together in their places to drink. No speeches or replies of any kind are undertaken. The basic procedure is generally as follows: The Director of Ceremonies will rise, sound his gavel, and ask his Wardens: 'How do you report your respective columns?' The Wardens reply appropriately, and are in fact reporting that all present have drinks in front of them. He then announces, each separately, that 'The Worshipful Master would be pleased to take wine with...'

1. His Wardens.
2. You all (members and visitors remain seated).
3. Grand Lodge Officers (if any present).
4. Holders of London Grand Rank, or holders of Provincial Grand Rank (as appropriate).
5. His Immediate Past Master.
6. The Initiate, or Initiates (if any). Often all present are requested to participate.
7. The Brother who was passed today (if any).
8. The Brother who was raised today (if any).
9. Our Guests (all visitors rise).
10. Companions of the Holy Royal Arch (all present rise).
11. Officers of the Lodge.
12. The Preceptor and Deputy Preceptor of a Lodge of Instruction (if any).
13. Any individual member, but only if the Master has a special reason.
14. His Tyler.

There is no further 'taking wine' after the Master has acknowledged his Tyler. Visitors will normally notice that a limited amount of wine is provided at each table. However, recipients of taking wine can rise with any drink they happen to have in front of them. Not all the taking wine toasts listed above will be used on any one occasion, as all the appropriate recipients are unlikely to be present at any one meeting. Some lodges use an abbreviated list, while others change the order of presentation. Of course, as already mentioned, a number of lodges do not use the taking wine procedure at all.

After the dinner is completed, or nearly completed, the Director of Ceremonies will then announce that the bar is open, whereupon further drinks will be served. He will then sound his gavel, and announce that the Master will propose the first toast of the evening. The toasts may begin before coffee is served, but all non-masonic catering staff must be excluded from the room while they proceed. A Masonic Fire will accompany many of the toasts. An example of a full Toast List is as follows:

1. The Loyal Toast (The Queen and the Craft). This is proposed by the Master, and is usually followed by the singing of the British National Anthem (*God Save the Queen*).
2. The Most Worshipful Grand Master. This is also proposed by the Master, and following it, the Director of Ceremonies will announce that the Master

grants his permission to smoke to those so desirous. It must be noted that smoking is not permitted once the dinner has commenced until after this announcement is made.

3. The Most Worshipful Pro Grand Master, and Officers of the Grand Lodge, Past and Present. If a Grand Lodge Officer is present, he will have previously been asked to respond.

4. Absent Brethren. This toast is proposed by the Master. Most lodges have a fixed time when they remember absent brethren, often 9 pm.

5. Holders of London Grand Rank, or Holders of Provincial Grand Rank (or both, if present).

6. The Worshipful Master (usually proposed by the immediate Past Master).

7. The Immediate Past Master (proposed by the Master, often only on Nights of Installation).

8. The Initiate, or Initiates. No set proposer, and each Initiate replies.

9. The Guests. The Visitors' Toast is proposed by a member, on prior notice. The responding visitor will also have received prior notice.

10. Past Masters and Officers of the Lodge. This proposition is usually delegated to a junior member. The response is given by a Past Master, or a Lodge Officer.

11. The Tyler's Toast. This is always the final toast of the evening, and no further proceedings may follow after its proposition.

Not all the toasts given above are always proposed, and the order of presentation can vary, except for the first three toasts. During the conduct of the toasts, a charity collection may take place. This will normally occur only in those lodges that do not have a collection associated with the closing ceremonies of the lodge inside the Temple. In any case, visitors are advised to have a small sum of money in their pockets to donate in this regard.

3. NIGHTS OF INSTALLATION
English lodges install a new Master every year in a month fixed by each individual lodge. Generally, Installations commence one to two hours earlier than a normal meeting. Therefore, in London lodges, an Installation night might well begin in the middle of the afternoon. Installation meetings are always well attended in England, and it is most desirable—indeed largely necessary—that a visitor inform the lodge whose Installation he proposes to visit of his intended presence. Methods of approach in this regard will be explained shortly. The dinner following an Installation will follow the same lines as a normal lodge dinner, but it will invariably be longer, and dining fees will be more expensive as a rule.

4. OF VISITING IN GENERAL
In the case of the majority of English lodge meetings, all masons attending, whether members or visitors, enter the lodge room prior to the opening of the lodge. When all are inside, the Director of Ceremonies will announce the coming of the Worshipful Master, who will enter with his Principal Officers. Thereafter, the lodge will be opened. Only an official visitor from the Grand Lodge, or the relevant Provincial Grand Lodge, will normally be admitted after the lodge is opened, as a matter of course. However, members and visitors arriving late may be admitted at appropriate

times by the Tyler, provided that no degree ceremony has commenced. Regardless, it is most inadvisable for an unknown visitor to be late. Aside from common courtesy, he must arrive early enough to be examined and avouched prior to entering the lodge. This will not normally be possible for a visitor arriving late.

Unlike many other jurisdictions, the cost of dining at the festive board is not always included as part of an English lodge member's dues. Therefore, an English lodge member will meet the costs of his own dinner when he attends his own lodge. The general English practice is for visitors to be invited by a member of a lodge. An invited visitor will have the cost of his meal met by his host. However, members and visitors alike are responsible for the purchase of their own drinks and refreshments. Nevertheless, a visitor attending an English lodge and not in the company of one of its members, will still not usually be called upon to contribute the costs of his meal. Such a visitor may well be inclined to offer payment. The Chief Steward of a lodge, or other lodge officer, usually collects dining fees at the festive board. Generally, an unaccompanied visitor's offer to pay will be politely refused. This is particularly so outside London. On the other hand, lodges meeting at Freemasons' Hall, London, tend to receive the bulk of overseas visitation, and so an offer to pay from a visitor attending such a lodge is more likely to be accepted. Of course, whereupon an unaccompanied visitor is not called upon to contribute, lodge finances must cover the cost of the meal provided. In some lodges, the Master will pay the dining fees of such a visitor. If a visitor is prevented from contributing to the costs of his meal, he may well feel inclined to contribute generously to any charity collection undertaken in connection with the lodge meeting he is attending.

English lodges, especially in London and other major cities, call in professional caterers for their festive board repasts. It is therefore necessary for a lodge to have an accurate idea of the number attending any meeting and dining at its festive board. A lodge will usually be required to pay for the number of meals ordered, regardless of whether they are taken, or not. It is the practice to charge members who order meals and fail to be present to receive them, unless there is some very good reason to the contrary. On the other hand, the provision of an extra meal at short notice to a visitor arriving unannounced does not usually pose a problem. Nevertheless, a few days notice to the relevant lodge secretary of any intended visit is very much appreciated. Of course, the problem is to know who to contact in this regard, and advise on this question is detailed below.

Regardless of the slight complexities of visiting just outlined, no visitor should be dissuaded from attending any English lodge meeting. Visitors are always made welcome, and will be most cordially received.

5. INTERESTING ASPECTS OF ENGLISH MASONRY

Many aspects of English masonry will provide the visitor with great interest, and some of these we will now proceed to examine:

The large majority of English lodges annually hold a Ladies' Festival. This often takes the form of a dinner dance, or formal ball. It is usually held at a hotel, or at other suitable public premises. In addition, many lodges hold social dances, or gatherings, three or four times per year to which ladies are invited. These socials are often held on lodge premises. As a rule, non-masons and their ladies may also be invited to these social functions.

Candidates for English lodges require a proposer and seconder, both of whom should be members of the lodge they seek to join. In a few lodges, a proposed candidate is first interviewed by a committee of the lodge appointed for that purpose, while in some the Master alone examines the applicant. If found acceptable in such a manner, the proposed candidate's name will then appear on the lodge summons (Notice Paper). A secret ballot will always be taken in open lodge prior to his acceptance as a candidate for Initiation.

Affiliating members of English lodges are called Joining Members, and they must officially be subjected to the same procedures as proposed candidates. In practice, the procedures involved tend to be more quickly effected, except if the proposed affiliate comes from a jurisdiction outside England, whereupon his home Grand Lodge may be asked for details concerning him prior to the matter proceeding.

Not surprisingly, the jurisdiction of the Premier Grand Lodge contains many masonic edifices of exceptional beauty and interest. Foremost of these is Freemasons' Hall, London. This large and magnificent building houses the Grand Temple, which is a most exquisite construction. It seats approximately 1,700, and is decorated with stained glass windows, a gold leaf mosaic ceiling, richly carved furniture, and many other features all of which have been wrought by the finest craftsmen. The Grand Temple is approached through several large anterooms, and entered through two huge bronze doors, each of which weighs several tons. In other sections of Freemasons' Hall are found the Grand Lodge library and museum. Both contain many treasures which will fascinate the masonic visitor. Tours of the Grand Temple are conducted regularly during business hours. They leave from the library, and are open to the public generally. Masonic visitors to the Grand Lodge library will find a visitors' book inside its entrance, which they are welcome to sign.

There are many buildings in London and other English cities with masonic connections, and therefore of direct interest to freemasons. Likewise, some of the masonic temples scattered throughout England and Wales are of great beauty and interest. Space makes it impossible to go into detail here, but the staff of the Grand Library and Museum will be happy to advise interested masonic tourists.

England possesses many Lodges of Instruction (LOI), which are attached to a normal Craft lodge, or specially licensed by certain lodges, such as the Emulation Lodge of Improvement, with Grand Lodge permission. Such lodges may meet monthly, fortnightly, or even weekly. They often meet in the early evening, usually between 7 pm and 8 pm. They are not warranted lodges, as such, and possess no number.

Lodges of Instruction are governed by a Preceptor and one or two Deputy Preceptors, who are elected annually from amongst its members, along with a Treasurer and Secretary. The purpose of Lodges of Instruction is to instruct and educate English masons in all aspects of masonic ritual and lodge work. Most elect a Worshipful Master at each meeting night to act over the proceedings. The Master of the Night then appoints his officers from amongst the members of the lodge to carry out a demonstration of a degree ceremony. Junior lodge officers who are visiting are instructed in the conduct of the work during the proceedings. The festive board, as it applies to normal Craft lodges, is not applied to Lodges of Instruction. However, a short social gathering of members is usual after a meeting. Visitors interested in attending a Lodge of Instruction are advised to make inquiries upon visiting a normal Craft lodge, whereupon they will readily receive an invitation.

6. LODGE WORKINGS, AND RITUAL

English ritual, as it exists today, largely stems from the Lodge of Promulgation which was erected after the Union of 1813 to accommodate the practices of the Antients and the Moderns. However, the United Grand Lodge has never attempted to lay down any standard ritual for use in lodges. Indeed, the diversity of English ritual practices would make any attempt to do so very unpopular. Today, English masonry possesses in excess of fifty different rituals in use in its lodges, bearing such names as *Emulation, Stability, Logic, West End, Bristol*, and so forth. The *Emulation* ritual is used by the majority of English lodges. Others are confined to smaller pockets of lodges in geographical locations, having no general currency. With the probable exception of the *Bristol* working and a few other minor exceptions, English rituals are quite similar. Between some the only difference is minor wording, although the adherents of each ritual form are often very loyal adherents, and it is therefore unwise to enter into a discussion as to the merits or otherwise of a particular ritual as against another when talking to English freemasons.

All English ritual practices are very similar in form, if not totally in accord on content. English lodges open and close, and conduct their ordinary business in the First Degree. A lodge will be taken into the Second or Third Degrees only when such a Degree is to be conferred. The usual order of proceedings is as follows:

1. The lodge is opened in the First Degree by the Master.
2. The Summons convening the Meeting is read (in abbreviated form). Nonetheless, there are a number of Lodges, probably the majority, that dispense with this particular procedure.
3. One of the Antient Charges of a Freemason is read (often by a Past Master), although it appears that only a small minority of lodges still follow this practice.
4. The Minutes of the last regular meeting are read, and confirmed. The Treasurer reports briefly on lodge finances.
5. Ballots for joining members, and for candidates for Initiation (if any). Notices of Motion are proposed, or if already on notice, are discussed and voted upon.
6. The Degree Ceremony (or the Installation Ceremony, on a Night of Installation).
7. The Master rises for the First Time (the Lodge having been resumed in the First Degree, if necessary). Grand Lodge, and Provincial Grand Lodge, correspondence is dealt with.
8. The Master rises for the Second Time. Propositions for candidates and joining members are read (if any).
9. Alms are collected (Charity Collection).
10. The Master rises for the Third Time. Fraternal Greetings are presented to the Master by all present as one group, and the lodge is closed.

The order of proceedings above serves as an example of the format of workings in an English lodge. However, this format tends to vary somewhat from lodge to lodge, or area to area. In some lodges, balloting is done after the degree ceremony, not all lodges read an Antient Charge, or read the summons convening the meeting. Likewise, not all lodges collect alms as part of a meeting, but rather take up a charity collection at the festive board.

As mentioned earlier, the *Emulation Ritual* is the most widely used under the English Constitution. Indeed, with some minor variations, many other Grand

Lodges, notably in Asia, Australia and Canada, permit the use of *Emulation*, or have adopted it as Official Ritual. However, there are probably a few more divergences in the form of presentation of the ritual between these jurisdictions, than there is in content. In England, the Tracing Boards are located on the floor in the centre of the lodge, while in Australian lodges they are generally located on a wall. It is quite common for a lodge Master to perform most of the Master's Work, whereas elsewhere Past Masters often provide heavy assistance. The content of the *Emulation Ritual* as practised in England is to be found in printed form, and most masonic libraries will possess at least one copy. Interested visitors can readily pursue their researches in this way.

Finally, it is as well to mention that English lodges do work the Chair Degree of Installed Master as part of an Installation ceremony, and the witnessing of this is restricted to Installed Masters. Visiting Past Masters will normally be able to see this ceremony.

7. THE GRAND LODGE

The United Grand Lodge of England meets on the second Wednesday of March, June, September and December. These meetings are normally held in the Grand Temple, at Freemasons' Hall, London.

Normally, only members of the Grand Lodge are permitted to attend. The members of the Grand Lodge are the Grand Master, all Grand Lodge Officers past and present, and all Masters, Wardens, and Past Masters of constituent lodges. Thus, the membership of the Grand Lodge is very large indeed, so much so that the Grand Temple cannot accommodate anywhere near the number of Grand Lodge members who wish to attend its meetings. The usual practice adopted is for Masters of lodges in various areas of the country to ballot amongst themselves for seats. The Grand Installation takes place in March each year.

With the exception of the Grand Master and Grand Treasurer, all Grand Lodge officers are appointed by the Grand Master. The Grand Master and Grand Treasurer are elected annually. However, in practice, the Grand Master is automatically re-elected, although the Grand Treasurer does change annually. The Grand Master is normally a member of the British Royal Family, and the highest Grand Lodge officers are often peers of the realm. Those appointed to Grand Lodge office must normally be Grand Lodge members, and hold their office for one year. The exceptions to this are the Grand Tyler, and administrative officers such as the Grand Secretary, who hold office at the pleasure of the Grand Master.

Visitors who wish to attend meetings of the Grand Lodge must be invited by the Grand Master, but in effect this will be arranged by the Grand Secretary. Generally, only the most senior members of Sister Constitutions receive such an invitation if visiting London, or a mason officially representing his own Grand Lodge.

The functions of the Grand Lodge are administered by the Board of General Purposes. It generally meets eight times per year. It consists of the most senior Grand Lodge officers, eight members appointed by the Grand Master, and twenty-four members elected for three year terms—half representing London lodges, and half representing Provincial lodges. This Board is responsible for all matters relative to the administration of the English Craft, and it answers only to the Grand Lodge.

Until very recent years, the second major administration unit within the Grand Lodge was the Board of Benevolence, and it was composed in much the same way as the Board of General Purposes. This Board functioned to administer relief, and to play a role in certain Masonic Benevolent Institutions. However, this Board has now been superseded by the Grand Charity, which performs much of the role of the Board of Benevolence, but it is basically independent of the Grand Lodge.

Finally, any discussion on Grand Lodge Government in England would not be complete without reference to Grand Rank and Past Grand Rank. It must be remembered that the English Constitution is the largest and most widely dispersed of any masonic organisation in the world. Consequently, it is largely impossible for an 'ordinary' mason to ever serve as an active Grand Lodge officer; and similarly, the hugeness of the English Craft has made local administration to be most necessary, in the forms of Provincial and District Grand Lodges. These bodies have already been discussed in our overview on the British Isles. One of the principal effects of the Provincial/District system in the English sense is that of Provincial/District Grand Rank. Every Grand Lodge office, and every Provincial/District Grand Lodge office may be conferred on English masons in a past sense. Thus the visitor will often observe a Past Provincial Grand Sword Bearer, or a Past District Grand Director of Ceremonies, and so on. The list of examples, of course, is almost endless. Generally, the holders of these ranks have never actually served actively in the position they hold, although this is not always true. Above the Provincial/District level is actual Grand Lodge Rank, and aside from those few who have actually served in an active Grand Lodge office, past Grand Lodge Rank is conferred sparingly. Obviously, the holder of a past Grand Lodge Rank, such as Past Senior Grand Deacon, or Past Junior Grand Warden, is more senior than the holder of Provincial or District Grand Lodge Rank, in most cases.

The astute observer of English masonry will immediately notice that lodges located in London (about 1,700) come directly under the ambit of the Grand Lodge, and therefore no Provincial Grand Lodge is involved. Of course, it naturally follows that in terms of conferred Provincial Grand Rank, the more senior members of London lodges miss out. This fact was recognised by the Grand Lodge, and several years ago London Grand Rank was introduced. It was also recognised that a number of overseas English lodges were not in Districts and therefore their senior members were not privy to District Grand Lodge Rank. Therefore, to cater for this need Overseas Grand Rank was introduced. In quite recent years, this system has been taken a step further with the introduction of Senior London Grand Rank, and Senior Overseas Grand Rank. All these ranks, whether Provincial, District, London, or Overseas all involve a system of Grand Lodge precedence, which is too complicated to explain here. In terms of regalia, English Master Masons wear a light blue trimmed apron with a triangular flap, and three rosettes placed in a triangular pattern within the white body of the apron. An Installed Master's apron is the same as that for a Master Mason, except the rosettes are replaced by silver 'levels'. Grand Lodge officers, past and present, wear aprons and collars of garter blue, with the particular symbol of the rank inscribed upon the apron. Certain jewels (medallions) are permitted to be worn by English masons, but the only jewels not applicable to Craft masonry that may be worn in a Craft lodge are those of the Holy Royal Arch.

8. THE OFFICERS OF CONSTITUENT LODGES

The following officers constitute an English Craft lodge: The Worshipful Master, Senior Warden, Junior Warden, Secretary, Treasurer, Senior Deacon, Junior

Deacon, Inner Guard, and Tyler. The Master may also appoint additional officers: a Chaplain, Director of Ceremonies, Assistant Director of Ceremonies, an Almoner, an Organist, Assistant Secretary, and Stewards. These optional offices are generally filled in most lodges. The Master and Treasurer are elected annually by lodge members, while the Tyler may be elected, or appointed by the Master, depending upon the provisions of an individual lodge's by-laws. All non-elective officers are appointed by the Master. In many lodges, especially those in London and other larger cities, Tyler's tend to be somewhat 'permanent' appointments, subject to the annual formalities of election or appointment. They also tend often to be actually paid for their services, and it is not uncommon for one brother to be Tyler to quite a number of different lodges. While most offices in English lodges are appointive, the principal offices are, without exception, progressive. The line of progression from bottom to top is as follows: Inner Guard, Junior Deacon, Senior Deacon, Junior Warden, Senior Warden, Worshipful Master. In some lodges, the Tyler needs to be included at the base of this list, but as has just been indicated the office of Tyler as a progressive office no longer exists in many English lodges. In addition, in most lodges it is usual for a member to have served as a Steward before joining the 'line' to the Chair. However, this is not a rigid list and even the Secretary is sometimes a progressive office towards the Master's chair.

List of Lodges

There are over eight thousand lodges warranted by the United Grand Lodge of England, and it is therefore completely impractical to even attempt to list them here. Of these lodges, about 1,700 meet in Greater London; 5,500 elsewhere in England and Wales; and about 700 overseas. Overseas lodges under the English Constitution are dealt with in their proper places elsewhere in this guide. Of the London lodges, several hundred meet at Freemasons' Hall, Great Queen Street. It can be readily stated that, except in the summer months of June, July and August when most English lodges (in England) recess, every available meeting room at Freemasons' Hall will be occupied with a lodge meeting on every night of the week (except Sundays). Many hotels, cafes, and guest houses of suitable size and quality in central London possess masonic meeting facilities, and cater for many lodges. Many of these meeting places are in easy walking distance of Freemasons' Hall. Visitors to London can readily make their enquiries at Freemasons' Hall, whereupon they will receive full assistance. The actual office is on the ground floor of the building, and if in doubt ask the doorman. Outside of London, each main Provincial Centre has a major Masonic Hall (usually they contain several others as well), and many are listed below. The visitor attending any of these centres will doubtless gain the necessary assistance to successfully visit.

Bath:	Masonic Hall, Old Orchard Street, Bath.
Birkenhead:	Masonic Temple, Clifton Road, Birkenhead.
Birmingham:	Masonic Temple, Clarendon Road, Edgbaston, Birmingham.
Blackpool:	Masonic Hall, Adelaide Street, Blackpool.
Brighton:	Sussex Masonic Temple, Queen's Road, Brighton.
Bristol:	Freemasons' Hall, 31 Park Street, Bristol.
Cambridge:	Freemasons' Hall, Bateman Street, Cambridge.
Cardiff:	Masonic Temple, Guildford Crescent, Cardiff, Wales.

Carlisle:	Masonic Hall, Portland Square, Carlisle.
Chester:	Freemasons' Hall, Queen Street, Chester.
Durham:	Masonic Hall, Old Elvet, Durham.
Leeds:	Masonic Hall, Great George Street, Leeds.
Leicester:	Freemasons' Hall, London Road, Leicester.
Liverpool:	Masonic Hall, 22 Hope Street, Liverpool.
Manchester:	Masonic Temple, Bridge Street, Manchester.
Newcastle upon Tyne:	Neville Hall, Westgate Road, Newcastle upon Tyne.
Nottingham:	Freemasons' Hall, Goldsmith Street, Nottingham.
Northampton:	Freemasons' Hall, St George Avenue, Northampton.
Norwich:	Masonic Hall, St Giles Street, Norwich.
Oxford:	Masonic Hall, 333 Banbury Road, Oxford.
Plymouth:	Davie Masonic Hall, North Hill, Plymouth.
Portsmouth:	Freemasons' Hall, 10 Guildhall Walk, Portsmouth.
Sheffield:	Tapon Hall, Shore Lane, Fulwood Road, Sheffield.
Southampton:	Masonic Hall, Albion Place, Southampton.
Swansea:	Masonic Hall, St Helens Road, Swansea, Wales.
York:	Masonic Hall, Duncombe Place, York.

Most English lodges working in England and Wales meet about six times per year, although some meet up to eight times annually, while others meet as few as four times. Lodges meeting infrequently often conduct more than one degree ceremony concurrently at the same meeting, although they never use the same candidate, bearing in mind the English constitutional requirements concerning the minimum time lapse between Degrees. For example, a particular lodge might work a 2nd Degree, and then proceed to work a 3rd Degree—one after the other.

English lodges meeting in England can be broadly placed into categories for the most part, and some of these are outlined below, with examples.

Military lodges
These lodges consist mainly of members who rank as personnel of the British Armed Forces, or retired servicemen. Examples: London Scottish Rifles Lodge No 2310; Royal Engineers Lodge No 2599; Navy Lodge No 2612; Air Force Lodge No 7335.

Professional Lodges
These lodges contain mainly members drawn from certain professions. Examples: London Hospital Lodge No 2845; Industrial Engineers Lodge No 7514.

Old School Lodges
These lodges consist mainly of former students of the schools for which they are named. Examples: Old Rugbeian Lodge No 3551; Old Harrovian Lodge No 4653; Old Etonian Lodge No 4500.

Expatriate Lodges
These lodges usually contain members mainly drawn from overseas countries living in Britain. Examples: Lodge of Erin No 2895; America Lodge No 3368; Canada Lodge No 3527; Australia Lodge No 6505.

Reunion Lodges
These lodges are generally composed of members who have served in other countries in the course of their professions. Examples: Anglo-Colonial Lodge No 3175; Anglo-South American Lodge No 3623; Star of India Lodge, No 3444.

Cultural Lodges
These lodges often consist of members associated with various cultural professions or pursuits. Examples: Incorporated Society of Musicians Lodge No 2881; Pen and Brush Lodge No 2909; Orchestral Lodge No 3028.

Language Lodges
These lodges tend to be composed of foreign nationals, and work in a language other than English, often with a non-English ritual. Examples: Pilgrim Lodge No 238 (German-speaking); Loge La France No 2060 (French-speaking); L'Entente Cordiale No 2796 (French); and Loggia Italia No 2678 (Italian).

Installed Masters' Lodges
These lodges are always composed of members who are Installed Masters in the Craft. Examples: City of London Lodge of Installed Masters No 8220; Isle of Wight Masters' Lodge No 8847.

Research Lodges
These lodges are specially formed for the purpose of masonic research, and generally conduct no degree conferment work, only lectures. Examples: Quatuor Coronati Lodge No 2076; Lodge of Research, Leicester No 2429.

There are several other categories into which various English lodges could be placed. In England, these lodges are often referred to as 'class lodges'. Of course, it must be immediately stated that there are a very large numbers of lodges not generally associated with any particular 'class', or type of person. Equally, it must be added that English lodges cannot constitutionally restrict the admission of members on the basis of class, religion, race, or any other similar reason. Nonetheless, many lodges have evolved with members sharing a community of interest and this, upon reflection, is quite understandable. Visitors who have the time to attend more than one lodge might well find it of interest to attempt to visit lodges in more than one category, as outlined. Of course, there are many other examples in each category in excess of the lodges mentioned above. Again, the staff at Freemasons' Hall, London, can provide the visitor with any advice in this regard.

While it will be noted that when we come to deal with Ireland and Scotland in the succeeding pages, several individual lodges are specifically discussed. However, to follow a similar course with respect to famous English lodges would virtually require a book in itself. Nonetheless, one important exception must be made. The Quatuor Coronati Lodge No 2076 is probably the single most well known lodge in the masonic world. It is the Premier Lodge of Masonic Research having been founded in 1884. Its full members (who currently number about thirty) are masons of great eminence in various scientific, academic and cultural areas outside freemasonry; as well as being renowned masonic scholars. In addition to its full membership (which is obtained strictly by invitation), the lodge has thousands of corresponding members (associate members), who annually receive the lodge's Transactions, and enjoy several other membership privileges. The Transactions of the Lodge—*Ars Quatuor Coronatorum*—are the most respected in the world of freemasonry, and are renowned for the highest scholarship. Members of the Correspondence Circle are welcome to attend meetings of the lodge when in London. It meets at Freemasons' Hall, Great Queen Street, on the 3rd Thursday in February; the 2nd Thursday in May, September and November; and the 4th Thursday in June. Installation: November. Inquiries concerning membership of the Correspondence Circle (which is open to every regular Master Mason) may be made in writing to the Secretary of the Lodge, at Freemasons' Hall, London.

IRELAND

The jurisdiction of the Grand Lodge of Ireland, the second oldest in the world, is unique in that it is spread over the borders of two sovereign nations. The Irish Grand Lodge is the sole regular masonic authority for the Republic of Ireland, and for Northern Ireland—the latter being politically a part of the United Kingdom. Again, as it is a major and wide-spreading jurisdiction, we must examine Irish masonry at some length.

The Grand Lodge of Ancient, Free and Accepted Masons of Ireland
Founded: 1725
Address: Freemasons' Hall, 17 Molesworth Street, Dublin 2, Republic of Ireland.
Telephone: 761337, or 762655.
Lodges: Circa 860   Permits Dual and Plural Membership.
Membership: Circa 55,000
Descent: Early Operative, and England.   *Government:* Elective Grand Lodge.
Courtesy Degrees: Permitted, but rarely conferred. Correspondence must be through Grand Lodges.
Minimum Time Lapse between Degrees: 28 days.   *Ritual:* Irish.
Major Publications: Annual Calendar and Directory (issued each January). Laws and Constitutions. Annual Report (Grand Lodge Proceedings).

History

There are several traces of the Craft working in Ireland prior to 1725, the accepted date of the foundation of the Grand Lodge. Records indicate that the Grand Lodge was working by June, 1725, but it probably existed somewhat earlier. The early history of the Grand Lodge is vague and disjointed from the records that remain extant.

Two schisms occurred in the Irish Craft, one in 1740, and the other in 1780. Both were healed with relative ease a few years after they occurred. The Grand Lodge of Ireland was unaffected by the great division of English masonry into the Antients and the Moderns, although it steadfastly supported the former until the English union of 1813.

The Grand Lodge of Ireland was the first Grand Lodge to issue a warrant to a military lodge, and was probably the most active of all Grand Lodges in this area. Indeed today, when military lodges have largely become stationary where they formerly existed under other constitutions, Ireland still possesses three.

The Irish Grand Lodge, unlike Scotland, governs only the three Craft Degrees.

However, there are several other additional orders in Ireland which work with the approval of the Grand Lodge, but operate separately from it. These are the Supreme Grand Royal Arch Chapter, the Grand Council of Knight Masons, the Great Priory of Knights Templar, and the Supreme Council of the Ancient and Accepted Rite for Ireland. No other Orders exist in Ireland in any regular sense, or are permitted by the Grand Lodge to be formed.

Today, the Grand Lodge of Ireland flourishes peacefully, with in excess of 860 lodges on its roll, of which about 70 are located outside Ireland. Lodges are organised into Provinces, as has already been indicated, with ten Irish Provinces being overseas. The Grand Lodge, as with those of England and Scotland, is well known for its charitable works. Organisations associated with the Grand Lodge include the Masonic Girls' Benefit Fund, the Masonic Boys' Benefit Fund, the Masonic Widows' Fund, and the Masonic Orphans' Welfare Committee.

Notes for Visitors to Ireland

1. MEETING TIMES, AND DRESS

Most Irish lodges meet at 7.30 pm in the cities of Ireland, while in the Provinces they may meet at any time between 7.30 pm and 8 pm. Visitors should arrive by 7 pm at the latest, in order to present their credentials. A visitor should make himself known to the Tyler and the Senior Warden, the latter of whom will generally be the one to vouch for him inside the lodge. The Tyler, or a lodge officer, will usually instruct a vouched visitor in pertinent aspects of Irish Workings, if he is unfamiliar with them.

Dress for all Irish lodges is a lounge suit. A visitor from outside Ireland who is not carrying a suit with him will be welcome in a sports jacket and tie. Shirts do not necessarily have to be white, and no gloves are worn. Dinner suits (tuxedoes) are usually worn on nights of Installation, but even in this case, an overseas visitor is not expected to wear a dinner suit if this is difficult.

2. LODGE AFTERPROCEEDINGS

In Dublin, and in most Irish cities, a festive board on the English model is not the norm. Most lodges have what is usually called light refreshments, or supper, after their meetings. This generally commences about 9.15 pm, and continues until about 10.45 pm. These suppers are characterised by informality, and toasts are limited to 'Ireland' ('The Queen' in Northern Ireland), the Grand Master and Grand Lodge, and any toast appropriate to the occasion, such as Visiting Brethren. Visitors are often seated at the Master's right hand, talk is general, and speeches limited. Drinks are served, and there is no charity collection at refreshment.

It is most unusual for a visitor to an Irish lodge to be asked to pay for his supper. However, towards the end of the evening, visitors will often notice the lodge Treasurer circulating amongst members to receive their contributions. A visitor may make an offer to contribute likewise, but invariably a polite refusal to accept will be tendered in reply. Nevertheless, should a visitor become a regular attender at any particular lodge, he should seriously discuss the matter with the lodge Treasurer. His offer to pay will probably be accepted if his visits are frequent. In the event that a visitor's toast is proposed, a reply is always called for. An overseas visitor, in particular, might be forewarned to respond. A speech in response should be very brief, and can be quite light hearted.

Toasts at Installation dinners are much more formalised, and follow a fixed pattern, similar to English practices. Visitors should also be aware that there are a very few lodges in Ireland that serve no alcohol at any supper associated with their proceedings. These 'Temperance Lodges', however, will rarely be encountered, and are getting fewer.

3. NIGHTS OF INSTALLATION
On nights of Installation, lodges generally meet at an earlier time, usually 6.30 pm or 7 pm. Most Irish Installation meetings occur in the months of January, February and March. Dinner suits are the normal dress at such meetings, but only if an actual formal dinner is to follow immediately afterwards. It should be noted that not all Irish lodges follow this practice, and that there are some which do not conduct their Installation dinner on the same night as their Installation meeting. If a lodge is planning not to dine after its Installation meeting, only lounge suits will be worn. However, dinner suits will be worn subsequently at the actual Installation dinner held at a later date.

Irish lodges, as with those of England and Scotland, do work the Chair Degree of Installed Master. Visiting Past Masters can be excluded from witnessing this part of an Irish Installation if they do not arrive early enough to be vouched as a Past Master. They must, of course, present a Past Master's Certificate, or equivalent documentation. It is most desirable for a visitor to provide notice to the lodge concerned, if he desires to attend its Installation. These functions are catered for, and lodges need to know the exact numbers attending. A visitor can readily approach the relevant lodge Secretary, if known, or make arrangements at the Grand Lodge Office in Dulbin when in personal attendance. Prior notice of a visitor's intended presence at a normal lodge meeting is not necessary, although this is recommended as a courtesy, where possible.

4. OF VISITING IN GENERAL
It is desirable that an overseas visitor proceeds in the first instance to Freemasons' Hall, Dublin; or to an appropriate Provincial Masonic Centre (the addresses of the main Temples are provided below). This method of approach is appreciated by the Grand Lodge. It is sometimes possible for a visitor, having presented his masonic credentials, to be examined as a freemason in the peace and quiet of Freemasons' Hall, prior to attending a lodge meeting. He will, as a consequence, be vouched for by the Grand Lodge office to any lodge he visits in Ireland. This will certainly save the visitor time when he actually visits, and will circumvent the necessity of his being examined at each and every lodge meeting he attends. Nonetheless, the visitor should not visit the Grand Lodge office at Freemasons' Hall expecting the procedure just outlined to occur automatically. Examination at the Grand Lodge office will depend on time available to appropriate office staff when the visitor arrives, and on other factors. In other words, it is a courtesy provided to the visitor, and he must be well aware of this fact.

It is unusual for a visitor's receipt for dues, or similar document, to be called for when he presents himself at an Irish lodge. However, a visitor is still well advised to have it with him, just in case. Of course, his Master Mason's Certificate (Diploma) will be called for, and it is a usual procedure for his signature on that document to be compared with his signature in the lodge attendance book. A usual feature of Irish visiting is that the visitor will be required to take 'The Tyler's Oath' during his masonic examination. This simple procedure is one whereby the visitor affirms that he is, indeed, a freemason. As will be noted later in this guide, a similar 'system' is used in the United States of America.

All masons attending an Irish lodge enter before the lodge is opened, with visitors having already been examined. There is no particular order of entry, and after all attending are inside the lodge, the Master and his officers will parade in to open the lodge. Grand Lodge officers, if present, will enter with the Master. All present should be seated before the Master enters, and will rise as he does so. Sitting Masters of other lodges, and Past Masters, should sit in the body of the lodge. After the lodge has been opened, the Master will then invite them to be seated in the East.

5. INTERESTING ASPECTS OF IRISH MASONRY

Many lodges hold a Ladies' Night annually, consisting of a buffet meal, dancing, raffles, and so on. Non-masons and their partners are usually welcome to attend. It is not common to have a lodge meeting prior to, or in connection with, these functions. They are often held on lodge premises, however, and visitors can normally be conducted over the masonic facilities where the function is held.

The Grand Lodge building in Dublin is a most attractive edifice, dating from 1869. The Temples within it are well worth visiting, as is the library and museum contained within its precincts. All Dublin Metropolitan lodges (except one) meet there, along with other masonic orders found in Ireland. Several other masonic buildings are worthy of note, and information concerning these may be readily obtained by interested visitors at the Grand Lodge office.

Candidates for Irish lodges must be proposed and seconded by two members of the lodge, both of whom should, and one of whom must, be personally acquainted with the candidate. On the meeting night that the proposition is put forward, three scrutineers are appointed to investigate the candidate. At the next lodge meeting night, the scrutineers report, and the lodge ballots. If the ballot is unanimous, the name of the candidate is submitted to a Committee of Enquiry which finally passes the candidate, who may then be initiated at the next, or a subsequent, meeting of the lodge.

A mason wishing to affiliate with an Irish lodge will pass through the same procedures as a candidate, except that there are some lodges that do not require a unanimous ballot for affiliation, although most do. He must be in good standing in some regular lodge, and inquiries may be directed to his home Grand Lodge, if he comes from outside Ireland. The Grand Lodge of Ireland permits plural membership both inside and outside Ireland. An affiliating Past Master joins an Irish lodge as junior Past Master.

6. THE GRAND LODGE OF INSTRUCTION

Ireland is the only regular constitution in the masonic world that does not print a Craft ritual in some form, or at least even permit its ritual to be printed. Even the American Grand Lodges which will not print a ritual as such, still print Monitors containing non-esoteric portions of their ceremonies. In Ireland, even this is not permitted. As a direct result of this policy, the Grand Lodge of Ireland has constituted a subordinate Grand Body. It was formed in the last century, and is known as the Very Worshipful Grand Lodge of Instruction. Membership of this is limited to fifty, including nine ex-officio members. The other forty-one members are elected from amongst Irish Past Masters of three, or more, years standing. Those elected must be known for their excellence in ritual work. Although they are not Grand Lodge officers (except for the Grand Secretary of Instruction, and his Assistant) members of it are styled Very Worshipful, wear Grand Lodge regalia, and receive Grand Lodge salutes. It holds eight meetings per year (four in Dublin, and four in Belfast), at which visiting lodges or lodge officers demonstrate complete degree ceremonies, or other ritual work. The audience is invited to ask questions, and these are answered by the Grand Secretary of Instruction. By old tradition, the Deputy Grand Master takes the Chair when present.

Two closed meetings of the Grand Lodge of Instruction are held annually, whereupon its members contemplate ritual matters. Decisions of the Grand Lodge of Instruction, when approved by the Grand Lodge (generally a formality) are binding. The Grand Lodge of Instruction does not itself conduct Classes of Instruction, but licenses a small number of classes in Dublin and Belfast. While these classes are conducted by masons of skill and ability, the class leaders do not necessarily have to be Grand Lodge of Instruction members. In Dublin, classes meet weekly, whereupon ritual is practised. Any interested visitors wishing to visit these classes, or the Grand Lodge of Instruction itself, must make inquiries at the Grand Lodge office.

7. LODGE WORKINGS, REGALIA, AND RITUAL

The ceremonies of Irish freemasonry are similar to those of England and Scotland in basic content, but their forms contain obvious differences to those witnessing them. The opening of an Irish lodge will pose the visitor with his first point of interest. All present are required to provide the Deacons of the lodge with the password of the First Degree. A similar procedure applies when the lodge is called up to the Second or Third Degrees. However, non-Irish visitors will have been instructed with the passwords at their earlier avouchment. It is also worthy of note that Irish lodges use Masonic Fire as part of their degree workings, as well as at lodge afterproceedings. A different Fire relates to each degree. As has already been explained, all members and visitors are seated in an Irish lodge prior to its opening. However, a late arrival can seek admission, via the Tyler. A member arriving late will be promptly admitted, whereupon he will take up a position level with the Junior Warden, salute the Master, and apologise for lateness. A visitor arriving late, subsequent to avouchment as necessary, will follow the same procedure on admission. Quite obviously, it is most unwise for a visitor to be late.

The Irish do have a most interesting procedure which is occasionally used for a late Irish visitor. After he has been admitted, the Master may challenge him after his apology. If so, the Master will ask: 'Whence come you, Brother?' If the visitor is an Installed Master, he will reply: 'From the East, Worshipful Master'. If he be a Master Mason, he will say: 'From the West, Worshipful Master'. The Master will then say: 'What tidings do you bring?' The visitor will then answer: 'Peace, love and harmony to all good and true masons, especially to you Worshipful Master, the Wardens and Brethren of this lodge'. The Master will then ask the visitor to be seated, and may call upon all present to salute him, whereupon the visitor will return the salute. However, it must be stressed that the foregoing procedure is included herein simply for the interest of the overseas visitor who may witness its use when visiting an Irish lodge. *Under no circumstances* will a *non-Irish* visitor arriving late, or for that matter arriving early, ever be called upon to undergo this procedure when entering an Irish lodge. Invariably, it will only be used on an Irish mason arriving late, and then invariably only on such a late-arriver who is person-ally known to the Master (and who the Master knows is aware of the procedure). Again, it is stressed that the visitor need have no fear in this regard. However, it is once again worth mentioning that, as with any lodge, it is not courteous to be late for an Irish lodge meeting. It must also be noted that no member or visitor will be admitted once a degree ceremony has commenced.

Unlike the English and Scottish Grand Lodges, the Grand Lodge of Ireland has long adopted a uniform ritual. However, while Irish ritual is nominally identical for all lodges, there are five or six lodges in the masonic province of Munster (which encompasses the City of Cork and nearby towns) which are 'allowed' to use a ritual that is quite different to the standard Irish version. There are historical reasons for this, and the ritual itself approximates the English *Bristol* Working. While the Grand Lodge regards this working as incorrect, it is permitted in view of the antiquity of certain Cork lodges. Approved Irish ritual contains many features that will interest visitors. Irish rules prohibit more than one candidate at a time to be taken through the First Degree, and the Third Degree (but not the Second). Part of the Irish First Degree is very dramatic, particularly at the point immediately following the obli-gation. Indeed, the English visitor will find that while the content of Irish ritual is fairly similar to that of his own experience, its order of presentation and the forms used are somewhat different.

The closing of an Irish lodge involves a statement by the Master that visitors may speak. At this point, visitors will rise and in turn present fraternal greetings from their lodge, naming it, and also its constitution if it be a non-Irish lodge. If there is more than one visitor from any one lodge, all members of that lodge present will rise together for the greeting, but only one of them will present greetings—usually the Master, or senior member in attendance. When all visitors have spoken, the Master will render masonic courtesies in return, and all visitors will rise again together, and return the courtesy. After the closing of the lodge, the Master and his officers form a procession out of the lodge in a manner similar to their entry.

Although he is welcome to do so, it is not necessary for a visitor to bring his own regalia to an Irish lodge. Working regalia is provided for all. Irish regalia is some-what different from the English or Scottish, but not markedly so. The wearing of Irish regalia is certainly not mandatory on visitors from outside Ireland. Indeed, Irish masons are most interested to view the regalia of other regular jurisdictions. Irish Craft aprons are worn inside the jacket, similar to Scottish practice. However, if a visitor wears his own personal regalia outside the jacket as normal practice, he is welcome to do so in Irish lodges. Likewise, a visitor is able to wear any appro-priate Craft jewels (medallions) consistant to his rank in his own jurisdiction. How-ever, it must be noted that ONLY Craft jewels may be worn in an Irish Craft lodge. It will be remembered from our discussions concerning England earlier in this guide that under that constitution jewels applicable to the Holy Royal Arch Degree may also be worn in English lodges, in addition to Craft jewels. This is not the case in Ireland. In short, the wearing of non-Craft regalia of any kind is prohibited in Irish lodges. Visitors will also notice that, unlike English practice, Irish Past Masters do not wear a Past Master's Collar. However, Irish Past Masters do wear a Past Master's Jewel, usually on a cord around the neck.

8. THE GRAND LODGE

The Grand Lodge of Ireland meets five times per year, and all regular Master Masons may attend. However, visitors desirous of attending should make application at the Grand Lodge office. Dress for Grand Lodge meetings is a lounge suit, or a dinner suit in the case of Grand Lodge officers. The Grand Lodge meets on the 1st Thursday in March, June, October and December at 8 pm. The fifth meeting is held at High Twelve (midday) on St John's Day, just after Christmas, to 'Install and Salute the Grand Officers'. A minimum of two of the first four meetings must be held in Dublin, and at least one must be held in Northern Ireland. The St John's Day meeting is usually held in Dublin, also. The offices constituting the Grand Lodge of Ireland are very similar to those of England. Interestingly, in June 1983, the Grand Lodge for the first time created the rank of Assistant Grand Master, bringing it even more closely in line with England in this area. Of course, previously it did possess a Deputy Grand Master (and still does).

Grand Lodge officers obtain their positions by merit, and usually serve for three years, holding a different office in each of those years. All offices are elective, except those of Deputy Grand Master and Grand Master's Standard Bearer, both of whom are appointed by the Grand Master. The Grand Secretary and Grand Treasurer tend to be re-elected indefinitely, generally until retirement. The Grand Master and Grand Wardens are, likewise, usually continually re-elected. The Grand Master, himself, invariably tends to be a British Peer, and this is certainly currently the case.

At meetings of constituent Irish lodges the Master, if present, must preside. Nevertheless, should the Grand Master be present, he must be offered the Chair, which he may accept. The Deputy Grand Master has the same right to preside. In addition, a Provincial Grand Master, or his Deputy, must be offered the Chair when he attends a lodge within his Province. It is traditional that an outgoing Master should install his successor if at all possible, or failing this some other Past Master. A Grand Lodge officer may be asked to act as Installing Master, and in doing so would take the Chair by invitation, not as a Grand Lodge officer but rather as a Past Master. In the Premier Lodge of Ireland (The Grand Master's Lodge), the Grand Master is the permanent Master of the lodge, and will take the Chair on any occasion that he is present. This is the only Irish lodge in which the Deputy Grand Master cannot preside as a right. This lodge annually elects an Acting Master, who presides in the Grand Master's absence.

9. OFFICERS OF CONSTITUENT LODGES

The officers of Irish lodges are as follows: The Worshipful Master, Senior Warden, Junior Warden, Treasurer, Secretary, Steward of Charities, Director of Ceremonies, Senior Deacon, Junior Deacon, Inner Guard, and Chaplain. Each lodge must have a Tyler, but he is not deemed an officer of the lodge. All officers are annually elected, and each non-administrative officer is usually elected to the next highest progressive office, until he reaches the Master's Chair. An Organist and Stewards may be appointed by the Master, and they sometimes are. The immediate Past Master has the traditional right, not always exercised, to take the Chair in the Master's absence. The right of the Master to appoint a Deputy to preside in his absence is almost invariably ceded to the lodge Secretary. It is interesting to note that while the majority of lodge offices are elective, no member of an Irish lodge can be installed without the written approval of the Grand Master (or if applicable, his Provincial Grand Lodge).

List of Lodges

As with England, the large number of Irish lodges forbids the inclusion of an expansive list here. Again, Irish lodges outside Ireland are dealt with in appropriate places elsewhere in this guide. As has already been stated, all Dublin lodges (except one) meet at Freemasons' Hall, Dublin. Visitors must also be aware that, as with England, Irish lodges recess in the northern summer months. No Irish lodge located in Ireland meets in June and July, and many fail to meet in May or August. Overseas Irish lodges tend to follow local practices in terms of months of meeting. The main meeting places in other Irish cities are listed below. A visitor can always be assured of full assistance should he care to make enquiries at any one of these locations.

Belfast: 15 Rosemary Street, Belfast. Arthur Square, Belfast. Crumlin Road, Belfast.

Cork: 27 Tuckey Street, Cork.

Londonderry: Bishop Street, Londonderry.

Limerick: 97 O'Connell Street, Limerick.

Nonetheless, there are several Irish lodges of special interest, which are detailed below. However, before proceeding to mention certain individual lodges, it is most interesting to examine briefly the Irish System of Lodge Numbering. It is a natural assumption that the lower a lodge's number—the older it must be, and therefore the greater is its seniority. By and large, in England and Scotland, and in many other constitutions, this is the case. However, not so in the case of Ireland, to anywhere near the same extent. Many of the earlier Irish lodges are greatly out of normal numerical sequence. The Grand Master's Lodge heads the Irish Roll of Lodges, but it carries no number and heads the list for special reasons. In any case, it is far from the oldest Irish lodge.

The oldest lodge in Ireland is the First Lodge No 1 (founded before 1731). Lodge No 2 (before 1731) appears to be assumed to be the second oldest, while Lodge No 6 seems to be credited as third oldest. Then comes the much respected Antient Union Lodge No 13, founded in 1732. It should now be quite obvious that there are a few gaps. Of course, other lodges hold the numbers in between those just mentioned. The cause of this mix-up had it origins in the nineteenth century.

As with any Grand Lodge, some lodges tend to become extinct for varying reasons. The general policy in England has always been to periodicialy close up the gaps by re-numbering—a policy which obviously had merit and proved most satisfactory. The policy in Ireland, however, was somewhat different. In the last century, the Grand Secretary of the era decided to try filling up his gaps by offering low numbers to new lodges, and inviting existing lodges (for a fee) the opportunity to exchange their existing warrant for a new warrant with a lower number, and therefore (in theory) raising the status of the lodge. Not every lodge embraced this idea, and after a while the practice was discontinued. Nonetheless, the result of this policy has meant that many Irish lodges are numerically out of step. Therefore, the observer must be careful in attempting to judge the antiquity or otherwise of any particular Irish lodge simply on the basis of its number. The Waterford Lodge No

5, proves a good example. It was originally warranted in 1757 as Lodge No 286, but it exchanged for the number 5 in 1814.

It is noteworthy that not all Irish lodges are named. A minority of Irish lodges, many of which are located in Northern Ireland, are known only by number. Ireland remains one of only two regular constitutions that possesses lodges without names (the other being Pennsylvania); although there are a few jurisdictions which, while ascribing names to their lodges, do not number them. Many Irish lodges possess long histories and rich traditions. A full list of all Irish lodges, with all meeting details, is found in the *Irish Freemasons' Calendar and Directory*, which is published by the Grand Lodge each January. It can usually be purchased when visiting Freemasons' Hall, Dublin, or alternatively an intending visitor's own Grand Lodge office may be able to secure a copy. It is as well to note that the Grand Lodge does not publish more copies than it considers necessary, and therefore it is often sold out within a few months of publication.

It now only remains to list the lodges of interest to which reference has already been made. Nonetheless, the following is only a very brief representative list, and there are many other lodges in Ireland well worth visiting—indeed, any Irish lodge must fall into this category.

The Grand Masters' Lodge. This lodge has already been largely discussed. It meets at Freemasons' Hall, Dublin, on the second Friday of every month (except June, July, August and September), at 8 pm.

The Lodge of Research No 200. Founded in 1914, the Lodge of Research is the only lodge of its type in Ireland, and after the Quatuor Coronati Lodge No 2076 (see under England), it is probably the best known in the masonic world. Its membership is restricted to Past Masters of the Irish Constitution, and any Irish Past Master may join it. There is no membership limit, as such; nor does an Irish Past Master need an invitation to join it. Nonetheless, the lodge does possess a worldwide 'Correspondence Circle', open to all regular Master Masons. Its *Transactions*, published at regular intervals, are renowned for their scholarship; and are available only to its members (whether full members, or corresponding members). The lodge meets four times per year, twice in Dublin, once in Belfast, and once elsewhere in Ireland. Inquiries concerning its Correspondence Circle are welcome, and can be directed to the Lodge Secretary, at Freemasons' Hall, Dublin.

The First Lodge No 1. This lodge dates from before 1731, and was probably in existence well before then, but no proof exists. It is located in the city of Cork, and is one of those lodges which uses a ritual of some antiquity, and to which reference has already been made. It meets at the Masonic Hall, Cork, on the first Monday of the month (except June, July and August), at 8 pm.

The Antient Union Lodge No 13. This very old lodge meets at the Masonic Hall, Limerick, on the second Friday of the month (except June, July and August), at 8 pm.

Ireland, alone among the three Grand Lodges of the British Isles, still has three military lodges under warrant. These lodges are not stationary, but meet where the military corps for which they are named, are posted at any particular time. On occasions, they meet outside of Ireland, notably in England. They are: *The 4th/7th Royal Dragoon Guards Lodge No 295; The 1st Battalion, the Worchester and Sherwood Foresters' Regiment Lodge No 322; The 1st Queen's Dragoon Guards Lodge No 571.*

SCOTLAND

The Grand Lodge of Scotland is the third oldest organised Grand Lodge in the masonic world by virtue of actual formation as such, although both the Grand Lodges of Massachusetts and Georgia claim earlier dates. Scotland is certainly second only to England both in terms of overall membership and the number of lodges it has under warrant. Once again, as Scotland is a major English-speaking constitution, an expansive view of it must be undertaken.

The Grand Lodge of Antient, Free and Accepted Masons of Scotland
Founded: 1736
Address: Freemasons' Hall, 96 George Street, Edinburgh EH2 4HQ, Scotland. *Telephone:* (031) 2255304.
Lodges: Circa 1,100.   Permits Dual and Plural Membership.   *Membership:* Circa 300,000
Descent: Early Operative.   *Government:* Elective Grand Lodge.
Courtesy Degrees: All correspondence must be through Grand Lodges.
Minimum Time Lapse between Degrees: Two weeks.   *Ritual:* Various Scottish forms.
Major Publications: Constitutions and Laws.   Annual Year Book.   Grand Lodge Proceedings.

History

At the time of the emergence of speculative freemasonry in England in the seventeenth century, Scottish operative masonry had already long since been well established. There were many operative lodges working in Scotland in this era, with a large mason trade organisation built up around them. While the sources of Scottish operative masonry were possibly English, wars between these two countries between the thirteenth and sixteenth centuries saw Scottish masonry look to the Continent for inspiration, and some Scottish buildings of the period show French influences. The wars themselves tended to lead Scotland as a nation into becoming somewhat insular in many fields of endeavour. In terms of masonry, this insularity and the uncertainty of the times would appear to have been the main impetus behind the emergence of lodges and trade organisations. The masonic trade organisations worked to provide training in the operative skills, and to preserve the integrity of the profession. Records indicate that at least twenty operative lodges were working in Scotland prior to 1700.

Extant records show that 'honorary members' were admitted to some Scottish lodges as early as the sixteenth century. However, unlike English masonry which had become largely speculative by the seventeenth century, Scottish lodges remained basically operative into the eighteenth century. While Scotland possesses by far the oldest lodges for which records exist, it was slow to adopt the Grand Lodge system, probably because of the trade organisations its masonry fostered over a lengthy period. It was not until 1736 that four old lodges met and acted as the catalyst for the formation of the Grand Lodge of Scotland. The Grand Lodge has developed steadily to this day, and remains one of the most respected in the world. The expanse of its history has been largely free of schism or internal discord, except for a period of seventy years when one of its lodges (Mother Kilwinning) broke away to operate independently. The masonic student can readily research Scottish masonic history at his leisure, there being a great many books and articles available on the subject. However, for the purposes of this guide, the brief introduction just provided must suffice.

Notes for Visitors to Scotland

1. MEETING TIMES, AND DRESS

The first point to be aware of concerning Scottish masonry is that the majority of its lodges meet regularly *twice* per month. There are, nevertheless, a percentage that meet only monthly, with many in this category being overseas. The second important point to mention is that all Scottish lodges, in Scotland itself, do recess in the northern summer months of June and July. The commencement time for most Scottish lodges is 7.30 pm, although some lodges located outside the main Scottish cities may meet later. The meeting times and other details concerning Scottish lodges overseas are dealt with elsewhere in this guide. Visitors should not fail to be early to a Scottish lodge meeting. Scottish avouchment procedures tend to be most thorough, so visitors are well advised to be in attendance by 7 pm, at the latest.

Dress for all Scottish lodges is a jacket and tie as a minimum requirement, but most wear a dark lounge suit. Many members wear a black suit, white shirt and black tie, and this is usually the case for lodge officers.

2. LODGE AFTERPROCEEDINGS

The 'festive board' in the English tradition is unknown in Scottish lodges, as is the term itself. However, a more formal festive board type arrangement always follows Installation meetings. At the conclusion of an ordinary lodge meeting, members gather together in the lodge premises for 'Harmony'. This is a most informal gathering, superintended by the Junior Warden. The only formal toast usually proposed is the Loyal Toast to the British Sovereign, although some lodges occasionally propose a toast to visitors. Any reply to a proposed toast should be very brief. A light supper consisting of hot drinks and sandwiches generally forms the repast. Visitors will never be required to contribute to the cost of the supper, as this is covered in members lodge dues. Most Scottish lodge buildings are licensed to serve alcohol, and possess their own bar facilities. Members pay for their own drinks, but the visitor will usually find that any drink he may require will be paid for him. The Harmony itself largely consists of singing songs and general light-hearted fellowship. A raffle, with the proceeds benefiting masonic charity, is quite usually a part of the Harmony. A Harmony can go on quite late into the evening after a lodge meeting, but members and visitors are certainly free to depart at any time after the lodge is closed. On occasions, one lodge will visit the meeting of another. On these visitation nights a more formal Harmony is usually invoked, and it is often funded by a levy (usually by a ticket donation) on members present. However, once again, visitors are never expected to contribute.

3. NIGHTS OF INSTALLATION

It is not common for Scottish lodges to begin proceedings earlier on nights of Installation, with most lodges still commencing about 7.30 pm. At the conclusion of an Installation, a special Harmony is usually held, often in the form of a formal-type dinner/banquet. While no special invitation is required for a visitor to attend a normal Scottish lodge meeting, the arrangements often differ for Installations. It is general practice in Scottish lodges to sell tickets to Installation dinners, and visitors who wish to attend are 'encouraged' to purchase one. The cost of the meal at an Installation is not met by a member's annual lodge dues, and the ticket method ensures that costs in this area are covered. Visitors should be aware that ticket costs are usually not refundable even in cases of last minute unavoidable non-attendance, as the lodge will invariably be required to pay its caterers for meals ordered whether they are taken, or not. In theory, no invitation or ticket is needed for a visitor to attend an actual Installation ceremony, but in practice those attending will normally hold tickets for the special Harmony following.

An Installation Harmony is accompanied by a formal Toast List, which usually includes the following toasts accompanied by short responses where applicable: The Loyal Toast. The Grand Master Mason, and Grand Lodge officers. The newly Installed Master. The Visitors. The Tyler's Toast. Dress for Installations is still normally a dark (often black) lounge suit, although in some lodges officers will wear a dinner suit (tuxedo). Visitors wishing to attend an Installation should express their desire at the Grand Lodge office in Edinburgh, or when they visit one of the main Temples in one of the other Scottish cities, as listed below. The visitor will readily receive either direct assistance, or will be referred to a relevant lodge Secretary from whom a ticket can be speedily obtained. Of course, this assumes that an Installation is to be held during the stay of the visitor, which, depending on the time of the year and the location, may not always be the case.

4. OF VISITING IN GENERAL
While not an absolute necessity, it is desirable that a visiting overseas mason proceeds to Freemasons' Hall in Edinburgh, at least in the first instance. This is a courtesy which is appreciated by the Grand Lodge of Scotland. Indeed, if for no other reason, such a visit provides a most interesting experience. The Grand Lodge building is a most attractive edifice, and the Grand Lodge library and museum housed therein are most highly recommended. The museum, in particular, contains many unique masonic relics which will engross any masonic visitor. A visitor to the Grand Lodge office can be assured of a warm welcome, and full assistance.

Upon entering the domain of a Scottish lodge for the purpose of visiting, the visitor should first approach the lodge Tyler, who will arrange the necessary avouchment procedures. All masons present, members and visitors, enter the lodge room prior to the opening. All present remain standing while the Master enters, and then all are seated. Visitors will then be asked to stand and each will be vouched for individually by a member of the lodge. Each visitor sits having been vouched for. Visitors who have not sat in open lodge with a member present will have already undergone a masonic examination prior to entering the lodge, and will be vouched for by their examiners. After all visitors have been vouched for, the Master will then invite Masters of other lodges and Past Masters who are visiting, to be seated in the East. They will then stand, proceed to the East, and be welcomed by the Master, who will also indicate their seats. The Master will then usually welcome all visitors with a very short address. Only then will the lodge be opened. It is not unusual for members of a Scottish lodge to give a round of applaude to the visitors after the Master has welcomed them.

The closing of Scottish lodges will be of interest to visitors or, more particularly, the procedures adopted immediately prior to the closure. Just prior to the closing of a Scottish lodge, members often take the opportunity to comment on the quality of the work undertaken during the course of the meeting. Some of these comments can be quite critical, but nevertheless polite. Visitors are welcome to speak at this point. They can convey fraternal greetings if they wish, or even comment on the proceedings themselves. However, as a visitor, considerable circumspection is strongly advised.

5. INTERESTING ASPECTS OF SCOTTISH MASONRY
There are quite a few aspects of Scottish masonry which will be of interest to the travelling freemason, some of which are outlined below.

The Master of a Scottish lodge is termed Right Worshipful Master, while the Wardens are termed Worshipful. Of course, these titles only apply to the appropriate incumbents while they hold office. Indeed, all Scottish masons are known simply as 'Brother ...', regardless of masonic rank. Thus, rank applies to the office held, not to the person holding it. For example, the Master of lodge will be known as: 'Brother ... Right Worshipful Master'. The Grand Master will be known as: 'Brother ... Grand Master Mason'. This is the reverse of the comparable English practice. Once a brother has served his term of office, the title he has held generally can no longer be applied to him. For example, a Past Master will not be 'Right Worshipful Brother ...' but simply Brother '... Past Master of Lodge ...'

The major social function held by many Scottish lodges is an annual ball. An old custom observed by many lodges on such occasions is the Grand March. At the beginning of the ball, masons and their ladies form a procession down the ballroom, led by the Right Worshipful Master. Each lady wears her husband's lodge apron for the duration of the March. After the procession is over, the regalia is put away and the ball continues. Of course, while non-masons may be present at an annual ball, they cannot take part in the Grand March. Many Scottish lodges also hold an annual Ladies' Night. In some lodges is might take the place of the annual ball, but in many lodges both functions are held—at different times, of course. The Ladies' Night might take several forms, but often involves a dance, a meal, or both. They are never held in combination with a lodge Installation—this is not permitted by Scottish masonic law—however, it is fairly common for Ladies' Nights to be held after a normal lodge meeting, in place of the normal Harmony.

Candidates for Scottish lodges (called Entrants) require only a proposer and a seconder, and no additional depositions are required as is the case in some other jurisdictions. A prospective candidate must meet with the lodge's Enquiry Committee prior to his name being placed on notice for a ballot. Every lodge must have an Enquiry Committee, and it must favourably report on every candidate referred to it prior to the matter being taken any further.

Scotland does not possess any lodges of instruction on the English or Irish models. However, rehearsals, as required, take place in open lodge. This interesting system of ritual training 'on the job', as it were, is largely confined to Scottish masonry.

It is not unusual for Scottish lodges to notify forthcoming meetings in local newspapers. Lodge meeting notices, which are usually called 'Billets' in Scotland, are rarely printed for ordinary meetings, although they are commonly produced for Installations. However, many Scottish lodges do print and distribute an annual card to their members; containing details of lodge Office Bearers, the addresses of principal officers, and meeting dates for the year.

Lectures on masonic subjects, while not uncommon in English lodges, are not nearly as prevalent in Scottish ones. Degree conferment work, therefore, predominates. Indeed, if for a particular meeting, a lodge does not have a candidate, it is far more likely to call a rehearsal than conduct a lecture.

Since 1952, the Grand Lodge of Scotland has issued a *Year Book*. Aside from printing general information concerning Scottish masonry, together with a list of lodges, the *Year Book* also contains many interesting research papers and articles of masonic interest. This publication is available directly from the Grand Lodge of Scotland, at its address recorded at the beginning of this section. It is in order for a mason to write directly to the Grand Lodge of Scotland to obtain a copy of the *Year Book*. However, if a non-Scottish mason wishes to communicate with the Grand Lodge for any other purpose, the letter must be directed via his own Grand Secretary. It must be noted that only the number of copies of the *Year Book* that are pre-ordered are printed, and the Grand Lodge therefore does not hold large stocks. It does, nonetheless, print an estimated number of copies in excess of orders, as it has become tradition to present every new Master Mason a free copy upon the occasion of his Raising. These extra copies are 'ear-marked' for that purpose. It must also be noted that a subscriber must re-apply every year for his copy, as no reminder notes are sent to old subscribers outside of the Scottish Constitution. Of course, Scottish masons receive their copies through the auspices of their own lodges. The cost of the *Year Book* tends to rise every year, in line with rising prices generally, so it is pointless to quote a subscription rate here.

6. *LODGE WORKINGS, REGALIA, AND RITUAL*

As with England, there is no standard ritual in use in Scottish masonry, and several printed forms are available through proper masonic channels. However, the Scottish rituals all tend to be similar in content, although their forms can be slightly more diverse than is generally the case with English rituals. Some of the points found in varying Scottish rituals include reference to the Holy Saints John in the first degree Obligation, a darkened temple for Initiation, and an extremely dramatic third degree ceremony which is acted out in quite spectacular fashion in some ritual forms. Visitors from English-type constitutions will also notice that music is often more frugally used in Scottish lodges than in their own.

A unique feature of Scottish masonry is that the degree of Mark Master Mason is worked in Scottish Craft lodges. In all other regular jurisdictions, only the three Craft degrees are worked in constituent lodges. In Scotland, the Mark degree is viewed as an adjunct to the Fellow Craft degree, although a member must first be a Master Mason to receive it. Scottish Craft lodges usually work the Mark degree ceremony once per year. Interestingly, the Mark degree can also be taken in a Chapter under the Supreme Grand Royal Arch Chapter of Scotland.

Lodge regalia in Scotland is by no means standard, as it tends to be in most other jurisdictions. Most Scottish lodges have long traditions of wearing various tartan-trimmed aprons. Sashes are also worn in some lodges. It should be noted that aprons are worn under the coat in Scotland. Nonetheless, visitors are both welcome to bring their own regalia and wear it as they would in their own lodge. However, it must be stated that only Craft jewels and medallions can be worn in Scottish lodges, and not those applicable to any additional Degrees.

7. THE GRAND LODGE

The Grand Lodge of Scotland meets quarterly, and consists of all Grand Office-bearers, and the Masters and Wardens of every Scottish lodge. Dress for the Grand Lodge is still a dark suit, although it is usual for Grand Officers to wear a dinner suit. The list of Grand Lodge Offices is similar to that of England and Ireland, although there are several variations. The majority of Grand Lodge Office-bearers are elected to office on an annual basis. However, it is usual for the Grand Master Mason (as the Scottish Grand Master is called) to remain in office for five years, although he is still subject to annual re-election. Salaried Grand Officers, such as the Grand Secretary and Grand Cashier (Treasurer) are appointed to office, and generally hold office from year to year, until retirement. The Grand Lodge, between its meetings, is administered by the Grand Committee consisting of senior Grand Lodge officers, and a number of elected members. There are several other Grand Lodge committees, including one responsible for benevolence. Unless officially representing a Sister Grand Lodge, it is unusual for a mason who is not a member of the Grand Lodge to attend its meetings.

It is of interest to note that the wearing of Grand Lodge regalia by a Grand Lodge officer in a constituent Scottish lodge is not normal under the Scottish Constitution. The only exception is an official visit by a senior Grand Lodge officer, and this is not particularly commonplace. Normally a Grand Lodge officer will only wear the regalia of his lodge even when visiting. By and large, Grand Lodge regalia is only worn by Grand Lodge officers in meetings of Grand Lodge itself.

A particular feature of Scottish masonry is the tendency of the Grand Master Mason, the Grand Secretary, and other Senior Grand Lodge officers to travel widely overseas to visit scattered Scottish lodges. Grand Master Masons often make such a trip annually, and endeavour to visit most areas of the world possessing Scottish lodges at least once during their term of office.

8. OFFICERS OF CONSTITUENT LODGES

Scottish lodges have several offices largely unknown in other regular jurisdictions. The full list of possible officers is as follows: The Right Worshipful Master, Immediate Past Master, Deputy Master, Substitute Master, Worshipful Senior Warden, Worshipful Junior Warden, Secretary, Treasurer, Almoner, Chaplain, Senior Deacon, Junior Deacon, Director of Ceremonies, Architect, Jeweller, Bible Bearer, Organist, Bard, Sword Bearer, Piper, Marshal, Inner Guard, Tyler (or Outer Guard), and Stewards. Not every lodge will elect (or appoint) every one of these officers—this depending to some extent on the form of ritual used, or simply tradition. Some of the additional offices have little in the way of defined duties. A Jeweller is largely responsible for lodge regalia, and its distribution and collection at meetings. The Bible Bearer, as the name suggests, is responsible for the care of the Lodge's Sacred Volume. The Sword Bearer in some Scottish riguals, precedes the candidate in a Degree Ceremony while he progresses around the lodge. Offices in Scottish lodges are largely elective. Any member of a Scottish lodge who has been admitted to it at least fourteen days prior to nomination, can be nominated and elected to office. However, he cannot be nominated and appointed to an appointive office (such as Secretary). In practice, the lodge committee generally recommends members to office, but they still must be proposed and seconded and, of course, elected. A nominee for the office of Master does not necessarily have to be Past Warden (as is the English practice).

List of Lodges
The very large number of Scottish lodges precludes any attempt being made here to list them. Lodges outside of Scotland will be found detailed in their proper place elsewhere in this guide. Within Scotland itself, most towns possess at least one lodge. The larger cities of Edinburgh, Glasgow, and Aberdeen have many. Each of these three cities possesses many lodge meeting places, servicing suburban areas. Listed below are the main meeting places in each (there are, of course, several others).

EDINBURGH
Aside from Freemasons' Hall itself, and meeting places immediately surrounding it in George Street, the three most frequented are as follows:
The Masonic Hall, 11 Morningside Drive, Edinburgh.
The Masonic Temple, 19 Hill Street, Edinburgh.
The Masonic Hall, 32a Broughton Street, Edinburgh.

GLASGOW
Glasgow is the largest Scottish city, and possesses in excess of eighty lodges. The major meeting place is Freemasons' Hall, 138 Butterbuggins Road, Glasgow.

ABERDEEN
Aberdeen is a popular tourist destination, and its main masonic meeting place is the Masonic Temple, Crown Street, Aberdeen.
There are several Scottish lodges of special interest, and some of these are detailed below:
Lodge Mother Kilwinning No 0 (pronounced 'nothing'). This lodge is arguably the oldest extrant lodge in the world, and it is certainly one of the most famous. It dates from 'before 1598'. In 1984, therefore, it can boast a recorded history of 386 years. The history of this lodge makes fascinating reading, but unfortunately any discourse in that area here is impractical. Interestingly, in very recent times, the lodge was created a Scottish Provincial Grand Lodge in its own right. It meets at the Masonic Hall, Kilwinning, Ayrshire, on the second and fourth Wednesdays every month. Visitors to this lodge are particularly advised to arrive early, as attendance at it is, quite naturally, extremely popular.
The Lodge of Edinburgh (Mary's Chapel) No 1. It remains a matter of contention between Mother Kilwinning and the Lodge of Edinburgh as to which is the oldest lodge, and certainly no opinion will be offered here! The Lodge of Edinburgh is certainly one of great traditions and fame. It meets at the Masonic Temple, 19 Hill Street, Edinburgh, on the second and fourth Tuesdays of the month, from October to April (inclusive).
The Lodge of Aberdeen is also another very old lodge, dating from before 1670. It meets at the Masonic Temple, Crown Street, Aberdeen, on the second and fourth Mondays, October to March.
Lodge St Andrew No 25, is an old lodge meeting at St Andrews, the town famous as the 'Home of Golf', and possessing the Royal and Ancient Golf Club. It meets

at the Masonic Temple, Town Hall, St Andrews, on alternative Fridays, from September to April.

The Operative Lodge No 47. This is the oldest lodge located in Dundee, and dates from 1745. It meets at the Masonic Hall, 161 Princes Street, Dundee, every Tuesday from November to February; and on the third Tuesday in September, October, March, April and May.

Lodge Montefiore No 753, is a most interesting lodge. Dating from 1888, its membership is comprised largely of adherents to the Jewish faith. It is renowned for the beauty of its ceremonial work, and tickets are often necessary to witness its third degree conferments, in particular. It meets at Langside Halls, 5 Langside Avenue, Glasgow, on the second Monday, September to May.

The above list affords only a very brief cross-section of some of the interesting Scottish lodges. However, all Scottish lodges are rich in history and tradition, and are equally recommended to the visitor. Full assistance to the intending visitor will be readily provided at the Freemasons' Hall in Edinburgh, or at the major temples in the large Scottish cities.

Section V

Visiting in Central America
and the Caribbean

Central America and the Caribbean

Of all parts of the habitable globe, Central America affords the most confused picture of masonic development. Both regular and irregular Grand Lodges abound, providing many notable insights for the visitor and the masonic student alike. Mexico, alone, has nearly thirty Grand Lodges. In the neighbouring Caribbean area, a sprinkling of Grand Lodges also exist; but outside these most lodges hold British charters. It is into this pot-pourri of freemasonry that the monologue must now descend.

BELIZE

Belize is located on the Gulf of Honduras, bordered by Mexico and Guatemala. While fairly sizable geographically, it possesses a population of only about 150,000. Formerly known as the British colony of British Honduras, it achieved independence in 1981. As a probable result of its small population, Belize currently has no lodge operating within its borders, regular or otherwise. Amity Lodge No 309 was formed at Belize in 1763, but it had expired by 1813. Two further attempts to establish English lodges were made with British Constitution Lodge No 723, in 1820; and Royal Sussex Lodge No 860, in 1831. However, both had vanished by the early 1860s, and apparently no further attempts to establish a lodge have been made with any success.

COSTA RICA

The Grand Lodge of Costa Rica has had a long and consistent history, unlike many of its neighbours. This happy state of affairs probably results from the relative political stability that Costa Rica has enjoyed in the past.

The Grand Lodge of Ancient, Free and Accepted Masons of Costa Rica:
Founded: 1899
Address: Masonic Temple, corner Central Avenue and 19th Street, San Jose.
Postal Address: P.O. Box 10060, San Jose, Costa Rica. Telephone: 225064.
Lodges: 11   Permits Dual and Plural Membership.
Membership: Circa 500.
Descent: Colombia.   *Government:* Appointive Grand Lodge.
Courtesy Degrees: rarely requested. All correspondence must be through Grand Lodges.
Minimum Time Lapse between Degrees: 12 months.
Ritual: Scottish (craft) Rite, and York Rite.
Main Publications: Constitutions. Annual Proceedings. History: *Freemasonry in Costa Rica.*

History
The history of the Craft on the 'Rich Coast' appears to begin in 1867, when the first lodge in Costa Rica was warranted by the Grand Lodge of New Granada

(Colombia). It would also seem that its main descent is from the Grand Orient of Central America established at San Jose in 1871. Despite sustained difficulties with the Roman Catholic Church, which saw the Craft in recess from about 1875 to 1883, it recovered with the formation of revived lodges after that date.

By 1899, the Costa Rican Craft was strong enough to form a Grand Lodge, with four lodges meeting for that purpose. Since that date, there has been no interruption to Costa Rican freemasonry, and the Grand Lodge has remained united, regular, and unchallenged as the masonic authority of the country; reporting eleven lodges in 1983.

Notes for Visitors to Costa Rica

Costa Rican freemasons have a reputation for hospitality towards visitors to their charming tropical country. The country itself has long remained a stable democracy and, indeed it is one of the few countries in the world that does not possess an army! Of its eleven lodges, ten work the Scottish Rite (Craft) ritual in Spanish, while one works the York Rite (English-type ritual), in English. Eight lodges meet at the main Temple in San Jose, while the remaining three meet in the provincial towns of Alajuela, Turrialba, and Cartago.

The Grand Temple houses a pleasant masonic museum, and the temple itself is picturesque internally. It is dominated by two huge pillars behind the Warden's chairs, the significance of which every mason will be familiar with. The Scottish Rite lodges meet at 8 pm, while the York Rite Lodge (La Luz No 3) meets at 7 pm. A festive board arrangement is usually only held for Installations, but varying sized informal repasts are often held prior to lodge meetings. A 'Week of Brotherhood' is held annually in April, with associated social functions. Of the 500 Costa Rican masons, about 300 are active members and regular attenders at their lodges, and this represents a higher active factor than in many jurisdictions. Dress for lodges is a collar and tie, or dark lounge suit. Nonetheless, it is to be recalled that Costa Rica is a hot, tropical country, and so dress requirements tend to be more casual than elsewhere. Visitors are welcome bring and wear their own regalia.

List of Lodges

The small number of Costa Rican lodges makes listing them here feasible. Detailed below are the eight lodges meeting at the Masonic Temple in the capital city, San Jose.

Regeneracion Lodge No 1	Meets every Wednesday at 8 pm.
Union Fraternal Lodge No 2	Meets 1st and 3rd Tuesdays at 8 pm.
La Luz Lodge No 3	Meets 1st and 3rd Tuesdays at 7 pm. (*English-speaking*)
Hermes Lodge No 7	Meets every Monday at 8 pm.
Hiram Lodge No 11	Meets 2nd and 4th Tuesdays at 8 pm.
Francisco Calvo Lodge No 15	Meets 2nd and 4th Thursdays at 8 pm.
Caridad Lodge No 16	Meets 1st and 3rd Thursdays at 8 pm.
Lautaro Lodge No 18	Meets 2nd and 4th Wednesdays at 8 pm.

EL SALVADOR

El Salvador, the smallest country in Central America, has a regular Grand Lodge, although it is not as widely recognised as some. Nonetheless, it maintains fraternal relations with England. The Grand Lodge, while small, seems to remain quite active despite the adverse political situation the country has suffered in recent years.

The Grand Lodge Cuscatlan of the Republic of El Salvador:
Founded: 1912
Address: Masonic Hall, 8a Avenida Sur No. 126, San Salvador. Telephone: 219793, or 227548.
Lodges: 14   Permits Dual and Plural Membership.   *Membership:* Circa 350.
Descent: Costa Rica.   *Government:* Appointive Grand Lodge.
Courtesy Degrees: Rarely conferred.   All Correspondence must be through Grand Lodges.
Minimum Time Lapse between Degrees: generally 12 months.
Ritual: Scottish (Craft) Rite, York Rite.
Main Publications: Constitutions.   Periodical: *Shittah* (published quarterly).

History

While El Salvador gained independence from Spain in 1821, it appears freemasonry did not reach its shores until the 1850s. After repression by several successive Governments, two lodges were formed in the 1880s from Costa Rica. In 1898, a Grand Lodge was established for both El Salvador and Honduras, with seven constituent lodges. This grand body was subsequently destroyed by the war between El Salvador, Honduras and Guatemala which broke out soon after.

In 1912, three lodges remaining El Salvador erected a Grand Lodge, only to see a breakaway group form a schismatic Grand Lodge. These re-united in 1919 to form the present Grand Lodge.

Notes for Visitors to El Salvador

Of the ten lodges currently working in El Salvador, six evidently work the Scottish Rite Craft ritual, while four practise the York Rite using an English-type Craft ritual. All lodges work in Spanish. El Salvador appears to have remained relatively free of the Scottish Rite Supreme Council domination that has often been seen in other Central American countries. Uncommonly for Central America, while most other Grand Lodges meet annually, the El Salvador Grand Lodge convenes five times per year. Of the ten lodges, six meet in the capital city, San Salvador, while two meet at San Miguel, one at Santa Ana, and one at Sonsonate. Interestingly, the last lodge to be consecrated (Chaparrastique Lodge No 11 at San Miguel) in El Salvador was formed in May 1975. Previous to that, the youngest lodge in the country (Resurreccion Lodge No 10 at San Salvador) was founded in 1948.

Dress for lodges is usually a coat and tie, or a lounge suit. While regalia is available for loan to visitors, they are welcome to wear their own. All the San Salvador based lodges work in Grand Lodge Temple. The political situation in the country is one of communist insurgency and epidemic unrest, and so visitors to El Salvador will probably be few at least until these problems are resolved. Nonetheless, the Grand Lodge continues to function largely unaffected, and any mason coming to El Salvador is welcome to contact the Grand Lodge office, where a warm welcome and every assistance awaits him.

GUATEMALA

Guatemala is a central American country that is not without its political difficulties, but nevertheless it has a regular Grand Lodge with constituent lodges working in Spanish, German and English.

The Grand Lodge of Guatemala:
Founded: 1903.
Address: Masonic Temple, 9 Avenida 3-65, Zone 1, Guatemala City.
Postal Address: Apartado Postal No 34, Guatemala City. *Telephone:* 21196, or 28121.
Lodges: 28. Permits Dual and Plural Membership. *Membership:* Circa 1,000.
Descent: Colombia, and the United States. *Government:* Modified Grand Orient.
Courtesy Degrees: Correspondence must be through Grand Lodges.
Minimum Time Lapse between Degrees: largely 12 months, although less for 'York Rite' Lodges.
Rituals: Scottish (Craft) Rite, York Rite, and Schroeder.
Main Publications: Constitution.   Proceedings.

History
Guatemala has had a most chequered political history, and this has affected its masonic development quite markedly. The first lodge in Guatemala was Constancia Lodge, warranted from Colombia in 1881. By 1886, this lodge had split into three new lodges, which in part formed the Grand Orient of Central America in the same year. Another lodge, called Union Lodge, also joined this Grand Body. It was supposed to have been chartered from America, but from which jurisdiction seems unclear. Nonetheless, this same lodge heads the Guatemala list of lodges today as No 1. It also works a Webb-type ritual in English, adding credence to its probable American ancestry. By 1903, eight lodges were working in Guatemala, and they succeeded in forming the Grand Lodge of the Republic of Guatemala in that year.

By 1908, a dictator had come to political power and the Craft was rigorously suppressed, leading eventually to the destruction and ransacking of Temples in 1917-18. The dictator was overthrown in 1920, whereupon the Grand Lodge re-formed. The year 1930 saw a new dictator assume power, and masonic activity was again restricted until his demise in 1944. After a short peace, two new and opposing dictators arose—Armaz and Arbenz—with the Grand Lodge largely caught up in the power play. Armaz dissolved the Grand Lodge in 1954, and this allowed a dissident group to organise a new Grand Lodge and seize the main temple, although the old Grand Lodge continued to meet. By 1958, dictatorship was replaced by a restoration of democracy, and this has brought relative political stability to the country since. It appears that the schism in Guatemalan masonry was later healed, whereby the Grand Lodge has since prospered, reporting 28 lodges in 1983. In very recent years, a right-wing military Government has taken power, but this occurrence does not appear to have affected masonic activity.

Notes for Visitors to Guatemala
Of Guatemala's 26 lodges, fifteen work in Guatemala City itself, while the remainder are located at provincial population centres. Two lodges work the York Rite, using Webb-type rituals. In addition to the English-speaking Union Lodge No 1, Mozart Lodge No 20 also works in the York Rite, although in Spanish. Both these lodges meet at Guatemala City. All other Guatemalan lodges operate a Scottish (Craft) Rite Ritual in Spanish, with the exception of the Archimedes Lodge No 35—a German-speaking lodge using the *Schroeder* Ritual.

The Scottish Rite lodges largely commence at 8 pm, while the York Rite lodges start at 7 pm. Dress is a dark lounge suit, but collar and tie are permissible in hotter months. December and January are recess months for most lodges. The majority meet twice monthly, but some lodges convene on a weekly basis.

Visitors to Guatemala wishing to attend a lodge are advised, at least in the first instance, to visit the main Masonic Hall in Guatemala City where they can be assured of full assistance. However, visitors should endeavour to remember not to turn up at the Temple during the siesta hours in the middle of the day, as it is unlikely that it will be staffed during these times.

HONDURAS

Honduras possesses both Caribbean and Pacific coastlines, and borders Guatemala, El Salvador and Nicaragua. It has a population of about four million, and remains the poorest nation in Central America. The first lodge in the country appears to have been Morazan Lodge No 14, warranted by the Scottish Rite Supreme Council of Central America. Two more lodges were rapidly erected by the same authority, and it formed the Grand Lodge of Honduras in 1922—the year after the country declared its independence from Nicaragua. After the formation of the Grand Lodge, the Supreme Council relinquished control over the three Craft degrees in Honduras, vesting them with the new Authority. The Grand Lodge of Honduras still exists, but it is not recognised by the Grand Lodges of England, Ireland and Scotland, although several of the United States Grand Lodges exchange recognition.

It is of interest to note that four Scottish lodges once existed in Honduras. Lodge Tela No 1196 was chartered in 1919; and this was followed by Lodge Ceiba No 1266 (1921); Lodge Puerto Castilla No 1293 (1922); and Lodge Cortes No 1315 (1923). These four lodges appear to have worked happily enough under Scotland until 1939, when three of them (Tela, Puerto Castilla, and Cortes) withdrew and formed the oddly named 'United Grand Lodge of Tela, Castilla, and Cortes No 1196'. Of course, this new Grand Body was not viewed with universal joy in Edinburgh. The one lodge that stood out—Ceiba—does not appear to have survived on its own. Evidently, this second Honduran Grand Lodge still survives, although little is known of it, and it is certainly not recognised outside Honduras.

MEXICO

Mexico is the most masonically diverse country in the world. It possesses nearly thirty Grand Lodges, most of which are not widely recognised, with the exception of the York Grand Lodge of Mexico.

The York Grand Lodge of Free and Accepted Masons of Mexico:
Founded: 1862
Address: Masonic Temple, Calle Hegel 416, Mexico 5, D.F. (Mexico City).
Address: Postal Address: P.O. Box 1986, Mexico 1, D.F.   Telephone: 5310784.
Lodges: 11.   Permits Dual and Plural Membership.   *Membership:* 632.
Descent: United States, Valle de Mexico.   *Government:* Elective Grand Lodge.
Courtesy Degrees: conferred on request.
Ritual: York Rite (Webb-form Craft Ritual).
Minimum Time Lapse between Degrees: 30 Days.
Main Publications: Constitution.   Annual Proceedings.

History

The task of producing even a synopsis of Mexican masonic history verges on the
encyclopaedic. This is due to its great complexity of development which, in turn,
was strongly tied to the political development (or lack of it) of the country. Mexico,
since its independence from Spain in 1810, has suffered approximately 100 Revolu-
tions and about eighty governments, so it is less than surprising that the Craft was
greatly affected as a result.

While tradition given an earlier date, the first lodges established in Mexico for
which extant evidence exists were chartered in the early nineteenth century from
Spain, Louisiana, Pennsylvania, and New York. The American jurisdictions
evidently disowned their offsprings not long after chartering, as most of them became extremely political in nature. Indeed, the various political factions which
battled for revoluntary control of Mexico during the first half of the nineteenth
century were largely comprised of 'masons'. The battle lines were drawn between
the York Rite masons on the one hand, and the Scottish Rite masons on the other.
In 1827, the Grand Masters of the two bodies of masonry actually battled in war
for the Presidency of Mexico! However, the story—one of the most interesting in
masonic history—is too long to relay here, except to say that the Scottish Rite won.

In an effort to unite the two factions, several well intentioned masons decided in
1830 to form a mixture of the two Rites, creating the Mexican National Rite. This
Rite contained nine degrees—the Craft degrees, plus selected Scottish degrees. While
the effort failed, there still exists an irregular Grand Lodge in Mexico today practising this Rite.

Masonry lay dormant between about 1833 and 1860, as a result of perpetual
political turmoil. In 1860, Scottish Rite lodges were established at Vera Cruz and
Mexico City from the United States. These bodies soon factioned, and a number of
State Grand Lodges were formed, all claiming to be independent Grand Bodies.
The next body to intervene appears to have been the Grand Lodge of New Grenada
(Colombia) which warranted a lodge at Mexico City in 1859. Out of this lodge soon
came a Supreme Council, and shortly afterwards the Grand Lodge Valle de Mexico.
By 1878, aside from the infant State Grand Lodges, the two main Mexican bodies
were the Grand Lodge Valle de Mexico, and the Grand Orient of Mexico (the latter
being the schismatic daughter of the former), together with two Scottish Rite
Supreme Councils. All four were in great competition, with some even offering
cut-rate initiations!

The Grand Lodge of Missouri warranted the Toltec Lodge No 520, at Mexico
City in 1883 for English and American residents. In 1890, the vast dispersion of

masonry that was Mexico at last came together, albeit only briefly, in a unifying reorganisation. The new body formed for this purpose was the Grand Diet of the States of Mexico. It brought virtually all Mexican masonry under its control, possessing 122 of the 125 lodges then operating in the country. Even the Toltec Lodge was prevailed upon by Missouri to exchange its charter. However, this unity was only fleeting. The Grand Diet Grand Master was accused (evidently on strong evidence) of initiating women, and there was a question concerning a shortfall of $10,000 in the accounts. It needs to be made plain that the Grand Diet was an 'apex' Grand Lodge, and that the then existing Grand Lodges still retained most of their identity within its structure. The Grand Diet shortly thereafter seems to have been lost in history. Aside from the small State-based Grand Lodges, the only Grand Lodge that was national in character at this time was Valle de Mexico. This Grand Lodge was extremely active in warranting lodges all over Mexico between 1891 and 1910, mostly English-speaking.

By 1910, Valle de Mexico, with a Scottish Rite Constitution, consisted of a majority of lodges and masons practising the York Rite. With this majority, the Yorkists changed the constitution to reflect more the main York Rite institutions. This resulted in the last great schism in Mexican masonry, whereupon the York and Scottish sections split. The Valle de Mexico continued as a Scottish Rite (Spanish-speaking Mexican) body, with the York body of lodges, renamed the York Grand Lodge of Mexico, going its own way.

The various State Grand Lodges recognised Valle de Mexico, while overseas just about the rest of the masonic world went with the English-speaking York Grand Lodge. These two remain the only Grand Lodges of a national sense in Mexico today. The argument between these two Grand Lodges remained until 1945, when intervisitation treaties started to be agreed upon. The York Grand Lodge's basic concern was its contention that Valle de Mexico was controlled by a Supreme Council. Valle de Mexico, however, came out strongly in 1939 favouring exclusive jurisdiction for itself over the three Craft Degrees. Since the War, a few of the State Grand Lodges, and Valle de Mexico, have entered into Visitation Treaties with the York Grand Lodge. These Treaties, certainly novel in terms of masonry, allow members from either allegiance, under certain conditions, to visit each other's lodges. This stops short of actual recognition. Nonetheless, in recent years two State Grand Lodges (Nuevo Leon and Tamaulipas) have exchanged recognition with the York Grand Lodge. Indeed, as late as 1979, the Grand Master of Valle de Mexico was invited to pay an official visit to the Annual Communication of the York Grand Lodge. It would appear, therefore, that in time it might be possible for amity to exist throughout the body of Mexican masonry. It will be noted that the York Grand Lodge is quite small in terms of membership. However, as it is so widely recognised outside Mexico, similar recognition for other Mexican Grand Lodges, to a large extent, depends on its blessings.

THE GRAND LODGES OF MEXICO

Aside from the Grand Lodge Valle de Mexico (with 154 lodges and 5,056 members in 1982), and the York Grand Lodge of Mexico, the country possesses nineteen State Grand Lodges. They are listed below, with basic details, in order of seniority by their dates of foundation.

State Grand Lodge	State	No of Lodges	Membership
Grand Lodge Unita Mexicana (1883)	Vera Cruz	70	2,000
Grand Lodge of Oaxaca (1883)	Oaxaca	15	400
Grand Lodge Oriental Peninsular (1883)	Yucatan	20	600
Grand Lodge of Campeche (1885)	Campeche	8	200
Grand Lodge 'Benito Juarez' (1890)	Caohuila	49	2,300
Grand Lodge 'El Potosi' (1896)	San Luis Potosi	14	400
Grand Lodge 'Cosmos' (1903)	Chihuahua	19	800
Grand Lodge Nuevo Leon (1905)	Nuevo Leon	72	4,000
Grand Lodge of Tamaulipas (1909)	Tamaulipas	83	3,500
Grand Lodge Occidental Mexicana (1912)	Jalisco	12	250
Grand Lodge 'Del Pacifico' (1923)	Sinaloa, and Sonora	12	400
Grand Lodge 'Restauracion' (1923)	Tabasco	10	200
Grand Lodge of Chiapas (1929)	Chiapas	11	500
Grand Lodge Guadaloupe Victoria (1932)	Durango	5	150
Grand Lodge of Baja California (1933)	Baja California	28	2,000
Grand Lodge of Queretaro (1934)	Queretaro	?	?
Grand Lodge of Hidalgo (1940)	Hidalgo	4	100
Grand Lodge Baja California Sur (1978)	Baja California	?	?
Grand Lodge Sur-Oeste (?)	Colima	?	?

The memberships figure provided above are approximate. There is also a Grand Lodge of the Mexican National Rite (with about 1,100 members), and two other obscure irregular bodies—the Valley of Anahuac, and the Ancient Valley of Anahuac. If a rough addition is undertaken, the approximate number of masons in Mexico, regular and irregular, totals about 32,000. This is based on 1973 figures (source: Proceedings of the York Grand Lodge, 1981), being the best available. The total number of lodges appears to be about 600.

Notes for Visitors to Mexico
The York Grand Lodge is the only Mexican Grand Lodge recognised as regular by the English, Irish and Scottish Grand Lodges, and therefore the only one open to discussion in the context of this guide. Until recent years, all its lodges were English-speaking and comprised mainly of non-Mexicans, although a number of bi-lingual Mexicans have joined it. The progress of the York Grand Lodge has been slow, simply because in Spanish-speaking Mexico there is a limit on the number of potential members available. Until very recent times, there has been a resistance within the York Grand Lodge to translate its ritual into Spanish to enable greater expansion. However, this was achieved in 1980.

Of its eleven lodges, nine work in English, one in Spanish, and one in German. The ritual for all is the York Rite, in this case a Webb-form ritual obviously derived from the United States. All lodges meet in the evening, generally about 7 pm. A meal is often included. Dress is a dark suit, and visitors are welcome to wear their own regalia.

List of Lodges
As the York Grand Lodge is largely English-speaking and possesses a small number of lodges, a full detailing of them is both desirable and practical.

Toltec Lodge No 1	Meets 1st and 3rd Mondays at Hegel 416, Mexico City.
Anahuac Lodge No 3	Meets 1st Wednesday at Hegel 416, Mexico City.
Guadalajara Lodge No 5	Meets 3rd Wednesday at Apartado 6–221, Guadalajara.
Monterrey Lodge No 13	Meets 1st Tuesday (except August) at Monterrey.
Aztec Lodge No 22	Meets 2nd Monday at Hegel 416, Mexico City.
Cuernavaca Lodge No 23	Meets 2nd and 4th Saturdays at Cuernavaca, Morelos.
Mexico Lodge of Research No 24	Meets 5th Wednesdays at Hegel 416, Mexico City.
Bahia Acapulco Lodge No 25	Meets 2nd Monday (April to November) at Tabachines 4–2, Acapulco, Guerrero.
Alexander Von Humboldt Lodge No 26	Meets 1st Tuesday at Hegel 416, Mexico City. (German-speaking lodge.)
Morelos Lodge No 27	Meets 1st and 3rd Thursdays, Cuernavaca, Morelos.
Tijuana Lodge No 28	Meets 1st Wednesday at Santa Maria del Mar 234, Tijuana. (Spanish-speaking Lodge.)

NICARAGUA

There is evidence of early English-warranted lodges in Nicaragua during the British occupation of the 'Mosquito Coast' (1740–86), including Bluefields Lodge No 875, and Eureka Lodge No 673, the latter of which appears to have been largely composed of Negroes. However, neither survived the British departure.

In 1882, the Grand Orient of Colombia granted a warrant for Lodge Progreso No 41 at Grenada City, but vigorous opposition from the Catholic Church forced its closure. However, it was re-formed in 1898. In 1905, Luz Lodge No 29 was formed by members of Progreso, but it had expired by 1912. The Supreme Council of Central America, which had been active in the area since about 1901, formed Estrella Meridional Lodge No 28, in 1906. A Grand Lodge of Nicaragua was formed by Progreso, Luz, and Estrella Meridional in 1907. In the 1970s, the Grand Lodge had its seat at Managua, and a membership of about 600 dispersed in about 10 lodges. In view of the fact that the Grand Lodge appears to have had a dubious relationship with a Supreme Council, and that there are doubts as to its regular descent, it is not recognised by the Grand Lodges of England, Ireland, and Scotland. Nonetheless, the advent of a Marxist government and civil war in Nicaragua in very recent years must have placed pressure on existing masonic institutions. Information on the current masonic situation does not appear to be available.

PANAMA

Panama is a country divided in half by the Panama Canal (or Canal Zone). It possesses a regular Grand Lodge, while the Canal Zone has a District under the Grand Lodge of Massachusetts. There are also two lodges working under warrant from Scotland.

The Grand Lodge of Ancient, Free and Accepted Masons of Panama
Founded: 1916
Address: Masonic Hall, 288th Street, Vista Hermosa, Panama City.
Postal Address: P.O. Box 84, Panama 1, Republic of Panama.
Lodges: 10.   Permits Dual and Plural Membership.   *Membership:* Circa 500.
Descent: Colombia, Venezuela, Massachusetts.   *Government:* Appointive Grand
Lodge.
Courtesy Degrees: conferred on request.   All correspondence through Grand
Lodges.
Minimum Time Lapse between Degrees: usually 12 months.
Ritual: largely Scottish (Craft) Rite.
Main Publications: Constitution.   Proceedings.

History

Panama's first lodge was formed by a group of masons petitioning the Grand Orient
of Spain in 1821. This lodge variously changed allegiance to France, New York and
Colombia over the succeeding years, but it had expired by 1840. A lodge appears to
have been chartered from Texas in 1850, but it lasted only four years.

Several lodges were established between 1854 and 1884, variously holding warrants from Colombia, the Grand Orient of France, and Massachusetts, most of
which expired. The only survivors were Fraternidad Lodge No 43, and Fidelidad
Lodge No 48, chartered from the Grand Orient of Cartegena (Colombia). Both of
these lodges were working when the Americans came to build the Panama Canal in
1903.

The influx of Americans brought new life to the two remaining lodges, but this
quickly evaporated when Scotland warranted the Sojourner's Lodge No 874. All the
Americans transferred to this new lodge, leaving the two Cartegena lodges high and
dry. Both these Colombian lodges had expired by 1905. In 1906, Scotland warranted
Lodge Thistle No 1013, at Colon; and the Grand Lodge of Massachusetts weighed
in with Isthmus Lodge in the same year.

The remaining Panamanian masons, with no lodge of their own working in the
country, now turned to Venezuela, which warranted six lodges between 1907 and
1913. By 1916, seven lodges had formed the Grand Lodge of Panama. On its
formation, the Grand Lodges of Panama and Massachusetts entered into a treaty
whereby the Panamanian Grand Lodge granted the Grand Lodge of Massachusetts
jurisdiction over the Canal Zone, while Massachusetts recognised Panama's jurisdiction over the balance of the country. Scotland warranted a second lodge in 1914,
its earliest 'Sojourner's Lodge' having exchanged for a Massachusetts charter.
Nonetheless, Scotland thereafter seemed to have respected the 'treaty', and has established no new lodges since that date. Panama has finished with six surviving lodges
in the Canal Zone, while the Grand Lodge of Panama now possesses ten lodges
under its jurisdiction. All the three governing bodies, and their constituent lodges,
work in amity. In 1982, the Panama Canal was returned to the Panamanian Government. As a result of this imminent occurrence, the Massachusetts and Panama
Grand Lodges involved themselves in protracted discussions as to future jurisdictional lines within the country—the old treaty now seen as outmoded. Evidently,
the negotiations bogged down, with Massachusetts declaring that unless agreement
was reached it would consider all of Panama to be open territory.

Notes for Visitors to Panama
Of the lodges working under the Grand Lodge of Panama, five work in Panama City, two at David, one at Colon, one at Puerto Armueeles, and one at Aguadulce. Pacific Lodge No 5 works in English at Panama City, evidently in the York Rite. All other Panamanian lodges work the Scottish (Craft) Rite in Spanish. Massachusetts and Scottish lodges, quite naturally, adhere to their mother rituals. Visitors to Panama are probably more likely to be interested in the English-speaking lodges, of which details are provided below. Massachusetts and Scottish lodges meet in the early evening, usually around 7 pm, and meetings twice monthly are the norm. With respect to afterproceedings, the practices of Massachusetts and Scotland, as appropriate, are largely followed. Dress is a dark suit. Of course, American and Scottish regalia is fairly dissimilar. Nonetheless, visitors are welcome to wear their own, regardless.

Scottish Lodges

Lodge Thistle No 1013	Meets 2nd and 4th Wednesdays monthly, at Building 15, Limon Avenue, Colon, Panama.
Lodge St Andrew No 1140	Meets 2nd and 4th Saturdays monthly, at 288th Street, Vista Hermosa, Panama City.

Massachusetts Lodges

Army Lodge	Meets 2nd Tuesday monthly, at Balboa, Canal Zone.
Canal Zone Isthmain Lodge	Meets 1st Wednesday monthly, at Ancon, Canal Zone.
Chagres Lodge	Meets 1st Monday monthly, at Balboa, Canal Zone.
Darien Lodge	Meets 2nd Thursday monthly, at Balboa, Canal Zone.
Sojourner's Lodge	Meets 1st Friday monthly, at Cristobal, Canal Zone.
Sibert Lodge	Meets 1st Wednesday monthly, at Gatun, Canal Zone.

Note: With America vacating the Panama Canal Zone, it would appear likely that the number of American nationals remaining in Panama will be lessened. It is therefore probable that some Massachusetts lodges will consolidate with others of that allegiance.

THE CARIBBEAN

As will soon be appreciated, the majority of lodges located in the Caribbean hold warrants from either England, Ireland or Scotland, although there are a few regular lodges warranted from France and the Netherlands. As the practices of these lodges largely parallel those of their respective home jurisdictions discussed elsewhere in this guide, no notes for visitors will be provided in this category. However, the meeting details of individual lodges will be provided. Nonetheless, for the three Regular Grand Lodges in the Caribbean, notes for visitors will remain a feature.

THE BAHAMAS (INCLUDING THE TURKS AND CAICOS ISLANDS)

The Bahamas is a former British Crown Colony located north of Cuba, and south east of Florida. It consists of several hundred islands, with the Turks and Caicos Islands at the easterly tail of the group. The first two English lodges in the Bahamas, warranted in the mid 1700s, did not survive much into the nineteenth century. Scotland met with the same lack of success with two lodges formed in the early nineteenth century. England met with permanent success with the establishment of the Royal Victoria Lodge No 443, erected at Nassau in 1837; and with Turk's Island Forth Lodge No 647, set up at Grand Turk Island in 1855. Scotland's first permanent lodge was Lodge St Michael, which opened at Nassau only in 1967. The English lodges are all governed by the District Grand Lodge of the Bahamas and Turks, while the two Scottish lodges in the country come under the Scottish District Grand Lodge of Jamaica and the Bahamas.

The District Grand Lodge of the Bahamas and Turks (English Constitution)
   Postal Address: P.O. Box N8424, Nassau, The Bahamas.

Lodges meeting at the Masonic Hall, McKinney Avenue, Nassau, New Providence:

Royal Victoria Lodge No 443	Meets 2nd Wednesday October to May. Inst: October.
Lodge of Unity No 8760	Meets last Thursday in February, May, September, and November. Inst: November.
Bahamas Lodge of Installed Masters No 8764	Meets last Saturday in February, April, June, and October. Inst: February.

Lodges meeting at the Masonic Temple, West Road, Freeport, Grand Bahama.

Lucayan Lodge No 8188	Meets 1st Tuesday September to June (except February). Inst:.December.
Arawak Lodge No 8877	Meets 3rd Thursday in February, April, June, September and November. Inst: September.

Lodges meeting at the Masonic Temple, Queen Street, Grand Turk, Grand Turk Islands:

Turk's Island Forth Lodge No 647	Meets 1st Wednesday monthly. Inst: 27th December.
Coral Lodge No 8888	Meets 3rd Thursday in February, May, August and November. Inst: November.

Scottish Lodges

Lodge St Michael No 1634	Meets at the Curfew Buildings, Nassau, New Providence. 1st Wednesday September to June.
Lodge St David No 1741	Meets at Masonic Hall, McKinney Avenue, Nassau, New Providence. 2nd Monday in March, April, June, July, August, October, November and December.

BARBADOS

Barbados is an island in the West Indies within the Windward Island group, but because of its masonic development it is dealt with separately here. Barbados contains both an English, and a Scottish, District Grand Lodge. An English Province was first formed about 1740, but it was not working in 1813. Similarly, two lodges had been formed under Irish warrants, forming a Province in 1804. It too later lapsed. The oldest surviving lodge is Albion Lodge No 196, established in 1790; and the earliest Scottish lodge is Lodge Scotia No 340 dating from 1799.

The District Grand Lodge of Barbados (English Constitution): with 8 lodges in the District of which 4 work in Barbados.
   Postal Address: P.O. Box 55, Bridgetown, Barbados.

Albion Lodge No 196	Meets at Masonic Hall, Spry Street, Bridgetown; 1st Wednesday monthly. Inst: December.

The remaining three English lodges meet at the Masonic Hall, Belleville, Barbados.

Victoria Lodge No 2196	Meets 2nd Thursday November to August. Inst: August.
St Michael's Lodge No 2253	Meets 3rd Thursday October to July. Inst: May.
Union Lodge No 7551	Meets 4th Tuesday February to June, and September to November. Inst: 3rd Tuesday, January.

The District Grand Lodge of Barbados (Scottish Constitution): with five lodges, all in Barbados.
   Address: Masonic Hall, Spry Street, Bridgetown, Barbados; at which meet all five Scottish lodges.

Lodge Scotia No 340	Meets 3rd Monday monthly.
Lodge Thistle No 1014	Meets 4th Wednesday monthly.
Lodge St John No 1062	Meets 2nd Monday October to July.
Lodge St Andrew No 1509	Meets 4th Monday January to November.
Lodge Unity No 1625	Meets 2nd Friday October to July.

BERMUDA

Bermuda is a British Crown Colony located in the western Atlantic about 900 km from the United States. The first lodge in Bermuda was Union Lodge No 266, warranted by England in 1761. This was followed by Bermuda Lodge No 507 in 1792. However, both these lodges expired. The oldest surviving lodge is Atlantic Phoenix Lodge No 224, formed under England in 1797. Scotland granted a warrant for Lodge St George No 266 (now No 200) in the same year, while Ireland's first lodge was Hannibal Lodge No 224, warranted in 1867. Currently, England has four lodges on the island, while Ireland and Scotland possess three each. As no constitution has enough lodges on Bermuda to support a District Grand Lodge, London, Edinburgh and Dublin have each appointed their own Grand Superintendent or Grand Inspector to act as local masonic governor.

The Grand Inspectorate of Bermuda (English Constitution): 4 Lodges.

Atlanic Phoenix Lodge No 224	Meets at Masonic Hall, Reid Street, Hamilton, Bermuda; Tuesday on or before the full moon; October to June (except December). Installation: 3rd Tuesday December.
Prince Alfred Lodge No 233	Meets at Freemasons' Hall, Somerset, Bermuda; 2nd Wednesday, October to June. Installation: March.
Lodge of Loyalty No 358	Meets at Masonic Hall, Reid Street, Hamilton; 4th Friday October to June (except December, when 2nd Friday). Installation: March.
Broad Arrow Lodge No 1890	Meets at Masonic Hall, Reid Street, Hamilton; 3rd Monday, October to June. Installation: April.

The Grand Inspectorate of Bermuda (Irish Constitution):

Abercorn Lodge No 123	Meets at Masonic Hall, Reid Street, Hamilton; 1st Monday monthly, October to June.
Hannibal Lodge No 224	Meets at Masonic Hall, St George's Island, Bermuda; 2nd Wednesday, October to June.
Bermuda Garrison Lodge No 580	Meets at Masonic Hall, Reid Street, Bermuda; 2nd Monday, October to June.

The District Superintendent of Bermuda (Scottish Constitution):

Lodge St George No 200	Masonic Hall, St George's Island, Bermuda; 1st Tuesday, October to June.
Lodge Civil and Military No 726	Meets at Masonic Hall, King Street, Hamilton; 1st Monday, September to June.
Lodge Somers Isles No 1503	Meets at the Somers Isles Temple, Bermuda; 2nd Tuesday, October to June.

CAYMAN ISLAND

This small British possession sits in the middle of Western Caribbean south of Cuba and west of Jamaica. It possesses one lodge, formed under England in 1967. It is administered as part of the District Grand Lodge of Jamaica (EC).

Cayman Lodge No 8153	Meets at Freemasons' Hall, Prospect Park, Cayman Island; 3rd Friday, September to June (except December). Inst: November.

CUBA

Cuba is a masonic enigma. It is the only Communist country on earth possessing a Grand Lodge, and a regular one at that. This unique situation alone makes for an interesting study.

The Grand Lodge of Cuba
Founded: 1859.
Address: Apartado Postal 72, Habana, Cuba.   Telephone: 75732 or 75065.
Lodges: 324.   Permits Dual and Plural Membership.

Membership: 19,728.
Descent: South Carolina, Spain, others.   *Government:* Appointive Grand Lodge.
Courtesy Degrees: rarely conferred.   *Ritual:* Scottish (Craft) Rite.
Minimum Time Lapse between Degrees: 12 months.
Main Publication: Annual Proceedings.

History

The masonic history of Cuba is probably second only to that of Mexico in terms of confusion. Masonry first appeared in Cuba with Le Temple des Vertus Theologales Lodge No 103, chartered by the Grand Lodge of Pennsylvania in 1804. A further ten lodges were established under the same authority up until 1820, but all of them had expired by 1827. The Grand Lodge of Louisiana warranted five lodges between 1815 and 1822, and South Carolina had two lodges under charter in 1819. In 1818, two Pennsylvania lodges and one South Carolina lodge organised the Gran Logia del Rito York at Habana. However, by 1828, the Spanish Government enforced a rigid ban on freemasonry in Cuba, and the Grand Lodge was suppressed.

The Craft revived in 1859, when three lodges arose to form the Independent Grand Lodge of Colon. A Supreme Council of the Scottish Rite was erected at the same time. These two bodies soon came into conflict, with the Supreme Council seeking to control the Grand Lodge. The dispute came to a head about ten years later, and left the Cuban Craft weak as a result. In addition, a revolution against Spain broke out in 1868, and freemasonry was again persecuted. Another Grand Lodge, the Gran Logia de la Isla de Cuba, sprang up about 1876, bringing condemnation from the Grand Lodge of Colon. Both these Grand Lodges appear to have prospered, despite the growing political troubles in the country. The Spanish–American War of 1898 brought Cuba under American protection, and the Craft was able to develop peacefully until the chaos wrought by the dictator Batista following his assumption of power in the late 1930s.

The relations between the two Grand Lodges were poor, although attempts were made about this time to unite them. However, by the late 1940s all the Isla de Cuba lodges, about seven, were on the Roll of the Grand Lodge of Colon. In 1951, the name Grand Lodge of Cuba was adopted, and by this time it had become the sole masonic authority on the island in terms of the Craft, and has continued to remain so. The expansion of both lodges and membership became rapid. In 1950, the Grand Lodge possessed 258 lodges and 22,000 members, and by 1959 this had risen to 339 lodges and nearly 35,000 members.

However, 1959 brought with it the rise to power of the Castro regime. Curiously, the Craft was not banned nor rigorously suppressed, although the relations between the Grand Lodge and the Communist government have never been warm. Nonetheless, government pressure has sometimes been applied, particularly in recent years. These pressures have seen the Grand Lodge's membership decline to about 19,500 in 1982. Just exactly how the Grand Lodge operates in a Communist state remains unclear, but nonetheless it has done so, and remains fully regular. It is recognised by the Grand Lodges of England, Ireland and Scotland, and by the majority of Grand Lodges in the regular masonic world.

Notes for Visitors to Cuba

All Cuban lodges work the Scottish Rite (Craft) Ritual in Spanish. There were four

English-speaking York Rite lodges operating under the Grand Lodge in 1959, but these have long since lapsed. The Grand Lodges erected a ten-storey masonic temple in central Habana in 1955, but it is not clear whether this building is still occupied by the Grand Lodge.

The position of the Grand Lodge has been made more difficult in recent years. In 1977, the government decreed new laws requiring all voluntary organisations, except religious organisations and agricultural co-operatives, to register with the government and provide details concerning their membership, officers, and property. These organisations are subject to regular inspection by government agents, and in the event of violations are subject to fines, suspension, or dissolution. Evidently, the right of appeal is severely limited.

In 1977, several constituent lodges of the Grand Lodge were found guilty of violations, and were fined from between $100 to $1,000 each, and the Grand Lodge was fined $95,000. The reason given by the Castro government was that the lodges concerned were guilty of having the names of masons who had fled Cuba on their membership rolls, and of giving assistance to the wives and daughters of masons who had been imprisoned or executed as enemies of the government. Despite these difficulties, the Grand Lodge carries on, and the resolve of Cuban masons to continue to practise their ancient Craft is undiminished.

The dress for all Cuban lodges is a dark suit, and working regalia is supplied to those attending. Cuban lodges do not operate any festive board type practices, but usually a light supper accompanies meetings. About 150 of Cuba's 324 lodges work in Habana, while the others are spread throughout the major population centres of the island. Masonic visitors travelling to Cuba are best advised to correspond with the Cuban Grand Secretary, via the auspices of their own Grand Lodge. This should be achieved well before departure to enable arrangements to be made.

It is interesting to note that one lodge chartered from Massachusetts still works on Cuba. However, it is located at the American naval base at Guantanamo Bay near the extreme west of the island. This base, however, is largely cut off from the rest of Cuba for political reasons. The lodge's details are as follows:

Guantanamo Bay Lodge   Meets at the Naval Base, Guantanamo Bay, 1st
                                          Wednesday, montly.

DOMINICAN REPUBLIC

The Dominican Republic shares about half of the Caribbean island of Hispaniola (with Haiti), and possesses a regular Grand Lodge dating from 1858.

The Grand Lodge of the Dominican Republic
Founded: 1858

Address: The National Grand Masonic Temple, Arzobispo Portes No 554, espuina Las Carreras, Santo Domingo. *Postal Address:* P.O. Box 209, Santo Domingo. Telephone: 682 4173, or 682 6973.

Lodges: 25.   Permits Dual Membership.   *Membership:* Circa 2,000.

Descent: Somewhat obscure, but probably England, Pennsylvania, and France.

Government: Modified Grand Orient.

Courtesy Degrees: rarely conferred.
Minimum Time Lapse between Degrees: 12 Months.   *Ritual:* Scottish (Craft) Rite.
Main Publications: Constitution.   Proceedings.

History

It is somewhat difficult to separate the masonic history of the Dominican Republic from that of Haiti. Originally, the entire island of Hispaniola was a Spanish possession, until 1697 when the west of the island was ceded to France. Not surprisingly, the Grand Orient of France soon warranted lodges in Haiti, but this will be discussed under that heading below. The Grand Orient of France controlled the Craft on the entire island of Hispaniola, it would seem, until the French Revolution, whereupon after much chaos, Haiti and Dominica became independent of colonial control at the start of the nineteenth century.

The Grand Lodge of Pennsylvania had warranted a lodge at Haiti as early as 1786, but this became extinct. Oddly enough, Pennsylvania chartered seven lodges on the island in the revolutionary period, between 1800 and 1806, none of which survived the chaos. England stepped in with four lodges about 1811, but all of them had been erased by 1824.

In 1844, San Domingo (now the Dominican Republic) finally became a republic, but still under the protection of Spain. A Grand Orient of San Domingo was formed in 1858, evidently largely using Haitian lodges working in its part of the island. A separate body, the Grand Lodge of the Dominican Republic, was opened in 1865. These two bodies merged in 1866, with ten lodges under its control. This number had grown to 25 by 1983.

Notes for Visitors to the Dominican Republic

As with virtually all Latin countries, the Dominican Grand Lodge works the Scottish (Craft) Rite, its Craft degrees being termed Apprentice, Craftsman and Master. Its lodges largely meet weekly or fortnightly, generally commencing at 8 pm. Of its 25 lodges, eight work in Santo Domingo, the capital city, at the National Grand Masonic Temple. The remainder work at other population centres, invariably one lodge per town. Dress for lodges is a dark suit, or a collar and tie during hotter weather. Visitors to the republic are advised to attend, at least initially, the National Grand Masonic Temple in Santo Domingo. All lodges work in Spanish, there being no York Rite lodges currently operating in the country.

HAITI

Haiti occupies the western portion of Hispaniola island, the other portion taken up with the Dominican Republic. Haiti was ceded from Spain to France in 1697. The Grand Orient of France formed two lodges in 1749, and about ten more lodges were erected by the same authority up until 1789. Pennsylvania warranted three lodges between 1786 and 1797, two of which lasted into the next century before expiring. The French Revolution brought about the independence of Haiti, but not until after the defeat of Napoleon. In the meantime, Pennsylvania again became active warranting seven lodges up until 1806, none of which survived long. Likewise, no French lodge survived the Revolution.

The saviour of Haitian masonry came in the form of four English lodges, warranted between 1809 and 1817. These lodges formed into a Provincial Grand Lodge, which in 1823 abandoned England and formed the Grand Lodge of Haiti. The Haitian Craft developed peacefully until 1830. In that year the Grand Orient of France invaded the island with its higher degrees, and by 1836 the Grand Lodge of Haiti had become the Grand Orient of Haiti controlled by a Scottish Rite Supreme Council. Thereafter, various struggles occurred between the Grand Orient and the Supreme Council for control of the Craft degrees. The situation in the second half of the twentieth century remains unclear, except to say that the Grand Orients of Haiti and France maintain fraternal relations. On that basis alone, the Haitian Craft remains irregular.

JAMAICA

Jamaica is one of the larger Caribbean islands. Located to the south of Cuba, it gained its political independence from Britain in 1962. The Grand Lodges of England, Ireland and Scotland were all active in Jamaica; and between them they erected a profusion of lodges. Some did not survive, but most did. The oldest extant English lodges are Royal Lodge No 207 (1794), and Friendly Lodge No 239 (1797), both at Kingston, the Jamaican capital city. The premier Scottish lodge is Lodge Glenlyon No 346 (1845). Ireland was less fortunate, with only one lodge, the South Carolina Lodge No 390, working at Kingston. It dates from 1927.

In 1983, nineteen English lodges worked in Jamaica, together with sixteen Scottish lodges, and the one Irish lodge. The English lodges come under the District Grand Lodge of Jamaica (EC), while the Scottish lodges come under the District Grand Lodge of Jamaica and the Bahamas. Rather than listing all 36 lodges here, the principal Masonic Halls in Jamaica will be detailed below instead. Visitors to the island can readily gain assistance at these addresses, particularly in Kingston.

Kingston: Freemasons' Building, 11-15 McGregor Square, Kingston (11 English, 8 Scottish, 1 Irish).

Mandeville: Masonic Temple, Ward Avenue, Mandeville (2 English).

Montego Bay: Masonic Temple, Davis Avenue, Red Hills, Montego Bay (1 English, 1 Scottish).

Spanish Town: Masonic Temple, 2 Ellis Street, Spanish Town (1 English, 1 Scottish). Either English or Scottish lodges (one lodge per location) meet in the towns of Lucea, Four Paths, St Ann's Bay, Port Maria, Morant Bay, Port Antonio, Savanna La Mar, Spalding, Linstead, and Duncans.

The relevant postal addresses are:

The District Grand Lodge of Jamaica (English Constitution), P.O. Box 555, Meadowbridge Post Office, St Andrew, Jamaica, West Indies.

The District Grand Lodge of Jamaica and the Bahamas (Scottish Constitution), P.O. Box 8, Kingston 10, Jamaica, West Indies.

LEEWARD ISLANDS

This large group of relatively small islands is located in the West Indies in an arc to the east of Puerto Rico. English lodges are located on Montserrat and Antigua, while a Scottish lodge works on St Kitts. In addition, a Netherlandic lodge is located on the island of St Martin (Sint Maarten). No other regular lodges currently operate in this part of the Caribbean, although irregular French lodges have long since worked on the large French island of Guadeloupe. The details of the regular Leeward Islands lodges are as follows:

ANTIGUA

St John's Lodge No 492 EC	Meets at the Masonic Hall, St John's Street, St John's, Antigua; on the Friday nearest to the full moon, February to November; on Maundy Thursday; and on the 2nd Friday January. Inst: 27th December.
Caribbee Lodge No 2869 EC	Meets at the Masonic Hall, St John's Street, St John's, Antigua; on the 1st Thursday November to July (except April, then 1st Wednesday). Inst: December.

MONTSERRAT

St Anthony Lodge No 4684 EC	Meets Masonic Temple, Jubilee Town, Plymouth, Montserrat; Friday nearest the full moon, February to December. Inst. January 17th annually.

ST KITTS

Lodge Mt Olive No 336 SC	Meets at the Masonic Hall, Taylor's Range, Basseterre, St Kitts; Thursdays nearest the full moon, October to June.

ST MARTIN

Union Lodge No 266 NC	Meets at the Juliana Airport Building, Thursdays, at 8 pm.

NETHERLAND ANTILLES

The Netherland Antilles consists of the islands of Curacao, Aruba, and Bonaire, located close to the Venezuela coast. It is self-governing integral part of the Netherlands. One old English lodge, dating from 1855, still works on Curacao. In addition, four Netherlandic lodges also operate in the islands. The oldest Netherlandic lodge is De Vergenoeging No 22, dating from 1785. Naturally, the Dutch lodges all work in the Dutch ritual. The various meeting details are as follows:

Igualdad Lodge No 653 EC	Meets Masonic Hall, Gravenstraat 3, Willemstad, Curacao; 2nd Saturday monthly. Inst: June. (P.O. Box 388.)
De Vergenoeging Lodge No 22 NC	Meets at the Masonic Temple, Rust en Burghlaan 17, Willemstad, Curacao; 2nd and 4th Thursdays monthly.
El Sol Naciente Lodge No 113 NC	Meets at the Masonic Temple, J G Emanstraat 39, Oranjestad, Aruba; Wednesdays and 3rd Fridays.
King Solomon's Lodge No 160 NC	Meets at the Masonic Temple, J G Emanstraat 39, Oranjestad, Aruba; 2nd Tuesdays monthly.
Phoenix Lodge No 227 NC	Meets at the Masonic Temple, Rust en Burghlaan 17, Willemstad, Curacao; 1st and 3rd Thursdays monthly.

PUERTO RICO

Puerto Rico has had a regular Grand Lodge since 1885. Formerly a Spanish colony, Puerto Rico has remained largely under the control of the United States since the Spanish–American War of 1898.

The Grand Lodge of Puerto Rico
Founded: 1885

Address: Masonic Hall, 107 Ponce de Leon Avenue, Santurce, San Juan, Puerto Rico.

Postal Address: P.O. Box 8385, Santurce, San Juan, Puerto Rico 00910.

Telephone: (809) 727 6780.

Lodges: 71.   Permits Dual Membership.   *Membership:* Circa 4,500

Descent: Cuba.   *Government:* Appointive Grand Lodge.

Courtesy Degrees: conferred on request.   *Ritual:* Scottish (Craft) Rite, and York Rite.

Minimum Time Lapse between Degrees: 3 months (Scottish Rite), 6 weeks (York Rite).

Main Publications: Constitution.   Annual Proceedings.

History

Freemasonry originally came to Puerto Rico in the early nineteenth century, with lodges gaining warrants from Massachusetts and the Grand Orient of France. As Puerto Rico was a Spanish colony, the Craft was suppressed, and membership of the Order was punishable by imprisonment and death. This suppression remained until 1859, when political conditions in Spain improved.

The Grand Lodge of Cuba warranted two lodges in Puerto Rico, in 1867 and in 1874. The Grand Orient of Spain also became active on the island after 1868, and was responsible for four lodges established between 1871 and 1874. Cuba again weighed in with the Adelphia Lodge No 40 in 1877. This lodge is the oldest extant in Puerto Rico, and today heads the roll of the Grand Lodge as Adelphia No 1.

Renewed pressure from Spain saw most lodges close in 1874, although by 1884 the Grand Lodge of Cuba was able to form a Provincial Grand Lodge, with ten constituent lodges. This body became the Grand Lodge of Puerto Rico in the following year. The new Grand Lodge still suffered from political pressure and was forced to close in 1896, reopening after the Spanish were ejected from Puerto Rico by the Spanish–American War of 1898.

Notes for Visitors to Puerto Rico

While most Puerto Rican lodges work the Scottish Rite Craft degrees in Spanish, there are a few lodges that work the York Rite in English. These lodges use American Webb-type rituals. As is usual for this area of the world, dress is a dark lounge suit. Lodges meet in the early evening, generally around 8 pm for Scottish Rite lodges, and 7 pm for York Rite lodges. Visitors arriving in Puerto Rico are best advised to make their first point of contact at the Grand Lodge building in San Juan, the capital city. San Juan and its suburbs house about one third of Puerto Rico's lodges.

TRINIDAD AND TOBAGO

Trinidad and Tobago is a former English colony at the tail of the Windward Islands, located just off the coast of Venezeula. The first lodge in Trinidad was Les Freres Unis Lodge No 77, warranted by the Grand Lodge of Pennsylvania in 1798. Ireland had a lodge working on the island between 1811 and 1858, when it expired. The Grand Orient of Spain granted warrants for five lodges early in the nineteenth century, but they were not survivors either. The oldest extant lodge is Lodge United Brothers, warranted by the Grand Lodge of Scotland in 1813. Indeed, Scotland appears always to have had a stronger masonic presence in Trinidad than England. The District Grand Lodge of Trinidad and Tobago (Scottish Constitution) has ten lodges in Trinidad, while the District Grand Lodge of Trinidad (English Constitution) possesses only seven. The oldest surviving English lodge is Royal Philanthropic Lodge No 405, erected in 1831.

The island of Tobago first had a Scottish lodge within its shores in 1868. This was lodge Scarborough No 488, which expired in 1906. However, Scotland made a second attempt in 1968 with Lodge Tobago Kilwinning No 1643. This lodge remains the only regular lodge working on Tobago. The meeting details of all lodges on Trinidad and Tobago are as follows:

There are six meeting places located in Trinidad and Tobago—Masonic Temple, 9 Herbert Street, St Clair, Port of Spain, Trinidad denoted (a) below; Masonic Temple, 7 Alexandra Street, Port of Spain, Trinidad denoted (b) below; Masonic Temple, 46a Piccadilly Street, Port of Spain, Trinidad denoted (c) below; Masonic Temple, Les Effort Avenue West, San Fernando, Trinidad denoted (d) below; Masonic Temple, Hosein Street, Arima, Trinidad denoted (e) below; and finally the Masonic Temple, Signal Hill, Lambeau Road, Tobago denoted (f) below.

English Lodges

Royal Philanthropic Lodge No 405	Meets (a); 4th Thursday January to November; 2nd Thursday December. Inst: January.
Royal Prince of Wales Lodge No 867	Meets (b); 3rd Wednesday monthly. Inst: December.
Royal Connaught Lodge No 3266	Meets (b); 1st Wednesday monthly. Inst: March.
Trinidad & Tobago Masters Lodge No 8057	Meets (a); 2nd Thursday February, May, August and November. Inst: February.
Daniel Hert Lodge No 9028	Meets (b); 4th Wednesday monthly. Inst: April.
St Andrew Lodge No 3963	Meets (d); 2nd Monday monthly. Inst: January.
Naparima Lodge No 7108	Meets (d); 3rd Thursday monthly (except December, then 2nd Thursday). Inst: February.

Scottish Lodges

Lodge United Brothers No 251	Meets (c); 1st Wednesday and 4th Saturday monthly.
Lodge Eastern Star No 368	Meets (a); 1st Friday monthly.
Lodge Rosslyn No 596	Meets (b); 2nd Friday January to November.
Loge Arima No 899	Meets (e); 1st Saturday monthly.
Lodge Alexandra No 1044	Meets (d); 1st Thursday monthly.

Lodge Caribbean Light No 1391	Meets (a); 1st Monday February, April, June, October and December; and 2nd Monday August.
Lodge Royalian No 1605	Meets (b); 3rd Monday monthly (except August), and 1st Friday in December in addition.
Lodge Tobago Kilwinning No 1643	Meets (f); 3rd Saturday monthly.
Lodge Felicity No 1681	Meets (c); 4th Wednesday January to October.
Lodge Trinity No 1733	Meets (b); 2nd Wednesday January to October.
Lodge Hesperus No 1738	Meets (a); 4th Saturday January to November.

VIRGIN ISLANDS

The Virgin Islands are located immediately to the east of Puerto Rico, at the start of the Leeward Island chain. Administratively, the islands are roughly divided in half. The eastern islands (nearest Puerto Rico) are an organised unincorporated territory of the United States, while the western islands form the British colony of the British Virgin Islands. Two lodges work on the Virgin Islands, both warranted from England. The oldest, erected in 1818, is located at St Thomas in the American Virgin Islands. It remains the only English lodge operating on American territory anywhere in the world, although there is a New Zealand lodge working at American Samoa in the Pacific. The second lodge, located in the British Virgins', is a recent arrival having been warranted only in 1980. Details are as follows:

Harmonic Lodge No 356	Meets at the Masonic Hall, Charlotte Amalie, St Thomas, American Virgin Islands; 1st Wednesday October to June (except April, then St George's Day—April 23rd). Inst: November.
St Ursula's Lodge No 8952	Meets at the Treasure Island Hotel, Road Town, Tortola, British Virgin Islands; last Friday monthly.

WINDWARD ISLANDS

The Windward Islands are located in the Eastern Caribbean to the south of the Leeward Islands and to the north of Trinidad. With the exception of the French island of Martinique, all the Windward Islands are British possessions or former British colonies. All the main islands in the group possess lodges, although generally only one, and most are warranted from England. The only exceptions are two lodges on Martinique holding charters from the regular Grande Loge Nationale Française (GLNF). The oldest lodge in the area is St George No 2616, warranted at St Vincent in 1896. Indeed, three of the five English lodges working in the Windward Islands bear the name St George. The lodges on St Lucia, St Vincent, and Grenada all come under the English District Grand Lodge of Barbados; while the lone English lodge on Dominica works directly under London. Of course, the two regular French lodges are governed from Paris. The two GLNF lodges are Abraham Lincoln No 152 (chartered in 1972), and the even more recent Vigilance Fraternalle No 230. Both these lodges meet at Ansegourad à Schoelcher, Fort de France, Martinique.

It must be noted that the political situation in Grenada, in very recent years, has

been unsettled, with a Marxist government in control of the island. The current situation of the island's two English lodges remains unclear, although they were still reported as working in 1982. The American 'invasion' of the island in October, 1983, and the eviction of the Marxist regime that followed it, may well have a beneficial effect in terms of masonry in Grenada.
The meeting details of the five English lodges are as follows:

St George Lodge No 2616

Meets at the Masonic Hall, Bentinck Square, Kingstown, *St Vincent*; 1st Thursday monthly. Inst: November.

Abercrombie Lodge No 2788

Meets at the Masonic Hall, Vigie, Castries, *St Lucia*; 2nd Friday monthly. Inst: March.

Lodge St George No 3072

Meets at the Masonic Rooms, 1 Hillsborough Street, St George's, *Grenada*; 1st Friday monthly. Inst: December.

St George Lodge No 3421

Meets at the Masonic Hall, Roseau, *Dominica*; 1st Monday monthly. Inst: April.

Conception Lodge No 8346

Meets at the Masonic Rooms, 1 Hillsborough Street, St George's, *Grenada*; 3rd Friday monthly. Inst: May.

Section VI

Visiting in
Continental Europe

Continental Europe

An Overview

For the freemason without previous experience, continental masonry can be a somewhat strange, but nevertheless interesting, experience. The Craft in Europe has over most of its history variously suffered repression, the effects of war, and a good deal of internal division. In all the countries of Europe suffering under either left wing or right wing dictatorship, the Craft has virtually ceased to exist, although from a few occasionally come spasmodic reports of 'underground' lodges. Certainly, any lodges that do exist in communist countries cannot be recognised as regular by the free Grand Lodges of the world, and therefore may not be visited by the regular freemason.

European masonry is certainly as old, if not older, than British masonry. Operative masonry can be traced back in France and Germany over many centuries. Regardless, the available evidence would suggest that speculative masonry as we now know it came to Europe from England in the early eighteenth century, whereupon it developed rapidly—particularly in France. However, this development was not uniform, nor was it in many cases similar. The Europeans tended to adapt the Craft as they received it into many varying forms, notably with the introduction of a profusion of additional or 'higher' degrees in excess of normal Craft freemasonry. This tendency for addition and change led to division and argument, making the history of the Craft in Europe quite turbulent. Breakaway lodges and Grand Lodges were not uncommon, and the residue of these unhappy outcomes is still to some extent evident in European masonry today.

The effect of repression and war on European lodges has been to make the European mason somewhat introspective, and European masonry more secretive than that of the English-speaking world. Whereas English-speaking masonry has in recent times moved to create better community understanding of its aims and objectives, European masonry has largely failed to emulate this pursuit. For the most part, the visitor will not recognise a masonic Temple or meeting place in Europe from its outside appearance—there generally being no trace of any masonic emblems to be seen. Unless the visitor knows the exact address, he will not find the place he seeks. In terms of external appearances, European masonic complexes usually look just like the buildings or apartment houses that surround them. Given the history of Continental masonry, this 'secrecy' is not altogether surprising, and it is certainly understandable. An English-speaking visitor should not be surprised to be asked questions concerning his views on the 'secrecy question'. Questions such as, 'Would you tell a non-mason of your membership in the Craft', are not uncommon. Indeed, many European masons will not admit their membership of the fraternity outside masonic circles. This is particularly true in catholic countries such as Austria and Italy, where the Craft has endured consistent religious opposition until very recent times. It should also be noted that in many European obediences, it is not done for a mason to enlighten any other person as to the masonic membership of another. Masonic membership, therefore, is considered a very personal matter.

The other main characteristic of European masonry is that it tends to be somewhat more exclusive than elsewhere. In many obediences, a high social, educational, and economic status are tacit prerequisities for masonic membership. For example, in Greece it is unusual for a candidate to enter freemasonry without possessing a university degree. In terms of economic requirements, the high membership dues largely prevalent in European masonry tend to preclude men below a certain financial position from considering membership. None of these requirements is statutory, but rather are simply a matter of convention. It is sometimes considered that the relatively small memberships of European masonic obediences when compared to those of English-speaking countries, are the result of religious antipathy and past repressions. However, this is only partly the case. The 'exclusive' nature of much of Continental masonry tends to deter high memberships. Indeed, the European Grand Lodges tend to have no great interest in large numbers. Rather, their interest lies in the quality of membership. Of course, that is not to say that non-European Grand Lodges have no interest in this area. The Europeans largely tend to lay stress on moral, ethical and philosophic study through the medium of freemasonry. Unlike English-speaking masonry, where the tendency is to pursue proficiency in ritual, Continental masons have little interest in this area. For example, a typical European lodge will meet weekly. Of an average four meetings per month, only one will be a degree conferment meeting, with the other three given over to lectures. When a ceremony is held, it is fairly common for the officers participating to read their parts, rather than recite them from memory. For candidates, progress from one degree to the next is commonly slow—often the minimum time lapse between degrees is twelve months. All these factors are manifestations of the desire by European obediences to imbue their memberships with a deep and thorough understanding of the teachings and principles of freemasonry. Indeed, it can be argued with some authority that the European masonic system achieves this objective with greater effect than does English-speaking freemasonry.

It is worthy of note that, except in English-speaking lodges, Continental freemasonry largely fails to follow the Anglo-Saxon custom of associating a meal with lodge meetings. Certainly, it is most rare for a repast to be provided for an informal/lecture meeting. For a formal degree ceremony, some lodges in some obediences will provide a repast either before or after a meeting—the latter being more usual. It will be noted that most European lodges meet at 8 pm, or later, thus allowing members to dine at home prior to attending a meeting. Nonetheless, many lodge members will gather informally after a meeting, whether formal or otherwise, for drinks and fraternal fellowship. Variations in these customs as they occur are mentioned in the text that follows.

Regardless of these complexities, which form part of the makeup of Continental masonry, it must be added that without exception the visitor will receive the warmest of welcomes. Europeans are a most hospitable people, and European masons very much so. A visitor need not fear any language problems either, as invariably any European lodge will possess members who speak fluent English. Quite common in many European obediences is a system of 'tagging', although it has no formal name. 'Tagging' simply means that a foreign visitor will be placed with a member who speaks the visitor's language. The 'tagging' member will sit with the visitor in the temple, and at any social function, to ensure his ease and comforts. Of course, the visitor will usually witness a ceremony in a language other than English. Nevertheless, although the ritual used may vary somewhat in form, the content will be basically the same, and fairly readily discernible to the masonic visitor regardless of the language used.

ALBANIA

As far as can be readily determined, freemasonry has never existed in Albania. In any case, this country has possessed a totalitarian government since the Second World War, and therefore the future prospects for masonry in Albania would appear non-existent.

AUSTRIA

Austria possesses a regular Grand Lodge which remains highly respected in the masonic world.

The Grand Lodge of Austria (Grossloge von Osterreich)
Founded: 1919
Address: Masonic Building, Dorotheergrasse 12, Vienna A 1010. Telephone: 527 422.
Lodges: 45. Permits Dual and Plural Membership. *Membership:* 1,800.
Descent: Probably Germany and France. *Government:* Modified Grand Orient.
Courtesy Degrees: rarely conferred. *Ritual:* Schroeder-form.
Minimum Time Lapse between Degrees: 12 months.
Main Publications: Constitution. Proceedings.

History
The first lodge in Austria was formed in Vienna in 1742, under the patronage of Duke Francis, husband of Maria Theresa, the Empress of Austria. The Craft expanded slowly until 1785, when under great religious pressure, the forty-five lodges then operating in the country were reduced to just three by imperial edict. Not surprisingly, the Craft moved into rapid decline, and by 1794 freemasonry was formally suppressed. Thenceforth, Austrian masonry remained mostly in darkness until 1867 when Hungary became a separate kingdom. It then became possible for Austrian masons to form lodges across the border. However, it was not until after the First World War that a Grand Lodge could be formed at Vienna. It contained 26 lodges by 1938, whereupon the Nazi takeover brought masonry to a quick end.

Following the Second World War, the Grand Lodge of Austria was revived, and it has since prospered to the point where it possesses forty-five lodges. Its membership continues to expand steadily and lodges now exist in all main population centres of the country.

Notes for Visitors to Austria
The vast majority of Austrian lodges meet in Vienna, at the Grand Lodge Headquarters at 12 Dorotheergrasse. Dorotheergrasse is a short street located right in the heart of old Vienna, and is a very short walk from the famous Spanish Riding School. As with most European masonic edifices, the building has no external masonic markings, and except inside the temples themselves the visitor will find little indication that he is inside a masonic centre. The dining rooms are on the first floor, the temples and meeting rooms on the second, and the third floor contains admin-

istration offices. Vienna has 31 lodges, all of which work in German, except one. This is Sarastro lodge, which works in English.

Austrian lodges meet for only nine months of the year—a common practice throughout Europe. June, July and August are the recess months. However, during the nine month season, all Austrian lodges (with few exceptions) meet weekly on a fixed day, with most commencing at about 7 pm. The evening's proceedings occasionally commence with a fully catered meal, with a lodge meeting following. Of the four or five meetings held in any one month, usually only one is an actual degree conferment. In Austria, it is rare for a mason to advance to the next degree in under twelve months. The non-degree-conferring meetings are taken up with members delivering lectures on masonic subjects and, indeed, a candidate in Austria must personally deliver at least one lecture to his lodge before he can advance to the next degree.

Dress for Austrian masons is a black lounge suit, black shoes, white shirt and long black tie. Visitors are welcome to wear any dark suit they may be carrying. It is also appreciated for visitors to bring and wear their own regalia, although regalia will be readily loaned to those without their own. The usual masonic documentation should be presented to the lodge officers when arriving, after the presentation of which a warm welcome is assured. The majority of Austrian masons speak English in addition to German, or at least understand it if they are not overly fluent. A visitor will usually be 'tagged' to an English-speaking member. The Austrian modes of recognition, while comparable to those of English-speaking jurisdictions, are somewhat different. While the visitor should be aware of this, it is quite in order for him to use the 'modes' he himself was taught, as these are known and recognised. Nevertheless, it will be useful for the visitor to have a private discussion with a lodge officer along these lines, prior to entering the lodge.

Austrian lodges use a form of the *Schroeder* ritual, inherited from Germany. As is usual across the gamut of Continental rituals, lodges are set out along operative lines, with the Master seated in the east and both Wardens seated in the west. The manner of entering an Austrian lodge is for all members and visitors, upon entering the temple, to walk between the two Wardens in the west, salute both Wardens and the Master in the process, and then move to their seat where they remain standing to order until the lodge is opened. Austrian lodges usually open in the First Degree. Visitors can expect to be welcomed by the Master, but to be actually called upon to speak is rare.

A meal associated with a meeting is very informal. The Master generally addresses the gathering, but no formal toasts are usually proposed. Visitors wishing to attend a lodge meeting are advised to visit the Grand Secretary's office during the day to discover which lodge meeting on that night, or in that week, is actually conferring a degree. The visitor will doubtless find the attendance at a degree conferment more interesting than a lecture, particularly if he is not German-speaking. It should be noted that visiting in Austria by Austrian masons is not nearly as common as visiting is in English-speaking jurisdictions. While Austrian masons may, of course, visit any other lodge; it is less common for them to do so because their own lodge will meet weekly in any case. In some Austrian lodges, therefore, visiting tends to be a little bit of a novelty. No charge is ever made on any visitor for any repast associated with a lodge meeting.

List of Lodges
Unlike most other jurisdictions, Austrian lodges are not numbered but, of course, each lodge carries a name. The following towns and cities outside Vienna possess lodges: Burgenland (one lodge), Graz (two lodges), Innsbruck (two lodges), Klagenfurt (four lodges), Linz (two lodges), Salzburg (one lodge), and Villach (one lodge).

The lodges in Vienna (all meet at Dorotheergrasse 12), with days of meeting, are as follows:

Mondays:	Freundschaft, Hiram, Zu Den Drai Rosen, Kosmos, Zur Wahrheit, Gleicheit.
Tuesdays:	Humanitas, Zukunft, Libertas Germine, Sapienta, Zur Toleranz, Pilgrim.
Wednesdays:	Fraternitas, Libertas, Zu Den Drei Lichtern, Donay Zu Den Friendlichen Ufern, Zur Bruderkette, Zur Bruderlichen Harmonie.
Thursdays:	Lessing, Mozart, Pythagoras, Eintracht, Libertas Oriens, Acacia, Zur Den Sieben Himmeln.
Fridays:	Sarastro, Concordia, Aux trois Canons.

Sarastro Lodge (English-speaking) meets only twice monthly (2nd and 4th Fridays).

BELGIUM

Belgium has had a fairly turbulent masonic history. It currently possesses three Grand Lodges, of which one is regular.

The Regular Grand Lodge of Belgium (Grande Loge Reguliere Belgique)
Founded: 1979
Address: Masonic Temple, Rue Royale 265, Brussels 1030.   Telephone: (02) 217 8400.
Lodges: 21.   Permits Dual and Plural Membership.   *Membership:* Circa 1,200.
Descent: The Grand Lodge of Belgium.   *Government:* Modified Grand Orient.
Courtesy Degrees: All correspondence must be through Grand Lodges.
Ritual: Scottish (Craft) Rite, and others.
Minimum Time Lapse between Degrees: mostly 12 months.
Main Publications: Constitution.   Annual Proceedings.

History
Belgium is a country that has seen frequent changes in sovereignty over the last three hundred years, and this has affected its masonic development. From 1714 (the Peace of Utrecht) until 1789 (the French Revolution) it was the Austrian Netherlands. From 1789 until 1814, it was a province of France. From 1814 until 1830, it was part of Holland, finally gaining its independence in 1830 as an sovereign kingdom.

There is scant evidence of freemasonry in Belgium in the early eighteenth century, but the antipathy of the then governing Austrian Empire towards the Craft seems to have precluded the formation of any lodges from Austrian sources. However, an English lodge was working in the Austrian Netherlands in 1765, and two more were subsequently formed—in 1768, and 1770, respectively. By 1784, sixteen English lodges were at work in Belgium, but by 1787 they had all closed as a result of an

Austrian edict. The coming of the French Revolution saw a fairly large number of lodges created under the Grand Orient of France, and at the same time, the introduction of many French higher degrees. Upon the demise of French political control over Belgium, its lodges came under the Netherlands, and by 1820 over thirty lodges were at work. Belgium gained its political independence in 1830, but the disturbances which accompanied the creation of the new country served to reduce the lodges to four in number. In 1833, these four lodges met and formed the Grand Orient of Belgium. Interestingly, the new Grand Body decreed that its lodges could work any Rite that they desired. As a result, many lodges opted to confer a myriad of higher degrees, in addition to the three Craft degrees. The Grand Orient sank into complete irregularity in 1854, when it moved to allow political discussion in its lodges. As well as being ostracised by other Grand Lodges, this move led to schism in the Grand Orient itself. In addition, the Grand Orient decreed that belief in the Supreme Being was an optional prerequisite for membership. The United Grand Lodge of England severed fraternal relations in 1877, and many other Grand Lodges followed suit.

Regular masonry again arose in Belgium in 1933 when Lodge Anglo-Belge, then under the Grand Orient of Belgium, was reconstituted as Lodge Wellington No 1385 under the Grand Lodge of Scotland, and meeting at Antwerp. In turn, this lodge sponsored a second Scottish lodge in Brussels in 1951. This was Lodge Allegiance No 1465.

The Second World War saw all freemasonry in Belgium suppressed by the Nazis, but subsequently the Grand Orient and the lone Scottish lodge at that time revived, although the former still persisted in irregularity. However, in 1959, five Grand Orient lodges which had always used the Sacred Volume withdrew from the Grand Orient and formed the Grand Lodge of Belgium. It was later joined by several more defecting lodges from the Grand Orient. This new body was consecrated by the regular Grand East of the Netherlands, and gained general fraternal recognition around the masonic world. Scotland granted recognition on the basis that its two lodges in Belgium would be preserved. By 1979, the Grand Lodge of Belgium had 35 lodges on its roll, and over 2,200 members.

Regrettably, in 1979, the Grand Lodge of Belgium followed the old Grand Orient into irregularity by requiring the abandonment of the necessity of a belief in God from its members. The result of this action was a schism within the Grand Lodge, whereupon nine lodges withdrew and formed the Regular Grand Lodge of Belgium. England, Ireland and Scotland, together with most other regular Grand Lodges around the world, promptly withdrew recognition from the old Grand Lodge, and instead recognised the new Regular Grand Lodge. This new Grand Body has since expanded to contain twenty-one lodges. Therefore, in total, Belgium today possesses three Grand Lodges, of which only the youngest is regular plus, of course, its two Scottish lodges.

Notes for Visitors to Belgium
With three Grand Lodges at work in Belgium, of which two are irregular, visitors must be quite certain as to which lodge they are visiting. Therefore, at least in the first instance, visitors are strongly advised to visit the office of the Regular Grand Lodge of Belgium at the Masonic Temple, Rue Royale 265, Brussels. Of the twenty-

lodges under the Regular Grand Lodge, six work in Brussels itself. Of the balance, three meet at Waterloo, two at Charleroi, and the remainder in other Belgian towns. Two lodges, namely King Leopold I Lodge No 3, at Mons-Shape; and Chevalier Ramsay Lodge No 4, at Waterloo, largely cater for English-speaking masons.

Belgian lodges largely work the Scottish Rite Craft degrees, although other rituals are in use. Lodges generally meet on a weekly basis, although there are a few that meet fortnightly. Most open proceedings at about 8 pm, with members occasionally dining together afterwards. Dress is a dark lounge suit, and visitors are welcome to wear their own regalia if they are carrying it. It should also be noted that Belgian lodges recess in the months of June, July and August. Belgium's two Scottish lodges meet on a monthly basis, and their meeting details are as follows:

Lodge Wellington No 1385	Meets at 33 Rue Van Maerlantstraat, Antwerp; 3rd Tuesday, September to May, 3rd Saturday in January.
Lodge Allegiance No 1465	Meets at the Masonic Temple, Rue Royale 265, Brussels; 4th Tuesday, September to May.

BULGARIA

While freemasonry was reputed to have existed in Bulgaria as early as 1820, the establishment of the first Bulgarian lodge occurred in 1879. This was Star of the Balkans Lodge No 13, warranted at Rasgrad by the Grand Orient of Portugal. Other lodges followed holding charters from Portugal, and from France. A Grand Lodge was formed in 1917 and it was still working in the 1930s, although it never received wide recognition. All masonry in the country was suppressed during the Second World War, and remains extinct today.

CHANNEL ISLANDS

The Channel Islands are all British possessions, and consist of the islands of Alderney, Guernsey, Jersey, and Sark. All are located in the English Channel close to France. Guernsey has ten English lodges, and Alderney one. These eleven lodges together constitute the English Provincial Grand Lodge of Guernsey and Alderney. Jersey is the seat of an English Provincial Grand Lodge in its own right, possessing eleven lodges. Some of the Channel Islands lodges boast considerable antiquity. For example, Mariner's Lodge No 168, dates from 1784; and is therefore about to celebrate its bi-centenary. The two main meeting places are as follows: Masonic Temple, Le Marchant Street, St Peter Port, Guernsey; and Masonic Temple, St Helier, Jersey.

CORSICA

This large Mediterranean island has been part of Metropolitan France since 1789. It has long possessed lodges owing allegiance to the irregular Grand Orient of France, and to the equally irregular Grand Lodge of France. It is therefore most pleasing to note that regular freemasonry has very recently been introduced to the

Island. In 1982, the Grande Loge Nationale Française (National Grand Lodge of France—GLNF) granted warrants for two lodges in Corsica. These are Corsica-Prima Lodge No 265, at Bastia; and I Jouanneli Lodge No 297 at Ajaccio.

CYPRUS

Cyprus is a large Greek-speaking island located in the western Mediterranean Sea, although it also possesses a substantial Turkish minority in its north. Cyprus has seven lodges warranted from Greece, while seven English lodges work under a District Grand Lodge. Needless to say, the Greek and English lodges work in harmony, and largely share meeting places.

The Greek lodges, all of which work in Greek, are located as follows Famagusta—*Evagoras Lodge No 77*. Larnaka—*Kimon Lodge No 53*. Limassol—*Zenon Lodge No 18*. Nicosia—*Adonis Lodge No 115, Koinon Kyprion Lodge No 126*, and *Solon Lodge No 55*. Paphos—*Kinyras Lodge No 64*.

The details of the English Constitution lodges are as follows:

St Paul's Lodge No 2277	Meets at the Masonic Rooms, Jerusalem Street, Limassol, Cyprus. 3rd Wednesday October to April. Inst: December.
St George's Lodge No 3135	Meets at the Masonic Rooms, 6 Haralambos, Michael Street, Nicosia, Cyprus. 2nd Wednesday October to May. Inst: April.
Lord Kitchener Lodge No 3402	Meets at the Masonic Hall, Dhekelia, Cyprus. 4th Wednesday September to June (except December). Inst: November.
Othello Lodge No 5670	Meets at the Masonic Hall, Dhekelia, Cyprus. 1st Wednesday October to June. Inst: April.
Lusignan Lodge No 7453	Meets at the Masonic Rooms, 6 Haralambos, Michael Street, Nicosia, Cyprus. 4th Tuesday September to May (except December). Inst: November.
Apollo Lodge No 7886	Meets at the RAF Base, Episkopi, Cyprus. 2nd Tuesday October to June. Inst: January.
Agapinor Lodge No 8905	Meets at the Masonic Rooms, 5 Hermes Street, Paphos, Cyprus. 1st Tuesday October to April. Inst: December.

CZECHOSLOVAKIA

Czechoslovakia was long a part of the Austro-Hungarian Empire, and so was bound up in the general masonic history of central Europe. Masonry appears to have arrived in the area from Austria, via the German Grand Lodges. Four lodges were working in Prague by 1775. The Craft in Bohemia (as modern Czechoslovakia was then known) was suppressed in the late 1700s, as it was in the rest of Austria-Hungary. Following independence after World War One, a small Grand Lodge was formed in Prague in 1919; only to be suppressed later by the Nazis, and then by the Communists.

FRANCE

France has possibly the most complex and diverse masonic history of any country in the world. It currently possesses three 'main' Grand Lodges (although there are others), of which only one is regular. This is the National Grand Lodge of France.

The National Grand Lodge of France (Grande Loge Nationale Française)
Founded: 1913
Address: 65 Boulevard Bineau, Neuilly-sur-Seine 92200, Paris. Telephone: 757 7575.
Lodges: 310. Permits Dual and Plural Membership. *Membership:* Circa 8,000.
Descent: England. *Government:* Appointive Grand Lodge.
Courtesy Degrees: Correspondence must be through Grand Lodges.
Ritual: Scottish (Craft) Rite, Rectified Scottish Rite, French Rite, several English-forms (notably *Emulation*), and several Webb-forms (notably the California and Texas Rituals).
Minimum Time Lapse between Degrees. varies between one and twelve months, depending upon the lodge and the ritual form used.
Main Publications: Constitution. Proceedings. *Annuaire* (Year Book—List of Lodges).

History

It is believed that freemasonry was introduced into France from England between 1725 and 1730, and there is some evidence to support this contention. It is probable that expatriate Scottish masons fleeing the failed Jacobin Revolution also had some influence. However, it is somewhat difficult to determine which lodges were first formed, or exactly when. Nonetheless, the English Roll of 1738 refers to three lodges then working in France. These lodges, with a few others, appear to have provided the core for the Grand Lodge of France which was erected in 1736.

Virtually from its introduction, masonry in France became the preserve of the French aristocracy, who considered it as a fashionable diversion. As a result of these affections, the French seemed to have derived great pleasure in inflicting wide innovations on masonry as they received it from England, particularly with the creation of a myriad of extra degrees and rites. In 1773, the Grand Lodge of France was superseded by the Grand Orient of France, reflecting the strong hold which 'higher' degrees has come to assert over the body of French masonry. Indeed, this profusion of extra rites caused great divisions and argument in the French Craft, and caused King Louis XV to decree the closure of the original Grand Lodge in 1768.

The French Revolution, beginning in 1789, somewhat halted these innovations, and most lodges closed. The aristocracy, which had hitherto used freemasonry as a plaything, were greatly decimated by the Revolution. It was not until the rise of Napoleon that the Craft began to recover—largely without its earlier excesses. Napoleon himself favoured the Craft, although no conclusive proof of his membership has ever been produced. After the fall of Napoleon, French masonry began to become somewhat radicalised, and progressively took on an anti-clerical stance. The Grand Orient, in fact a Scottish Rite Supreme Council, eventually moved in 1877 to remove from its constitution the affirmation of the existence of the GAOTU. The United Grand Lodge of England immediately withdrew recognition, and was followed in this course by most other Grand Lodges. This move was not met with complete joy within the Grand Orient itself. In 1880, the main Scottish Rite Supreme Council (formed back in 1804 largely in competition with the Grand Orient) sponsored the Grand Lodge of France. This new body was spawned out of disagreements within the Grand Orient. Nonetheless, it still retained the agnostic tendencies of the older body.

It was not until 1913 that regular freemasonry finally came to France. In that year, two lodges under the Grand Orient decided to secede and form a new Grand Lodge on a regular basis. These were Le Centre des Amis Lodge (dating from 1793), Lodge L'Anglaise 204—a very old lodge located at Bordeaux, which was originally on the English Roll. These lodges were to become the first two on the Roll of the Grande Loge Nationale Française (The National Grand Lodge of France). The United Grand Lodge of England gave great support to this new body, although its initial progress was quite slow. The intervention of the First and Second World Wars also served to dampen rapid progress. However, rapid expansion did take place after the Second World War. The early lack of progress was largely the outcome of the bad name freemasonry possessed amongst the French populace as the result of years of observing irregular Grand Orient masonry. However, time has convinced a growing number of Frenchmen that regular French masonry, in the form of the National Grand Lodge of France, is worthy of their participation. The National Grand Lodge was also assisted numerically in 1965, when over 1,000 members of the irregular Grand Lodge of France seceded and joined the regular French body. The National Grand Lodge continues to grow in strength, although its numbers do not yet approach those of the irregular bodies. Originally there were more English-speaking members of the National Grand Lodge than there were Frenchmen, but this situation is now reversed and the trend continues strongly.

Notes for Visitors to France
The National Grand Lodge of France (GLNF) has expanded to possess over 300 lodges, of which over 20 are located outside of France. Of these lodges, over 80 meet at the Grand Lodge complex at 65 Boulevard Bineau, Paris. Early in its career, most lodges worked in the English language, but French-speaking lodges hold a comfortable majority today. Most of the English-speaking lodges work in Paris. There is also one lodge in Paris (Eleusis No 210) working in German.

A wide variety of rituals are in use in the GLNF lodges. English-speaking lodges largely prefer the *Emulation* Ritual, and there are several French-speaking lodges which work *Emulation* in translation. The Rectified Scottish Rite, and the Scottish Rite Craft degrees also have their share of popularity amongst French-speaking lodges. In very recent years, the French Rite (Rite Français Moderne) Craft degrees have been adopted by a few French-speaking lodges, having been first purged of irregular innovations. There are also a few lodges largely composed of American Servicemen located in Spain, using the Californian or Texas Webb-form rituals. Regular French-chartered lodges located outside France are discussed elsewhere in this guide. It is interesting to note that, unlike the rest of Continental Europe, all GLNF lodges require their officers to actually learn and recite their ritual. This even applies to French-speaking lodges using a Continental Rite. The strong British influence in regular French masonry doubtless provides an explanation in this area.

The meeting days of lodges under the GLNF vary somewhat, largely in consequence of the language and ritual used. Generally, English-speaking lodges meet on a monthly basis, as do French-speaking lodges using *Emulation*. Lodges using a Continental Rite tend to meet fortnightly. It must also be noted that most lodges, regardless of their ritual practices, recess in June, July, August and September, and some fail to meet in December, in addition. Meeting times are also apt to vary. English-speaking lodges tend to convene about 7.30 pm, following proceedings with a festive board. French-speaking lodges using Continental Rites tend to meet later at about 8-8.30 pm. Afterproceedings for these lodges, often of an informal nature, will generally only follow a formal degree conferment meeting. There are, in addition, a small number of lodges in Paris that meet in the afternoon, such as Attar No 157 (meeting 3.30 pm on 2nd Thursdays), and La Belle Page No 217 (meeting 4 pm on 1st Thursdays). Dress for all GLNF lodges is a black or dark business suit, and visitors are welcome to bring and wear their own regalia. As most visitors to France will enter via Paris, they should find a visit to the Grand Lodge complex quite practical. 65 Boulevard Bineau is not recognisable as a masonic centre from its outside appearance—indeed, it looks very similar to the buildings surrounding it. The entrance is to the side of the building, not to the front. The Grand Temple is on the ground floor, with the Grand Lodge office on the first floor. Office staff are happy to guide interested visitors over the complex, and advise them with lodge meeting times. Except in recess months, it is accurate to say that there are few weeknights whereupon at least one lodge will not be meeting.
The addresses of the main meeting places in the main French cities are as follows:

Bescancon:	Hotel du Lion d'Or, 5 Rue Jean-Petit.
Bordeaux:	8 Rue Segalier.
Clermont-Ferrand:	3 Rue des Petits Gras.
Dieppe:	29 Rue Paramentier.
Lyon:	22 Rue Montesquieu.
Le Mans:	9 Rue Gastelier.
Marseille:	Club Ecossais, 78 cours Lieutad.
Metz:	9 Rue des Etats-Unis, Montigny-Les-Metz.
Nice:	32 rue de Postes.
Orleans:	94 Rue de Hameau.
Perpignan:	3 rue Adam.
Poitiers:	51 Grand Rue.
Rouen:	48 Rue Stanislas Girardin.
Strasbourg:	1 Rue du Pints.
Toulouse:	34 Rue Gabriel Peri.
Tours:	8 Rue de la Bourde.

GERMANY (EAST)

The masonic history of this area of Germany, now the German Democratic Republic, is that of Germany as a whole until the Second World War. Subsequent to that War, and the build-up of a Communist state, freemasonry was not able to revive.

GERMANY (WEST)

Uniquely, German masonry is made up of a combination of five distinct and largely independent Grand Lodges which are under the United Grand Lodges of Germany. These are the Grand Lodge AF & A. Masons of Germany, the Grand Landslodge of Freemasons in Germany, the Grand Lodge Zu Den Drei Welkugeln, the American–Canadian Grand Lodge, and the Grand Lodge of British Freemasons. The first three are German-speaking, while the last two are English-speaking.

The United Grand Lodges of Germany (*Brotherhood of Freemasons*)
Founded: 1958
Address: Grand Lodge Building, Emserstrasse 12–13, 1000 Berlin 31.   Telephone: (030) 861 4796.
Lodges: 388.   Permits Dual and Plural Membership.   *Membership:* 21,000.
Descent: originally England and France.
Ritual: Schroeder, Swedish Rite, English and Webb forms, Fessler.
Minimum Time Lapse between Degrees: 12 months (German-speaking lodges), 30 days (English-speaking lodges).
Courtesy Degrees: All transactions must be through Grand Lodges.
Government: Appointive Grand Lodge.   *Main Publications:* Constitution. Proceedings.

History

Freemasonry arrived in Germany from England, and probably France, in the first half of the eighteenth century. The first recorded lodge was one erected in Hamburg in 1737, in which the Emperor Frederick the Great was initiated. Several other lodges followed, all originally holding warrants from London. From 1750, and for some thirty years, German masonry came to be dominated by the Rite of Strict Observance propagated by one Baron Von Hund. While space here prevents lengthy discussion on this occurrence, it is sufficient to say that German masonry became filled with innovation in this period, leading to great fragmentism.

By the First World War there were no fewer than eight Grand Lodges in Germany, with three more being formed by 1930. These eleven Grand Lodges, with their locations and years of foundation, are as follows:

1. The Grand Mother Lodge of the Three Globes, at Berlin. (1740)
2. The Grand Lodge of Prussia. (1760)
3. The National Grand Lodge of German Freemasons, at Berlin. (1770)
4. The Grand Lodge of Hamburg. (1743)
5. The Grand Lodge of the Sun, at Bayreuth. (1741)
6. The Mother Grand Lodge of the Eclectic Union, at Frankfurt. (1742)
7. The National Grand Lodge of Saxony, at Dresden. (1811)
8. The Grand Lodge 'Concord', at Darmstadt. (1846)
9. The Grand Lodge 'Chain of German Brotherhood', at Leipzig. (1924)
10. The Grand Lodge 'Freimaurerbund' at Nurnburg, later at Hamburg. (1907)
11. The Symbolic Grand Lodge at Hamburg, later at Berlin. (1930)

The first three of these Grand Lodges, all based at Berlin, were called the Old Prussian Lodges, and they generally enjoyed the protection of the Prussian Kings. They only admitted men professing the Christian Faith. The National Grand Lodge adopted the Swedish Rite quite early in its career.

The Grand Lodges, number four to nine above, admitted men of any monotheistic faith, and have been called the Humanitarian Lodges. All the first nine Grand Lodges recognised each other and enjoyed fraternal relations. The last two Grand Lodges (numbers ten and eleven) were not recognised by the other nine, evidently because they did not conform to several of the ancient landmarks of the order.

By 1930, there were an estimated 100,000 freemasons in Germany, indicating that the Craft had taken root amongst the Germans with far greater success than in any other Continental country at that time. The rise to power of the Nazis in 1933 saw this happy situation quickly reversed. By 1935, all lodges in Germany had been dissolved, and their property confiscated. Thereupon, freemasonry remained completely suppressed until 1945.

After the War, the Craft rapidly re-established itself, although its membership had been greatly lessened by the War. It was widely recognised by surviving German masons that the old system of eleven independent Grand Lodges was unsatisfactory, and indeed, several of these were not to rise again from the ashes of the War. Aside from a lack of unity, the old system had meant that German masonry had remained largely unrecognised outside the country. This unity was not easily achieved, as it needs to be appreciated that the surviving German masons grew up masonically under a number of differing Grand Lodge systems and rites.

By 1949, a good start had been achieved, when representatives of 151 German lodges met at Frankfurt and founded the United Grand Lodge of German Freemasons. However, complete unity was still not gained, as former members of the old National Grand Lodge at Berlin stood out. Members of this Grand Lodge were nurtured under the Swedish Rite system, and they found that assimilation presented them with governmental and ritualistic difficulties. Instead, the Swedish Rite lodges erected the Grand Lodge of the Freemasons' Order (GLFD). Nonetheless, the idea of unity was far from dead, and protracted negotiations ensued between the two Grand Lodges. In 1958, these negotiations led to the formation of the United Grand Lodges of Germany. Particular attention should be paid to the word 'Lodges'. At the convention forming the United Grand Lodges, 264 lodges of the Grand Lodge AF & AM were represented, together with 82 GLFD lodges. The basis of the unity was a Magna Charta, which passed sovereignty to the United Grand Lodges, but maintained the two forming bodies as Provincial (Land) Grand Lodges. Each 'Land' lodge remained largely administratively independent, with external relations and general policy ceded to the United Grand Lodges. A Senate was formed for the United Grand Lodges, with each party having five members of it.

There still remained outside the Union the original Grand Lodge of the Three Globes, which had been resuscitated at West Berlin. This situation was rectified after the Union, when it joined the United Grand Lodges and took a seat in the Senate. Meanwhile, a large number of English-speaking lodges had been formed in Germany after the War by stationed American, Canadian and British troops. These lodges formed themselves into two Provincial Grand Lodges, namely the American Canadian Grand Lodge, and the Grand Lodge of British Freemasons, whereupon they both affiliated with the United Grand Lodges. In 1970, the status of the three latterly joining Grand Lodges was raised under an amended Magna Charta. Each Grand Lodge now has two members of the Senate, except the Three Globes which has one member. Finally then, German masonry has become totally united with a unique stystem of five largely independent Grand Lodges bonded together under the umbrella of the United Grand Lodges of Germany. As each of the five Grand Lodges forming the Union is somewhat divergent, each will now be examined separately.

The Grossloge Ancient, Free and Accepted Masons of Deutchland
(The Grand Lodge AF & AM of Germany).

Founded: 1947

Ritual: Schroeder-form.

Address: Grand Lodge Office: Ettighoffer Strasse 64, 5300 *Bonn* 1.   Telephone: (0228) 626 230.

Notes for Visitors

This Grand Lodge was formed out of the majority of masons surviving the Second World War, and its lodges mostly work in the *Schroeder* Ritual. Its lodges usually meet weekly during the masonic season, although a few meet on a fortnightly basis. As is common throughout Europe, most German lodges recess in the months of June, July, and August. An example of a monthly programme in a lodge might be— Meeting 1: an informal meeting. 2: a lecture with discussion. 3: an informal meeting, with lectures. 4: a formal lodge meeting, with a degree ceremony. For a meal to be associated with any German-speaking lodge meeting is not particularly common, and where this occurs such a repast will accompany a formal lodge meeting, never an informal/lecture meeting. Sometimes, when a meal is scheduled, a short toast list will be used. Toasts often included are those to the Grand Master, to the Grand Lodge AF & AM, and to the United Grand Lodges. Visitors may be called upon to speak. If a repast is associated with a degree conferment meeting, the candidate of the evening is sometimes called upon to give his thoughts on the degree ceremony he has just experienced. As is usual German custom, all toasts are given and re-sponded to while seated. Visitors, while not often speaking at lodge afterproceed-ings, will usually be called upon to speak near the close of a formal lodge meeting, whereupon fraternal greetings will be exchanged. In addition, it is not uncommon for a charity collection to be taken inside the Temple. AF & AM lodges largely meet either at 7.30 pm or 8 pm. Dress is a dark or black business suit, and regalia will be lent to visitors who are not carrying their own. Some matters relative to the *Schroeder* Ritual have been dealt with earlier in this guide under the heading of Degrees and Rites.

The Grosse Landsloge Der Freimaurer von Deutschland
(The Grand Land Lodge of Freemasons in Germany).

Founded: 1770, revived: 1947

Ritual: Swedish Rite.

Address: Masonic Temple, Peter-Lenne-Strasse 1–3, Berlin.   Telephone: (030) 831 1877.

Notes for Visitors

This Grand Lodge works the Swedish Rite, imported originally from Scandinavia. It is a system of ten degrees in Germany, and it has been modified in part from the Swedish original, although evidently the Grand Lodge has recently aligned their system more to that of Sweden. A fuller discussion of the Swedish Rite is found later in this guide under the heading of Sweden. Swedish Rite lodges meet weekly, with a typical monthly programme being lectures at three meetings, and a formal degree ceremony once per month at the fourth meeting. It is uncommon for a repast to be associated with lodge meetings, although 'drinks' afterwards are fairly usual. Where a repast is held, it will normally follow a formal degree ceremony. A visitor will never be expected to contribute to any repast he may attend. Swedish Rite lodges largely meet at 8 pm, with members having dined at their homes beforehand. Dress is a dark business suit, and regalia tends to follow the Swedish pattern, including the use of sashes.

The Grosse National-Mutterloge 'Zu Den Drei Welkugeln'
(The National Grand Mother Lodge of the Three Globes).
Founded: 1740, revived: 1947

Ritual: Fessler.
Address: Masonic Temple, Heerstrabe 28, Berlin.   Telephone: (030) 304 2806.

Notes for Visitors

The Grand Lodge of the Three Globes, virtually from its outset, has been centred in Berlin. It was re-formed after the War, and had nineteen lodges when it entered the United Grand Lodges. It was heavily affected by the Rite of Strict Observance in its early history, but later came to use the Fessler Ritual. Brother Fessler was a contemporary of Brother Schroeder, and he was possessed with the same idea of purging the then German ritual of irregularities. Indeed, the Fessler Ritual is not unlike the Schroeder version. The basic notes for visiting are much the same as those for the Grand Lodge AF & AM.

The American–Canadian Grand Lodge, Ancient, Free and Accepted Masons
Founded: 1962

Address: Grand Lodge Office, Hermannstrasse 39, Frankfurt/Main. Telephone: (0611) 593 262.

Notes for Visitors

The Second World War left a large number of American, Canadian and British troops stationed in Germany. Of course, a number of these servicemen were masons, and attempts to erect English-speaking lodges soon followed the War. These new lodges initially took various US or German charters, eventually leading to the formation of the American–Canadian Provincial Grand Lodge, and the Provincial Grand Lodge of British Freemasons (the latter of which is reviewed below).

American lodges were initially military lodges meeting at military bases, but US military policy changed in the late 1960s, whereupon lodge meetings at bases became discouraged. These lodges were then forced to become stationary in various German population centres, and this quickly spurred the formation of the American–Canadian Grand Lodge (ACGL). Over forty lodges now work under the ACGL, all using various American rituals. The Webb-form rituals in use include the Rhode Island, New York and Oregon workings, and several others. Of course, the various US rituals are quite similar.

It is, therefore, hardly surprising to discover that general American masonic practices are fairly closely followed in ACGL lodges. Dress is a dark business suit, sports jacket, or even more informal; although in some lodges, officers will wear a dinner suit. The visitor arriving in a dark suit will cover all contingencies. Visitors should first approach the lodge Tyler, who will arrange for an examination by Past Masters. Usual American practices such as the 'Open Installation', the 'Collation' after a meeting, the lack of toasts at afterproceedings, and holding a repast in the middle of proceedings are all found under the ACGL. Indeed, the general text for visitors found under the heading of the United States elsewhere in this guide largely applies to ACGL lodges in Germany. Again, as with usual American practice, members contribute to every meal taken in association with lodge meetings. While not particularly common, visitors may also be asked to contribute.

Any repast under an AGCL lodge is informally structured, under the superintendence of the Junior Warden. While no toasts, as such, are proposed, various members and visitors will be called upon to speak. A charity box is always present, and visitors are welcome to contribute. Unlike general practice in the United States, there is no prohibition against the serving of alcohol in association with an ACGL lodge repast. Each member and visitor is responsible for purchasing his own needs in this regard. Usual practice is for the custodian of each 'Logenhaus' (Masonic Temple) to have a range of drinks available for purchase. The lodge itself is not involved. This applies to all lodges in Germany, regardless of their affiliations.

Visitors and joining members are eagerly sought by ACGL lodges, particularly the latter. Most lodge members are servicemen stationed in the country for only three to five years, and so a considerable turnover of membership is experienced. This occurrence sometimes robs lodges of experienced officers. Again, as is common in the United States, ACGL lodges conduct a Stated Meeting once per month, and extra, special meetings as needed. The meeting time for most lodges is 7.30 pm.

The Grand Lodge of British Freemasons in Germany
Address: Masonic Temple (Logenhaus), Uhlandstrasse 38, Dusseldorf.

Notes for Visitors

The Grand Lodge of British Freemasons is the smallest of the five constituents of the United Grand Lodges, but nevertheless it possesses lodges throughout Germany. As one would suspect, the British lodges closely follow British masonic practices, and those of England in particular. The most popular ritual is the English *Emulation* working. A festive board, with Toast List, generally follows a lodge meeting. A charge is levied on members attending a festive board, and visitors are not always exempt from this. Dress for British lodges is a dark lounge suit, and visitors should attend with their own regalia where possible. Most British lodges meet at around 7.30 pm, on a fixed day each month. However, there are a small number that meet in the afternoon (for example: Anglo-Hanseatic Lodge No 850, which meets at the Logenhaus, Moorweidenstrasse 36, Hamburg 13; at 2.30 pm, on the 3rd Saturday October to May).

List of Lodges—Germany

While no attempt can be made here to list all German lodges, below are English-speaking lodges located in the main German cities, together with the main meeting places at most well known German destinations. A complete list of all German lodges is to be found in the *Taschenbuch* (Pocket Book) published annually by the American–Canadian Grand Lodge. Not only does it contain details for every lodge in Germany under the five constituent Grand Lodges of the United Grand Lodges, it also details every German-speaking lodge in the regular masonic world, as well as providing details for many lodges under other regular European Grand

Lodges. In short, it is a most useful book for the masonic traveller provided he has a rudimentary knowledge of German, as the book is largely printed in that language. It is available for a modest price from the American–Canadian Grand Lodge. However, visitors wishing to purchase it should make their request to the ACGL office through the auspices of their own Grand Lodge office.

Other publications which might be of interest to the visitor are a Year Book, and a periodical magazine—*Humanitaet*. Both are published in German by the Grand Lodge AF & AM.

ASCHAFFENBURG

Spessart Lodge No 875 ACGL	Meets at Elisenstrabe 31, Aschaffenburg; 1st Tuesday, at 7.30 pm (Stated Meeting).

AUGSBURG

Lebanon Lodge No 831 ACGL	Meets at the Logenhaus, Schiebgrabenstrasse 30, Augsburg 11; 1st Monday at 7.30 pm (Stated Meeting).

BADEN-BADEN

Dominion Lodge No 848 ACGL	Meets at the Logenhaus, Vincentistrasse 8, Baden-Baden; 1st Monday at 7.30 pm (Stated Meeting).

BAMBERG

Bamberg Acacia Lodge No 832 ACGL	Meets at the Logenhaus, Franz-Ludwig-strasse 16, Bamberg; 1st Thursday at 7.30 pm (Stated Meeting).

BAYREUTH

Bayreuth was once the site of a now extinct German Grand Lodge. It contains no English-speaking lodges as yet, but does possess two of the German-speaking variety. One of these lodges is Germany's only currently warranted research lodge. This is the Forschungsloge (Research Lodge) Quatuor Coronati No 808, named after the Premier Lodge of Masonic Research in London.

Bayreuth's other claim to masonic fame is a superb masonic museum, located at the Logenhaus, Horgarten 1, Bayreuth. A display of particular interest is that of Nazi anti-masonic propaganda from the Second World War.

BERLIN

Berlin is the headquarters of two of Germany's Grand Lodges, as noted above. It contains over forty lodges, with all five Grand Lodges being represented. The English-speaking lodge details are as follows:

Phoenix Lodge No 847 GLBF	Meets at the Masonic Rooms (Block 13), Flugplatz Gatow, Berlin 22; 2nd Monday October to June.
Outpost Lodge No 895 ACGL	Meets at the Logenhaus, Heerstrasse 28, Berlin 19; 2nd Thursday, at 7.30 pm (Stated Meeting).
Berlin 46 Lodge No 933 ACGL	Meets at the Logenhaus, Emserstrasse 12–13, Berlin; 2nd Thursday, at 7.30 pm (Stated Meeting).

BIELEFELD

Britannia Lodge No 843 GLBF	Meets at the Logenhaus, Lessingstrasse 3, Bielefeld; 3rd Tuesday at 7 pm.

BONN
Bonn is the federal capital city of West Germany, and it currently possesses four lodges, of which one is English-speaking.

Bond of Friendship Lodge No 890   Meets at the Logenhaus, Dyroffstrasse 2, Bonn;
GLBF   3rd Thursday, November to June, and 2nd Saturday in October (Installation).

BREMEN
Bremen currently possesses no English-speaking lodges, although it does contain seven German-speaking lodges. All these lodges meet at the Logenhaus, Kurfurstenallee 15, Bremen.

BREMERHAVEN
Nth Sea Armed Forces Lodge No 829   Meets at the Logenhaus, Lange Strasse 147,
ACGL   Bremerhaven; Thursdays, at 7.30 pm.

BUTTELBORN
US Hessen Lodge No 844 ACGL   Meets at Hauptstrasse 33, Buttelborn; 1st Thursday, at 7.30 pm (Stated Meeting).

CELLE
Saxony Lodge No 842 GLBF   Meets at the Logenhaus, Magnusstrasse 2a, Celle; Last Wednesday (except August and December).

DUSSELDORF
Niederrhein Lodge No 892 GLBF   Meets at the Logenhaus, Uhlandstrasse 38, Dusseldorf; 1st Monday, at 7 pm.

FRANKFURT
Frankfurt is one of the larger German cities. It currently possesses ten lodges, meeting variously at three locations. It is the base location of the ACGL. The three English-speaking lodges in Frankfurt come under the ACGL.

Frankfurt on the Main Lodge No 861   Meets at the Logenhaus, Kaiserstrasse 37, Frankfurt; 1st and 3rd Mondays, at 7.30 pm.

Oregon Military Lodge No 936   Meets at the Logenhaus, Kaiserstrasse 37, Frankfurt; 1st Tuesday, at 7.30 pm (Stated Meeting).

ACGL Past Masters Lodge No 950   Meets at Hermannstrasse 36, Frankfurt; four times annually by summons.

FURTH
Truth and Friendship Lodge No 828   Meets at the Logenhaus, Dambacherstrasse 11,
ACGL   Furth; 1st and 3rd Wednesday, at 7.30 pm.

GIESSEN
Friends on the lahn Lodge No 860   Meets at the Logenhaus, Bruhlsbachstrabe,
ACGL   Giessen; 1st Thursday, at 7.30 pm (Stated Meeting).

HAMBURG
One of the largest German cities, Hamburg contains over forty lodges, of which only one is English-speaking. This is the Anglo-Hanseatic Lodge No 850 (GLBF), which has already been detailed. The two main Logenhauses in Hamburg are located

at Welckerstrasse 8, Hamburg 36 (Telephone: (040) 344 267), and at Moorweiden-strabe 36, Hamburg 13 (Telephone: (040) 443 723).

HANAU
Ashler Lodge No 894 ACGL

Meets at Schlob Phillipsruhe 6450, Hanau; 1st Wednesday, at 7.30 pm (Stated Meeting).

HEIDELBERG
Alt Heidelberg Lodge No 821 ACGL

Meets at the Logenhaus, Klingenteichstrasse 8, Heidelberg; 1st Tuesday, at 7.30 pm (Stated Meeting).

HEILBRONN
Forget me Not Lodge No 896 ACGL

Meets at the Logenhaus, Moltkestrabe 8/2, Heilbronn; 1st Tuesday, at 7.30 pm (Stated Meeting).

KAISERSLAUTERN
Galilei Lodge No 810A ACGL

Meets at the Logenhaus, Augustastrabe 2, Kaiserslautern; 1st Monday, at 7.30 pm.

George Washington Lodge No 820 ACGL

Meets at the Logenhaus, Augustastrabe 2, Kaiserslautern; 1st Thursday, at 7.30 pm.

KARLSRUHE
Fidelitas Lodge No 830 ACGL

Meets at the Logenhaus, Bismarckstrabe 83, Karlsruhe; 1st Tuesday, at 7.30 pm (Stated Meeting).

KOLN (COLOGNE)
Cologne possesses no English-speaking lodges as yet, but does contain five German-speaking lodges. The two main meeting places in use are located at Hardefuststrasse 9, Koln; and at Lindenallee 58, Koln.

KRONWEILER
Nahe Temple Lodge No 824 ACGL

Meets at the Kronweiler Schulhaus, Kronweiler; 1st and 3rd Mondays, at 7.30 pm.

LAHR
Black Forest Lodge No 901 ACGL

Meets at the Logenhaus, Friedrichstrasse 9, Lahr; 1st Wednesday, at 7.30 pm (Stated Meeting).

LUDWIGSBURG
Hiram Lodge No 819 ACGL

Meets at the Logenhaus, Aspergerstrasse 37, Ludwigsburg; 2nd Monday, at 7.30 pm (Stated Meeting).

MANNHEIM
Mannheim possesses seven lodges, of which one is English-speaking, five are German-speaking, and one is Czech-speaking. The latter of these lodges is unique (thus far) in German masonry. It was formed in 1981 to cater for Czech masonic 'exiles'. All Mannheim lodges meet at the same location.

Triangle Lodge No 834 ACGL

Meets at the Logenhaus, Block L 9, 9, Mannheim; 1st Tuesday, at 7.30 pm (Stated Meeting).

TG Masaryk Lodge No 957A.F. & A.M.

Meets at the Logenhaus, Block L 9, 9, Mannheim; 3rd Saturday, at 8 pm (Czech-speaking).

MINDEN
The Rose of Minden Lodge No 918 GLBF	Meets at the Logenhaus, Prinzenstabe 3, Minden; 1st Monday, September to April (except January), at 7 pm; and 2nd Saturday May, at 11 am (Installation).

MONCHENGLADBACH-RHEINDAHLEN
New Absalom Lodge No 841 GLBF	Meets at the Logenhaus, 33a Stadtwaldstrasse; last Thursday (except March, July and August), at 6.30 pm.
Star of Saxony Lodge No 853 GLBF	Meets at the Logenhaus, 33a Stadtwaldstrasse; 3rd Wednesday, October to June at 7 pm.

MOTSCH/BITBURG
Eifel Lodge No 855 ACGL	Meets at Sportsplatz 2; 1st Tuesday at 7.30 pm (Stated Meeting).

MUNICH (MUNCHEN)

This large Bavarian city possesses eleven lodges, of which one is English-speaking. Most of the German-speaking lodges meet at the large Logenhaus located at Schwanthalerstrasse 60, Munich (Telephone: 533 477).

Bavaria Lodge No 935 ACGL	Meets at McGraw Kasern, Building 364, top floor; 1st Thursday at 7.30 pm (Stated Meeting).

MUNSTER
Keys of Munster Lodge No 881 GLBF	Meets at Blucherstuben, Diepenbrockstrabe 30, Munster; 2nd Friday (except July and August) at 7 pm.

NIENBURG
Bridge of Fellowship Lodge No 929 GLBF	Meets at Neuestrasse 5, Nienburg; 2nd Tuesday at 7.15 pm.

NURNBERG

This large German city possesses no English-speaking lodges. Its seven German-speaking lodges all meet at the Logenhaus, Hallerwiesse 16, Nurnberg (Telephone: (0911) 339 996).

PIRMASENS
Mount Moriah Lodge No 823 ACGL	Meets at the Logenhaus, Beckenhofstrabe 36, Pirmasens; 1st and 3rd Mondays at 7.30 pm.

RAVERSBEUREN
Hunsruck Lodge No 839 ACGL	Meets at Raversbeuren Hahn AB, 6541 Flugsplatz Hahn; 2nd Thursday at 7.30 pm (Stated Meeting).

SCHWEINFURT
More Light Lodge No 874 ACGL	Meets at the Logenhaus, Neutorstrabe 4, Schweinfurt; 1st Tuesday at 7.30 pm (Stated Meeting).

STUTTGART
Solomon Lodge No 822 ACGL	Meets at the Logenhaus, Herdweg 19, Stuttgart; 1st and 3rd Wednesdays at 7.30 pm.

● = A.C.G.L

O = G.L.B.F

Hamburg

Bremerhaven

Nienburg

Osnabrück   Celle

Minden

Münster O   O Bielefeld

Sennelager

Werl

Düsseldorf

Mönchengladbach-Rheindahlen   Bonn

EAST GERMANY

Berlin

Giessen

Raversbeuren (nr. Hahn A.B.)

Bitburg.(Mötsch)   Frankfurt

Wiesbaden   Hanau

Aschaffenburg   Schweinfurt

Bad Kreuznach   Wuerzburg   Bamberg

Kronweiler ●   Worms   Darmstadt

Kitzingen

Kaiserslautern   Mannheim

Zweibruecken   Heidelberg   Fuerth

Pirmasens

Heilbronn   Sorghof

Karlsruhe   Ansbach

FRANCE

Ludwigsburg

Baden-Baden   Stuttgart   WEST GERMANY

Lahr

Ulm-Donau

Augsburg

Munich

Bad Tolz

(Bad Heilbrunn)

ULM
Munster Lodge No 833 ACGL   Meets at the Logenhaus, Schuelinstrabe 11, Ulm;
                                     1st Tuesday at 7.30 pm (Stated Meeting).

WIESBADEN
Luftbrucke Lodge No 838 ACGL   Meets at the Logenhaus, Friedrichstrasse 35,
                                     Wiesbaden; 1st Wednesday at 7.30 pm (Stated
                                     Meeting).

WORMS
Peter M Rasmussen Lodge No 916   Meets at Friedrich-Ebert-Strasse 1, Worms; 1st
*   ACGL*   Wednesday at 7.30 pm (Stated Meeting).

WURZBURG
Cornerstone Lodge No 836 ACGL   Meets at the Logenhaus, Valentin-Beckerstrasse 3,
                                     Wurzburg; 1st Wednesday at 7.30 pm (Stated
                                     Meeting).

ZWEIBRUCKEN
Two Bridges Lodge No 877 ACGL   Meets at the Logenhaus, Ixheimer Strasse 89,
                                     Zweibrucken; 1st and 3rd Thursdays at 7.30 pm.

Reminder Visitors to Germany are again reminded that most German-chartered lodges recess in June, July and August, and some in September and December. Visitors should be sure to obtain exact information from a German Grand Lodge office when in Germany, prior to visiting in these months.

GIBRALTAR

The Rock of Gibraltar is a British Crown Colony and important naval base, located at the mouth of the Mediterranean Sea. It possesses eight lodges under the English District Grand Lodge of Gibraltar, three lodges under the Scottish District Grand Lodge of Gibraltar, and one Irish lodge governed directly from Dublin. All lodges meet at the Gibraltar Masonic Institute, 47A Prince Edward Road, Gibraltar. Meeting details are as follows:

Lodge of St John No 115 EC   Meets 4th Thursday, September to May (except
                                     December). Inst: 24th June annually.

Inhabitants Lodge No 153 EC   Meets 3rd Saturday, October to May (except
                                     December, then 2nd Saturday). Inst: January.

Royal Lodge of Friendship No 278 EC Meets 1st Wednesday October to June (except
                                     January). Inst: March.

Robert Freke Gould Lodge No 2874   Meets 1st Tuesday October to April (except
*   EC*   January). Inst: December.

Connaught Lodge No 2915 EC   Meets 1st Friday October to June (except January).
                                     Inst: November.

Letchworth Lodge No 3505 EC   Meets 2nd Thursday February (Inst.); 4th Tuesday,
                                     September; and 1st Wednesday, December.

United Services Lodge, Gibraltar No Meets 3rd Thursday September to May (except
3813 EC   December). Inst: November.

Gibraltar Masters Lodge No 3825 EC Meets 3rd Tuesday February (Inst.), May and
                                     November.

Calpe Lodge No 325 IC   Meets 2nd Monday October to May.

Lodge St Thomas No 576 SC   Meets 3rd Monday October to June.
Lodge Al Moghreb Al Aksa No 670   Meets 2nd Tuesday October to June.
SC
Lodge Coronation No 934 SC   Meets 4th Friday October and November; and
March to June.

GREECE

Greece possesses a regular Grand Lodge of some strength, as well as a very old English lodge dating from 1861.

The Grand Lodge of Ancient, Free and Accepted Masons of Greece
Founded: 1811
Address: Masonic Hall, 19 Archarnon Street (corner Sourmeli Street), Athens.
Telephone: 881 2182, 822 3120, 822 9950.
Lodges: 68.   Permits Dual and Plural Membership.   *Membership:* Circa 2,500.
Descent: France, England, and Italy.   *Government:* Modified Grand Orient.
Courtesy Degrees: rarely conferred.   *Ritual:* French Rite-type Craft Degrees.
Minimum Time Lapse between Degrees: 12 months (1st to 2nd Degree), 6 months (2nd to 3rd Degree).
Main Publications: Constitution.   Proceedings.

History
During the Ottoman Empire's control of mainland Greece, it was not possible to introduce freemasonry. However, the Ionian islands located to the west of the Peloponnese were not in Turkish hands, but controlled from Venice. It appears that the first lodge in Greek territory was erected in the Ionian Islands from Venice in 1714. This lodge was called Benefizena (Benevolence), and it worked in the Greek language. When, in 1799, the Russians came to control Ionia, this lodge declared its independence, although nothing appears to have been heard of it subsequently.

The year 1807 saw Napoleon assume control over Ionia, and within three years two lodges had been established at Corfu (the most northern of the Ionian islands) under the Grand Orient of France. By 1811, these lodges had formed the National Grand Lodge of Greece in Corfu, but it had expired by 1814. Another Grand Lodge, The Serene Grand Orient of Greece in Corfu was formed in 1814, but after a chequered career it was extinct by 1843.

The fall of Napoleon saw England assume political control over Ionia, with the occupation forces having a hand in forming Pythagorus Lodge at Corfu, and Phoenix Lodge at Zante. Both these lodges later expired, but the Grand Lodge of Greece has maintained Phoenix Lodge No 1 on its roll of lodges, evidently as a token of masonic gratitude for the restitution of Ionia to Greece.

During the Greek War of Independence (1821-1833) from the Ottomans, masonic records are scant, and remain so until 1863. In this period those lodges surviving appear to have remained independent, or worked under the Italian Grand Lodges at Turin. In 1867, Greece became a masonic province of the Grand Orient of Italy, and in the following year eight Italian-chartered lodges formed the Grand Orient of Greece at Athens, but whether this new Grand Body was a successor of the earlier Corfu body remains obscure. Nevertheless, 1811 is claimed by the current Grand Lodge of Greece as its foundation year, rather than 1868. The Greek Grand Orient, as was fairly typical of European nineteenth century masonry, was controlled by a Scottish Rite Supreme Council.

The Grand Orient of Greece expanded steadily, but without much in the way of fraternal recognition outside Greece. This changed after 1940, whereupon the Supreme Council surrendered its control over the three Craft degrees, and the Grand Orient became the Grand Lodge of Greece. It has since been recognised as regular throughout the masonic world.

Notes for Visitors to Greece

Greek freemasonry has its own ritual, which is basically the French Rite Craft degrees translated into Greek. Interestingly, the only degrees available to Greek masons outside the Craft degrees are those of the Greek Scottish Rite Supreme Council. However, English-speaking masons should be aware that while the Grand Lodge of Greece is regular, the Greek Supreme Council is not recognised by the Supreme Councils of England, Ireland, and Scotland.

As is somewhat the tendency in Europe, the Greek Craft tends to be somewhat exclusive, with a high social and educational standard being a general prerequisite for membership. Greek lodges meet weekly, although an actual degree conferment ceremony is usually performed only once per month. Other meetings are taken up with lectures, and instruction. Each Greek Entered Apprentice must have served at least twelve months at that rank before he may receive the Fellow Craft Degree. In addition, he must deliver at least one lecture on the First Degree in his lodge prior to being passed, and he must satisfactorily complete a written examination. These practices follow usual Continental patterns. The time lapse between the second and third degrees is a minimum of six months, with the same proficiency requirements applying. Greek lodges, as is common throughout Europe, recess in June, July and August, although some lodges hold unofficial social meetings in the open air during this period.

The structure of Greek masonry is that of a modfied Grand Orient System. Each year at their annual elections, lodges elect three Past Masters as their representatives to the Grand Lodge. Every three years these lodge representatives elect the Council of the Grand Lodge (its Grand Orient). In turn, the Grand Orient elects the Grand Master, and other Grand Lodge officers. Thus the Greek system of masonic government uses indirect democracy, unlike the more autocratic forms of Grand Orients.

Dress for Greek lodges is a dark business suit, but the carrying of personal regalia is a good idea, although those without will be catered for. Lodges meet in the evening, at any time between 7.30 pm and 9 pm, depending on the individual lodge. As a result of these divergent meeting times, visitors are best advised to make themselves known at the Grand Lodge building in Athens prior to visiting, where they will receive every assistance.

It is usual for the principal officers of Greek lodges to meet separately before their lodge meeting, and undertake a preview of the evening's proceedings. The lodge members will already be inside the Temple, and the Master and his Wardens will enter later. Visitors, having previously been masonically examined if unknown, will often enter with the Master's party. The use of printed rituals inside the lodge is the norm. To the Greek freemason, excellence in ritual is not as important as masonic knowledge and behaviour. Indeed, 'Lodges of Research' are conducted by every Greek lodge, and masonic orators and scholars are called upon to impart their knowledge. Grand Inspectors, appointed by the Grand Lodge, are present at every Greek lodge meeting to assist the Master and his members on points of masonic knowledge and procedure.

Greek lodges have an interesting method of electing a new Master. The elections are held annually, in the Third Degree. The retiring Master, together with two qualified Master Masons (usually the Wardens) are elected to stand for the position. The lodge is then returned to the First Degree, and all members present elect a new Master from those three, together with other lodge officers.

Another absorbing Greek masonic practice is called the White Ceremony. Each lodge usually holds such a ceremony, on an annual basis, and most impressive it is. It is, in fact, a ceremony of masonic mourning in recognition of members deceased during the year; of celebration for members married during that year; and for the adoption of Lewises by the lodge. This latter practice hails back to old French usage, whereupon a lodge 'adopts' the twelve-year-old sons of masons and pledges itself to their welfare. The White Ceremonies are semi-public occasions, with brides attending in their bridal attirement, Lewises in their special attirement, with members of their family, and friends. Visitors who would like to attend these ceremonies can readily enquire at the Grand Lodge office.

Lodges in Greece are involved in some excellent charitable work, a feature of which are night schools run by lodges for poor children. There is also a Masonic Archaeological Club which visits sites of masonic interest and conducts lectures for the general public.

Of the 68 current Greek lodges, 27 work in Athens, seven in Cyprus, six in Thessalonika, three in Crete, and the remainder in other centres throughout mainland Greece and the Greek islands. One English-speaking lodge works in Athens (Parthenon No 112), together with an Italian-speaking lodge (Garibaldi No 130), a French-speaking lodge (La Tradition Française No 125), and two German-speaking lodges (Apollo No 98, and Harmonia No 118).

Greece also possesses an old English-warranted lodge, formed in the days when England held sway in Ionia. This is Star of the East Lodge No 880 EC, erected in 1861. It meets at Zante (Zakinthos), which is the southernmost of the Ionian lodges. It meets on the 1st and 3rd Fridays in February, April, May, October and November; the 1st Friday in June and December; the 4th of April, and installs on the 7th of January each year. It convenes at the new lodge building in Zante, which it shares with the Greek Lodge Helios No 99.

HUNGARY

As a part of the Austro-Hungarian Empire, the history of the Craft in this area parallels that of all Central Europe. The first Hungarian lodges came from Austria, and several appeared to have been working there by the 1770s. While freemasonry in Central Europe was suppressed by Imperial Edict in 1795, Hungary became a separate kingdom in 1867, thus allowing the Craft to re-establish. In 1870, a National Grand Lodge was formed (often called the Grand Lodge of St John) by seven lodges of German origin. A Grand Orient was erected separately in 1872 by lodges then under the Grand Orient of France. These two bodies united in 1886 to form the Symbolic Grand Lodge of Hungary. It was dissolved by decree in 1920. After suppression by the Nazis during the Second World War, the Grand Lodge was revived in 1946, only to be permanently dissolved by the Communists in 1950.

ITALY

Freemasonry in Italy has historically been afflicted with a wide variety of innovations, repression, and religious opposition. Its regular Grand Body is the Grand Orient of Italy, dating from 1805.

The Grand Orient of Italy
Founded: 1805

Address: Grand Lodge Office, Via Giustiniani 5, Rome.   Telephone: 656 9453, 654 1388.

Lodges: 562.   Permits Dual Membership outside Italy, only.   *Membership:* Circa 24,000.

Descent: England and France.   *Government:* Modified Grand Orient.

Courtesy Degrees: Correspondence must be through Grand Lodges.

Ritual: Largely the Scottish (Craft) Rite.

Minimum Time Lapse between Degrees: 12 months.

Main Publications: Constitution.   Proceedings.   Periodical: *Revista Massonica.*

History

The early history of Italian freemasonry is particularly obscure. It is traditionally supposed that masonry came to Italy about 1733 from England, and that lodges were established at Florence, Rome, Siena, and other places. Certainly, it must have been well established by 1738, when Pope Clement XII issued the first Papal Bull against it. This prohibition appears to have had only limited impact. Nonetheless, the Inquisition certainly prevented rapid progress, to say the least. A National Grand Lodge Zelo was formed at Naples in 1764, but it was closed by Royal Decree in 1775. The first Grand Orient of Italy appears to have emerged about 1784 under the influence of the Grand Orient of France, but its career was also short. There were, in addition, several weak and short lived Grand bodies of various names set up around this time in Turin, Rome, Naples and Sardinia.

A new Grand Orient was formed at Milan in 1805, and it is from this body that the current Grand Orient of Italy claims its direct descent. This body expired in 1814. At this time, the Scottish Rite was introduced from France, and a Supreme Council was erected 1809. By 1861, there were three Grand Orients in Italy, at Naples, Turin, and Palermo. These three were temporarily united in 1867 by Garibaldi, the 'father' of modern Italy, and probably the country's most famous freemason. This was achieved at a meeting of all lodges in Italy, and out of it came the Grand Orient of Italy to govern the Craft degrees, and a Scottish Rite Supreme Council. These two bodies endured with mixed success until 1925, when all lodges were dissolved by the Fascist regime of Mussolini. The Craft was then ruthlessly repressed, and many prominent masons were killed. The Grand Orient revived in 1945, but suffered schisms in 1947 and 1951.

After the Second World war, the Grand Orient of Italy moved into regularity, and was finally recognised by the United Grand Lodge of England in 1972. It has since been recognised by virtually all other regular Grand Lodges around the world. In 1974, the Roman Catholic Church softened its long standing hard line opposition to masonry, which had been backed up several times in the past by anti-masonic Papal Bulls. This happy outcome was seriously compromised in 1976/77 when sustained attacks by the secular press in Italy against masonry caused great concern in world masonic circles, and some American Grand Lodges temporarily withdrew recognition. In 1980, the P-2 'Masonic Lodge' scandal broke in Italy, and resulted in the fall of the Italian Government of the day. It was discovered that this bogus lodge, which had engaged in deep political intrigues, was originally under the Grand Orient, but was suspended by it in 1976. While this explanation satisfied other Grand Lodges, the P-2 Affair brought the Craft bad press around the world, and resulted in the Vatican hardening its line against masonry after the softening of 1974. Despite these recent disturbances, it must be stressed that the Grand Orient of Italy had no complicity in them, and it remains a fully regular Grand Lodge, as attested by its very wide recognition as such.

Notes for Visitors to Italy

Italian masonry is the most 'secretive' in the masonic world. Given the sustained religious, political, and popular opposition it has received in the past, this is somewhat understandable. Indeed, with exception of the Grand Master, Italian freemasons are not permitted to make public statements concerning the Craft. Such statements as have been made in years gone by appear to have often been distorted. It is extremely rare for an Italian mason to admit his membership outside masonic circles, and it is certainly taboo for one mason to comment on the masonic membership, or otherwise, of another. Nonetheless, provided the visitor appreciates these points, he will encounter no problems in his sojourn amongst his Italian brothers. Indeed, foreign masonic visitors are always made most welcome when attending an Italian lodge meeting.

However, the visitor is advised, where possible, to attend the Grand Orient's office at Giustiniani 5, Rome—at least in the first instance. Giustiniani is a short narrow street, and the entrance to the masonic complex is totally unmarked, except for the number '5' above the door. The G O Office is on the first floor. The building also contains a number of temples and ancillory facilities. Indeed, no masonic meeting place in Italy is recognisable as such from its outside appearance. Without an exact address, the visitor may not find his destination.

Most Italian lodges use a Scottish Rite Craft ritual. As is quite common in Europe, progress through the three degrees is slow, with candidates being required to present lectures and undergo a written masonic examination prior to advancement. Most lodges meet about 8 pm, and dress is a dark business suit. Regalia will be supplied on loan to visitors attending without their own. A meal, gratis to visitors, accompanies some Italian lodge meetings. Lodges largely meet on a weekly basis, although a temple ceremony is often only performed once per month. It should be noted that most Italian lodges recess in June, July, and August.

There are eight Craft lodges under the Grand Orient which work in English. These lodges use American or English Rituals, as appropriate, and cater largely for servicemen stationed in Italy. These lodges are Loggia Aviano No 643 (at Aviano), Loggia Fiorello la Guardia No 653 (at Bologna), Loggia Benjamin Franklin No 591 (at Livorno), Loggia Harry S. Truman No 649 (at Naples), Loggia

Colosseum No 602 (at Rome), Loggia Keats and Shelley No 900 (at Rome), Loggia J L McClellan No 780 (at San Vito dei Normanni), and Loggia George Washington No 585 (at Vincenza).

The main meeting places in the main Italian cities are as follows:

Naples:	Galleria Umberto 27, Napoli. (12 Lodges)
Bologna:	Via Castiglione 6, Bolonga. (8 Lodges)
Ravenna:	Via Matteotti 35, Ravenna. (4 Lodges)
Rimini:	Circolo Europa, Via Ampere 28, Rimini. (2 Lodges)
Trieste:	Circolo Gymnasium, Via Saint Nicolo 30, Trieste. (7 Lodges)
Genoa:	Associazione Studi Liguri, Via Porta d'Archi 12, Genova, and Stanze di Cultura G Rensi, Via Rome 4/3, Genova. (15 Lodges)
Milan:	Circolo Culturale Olona, Corso di Porta Nuova 16, Milano. (21 Lodges)
Turin:	Piazza Vittorio Veneto 8, Torino; and Piazza Vittorio Veneto 17/19, Torino; and Via Cernaia 15, Torino; and Corso Vittorio Emanuele 83, Torino. (35 Lodges)
Bari:	Corso Cavour 198, Bari. (5 Lodges)
Messina:	Via Saint Cecilia 119, Messina, Sicily. (10 Lodges)
Palermo:	Corso Vittorio Emanuele 137, piano 2, Palermo, Sicily. (21 Lodges)
Florence:	Borgo degli Albizi 18, Firenze; and Via Tornabuoni 5, Firenze. (43 Lodges)
Siena:	Via dei Montanini 101, Siena. (3 Lodges)
Perugia:	Via Saint Galigano-Rimbocchi 30, Perugia; Piazza Biordo Michelotti 5, Perugia; and Piazza Piccinino 9, Perugia. (15 Lodges)
Venice:	San Marco 4325 (Campanello Jevolella), Venezia; Saint Croce 664/A (Campanello Urbani); Venezia; Via Emilei 9 (Campanello Circolo Ricerche Storiche), Venezia; and Cannaregio 6270/a (L'Adriatica), Venezia. (5 Lodges)
Vicenza:	Via Tornieri 103, Vicenza. (2 Lodges)
Rome:	Via Giustiniani 5, Roma. (38 Lodges)

LIECHTENSTEIN

This tiny Principality wedged between Switzerland and Austria appears to have never had a lodge, although if one were to be established it is likely that the Swiss would have best claim to jurisdiction.

LUXEMBOURG

Luxembourg has the distinction of possessing the smallest Grand Lodge in Europe, and arguably the smallest in the world.

The Grand Lodge of Luxembourg
Founded: 1868

Address: Masonic Temple, 5 Rue de la Loge, Luxembourg. *Telephone:* 29451.
Lodges: 4. Permits Dual Membership. *Membership:* Circa 200.
Descent: Probably French. *Government:* Modified Grand Orient.
Courtesy Degrees: Situation unknown.

Ritual: The French Rite Craft Degrees.
Minimum Time lapse between Degrees: 12 months.   *Main Publication:* Constitution.

History

The early history of the Grand Lodge of Luxembourg is obscure. Some accounts indicate that a Grand Orient existed in Luxembourg between 1774 and 1812. However, the earliest lodge in the country can be definitely stated to have been La Parfaite Union, dating from 1770. Its origin was probably Belgian. The second lodge in Luxembourg was Les Enfans de la Concorde Fortiffee. It appears to date from 1803, and its origin the Grand Orient of France. The remaining two lodges would appear to be daughters of those two already existing. The date of erection of the Grand Lodge is equally obscure, but the date given above seems the most likely.

Luxembourg is a Grand Duchy wedged between Belgium, Germany and France. It is almost wholly Catholic in religion which probably accounts for the very slow development of the Craft within its boundaries. However, its fourth lodge, erected in 1974, would seem to indicate that membership is now expanding. There was for many years questions concerning the authenticity of the Grand Lodge, and it was not recognised by England until as late as 1969. The Grand Lodge is still not as widely recognised as it would probably hope, particularly among the American Jurisdictions. An irregular Grand Orient of Luxembourg also exists in the country, about which little is known.

Notes for visiting in Luxembourg

All Luxembourg lodges meet at 6.30 pm. It is evidently uncommon for a repast to accompany a meeting. Unlike many other European lodges, those of Luxembourg only meet monthly. Dress is a dark suit, but visitors are welcome in jacket and tie. Craft government is by a form of modified Grand Orient, but the small number of lodges under warrant would appear to make Luxembourg masonry quite tightly knit in any case. Visiting by members between lodges is quite commonplace in Luxembourg, probably more so than elsewhere in Europe.

List of Lodges

The small number of Luxembourg lodges readily allows the listing of the relevant details of each. All four lodges meet at 5 Rue de la Lodge, so obviously any mason visiting in Luxembourg will also be attending the Grand Lodge office concurrently.

La Parfaite Union Lodge No 1	(The Perfect Union). Meets second Friday monthly.
Les Enfans de la Concorde Fortifee Lodge No 2	(Lodge of the Children of Concord Fortified) Meets first Friday monthly.
Saint Jean de l'Esperance Lodge No 3	(Saint Jean of Esperance). Meets 3rd Friday monthly.
Friendship Lodge No 4	Meets on the last Saturday of the Month in January, April, June, and October.

It should also be noted that the first three Luxembourg lodges recess in the northern summer months.

MALTA

Malta is a small island located in the central Mediterranean Sea. It was a British possession prior to its independence, so not surprisingly its masonry is derived from that source. Six English lodges work in Malta under an English District Grand Lodge. Scotland has one lodge under warrant, while Ireland has two. All the English lodges meet at the Masonic Hall in Valetta, while the Scottish and Irish lodges meet at the Masonic Hall, Villa Blye, Pawla. Meeting details are as follows:

Lodge of St John and St Paul No 349 EC	Meets 1st Monday October to May. Inst: December.
Union Lodge No 407 EC	Meets 1st Saturday in March (Inst.), April, October and November.
Zetland Lodge No 515 EC	Meets 2nd Monday in October, December, February (Inst.), and April.
Wayfarers Lodge No 1926 EC	Meets 3rd Wednesday, November, January, February (Inst.), and April
Waller Rodwell Wright Lodge No 2755 EC	Meets 4th Saturday in April (Inst.), June, and October; and 1st Saturday in September.
Royal Naval Lodge No 2761 EC	Meets 3rd Monday in February, March, May, October, and December (Inst.).
Abercorn Lodge No 273 IC	Meets 4th Wednesday monthly except June and July.
Leinster Lodge No 387 IC	Meets 1st Tuesday monthly except July, August, and September.
Lodge St Andrew No 966 SC	Meets 1st Friday in April, October and February; and 4th Friday in November.

MONACO

This small Principality is located amidst the French Riviera. It does not possess a regular French lodge (GLNF) as yet, although the irregular Grand Orient of France reportedly has a lodge working in Monte Carlo. However, there is one English lodge working in Monaco, erected in 1924, and this remains the only lodge of that obedience still remaining in 'French' territory. Its details are as follows:

Port of Hercules Lodge No 4626 EC	Meets at the Library of St Paul's Church House, Avenue de la Grande Bretagne; 2nd Thursday in November, January, February and March; and on April 23rd each year. Installation: February.

THE NETHERLANDS

Dutch freemasonry possesses a Grand Lodge dating from 1756, making one of the oldest in Europe. One of the main features of Dutch masonry has been its relatively tranquil development—a trait not generally shared with other Continental obediences.

The Grand East of the Netherlands
Founded: 1756
Address: Masonic Hall, 22 Fluwelen Burgwal, 2511 CJ, s'Gravenhage (The Hague), Netherlands. *Telephone:* (070) 460046.

Lodges: 148.   Permits Dual Membership.   *Membership:* 6,800.
Descent: England.   *Government:* Appointive Grand Lodge.
Courtesy Degrees: Correspondence must be through Grand Lodges.
Ritual: Dutch.
Minimum Time Lapse between Degrees: One month (1st to 2nd degrees), 12 months (2nd to 3rd).
Main Publications: Constitutions.   Proceedings.

History

The first lodge to meet in Holland was the Lodge of the Grand Master, in 1734. It gained an English warrant in the following year. Several other lodges followed, although local opposition to the Craft was not slow to rear its head. An English lodge in Amsterdam was pillaged by a riotous mob in 1735, and this led to a ban on masonic activity. By 1744, the effects of this prohibition appears to have vanished, and in 1756, fourteen lodges united to form the Grand Lodge of Holland. Of these, thirteen were warranted from England, while one held a Scottish charter.

The Grand Lodge of England recognised the Dutch Grand Lodge in 1770, and thereafter ceased to warrant new lodges in Holland. All English lodges not then incorporated into the Grand Lodge of Holland progressively joined it or eventually became extinct, so that by the time of the English Union in 1813, no extant lodge in Holland remained on the English roll.

The most interesting feature of Dutch masonry is that it has remained largely free of control from the 'higher degrees' which have so often plagued other Continental obediences. Consequently, Dutch masonry has enjoyed a long reign of stability. Until 1807, there were virtually no additional degrees available to the Dutch mason, but in that year the Grand Lodge bowed to growing pressure and accepted a simple form of 'supplementary Rites'. Today, the three Craft degrees are worked under lodges warranted by the Grand East of the Netherlands (as the Grand Lodge came to be styled), while the French Rite Ecossais degrees and Rose Croix are worked under a Grand Chapter of the Higher Degrees. There is also a Scottish Rite Supreme Council which is in amity with the corresponding English body—in itself a rare feat in terms of Continental masonry as a whole. In recent years, the Royal Arch, Mark Master Mason, and Royal Ark Mariner. Degrees have been introduced from England. It should be noted that the controlling bodies of none of these additional degrees have ever come to exercise control or authority over the Grand East.

It is worthy of note that Belgian lodges were once controlled from the Netherlands, but that control was relinquished in 1837, whereupon Belgian masonry followed its separate course. The peaceful development of Dutch masonry was interrupted by the Second World War which saw all lodges closed, and its membership persecuted. A rapid recovery was made after the War.

The Grand East of the Netherlands has in the past warranted many lodges outside Holland, notably in Southern Africa, the Dutch West Indies and Rhodesia. In 1961, the Dutch lodges in South Africa (except one) formed the Grand Lodge of Southern Africa. Eight Dutch lodges still work happily in the West Indies, while seven still hold warrants in Rhodesia (now Zimbabwe).

Notes for Visitors to the Netherlands

As is fairly usual European practice, Dutch lodges meet weekly, except in the northern summer months of June, July, and August. Dress is a dark, usually black, business suit, with white shirt and long black tie. Visitors are welcome to wear a jacket and tie, if they are not carrying a suit with them. Almost without exception, Dutch lodges open at 8 pm.

While Dutch lodges meet weekly, only once per month is a 'Temple meeting' usually held for the purposes of degree conferment. The other meetings are taken up with lectures. Lecture topics may be masonic, social, cultural or spiritual (although religion and politics are never discussed). A Dutch mason must personally present at least one lecture to his lodge prior to being admitted into a superior degree. The minimum time lapse between the first and second degrees is one month, while twelve months is the requirement between the second and third degrees. In practice, it is rare for progression from any degree to the next to occur under twelve months. Indeed, a Fellow Craft does not receive the Master Mason degree as a right, but strictly on merit. The resolution of the Master Masons of a lodge is necessary before any Fellow Craft may be raised. As with some other Continental obediences, Dutch lodges generally enforce a system of compulsory attendance, and a member who fails to live up to expectations in this regard will find his rate of progression greatly slowed.

An informal dinner is usual after some formal meetings, and visitors are always most welcome to dine with members. Visitors are treated as honoured guests, as is the case anywhere in Europe, and under no circumstances will a visitor be called upon to pay. The costs of repasts are borne as part of each Dutch mason's lodge dues, which by English standards are quite hefty. No speeches of any kind are usually associated with these dinners.

The procedures for entering a Dutch lodge vary somewhat from English-type practices. In many Dutch lodges, the Master and Wardens remain in the lodge ante-room ('Voorhof', in Dutch), while all other members enter the lodge room. Only then will the Master and Wardens enter to open the lodge. However, in some Dutch lodges the reverse procedure applies, whereupon the Master and Wardens enter the lodge, and when ready summon the remainder inside. When the former approach is used it is not uncommon for visitors, as honoured guests, to enter with the Master. Of course, all necessary avouchment procedures must first have been completed with respect to any unknown visitor.

All who enter a Dutch lodge hold the Sign of the Faithful (indentical to the English Sign of Fidelity), and communicate the password of the degree concerned as they enter. Visitors should make appropriate enquiries in this regard, subsequent to avouchment. It must be noted that Dutch lodges open and close in whatever degree is to be worked on any particular occasion. Thus, to the Dutch, there is no such thing as calling the lodge up or down from one degree to another. The normal business of the lodge is not conducted in the Temple but rather at a separate meeting, equivalent to the standing committee of English-type lodges. It is extremely rare for a visitor to called upon to speak during any Dutch 'Temple meeting'.

The regalia used in Dutch lodges is very similar to that generally adopted on the Continent, and somewhat similar to American regalia. Dutch aprons are plain white, with a triangular flap—which closely resembles the English Entered Apprentice Apron. The same apron is used in each of the three degrees, with it being arranged in certain different ways to distinguish the degree being worked. However, visitors are welcome to wear the regalia of their own jurisdiction appropriate to their rank.

Dutch ritual is somewhat unusual in terms of wider Continental masonry. To begin with, unlike most other European obediences, it is uniform for all Dutch lodges, as prescribed by the Grand East. In addition, Dutch ritual is largely 'clean' of the contental innovations found elsewhere in Europe. Nonetheless, it must be remembered that Dutch practice stems from eighteenth-century English ritual, not from the post 1813 Union English rituals in use in English masonry today. Indeed, Dutch ritual is more comparable with the German *Schroeder*-Type rituals rather than with *Emulation*.

The ceremonies of the three degrees in Dutch working are similar to continental practices in terms of their brevity, being far shorter than English-types. Some of the interesting features of Dutch ritual include: the similarity of the opening and closing of each degree; the Sacred Volume is always opened at the 1st Chapter of St John's Gospel; the 'Mason's Applause' is given at the end of the opening, and corresponds to a Masonic Fire in English-type practices; a candidate is only obligated in the first degree, and it is taken towards the end of the initiation, rather than near the beginning; a catechism for each degree must be learnt by every candidate.

Certain other aspects of Dutch masonry will be of interest to visitors. Certificates are issued for each degree completed with the lodge seal attached, and these are issued by the lodge itself. However, the Master Mason's Certificate is issued by the Grand East, and is countersigned by the lodge officers. Any Master mason may be elected to the Master's Chair in the Netherlands without ever having served in any other office, and there is no limit to the time he may occupy the chair. Indeed, many Dutch Masters serve for serveral years.

The layout of a Dutch temple largely follows old Operative-type lines, with both Wardens seated in the West. A typical Dutch lodge will feature an altar in the form of a double cube of white marble. Many temples feature walls and ceilings which are richly decorated with zodiacal signs and masonic symbols. An all-seeing eye often adorns the ceiling above the Master in the East, and the entire lodge floor is mosaic. Another common practice is for Dutch temples to have a concealed spot-light in the ceiling which illuminates the Sacred Volume on the altar, as appropriate.

The form of government employed in Dutch masonry is largely that of an appointive Grand Lodge with Masters and Wardens of all Dutch lodges being members of the Grand East, although some European characteristics are evident. Most Grand offices are appointive, of which the main ones are: the Grand Master, Deputy Grand Master, Grand Overseer, Grand Orator, Grand Treasurer, Grand Secretary, Grand Almoner, Grand Librarian, Assistant Grand Secretary, Grand Master of Ceremonies, Grand Examiner, and Grand Steward.

List of Lodges

Most Dutch cities and towns of any size possess lodges. Visitors are advised to make themselves known at the Grand Lodge office in The Hague if at all possible. However, as The Hague may well not be a visitor's initial or main destination in the Netherlands, listed below are lodges meeting in the four largest Dutch cities.

s'Gravenhage (The Hague)	All lodges meet at the Masonic Hall, Fluwelen Burgwal 22, s'Gravenhage, and most meetings commence at 8 pm.

Mondays—L'Union Frederic No 106; Het Zuiderkruis No 152; De Clammende Ster No 169; Het Westelijk Venster No 242.

Tuesdays—L'Union Royale No 1; De Oude Plichten No 136; De Ruwe Steen No 210; Het Schietlood No 215; Driehoek No 251.

Wednesdays—De Vriendschap No 35; Hiram Abiff No 68; Via Lucis No 161; De Broederketen No 199.

Thursdays—Groot Nederland No 118; Sint Jan No 178; Vincent La Chapelle No 180.

Amsterdam

Most Amsterdam lodges meet at the Masonic Hall, Vondelstraat 39–41, Amsterdam; and all meet at 8 pm.

Mondays—La Charite No 6.

Tuesdays—La Bien Aimee No 2; Nos Vinxit Libertas No 69.

Wednesdays—Wending, No 186; Post Nubila No 236.

Thursdays—La Paix No 4; Concordia Vincit Animos No 5.

Fridays—Willem Fredrik No 36; Eendracht No 107.

Rotterdam

All Rotterdam lodges meet at Delftsestraat 9, Rotterdam; and all meet at 8 pm.

Mondays—Concord No 134; Eensgezindheid No 150; De Drie Licten No 197.

Tuesdays—Frederic Royal No 8; Acacia No 56.

Wednesdays—Nil.

Thursdays—De Drie Kolommen No 13; De Eendragt No 233; Tamarisk No 248.

Utrecht

All lodges in Utrecht meet at the Masonic Hall, Lange Jufferstraat 4, Utrecht, at 8 pm; except one as noted.

Mondays—De Unie van Utrecht No 146 (Meets at Sweelincklaan 48, Bilthoven, Utrecht).

Tuesdays—De Stichtse Broederschap No 200.

Wednesdays—Hermannus Van Torgeren No 204.

Thursdays—Nil.

Fridays—Ultrajectina No 42.

POLAND

The first lodge erected in Poland was The Three Brothers lodge, of unknown origin. Other lodges followed, despite some early religious repression, culminating in the constituting of the Grand Lodge of Poland in 1769. Its founding lodges were largely of English origin. This Grand Lodge became extinct in 1772 with the first partitioning of Poland. In 1784, a new National Grand Orient of Poland was established, with twelve constituent lodges of German and French origin. Poland was again partitioned in 1794, and most lodges were dissolved. Poland again gained independence in the Napoleonic era, and another Grand Orient was erected under French influence in 1810. The defeat of Napoleon saw the Russians take over Poland, and the Grand Orient was closed by degree of the Czar in 1821. This situation remained unchanged until Polish independence in 1918, whereupon several lodges were formed under the Grand Orient of Italy. In 1921, these lodges established a National Grand

Lodge. This Grand body remained intact, although without much in the way of foreign fraternal recognition, until 1938 when it was outlawed by the Polish government. The Second World War quickly followed, and the subsequent advent of communism in Poland has prevented any further masonic activity.

PORTUGAL

The first warrant issued for a lodge in Portugal came in 1735, from England. The Papal Bull (1738) was heeded in Portugal, and the Craft had to develope on an underground basis until about 1807. The Grand Orient of Lusitania was nonetheless erected in 1804. In 1807, the French captured Lisbon and masonry was able to come out into the open, although it was subjected to the influence of the Grand Orient of France. By 1824, the Portugese monarchy was firmly back in control, and freemasonry was again strenuously suppressed. However, the Craft managed to survive, and a Grand Orient of Portugal, together with several other rival Grand Bodies, were soon to spring up—all working the French rite. The Grand Lodge of Ireland also had chartered four lodges by 1844. Several schisms and unions occurred within the body of Portuguese masonry over succeeding years, all of which did little for the harmony of the Portuguese Craft, or endear it to government authorities.

By 1869, the United Grand Orient of Portugal had emerged as the dominant Grand body, reporting about forty-eight lodges at this time. The Irish lodges joined it in 1872. By 1885, it had grown to possess over seventy lodges, not a small number of which were located in overseas colonies. In 1926, a right wing dictatorship assumed control in Portugal, and the craft was suppressed, to be finally dissolved by the governing regime in 1935.

The Grand Orient was revived in 1978, upon the restoration of Portugal to a democracy. It currently remains small, possessing about 250 members. Regrettably, the Grand Orient has chosen to align itself with the Grand Orients of France and Belgium, and so remains irregular. No regular masonry currently exists in Portugal.

RUMANIA

Rumania gained its first lodge in 1856, when the Grand Orient of France warranted Star of the Danube Lodge at Bucharest. Other lodges followed with charters from Italy, Germany, and Hungary. The Craft in Rumania appears to have not suffered the repression of elsewhere in Europe. In 1880, a National Grand Lodge of Rumania was formed by twenty lodges then under the Grand Orient of France, and other Grand bodies. However, Rumanian masonry did suffer the excesses of the 'Higher Degrees'. A period of degeneration followed, and by 1905 only one lodge was still working, with the Grand Lodge extinct by 1913.

The First World War served to prevent any early masonic recovery, but by 1926, a Grand Orient of Rumania was established by seven lodges then under the Grand Lodge of New York. It was joined by four lodges which had revived under the Grand Orient of France. A spurious Scottish Rite Supreme Council also existed about this time. By 1937, masonry in Rumania was repressed, and it certainly did not survive the Second World War to any extent. The Grand Orient was re-activated late in 1944, only to be closed by the communists in 1948.

RUSSIA

It would appear that the first lodge in Russia operated at St Petersburg (now Leningrad) about 1732. An English lodge, Perfect Unity No 414, was erected at St Petersburg in 1771, and four other lodges quickly followed. By 1775, a National Grand Lodge was formed with a reputed 18 lodges, and it abandoned the English system to work the Swedish Rite. Regrettably, Russian masonry appears to have degenerated into political intrigue. Government pressure began in 1782, and by 1794 all lodges were forced to close. The Craft was allowed to revive under the Liberal Czar Alexander I, who ascended the throne in 1801. However, by 1820 he had been persuaded that masonry was a danger to the State, and all lodges were again closed. Thereafter, the Russian Craft existed in limbo. There are stories of continuing masonic activity up until the Bolshevik Revolution, which the Craft most certainly did not survive.

SARDINIA

Sardinia is a large Mediterranean Island located to the south of Corsica, and it is an Italian possession. Quite naturally, all regular masonry in Sardinia stems from the Grand Orient of Italy. Indeed, the Grand Orieht has been quite active on the Island, and is now represented there in some strength. The addresses of the four current meeting places in Sardinia are as follows:

Cagliari: six Lodges, all meeting at Piazza Carmine 22, Cagliari.
Carbonia: two Lodges, all meeting at Via Gramsci 8, Carbonia.
Nuroro: one Lodge, meeting at Via Veneto 27 (Mura), Nuoro.
Sassari: one Lodge, meeting at Viale Umberto 110, Piano 4, Sassari.

SPAIN

Freemasonry came to Spain from England about the 1730s. Just what lodges were first erected remains obscure, but it seems that at least two were working in Madrid in the early 1750s. King Philip V of Spain supported the anti-masonic Papal Bull of 1738, and turned the Spanish Inquisition against the Craft. Under the greatest of difficulties, Spanish masonry continued, and in 1767 a Grand Lodge (later Grand Orient) was formed. The coming of the Napoleonic Era saw Spain briefly come under French control, and a National Grand Orient was set up in 1809 under the auspices of the Grand Orient of France. A Scottish Rite Supreme Council appears to have also been erected about this time, and by 1820, the original Grand Orient was under Scottish Rite control.

The suppression of masonry continued unabated, with the harshest measures employed against masons, including capital punishment. Finally, the death of Ferdinand VII in 1853 saw these persecutions cease, as the following Civil War saw the Catholic Church lose much of its influence. However, the Craft soon became its own worst enemy in Spain. By 1874, there were at least four Grand Orients in the country, with others being established in 1881 and 1889. In 1922, the old Grand Orient dissolved into no less that seven separate Grand Bodies. The Spanish Craft was in a most dis-united state and in no position to resist the right wing dictatorships that developed in the 1920s. Freemasonry was ruthlessly repressed under General

Franco, and it is reputed that since the Second World War over 10,000 Spaniards have been arrested for supposed masonic membership. The Grand Orient of Spain went into exile in Mexico.

The death of Franco and the restoration of democracy enabled the Grand Orient to reform in Madrid in 1978, as the United Grand Lodge Orient of Spain. Evidently, this body is a fusion of the Craft and the Scottish Rite. In the meantime, the regular French National Grand Lodge (GLNF) commenced chartering lodges in Spain. The Grand Orient allied itself with the equally irregular Grand Orient of France, and subsequently, a large proportion of its members 'defected' to the regular French-warranted lodges. On 6 November, 1982, the GLNF constituted the regular Grand Lodge of Antient, Free and Accepted Masons of Spain, in Madrid.

All twelve civilian GLNF lodges then in Spain transferred to the new Grand Lodge. Of these lodges, four work in Barcelona, and three in Madrid. It appears that about another eight lodges have since been established. All lodges work in Spanish, save one which operates in German using the *Schroeder* Ritual. Other rituals used are *Emulation*, the Scottish Rite Craft Degrees, and the rectified Scottish Rite Craft Degrees. Five military lodges previously warranted by the GLNF remained under that allegiance. All five meet at military bases in Spain, and are largely composed of American masons using Webb-form ritual. Most of the Grand Lodges of Europe, and many in North America, have extended recognition to the new Grand Lodge of Spain, and the list of those extending recognition continually grows. At the time of writing, the United Grand Lodge of England had not followed suit, but doubtlessly this will be effected in due course. Intending masonic visitors to Spain should enquire from their own Grand Lodge office whether, or not, the Grand Lodge of Spain has been recognised. If this is the case, the address of the Spanish Grand Lodge Office will be readily available.

SWITZERLAND

This picturesque European country has had a somewhat confused masonic history, but nonetheless possesses a regular Grand Lodge, dating from 1844.

The Grand Lodge Alpina of Switzerland
Founded: 1844
Address: The Grand Chancellory, Rue du Petit-Beaulieu 1, Lausanne Ch-1004, Switzerland. *Telephone:* (021) 383 070.
Lodges: 58. Permits Dual Membership. *Membership:* 3,642.
Descent: England and France. *Government:* Modified Grand Orient.
Courtesy Degrees: Rarely conferred. Correspondence must be through Grand Lodges.
Ritual: Mainly Scottish (Craft) Rite, and Schroeder.
Minimum Time Lapse between Degrees: Generally 12 months. *Main Publications:* Constitutions. Proceedings. Periodical: *Alpina*.

History
The first lodge in Switzerland was erected by English masons at Geneva in 1736. Several further English lodges appeared in various parts of the country, but the mortality rate was high. This was in no small way due to official opposition, with lodges in Geneva being suppressed in 1738. However, by the 1760s the climate had

become more favourable, and nine lodges met in Geneva in 1769 to form the Independent Grand Lodge of Geneva, working an English ritual in English. Soon thereafter, French and German 'Higher Degrees' entered the country; and a resultant Grand Orient was formed at Geneva by eight lodges. By 1822, there were four different Grand Lodges working in Switzerland, each with various 'Higher Degree' systems. The two main bodies were a Grand Orient, and a National Grand Lodge largely composed of former English lodges.

A sustained effort was made to unite Swiss masonry, beginning in 1822, when the then English Provincial Grand Lodge and a Grand Lodge at Lausanne merged to form the National Grand Lodge of Switzerland. However, after repeated attempts, it was not until 1844 that a greater union was effected, with the formation of the Grand Lodge Alpina of Switzerland. This new Grand Lodge adopted constitutions similar to those of England, but with some Grand Orient type forms. A Scottish Rite Supreme Council was erected in 1876, separate from, but in amity with, the Grand Lodge.

Swiss masonry thereafter has enjoyed a relatively tranquil and prosperous existence, although there have been three noteworthy hiccups. The first of these occurred in the late 1920s when questions concerning the use of the Sacred Volume were raised, but the Grand Lodge fortunately remained firm in its regularity.

The second testing time for the Swiss Craft occurred shortly thereafter in the 1930s with the rise of anti-masonic feeling, stemming largely from Germany. A large petition presented to the Government forced a referendum calling for freemasonry to be banned, but it was defeated in the popular vote. This is the only occasion in masonic history where masonry has been the subject of a plebisite.

The third hiccup occurred in 1966, with England taking a dim view of the fact that the Swiss Grand Lodge had recognised the irregular Grand Orient of France. Pressure from the three British Grand Lodges persuaded 'Alpina' of its folly, and a breach between British and Swiss masonry was avoided. Regrettably, a similar occurrence manifested itself in 1971, and on this occasion England did temporarily withdraw recognition. However, relations were fully restored in the following year when 'Alpina' barred irregular French Masons from attending its lodges. Swiss masonry has happily followed a regular path since, although these former tensions appear to have resulted in the regular French Grand Lodge (The Grande Loge Nationale Française) and the Swiss body not maintaining fraternal relations, and this situation remained unchanged in 1983.

Notes for Visitors to Switzerland

The first point to note about Switzerland itself is that it is a country of several languages. In the western areas around Geneva, French is the predominate language; in the north, German; and in the south the main language is Italian. Not surprisingly therefore, each of these languages is well represented in Swiss masonry. Similarly, Swiss ritual is not uniform. French-speaking lodges largely prefer the Scottish Rite Craft Degrees, while German-speaking lodges mostly practice the *Schroeder* Ritual. There are two English-speaking lodges in Switzerland, one at Geneva and one at Zurich. There is even a lodge at Berne (Bon Accord No 41) which works the *Emulation* ritual in German.

Dress for Swiss lodges is a dark, or black, business suit; and visitors are welcome to wear their own regalia. Visitors will notice that most Swiss lodges use the plain white aprons common in many other European obediences. The majority of Swiss lodges meet at 8 pm, although there are some that meet as late as 8.30 pm. An informal dinner accompanies a few Swiss lodge meetings. Some lodges dine afterwards—particularly those following English-type practices. Visitors will never be asked to contribute to any repast of which they may partake.

As is common European practice, the majority of Swiss lodges meet weekly, except in the summer months of June, July and August. Generally, only one degree conferment is held per month, with other meetings taken up with lectures. Again, the progression from one degree to the next is slow, and it may take a Swiss mason up to five years to achieve the Master Mason degree. The general continental practices discussed in this guide as obtaining to European obediences are largely applicable to Swiss masonry.

List of Lodges

While a visit to the Grand Chancellor's Office in Lausanne is recommended, this town may not prove to be a visitor's main destination. Therefore, listed below are details of Swiss lodges meeting in the main cities and towns. The language used in each lodge is noted.

Basel

All Basel lodges meet at the Masonic Temple, Byfangweg 13, 4051 Basel. *Telephone:* 239 293. All meet at 8.15 pm, unless otherwise stated. All work in German.

Mondays—Panta Rhei No 47 Meets at 8 pm.
Tuesdays—Zur Freundschaft und Bestandigkeit No 4.
Wednesdays—Zum Fels am Rhein No 5.
Thursdays—Osiris No 6.

Berne

The two Berne lodges meet at the Masonic Temple, Brunngasse 30, Berne 3011. Both work in German. *Telephone:* 220 474.

Wednesdays—Zur Hoffnung No 7 (at 8.15 pm).
4th Fridays—Bon Accord No 41 (at 7.30 pm).

Geneva:

All Geneva lodges meet at the Masonic Temple, Rue de la Scie 4 & 6, Geneva denoted (a) below, telephone: (022) 292 203; or at the Masonic Temple, 3 Rue Massot Denoted (b) below. With the exception of Masonry Universal Lodge No 40 which works in English, Geneva lodges work in French.

Mondays—Perseverance No 17 meets (a), 8.15 pm; Masonry Universal No 40 meets (b), 7 pm.
Tuesdays—Cordialite et Verite No 15 meets (a), 8.30 pm.
Wednesdays—Union des Coeurs No 18 meets (a), 8.30 pm.
Wednesdays—Union des Coeurs No 18 meets (b), 6.45 pm; Union et Travail, No 19 meets (a), 8.30 pm.
Thursdays—Fidelite et Prudence No 16 meets (a), 8.30 pm; Tolerance et Fraternite, No 46 meets (b), 8.15 pm.
Fridays—Les Amis Fideles No 14 meets (a), 8.15 pm.

Lausanne
All Lausanne lodges meet at the Masonic Temple, 17 Avenue de Beaulieu, Lausanne. *Telephone:* (021) 375 484. All lodges work in French.
Mondays—Liberte No 21 (at 8.30 pm).
Tuesdays—Le Progres No 22 (at 8.30 pm).
Wednesdays—Esperance and Cordialite No 20 (at 8.30 pm).
Thursdays—Tradition No 51 (1st and 3rd Thursdays at 8.15 pm).

Lugano
Il Dovere No 24. Meets Wednesdays, at Via Pretorio 20, Lugano. (8.30 pm, in Italian).

Lucerne
Fiat Lux No 25. Meets Wednesdays, at Murbacherstrasse 15, Lucerne. (8.15 pm, in French).

Zurich
All Zurich lodges meet at the Masonic Temple, Lindenhof 4, Zurich 8001. All lodges meet at 8 pm, and work in German; except Cosmopolitan Lodge, which works in English and meets at 7.30 pm.
Mondays—In Labore Virtus No 36.
Tuesdays—Nil.
Wednesdays—Catena Humanitas No 44.
Thursdays—Libertas et Fraternitas No 37; Cosmopolitan No 43.
Fridays—Sapere Aude No 39.
Saturdays—Modestia cum Libertate No 38.

TURKEY

Turkey possesses a regular Grand Lodge which was recognised by England in 1970, although it dates from 1909.

The Grand Lodge of Free and Accepted Masons of Turkey
Founded: 1909
Address: Masonic Hall, Nur Ziya Sokak 25, Beyoglu, Istanbul. *Telephone:* 492 451.
Lodges: 65. Permits Dual and Plural Membership. *Membership:* 4,766.
Descent: France, England, Scotland, & others. *Government:* Modified Grand Orient.
Courtesy Degrees: Correspondence must be through Grand Lodges.
Ritual: French Rite, & others.
Minimum Time Lapse between Degrees: 7 months (1st to 2nd Degree), 5 months (2nd to 3rd).
Publications: Constitutions. Proceedings. Year Book.

History
There is documented reference to the existence of lodges in Turkey in 1738. These lodges appear to have emanated from various European sources. There is also evidence of a Scottish lodge being formed at Aleppo about 1748. A Supreme Council of the Ottoman Empire was erected in 1861, probably under auspices of the Grand

Orient of France. It was extinct by 1871. However, the expansion of the Craft came slowly. Various Ottoman Sultans issued edicts suppressing freemasonry. This repression became particularly harsh during the reign of the Sultan Abdulhamid II (1876-1909). Many Turkish masons were forced to flee the country.

However, this repression did not appear to extend to lodges warranted from foreign countries. An English lodge (Oriental No 988) was formed in Turkey in 1856, and another ten English lodges were established between 1860 and 1870. Ireland, Scotland, and the Grand Orients of Italy and France also had lodges in Turkey in this period. Most English-speaking lodges had expired by the First World War, although a few held on until 1938.

Upon the coming of constitutional government to Turkey, Turkish masonry was revived in 1909, in the form of a resurrected Scottish Rite Supreme Council warranted from Egypt. The Supreme Council sponsored the National Grand Orient of Turkey, constituted by 14 lodges then holding either French, Italian or Spanish charters. It modelled its constitution on that of the Grand Orient of France. The Grand Orient enjoyed a period of sustained expansion, erecting 65 lodges up until 1935. However, the political climate in Turkey had been deteriorating, and the Grand Orient became dormant in 1935. The Turkish Supreme Council revived in 1948, and controlled Turkish Craft lodges until it divested control to The Grand Lodge of Turkey, founded in 1956 on a regular basis. The Turkish Grand Lodge was recognised by England in 1970, and today enjoys fraternal relations with most regular Grand Lodges around the world.

Notes for Visitors to Turkey
The Grand Lodge of Turkey is quite a strong masonic body. Of its current 64 lodges, all but two work in its three largest cities. 34 lodges meet at Instanbul, 19 at Ankara (the capital city), and nine at Izmir. While most lodges, quite naturally, work in Turkish, there are a few which operate with foreign languages and rituals. Lodge Dikmen No 22 (at Ankara), Lodge Freedom No 35 (at Instanbul), and Lodge Ephesus No 42 (at Izmir) all work in English and cater largely for NATO Servicemen stationed in the country. In addition, each of the three main cities possesses at least one French-speaking lodge, while two Greek-speaking lodges, and one German-speaking lodge meet in Instanbul. Turkey also has one Lodge of Research (Mima Sinan No 43) working in Istanbul.

Turkish-speaking lodges use a French Rite-type ritual for the three Craft degrees, and largely follow typical continental practices. They require such things as a long time lapse between degrees, compulsory attendance, candidates presenting lectures and written assignments prior to progression, and operative-style lodge layouts.

Dress for Turkish lodges is a dark suit, and working regalia will be supplied to visitors without their own. Most lodges meet weekly at about 8 pm, although some meet on a fortnightly basis. Lodges largely recess in June, July and August. It is recommended that visitors in the first instance call at the Grand Lodge office at the Masonic Hall in Istanbul, where ready assistance will be obtained.

YUGOSLAVIA

As with Austria and Hungary, Yugoslavia (then called Bosnia) was part of the Austro-Hungarian Empire in the last century. Several lodges existed in Bosnia, tenuously, prior to World War One. After that war Yugoslavia largely gained independence, and a Grand Lodge was erected in 1919 by six lodges then variously under the Grand Lodges of Hungary, Hamburg, and the Grand Orient of Italy. Nazi occupation saw the speedy demise of the infant Grand Lodge, but it appears to have recovered on a clandestine basis since the war. Yugoslavian communism has proved less repressive than versions elsewhere, and this may account for the limited masonic activity. It also appears that an irregular Grand Lodge still exists, about which little is known.

Section VII

Visiting in
The Middle East

Middle East

An Overview
The first lodge erected in the Middle East was established by Scotland at Aden in 1850. This appears to have been followed by a lodge in Palestine about 1873. However, most masonic development was spawned in this century, beginning with English lodges located in Iraq shortly after the First World War. Unfortunately, the lot of the Craft in the Middle East has not generally been a happy one. Only in Israel has masonry flourished, with that country possessing a regular Grand Lodge.

Outside of Israel very few lodges remain, with the oldest survivor being a Scottish lodge in Jordan, dating from 1925. British-warranted lodges that formerly existed in Iraq, South Yemen (Aden), and elsewhere on the Arabian Penninsula have all been extinguished as the result of political pressure. A few German-warranted lodges work in Arabia, having been set up in only very recent years. However, their longer term future must be uncertain. In Iran, which has lately had a regular Grand Lodge, freemasonry has been destroyed, almost literally, and this occurrence must rate as one of the greatest tragedies in masonic history. In short, in view of the turbulent political and religious situation in the Arab world, it would appear most unlikely that the Craft will expand in the Middle East in the foreseeable future. Having gained a general view of the masonic situation in the Middle East, a more detailed examination of what the visitor will likely experience can now be undertaken.

BAHRAIN

This oil rich Arab State on the Persian Gulf has until very recently possessed an English lodge. This was Lodge St George Bahrain No 7389, founded in 1954. It consisted largely of British who had come to work in the oil fields. However, the Bahrain Government would appear to have not been benignly disposed towards the Craft, and this lodge ceased operation in that country. It has now moved to Ashford, England, where it continues to meet.

IRAN (PERSIA)

The fate of the Craft in Iran forms the greatest masonic catastrophe since the Second World War. The discovery of oil in Persia brought in many British workers and traders, a percentage of whom where masons. Scotland was the most active in issuing warrants, and it began with Lodge Light in Iran No 1191, at Shiraz in 1919, although this lodge later moved to Teheran. Three other Scottish lodges followed prior to World War Two. England weighed in with St George Abadan Lodge No 6058, at Abadan in 1945. This lodge later moved back to England, where it still works happily at Rochester. Regular French (GLNF) and German lodges were also erected in the country after the War.

Subsequently, the growth of the Craft in Iran led to moves to form a Grand Lodge, and this was achieved with Scottish sponsorship in 1969. As at 1978, the Grand Lodge of Iran possessed forty three lodges, and 1,035 members. This year was the last time that the Craft in Iran was heard of in the outside masonic world.

The Islamic Revolution in Iran saw freemasonry swept away rapidly, and it would appear that a number of masons suffered execution at its hands. Whether these deaths were occasioned for political or anti-masonic reasons will probably never be known, and the fate of many Iranian masons may equally remain a mystery. One thing is certain, the Craft in Iran is destroyed. One can only hope that at some time in the future it will rise again.

IRAQ

Iraq's first lodge was establihsed in 1919. This was Baghdad Lodge No 4022, warranted from England. By the 1950s, Iraq possessed nine lodges under an English District Grand Lodge. A Scottish lodge, Lodge Faiha No 1311, was erected at Basrah in 1923. However, the coming of Iraqi independence, and the subsequent left wing government attained by this country, have made the continuance of masonry impossible. All lodges in the country were forced to close their doors, and it would appear unlikely that they will be re-opened.

ISRAEL

The Jewish State of Israel has possessed a regular Grand Lodge since 1953. Here, in the land of the legendary birthplace of freemasonry, the Craft has flourished, particularly since the Second World War.

The Grand Lodge of the State of Israel
Founded: 1953
Address: P.O. Box 33206, Tel Aviv, Israel.
Principal Temple: Masonic Temple, 5 Weizman Street, Tel Aviv.   *Telephone:* (03) 251805.
Lodges: 59.   Permits Dual and Plural Membership.   *Membership:* 3000.
Descent: Largely Scottish.   *Government:* Elective Grand Lodge.
Courtesy Degrees: Correspondence must be through Grand Lodges.
Minimum Time Lapse between Degrees: One month.
Main Publications: Constitution.   Annual Proceedings.

History

There can be no doubt that operative masons worked in the Holy Land in ancient times and, of course, the circumstances surrounding the erection of Solomon's Temple at Jerusalem forms the basis of most masonic Craft ritual. However, masonry of the speculative kind arrived in Israel some time later. The first symbolic lodge was formed at Jerusalem about 1873, where it met until it expired in 1903. This was the Royal Solomon Mother Lodge, which was established by Canadian archaeological engineers under a charter from Canada. One of the greatest legacies left by this lodge was its admission of many residents of Palestine. Subsequently, several lodges were established in the Holy Land by the then regular National Grand Lodge of Egypt, which in turn formed themselves into the National Grand Lodge of Palestine in 1933.

In the years between 1930 and 1940, the United Grand Lodge of England warranted three lodges in the area, and Scotland chartered eleven in the same period. In addition, five German lodges were established in the 1930s by German masons who had fled the Nazi tyranny.

In 1948, the British mandate over Palestine ended and all English lodges withdrew from the Holy Land. A general desire for administrative and fraternal unity among lodges in what was now the State of Israel was felt at this time. In 1953, the Grand Lodge of the State of Israel came into being largely under Scottish sponsorship. Its thirty-one founding lodges consisted of all those in Israel holding Scottish charters, those under the National Grand Lodge of Palestine, and the five German lodges. Rarely in the formation of a new Grand Body has such unanimity of purpose been seen as it was in Israel. The Grand Lodge has since expanded steadily, and in 1983 it reported 61 lodges with a membership of three thousand.

Notes for Visitors to Israel

1. MEETING TIMES, AND DRESS
The large majority of lodges in Israel meet at or about 6 pm. However in the past the Government of Israel has on occasions found it necessary to impose curfews. Where this has occurred, lodges moved to meet in the mid-afternoon to enable members to be home by nightfall. The dress for Israeli lodges is a dark lounge suit, white shirt, and black tie. Visitors are welcome to bring and wear their own regalia.

2. LODGE AFTERPROCEEDINGS
The afterproceedings of Israeli lodges stem largely from Scottish practices. The proceedings following ordinary meetings consist of a light meal, and visitors are never required to contribute its costs. Limited toasts and responses are honoured; and these those proposed to the President and State of Israel, the Grand Master and Grand Lodge, and the Visitors. On nights of Installation, a formal dinner and more extensive Toast List is the norm. In addition, it is not uncommon for the ladies of members and visitors to attend an Installation dinner.

A custom in some lodges is for the visitor who resides the furthest away to respond to the Visitors' Toast. A charity collection is often associated with lodge afterproceedings in Israel.

3. OF VISITING IN GENERAL
The masonic visitor will find that attending a lodge in Israel is a most interesting and stimulating experience. The masons of Israel come from many religious faiths, and work together in complete harmony—an experience which is unfortunately not widely enjoyed elsewhere in this often troubled area of the world.

Israeli lodges work variously in Hebrew, Arabic, German, French, English, Rumanian and Spanish. It is, therefore, quite usual to see at least three Sacred Volumes open in Israeli lodges—the Old Testament of Hebrews, the New Testament Bible of the Christians, and the Koran of the Muslims. Quite a number of lodges work in more than one language, but usually only one at any single meeting. For example, at one meeting a particular lodge might work in Hebrew, whereas at its next meeting it might work in English. Therefore, a visitor to Israel is well advised to enquire just what language the lodge he seeks to visit will be working in when he attends it. Nevertheless, regardless of the lodge visited, a visitor will generally find at least several members present who can speak his own language. Certainly, an English-speaking visitor will not experience any difficulty in this regard.

4. INTERESTING ASPECTS OF MASONRY IN ISRAEL
The seal of the Grand Lodge of Israel is of particular interest. It is unique in

design and includes the square and compasses, together with the emblems of the three great faiths to which the great majority of members belong—the Star of David of the Jews, the Crescent of the Muslims, and the Cross of the Christians.

In some Arabic-speaking lodges, an old Arab custom is observed after toasts, whereby all present drain their glasses and turn them upside down on the table. Alcohol is available at the afterproceedings of many lodges.

In some Arabic-speaking lodges, an old Arab custom is observed after toasts, whereby all present drain their glasses and turn them upside down on the table. Alcohol is available at the afterproceedings of many lodges.

The Grand Lodge meets annually, towards the end of June each year. All offices are elective, although the Grand Master to be eligible for election must first have served at least one year as Deputy Grand Master. In practice, it is usual for the recommendations of the Grand Committee to be accepted for the offices of Junior Grand Warden, and above. The Constitution of the Grand Lodge is based largely on that of Scotland. It is not unusual for a Grand Master to be re-elected to serve a second, or sometimes a third, consecutive year of office. Interestingly, in 1981, a Christian Arab was elected Grand Master, which is somewhat indicative of the harmony that prevails throughout masonry in Israel.

The Grand Lodge of Israel involves itself in some excellent charitable works. Its Fund of Benevolence operates an aged people's home, and awards various scholarships to students.

5. LODGE WORKINGS, REGALIA, AND RITUAL

The ritual employed by Israeli lodges is nominally uniform as laid down by the Grand Lodge, and follows, quite closely, Scottish Ritual. However, there is still to be found in some older lodges traces of rituals and customs of other constitutions, which reflect of origins of their members.

The regalia worn by Israeli masons, both at Grand Lodge and lodge level, is again fairly similar to that of Scotland. Nevertheless, some of the founder lodges still use regalia incorporating the design and colours used by them during their existance prior to the erection of the Grand Lodge.

6. THE SPECIAL INTEREST OF JERUSALEM

There is absolutely no doubt that the ancient and Holy City of Jerusalem possesses much of interest to the pilgrim and tourist alike. In addition, for the freemason, it has delights which only he can fully appreciate. Near the centre of the old city is Temple Mount, the site of the Temples of Solomon, Zerubbabel, and Herod. Of the old Temples, only the foundations remain, but to the mason it is an inspiring sight, as are many other features of the ancient city. Chief among these is King Solomon's Quarries, or the Caves of Hezekiah. They are located close to the Damascus Gate, under the walls of the Old City. In the depths of the caves is a large chamber which can seat up to two hundred. In this chamber, masonic ceremonies are intermittently held, although since the re-unification of the City of Jerusalem in 1967, only the degree of Mark Master Mason has been worked. The Chamber floor is covered in rubble indicating its ancient use as a stone quarry, and it is located about one hundred and thirty feet underground almost below Temple Mount—a fact that will hold special significance to holders of the Holy Royal Arch Degree. The Caves of Hezekiah are generally open to the public, but by special arrangement with the city government they are closed on days of masonic meetings.

List of Lodges

The fairly large number of Israeli lodges prevents a full detailed list from being included here. However, the large majority of lodges in Israel meet at its three main cities—Haifa, Jerusalem, and Tel Aviv. Prior to visiting a lodge in Israel it is an appreciated courtesy for a visitor to call at the Freemasons' Hall in Tel Aviv, where full assistance and a very warm welcome will be obtained. Identical assistance can be obtained in Jerusalem or Haifa. The addresses of the three pertinent temples are as follows:

Masonic Temple, 5 Weizman Street, Tel Aviv.
Masonic Temple, 13 Esrath-Israel Street, Jerusalem.
Masonic Temple, 119 Hanassi Street, Haifa.

The bulk of Israeli lodges meet twice per month, for nine months of the year—recessing in the three hot summer months. Of these lodges, some are of special interest. Elijah the Prophet Lodge No 16, at Haifa, has a long standing tradition of working in both Hebrew and Arabic at every ceremony it conducts. The Bnei Or Lodge (Sons of Light) No 66, is a military lodge. It consists of men serving in the Israeli Defence Forces, and has a travelling warrant enabling it to meet anywhere in Israel. Members attending this lodge invariably dress in their military uniforms. The Alumin (Youth) Lodge No 58, located at Tel Aviv, requires that every candidate to come before it must be a Lewis. It is the usual practice for the father and grandfathers of a candidate to be invited to act as Deacons of the lodge during the appropriate initiation, even if they are not members of the lodge. Another interesting lodge is the Gazit Lodge No 30, meeting at Tel Aviv, which acts as a Lodge of Instruction.

JORDAN

Jordan, formerly the British protectorate of Trans-Jordan, is now an independent Monarchy. It would seem that Jordan, based on its present boundaries, has never possessed many lodges. The only remaining lodge is Lodge Jordan No 1339 SC. It was originally chartered by the Grand Lodge of Scotland in 1925 at Jaffa (Tel-Aviv), but it moved to Amman in 1935, where it has worked since. Lodge Jordan now has the unhappy distinction of being the only British-warranted lodge still working anywhere in the Middle East, and one of the very few left in this area outside Israel. Its details are as follows:

Lodge Jordan No 1339 SC   Meets at the Masonic Hall, Jabal Amman,
                                 Amman, Jordan; 1st and 3rd Mondays, monthly,
                                 except July, August and September.

KUWAIT

Another small Arab State bordering the Persian Gulf, oil-rich Kuwait had, until recently, two English lodges. These were Kuwait Lodge No 6810, and the Rowland Chadwick Lodge No 7472. The former was erected in 1949, the latter in 1956. Strong opposition from the Kuwait Government saw both these lodges become dormant, and sadly, neither re-appeared on the English Roll of Lodges in 1982.

LEBANON

Lebanon provides us with an unparallelled masonic history. It has been the Grand Lodge of Scotland, and somewhat amazingly, the Grand Lodge of New York, which have been responsible for the lodges located in this country of any regular nature. The first Scottish lodge was Lodge Palestine No 415, formed at Beirut in 1861. Four other Scottish lodges were erected in Lebanon up until the time of the First World War, but only some of these revived thereafter. The irregular Grand Orient of France also had lodges in Beirut in the 1860s, but they appear to have been devoid of longevity.

Until recent years, five Scottish lodges had survived in Lebanon, with a few others being less fortunate. Those surviving were: Lodge Peace No 908 (founded: 1900), at Beirut; Lodge Kadisha No 1002 (1906), at Beirut; Lodge Zahle No 1047 (1908), at Zahle; Lodge El Mazab No 1130 (1914), at Tripoli; and Mount Lebanon Lodge No 1312 (1923), at Beirut. The three lodges in Beirut met at the aptly named Peace Lodge Building, Beshara Street, Beirut. With the arrival of the Lebanese Civil War in 1974, the Scottish lodges found continuence impossible and all five became dormant, although they still appeared on the Scottish Roll of Lodges in 1984.

The first New York-chartered lodge was the Syrio-American Lodge No 1. Nine other lodges were added subsequently, allowing the Grand Lodge of New York to form its only District outside its geographical jurisdiction. With the exception of one lodge originally erected in Syria, all New York chartered lodges in its Syria-Lebanon District still appearred on the New York Roll of Lodges in 1983. However, given the very sad political and civil state existing currently in Lebanon, these lodges are dormant.

OMAN

As far as can be determined, no regular lodge has ever been erected in Oman.

SAUDI ARABIA

One would suspect that Saudi Arabia, being a very traditional Islamic Monarchy, would be devoid of masonic lodges. Indeed, that was the case until 1962, when the American Canadian Grand Lodge (within the United Grand Lodges of Germany) erected Arabian Lodge No 882. This was followed by Nejma Lodge No 897 (1966); Red Sea Lodge No 919; Milo Lodge No 938; and the Pyramid Lodge of Past Masters No 962 (1982). All these lodges cater for foreigners in the country, mainly North American and British masons in Saudi Arabia as a result of its oil. Most of these lodges are currently operating with the exception of Red Sea Lodge, which was in recess in 1981.

It is the policy of the American Canadian Grand Lodge not to publish the addresses of its lodges in Saudi Arabia, and no variance of that position will be undertaken here. Visitors intending to travel to Saudi Arabia are advised to correspond with the Grand Secretary, American Canadian Grand Lodge, Hermannstrasse 39, Frankfurt 6000, West Germany; from whom full details may be obtained. Such a letter must be sent via the inquirer's own Grand Lodge office.

SYRIA

The initial lodges erected in Syria, once part of the Turkish Ottoman Empire, were established in the 1860s by the Grand Orients of Italy and France. The French lodge, Lodge le Liban, in particular seems to have involved itself political activities. The Italian and French lodges had expired by the turn of the century.

Scotland chartered Lodge Light in Damascus No 1058, in 1909; and the Grand Lodge of New York had Ibrahim el Khalil Lodge No 4, at the same location under its Syria-Lebanon District. Subsequent to the Second World War and Syrian Independence, the political situation in the country forced all lodges to close, and there was no change in this situation in the 1980s.

UNITED ARAB EMIRATES

This oil-based Persian Gulf country is made up of several small Arab Emirates, which used to collectively be referred to as Trucial Oman. Its first and only lodge was erected by England at Sharjah, in 1967. This was Trucial Lodge No 8160, and it largely serviced masons who were British oil workers. However, this lodge has become dormant in recent years. It remains the only Persian Gulf lodge still on the English Roll in 1983, although one would suspect that its erasure to be fairly imminent.

YEMEN (NORTH)

North Yemen is an Arab country located almost in the south-west corner of the Arabian Penninsula, and it appears to have never possessed a regular lodge.

YEMEN (SOUTH)

South Yemen was formerly known simply as Aden, or more correctly, the British Protectorate of South Arabia. Aden had the honour of receiving the first charter for a lodge in the Middle East. This was granted by the Grand Lodge of Scotland in 1850 to Lodge Felix No 335. Lodge Centenary No 1449, was erected under the same authority in 1900. England stepped in with Lodge Light in Arabia No 3870, in 1918. This lodge now works at Croydon, England. The Independence of South Yemen brought it soon under the control of a totalitarian government, which made the conditions for freemasonry untenable. The two Scottish lodges were eventually erased.

Section VIII

Visiting in
North America

Canada

Canada possesses ten political divisions known as 'Provinces', with each having a Provincial Government similar to each of the United States of America. Of these Provinces, nine have regular Grand Lodges. Lodges in the tenth Province, Newfoundland, are still governed by the Grand Lodges of England and Scotland. The masonic scene in Canada can, in a broad sense, be described as an amalgam of American and British practices and customs. In some Canadian jurisdictions, both Webb-type and English-type rituals are used.

Historical Overview

The first settlers in Canada were the French. Quebec became a French colony in 1608, and remained so until 1763, when all of Canada became a British possession. The geopolitical history of Canada is rather confused, but it is enough to say here that the several Provinces underwent various groupings, separations and regroupings. Canada became a Dominion in 1867, uniting Nova Scotia, New Brunswick, Quebec, and Ontario. Other Provinces later joined. The first lodges in Canada emerged about 1740 in Nova Scotia, and about 1750 in Quebec. Many of the earliest lodges were military. Warrants came from both the United States and Britain. In 1858, a Grand Lodge of Canada was formed in Ontario, claiming jurisdiction over the whole of Canada, which at that time comprised Ontario and Quebec. After Canadian independence, and the progressive formation of other Provinces, other Grand Lodges were erected accordingly. The original Grand Lodge became the 'Grand Lodge of Canada in the Province of Ontario'.

ALBERTA

The Grand Lodge of Alberta, Ancient, Free and Accepted Masons
Founded 1905
Address: Grand Lodge Office: 330 12th Avenue South West, Calgary, Alberta. T2R 0H2. *Telephone:* (403) 262 1149, or 262 1140.
Lodges: 162   Permits Dual Membership.   *Membership:* 14,350.
Descent: Manitoba   *Government:* Elective Grand Lodge.
Courtesy Degrees: Correspondence must be through Grand Lodges.
Minimum Time Lapse between Degrees: 28 days.
Ritual: Canadian (English-type), and *Ancient York* (Webb-type).
Main Publications: Constitution. Annual Proceedings. Periodical: *The Grand Lodge Bulletin.*

History

The first lodge formed in Alberta was Saskatchewan Lodge No 17, chartered by the Grand Lodge of Manitoba at Edmonton in 1882. It had expired by 1890. The oldest extant lodge in Alberta is Bow River Lodge, chartered as No 28, at Calgary in 1884, by Manitoba. This was followed shortly afterwards by Medicine Hat Lodge No 31, at Medicine Hat. Sixteen lodges met together in a Convention of Delegates in 1905, and established the Grand Lodge of Alberta. The Province of Alberta had been created in that year, being formed by splitting off the Alberta territory from Manitoba.

Notes for Visitors

Alberta lodges are permitted to work either of two Craft rituals approved by the Grand Lodge. These are the *Canadian* ritual, and the *Ancient York* ritual. The former is English-type derived subsequent to the English Union of 1813, while the latter is an American Webb-form ritual. As a result, meeting procedures vary between lodges. Lodges using the *Ancient York* ritual open in the Third Degree, as is usual Webb-form practice. Interestingly, the Alberta Constitution requires that all lodges conduct their regular business in the Third Degree. This has meant that lodges using the *Canadian* ritual must open in the first, second and third degrees for this purpose, regardless of which ceremony is to be conferred at any given meeting.

Dress for Alberta lodges varies from lodge to lodge. The minimum requirement is a dark business suit, but in many lodges officers will wear a dinner suit (tuxedo). Again, lodge afterproceedings vary depending on the ritual form employed. In lodges using the *Canadian* ritual, it is usual for a Toast List to be followed at a formal festive board following a meeting. Toasts will invariably include propositions to 'The Queen', 'The Grand Master and his Officers', and 'The Visitors'. At least one pre-warned visitor will be called upon to respond to a Visitor's Toast. Afterproceedings in this form tend to be composed of a substantial meal.

In lodges using the *Ancient York* ritual, the American practice of having a very light supper after a meeting is largely followed. Normally, no formal Toast List is used. Nonetheless, regardless of which ritual form is employed, most Alberta lodges tend to prefer a substantial repast and full Toast List following a Night of Installation. While members are sometimes called upon to contribute to the costs of any substantial meal provided in association with a lodge meeting, it is unusual for a visitor to be asked to pay.

All Alberta lodges meet regularly on a monthly basis, although most recess in the months of June, July and August. It is also fairly common for lodges to hold at least one 'Emergent Meeting' per month, particularly those lodges using the *Ancient York* working. Again, meeting times tend to vary between lodges, somewhat according to the ritual form used, but most convene about 7.30 pm. Unknown visitors should arrive early to complete the appropriate examination procedures, which will often include a 'Tyler's Oath'. Despite the fact that two divergent ritual forms are approved, it appears that both have influenced each other somewhat. For example, a procedure employed in both openings includes the 'Purging of the Lodge' to collect certain modes of recognition. In addition, the proficiency tests for candidates tend to be quite extensive, and compare more with American than English practices. It is also not unusual for a charity collection to be taken inside the lodge, often during the closing ceremonies. The regalia used in Alberta lodges is quite similar to that of England, rather than to that of the United States. Indeed, the regalia used by Grand Lodge officers, in particular, is largely indistinguishable from the English.

The Grand Lodge of Alberta is basically an Elective Grand Lodge on the American model, but nonetheless many of its Constitutional statutes compare strongly to those of England. Indeed, its two main administrative bodies are a Board of General Purposes, and a Board of Benevolence.

Alberta possesses two 'Masonic Tourist Attractions' which will be of interest to the visitor. In the Heritage Park in Calgary is a replica of an old Lodge Room (prior to 1914). A similar historical site has recently been erected in Edmonton, depicting a lodge from the earliest days of Alberta. Both attractions are open to the public.

List of Lodges
The fairly large number of Alberta lodges precludes the possibility of providing meeting details here. Alberta possesses two large cities, Calgary (the Grand Lodge seat, with 21 lodges), and Edmonton (with 25 lodges). The Address of the Grand Lodge Temple in Calgary is provided above. The main Masonic Temple in Edmonton is located at 10318, 100th Avenue, Edmonton. Visitors are directed to either of these two locations, where full details of lodge meetings in Alberta can readily be obtained. Outside of Calgary and Edmonton, there are few towns in Alberta that do not possess at least one lodge. A research lodge has also been recently formed in Alberta. This is the Fiat Lux Lodge of Research 1980. It meets at Calgary at irregular intervals. Finally, it is worth noting that of the 162 lodges currently comprising the Grand Lodge of Alberta, just over 100 work the *Canadian* ritual, while about 60 use the *Ancient York* working.

BRITISH COLUMBIA

The Grand Lodge of Antient, Free and Accepted Masons of British Columbia
Founded: 1871
Address: Freemason's Hall, 1495 West 8th Avenue, Vancouver V6H 1C9. *Telephone:* 736 8941.
Lodges: 173 Permits Dual and Plural Membership. *Membership:* 22,480.
Descent: England and Scotland. *Government:* Appointive Grand Lodge.
Courtesy Degrees: All correspondence must be through Grand Lodges.
Minimum Time Lapse between Degrees: 14 days.
Ritual: Emulation, Canadian, Ancient.
Main Publications: Constitution. Annual Proceedings. Periodical: *The Masonic Bulletin.*

History
Prior to 1858, British Columbia remained almost devoid of white settlement. In that year, gold was discovered in the area and its population suddenly boomed as a consequence. A number of lodges quickly followed, variously holding either English or Scottish warrants. By 1871, England had four lodges in British Columbia, and Scotland possessed five. District Grand Lodges had been formed for both. In that year, all English and Scottish lodges united to form the Grand Lodge of British Columbia.

Initially, the development of the new Grand Lodge was slow. The fluid population of the area as a result of its mining industry was the main cause. Nonetheless, time saw expanding permanent settlements develop, and British Columbian masonry established on a sound footing. Right from its foundation, the Grand Lodge permitted its constituent lodges to work any regular Craft ritual they wished, rather than possibly prejudice the union of English and Scottish lodges then effected. This policy has seen masonry in British Columbia employ a wider variety of ritual forms than any other North American Jurisdiction.

Notes for Visitors

As has just been premised, lodges in British Columbia are largely free to use any regular ritual they choose. The three main rituals in use are the English *Emulation* working, the *Ancient* ritual (basically a Webb-type ritual), and the *Canadian* ritual. The last named is an English-type ritual originally emanating from Ontario, although the *Canadian* working has a number of Scottish features. Other rituals in minor usage are the English *Oxford* ritual, the *Revised* English ritual, and the *Australian* ritual. The *Australian* ritual is actually the ritual used under the United Grand Lodge of New South Wales (Australia), which is itself an English-type ritual. Two lodges located at Vancouver (Southern Cross Lodge No 44, and Commonwealth Lodge No 156) use the *Australian* ritual, and both were originally formed by expatriates from that country.

The standard dress in British Columbian lodges is a dark business suit, although it is largely usual for Lodge Officers to wear a dinner suit (tuxedo). Afterproceedings tend to vary from lodge to lodge, but generally a very simple supper is served, although a full meal more commonly follows an Installation Meeting. A toast list will generally accompany any afterproceeds. Toasts commonly used include: 'The Queen', 'The Grand Master and Grand Lodge', 'The Visitors', and 'The Tyler's Toast'. Again, toast lists often are more expansive on nights of Installation. Visitors are asked to respond to the Visitors' Toast, and a visitor from outside British Columbia can usually consider himself unlucky if he does not get the visitor's response. Visitors will not be charged for any repast they attend following a lodge meeting. Alcohol is permitted to be served in association with afterproceedings in British Columbia, although under strict rules laid down by the Grand Lodge. Indeed, unlike common American practice in this area, the limited consumption of alcohol following lodge meetings is largely permitted under most Canadian Grand Lodges. A majority of lodges have a bar attached to their dining facilities, and the vast majority of lodges at least serve wine for Toasts, although there are a few temperance lodges. It is the policy of the Grand Lodge that lodge funds not be used to subsidise a bar, so generally each member and visitor will be responsible for his own purchases in this area.

The regalia used in British Columbia is quite similar to that employed in England, and visitors are certainly welcome to wear their own. Interestingly, despite its British origins, the Grand Lodge of British Columbia is basically an Elective Grand Lodge, with its constitution being somewhat closer in nature to those of America, rather than to that of England. It possesses the large range of Grand Lodge Committees common in American jurisdictions, and uses a 'Grand Lodge Line' system, by convention, for its highest Officers.

Lodges in British Columbia meet on a monthly basis, although most recess in July and August, and some in September. The vast majority of lodges open at 7.30 p.m. Every unknown visitor can expect a masonic examination, and so an early arrival is advised. Of the 173 lodges currently on the British Columbia roll of lodges, 50 meet in Vancouver. Of all lodges, about 85 use the *Canadian* working, about 75 the *Ancient* working, and about a dozen employ the *Emulation* ritual. Similar to usual American practice, the British Columbia jurisdiction is divided into masonic districts (currently 27), each under a District Deputy Grand Master.

List of Lodges
The Grand Lodge of British Columbia does not publish a directory of lodges, as is common to many English-speaking jurisdictions. However, a sheet entitled *The Trestle Board Directory* is regularly produced providing all meeting details for lodges in Vancouver and District. It is available at the Grand Lodge office within Free-masons' Hall, Vancouver. Indeed, this imposing building also houses a fine Grand Lodge library and museum which will be of interest to visitors. Visitors can readily gain the meeting details of all lodges in British Columbia at this address.

MANITOBA

The Grand Lodge of Manitoba, Ancient, Free and Accepted Masons
Founded: 1875
Address: Masonic Memorial Temple, 420 Corydon Avenue, Winnipeg, Manitoba.
Telephone: (204) 453 7410.
Lodges: 98   Permits Dual and Plural Membership.   *Membership:* 10,432.
Descent: Ontario.   *Government:* Elective Grand Lodge.
Courtesy Degrees: Correspondence must be through Grand Lodges.
Minimum Time Lapse between Degrees: 28 days.
Ritual: Canadian, and *Ancient York.*
Main Publications: Constitutions. Annual Proceedings.

History
Originally, Manitoba included all of Western Canada, except British Columbia. The initial lodge in the area was chartered at Fort Garry (now Winnepeg) by the Grand Lodge of Minnesota in 1864, but it soon expired. The first permanent lodge in Manitoba was formed under a warrant from Ontario. This was Prince Rupert Lodge No 240, established at Winnipeg in 1871. This lodge now holds the No 1 in the Manitoba *Directory of Lodges.* Two further Ontario lodges subsequently followed, and in 1875 these three lodges sent representatives to a Convention and formed the Grand Lodge of Manitoba. Upon the erection of the Province of Alberta in 1905, 18 lodges in that territory split off to form a new Grand Lodge. Similarly, in 1906, upon the formation of the Province of Saskatchewan, 29 lodges in that area followed the Alberta example.

Notes for Visitors
Manitoba lodges are permitted to choose between two official rituals. By far the most popular is the *Canadian* Working, which is an English-type ritual derived from Ontario. Ten Manitoba lodges, however, work an *Ancient York* ritual, often referred to locally simply as the *American Work.* It is, of course, a Webb-form ritual.
    The dress employed in all Manitoba lodges is a dark business suit, with officers in many lodges attending in a black dinner suit (tuxedo). As with the other Canadian jurisdictions already reviewed, the regalia employed in Manitoba closely resembles English types. Visitors are certainly welcome to wear their own regalia when attending a Manitoba lodge meeting. All lodges meet at least on a monthly basis, except

during the recess months of June and July. Afterproceedings in Manitoba largely consist of a light supper, incorporated with a short toast list. On Installation nights, afterproceedings tend to comprise of a more substantial meal, as a rule. Alcohol is often available. Visitors are not required to contribute to the costs of any supper or meal they might attend.

Most Manitoba lodges convene at 7.30 pm, and prior examinations for unknown visitors tend to be quite thorough. An early arrival is therefore necessary. Of the 98 lodges in Manitoba, 29 meet at Winnipeg. Again, Manitoba uses a District system largely on the American model, headed by District Deputy Grand Masters. Indeed, the structure of the Grand Lodge compares strongly to those of the United States, with all senior Grand Lodge offices being elective. Nonetheless, while using an expansive American-type committee system, Manitoba still employs a Board of General Purposes which is formed and operates in an analogous way to that of England.

List of Lodges
Alberta possesses only one large city—Winnipeg. The address of the Masonic Memorial Temple in that city has already been provided. It contains the Grand Lodge office, at which visitors will receive the meeting details of all lodges in Manitoba, plus an excellent Grand Lodge library.

NEW BRUNSWICK
The Grand Lodge of Free and Accepted Masons of New Brunswick
Founded: 1867
Address: Masonic Temple, 92 Germain Street, Saint John, New Brunswick, E2L 4R8.
Lodges: 51.   Permits Dual and Plural Membership. *Membership:* 7,453.
Descent: Nova Scotia, New York, and England. *Government:* Elective Grand Lodge.
Courtesy Degrees: Correspondence must be through Grand Lodges.
Minimum Time Lapse between Degrees: 28 days.
Ritual: Ancient York (Webb-form).
Main Publications: Constitution. Annual Proceedings.

History
The first lodge erected in New Brunswick was St George's Lodge No 2, warranted as a military lodge by the Provincial Grand Lodge of New York in 1783. This lodge subsequently became stationary, but still continued to meet under its original Warrant until 1788, when the Provincial Grand Lodge of Nova Scotia granted it a new charter. A second lodge was chartered from Nova Scotia at St John 1784. In 1789, the Modern's Grand Lodge of England warranted New Brunswick Lodge No 541, at Fredericton, and this was the only lodge in New Brunswick to receive a Warrant from that source. The source of further charters was Nova Scotia, but it was not until 1867 that the Grand Lodge of New Brunswick was established. This was achieved at a Convention of 19 lodges in that year.

Notes for Visitors
New Brunswick is a relatively small Grand Lodge. Unlike most other Canadian

Grand Lodges, the Grand Lodge of New Brunswick has only one official ritual for its lodges. This is the *Ancient York* working, inherited from Nova Scotia. It is a Webb-form American Ritual. Not surprisingly, masonry in New Brunswick is far more comparable to the United States than to England. Its Grand Lodge is elective, and its Constitution reflects its American heritage. A District system on the American model is used. New Brunswick currently possesses seven Districts, each headed by a District Deputy Grand Master.

Most lodges in Manitoba meet at 7.30 pm, invariably holding a regular meeting each month, except in June and July. 'Emergent' meetings are sometimes held between regular meetings. Dress is a dark business suit, although lodge officers and Grand Lodge officers usually attend meetings in a black dinner suit (tuxedo). Regalia, in common with other Canadian jurisdictions, compares stongly with that of England, rather than with that of America.

Lodge afterproceedings in New Brunswick usually consist of a light supper. A toast list is sometimes used following regular meetings, but this practice is far more common in association with a night of Installation. Again, visitors will not often be required to contribute to any repast attended by them.

List of Lodges

Of New Brunswick's 51 lodges, six meet in Saint John, the largest population centre of the Province. Virtually every town in New Brunswick possesses at least one lodge. All meeting details of all New Brunswick lodges can be gained at the Grand Lodge office located in the Masonic temple at Saint John.

NEWFOUNDLAND

Newfoundland does not possess a Grand Lodge, and remains the only Canadian Province in this position. All lodges working in Newfoundland operate either under English or Scottish Warrants.

The District Grand Lodge of Newfoundland
(under the United Grand Lodge of England)
Address: P.O. Box 9114, St John's, Newfoundland.
Lodges: 24.

The District Grand Lodge of Newfoundland
(Under the Grand Lodge of Scotland)
Address: P.O. Box 1164, St John's, Newfoundland.
Lodges: 15.

History

The first point to appreciate about Newfoundland is that it did not become a Province of Canada until 1949. The political history of the area has been turbulent, although such a study is outside the scope of the text provided here. The first lodge erected in Newfoundland was St John's Lodge No 186, warranted by the Antient's Grand Lodge of England in 1774. It had expired by 1832. Several further lodges were formed in the area either under the Antients, or the Moderns, but by the time of the English masonic union in 1813, only two lodges remained. These were St John's No 186 (now revived), and Benevolent No 247. However, again, both these lodges failed to survive. The oldest English lodge now working in Newfoundland is

St John's Lodge No 579, dating from 1850. This was followed in Avalon Lodge No 776 in 1858.

The premier Scottish lodge in Newfoundland is Lodge Tasker No 454, established at St John's in 1866. An English District Grand Lodge was formed for Newfoundland in 1871, and this was followed by one for the Scottish lodges. In 1876, moves were made to establish an independent Grand Lodge, which was met with opposition within the area, as well as from the United Grand Lodge of England. Subsequently, no successful move has ever been made to erect a Grand Lodge of Newfoundland. In 1983, England had 24 lodges in the Province, with the latest (Trinity Lodge No 9039) being formed as late as 1982. Scotland currently has 15 lodges in Newfoundland, with its youngest lodge (McLeod No 1725) dating from 1978.

Notes for Visitors

The practices and customs of lodges in Newfoundland stem directly from those of England and Scotland, and therefore it is unnecessary to become involved in a copious repetition here. Most towns in Newfoundland now possess at least one lodge, with the capital city of St John's accounting for eight of the Province's 39 lodges. A visitor calling at the Masonic Temple in St John's will receive all necessary meeting details.

List of Lodges

As they are small in number, it is possible to list the details of lodges meeting in St John's. Unless otherwise stated, all eight lodges detailed below meet at the Masonic Temple in St John's generally commencing about 7.30 pm.

Saint John's Lodge No 579 EC.	Meets 2nd Wednesday monthly (except July and August). Inst: January.
Avalon Lodge No 776 EC.	Meets 2nd Thursday monthly (except July, August, and November). Inst: 1st Tuesday, November.
Whiteway Lodge No 3541 EC.	Meets 2nd Monday monthly (except July and August). Inst: April.
St George's Lodge No 6739 EC.	Meets 1st Monday monthly (except July and August). Inst: 3rd Tuesday, April.
Neptune Lodge No 8465 EC.	Meets 3rd Wednesday monthly (except July, August, and February). Inst: Friday before 3rd Weds., February.
Lodge Tasker No 454 SC.	Meets 3rd Thursday monthly (except July and August).
Lodge St Andrew No 1139 SC.	Meets 3rd Monday monthly (except July and August).
Lodge Westmorland No 1689 SC.	Meets at the Church of Ascension, Mt. Pearl, St John's 4th Wednesday, monthly (except July and August).

NOVA SCOTIA
The Grand Lodge of Ancient, Free and Accepted Masons of Nova Scotia
Founded: 1866
Address: Freemasons' Hall, 1533 Barrington Street, Halifax, Nova Scotia. Postal
Address: P.O. Box 214, Halifax, B3J 2M4. Telephone: (902) 423 6149.
Lodges: 116   Permits Dual and Plural Membership. *Membership:* 10,444.
Descent: England and Scotland. *Government:* Elective Grand Lodge.
Courtesy Degrees: All Correspondence must be through Grand Lodges.
Minimum Time Lapse between Degrees: 28 days.
Ritual: Antient York, and *Emulation.*
Main Publications: Constitution. Annual Proceedings.

History
There are records of masonic activity in Nova Scotia as early as 1740, when a
dispensation was issued by the Provincial Grand Lodge of Massachusetts for the
erection of a lodge. This lodge would appear to have been military. The first stationary lodge in Nova Scotia was First Lodge, which received a Moderns warrant
about 1750. This lodge subsequently turned Antient, and it received a Charter as an
Antients Provincial Grand Lodge in 1757. Today, this lodge is St Andrew's Lodge,
No 1 on Nova Scotia roll of lodges.
Up until 1866, both England (Antients) and Scotland warranted a number of
lodges in Nova Scotia, although many had a chequered history. At that date, most
lodges in Nova Scotia united to form a new Grand Lodge, although many English
lodges stood out until 1869. One English lodge has survived in Nova Scotia. This
is Royal Standard Lodge No 398 EC working at Halifax. It dates from 1815.

Notes for Visitors
Virtually all lodges in Nova Scotia work its *Ancient York* ritual, which is most
analogous to the Webb-form rituals of the United States (being largely the Antients
pre-1813 English Union working). Nonetheless, the Constitution of the Grand
Lodge does permit lodges originally working the English *Emulation* ritual to continue using it.
The dress for lodges in Nova Scotia is a black dinner suit (tuxedo), but a dark
business suit is a permitted alternative. Lodge afterproceedings are quite comparable
to those of the United States, and generally consist of a very light meal. Toasts are
only rarely proposed at regular meetings, although brief speeches are sometimes
employed. A toast list is, however, sometimes used at a repast following an Installation meeting. All Nova Scotia lodges meet on a monthly basis, although most
recess in the months of July and August. Largely, meetings commence at 7.30 pm.
In addition, it is not uncommon for lodges to hold emergent meetings. The private
business of a lodge is always dealt with in the third degree at a regular meeting.
Emergent meetings are usually called for extra degree conferments. It should also be
noted that the use of alcohol at any masonic function in Nova Scotia is prohibited
by Grand Lodge statute. As with most other Canadian Grand Lodges, the regalia
used in Nova Scotia approximates English-types. Again, visitors are welcome to
wear their own regalia at a lodge meeting in Nova Scotia.
The Grand Lodge of Nova Scotia is quite comparable to those of the United

States. It is an Elective Grand Lodge, makes extensive use of a Grand Lodge committee system, and divides its jurisdiction into masonic districts headed by District Deputy Grand Masters. Nova Scotia is the only Canadian Jurisdiction possessing a masonic home for the elderly. The Nova Scotia Freemasons' Home is located at Windsor, about 45 miles from Halifax. Dating from 1908, the Nova Scotia home has a current capacity of 60, and in recent years the majority of residents have been women. Of course, it is heavily supported by the body of Nova Scotia freemasonry. Visitors are welcome to inspect the home, for which purpose application can be made at the Grand Lodge office in Halifax.

List of Lodges

Of Nova Scotia's current list of 116 lodges, 14 meet at Halifax. Details of all lodge meetings in Nova Scotia are obtainable upon personal application at Freemasons' Hall, Halifax.

Indeed, Freemasons' Hall will be of interest to visitors. It is over 100 years old, and well worth inspecting. Details of the 14 Halifax lodges under Nova Scotia and meeting within it, are as follows:

St Andrew's Lodge No 1	Meets 1st Tuesday monthly.
St John's Lodge No 2	Meets 1st Monday monthly (except July and August).
Virgin Lodge No 3	Meets 4th Monday monthly (except July and August).
Royal Sussex Lodge No 6	Meets 1st Thursday monthly (except July and August).
Burm Lodge No 10	Meets 1st Wednesday monthly (except July and August).
Acadia Lodge No 14	Meets 2nd Monday monthly (except July and August).
Keith Lodge No 17	Meets 1st Monday monthly (except July and August).
The Lodge of Saint Mark No 38	Meets 2nd Friday monthly (except July and August).
Composite Lodge No 105	Meets 4th Saturday monthly (except July, August, and December), and 3rd Thursday in December.
Equity Lodge No 106	Meets 3rd Monday monthly (except August).
University Lodge No 110	Meets 3rd Tuesday monthly (except June, July and August).
White Ensign Lodge No 129	Meets 3rd Wednesday monthly (except July and August).
Ad Astra Lodge No 130	Meets 4th Wednesday monthly (except July and August.

Of special interest to visitors will be the sole remaining English lodge in Nova Scotia. Its meeting details are as follows:

Royal Standard Lodge No 398	Meets at Freemasons' Hall, Halifax; 2nd Tuesday (except July and August). Installation: May.

ONTARIO

The Grand Lodge, Ancient, Free and Accepted Masons of Canada in the Province of
Ontario
Founded: 1855
Address: Grand Lodge Office, 363 King Street West, Hamilton, Ontario.
Postal Address: P.O. Box 217, Hamilton. L8N 3C9. Telephone: (416)
528 8644.
Lodges: 647 Permits Dual and Plural Membership. *Membership:* 103,167.
Descent: England, Quebec, New York. *Government:* Elective Grand Lodge.
Courtesy Degrees: Correspondence must be through Grand Lodges.
Minimum Time Lapse between Degrees: four weeks.
Ritual: Canadian.
Main Publications: Constitution, Proceedings. Periodical: *Grand Lodge Bulletin.*

History
Ontario probably has the most confused history of any Canadian jurisdiction. Ontario first became the object white settlement in the 1760s and 1770s. By 1790, ten
lodges were operating in the territory. Of these, five held English warrants, three
held warrants from the Provincial Grand Lodge of Quebec (Antients), while one
owed allegiance to the Provincial Grand Lodge of New York (Antients). Soon
afterwards, the division of Upper Canada and Lower Canada occurred, and this
resulted in a good deal of territorial acrimony between lodges in both areas. Political
conditions in both areas were less than satisfactory, and in 1840 England re-united
both territories. In 1843, a convention of lodges formed the Grand Lodge of Canada
West. Continuing masonic difficulties occurred with England, and in the territories.
Finally, a Grand Lodge of Canada was formed in 1855, uniting most lodges in both
Upper and Lower Canada. It must be appreciated that this area then covered
Ontario and Manitoba, and from 1858, Quebec. Subsequent to the creation of the
Dominion of Canada in 1867, a Grand Lodge of Quebec was formed in 1869, with
lodges in Manitoba going their own way in 1875. The Grand Lodge of Canada now
only controlled lodges in Ontario, and in 1888, it therefore changed its name to The
Grand Lodge of Canada in the Province of Ontario.

Notes for Visitors
Ontario possesses by far the largest masonic jurisdiction in Canada, and one of the
largest in North America. The prescribed ritual for Ontario is the *Canadian* work
which, as has previously been alluded to, is reasonably similar to present day
English-type ritual. As with most other Canadian jurisdictions, Ontario prints its
ritual in plain English for sale to qualified members.
 The usual dress for lodges in Ontario is a dark business suit or a black dinner
suit (tuxedo), with the latter favoured by lodge officers and Grand Lodge officers
for the most part. Again, Ontario regalia resembles English types. Visitors are
welcome to attend any lodge meeting, and wear their own personal regalia if they
have it with them. Afterproceedings in Ontario lodges largely tend to be informal,
and consist of a light supper. A toast list is often only employed on special occasions,
such as at the festive board following a Night of Installation. Nonetheless, speeches
are not uncommon, and visitors are often given an opportunity to speak. Visitors

are never expected to contribute to the costs associated with any repast at an Ontario lodge.

All Ontario lodges meet on a monthly basis, usually about 7.30 pm. The large majority of lodges conduct their Installation meetings on or near the Festival (Feast Day) of St John the Evangelist, which in effect means at a meeting between October and March. The minority install on or near the Festival of St John the Baptist, in effect, at a meeting between April and September.

Whie the Grand Lodge of Canada in Ontario is basically an 'Elective Grand Lodge' on the American model, its Constitution possesses a number of English influences. Typical American forms include delegates to Grand Lodge from lodges, the use of many Grand Lodge Committees, and an extensive District system under District Deputy Grand Masters. Currently, Ontario is divided into 43 Masonic Districts. English influences include the use of large Board of General Purposes with nearly 100 members.

List of Lodges

Ontario possesses a number of substantial population centres, of which the largest are Toronto (with 63 lodges), Ottawa (the Canadian Capital City, with 16 lodges), and Hamilton (the Grand Lodge seat, with 19 lodges). Visitors to Ontario are best advised to call at the main Temple in one of these cities, whereupon full assistance can be obtained. The main Temple in Toronto is located at 888 Yonge Street, Toronto (Telephone: (416) 922 1248), while Ottawa's main Temple is at 2140 Walkley Road, Ottawa (Telephone: (613) 521 8636). The address of the Grand Lodge Building in Hamilton is provided above.

PRINCE EDWARD ISLAND

The Grand Lodge of Prince Edward Island, Ancient, Free and Accepted Masons
Founded: 1875
Address: Grand Lodge Office: 204 Hillsboro Street, Charlottetown, Prince Edward Island.
Postal Address: P.O. Box 337, Charlottetown. *Telephone:* 894 9326.
Lodges: 16   Permits Dual Membership. *Membership:* 1,292
Descent: England and Scotland. *Government:* Elective Grand Lodge.
Courtesy Degrees: Correspondence should be through Grand Lodges.
Minimum Time Lapse between Degrees: four weeks.
Ritual: English-type.
Main Publications: Proceedings. Constitution.

History

The Provincial Grand Lodge of Nova Scotia (Antients) granted the first warrant for a lodge in Prince Edward Island. This was for St John Lodge No 26, founded at Charlottetown in 1797, and it became No 833 on the Roll of the United Grand Lodge of England subsequent to 1813. In 1858, Victoria Lodge No 383 was chartered at Charlottetown by the Grand Lodge of Scotland. These two lodges remain the only lodges working at Charlottetown. Another six lodges received English warrants up until 1869, and in 1875, all eight lodges then working met and erected the Grand Lodge of Prince Edward Island.

Notes for Visitors
The Grand Lodge of Prince Edward Island is not only the smallest Grand Lodge in Canada, it is the smallest in North America, possessing only sixteen lodges. All lodges hold a regular meeting on a monthly basis, although the two lodges in Charlottetown recess in July and August. Dress for lodges is a dark business suit, or dinner suit (tuxedo), with the latter being favoured, particularly by lodge officers. Regalia is largely identical to England. Most lodges open at 7.30 pm, and follow their meetings with a light supper. A toast list is sometimes employed, especially on Installation Nights, when a full meal is usually provided.

It is not uncommon for Prince Edward Island lodges to convene a special meeting between regular meetings for a variety of reasons. Annual Ladies' Nights, and an Annual Church Service are a feature of the programmes of most lodges. Visitors, particularly those from outside the Island, will usually be given an opportunity to speak at the festive board. Again, no visitor will be asked to contribute to any repast attended.

The ritual prescribed by the Grand Lodge exhibits a number of American forms, although it is basically of an English-type. Likewise, the Grand Lodge's Constitution is largely that of an Elective Grand Lodge, with all senior Grand Offices filled by ballot at the Annual Grand Lodge Communication. The American-type Grand Lodge Line also prevails. Nonetheless, English forms such as a Board of General Purposes are features of the Grand Lodge structure.

List of Lodges
Virtually every town on Prince Edward Island possesses one lodge, with Charlotte-town, the Provincial Capital and Grand Lodge seat, having two. The Charlottetown lodges meet in the Grand Lodge Temple, as follows:

Saint John's Lodge No 1   Meets 2nd Tuesday monthly (except July and August).

Victoria Lodge No 2   Meets 1st Monday monthly (except July and August).

The meeting details of all other lodges in Prince Edward Island can readily be gained at the Grand Lodge Office.

QUEBEC

The Grand Lodge of Quebec, Antient, Free, and Accepted Masons
Founded: 1869
Address: Masonic Memorial Temple, 2295 St Mark Street, Montreal, Quebec. H3H 2G9. *Telephone:* (514) 933 6739.
Lodges: 101   Permits Dual and Plural Membership. *Membership:* 11,835.
Descent: England. *Government:* Elective Grand Lodge.
Courtesy Degrees: All correspondence must be through Grand Lodges.
Minimum Time Lapse between Degrees: four weeks.
Ritual: Canadian.
Main Publications: Proceedings. Constitution. Periodical: *The Trowel.*

History

Quebec is a largely French-speaking Province of Canada, and was one of the first areas of the country to be settled. The first lodges in Quebec were military, the members of which formed part of the forces which captured it for the British in 1760. Five military lodges appear to have formed a Grand Lodge of Quebec about this time, which in 1768 apparently became a Provincial Grand Lodge under the English Moderns. However, by about 1791, lodges in Quebec had defected to the Antients. By the time of English Union in 1813, Quebec possessed seven military lodges and 13 stationary lodges.

It must be remembered that at this time Quebec was not an individual political entity. In 1855, the Grand Lodge of Canada was formed, and in 1858 a majority of Quebec lodges joined this body. Upon the creation of the Dominion of Canada in 1867, many Quebec lodges decided to form their own Grand Lodge, and this was duly effected with the creation of the Grand Lodge of Quebec in 1869. By the early 1880s, no Quebec lodges remained under the Grand Lodge of Canada (Ontario). However, a small number of lodges chose to remain under the United Grand Lodge of England, of which two survive today. St. Paul's Lodge No 374 EC, and St George's Lodge No 440 EC still work happily in Montreal, and together with one other English lodge at Halifax, Nova Scotia, remain the only English-warranted lodges in North America.

Notes for Visitors

Lodges in Quebec use the *Canadian* ritual as briefly discussed under earlier headings. It is reasonably similar to post-1813 English ritual, but possesses several features which are analogous to Webb-form and Scottish practices. It is of interest to note that in very recent years the Quebec ritual has been translated into French. It is notable that masonic membership in Quebec is relatively small when compared to the total population of the Province. The answer to this is found in the fact that about 80% of the populace of Quebec are French-speaking. It is only in fairly recent times that English-speaking Quebec masonry has moved to pave the way for increasing French Involvement. A handful of lodges, notably in Montreal, now work in the French language, and it would appear that this trend will continue into the future.

Dress for Quebec lodges is a dark business suit as a minimum requirement, but many members wear a black dinner suit (tuxedo), particularly lodge officers. Most lodges convene at about 7.30 pm, and meet on a monthly basis for a regular meeting. At these meetings, the business of the lodge is dealt with in the third degree, and a degree conferal will usually be performed as well. Many lodges will also, on occasions, hold an emergency meeting between regular meetings, often for an extra degree conferal, or for some other special reason. The annual Installation Meeting in Quebec lodges is either held on or near the Festival of St John the Evangelist (December 27th) or the Festival of St John the Baptist (June 24th). Again, most lodges recess in the months of July and August, and some fail to meet in June as well.

The festive board following a Quebec lodge meeting, as is quite common throughout Canada, tends to consist of a simple supper and an informal structure. A toast list is generally only used following an Installation or on some other special occasion. Nonetheless, speeches are not unusual, and a visitor may be called upon to speak, although prior notice is normal. Visitors are never expected to contribute to any repast associated with a Quebec lodge meeting.

The Grand Lodge of Quebec is fairly typical of wider Canadian practices in terms of its organisation. It is basically an Elective Grand Lodge, although it retains such English-type customs as a Board of General Purposes. Quebec is divided into nine masonic districts, each under a Deputy District Grand Master whose functions closely parallel those of the American Jurisdictions. Once again, the regalia employed in Quebec lodges largely compares with that of England.

List of Lodges

Of the current 101 lodges in Quebec, 28 work in Montreal, which is the largest city in Canada, as well as in Quebec. The Masonic Memorial Temple in Montreal is centrally situated, and contains a fine library in addition to the Grand Lodge office, and several lodge rooms. A visit to the Grand Lodge office will quickly gain the visitor the meeting details of all lodges working in Quebec.

SASKATCHEWAN

The Grand Lodge of Saskatchewan, Ancient, Free and Accepted Masons
Founded: 1906
Address: Masonic Temple, 1930 Lorne Street, Regina, Saskatchewan. S4P 2MI.
Telephone: 522 5686.
Lodges: 159   Permits Dual Membership. *Membership:* 11,402.
Descent: Manitoba   *Government:* Elective Grand Lodge.
Courtesy Degrees: All correspondence must be through Grand Lodge.
Minimum Time Lapse between Degrees: 28 days.
Ritual: Canadian.
Main Publications: Annual Proceedings. Constitution.

History

The first lodge in Saskatchewan was warranted from the Grand Lodge of Canada in 1880, having been founded under dispensation in the previous year. This was Kinistino Lodge No 381, at Prince Albert. In 1882, this lodge transferred its allegiance to the Grand lodge of Manitoba, and subsequently came to head the directory of lodges of the Grand Lodge of Saskatchewan. By 1906, the year after the creation of the Province of Saskatchewan, 24 lodges were working in the territory under charters from Manitoba. In that year, most of these lodges came together in Convention and formed the Grand Lodge of Saskatchewan.

Notes for Visitors

Saskatchewan uses a form of the *Canadian* ritual inherited from Ontario, via Manitoba. The basic details of this working have already been mentioned. The dress for Saskatchewan lodges is a dark business suit, although lodge officers largely prefer a dinner suit (tuxedo). All lodges meet on a monthly basis for a regular meeting, although many recess in the months of July and August. In addition, a number of lodges convene emergency meetings as necessary. Most lodges commence their proceedings about 7.30 pm. About 50 Saskatchewan lodges conduct their annual Installation Meeting on or about the anniversary (Feast Day) of St John the Baptist, while the rest prefer St John the Evangelist Day.

In common with most other Canadian Jurisdictions, the festive board following a regular Saskatchewan lodge meeting tends to consist of a light and simple supper. A toast list is usually only used on special occasions, such as at the festive board following an Installation. Even then, the list is often limited to only a handful of toasts, such as 'The Queen', The Craft', and 'The Visitors'. Nonetheless, it would be an unusual Saskatchewan festive board that did not contain a few brief speeches. Opportunities are usually afforded to visitors to speak if they so desire. It should also be noted that visitors are never expected to contribute financially at any Saskatchewan festive board.

The government of the Grand Lodge of Saskatchewan approximates other Canadian Jurisdictions. It is basically an elective Grand Lodge, with both English and American type forms in its constitution. Both Grand Lodge and constituent lodge regalia, again, closely resembles that of England.

Visitors to a lodge in Saskatchewan, particularly if they are unknown, should be certain to arrive early. Lodges in this jurisdiction are particularly vigilant with their avouchment procedures, although these will pose no problems to the regular mason. These procedures also include the requirement that a visitor recite the 'Tyler's Oath' (for the wording of this oath, see under the heading of the United States). In addition, the *Canadian* ritual requires both visitors and members to provide certain modes of recognition inside the temple when the Deacons 'Purge the Lodge' at appropriate points. A visitor can usefully make inquiries in this area after he has been examined, if he is unfamiliar with this procedure.

List of Lodges

Saskatchewan is largely a rural Canadian province, and does not possess any large cities. Nonetheless, there are few towns within its boundaries that do no have at least one lodge. The largest population centre in the Province is Regina (with 10 lodges). Visitors are directed to the Grand Lodge Temple in Regina, where lodge meeting details will be happily supplied.

The United States of America

The United States of America possesses fifty regular Grand Lodges governing between them approximately fifteen thousand lodges and four million freemasons. Every State of the Union, except Hawaii, has a Grand Lodge. In addition, there is a Grand Lodge for the District of Columbia centred on Washington DC, the American capital city. Lodges in Hawaii come under the Grand Lodge of California.

With fifty jurisdictions, the United States accounts for nearly half of all the regular Grand Lodges recognised by the Grand Lodges of England, Ireland and Scotland. In an effort to maintain decorum in terms of the length of this guide, each of these jurisdictions will not be found detailed below at great length. Instead, an expansive general text of American freemasonry as a whole will be provided. This will be followed by an abbreviated detailing of each individual jurisdiction, with special notes for visitors provided for each.

In a broad sense, it is possible to adopt this approach as a great many similarities do exist between the American Jurisdictions. Of course, there are differences in usages and customs, but for the most part these are fairly minor. Nonetheless, it must be made perfectly clear that it is impossible to minutely detail the practices of all American Jurisdictions in these pages, as they may affect or interest the visitor. Rather, the aim here is to provide the visitor with a wide and reasonably detailed impression of what he may expect in the majority of cases. The visitor must be aware that much of the information about to be provided is not necessarily applicable America-wide. Where this is the case, varying degrees of qualification are added to the general text as appropriate.

The United States—an Historical Overview
A brief history of each of the American Jurisdictions is provided under jurisdictional headings following the general text. It is therefore unnecessary to provide an historical overview at this point. For a brief explanation of the introduction of freemasonry into the United States, readers should refer to the historical notes under the headings of Massachusetts, New York and Pennsylvania. Reference is often made in the brief histories of the Morgan Affair and Anti-Masonry. The brief history provided under the heading of New York supplies a short explanation of these aspects.

Notes for Visiting in the United States—A General Text

1. MEETINGS
As a general rule, lodges in the United States meet at least twice per month, often on a fortnightly basis. One meeting is called the 'Stated Meeting' or 'Regular Communication', while other meetings are referred to as 'Special', 'Called', or 'Emergent'.

Recess Months: Visitors should note that most American lodges, regardless of jurisdiction, recess in the northern summer months of July and/or August. A small number of lodges will also fail to meet in June and/or September. An increasing number of lodges in northern American areas are recessing in January and February instead of, or in addition to, July and August in order to avoid the expence of heating their Temple.

Stated Meetings: These meetings are often held monthly at a fixed time (for example: 2nd Monday, 3rd Thursday, 4th Tuesday). They do not necessarily involve a degree conferment ceremony, but are more usually business meetings adopted for the conducting of the routine affairs of the lodge. This includes such things as reading minutes, correspondence, receiving reports, and conducting ballots. For these meetings, the lodge will be opened in the third degree. Indeed, regardless of jurisdiction, no lodge in the United States will open proceedings in the first or second degrees except when they are to be actually conferred. Quite obviously, only Master Masons can attend business meetings and indeed, a mason is not constituted as a member of an American lodge until he has taken that Degree.

The American Stated meeting, as a purely business meeting, is somewhat analogous to the Standing Committee or Committee of Past Masters which forms the administrative body of an English-type lodge. However, two major differences are noteworthy. Firstly, the administrative body of an English lodge does not meet as part of a regular, tyled meeting. Secondly, in English Lodges, administration devolves largely on Past Masters, whereas in the United States every Master Mason has an equal say, and vote, in the running of his lodge through its business meetings.

Nonetheless, it must be clearly indicated that in many American Jurisdictions, a business meeting and a degree conferment are undertaken, on occasions, within the totality of a stated meeting. Procedures in this regard may even vary between lodges within a single jurisdiction. In many lodges, a degree conferment and a business meeting will be held together at a stated meeting on the basis of available work. An example might be that if one conferment of a degree is available to a lodge in a given month, then it will have a stated meeting, without degree work, followed two weeks later by a special meeting for the degree conferment. If two conferments are available, one might be done at the stated meeting, and the other at a special meeting. Of course, a number of variations to this pattern are in use.

Special Meetings: While stated meetings are held monthly on a day fixed by a lodge's by-laws, special meetings are held when convenient in many jurisdictions. Such a meeting might be held one or two weeks before or after a stated meeting, and they are most often called specifically to conduct a degree conferment. The lodge will open directly into the degree to be conferred. In the majority of jurisdictions, special meetings are only called when there is degree work to be undertaken, or for some other special reason such as an Installation, or for the visit of a Grand Lodge officer. Often, there is no set limit to the number of special meetings that may be called in any one month. As the need arises, a lodge might call two or more such meetings between its stated meetings, although this is not overly common. It must also be noted that in some jurisdictions, lodges are required to fix regular dates for two meetings per month (one stated, one special) in their by-laws. Again, in some States this is optional, so that the visitor might find some lodges advertising two regular meetings, and others only one. Where a lodge has two fixed meetings per month, these are invariably held at fortnightly intervals.

2. MEETING TIMES

The meeting times of American lodges are not easy to detail simply because, as with days of meeting, there are few constants. Meeting times are largely linked to the type of meeting, the work of the lodge, and to its repast. In broad terms, meeting times can be grouped into three categories, as follows:

A Stated Meeting, without Degree Work: Lodges generally meet at a time between 7 pm and 8 pm, open directly in the third degree, conduct a business meeting, and close in the third degree. In a minority of jurisdictions, lodges are required to state the time of opening of their stated meeting in their by-laws. Often this will be 7.30 pm. Where this occurs, visitors will often find that this category of meeting is the norm.

A Stated Meeting, with Degree Work: Lodges often open between 5.30 pm and 6 pm directly in the degree to be worked (whether first, second or third), and conduct the first part of the ceremony. The lodge will then adjourn for a repast between about 6.30 to 7 pm. At about 7.30 to 8 pm, the lodge will open in the third degree for its business meeting, which will usually consume about half an hour. At the conclusion of the business, the lodge will then be resumed in the degree of the ceremony commenced prior to the repast, and the ceremony will be finished. There are a number of varying patterns to this format. In some areas or jurisdictions, the repast will be taken prior to the opening of the lodge, while in others, the business meeting might be held before or after the degree ceremony, rather than breaking in the middle for this purpose. This later occurrence is not particularly common, as Americans tend to prefer to work degree ceremonies in two parts. Indeed, American (Webb-Form) rituals are largely structured in this manner, as will be outlined below.

A Special Meeting: The meeting times of special meetings tend to largely follow those of stated meetings, with degree work. The lodge will often be opened in the degree to be worked at or about 6.30 pm, whereupon the first part of the ceremony will be conducted. Again, the ceremony will usually be broken by a repast, often commencing at about 7.30 pm.

Visiting in terms of Meetings, and Meeting Times
In view of the foregoing, the visitor will now doubtlessly appreciate that planning ahead to visit an American lodge involves specific local knowledge. The only lodge meeting for which a date is often fixed is the stated meeting, and depending on the lodge or the jurisdiction, a visitor attending such a meeting might well find no degree work being performed. As special meetings are not often fixed, it can be fairly difficult to plan a visit well in advance without specific information. Again, the variations of meeting times do not add to the visitor's cause.

Nonetheless, with these matters identified, visiting any American lodge does not pose any real problem. However, a visit to the appropriate Grand Lodge office, or to the main temple in any of the larger American cities, is virtually a basic prerequisite to expeditious visiting. Upon such a visit, the travelling mason can be assured of every courtesy and assistance. It will be noted that not all Grand Lodge offices are located in the largest city or population centre of a State. Where this is the case, the addresses of Temples in the larger cities are provided under jurisdictional headings below.

3. DRESS
In general terms, the dress required for attending American lodges is often of a far more relaxed nature to that which is normal in Britain and Europe. Indeed, the

majority of American Jurisdictions do not impose dress regulations by Grand Lodge statute, but rather rely on convention. In a number of jurisdictions, business suits are worn, but usually sports coats and open neck shirts are also acceptable for ordinary members. It is more standard for lodge officers to wear a business suit to meetings, and even dinner suits (tuxedoes) especially to 'special nights', such as an Installation. Generally, the more southerly the jurisdiction (and therefore the more climatically warmer), the more relaxed will be the dress worn by members attending lodge meetings. In order to cover all contingencies, unless a visitor has specific local knowledge to the contrary; the best advice is for him to visit in a dark business suit. White gloves are worn by lodge officers in some jurisdictions, but it is unlikely a visitor will have any need of these.

4. REGALIA

The regalia worn by American masons is reasonably dissimilar to that of Britain. The first point to note is that most lodges in most American Jurisdictions supply aprons for members and visitors. Generally, only a Past Master will own his own apron. Nonetheless, a visitor from outside America who owns his own apron is certainly most welcome to bring and wear it in an American lodge. Aprons are generally blue trimmed, and in the first and second degrees, the position in which the apron is worn indicates the rank of the wearer. This system is more reminiscent of Continental practice, rather than those of the British Isles. The Master Mason's apron usually has two tassles hanging down its front. An interesting custom in many parts of America is associated with the Entered Apprentice apron. In this practice, the initiate is presented with a lambskin apron and is instructed to put it away, and that it will only be used again for his funeral. Grand Lodge regalia throughout the American Jurisdictions tends to be far less ornate than the gold-trimmed aprons of the British type.

In short, having assimilated the position regarding American regalia, the visitor should have no hesitation in attending a lodge, regardless of whether he is carrying regalia, or not.

5. LODGE AFTERPROCEEDINGS

A heading of afterproceedings, in the American masonic sense, is to some extent a misnomer. The term festive board or refectory, common in English usage, is unknown in America. As has already been indicated, American lodges commonly hold a repast in the middle of proceedings. The repast can take the form of a dinner or a supper, depending largely on the preferences of the lodge and the work to be undertaken. Some lodges rarely hold a dinner, except perhaps on Nights of Installation, but instead hold a supper. In addition, a not insignificant number of lodges have neither a dinner or a supper associated with lodge meetings. Again, in some lodges, a dinner will only be held at a stated meeting, or when the Master Mason degree is conferred, or perhaps only at a special event. It is, therefore, something of an understatement to say that dining arrangements associated with American lodges vary widely.

Regardless of whether or not a particular lodge engages in a dinner or supper as an adjunct to any meeting, the vast majority of American lodges, regardless of jurisdiction, provide a very light repast after proceedings have concluded. This is usually referred to as a 'collation', and the food provided generally only includes savouries and snacks.

In virtually every jurisdiction of the United States, the provision of alcohol at any dinner or supper associated with a lodge meeting, or any masonic function, is not permitted. In some, this ban is simply achieved by not allowing alcohol onto masonic premises. However, a very small number of jurisdictions do permit alcohol to be available to members and visitors after a lodge meeting has closed, in other words, at the 'collation'. In the States where this is permissible, the matter is left to the discretion of individual lodges, but always under strict conditions. Nonetheless, it is often only a small majority which avail themselves of this option. In addition, a small number of jurisdictions do not oppose the provision of wine at a table lodge. The table lodge ceremony will be examined shortly.

Another factor which may appear somewhat strange to the non-American visitor is that no toasts of any nature are proposed during the normal repasts of American lodges—the table lodge being the only exception. There is certainly no prohibition to the proposition of toasts in any American Jurisdiction. Rather, toasting appears to have never found its way into general American custom. Nonetheless, at a dinner or supper, visitors are sometimes called upon to speak. A visitor from outside the United States is more likely to be called upon in this way, than a local visitor.

It is unusual in the United States for lodge dues to cover the costs of any repast associated with meetings except, perhaps, the 'collation'. It is far more usual for members to contribute to the expenses of dinners and suppers on each occasion that they are provided. Thus, general American practice in this area parallels those of England. Members are usually encouraged to purchase tickets for major lodge repasts, which depending on the expanse of the meal provided may cost anything from five to ten dollars, or more. As a result of this system, pre-booking for meals is the norm. While this is appreciated on the part of visitors, no visitor will be prevented from attending any meeting without prior notice, but alternatively will be warmly welcomed. It can clearly be seen that the issuance of invitations to visitors to attend American lodges is quite rare —visitors are most welcome to attend any lodge meeting without any forewarning being provided to the lodge concerned, subject to the usual proofs of regularity and good standing. Regardless of whether a visitor has pre-booked for a meal, or not, it is extremely rare for him to be asked to contribute. However, should a visitor become a regular visitor at any particular lodge, he may then be expected to pay. As has already been indicated, most visitors will find it a practical necessity to gain meeting details at an appropriate Grand Lodge office, or Major Temple, to facilitate a lodge visit. The visitor will then invariably find that the lodge he intends to visit will receive some forewarning of his imminent presence.

6. THE TABLE LODGE
A most interesting custom associated with modern American masonry is the Table Lodge Ceremony. This ceremony has many similarities to English festive board practices, as well as several obvious differences.

The Table Lodge is an old masonic custom dating back several centuries and stems at least from the earliest speculative times, and probably earlier, when it was common practice in England for lodges to convene in taverns and inns. In England, Table Lodge practices of these earlier times have evolved into the festive board—so familiar to English masons. In America, it would appear that Table Lodges in varying forms were certainly characteristic of early lodge meetings. However, it would seem that by the nineteenth century these practices has died out in favour of the current American system. In relatively recent years, American jurisdictions have largely supported the revival of Table Lodges, and their use has now spread throughout much of American masonry. The revived Table Lodge ceremony is a translation from an early French ceremony, which itself derives from England prior to the English Union of 1813. Various regulations adopted for it by the American Grand Lodges have led to some divergences in its practice across the spectrum of American Masonry, but basically the ceremony used is similar throughout the United States.

The Table Lodge ceremony varies from an English festive board in several major ways. Firstly, it is a tyled meeting, and only masons may be in attendance. Secondly, it involves a ritual catechism for its opening and closing. It must be held on masonic premises, invariably in a dining room. The opening and closing of the Table Lodge is roughly analogous to the opening and closing of an actual English lodge, although in a much more abbreviated form. The catechism involved is almost solely between the Master and the Senior Warden. Hereafter, the ceremony differs somewhat depending on the jurisdiction.

There are two main forms. In the first form, dinner follows the opening. After the repast, those present are welcomed by the Master, who then introduces a guest speaker. Thereafter follows a toast list, generally limited to seven toasts, which are similar to the toast programme of an English festive board. The main point of difference is that the wording of the toasts is often prescribed in the *Table Lodge Ritual,* and where this occurs this wording must be used. The form of layout of the Table Lodge is quite similar regardless of which type of ritual is used. An example layout follows. Extra tables are added parallel to the side tables shown in the diagram on the facing page.

An example of a toast list used in the first main form is hereinafter set out. Each toast is followed by a unison response.

1. *To our Country.* This toast is always proposed by the Master, and followed by a pledge of allegiance to the American flag.
2. *To the Craft.* This toast may be proposed by any member who is so designated by the Master. It may be followed by a short talk on some significant aspect of masonry.
3. *To the Memory of Departed Brethren.* Again, this toast may be delegated to any member.
4. *To the Grand Lodge of............* This toast is often proposed by a Past Master. If a Grand Lodge officer is present, he may be called upon to respond.
5. *To the Lodge.* This toast is proposed by the Junior Warden.
6. *To our Visiting Brethren.* This toast is proposed by the Senior Warden. A reply is made by a forewarned visitor.
7. *To all Freemasons Wheresoever Dispersed.* This is the Tyler's Toast, and the wording is almost identical to that used in England.

In the second main form, the toasts are spaced throughout the repast, and not given afterwards. After the opening, the first two toasts of this form will often be given before the meal commences. The first five toasts are different, and are: 1. To the President of the United States. 2. To the Grand Master and the Grand Lodge.

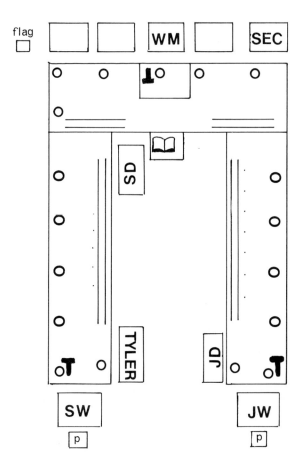

3. To the Master. 4. To the Wardens. 5. To our Brothers in the Armed Forces. The sixth and seventh toasts are the same in both the main forms.

After the toast list is completed, regardless of the form, the Table Lodge is then closed according to the ritual. Indeed the opening and closing rituals are largely identical across the United States. The first form just described is more common in the middle-Western Jurisdictions, while the second form is commonly used in the Eastern States. It is interesting to note that most toasts are accompanied by Masonic Fires, some of which are quite spectacular. In a number of Jurisdictions, the use of the Table Lodge is restricted to once per year. Even in those jurisdictions where this restriction does not apply, it is unusual for frequent use to be made of it. Indeed, some lodges fail to use it at all, even though they are entitled to do so. There is evidence to suggest that its use is becoming increasingly popular. Other regulations sometimes associated with a Table Lodge include the necessity of obtaining Grand Lodge permission before it is held, and the necessity of having a Grand Lodge Officer present when it is presented.

In almost all jurisdictions, the general ban on alcohol at masonic occasions equally applies to Table Lodges. However, some Grand Lodges do permit a small quantity of wine to be available for toasts—invariably under strict regulations. It is rare for there to be any restrictions as to the type of meeting to which a lodge may associate a Table Lodge, although in practice may lodges call a special meeting for the purpose.

As visitors will readily appreciate, the intermittent use of the Table Lodge Ceremony in American masonry makes it difficult to plan a visit to witness one. Interested visitors are advised to make enquiries at any Grand Lodge office they happen to attend, whereupon they will readily receive details of any lodge which will be using the ceremony during their stay.

7. NIGHTS OF INSTALLATION

Nights of Installation in American lodges vary considerably from the English pattern. The first point to note is that virtually nowhere in America is a Night of Installation assigned to a specific date, as such. Instead, it is the night of Election that is often fixed. The actual Installation will be held perhaps two or three months later, at a special meeting.

The Night of Election: This occasion is held annually for the purposes of electing a new Master, and certain other senior officers of the lodge. The date of it is usually fixed, and it takes place at a stated meeting. The Master-elect then has two or three months to plan his year in office prior to his Installation. Another common feature of most American jurisdictions is the Annual Meeting or more correctly, the Annual Business Meeting. This is sometimes held on the Night of Installation, just prior to the event, but certainly not always. Another practice in this regard, although less common, is to hold the Annual Meeting in concert with the Election. The Annual Meeting will receive annual reports from various sources, and at it the Lodge Committees for the ensuing twelve months will be elected or appointed.

The Night of Installation: As has already been mentioned, a Night of Installation is keyed to a Night of Election. Therefore, while its date is rarely fixed as such, it is held in each lodge at about the same time every year. In not a small number of jurisdictions, Installations are required to be held on or near the festival of St John the Baptist, or St John the Evangelist. These two Patron Saints of Freemasonry figure in Webb-form ritual, and are viewed with special affection by the body of American masonry. Again, in not a few jurisdictions all lodges are required to install in one particular month, or before a certain date each year. Two main features characterise an American Installation, both of which are opposite in nature to British-type practices. Firstly, common in the United States is the Public Installation. Secondly, the Chair Degree of Installed Master has no prominent place in an American Installation Ceremony.

The 'Public Installation': To the non-American mason, the 'Public Installation' of a new Master will at first view appear most strange indeed. To begin with, the term 'Public Installation' is not strictly correct, although it is the usual American designation. Actually, only part of the ceremony is public, and even then non-masons in attendance are present only by invitation. Invitations are only extended, as a rule, to the relatives and friends of members. Of course, invitations are necessary only for non-masons, and not for masonic visitors, who may freely attend. Public Installations are not only permitted by all American Grand Lodges—in many they are actively encouraged. No lodge is under any compulsion to 'open' its Installation, but nevertheless there are few that do not.

An English mason will be interested to know, perhaps with some relief, that not all parts of an American Installation are open to non-masons. The opening of the lodge is restricted to masons. An example of an Installation programme might be: opening at 5 pm in the third Degree for a Business Meeting, followed by an adjournment. At maybe 6.30 pm, a dinner will be held, attended by members and visitors—masonic and non-masonic. At 8 pm, the lodge will resume for the 'Public' Installation of the Master, and Investiture of Officers. This part of the ceremony has been adapted somewhat. Of course, during the 'public' proceedings the use of any esoteric ceremonial is avoided.

The example programme just outlined is subject to fairly wide variations. Often a dinner will be held after the meeting rather than in the middle, or no dinner will be held at all. If the latter occurs, the 'collation' available afterwards might well be more substantial than usual. Again, meeting times are apt to vary from lodge to lodge, often depending on the Installation Programme.

Qualifying the Master-Elect: While the Chair Degree of Installed Master forms no part of an actual American Installation, it is nonetheless a prerequisite for the Master's Chair. All American Grand Lodges require that a Master-Elect possesses the secrets of an Installed Master prior to his Installation. This procedure is often called Qualifying the Master-Elect. There are two ways this may be achieved. The Installed Master's Degree may be conferred at a Lodge of Qualification, or on an actual Night of Installation in a side room. The first method is by far the most common. A Lodge of Qualification will bring together the Masters-Elect of a number of lodges, usually on a District basis, whereupon the degree will be conferred on them collectively. Where the degree is conferred on an individual Master, this will be done in camera at an appropriate point on his Night of Installation. Regardless of the method used, only Installed Masters may be present. The method employed varies between jurisdictions, but in most the Lodge of Qualification is favoured, with the degree only being conferred on a Master-Elect at his actual Installation if he for some reason was unable to be present at the Lodge of Qualification.

This Degree in America is universally called the Actual Past Master Degree. The reason for this is that the same, or a similar, degree is conferred in Royal Arch Chapters as part of the York Rite. In that context it is called the Virtual Past Master Degree. The holder of the York Rite degree certainly has none of the rights or privileges of a mason who is an actual Installed Master of a Craft lodge. The York Rite will be examined in some detail below.

In terms of the visitor, he will experience no problems in attending an American Installation, in excess of those he may find in attending a normal meeting. Once again, as Installations in the United States are not often held on fixed dates as such, the visitor is well advised to make his inquiries at a Grand Lodge office.

8. Of Visiting in General
The Initial Approach, and the Dues Card: Upon entering the domain of an American lodge, the visitor will first approach the Tyler's table. An American or Canadian Visitor will present his current Dues Card, and seek admission. The Dues Card is another practice largely peculiar to North America. While all American Grand Lodges prescribe a Master Mason's Diploma (certificate), it is most unusual for an American mason to carry this document when visiting. The Dues Card is universally accepted in America as proof of current financial membership of a Craft lodge. Of course, many jurisdictions do not issue Dues Cards. Visitors from these areas should present their Grand Lodge Certificates, a letter of Introduction from their Grand Lodge if they possess one, and some form of receipt of dues to show that they are currently fully paid up members in a Craft lodge. It is this receipt of dues that will be of greatest interest to the hosting American lodge.

Recognition and the Tyler's Oath: In having produced his credentials to show that he is, indeed, a financial mason, it will still be necessary for the Tyler to determine if the visitor comes from a recognised jurisdiction. Of course, this will usually be 'taken as read' for an American or Canadian visitor, but for 'foreign' visitors, reference is often made to a book on the Tyler's table which lists every regular lodge and Grand Lodge in the world, and cross-references the various Grand Lodge recognitions. This is invariably the *List of Lodges—Masonic*, published annually, in the United States, and circulated to every lodge which cares to purchase it, which is most. Once the visitor has satisfied the Tyler as to his bona-fides, he will then usually be passed over to one or two Past Masters of the lodge, to take a brief masonic examination. The Americans are generally particularly vigilant in this area, and the examination will be thorough, but of course, it will pose no problems to the true and lawful brother. At the examination, the visitor will usually be called upon to take the Tyler's Oath. While this procedure is unknown in England, the oath used is similar to that required under the same circumstances when visiting a lodge under the Grand Lodge of Ireland. The Tyler's Oath, in some American Jurisdictions simply referred to as a 'Test Oath', is considered as Monitorial in the United States, and so can properly be repeated here. It reads as follows:

'I, ..., in the presence of God and these witnesses, do hereby and hereon, solemnly and sincerely swear: that I have been regularly initiated as an Entered Apprentice Mason, passed to the degree of a fellow Craft and raised to the sublime degree of a Master Mason in a just and legal manner; that I do not stand suspended or expelled from any Lodge of Masons, nor do I know of any reason why I should not hold masonic communication with my brethren. So help me God'.

Entry into the Lodge, and the Flag Ceremony: Having passed the necessary avouchment procedures, the visitor may now enter the lodge room. He will be supplied with regalia, should he not be carrying his own. All members and visitors assemble in the lodge room for the opening. Generally, only the visit of a Grand Lodge officer, or another lodge on an official visit, will occasion an admittance once the lodge is opened, latecomers excepted. Even so, procedures in this regard do vary between jurisdictions. Generally, the lodge will be opened directly in the Master Mason degree. During the opening procedures, it is not uncommon for the lodge deacons to 'purge the Lodge', demanding certain modes of recognition from those present.

An interesting ceremony sometimes applied during the opening of a lodge in America is the Flag Ceremony, or more correctly, the Reception of the Flag of our Country. All American lodges must display the American Flag within the lodge room. The ceremony involves certain lodge officers retiring from the lodge to collect the flag, and re-entering to present it to the Master. The Master then leads those present in a Pledge of Allegiance, which is usually accompanied by the singing of *America* or the *Star-Spangled Banner*. During the closing of the lodge, the flag will be retired with similar ceremony. It should be noted that in most jurisdictions the Flag Ceremony is only used, as a rule, at certain meetings such as the annual election, and the lodge Installation. However, in every jurisdiction, a flag Ceremony is always used at the opening and closing of a Grand Lodge meeting.

The Closing of a Lodge: Towards the closing of an American lodge, it is not uncommon for visitors to be asked to speak although if time is running late this might be dispensed with. Visitors will be asked to rise, and state their name, lodge and jurisdiction. Visitors from some distance are more likely to be asked if they wish to speak. It is most desirable to be brief.

Special Visits: There are two other occurrences which the visitor may encounter at American lodges—a Fraternal Visit, and an Offical Visit. A Fraternal Visit can mean differing things, depending on the jurisdiction. Either it is the visit of one lodge to another (Master, Officers, and members) or, it is the visit by the local Grand Lodge officer. It is quite common in the large majority of American Jurisdictions for lodges to be grouped into Districts under a local Grand Lodge officer. It is usually incumbent upon this officer to visit each of his lodges at least once per year. The American District system will be more fully examined below.

An official visit in a number of jurisdictions consists of the attendance at a lodge by the local Grand Lodge officer for the purposes of 'inspecting' the lodge. Upon entry, he will examine the lodge charter, its by-laws, and its records to ensure that they are in order, and he will receive the annual dues payable to the Grand Lodge. He will also witness an exemplification of a degree ceremony. In practice, his inspection of lodge records is usually a symbolic ceremony to a great extent, as the official purposes of the visit will normally have been already dealt with in a meeting with the lodge's Master and Secretary. An Official or Fraternal Visit largely affords the only examples whereupon a group of masons will be admitted, with some ceremony, into an American lodge after it has been opened. In many jurisdictions, it is usual to call a special meeting for the purpose of receiving such a visit. Of course, the official visit of a Grand Master or Senior Grand Lodge officer will also be received with great ceremony, but in most jurisdictions—particularly those with a large number of lodges—such visits tend to be infrequent. It must be noted, in addition, that the terms Fraternal Visit and Official Visit can be found to be interchanged between some American Jurisdictions in terms of the occasion to which the name is applied.

As with usual British-type practices, a visit from a local Grand Lodge officer often coincides with a lodge Installation. The American system of lodge inspection is largely a reflection of another difference between American and British-type customs. In America, with some exceptions, there is no such thing as a Past Grand Lodge Officer, or Past Grand Lodge Rank.

Limitations of Visiting American Lodges: In addition to general limitations imposed on any mason visiting from one lodge to another (as discussed near the beginning of this guide), there is a further limitation that the visitor may encounter in America. In some jurisdictions, a visitor will not normally be present during a Business Meeting, and more particularly during an Annual Meeting. Of course, such a restriction will not apply to a visitor attending a degree ceremony, or other type of meeting. Nonetheless, even in those jurisdictions where attendance at a Business Meeting by a visitor is not totally usual, many lodge masters will grant permission to allow visitor attendance. In this area, the visitor is advised to approach these matters with circumspection.

9. THE FAMILY AND AMERICAN MASONRY

It is difficult to delve much further into the realms of American masonry without discussing it in the context of the family. Probably one of the first things that will become apparent to the non-American visitor is that freemasonry in the United States is not simply for the man alone, but rather it involves the entire family. The male freemason will be a member of one or more Craft lodges. In America, these are consistently referred to as Blue Lodges. He will often be a member of a number of additional degrees, as well. For his wife, there are several 'masonic' orders, such as the Order of the Eastern Star, the Order of Amaranth, and others. For girls, there is the Order of Job's Daughters, and the Order of the Rainbow. For boys up to the age of twenty-one, there is the Order of DeMolay. These organisations for the masonic family are not 'masonic as such—they contain no ritual or forms in any way imitative of freemasonry. However, in America, these bodies are certainly associated or identified with masonry. For the women's orders such as the Eastern Star, a definite masonic relationship is a prerequisite for membership. In other words, the female candidate for the Eastern Star must be wife, mother, sister, aunt, dauther, or some other relative of a freemason. A masonic relationship is not necessary for the children's orders, but nevertheless the vast majority of children involved tend to be related to Freemasons. Masons may be members of the essentially female orders, such as the Eastern Star. In addition, masons and Eastern Star Sisters tend to act as organisers and guardians for the various children's orders.

It must be noted that outside North America these organisations for the masonic family are not often approved by Grand Lodges, particularly those of Britain or of direct British descent. Indeed, the Grand Lodges of England, Ireland and Scotland look upon them with consistent dissapproval, and will not permit their memberships to belong to them. It is therefore most advisable for the non-American visitor to be well aware of his own Grand Lodge's policies and statutes in these matters.

10. The Matter of Membership

Another fact which may well surprise the non-American visitor is that lodge memberships in the United States tend to be very large. In the larger cities of America, it is far from uncommon to find lodges with memberships of more than one thousand. Naturally, in smaller centres these huge memberships are not reached, but nevertheless across the national masonic spectrum, most lodges will fit into a two hundred to eight hundred membership range. Indeed, in many jurisdictions, should a lodge find itself reduced to one hundred members, it will generally be looking to merge with some other lodge. Conversely, of course, in many jurisdictions outside of North America a lodge possessing more than one hundred members will be considered large.

The Reasons for Large Membership: It would appear that there are two main reasons for the somewhat mammoth memberships of American lodges. Firstly, the costs of running lodges and maintaining lodge buildings in America are very high. This is accentuated by the fact that individual lodges tend to own individual Masonic Temples. Therefore, a large membership is usually needed to maintain a sound financial position.

Secondly, high lodge memberships are often enforced by the territoriality of American lodges, and by regulations relating to dual and plural membership. The majority of American lodges, either by statute or custom, have custody over candidates in their immediate geographical area. This custody may be shared by one or more other lodges in the same area, whereupon it becomes joint custody. In other words, a man seeking to join freemasonry may only petition a lodge located in the vicinity of his residential address. Indeed, often larger cities are divided into territories for masonic purposes. In addition, it is far from uncommon for a lodge to object to a new lodge being formed in its territory as this will, it is argued, limit its potential membership.

Dual and Plural Membership: In terms of dual and plural membership, American practices in this area also assists in ensuring large lodge memberships. A number of Grand Lodges only permit single membership—in other words a mason may belong to only one Blue lodge. Some Grand Lodges do allow dual membership, but more commonly permit members to belong to one lodge in its jurisdiction and one lodge in another, rather than to two lodges within its own boundaries. Only a minority of American Grand Lodges permit plural membership.

The sum total of all these factors means that the actual number of lodges is kept relatively low in most jurisdictions of the United States, and this in turn forces high memberships. In addition, the American system for convening a virtually unregulated number of special meetings allows for a great many men to join freemasonry.

The Higher Degree Factor: A rather obvious effect of large memberships is that the average mason might be excused for thinking that his personal scope for involvement in lodge activities is somewhat limited. This is doubtlessly one of the main reasons why the higher degrees are extremely popular in the United States. Curiously, the large number of masons who become members of these additional degrees and get involved as such, tend to greatly lessen the active membership of Blue lodges. A natural question coming from a non-American visitor might well be: 'With lodge memberships as many as one thousand, how can one ever attain office and become Master of his lodge?' The answer, it can now be appreciated, lies in the fact that active membership is comparatively low. All the Master Mason has to do is express interest, and he will soon find himself in office, or to use the American term—in the Lodge line. Of course, these factors cannot be applied equally across the breadth of American masonry, but nevertheless, the higher degree factor unintentionally aids progression in Blue lodges.

11. The Scottish Rite, the York Rite, and the Shriners

There are two major progressions beyond the Craft in American masonry—the Scottish Rite and the York Rite. Both involve a system of degrees which are eagerly sought, and fairly readily attained, by a large number of American freemasons.

The Ancient and Accepted Scottish Rite: The Scottish Rite is probably the most powerful masonic organisation in the United States, and 'above the Craft' it is certainly the most popular. In the United States, the Rite is governed by two independent Supreme Councils—those of the Northern and Southern Jurisdictions—which between them control the Rite in America and part of Canada. The Scottish Rite is a system of 33 degrees. The first three degrees are the Craft degrees, taken in a Blue lodge. Within the American Scottish Rite, under the Northern Jurisdiction, there then follows five stages of advancement—The Lodge of Perfection (4th to 14th degrees), The Princes of Jerusalem (15th and 16 degrees), Chapters Rose Croix (17th and 18th degrees), the Consistory (19th to 32nd degrees), and finally the Supreme Council (33rd degree). The system under the Southern Jurisdiction is similar. Progress up to the 32nd degree is readily obtainable and reasonably rapid. However, the 33rd degree is considered an honour and is only held by members of the Supreme Council (limited in number to 33), and awarded on an honorary basis to small numbers of 32nd degree masons for distinguished service to the Rite.

A commonly heard statement made in American freemasonry is that a brother is a '32nd Degree Mason and a Shriner'. Indeed, the attainment of the 32nd Degree and membership of the Shriners is considered in America to be the pinnacle of freemasonry. The Shriners will be discussed shortly.

The conferment of the degrees of the Scottish Rite is achieved with great pageantry. Without doubt, the largest masonic edifices in the United States are Scottish Rite temples. Basically, they are in fact large theatres, with stages, props, scenery, elaborate lighting and sound, dressing rooms, and all the trappings one would expect to find associated with a huge dramatic production. Indeed, a huge production is exactly what a session of degree conferment involves. Groups of degrees are often conferred at any one session, and there may be up to one hundred or more candidates. Usually, only one of the degrees to be conferred will actually be worked in full, with the others being communicated in brief form. Often, only one candidate is chosen to take part in the ceremony, with all others watching they will all take their obligations as a group. The work is conducted by a team of officers acting out the ceremony as one would a dramatic play.

Membership of the Scottish Rite is very high, and about one mason in five in America holds the 32nd degree. It is usual for there to be only one Scottish Rite Cathedral in any one city, and as a result some valleys (as single units of the Rite are often called) have memberships up to 30,000, or more. Doubtlessly, these huge numbers are needed to maintain the massive buildings that are usually the Scottish Rite Cathedrals. Appropriately qualified visitors may readily visit the Scottish Rite in America. The two American Supreme Councils maintain fraternal relations with the English, Irish and Scottish Supreme Councils of the Rite. Nonetheless, overseas visitors are still advised to seek advice from their own Supreme Council prior to visiting under the Scottish Rite in America.

The York Rite: The York Rite is the second system of masonry beyond the Craft to claim our attention. It covers a series of eleven degrees, all of which are worked in full. These degrees are grouped into three tiers, or sub-Rites, as follows: conferred in a Royal Arch Chapter—the Mark Master Mason Degree, the (Virtual) Past Master Degree, the Most Excellent Master Degree, and the Degree of Royal Arch Mason. Together these four degrees form what is known in America as the Capitular Rite. Conferred in a Council of Royal and Select Masters—the Royal Master Degree, the Select Master Degree, and the Super Excellent Master Degree. Together these three degrees form the Cryptic Rite. Conferred in a Knights Templar Commandery—the Red Cross Order, the Knights of Malta Order, and the Knight Templar Order. Together these three Orders form the Chivalric Rite.

The Scottish Rite and the York Rite both tend to engage in friendly rivalry for membership. Both systems are well established throughout America. In some jurisdictions, the York Rite is stronger, but in many the Scottish Rite predominates. Of course, a mason may belong to both Rites, and many do. Again, York Rite bodies tend to maintain fraternal relations with Grand Bodies working the same degrees in other parts of the world. This certainly applies to the comparable Grand Bodies in England, Ireland, and Scotland. However, once again, qualified visitors should consult their own home Grand Bodies prior to visiting a York Rite 'lodge' in America.

The Shriners: A North American mason who holds the 32nd degree in the Scottish Rite, or who is a Knight Templar in the York Rite, is in a position to join the Shriners. The full title of this order is the Ancient Arabic Order, Nobles of the Mystic Shrine. It is considered the apex of freemasonry in the United States. Actually, it is in every sense a non-masonic order, except that it requires the prerequisites just stated. It was invented as an order—quite literally—in New York in the 1870s and later spread throughout North America. Its ceremonies are extremely extroverted and somewhat bazarre. The Shriners as an organisation is devoted entirely to charity and social activities. Membership of the Shriners is keenly sought, and it appears to grant a certain social status in America. The charitable work of the order is outstanding. The Shriners operate 22 huge hospitals for crippled children in major cities across the United States, Canada and Mexico; together with institutes for research and treatment of the severely burned. Membership of the Shriners is about one million. It does not exist to any extent outside North America, although there is a Shrine Temple (called a Mosque) in West Germany. It must be noted that the Shriners are not countenanced by the Grand Lodges of England, Ireland and Scotland, and some other non-American Grand Lodges. Masons belonging to these jurisdictions may not join the Shriners. Visitors from outside North America are advised to be aware of their own Grand Lodge policy in this area.

12. LODGE WORKINGS, AND RITUAL

American Craft ritual is reasonably similar to British rituals. The content is much the same, but the forms used show variations. Indeed, American ritual is older than English ritual currently in use. English ritual, to a very large extent, was standardised upon the union of the rival Antients and Moderns Grand Lodges in 1813. This standardisation, or amalgamation, of two rituals meant that certain symbolic features of both were lost in the process. American ritual, on the other hand, retains many of those features that were lost to the English. There is no question that American ritual originated from the workings of England, Ireland, and Scotland. Indeed, not only in terms of ritual but in many other customs, the visitor will note many facets of American masonry which are grafts from the old usages of the British Isles.

American ritual, in a broad sense, was itself standardised. This was achieved in the late 1790s by one Brother Thomas Smith Webb who is often described as the 'Father of American Ritual'. Basically, Webb took the English Antient ritual of the time, and with a few minor changes, the *Webb* Ritual emerged, whereupon it became generally adopted in the United States. Of course, barely twenty years later the English Union occurred, and English ritual was thereupon moulded into its present form. The term *Webb* ritual has long been used to describe the spectrum of American Craft rituals. There are a range of differences between the workings of the fifty American Grand Lodges, just as there are between the various English rituals in current usage. For example, while in most jurisdictions lodges open and close in the Master Mason degree, some do so in the first degree, while some only open in the degree to be conferred. In some eastern jurisdictions, and Pennsylvania is a notable example, ritual forms tend to be somewhat more English than Webb. Clearly, there is no such thing as the *Webb Ritual* as such, as each American jurisdiction has its own prescribed ritual. The term Webb Form is probably more appropriate to encompass the gamut of American ritual.

Probably the first thing that the overseas visitor will notice about American ritual is that it retains many symbols no longer found in English forms. For example, symbolic use is made of such things as the hour-glass, beehive, scythe, and anchor. In addition, great use is made of catechismic lectures which have been largely lost to English usage. The signs of the three degrees are largely similar to those of England, except that the Scottish first degree sign is favoured. The second degree is probably more elaborate than the English, while the third degree in many Webb Forms is closer in character to Scotland than England.

All American Grand Lodges prescribe a standard ritual for their lodges, and generally only this ritual may be used. The Americans go to some lengths to safeguard their rituals. Only about a dozen Grand Lodges actually published a ritual, or 'The Work' as it is commonly called in the United States. In those that do, it is always in cipher (code). However, most American Grand Lodges, whether they publish a ritual or not, produce a monitor. The monitor contains monitorial or explanatory parts of the ritual, such as symbolical lectures, as opposed to esoteric portions. These monitors are printed in plain language.

The American District System: As with the system in Ireland, which also prohibits a printed ritual, innovations in America are guarded against by the extensive use of Inspectors or lecturers. Brief reference has already been made to the American District system. Nearly all American Grand Lodges use such a system, all of which are quite similar. Basically, every lodge in a jurisdiction is placed in a District, which might contain anything from five to twenty lodges. Each District is placed under a local Grand Lodge officer, usually named a District Deputy Grand Master, or District Inspector. It is pertinent to add that American Districts bear no real comparision to a Provincial or District Grand Lodge of the British type. American Districts are not District Grand Lodges, and a District Deputy Grand Master has only limited administrative powers. Instead, American Districts basically exist to perpetuate the ritual prescribed by the Grand Lodge. A District Deputy Grand Master, therefore, acts largely as an Inspector of Workings. The District Deputy generally acts as a co-ordinator of masonic instruction and education in his district. This is done through classes for lodge officers, exemplifications, and other methods. Many jurisdictions decree lodges of instruction organised on a District basis. Generally, attendance at instruction classes is compulsory for lodge officers.

Perhaps the most striking feature of the *Webb* ritual is its proficiency tests. Each Grand Lodge has its own standards in this area, but all tend to be most rigorous. In the United States, it is obligatory for a candidate to pass an extensive proficiency test in the previous degree before being advanced to the next. This also includes passing a proficiency test in the Master Mason Degree. Passing a proficiency test may involve answering by memory up to eighty questions in catechismic form by memory, including the recital of the obligation. In some jurisdictions, these tests will be taken in open lodge, while in others they are taken privately with examiners and progress is reported to the lodge.

Of course, the lack of a printed ritual does not make achieving proficiency a simple task for candidates. Many jurisdictions hold instruction classes for candidates to assist in this regard. In addition, many Grand Lodges require that senior lodge officers attain proficiency in aspects of the work prior to achieving a higher office. For example, a Junior Warden might be required to prove his proficiency as a Senior Warden before he can be elected to that office. Instructors must also achieve proficiency in what they instruct. Many Grand Lodges offer an extensive series of proficiency certificates to qualifying masons.

13. THE AMERICAN LODGE, ITS LAYOUT, AND ITS OFFICERS

The layout of American lodges differs only slightly between jurisdictions, and like many features of American Masonry it can be viewed as an amalgam of English, Irish and Scottish usages. Typical features of an American lodge are the location of an altar in the middle of the lodge room, and a concealed light to illuminate it at appropriate times. In many lodges, only the Master's chair will be located in the East, while in others a chair will be available for the Chaplain. As a rule, the immediate Past Master has no 'official status' in an American lodge. An interesting point concerning the Master is that in American lodges he often wears a hat. The hat is briefly removed when the name of the GAOTU is mentioned. Not all Grand Lodges approve the hat, but in those that do a variety of types can often be seen in use in lodges.

The standard officers of an American lodge are: The Worshipful Master (often referred to as Worshipful Sir), the Senior Warden, the Junior Warden, the Treasurer, Secretary, Chaplain, Senior Deacon, Junior Deacon, Marshall, Senior Steward, Junior Steward, and Tyler. Most lodges also possess an Organist. In some jurisdictions, other officers may be appointed, such as a Ritualist, Orator, Electrican, and Inner Sentinal; but these appointments are not particularly common. In every American jurisdiction, the Master, Wardens, Secretary, and Treasurer are elective officers. The balance of the offices are held by the Master's appointees. Nevertheless, in practice both elective and appointive offices tend to the progressive, with the more obvious exceptions of Secretary and Treasurer, who generally hold office, subject to re-election, for as long as they wish to serve. It is most unusual, for example, for a Junior Warden to fail to be elected as Senior Warden subsequently. Again, the titles and functions of certain offices show Irish or Scottish influences, in particular. The offices of Senior and Junior Steward are unknown in English-type lodges, and they certainly do not function as Stewards in the English sense. Rather, their duties tend to parallel the Senior and Junior Deacon of an English lodge to some degree. The Junior Deacon in an American lodge sits inside the door to the lodge room, and his functions largely match those of an English Inner Guard. In those jurisdictions that appoint an Inner Sentinel, he basically functions as a door opener to the Preparation Room. Similarly, a Ritualist, often a Past Master, acts as the prompter of ritual work, while an Electrican controls the lighting of the Temple. In many jurisdictions, while these extra officers are not appointed or given a title, designated masons are often placed to perform analogous functions.

14. ASPECTS OF AMERICAN MASONRY

While American lodges involve themselves in a diverse range of charitable pursuits, probably the most popular charity is the Blood Bank. The giving of blood to Blood Banks and hospitals is greatly favoured by American masonic authorities, particularly in the Eastern States. In some jurisdictions, actual Masonic Blood Banks are maintained.

There are few American Grand Lodges that do not possess a masonic home for the elderly. Those that do not generally tend to be too small numerically to afford one. American masonic homes tend to be very large institutions, and heavily supported by the general masonic fraternity. Some jurisdictions have also endowed children's homes, and Masonic hospitals. Charitable pursuits of this nature, where they occur, are mentioned under the jurisdiction headings following this general text.

Perhaps the best known masonic charitable organisation is the Masonic Relief Association of the United States and Canada. It is supported by all North American Grand Lodges, and there is scarcely a major city in North America that does not possess an affiliated Masonic Relief Committee, Masonic Service Bureau, or Masonic Employment Association.

The other major inter-jurisdictional masonic organisation is the Masonic Service Association. Again, it is supported by all American Grand Lodges. It was founded in 1919, and its basic aims are those of masonic education and the dissemination of masonic information. It is also involved in benevolent activities. It has field agents in most jurisdictions, and co-ordinates a nation-wide hospital visiting program for masons and their family members. Its periodical, the *Short Talk Bulletin* has a very wide circulation. The Association meets annually.

Inter-jurisdictional co-operation in North America is aided by several annual conferences. Firstly, there is the Annual Conference of Grand Masters of North America. In concert with this is always held the Annual Conference of Grand Secretaries of North America. There are also several regional Conferences of Grand Masters held on a regular basis. The Conference of Grand Masters has several Committees attached to it, the most influential being the Commission on Information for Recognition.

In a number of American Jurisdictions, lodges have been specifically formed for the sole purpose of conducting masonic funerals. These lodges are usually known as Memorial Lodges. Their functions are self-evident. They meet only as required, and while they possess the officers of a normal lodge, they perform no degree work whatsoever.

In some jurisdictions, smoking is permitted in lodge rooms. However, where this is permitted, it is often restricted to the body of the lodge, and the privilege rarely extends to lodge officers for obvious reasons. Nonetheless, the number of Grand Lodges continuing to permit smoking in its Temples is diminishing.

The titles assumed in American masonry warrant some comment. General practice in America is to omit the word brother for Worshipful Masters and Grand Lodge officers. Thus, a Master will be referred to as 'Worshipful John Smith', and a Grand Master as 'Most Worshipful John Smith'. Nonetheless, there are a few jurisdictions, mainly in the East, that do use the word 'brother' for these types of titles. In addition, one or two Grand Lodges (for example, New Hampshire) use the Scottish system, whereby the title is attached to the office, not to its incumbent. Thus, a Grand Master in this usage will be referred to as Brother John Smith, Most Worshipful Grand Master.

In some jurisdictions, a not unusual practice is for a dispensation to be obtained to work a degree ceremony (suitably tyled) in the open air—usually on a private farm. Often the ceremony worked will be the Master Mason degree.

It is not uncommon for many American lodges to hold ladies' nights. As one might expect a wide variance of usage is prevalent in this area. Often they are not associated with any lodge meeting, but when they are a special meeting is usually called for the purpose, although no masonic meeting as such will be held. Ladies' Nights often consist of a dinner or a dance.

Language lodges are permitted in a number of American jurisdictions. A number of American cities tend to be fairly cosmopolitan in nature, and this doubtlessly accounts for practices in this area. As many as twenty American jurisdictions possess this type of lodge, whereupon members work in a language other than English. New York City has quite a number of these lodges, and many large cities often possess at least one or two. Visitors interested in attending such a lodge will readily gain assistance at a Grand Lodge office.

15. MASONIC GOVERNMENT

The forms of Grand Lodge government in the United States are remarkably similar to one another. With the exception of only two eastern jurisdictions (Massachusetts and Pennsylvania, which meet in Quarterly Communications), all other American Grand Lodges meet annually. The annual session usually lasts two to three days. At the Annual Communication all business of the Grand Lodge is considered, and the new Grand Lodge officers are elected and installed.

The Elective Grand Lodge: All Grand Lodge officers, including the Grand Master, usually hold their positions for only one year, with the exceptions of the Grand Secretary and Grand Treasurer. It is not common for a Grand Master to serve a second year in office. In all American jurisdictions, the Grand Master, Deputy Grand Master, Senior Grand Warden, Junior Grand Warden, Grand Treasurer, and Grand Secretary are elected annually. In a very small number of cases, the offices of the Grand Secretary and Grand Treasurer are combined. All other Grand Lodge officers are, as a rule, appointed by the Grand Master. The Grand Secretary and Grand Treasurer tend to be re-elected every year until retirement. Of course, they are invariably paid, full time employees of the Grand Lodge; although in smaller Grand Lodges the latter may be part-time.

The Grand Lodge Line: Aside from the Grand Secretary and Grand Treasurer, the elective Grand Lodge offices in the United States tend to be progressive. For example, it would be most unusual for a Senior Grand Warden to fail to be subsequently elected as Deputy Grand Master, and so on. In America, this is usually called the Grand Lodge Line, and the high officers of the Grand Lodge are called Line Officers. Of course, this progressiveness is quite distinctive of American masonry, and is unknown in British-type practices. In many American jurisdictions, but certainly not all, most appointive Grand Lodge offices also tend to be progressive—leading in time to the elective offices at the top, and eventually to the

Grand Mastership. The appointive Grand Lodge offices in the United States closely resemble those of the British Grand Lodges.

The Equal Representation System: The actual membership of American Grand Lodges, for the most part, is based on equal representation. The usual members of an American Grand Lodge are its Grand Lodge officers, past Grand Lodge officers (which are usually few), and the Masters and Wardens of each constituent lodge. Generally, every lodge is entitled to three votes in the Grand Lodge, alloted to the three lodge officers just mentioned. Many jurisdictions also employ a proxy system, whereupon a lodge may appoint a mason other than its three usual representatives to attend the Grand Lodge should one or more of these three be unable to attend. It is also quite usual that if only one lodge delegate is attending, he exercises all three votes to which his lodge is entitled. By these methods this system ensures, at least in theory, that every lodge has an equal say in the running of the Grand Lodge. Of course, the system tends to break down if a lodge's representatives fail to attend the Annual Communication, or fail to appoint proxies, and this sometimes occurs.

Past Grand Lodge Officers: Past Grand Lodge officers are not common in American Grand Lodges. Generally, only past elective Grand Lodge officers retain their rank as such, and thus maintain Grand Lodge membership. Of course, as the offices of Deputy Grand Master, Senior Grand Warden, and Junior Grand Warden are progressive, it is rare for a Grand Lodge to possess masons holding these offices in a 'past' sense. Occasionally, there will be a Past Grand Secretary, or a Past Grand Treasurer, but as the incumbents of these offices tend to serve for long periods, this occurrence is equally rare. In addition, in many jurisdictions, a Past Grand Secretary (or Treasurer) is usually termed as 'Grand Secretary Emeritus'. Therefore, it is generally only Past Grand Masters who hold a 'Past Office'. Appointive Grand Lodge officers who leave the Grand Lodge Line often gain no past rank, but merely revert to being Past Masters. The conferment of Past Grand Rank in the English sense is largely unknown in the United States, except occasionally to distinguished brethren from other jurisdictions in a purely honorary capacity.

The Past Master: Of course, the Past Master is a universally recognised rank in all United States Grand jurisdictions. The distinction between an 'Actual' and 'Virtual' Past Master in the American sense has already been explained. Generally, a candidate for an office in a Grand Lodge (whether it be elective or appointive) must be an actual Past Master. There are a small minority of Grand Lodges (mostly in the east) in which Past Masters of constituent lodges are members of the Grand Lodge in their own right, generally in addition to the representative system already outlined. Of course, the Grand Lodge membership of Past Masters parallels usual English-type practice.

The Committee System: Between Annual Communications, an American Grand Jurisdiction is administered by a myriad of Grand Lodge Committees, many of which are permanent, although some are Ad Hoc. Generally, the membership of each is elected or appointed (varying methods are employed depending on the jurisdiction) at the Annual Communication. It is not uncommon for a Grand Lodge to possess over twenty committees, such as Masonic Education, Fraternal Relations, Public Relations, Necrology, Finance, and so on. In most Grand Lodges, it is the Committee on Jurisprudence which tends to be the most 'powerful'. Very few American Grand Lodges employ a Board of General Purposes on the 'English Model'.

16. THE FIFTY AMERICAN GRAND LODGES—AN INTRODUCTION

In having completed this extensive, although broad, synopsis of American masonry, it is now possible to proceed to very briefly examine each of the American Jurisdictions individually, and it is to that pursuit which the pages immediately following will encompass. However, it is first necessary to make several points by way of explanation. As has already been mentioned, the common practice in the United States is that of 'one temple—one lodge'. Of course, there are a great many exceptions to this practice, particularly in the largest cities. However, even in many of these the practice applies. One must hasten to add that the 'one temple—one lodge' practices in America have occurred as the result of history and tradition, and not as the result of any Grand Lodge statute. In the following pages, the address of the various Grand Lodge offices are listed, plus the main Temple in the main cities of the United States. The word *main* Temple is stressed. Without exception, there are several other Temples in every city listed. The address given is simply that of the one which, by and large, houses the most lodges in that particular city. In some cities, each lodge does own its own Temple, and it is therefore impossible to designate a main Temple. Where this occurs, the fact is stated and readers are referred to local telephone directories.

Indeed, right across the United States it is quite usual for lodges to be listed in local telephone directories. In the 'white pages' they are listed under the heading 'Masonic', while in 'yellow pages' the heading 'Fraternal Organisations' should be consulted. Of course, these directories do not give any meeting details, but they do provide addresses and a phone number.

One further point is most worthy of note. As is usual in most of the masonic world, American lodges do print meeting notices for each meeting, for distribution to members. Of course, these are not much use to intending visitors. However, one American practice in this area is of distinct use. In many jurisdictions, lodges actually advertise their meetings in the Public Notices columns of local newspapers. Visitors are well advised to make use of this facility, where they find it to occur.

Lastly, the matter of Grand Lodge offices themselves must be explained. Every American Grand Lodge has a Grand Lodge office, wherein is housed the Grand Secretary and his staff. Obviously, the size of the office and the number of staff tends to parallel the numerical strength of the jurisdiction. However, it is relatively rare for a Grand Lodge office building to possess masonic temples and meeting rooms. In other words, these buildings tend to be purely administrative. Nonetheless, not a few of them do house a Grand Lodge library and museum. In addition, in quite a few jurisdictions, the Grand Lodge building will be on the campus of its masonic home, or form part of its masonic home complex.

The Grand Lodges of the United States of America

ALABAMA

The Grand Lodge of Free and Accepted Masons of Alabama
Founded: 1821
Addresses: Grand Lodge Office: Masonic Home, 3033 Vaughn Road, Montgomery 36106. Postal Address: P.O. Box 6195, Montgomery, Albama 36106. *Telephone:* (205) 272 8961.
Birmingham: Masonic Temple, 215 24th Street North, Birmingham.

Lodges: 409. Permits Dual Membership, but 2nd Lodge must be outside the State of Alabama.
Membership: 64,537.
Descent: Kentucky, Tennessee, North Carolina, and others.
Government: Elective Grand Lodge.
Courtesy Degrees: Conferred on request.   *Ritual:* Webb form.
Minimum Time lapse between degrees: 24 hours.
Major Publications: Annual Proceedings.   Constitution.

History
Alabama's first lodge was established at Huntsville in 1811, under dispensation from the Grand Lodge of Kentucky. A Grand Lodge was formed in 1821 by a convention of delegates from nine lodges, variously holding charters from Kentucky, North Carolina, South Carolina, Georgia and Tennessee.

The anti-masonry which swept America in the wake of the Morgan Affair had a great effect in Alabama. While a great many lodges were formed in the early years following the erection of the Grand Lodge, by 1829 a third of all Alabama lodges had closed. The Grand Lodge failed to meet at all in 1832, such was the decline of masonry in that State. By 1836, the Grand Lodge was able to re-establish itself, and thereafter followed a long period of sustained expansion. By 1860, Alabama had 236 lodges on its roll, and this number had risen to 409 in 1983.

Special Notes for Visitors
Alabama is a largely rural southern State, without the large population centres found in other parts of America. Virtually every small town in Alabama has a lodge, each with its own temple, as a rule. In Alabama, it is usual for lodges to list two regular meetings per month, which are usually on the same days—for example: 1st and 3rd Mondays; 2nd and 4th Thursdays, and so forth. As with most other American Jurisdictions, Alabama lodges are grouped into Districts (currently forty), under District Inspectors. The masonic home at Montgomery (also the seat of the Grand Lodge) represents the great emphasis masonry in Alabama places on benevolent pursuits.

ALASKA

The Grand Lodge of Free and Accepted Masons of Alaska
Founded: 1981
Address: Grand Lodge Office: 540 International Airport Road, Anchorage 99502.
Postal Address: P.O. Box 6668, Anchorage.   *Telephone:* (907) 277 5414.
Anchorage: Masonic Temple, 606 West 4th Avenue, Anchorage.
Lodges: 12.   Permits Dual Membership inside Alaska, and Plural Membership outside Alaska.
Membership: 1,863.
Descent: Washington.   *Government:* Elective Grand Lodge.
Courtesy Degrees: Conferred on request.   *Ritual:* Webb form.
Minimum Time Lapse between Degrees: 14 Days.
Major Publications: Constitution.   Annual Proceedings.

History

Alaska is the youngest regular Grand Lodge in North America, being formed in 1981. Until that year, all lodges in Alaska held charters from the Grand Lodge of Washington. It was formed by twelve lodges with the blessing of the Washington Grand Lodge, although seven lodges located in south Alaska close to Washington State decided to maintain their current allegiance. The net result of this occurrence means that Washington is the only Grand Lodge in the United States with lodges in another American Jurisdiction. Subsequent to its formation, the Grand Lodge of Alaska has secured the fraternal recognition of virtually all the regular Grand Lodges of the world, including England, Ireland and Scotland. Quite naturally, the Alaskan Grand Lodge has adopted a constitution and other forms closely identified with the Grand Lodge of Washington.

Special Notes for Visitors

As Alaska is such a new jurisdiction, its practices as yet closely follow those of the Grand Lodge of Washington. Masonic visitors to lodges in southern Alaska should make their enquiries to the Grand Lodge of Washington office in Tacoma. Otherwise, a visit can be readily made to the Grand Lodge office in Anchorage.

ARIZONA
The Grand Lodge of Free and Accepted Masons of Arizona
Founded: 1882
Address: Grand Lodge Office: Masonic Temple, 345 West Monroe Street, Phoenix, Arizona. 85003. *Telephone:* (602) 252 1924.
Lodges: 71. Permits Dual and Plural Membership.
Membership: 16,302.
Descent: California and New Mexico. *Government:* Elective Grand Lodge
Courtesy Degrees: Conferred on request. *Ritual:* Webb form.
Minimum Time Lapse between Degrees: None, candidates may advance when proficient.
Major Publications: Constitutions. Annual Proceedings. *Periodical: Arizona Masonry.*

History

The first lodge established in Arizonia was Azatlan Lodge No 177, formed in 1866 under the Grand Lodge of California. This was followed by Arizona Lodge No 257, in 1879, also under Californian charter. New Mexico chartered White Mountain Lodge No 5 in 1881. Today, these three lodges head the Arizona roll of lodges. In 1882, these three lodges sent delegates to a Convention at Tuscon, and formed a new Grand Lodge. The Grand Lodge of Arizona has expanded steadily since that date, reporting seventy lodges in 1982, its Centenary Year.

Special Notes for Visitors

Arizona is largely a desert State, with its history steeped in the Wild West tradition. Its two main population centres are Phoenix and Tuscon, which possess ten lodges each. The Grand Lodge office is centrally located in Phoenix, and is readily accessible to visitors. Nothing further needs to be added to the general text on America, in terms of Arizona.

ARKANSAS

The Grand Lodge of Free and Accepted Masons of Arkansas
Founded: 1838
Address: Albert Pike Memorial Temple, 700 Scott Street, Little Rock, Arkansas. 72201. *Telephone:* (501) 374 6408.
Lodges: 354. Permits Dual Membership.
Membership: 46,367.
Descent: Louisiana, Tennessee and Alabama. *Government:* Elective Grand Lodge.
Courtesy Degrees: Conferred on request. *Ritual:* Webb form.
Minimum Time Lapse between Degrees: None, candidates may advance when proficient.
Major Publications: Annual Proceedings. Constitution.

History
The first lodge erected in Arkansas received its charter from Kentucky in 1819, and was named Washington after the first American President. By 1838, three lodges were working in Arkansas chartered from Louisiana, Tennessee and Alabama, and it was these lodges that joined together in that year to establish a new Grand Lodge. The original Washington Lodge has expired in 1822. The early history of the Grand Lodge is somewhat scant, largely as the result of records being lost in fires in 1864 and 1876. The Grand Lodge has expanded continually since its inception, and today there remain few places in Arkansas without a masonic temple.

Special Notes for Visitors
Arkansas (pronounced *Ar-can-saw*) is a largely rural mid-west American State, with the city of Little Rock being the only population centre of any real size. Nevertheless, Little Rock possesses only ten lodges out of a total of 354 for the State. Almost without exception, every town in Arkansas possesses a lodge, but rarely more than one. Again, in terms of general American practices, there is little to mention by way of special notes for Arkansas outside the main text.

CALIFORNIA

The Grand Lodge of Free and Accepted Masons of California
Founded: 1850
Addresses: Grand Lodge Office: California Masonic Memorial Temple, 1111 California Street, San Francisco. 94108. *Telephone:* (415) 776 7000.
Los Angeles: Masonic Temple, 4357 Wilshire Boulevard, Los Angeles. 90010.
Long Beach: Masonic Temple, 3610 Locust Avenue, Long Beach. 90807.

Sacramento: Masonic Temple, 1123 'J' Street, Sacramento, 95814.
San Diego: Masonic Temple, 1895 Camino de Rio Street, San Diego. 92108.
Lodges: 626. Permits Dual and Plural Membership.
Membership: 188,535.
Descent: Missouri, Louisiana, Illinois, Connecticut, and others. *Ritual:* Webb form.
Courtesy Degrees: Conferred on request. *Government:* Elective Grand Lodge.
Minimum Time Lapse between Degrees: None, candidates may advance when proficient.
Major Publications: Constitutions. Monitor & Officers Manual. Annual Proceedings. Roster of Lodges. *Periodical: The California Freemason.*

History

The history of Craft in California closely parallels the discovery of gold in 1848. The first lodge was born in that year, and incredibly, the Grand Lodge of California was formed only two years later in 1850. Of course, the vast population influx occasioned by the gold discovery largely accounts for these events.

The first lodge in California, chartered in 1848, was Western Star Lodge No 98, formed under the Grand Lodge of Missouri. It commenced operations late in 1849. In the next two years, about fifteen further charters were issued for California, coming from a variety of Grand Lodges including Louisiana, Connecticut, Indiana, Illinois, and Wisconsin. The Grand Lodge was formed by four lodges on 19 April 1850, after which it expanded rapidly. Today, it remains one of the largest jurisdictions in the United States, and in the world.

Special Notes for Visitors

California possesses several large population centres, and to assist visitors the main temple in the five largest cities are listed above. Of course, each city has several other temples within its precincts. All the noted temples possess an office, and the visitor will find each staffed during daylight hours, whereupon he may readily obtain assistance. While these temples are large, it is invariably the Scottish Rite temples in particular which are, indeed, huge and magnificent edifices. The Scottish Rite Memorial Temple in San Franciso, for example, falls into this category and is well worth visiting. It is located at 2850—19th Avenue, San Francisco. Telephone: 664 4700.

There is little concerning Californian masonry which does not fit into parameters of the general text. Noteworthy is the extensive use in California of the District system for grouping lodges, with each District under a District Inspector. Each District has between three to five lodges within it, and currently there is in excess of 150 Districts within the Grand Lodge of California.

Of interest to visitors will be the old masonic hall, located at 416½ North Main Street, in central Los Angeles. It was first used in 1854, and has been refurbished by the State of California as an historic monument. It is open for public inspection on four afternoons per week. One lodge, Plaza de Los Angeles No 814, still uses the temple. Its regular meeting is the first Wednesday of the month. The old masonic temple at 25 Van Ness Avenue, San Francisco, will also be of interest to visitors to that city. It must also be mentioned that the Grand Lodge library and museum at the Masonic Memorial Temple in Los Angeles is well worth a visit when the visitor calls at the Grand Lodge office.

In the area of charity and benevolence, the Grand Lodge is particularly active. The masonic home at Union City is a very large establishment, catering for well over 300 aged residents. In addition, the Grand Lodge dispenses benevolence through various foundations and charitable funds.

The Grand Lodge publishes a particularly fine periodical magazine—the *California Freemason*. It is the official organ of the Grand Lodge, and is released quarterly.

COLORADO

The Grand Lodge of Ancient, Free and Accepted Masons of Colorado
Founded: 1861
Addresses: Grand Lodge Office: 1130 Panorama Drive, Colorado Springs. 80904.
Telephone: (303) 471 9587.
Denver: Masonic Temple, 1614 Welton Street, Denver.
Lodges: 168.　Permits Plural Membership within the State, and Dual Membership outside the State.
Membership: 33,402.
Descent: Kansas and Nebraska.　*Government:* Elective Grand Lodge.
Courtesy Degrees: Conferred on request.　*Ritual:* Webb form.
Minimum Time Lapse between Degrees: two weeks.
Major Publications: Constitution.　Annual Proceedings.　Periodical: *Colorado Masonic Craftsman.*

History
The early masonic history of Colorado was largely uneventful. The first lodge to receive a charter in Colorado was Golden City Lodge No 34; which was established from Kansas in 1860. This was followed in 1861 by the Nebraska-chartered Summit Lodge No 7; and Rocky Mountain Lodge No 8. In the same year these three lodges meet and erected the Grand Lodge of Colorado. Summit and Rocky Mountain Lodges subsequently expired, but the Grand Lodge itself continued to grow in strength, reporting 168 lodges in 1983.

Special Notes for Visitors
Colorado is another mid-west State largely composed of dry areas, whose principal tourist attractions include the southern Rocky Mountains. Masonically, Colorado's usages and customs largely fit within the scope of the general text on the United States. Visitors will receive every assistance in visiting upon attending either address listed above.

CONNECTICUT

The Grand Lodge of Ancient, Free and Accepted Masons of the State of Connecticut
Founded: 1789
Addresses: Grand Lodge Office: Masonic Home, Masonic Avenue, Wallingford. Postal Address: P.O. Box 250, Wallingford. 06492. *Telephone:* (203) 269 8757.
Bridgeport: Masonic Temple, 3045 Fairfield Avenue, Bridgeport.
Hartford: Masonic Temple, 201 Ann Street, Hartford.
New Haven: Masonic Temple, 285 Whitney Avenue, New Haven.
Lodges: 133.   Permits Dual Membership.
Membership: 32,310.
Descent: England (Moderns), and Scotland.   *Government:* Elective Grand Lodge.
Courtesy Degrees: Conferred on request.   *Ritual:* Webb form.
Minimum Time Lapse between Degrees: 24 hours, but candidates must be proficient.
Major Publications: Constitution.   Annual Proceedings.   Periodical: *Connecticut Square & Compasses.*

History
Connecticut is one of the oldest masonic jurisdictions in America. Its first lodge was warranted by the Provincial Grand Master at Boston, Massachusetts (under the English Moderns). This was Hiram Lodge, today heads the Connecticut roll of lodges. Other lodges were warranted from Scotland (via Massachusetts), and New York (English Moderns), as well as another five from Boston. By the end of the American Civil War, sixteen lodges existed in Connecticut; of which thirteen joined together in convention in 1789 to form a Grand Lodge.
As with all the New England areas, Connecticut masonry suffered during the anti-masonry of the 1830s. In 1831, almost all Grand Lodge officers resigned, and many lodges closed. It was not until the 1860s that masonry made a recovery in the State. Since those times, the Craft in Connecticut has expanded continually, and in 1983 it reported 133 lodges.

Special Notes for Visitors
Connecticut is one of the minority of US jurisdictions wherein most of its lodges list two stated communications per month. Again, as with elsewhere in the United States, few lodges in Connecticut meet during July and August. For the most part, lodges meet at 7.30 pm, although a small number open as late as 8 pm. Connecticut also possesses two lodges of research, one meeting at Bridgeport, the other at Wethersfield.
Full assistance will be received by visitors at the Grand Lodge office, which also has a very good library attached to it.

DELAWARE

The Grand Lodge of Ancient, Free and Accepted Masons of Delaware
Founded: 1806
Address: Grand Lodge Office, 818 Market Street, Wilmington. 19801.
Telephone: (302) 652 4614.
Lodges: 31. Permits Dual Membership outside the State.
Membership: 8,698.
Descent: Pennsylvannia (Antients), and Maryland. *Government:* Elective Grand Lodge.
Courtesy Degrees: Conferred on request. *Ritual:* Webb form.
Minimum Time lapse between Degrees: One lunar month.
Major Publications: Constitution. Annual Proceedings.

History

The first lodge established in Delaware was warranted by the Provincial Grand Lodge of Pennsylvania (under the English Antients Grand Lodge) in 1765, but it would appear that it did not survive. The second lodge in the area, and the oldest remaining, was Washington Lodge, No 14, also warranted from Pennsylvania, this time in 1769. This lodge now heads the Delaware roll of lodges as Washington No 1. Four more lodges were warranted from Pennsylvania up until 1802, of which two survived. The Grand Lodge of Maryland weighed in with two lodges 1792 and 1806.

Four lodges held a convention in 1806 for the purposes of forming a Grand Lodge, which was duly established on 7 June of that year. However, the Washington Lodge failed the pay its outstanding dues to Pennsylvania prior to joining the new Grand Lodge. The Grand Lodge of Pennsylvania, as it now was, voiced strong objections, and was less than happy with other procedures concerning the erection of the Delaware Grand Lodge—declaring it illegal. The Grand Lodge of Maryland adopted the same course. However, other Grand Lodges, such as Virginia, supported Delaware. With the passing of time the acrimony abated, and the Grand Lodge of Delaware was generally recognised as regular.

Special Notes for Visitors

Delaware is one of the smaller Grand Lodges in the United States, currently possessing thirty-one lodges. Of these, seven meet in Wilmington, the major population centre of the State. A visitor will readily receive every assistance upon visiting the Grand Lodge office in that city.

DISTRICT OF COLUMBIA

The Grand Lodge of Free and Accepted Masons of the District of Columbia
Founded: 1811
Address: Masonic Temple, 801—13th Street North West, Washington, D.C. 20005. *Telephone:* (202) 393 0121.
Lodges: 37. Permits Dual Membership.
Membership: 9,800.
Descent: Maryland, Pennsylvania, and Virginia. *Government:* Elective Grand Lodge.

Courtesy Degrees: Conferred on request.   *Ritual:* Webb form.
Minimum Time lapse between Degrees: One Lunar Month.
Major Publications: Constitutions. Annual Proceedings. Grand Lodge Bulletin.

History

The District of Columbia, of course, is not an American State, but it is nevertheless treated as one for masonic purposes. The District of Columbia is that area which surrounds the American capital city of Washington DC. The first lodge in the District was chartered by the Grand Lodge of Maryland in 1789, but it expired in 1794. The Grand Lodge of Pennsylvania established Alexandria Lodge in 1783, but after the formation of the District of Columbia in 1790, this lodge exchanged its charter for one under the Grand Lodge of Virginia and became Alexandra-Washington Lodge No 22. Virginia formed another lodge in 1796, and Maryland weighed in with a further four lodges between 1783 and 1806, giving the area six lodges in total. These lodges, with the exception of Alexandra-Washington, met in convention in 1811 and formed a Grand Lodge.

Today, the Grand Lodge of the District of Columbia possesses thirty-seven lodges, all of which meet in Washington.

Special Notes for Visitors

As the jurisdiction of the Grand Lodge of the District of Columbia centres on one city, the visiting of its lodges is a relatively easy pursuit for the travelling mason. In addition to the Grand Masonic Temple containing the Grand Lodge office, the other main masonic edifice in Washington is the Scottish Rite Temple. This is located 2800-16th Street North West, Washington. Both meeting places are large, attractive structures, and possess excellent libraries.

Without doubt, the highlight of any visitor's trip to the American capital will be an excursion to the George Washington National Monument located at Alexandria just to the south of Washington. The monument was built between 1922 and 1932, with the financial support of all the American Jurisdictions, at a cost of about five million dollars. The monument was dedicated in 1932 at one of largest masonic meetings ever held, with the President of the United States and all American Grand Masters present. Alexandria, itself, is actually within the State of Virginia.

The momument is on a site of 36 acres, and rises seven storeys. Its design is that of a Chaldeen Ziggarut, built entirely of stone masonry without the use of steel. Its contents consist of assembly rooms, dining rooms, museums, libraries, an auditorium with a seating capacity of 1200, archives, and a variety of masonic temples. A major feature is the statue of Washington in the Memorial Hall, which is over seventeen foot high in bronze and weighs nearly eight tons.

The District of Columbia is one of the few American Grand Lodges which does not use a District System, doubtessly because of the concentration of all its lodges in Washington. The Grand Lodge maintains a masonic home for the aged, and is heavily involved in a masonic blood bank program. A Lodge Activities Bulletin is regularly published for circulation to lodge officers, Past Masters, and Grand Lodge officers. The Past Masters Association of the District of Columbia publishes a bi-monthly newsletter, in addition, which is mailed to all its members.

FLORIDA

The Grand Lodge of Free and Accepted Masons of Florida
Founded: 1830

Addresses: Grand Lodge Building, 220 Ocean Street, Jacksonville. 32201. *Postal Address:* Grand Secretary, P.O. Box 1020, Jacksonville. 32201. Telephone: (904) 354 2339.
Miami: Several Temples (no main one). Check local telephone directory.

Lodges: 326. Permits Dual Membership.

Membership: 83,158.

Descent: Scotland, South Carolina, Alabama, Georgia. *Government:* Elective Grand Lodge.

Courtesy Degrees: Conferred on request. *Ritual:* Webb form.

Minimum Time Lapse between Degrees: One Lunar Month.

Major Publications: Constitutions. Annual Proceedings.

Periodical: *The Florida Mason.*

History

The territory that comprises Florida spent its early colonial career being ceded between varying nations. Originally a Spanish colony, it was ceded to Britain in 1763, ceded back to Spain in 1783, and finally the whole territory was ceded to the United States in 1819. It became a State of the Union in 1845.

The first lodge in the area was warranted from Scotland in 1768. This was Grant's East Florida Lodge No 143 SC. A military lodge was also warranted by Scotland in 1771. Both these lodges expired in Florida on the Spanish takeover. In the years between 1804 and 1809, four lodges were chartered in Florida variously by the Grand Lodges of South Carolina and Georgia, but none survived. However, once United States control was firmly established from 1819, a number of new lodges sprang up. After several more false starts with short lived lodges, Jackson Lodge No 23 was chartered at Tallahassee by the Grand Lodge of Alabama in 1825. This lodge now heads the Florida roll of lodges. The Grand Lodge of Georgia chartered lodges in 1828 and 1829. These three lodges met and formed the Grand Lodge of Florida on 6 July 1830. Today, virtually every town in Florida possesses a lodge, with the greatest concentrations being at Miami (with 22 lodges), and Jacksonville (with 17 lodges).

Special Notes for Visitors

The Grand Lodge of Florida is one of the larger American Jurisdictions, and as one would suspect its uses a District system with each District headed by a District Deputy Grand Master. Presently, Florida comprises 33 masonic Districts under the Grand Lodge, with each possessing ten to fifteen lodges. Florida is also one of those American Jurisdictions wherein lodges have two regular communications per month permanently fixed.

The Grand Lodge is heavily involved in charitable pursuits. Among these are the masonic home at St Petersburg catering for about 150 residents, and a masonic blood bank. Visitors to Florida can readily gain assistance in either Jacksonville or Miami at the addresses given above. It is also interesting to note that Florida possesses three lodges (at Key West, Miami, and Tampa) which are Spanish-speaking. These lodges cater for, among others, Spanish-speaking Cuban masons who have found it necessary to leave the Caribbean.

GEORGIA

The Grand Lodge of Georgia, Free and Accepted Masons
Founded: 1735
Addresses: Grand Lodge Office, 811 Mulberry Street, Macon, 31298. *Telephone:* (912) 7421475.
Atlanta: Masonic Temple, 1690 Peachtree Road North West, Atlanta.
Lodges: 468. Permits Dual Membership by dispensation only.
Membership: 89,060.
Descent: England and Pennsylvania. *Government:* Elective Grand Lodge.
Courtesy Degrees: Conferred on request. *Ritual:* Webb form.
Minimum Time Lapse between Degrees: Two weeks.
Major Publications: Annual Proceedings. Constitution. Periodical: *Masonic Messenger.*

History
The early history of masonry in Georgia is somewhat obscure. The first lodge established in the area was Solomon's Lodge, under the Grand Lodge of England (Moderns). It would seem that this lodge was meeting in 1735, but records do not appear to exist prior to 1756. This lack of information was not assisted by the destruction of the records of the Grand Lodge in a fire in 1820. The Moderns warranted two further lodges in 1774 and 1775, but both had short lives. In 1784, the Grand Lodge of Pennsylvania issued a Charter for Hiram Lodge No 42, at Savannah. The Pennsylvania Grand Lodge was of Antients stock and, possibly as a prelude to union, Solomon's Lodge resolved to become Antient in 1785.

In 1786, these two lodges organised the Grand Lodge of the Most Ancient and Honourable Fraternity of Free and Accepted Masons according to the Old Institutions in the State of Georgia. This title was later changed to that in current usage. It will be noted that the Grand Lodge of Georgia was formed by only two lodges, instead of by three as the minimum requirement stated by masonic custom. However, this deficiency never seems to have been quetioned. In the 1980s, the Grand Lodge of Georgia remains one of the larger American Grand Lodges, with 468 Constitutent lodges under allegience to it in 1983.

Special Notes for Visitors
As with many other American Jurisdictions, Georgia is divided masonically into Districts, under District Deputies to the Grand Master. Lodges themselves meet at two stated communications per month. In terms of charitable activities, the Grand Lodge runs a masonic home, among other benevolent endeavours. There is also a large Scottish Rite hospital in Atlanta.

Georgia also produces a particularly fine periodical entitled *The Masonic Messenger*, containing a wealth of interesting information. It is available on subscription to interested visitors.

HAWAII

Hawaii does not possess a Grand Lodge, and remains the only American State in this category. It has ten lodges currently working under charters from the Grand Lodge of California. Discussions have taken place in recent years concerning the formation of an Hawaiian Grand Lodge, but the situation remains unchanged in 1983. Visitors to Hawaii are advised to attend the Makiki Masonic Temple, located at 1227 Makiki Street, Honolulu (telephone: 949 7809). Full assistance can be readily attained at that address.

IDAHO

The Grand Lodge of Ancient, Free and Accepted Masons of Idaho:
Founded: 1867
Address: Grand Lodge Office: 215 North 10th Street, Boise. Postal Address: P.O. Box 1677, Boise, Idaho 83701. *Telephone:* (208) 343 4562.
Lodges: 84. Permits Dual Membership.
Membership: 10,559.
Descent: Oregon and Washington. *Government:* Elective Grand Lodge.
Courtesy Degrees: Conferred on request. *Ritual:* Webb form.
Minimum Time Lapse between Degrees: None, but candidates must be proficient.
Major Publications: Constitution. Annual Proceedings. Masonic Directory.

History

The initial lodge established in Idaho was formed by the Grand Lodge of Washington in 1863. This was Lewiston Lodge No 10, but it lasted only a few months. The Grand Lodge of Oregon had more success with Idaho Lodge, chartered in 1864. This lodge currently heads the register of the Grand Lodge of Idaho. In the following two years Oregon chartered three more lodges, and the Grand Lodge of Washington finally had success with Pioneer Lodge No 12, in 1867.

These five lodges met on 17 December, 1867, and formed the Grand Lodge of Idaho, which has prospered since that time. Idaho is one of the smaller American States in terms of population, but nevertheless there are few towns within its borders today that do not possess at least one lodge.

Special Notes for Visitors

Idaho is divided masonically into fifteen Districts, with between four to seven lodges in each. Visitors will find the Grand Lodge library in Boise of particular interest. It is largely maintained by the Idaho Lodge of Research. Two old temples in Idaho may be of interest to the visitor. These are the temples at Idaho City and Silver City, both of which have been designated as masonic memorials.

ILLINOIS

The Grand Lodge of Ancient, Free and Accepted Masons of the State of Illinois
Founded: 1840
Addresses: Grand Lodge Office: 2866 Via Verde Street, Springfield. Postal Address: P.O. Box 4147, Springfield 62708. *Telephone:* (217) 529 8900.
Chicago: Masonic Building, 1210 North Waller Avenue, Chicago.
Lodges: 735. Permits Dual Membership.
Membership: 146,481.
Descent: Kentucky, Missouri, and others. *Government:* Elective Grand Lodge.
Courtesy Degrees: Conferred on request. *Ritual:* Webb form.
Minimum Time Lapse between Degrees: One day.
Major Publications: Annual Proceedings. Constitution. Bi-Monthly Grand Lodge Newsletter.

History

The early history of freemasonry in Illinois was somewhat chequered. The first lodge in this area was formed in 1805 under charter from Pennsylvania. This was quickly followed by lodges from Indiana, Tennessee, Kentucky, and four lodges from Missouri. These eight lodges came together to erect a Grand Lodge in 1823. However, shortly after its formation the anti-masonic fervour accompanying the Morgan Affair (see section on New York) arose, and by 1827 the infant Grand Lodge ceased to operate, with none of its constituent lodges surviving.

By 1835, the hysteria surrounding Morgan's disappearance had waned, and the Grand Lodge of Kentucky chartered Bodley Lodge, which was later to assume the head of the Illinois directory of lodges as No 1. Another ten lodges followed prior to the erection of new Grand Lodge, holding charters variously from either Kentucky or Missouri. Six of these lodges joined together in 1840 to form the Grand Lodge of Illinois, but not without some difficulty. Several lodges held out of the union, the last of which waited until 1845 to join. However, these problems were soon overcome and by the 1890s Illinois possessed nearly 700 lodges. Today, it remains one of the largest jurisdictions in North America.

Special Notes for Visitors

In being such a large jurisdiction, Illinois follows an extensive District system, with nearly 100 Districts under District Deputy Grand Masters. The Grand Lodge runs a very large Masonic Home for the aged at Sullivan, Illinois; which includes a hospital. There is also a large Illinois Masonic Childrens Home. A Blood Sharing Program is among the many other charitable pursuits of Illinois masonry. While the Grand Lodge office in Springfield can be readily visited, most masons coming into Illinois will probably do so by way of Chicago. Full assistance can be obtained by visitors at the main temple in that city, the address of which is noted above.

INDIANA

The Grand Lodge of Free and Accepted Masons of the State of Indiana
Founded: 1818
Address: Grand Lodge Office, Masonic Temple, 525 North Illinois Street, Indianapolis. Postal Address: P.O. Box 44210, Indianapolis, Indiana 46204. *Telephone:* (317) 634 7904.
Lodges: 543. Permits Dual Membership.
Membership: 142,229.
Descent: Kentucky and Ohio. *Government:* Elective Grand Lodge.
Courtesy Degrees: Conferred on Request. *Ritual:* Webb form.
Minimum Time Lapse between Degrees: None, candidates may advance when proficient.
Major Publications: Book of Masonic Law (Constitution). Annual Proceedings. Periodical: *The Indiana Freemason.*

History
Kentucky was the source of the first charter issued in Indiana. This was given in 1809 for Vincennes Lodge No 15; although it had been operating in the two previous years under dispensation. Kentucky chartered another seven lodges between 1815 and 1817, while the Grand Lodge of Ohio chartered Brookville Harmony Lodge in 1817. With one exception, these lodges held a convention in 1818, and formed the Grand Lodge of Indiana. The subsequent history of masonry in Indiana has been largely uneventful in any extraordinary sense. The Grand Lodge has expanded steadily to become one of the largest in the United States.

Special Notes for Visitors
In addition to the Grand Lodge building in Indianapolis, that city also possesses one of the larger Scottish Rite Cathedrals in the United States. Both edifices are of great architectural interest, and well worth visiting. The Indiana Masonic Home at Franklin is also most worthy of a visit. A very large establishment, it caters for over 400 mostly elderly residents. Interestingly, in recent years Indiana has become one of the growing number of American Jurisdictions to charter new lodges to meet during the day—otherwise known as 'Daylight Lodges'. These lodges may prove useful to the visitor, and specific inquiries in this area are welcome at the Grand Lodge office.

IOWA

The Grand Lodge of Ancient, Free and Accepted Masons of Iowa
Founded: 1844
Addresses: Grand Lodge Office: Grand Lodge Library, 813 1st Avenue South East, Cedar Rapids. Postal Address: P.O. Box 279, Cedar Rapids 52406, Iowa. *Telephone:* (319) 365 1438.
    Des Moines: Masonic Temple, 1011 Locust Street, Des Moines.
Lodges: 463. Permits Dual Membership.
Membership: 59,618.

Descent: Missouri. *Government:* Elective Grand Lodge.
Courtesy Degrees: Conferred on request. *Ritual:* Webb form.
Minimum Time Lapse between Degrees: None, candidates may advance when proficient.
Major Publications: Constitution. Annual Proceedings. Periodical: *Grand Lodge Bulletin.*

History
The Grand Lodge of Missouri was responsible for the charters of all the lodges which formed the Grand Lodge of Iowa. The first charter was issued in 1840 for Des Moines Lodge No 41, at Burlington. This lodge now heads the Iowa Register as No 1. Missouri chartered a further lodge in 1841, and two more in 1843. These four lodges met and established the Grand Lodge of Iowa in 1844.

Special Notes for Visitors
There is little outside the parameters of the general text on the United States to add here. However, special mention must be made of Iowa Masonic Library located at Cedar Rapids. It is probably the largest masonic library in the world, and as such will be of particular interest to visitors.

KANSAS
The Grand Lodge of Ancient, Free and Accepted Masons of Kansas
Founded: 1856
Addresses: Grand Lodge Office: 320 West 8th Street, Topeka 66617, Kansas. Postal Address: P.O. Box 1217, Topeka. *Telephone:* (913) 234 5518.
Kansas City: No Main Temple—several in use—check Telephone Directory.
Wichita: Masonic Temple, 332 East 1 Street, Wichita.
Lodges: 372. Permits Plural Membership inside the State of Kansas, and Dual Membership outside Kansas.
Membership: 66,784.
Descent: Missouri. *Government:* Elective Grand Lodge.
Courtesy Degrees: Conferred on request. *Ritual:* Webb form.
Minimum Time Lapse between Degrees: Two weeks.
Major Publications: Laws of Masonry (Constitution). Annual Proceedings. Periodical: *The Kansas Mason.*

History
The first lodge erected in Kansas was Wyandotte Lodge, which was formed under dispensation in 1854 from the Grand Lodge of Missouri. This was followed by two more Missouri lodges in 1854, and another in 1855. The Grand Lodge was opened in 1856, by representatives of three of these lodges. Since that date it has expanded steadily, with virtually every town in Kansas having at least one lodge.

Special Notes for Visitors
The Kansas Masonic Home will be of interest to visitors. This huge complex is located at Wichita, catering for over 200 elderly residents. A 120 bed skilled nursing section was opened in 1981. The Grand Lodge library in Topeka is another point of interest for the visitor. Other matters of interest to visitors will be that most Kansas lodges hold two stated meetings per month, although only one will include a business meeting. Kansas recently formed a lodge of research, thus leaving the ranks of those few American Grand Jurisdictions without such a body. Kansas is, in addition, one of the few American Grand Lodges which issues a printed degree ritual (although in cipher). Kansas publishes a quarterly magazine entitled the *Kansas Mason*. It is available on subscription.

KENTUCKY

The Grand Lodge of Free and Accepted Masons of Kentucky
Founded: 1800
Addresses: Grand Lodge Office: Masonic Home, Louisville. 40041. *Telephone:* (502) 893 0192.
Louisville: Masonic Temple: 1000 South 4th Street, Louisville.
Lodges: 463. Permits Dual and Plural Membership.
Membership: 94,311.
Descent: Virginia. *Government:* Elective Grand Lodge.
Courtesy Degrees: Conferred on request. *Ritual:* Webb form.
Minimum Time Lapse between Degrees: 28 Days.
Major Publications: Constitution. Annual Proceedings.

History
As Kentucky was a part of Virginia until 1792, it is not surprising to discover that all its early lodges came from that source. The first lodge chartered from Virginia was Lexington Lodge No 25, in 1788. This lodge now heads the Kentucky register of lodges. This was followed by four more Virginia lodges up until 1800. These five lodges sent representatives to a Convention on 16 October 1800, and thereupon formed the Grand Lodge of Kentucky. The Grand Lodge survived the anti-masonic excitement of the 1830s, and developed into a large body.

Special Notes for Visitors
Kentucky is a large southern jurisdiction, with virtually every town in the State possessing a lodge. Louisville is the only population centre in Kentucky of any real size, and currently it is the home of twenty-seven lodges. Louisville also is the location of the Kentucky Masonic Home, a visit to which is recommended to any travelling freemason.

LOUISIANA

The Grand Lodge of the State of Louisiana, Free and Accepted Masons
Founded: 1812
Address: Grand Lodge Office: 1300 Masonic Temple, 333 St Charles Avenue, New Orleans 70130. *Telephone:* (504) 523 4382.
Jefferson: Masonic Temple, 232 Industrial Avenue, Jefferson.
Lodges: 286. Permits Dual and Plural Membership.
Membership: 43,889.
Descent: France, Mississippi, and others. *Government:* Elective Grand Lodge.
Courtesy Degrees: Conferred on request. *Ritual:* Webb form (York Rite) and Scottish Rite (Craft).
Minimum Time Lapse between Degrees: None, candidates may advance when proficient.
Major Publications: Handbook of Masonic Law (Constitution). Annual Proceedings. Masonic Directory. Periodical: *The Louisiana Freemason.*

History
The history of freemasonry in Louisiana poses a complicated picture, characterised by great disharmony. The basic problem was a French inspired struggle between Craft masonry and the Scottish Rite for control. In seeking to understand this, it must be first noted that Louisiana was originally a French colony and, not surprisingly, largely colonised by Frenchmen. Indeed, the masonic history of Louisiana in some ways forms a parallel with that of France.

The first lodge in the area was formed by a group of refugee Frenchmen in 1794, under a charter from the Grand Lodge of South Carolina. This was La Parfaite Union Lodge which, of course, worked in French. This was followed by L'Etoile Polaire Lodge, originally chartered by the Provincial Grand Lodge of Marseilles, but it was reconstituted in 1804 by the Grand Orient of France. Three further French lodges were chartered by Pennsylvania but they appear to have not survived.

The first English language lodge was Louisiana Lodge, chartered from New York in 1807. By the time of the admission of Louisiana into the Union of the United States in 1812, there were seven lodges in the new State. These were Charity, Concord, Perseverance, Harmony and L'Etoile Polaire (The Polar Star) Lodges, all under Pennsylvania; Parfait Union (Perfect Union) under South Carolina; and Louisiana Lodge under New York. Polar Star Lodge had left the umbrella of the Grand Orient of France and took a Pennsylvania Charter in 1811. Louisiana and Harmony Lodges were the only ones to work in English at this time, although all seven lodges were working in the York Rite. The seven lodges meet in 1812 to form a Grand Lodge, but the English-speaking lodges withdrew, leaving the French-speaking lodges to form the Grand Lodge of Louisiana. In 1818, the Grand Orient of France again became active, warranting a lodge in 1820. The two English-speaking lodges failed to flourish, with one becoming extinct. By 1820, the Grand Orient had three lodges in the State, and it appears to have greatly effected the attitudes of the Grand Lodge, which in that year permitted its lodges to work either the York, Scottish or French Rites. Several new English-speaking York Rite lodges sprang up under the Grand Lodge about this time, creating English and French factions within it. A protracted struggle was then undertaken between these two factions leading to the formation of a Council of Rites in 1836, which had all the hallmarks of a Grand Orient on the French model. In short, the French faction had progressively 'won the day'. However, the degeneration of organisation inherent in the factionalism brought the Grand Lodge to virtual dormancy by this time. About this time there were also incursions into the Grand Lodge's affairs by higher bodies, including a Grand Consistory, and a Supreme Council. In the face of this mire, Louisiana Lodge seceded, but it expired soon afterwards.

In 1844, the Grand Lodge adopted a new constitution, but still kept its French Grand Orient structure largely in tack. In the meantime, the Grand Lodge of Mississippi weighed into the Louisiana scene and chartered seven lodges up until 1848. In that year, these lodges formed the Louisiana Grand Lodge, which in two years had a further 18 lodges within in ranks. Not surprisingly, the old Grand Lodge was less than impressed. It severed relations with Mississippi and declared the new Grand Lodge to be clandestine. Various Grand Lodges took differing sides in this struggle.

Union was finally effected between the two Grand Lodges in 1850, although the question of what to do with Craft lodges working French or Scottish Rite higher degrees caused problems for several years. This problem was eventually solved, but not without a bogus Supreme Council causing considerable trouble, in alliance with the Grand Orient of France. This alliance took place in 1867, and it was directly responsible for all American Grand Lodges severing relations with the Grand Orient following an appeal from the Grand Lodge of Louisiana. Since that time the Grand Lodge has maintained harmony within its ranks. It has long since adopted a Code or Constitution of the elective Grand Lodge Type, similar to other American Jurisdictions. However, some of its lodges still work the Craft degrees of the Scottish Rite, instead of the more usual York Rite with a Webb form of ritual. Nevertheless, the modes of recognition and certain other ritual points must be uniform between lodges regardless of ritual. In addition, there are a small number of lodges which work in other languages, notably Spanish.

Special Notes for Visitors

Louisiana is a medium-sized American Jurisdiction, which is today quite similar to others in the United States. It uses a District system for masonic education and ritual proficiency similar to other States, each under a District Deputy Grand Master. It runs a large masonic home for children, underwrites its own masonic cemetery, and publishes an excellent periodical magazine—*The Louisiana Freemason*. The Grand Lodge Library in New Orleans is also worthy of mention, and visitation. Louisiana also possesses four chartered 'Relief Lodges', which dispence charity, and conduct masonic funerals.

MAINE

The Grand Lodge of Ancient, Free and Accepted Masons of the State of Maine
Founded: 1820
Address: Grand Lodge Office: Masonic Temple, 415 Congress Street, Portland 04101, Maine. *Telephone:* (207) 773 5184.

Lodges: 202.   Permits Dual Membership outside the State, only.
Membership: 38,680.
Descent: Massachusetts.   *Government:* Elective Grand Lodge.
Courtesy Degrees: Conferred on request.   *Ritual:* Webb form.
Minimum Time Lapse between Degrees: Two weeks.
Major Publications: Constitution.   Annual Proceedings.   Periodical: *The Maine Mason.*

History
All the early lodges in Maine were chartered from Massachusetts, which was far from surprising, considering that Maine was part of Massachusetts until 1820. The first lodge formed in Maine received its charter in 1769. This was the Triangle Lodge, which now heads the Maine list of lodges. Four more lodges were established in Maine between 1778 and 1796, all of which still exist. By the time of independence from Massachusetts in 1820, there were 31 lodges in Maine, of which 24 met in convention in that year and formed the Grand Lodge of Maine.
Maine, as with all other eastern American Jurisdictions, was hard hit by the anti-masonry of 1830s, following the Morgan Affair. The Grand Lodge was placed under great pressure as a result, and several lodges closed. However, it recovered, and continually expanded from the 1840s onward.
It is interesting to note that Maine masonry is stronger than anywhere else worldwide, except Scotland. On 1982 figures, Maine had a ratio of one mason to very 29 persons in the State. In other words, approximately one male in every fifteen is a freemason in Maine, Maine's population (1982 est) was 1,133,000; with a masonic membership of 38,680. Thus 1,133,000 divided by 38,680 = 29.29.

Special Notes for Visitors
Although Maine does not possess a masonic home as such, the Grand Lodge is heavily involved in charity programs, through its Charity Fund, and its Blood Bank activities, among others. Maine also possesses an excellent Grand Lodge library at Portland, and a recently chartered lodge of research. A most interesting feature of Maine masonry is its Grand Lodge Travel Program. In recent years, masons from this jurisdiction have visited many overseas jurisdictions, notably in Europe, and received return visits. This most commendable program is fully supported by the Grand Lodge. A periodical magazine, *The Maine Mason,* is published quarterly by the Grand Lodge.

MARYLAND

The Grand Lodge of Ancient, Free and Accepted Masons of Maryland
Founded: 1787
Address: Grand Lodge Office: Masonic Temple, 225 North Charles Street, Baltimore 21201.   *Telephone:* (301) 752 1198.
Lodges: 129.   Permits Dual membership outside Maryland.
Membership: 38,746.
Descent: Pennsylvania.   *Government:* Elective Grand Lodge.

Courtesy Degrees: Conferred on request.   *Ritual:* Webb form.
Minimum Time Lapse between Degrees: None, candidates may advance when proficient.
Major Publications: Constitution.   Annual Proceedings.   Periodical: *The Free State Freemason.*

History

The early history of freemasonry in Maryland is somewhat hazy. A lodge was purported to have met at Annapolis under a charter from Boston in 1750, but evidence is scant. The first lodge for which records exist was an English (Moderns) lodge, warranted in 1765. In 1782, it became 'Antient' by taking a charter from the Provincial Grand Lodge of Pennsylvania. Between 1766 and 1782, ten lodges were chartered from Pennsylvania. Following the American Revolution, five lodges met in 1783 with a view to forming a Grand Lodge, but this was not achieved until 1787.

Interestingly, of the first half dozen lodges warranted in Maryland, only one has survived. This is Washington Lodge No 3 at Baltimore, which remains the oldest lodge in the jurisdiction. Of course, the anti-masonry of the 1830s had its effect on Maryland, as it did elsewhere. However, the Grand Lodge of Maryland survived to become a large jurisdiction.

Special Notes for Visitors

Baltimore is the largest city of Maryland, and is the home of about 35 of its lodges. The Masonic Temple in Baltimore is a large edifice, and well worth a visit. It houses the Grand Lodge offices and a fine library. Maryland also possesses a large masonic home just outside Baltimore.

MASSACHUSETTS

The Grand Lodge of Ancient, Free and Accepted Masons of the Commonwealth of Massachusetts
Founded: 1733
Address: Masonic Temple, 186 Tremont Street, Boston 02111, Massachusetts.
Telephone: (617) 426 6040.
Lodges: 329   Permits Dual and Plural Membership.
Membership: 88,440.
Descent: England.   *Government:* Elective Grand Lodge.
Courtesy Degrees: Conferred on request.   *Ritual:* Webb form.
Minimum Time Lapse between Degrees: Four weeks.
Major Publications: Constitutions and Regulations. Annual Proceedings. Directory of Lodges.   Periodical: *The Trowel.*

History

The Grand Lodge of Massachusetts is the oldest Grand Lodge in North America in terms of the age of its earliest lodges. The Grand Lodge of Virginia is older in terms of continuous existence. In April, 1733, the Grand Lodge of England appointed one Brother Henry Price 'Provincial Grand Master of New England and Dominions and Territories thereunto belonging'. Henry Price thereafter organised the Provincial Grand Lodge of Massachusetts. This body constituted the 'First Lodge' in Boston, which became known as Saint John's Lodge in 1783. The Provincial Grand Lodge was also responsible for chartering a large number of lodges in other American colonies during its history, but these will be dealt with in their proper place.

The next lodge formed in Massachusetts was the Master's Lodge, warranted at Boston in 1738, but it had expired by 1783. A second and a third lodge were erected in 1750. The 1750s saw the incursion of the Antients into American masonry. A Lodge of St Andrew, under the Grand Lodge of Scotland, was warranted at Boston in 1756. The relations between this new lodge and the English Provincial Lodge were fairly hostile, and to counter this St Andrew's Lodge secured their own Provincial Grand Lodge from Scotland in 1769. This body managed to charter thirty lodges in the next 22 years, many of which were erected in other American colonies.

Thus, Massachusetts had two Provincial Grand Lodges, one Modern (England), and one Antient (Scotland), both of which, in effect, acted as full Grand Lodges. Subsequent to the American Revolution, the Antient body elected a new Grand Master in 1777, and authorised the draughting of Constitutions in 1782, thereupon becoming, in fact, a separate Grand Lodge. However, dissent from this course of action soon arose, and in 1784 a vote was taken marginally favouring staying under Scottish allegience in the Lodge of St Andrew. Members of this lodge voting to stay with the Massachusetts Grand Lodge were expelled from the lodge. The expelled members formed a new lodge under Massachusetts. Thus between 1784 and 1792, the body of masonry in Massachusetts remained divided between the two independent Grand Lodges, with the Lodge of St Andrew under Scotland.

During this period, the Moderns had not fared overly well. In 1783, the first and second lodges united into St John's Lodge', the third lodge having totally expired. In this weakened position the idea of Union became attractive, and in 1792 this was happily effected. Thus the Saint John's Grand Lodge (Moderns dating from 1733), and the Massachusetts Grand Lodge (Antients dating from 1769) formed the Grand Lodge of the Commonwealth of Massachusetts. The Lodge of St Andrew finally affiliated with Massachusetts in 1809.

Even after the amicable formation of the Grand Lodge through union, the subsequent history of masonry in Massachusetts was far from uneventful. In 1820, upon the creation of the State of Maine, the 31 Massachusetts-chartered lodges therein formed a new Grand Lodge. The anti-masonic storm following the Morgan incident in New York had a devastating effect on Massachusetts. Many lodges closed, never to reopen. Nevertheless, the Grand Lodge resolutely continued to meet under very difficult circumstances. The magnificent Grand Lodge Temple in Boston was built in this period in very precarious circumstances. Nonetheless, every crisis was met, and the Grand Lodge eventually emerged to become one of the strongest in America.

Special Notes for Visitors

As just mentioned, the Grand Lodge Temple in Boston rates as one of the most outstanding in freemasonry, and any visitor to Massachusetts would be ill advised to miss seeing it. The Grand Lodge Library within it, dating from 1815, is also most highly recommended. The Masonic Home at Charlton, established in 1908, is a tribute to the charitable activities of the Grand Lodge; as is the Massachusetts Masonic Blood Bank.

The administration of the Grand Lodge, while quite similar to others in the United States, exhibits some patterns more reminiscent of English forms. For example, with the only other exception being Pennsylvania, the Grand Lodge of Massachusetts meets in quarterly communications; rather than annually as is the more usual American pattern. Aside from the usual wealth of Grand Lodge Committees which characterise all American Jurisdictions, Massachusetts possesses a Grand Lodge Board of Directors to govern administrative matters. This body can to some extent be compared with the English-type Board of General Purposes.

It is interesting to note that alone among the American Jurisdictions, Massachusetts has never given its lodges numbers, and remains one of the very few Grand Lodges not to follow a number system. This situation stems from the Union of the two Grand Lodges in 1792, whereupon it could not be agreed between the parties as to which lodge would get number one. The problem was simply solved by not numbering lodges at all.

Massachusetts has, since its beginnings, been a 'Missionary Grand Lodge'. It has been directly responsible for chartering many of the early lodges in America, and was never restrained from granting charters outside America. Today, it has five lodges under charter in Panama, three in Chile, one at Tokyo, Japan; and one at the Naval Base at Guantanamo Bay, Cuba. These lodges will be mentioned under the appropriate headings elsewhere in this guide.

MICHIGAN

The Grand Lodge of Free and Accepted Masons of Michigan
Founded: 1826
Addresses: Grand Lodge Office: Masonic Temple, 233 East Fulton Street, Grand Rapids 49503.   *Telephone:* (616) 459 2451.
Detroit: Masonic Temple, 500 Temple Avenue, Detroit.
Lodges: 490.   Permits Dual Membership.
Membership: 111,386.
Descent: England and New York.   *Government:* Elective Grand Lodge.
Courtesy Degrees: Conferred by request.   *Ritual:* Webb form.
Minimum Time Lapse between Degrees: 28 days between the 1st and 3rd Degrees.
Major Publications: Constitution.   Annual Proceedings.

History
Freemasonry came to Michigan at a reasonably early date, mainly because Detroit was a key town on the track between Canada and the Mississippi River. The first lodge in the area was chartered at Detroit in 1764, under a warrant from the English Provincial Grand Master at New York. This was Union Lodge No 448 on the English roll. A number of lodges were erected between 1772 and 1824, few of which survived. Some were Irish Military lodges, others were chartered from Canada and New York.

In 1823, Union, Zion and Detroit lodges, all meeting at Detroit, formed a Provincial Grand Lodge to lay the cornerstone of the Territory Capitol. In 1826, a Grand Lodge was formed, only to become dormant in the anti-masonic excitement of the 1830s. By 1843, seven lodges were again active. However, it was not until 1844 that the Grand Lodge was actually revived. Since that time the Grand Lodge of Michigan has developed into one of the largest jurisdictions in the United States.

Special Notes for Visitors
Michigan, as one of the largest jurisdictions in the United States, makes great use of a District system, similar to most of its American peers. The State has several large towns, but of course its biggest population centre is the huge industrial city of Detroit, which itself possesses over 40 lodges. Michigan has long been the proud possessor of a very large masonic home complex, which with its associated hospital, caters for over 300 elderly residents.

MINNESOTA

The Grand Lodge of Ancient, Free and Accepted Masons of Minnesota
Founded: 1853
Addresses: Grand Lodge Office: St Paul Masonic Center, 200 East Plato Boulevard, St Paul 55107. Telephone: (612) 222 6051.
Minneapolis: Masonic Temple, 1940 Hennepin Road, Minneapolis.
Lodges: 238.   Permits Dual Membership.
Membership: 45,540.
Descent: Wisconsin and Illinois.   *Government:* Elective Grand Lodge.
Courtesy Degrees: Conferred on request.   *Ritual:* Webb form.
Minimum Time Lapse between Degrees: Two weeks.
Major Publications: Annual Proceedings. General Regulations (Constitution).   Periodical: *The Minnesota Mason.*

History
The first lodge to be located in Minnesota was St Paul Lodge, erected under dispensation from the Grand Lodge of Ohio in 1849. It received its formal Ohio charter in 1852. However, as this lodge was somewhat removed from Ohio, it sought to change its allegience to Wisconsin, receiving a new charter in 1853. In the meantime, two other lodges were chartered, namely St John's Lodge No 39 from Wisconsin, and St Anthony Falls (later Cataract) Lodge from Illinois.
Consequently, when these three lodges met in convention to form the Grand of Minnesota in 1853, St Paul Lodge became No 3, with St John's and Cataract preceding it. Today, the Grand Lodge maintains great strength, with lodges in every corner of the State.

Special Notes for Visitors
As with many other American Jurisdictions, Minnesota uses a District system, each under a Grand Lodge District Representative. Currently, Minnesota possesses 30

Districts with each consisting of between four and 12 lodges. The two largest population centres in the State are the cities of St Paul and Minneapolis, having
currently 15 and 18 lodges, respectively. Visitors can readily gain assistance at the
main Masonic Temple in either of these cities. The outstanding charitable pursuit
of Minnesota masonry is the Masonic Memorial Hospital. It consists of a hospital,
laboratories and an outpatient clinic in association with the University of Minnesota. Recently designated as the Masonic Cancer Center, it is endowed and supported by the Grand Lodge, and carries out great work into cancer research.

MISSISSIPPI

The Grand Lodge of Mississippi, Free and Accepted Masons
Founded: 1818
Address: Grand Lodge Office: Campus of the Masonic Home for Children, 2400
23rd Avenue, Meridian, Mississippi. *Telephone:* (601) 482 4543 or 482
2914. Postal Address: P.O. Box 1030, Meridian 39301.
Lodges: 301. Permits Single Membership only.
Membership: 45,570.
Descent: Kentucky and Tennessee. *Government:* Elective Grand Lodge.
Courtesy Degrees: Conferred on request. *Ritual:* Webb form.
Minimum Time Lapse between Degrees: One Stated Meeting until the next.
Major Publications: Annual Proceedings. Grand Lodge Statutes (Constitution).

History
The early history of masonry in Mississippi is fairly straightforward. The first lodge
in the area was Harmony Lodge No 7, chartered at Natchez in 1801 by the Grand
Lodge of Kentucky. However, this lodge had expired by 1814, only to be re-chartered in 1816 as Harmony Lodge No 33. Interestingly, the re-chartered lodge took
its warrant from the Grand Lodge of Tennessee. The second lodge in Mississippi
was also chartered from Tennessee, and also at Natchez. This was Jackson Lodge
No 15, erected in 1816. These two lodges are now No 1 and No 2, respectively of
the Grand Lodge of Mississippi, and remain the only two lodges located at Natchez.
The third lodge to enter the scene was Washington Lodge No 17, chartered from
Tennessee in 1817. These three lodges met in Convention in 1818, and formed the
new Grand Lodge.

Special Notes for Visitors
Mississippi is largely a rural State, having no huge cities. The two larger population
centres in the State are Jackson and Meridian, currently possessing six and eight
lodges respectively. Mississippi is divided into thirty Districts under Deputy District
Grand Lecturers. Aside from attending a lodge meeting, without doubt the facet of
Mississippi masonry that will be of great interest to visitors is the Mississippi
Masonic Home. This home is not a home for aged persons, but rather a home for
children. It usually has about 25 children in residency. As the Grand Lodge office
building is on the campus of the Masonic Home, visitors will readily be in a position
to view it.

MISSOURI

The Grand Lodge of Ancient, Free and Accepted Masons of the State of Missouri
Founded: 1821
Addresses: Grand Lodge Office: 800 Highway 63 North, Columbia 65201-6697, Missouri. *Telephone:* (314) 474 8561.
Kansas City: Scottish Rite Temple, 1330 Linwood Boulevard, Kansas City. 64109.
St Louis: Scottish Rite Temple, 3633 Lindell Boulevard, St Louis. 63108.
Lodges: 526. Permits Plural Membership.
Membership: 92,000.
Descent: Tennessee. *Government:* Elective Grand Lodge.
Courtesy Degrees: Conferred on request. *Ritual:* Webb form.
Minimum Time Lapse between Degrees: 28 days.
Major Publications: Constitution and By-Laws. Annual Proceedings. Periodical: *The Freemason*—issued quarterly.

History
The first two lodges in Missouri were chartered by the Grand Lodge of Pennsylvania in 1807 and 1808, but evidently both expired. The third lodge in Missouri, and the oldest surviving, was Missouri Lodge No 12, chartered at St Louis by the Grand Lodge of Tennessee in 1816. This was followed by three more lodges constituted from Tennessee, and one each from Kentucky and Indiana. In 1821, Missouri, Joachim, and St Charles Lodges, all stemming from Tennessee, met in Convention and formed the Grand Lodge of Missouri. The earliest days of the new Grand Lodge were not particularly buoyant, and it was not until the 1850s that the Grand Lodge became secure. Its early problems came as a direct result of the anti-masonic excitement accompanying the Morgan Affair. After this unsteady start, the Grand Lodge of Missouri has developed into a large jurisdiction, containing nearly 530 lodges in 1983.

Special Notes for Visitors
Of recent interest concerning Missouri is the Grand Lodge's decision to permit plural membership. Formerly, it permitted only single membership. The two largest population centres in Missouri are Kansas City and St Louis, possessing twenty and twenty-two lodges, respectively. In terms of masonic charity, Missouri has a large masonic home at St Louis catering for over 300 residents, of which more than 250 are women.

MONTANA

The Grand Lodge of Ancient, Free and Accepted Masons of Montana
Founded: 1866
Address: Grand Lodge Office: 425 North Park Avenue, Helena. Postal Address: P.O. Box 1158, Helena 59624. *Telephone:* (406) 442 7774.
Lodges: 130. Permits Dual Membership.

Membership: 15,332.
Descent: Colorado and Kansas. *Government:* Elective Grand Lodge.
Courtesy Degrees: Conferred on request. *Ritual:* Webb form.
Minimum Time Lapse between Degrees: None, candidates may advance when proficient.
Major Publications: Annual Proceedings. Constitution. Periodical: *The Montana Masonic News.*

History

The first lodge in Montana was formed under the Grand Lodge of Nebraska in 1863. This was the Idaho Lodge, established at Nevada City. Unfortunately, it expired in 1865. This was followed in the same year by Virginia City Lodge No 43, under the Grand Lodge of Kansas. The Grand Lodge of Colorado weighed in with Montana Lodge No 9, and Helena City Lodge No 10, both in 1865. These three lodges met in 1866, and formed the Grand Lodge of Colorado. The Grand Lodge has expanded comfortably since its formation, to find lodges under its banner in all parts of the State.

Special Notes for Visitors

Montana is one of America's largely rural States, possessing no huge cities. The most lodges located at any one place is five, at Great Falls. In being largely rural, the population of the State is not relatively big, and as a result the membership of the Grand Lodge of Montana forms one of the smaller American Jurisdictions. Nevertheless, Montana has been able to erect and maintain a substantial masonic home for the aged at Helena, dating from 1909. Visitors will be made most welcome at the Grand Lodge in Helena, and receive full assistance in any visitation they may care to make.

NEBRASKA

The Grand Lodge of the Most Ancient and Honorable Fraternity of Free and Accepted Masons of Nebraska
Founded: 1857
Address: Grand Lodge Office: 201 Masonic Temple, 119 South 19th Street, Omaha 68102. *Telephone:* (402) 342 1122.
Lodges: 230. Permits Dual Membership.
Membership: 30,621.
Descent: Illinois, Missouri, and Iowa. *Government:* Elective Grand Lodge.
Courtesy Degrees: Conferred on request. *Ritual:* Webb form.
Minimum Time Lapse between Degrees: 28 days.
Major Publications: Annual Proceedings. Constitution and By-laws.

History

The early development of masonry in Nebraska followed lines similar to most other American Jurisdictions. The first lodge in the area was Nebraska Lodge No 184, chartered by the Grand Lodge of Illinois in 1855. This was followed in the Giddings Lodge No 165 (later named Western Star Lodge) in 1856, under the Grand Lodge of Missouri. The Grand Lodge of Iowa chartered the third lodge in Nebraska in 1857. This was the Capitol Lodge No 101. These three lodges met in convention in September, 1857, and formed the Grand Lodge of Nebraska. All three original lodges have survived, and continue to occupy the first three places on the Nebraska roll of lodges.

Special Notes for Visitors
Nebraska forms a medium sized masonic jurisdiction in terms of America. The State forms a mixture of urban and rural communities, with Omaha (14 lodges) and Lincoln (nine lodges) being the larger population centres. As is usual throughout America, virtually every town in Nebraska possesses at least one lodge. Nebraska uses a District system, in common with most other Grand Lodges in the United States. In Nebraska, the Grand Custodian (of the Work) is the overseeing official, with a Deputy Grand Custodian appointed to each District. Nebraska is blessed with two masonic homes. The Nebraska masonic home (for the Aged) at Platts-mouth serves about 60 residents, while the Masonic/Eastern Star Home for children at Fremont, houses about 30 children.

NEVADA
The Grand Lodge of Free and Accepted Masons of the State of Nevada
Founded: 1865
Addresses: Grand Lodge Office: Masonic Temple, 40 West 1st Street, Reno 89501. *Telephone:* (702) 786 5261.
Las Vegas: Masonic Temple, 2200 West Mesquite Avenue, Las Vegas. *Telephone:* (702) 382 6055.
Lodges: 42. Permits Dual and Plural Membership.
Membership: 7,613.
Descent: California. *Government:* Elective Grand Lodge.
Courtesy Degrees: Conferred on request. *Ritual:* Webb form.
Minimum Time Lapse between Degrees: None, candidates may advance when proficient.
Major Publications: Annual Proceedings. Constitution (Masonic Code).

History
Somewhat unusually in terms of overall American masonic history, all the early lodges in Nevada were chartered from California. The first lodge in Nevada was Carson City Lodge No 154, formed in 1862. Another ten lodges were erected between 1862 and 1864, some of which were quite short lived. The Grand Lodge of Nevada was constituted in 1865. Of the early lodges, only four have survived until the present day. These are Carson City Lodge No 1; Amity Lodge No 4 (at Silver City); Escurial Lodge No 7 (at Virginia City); and Lander Lodge No 8 (at Austin). After this slow start, the Grand Lodge expanded steadily, spreading its lodges throughout Nevada.

Special Notes for Visitors
The Grand Lodge of Nevada is one of the numerically smallest of the American Grand Lodges. In explanation of this, it needs to be remembered that Nevada is

largely a desert area with relatively few population centres. Of course, the larger towns of Las Vegas and Reno are international tourist destinations, famous for their casinos. The Grand Lodge office has recently moved to the Reno Masonic Temple, and together with the Grand Lodge Library and Museum, is located on the third floor. Nevada has no masonic home, but charity relief is available through its lodges.

NEW HAMPSHIRE

The Grand Lodge of Free and Accepted Masons of the State of New Hampshire
Founded: 1788
Address: Grand Lodge Office: 813 Beech Street, Manchester 03104. *Telephone:* (603) 668 8744.
Lodges: 80.   Permits Dual and Plural Membership.
Membership: 13,368.
Descent: Massachusetts (England and Scotland). *Government:* Elective Grand Lodge.
Courtesy Degrees: Conferred on request. *Ritual:* Webb form.
Minimum Time Lapse between Degrees: Four weeks.
Major Publications: Constitution.   Annual Proceedings.

History
The first lodge in New Hampshire was warranted by the Provincial Grand Lodge (English) at Massachusetts about 1736. This was St John's Lodge, which now heads the New Hampshire list of lodges. It would appear that it was not until 1780 that a second lodge was formed. This was St Peter's Lodge, warranted by the Massachusetts Grand Lodge (under Scotland). This body issued warrants for another five lodges up until 1788, but few survived. In 1788, delegates from St John's Lodge and Rising Sun Lodge (formed in 1784) met and constituted the Grand Lodge of New Hampshire. New Hampshire suffered, as did all Eastern Grand Lodges in America, during the anti-masonry of the 1830s, and this somewhat explains the mortality rate of some of its earlier lodges.

Special Notes for Visitors
New Hampshire is a small mountainous State located in the north-east of the United States. Its population is not large, and consequently the Grand Lodge is one of the smaller ones in North America. Nevertheless, it still possesses eighty lodges located widely throughout the State. Somewhat unusually for a smaller Grand Lodge, and therefore one with presumably lower financial resources, New Hampshire possesses a substantial masonic home for the aged. It was established at Manchester in 1903, and today caters for about 30 residents. Visitors are welcome at the home, and inquiries can readily be made at the Grand Lodge office in Manchester. New Hampshire is organised into eight masonic Districts, each under a Deputy District Grand Master and Deputy District Grand Lecturer. The Grand Lodge publishes quarterly the *Grand Lodge Bulletin*. This magazine has, in recent years, been mailed to every member in the jurisdiction. New Hampshire also possesses a lodge of research, meeting at Portsmouth, and dating from 1964.

NEW JERSEY

The Grand Lodge of the Most Ancient and Honorable Society of Free and Accepted Masons for the State of New Jersey
Founded: 1786
Addresses: Grand Lodge Office: Grand Lodge Building, Jacksonville Road, Burlington 08016. Postal Address: P.O. Box 460, Burlington 08016, New Jersey. *Telephone:* (609) 386 5115.
Trenton: Masonic Temple, corner South Willow and West Front Streets, Trenton.
Lodges: 217. Permits Dual Membership.
Membership: 66,901.
Descent: New York, Massachusetts, Pennsylvania. *Government:* Elective Grand Lodge.
Courtesy Degrees: Conferred on request. *Ritual:* Webb form.
Minimum Time Lapse between Degrees: Four weeks.
Major Publications: Annual Proceedings. Constitution. Periodical: *New Jersey Freemason.*

History

As New Jersey was one of the earliest colonies in America, it is not surprising to learn that freemasonry entered it at an early date. The first lodge in New Jersey was formed at Newark under warrant from the English Provincial Grand Lodge in New York, in 1761. This lodge became dormant during the American Revolution, but revived thereafter. Two further lodges were warranted from Massachusetts in 1762 and 1763, but these failed to survive the Revolution. Two lodges warranted from Pennsylvania, Baskingridge and Burlington Lodges, did manage to survive those troubled times.

The formation of the Grand Lodge of New Jersey was unique. For the first time, a Grand Lodge was erected not by a group of lodges or a convention of lodges, but rather by a general assembly of freemasons. It is probable that the move was originated in the Baskingridge Lodge, but nonetheless the Grand Lodge was constituted in 1786. Interestingly, it was the Baskingridge Lodge, rather than the older St John's Lodge (of 1761), which was placed at the head of the New Jersey roll of lodges. St John's Lodge became No 2. Baskingridge Lodge moved to Bedminster about the time the Grand Lodge was formed, and it changed its name accordingly. However, St John's Lodge in due time received 'justice', as Bedminster Lodge expired, and in a re-numbering of lodges in 1842 it ascended the head of the roll, a position it retains to this day.

Special Notes for Visitors

New Jersey is located immediately to the south of New York City. While geographically small, it has a fairly substantial population, and this is reflected in masonic membership. Nevertheless, New Jersey does not possess any large cities, with the largest population centre being the city of Trenton. There are several aspects of masonry in New Jersey that will be of interest to visitors. In terms of benevolence, New Jersey possesses a masonic home dating from 1898 and located at Burlington.

It caters for about 200 residents. An excellent Masonic Blood Bank programme is also supported by the Grand Lodge.

In recent years, it has come to the notice of the Grand Lodge that many Cuban masons in exile were resident in New Jersey. After exhaustive enquiries, large numbers of Cuban masons have been enabled to affiliate with New Jersey lodges. Plans have been advanced for chartering a new lodge to specifically cater for Cuban brethren.

Of great interest to visitors will be the most attractive Grand Lodge building in Burlington. The library and museum contained therein are of great quality, and are highly recommended.

While it has not generally been the practice in this guide, in terms of American Jurisdictions, to single out individual lodges for detailed discussion, an exception can justly be made for one lodge in New Jersey. This is the Alpha Lodge No 116. The interesting feature of this lodge is that it is entirely composed of Negroes. It was warranted in 1871, specifically to admit Negroes to membership. While it was originally a 'mixed lodge', since 1929 it has been entirely Negro. Great controversy surrounded its formation, and early history. Outside of New Jersey, several Southern Grand Lodges strongly disapproved. However, all these storms have been weathered, and Alpha Lodge remains happily working in New Jersey to this day, with a membership of over 200. The lodge meets at the Masonic Temple, 56 Melmore Gardens, East Orange, New Jersey. Its regular meetings are held on the 2nd and 4th Wednesdays monthly, except July and August, holidays, the 4th Wednesday in December, and the Annual Communication of the Grand Lodge. Visitors are most welcome to attend. Details of other New Jersey lodges can readily be obtained from the Grand Lodge office in Burlington.

NEW MEXICO

The Grand Lodge of Ancient, Free and Accepted Masons of New Mexico
Founded: 1877
Address: Grand Lodge Office: 1638 University Boulevard North East, Alberqu-
erque. Postal Address: P.O. Box 25004, Albuquerque 87125, New
Mexico. *Telephone:* (505) 243 4931.
Lodges: 67. Permits Dual and Plural Membership.
Membership: 11,916.
Descent: Missouri. *Government:* Elective Grand Lodge.
Courtesy Degrees: Conferred on request. *Ritual:* Webb form.
Minimum Time Lapse between Degrees: 28 days.
Major Publications: Annual Proceedings. Constitution. Periodical: *New Mexico Freemason.*

History
Freemasonry was first introduced into New Mexico during the American–Mexican War, in the form of two military lodges. Both these lodges, chartered from Missouri, did not survive after the war ended. The first permanent lodge in New Mexico opened in Santa Fe in 1851. This was Montezuma Lodge No 109, holding a Missouri charter. Indeed, all the lodges erected in New Mexico prior to the formation

of its Grand Lodge held Missouri charters. The second lodge in New Mexico was Bent Lodge No 204, chartered in 1860. The claim to fame of this lodge is that one of its members was the famous frontiersman, Kit Carson. It expired in 1865, but a lodge of the same name was erected in 1909. Another six lodges were chartered from Missouri up until 1875, and most of these have survived. The Grand Lodge of New Mexico was formed at a convention of Montezuma, Chapman, Aztec, and Union Lodges, held in 1877. These lodges, in the order indicated, hold the first four places in the New Mexico list of lodges.

Special Notes for Visitors
New Mexico is a southern mid-western State, bordering onto Mexico. It is composed largely of desert areas, and consequently it is not heavily populated. The only city of any real size is Albuquerque, which is the seat of the Grand Lodge, and itself possesses eight constituent lodges. New Mexico does not have a masonic home, but it is nevertheless engaged in a range of charitable activities. However, it does possess an excellent periodical magazine, the *New Mexico Freemason*, published regularly by the Grand Lodge. New Mexico also has two 'Daylight' lodges under charter, as well as a Lodge of Research. Zia Daylight Lodge No 77 (chartered 1976) meets in Albuquerque on the 1st Tuesday; while the Dona Ana Daylight Lodge No 78 (chartered 1977) meets in Mesilla on 2nd and 4th Saturdays. Both these lodges commence at 10 am. The Lodge of Research (unnumbered) meets at various locations within New Mexico on the 2nd Saturdays in January, May and September.

NEW YORK
The Grand Lodge of Free and Accepted Masons of the State of New York
Founded: 1781
Address: Grand Lodge Office: Masonic Temple, 71 West 23rd Street, New York City 10010. *Telephone:* (212) 741 4500.
Lodges: 848. Permits Dual and Plural Membership.
Membership: 153,294.
Descent: England. *Government:* Elective Grand Lodge.
Courtesy Degrees: Conferred on request. *Ritual:* Webb form.
Minimum Time Lapse between Degrees: Two weeks.
Major Publications: Constitution. Annual Proceedings. Periodical: *The Empire State Mason.*

History
The Grand Lodge of England appointed one Daniel Coxe as Provincial Grand Master of North America, based at New York, in the 1730s, but the surviving evidence of early activities is very scant. The first lodge in New York for which records exist was St John's Lodge, warranted in 1757. Today, this lodge heads the New York roll of lodges. Approximately twenty further lodges were warranted up until 1771 by the Provincial Grand Lodge, many of which were located outside of New York.
The Independence War of the late 1770s brought unsettled times to New York

masonry. The main characteristic of the period was the transition by lodges from Moderns allegiance to the Antients. Three Antient lodges were operating in New York by 1781, and in that year an Antient Provincial Grand Lodge was organised. By 1786, most New York lodges had transferred allegiance to the Antients, whose local administration would appear to have been superior. The formation of the Grand Lodge of New York was unique. In 1787, a committee was appointed to consider methods for forming an independent Grand Lodge. The Committee determined that the Provincial Grand Lodge (Antient) exercised all the powers of a Grand Lodge and had done so since its formation in 1781, and that all that was required was a name change! The Grand Lodge of New York was thus formed. As the Moderns Provincial Grand Lodge had by this time faded away, the 'new' Grand Lodge remained undisputed as the masonic authority in New York.

The subsequent history of masonry in New York was less than happy. Mounting friction arose between lodges in New York City and lodges located in up-country areas of New York State concerning voting in the Grand Lodge and related matters. The discontent came to a head in 1823 when the city lodges effectively seceded and formed their own Grand Lodge. Reunion was achieved in 1827, on the basis that in future Grand Lodge officers must be evenly divided between city and country.

Hardly had the reunion been happily effected, when the Morgan Affair occurred. In autumn, 1826, one William Morgan disappeared and was presumed to have been murdered. Prior to this, Morgan had conspired to publish an exposure of freemasonry after being refused admission to a lodge in Batavia, New York State. It was his supposed murder by masons which largely gave rise to the anti-masonic movement, which had built up full steam by 1830 and lasted to about 1840. Despite public denials by the Craft of any complicity with Morgan's disappearance, public outrage was immense—greatly spawned by most effective propaganda from the opponents of masonry. A very large number of lodges closed down throughout eastern America, temples were sacked, and it was most dangerous for any man to admit masonic membership. Of course, New York was the scene of the 'crime', and it felt the full force of the attack. The number of lodges under the Grand Lodge fell from 480 to about 70 in the period. During this period, to make matters worse, a schism occurred in the Grand Lodge. York Lodge in New York City withdrew from the Grand Lodge and with nine others formed its own Grand Body. It had 27 lodges when it reunited with the regular Grand Lodge of New York in 1850.

No sooner had this schism been happily mended when another occurred. In 1848, the Grand Lodge resolved to disfranchize Past Masters in favour of elected delegates for the purpose of Grand Lodge membership. In other words, this was a move from the English system to the elective Grand Lodge system current throughout American Jurisdictions today. Needless to say, the Past Masters were less than impressed, and they withdrew en masse in 1849 and formed a rival Grand Lodge. This schism lasted nine years before an amicable reunion was effected. Fortunately, disharmony in the Grand Lodge appears to have faded away after this last incident. The Grand Lodge of New York recovered speedily from these schisms and the Morgan Affair, and today rates as one of the largest in North America.

Special Notes for Visitors
New York City probably possesses more lodges than any other city in the United
States, but of course, virtually every town throughout New York State has at least
one lodge meeting within it. The Grand Lodge building in New York is huge, and
will be of very great interest to visitors. It contains a particularly fine library and
museum. Understandably, New York employs a very extensive District system for
masonic education. New York is one of the small minority of jurisdictions that does
publish a ritual for use by its members, although of course, it is in cipher. The
Masonic Home at Utica, founded in 1891, is one of the largest such establishments
in the United States. The Soldiers and Sailors Memorial Hospital was established
on the site in 1922, and this was followed in 1956 by the huge Masonic Medical
Research Laboratory.

Perhaps the most interesting point concerning New York masonry is the large
number of so called language lodges it contains. There are about thirty such lodges
in the jurisdiction, all of which are located within greater New York City. The
oldest lodge among them is L'Union Française Lodge No 17, which has worked in
French since its creation in 1797. New York also possesses a fair number of
German-speaking lodges, mostly located in the Manhattan area. There are also
lodges working in Italian, Spanish and Greek. Therefore, it is doubtlessly desirable
for any visitor to enquire as to the language used by a lodge he proposes to visit.
All these enquiries and any others concerning visiting under the Grand Lodge of
New York will be readily answered at the Grand Lodge office.

It is of some interest to note that the Grand Lodge of New York, like Massachusetts, has chartered lodges outside the United States. Currently, it has ten lodges
located in Lebanon in the Middle East. However, the civil war that has raged in
that country in recent years has forced all these lodges into recess.

NORTH CAROLINA

The Grand Lodge of Ancient, Free and Accepted Masons of North Carolina
Founded: 1787
Address: Grand Lodge Office: 2921 Glenwood Avenue, Highway 70 West, Ral-
eigh. Postal Address: P.O. Box 6506, Raleigh 27628, North Caro-
lina. *Telephone:* (919) 787 2021.
Lodges: 394. Permits Dual Membership.
Membership: 73,076.
Descent: England (Moderns). *Government:* Elective Grand Lodge.
Courtesy Degrees: Conferred on request. *Ritual:* Webb form.
Minimum Time Lapse between Degrees: None, candidates may advance when
proficient.
Major Publications: Annual Proceedings. Constitution. Periodical: *The North
Carolina Mason.*

History
The early masonic history of North Carolina is somewhat obscure. It would appear
freemasonry was active in the area about 1736, but records are scant. The oldest
lodge for which records exist is Wilmington Lodge No 213, which appeared on the

English roll of lodges in 1754. It is now St John's Lodge No 1 on the roll of the Grand Lodge of North Carolina. The Royal White Hart Lodge, now numbered No 2, appeared on the English roll as No 403 in 1767. This remains the second lodge of North Carolina. In 1771, the Moderns Provincial Grand Master for North America became actively involved in North Carolina, and warranted several lodges between that date and 1787. It would appear that about four lodges were erected by the Moderns in this period, while about the same number came into being through other sources—their origins being largely obscure.

In December, 1787, eight lodges met in convention and formed the Grand Lodge. It is noteworthy that at this time North Carolina also included Tennessee. Tennessee became a State of the Union in 1796, but it was not unil 1813 that a Grand Lodge was formed in that State. The establishment of the Grand Lodge of Tennessee by North Carolina will be dealt with under the former heading.

Special Notes for Visitors
North Carolina is one of the oldest jurisdictions in the United States, and while its ritual and masonic government largely parallels those of other American Jurisdictions, a few of its forms hark back to its original English ancestry. For example, North Carolina possesses a Board of General Purposes consisting of the most senior Grand Lodge officers, which has an overall administrative function. Of course, the large number of other Grand Lodge Committees which characterise American masonry also prevail in North Carolina.

The Craft in North Carolina is involved in some quite outstanding charitable pursuits. The Oxford Ophanage, established in 1872, also includes a hospital. It caters for about 200 children. The Masonic and Eastern Star Home at Greensboro, houses about 130 elderly persons. Both of these institutions are large, and well worth visiting.

NORTH DAKOTA

The Grand Lodge of Ancient, Free and Accepted Masons of North Dakota
Founded: 1889
Address: Grand Lodge Office: 201 14th Avenue North, Fargo 58102, North Dakota. *Telephone:* (701) 235 8321.
Lodges: 97. Permits Dual and Plural Membership.
Membership: 8,394.
Descent: Iowa, Minnesota. *Government:* Elective Grand Lodge.
Courtesy Degrees: Conferred on request.
Ritual: Webb form.
Minimum Time Lapse between Degrees: Four weeks.
Major Publications: Annual Proceedings. Constitution.
Periodical: *The North Dakota Mason.*

History
It is largely impossible to separate the masonic histories of North and South Dakota. These two States originally comprised the Dakota Territory, which was divided by an Act of the United States Congress in 1889 for the purposes of creating two new States of the Union.

The first lodge in the Dakota Territory was chartered by the Grand Lodge of Iowa in 1862. This was St John's Lodge, which now heads the roll of lodges of South Dakota. Four other lodges, also chartered from Iowa, were quickly formed, and together these five lodges established the Grand Lodge of Dakota in 1875. At the division of Dakota into two States in 1889, the Grand Lodge of Dakota became the Grand Lodge of South Dakota, with 73 lodges under its jurisdiction at that time. The 26 lodges then working in North Dakota formed a new Grand Lodge— the Grand Lodge of North Dakota. The division was effected with total harmony, with both Grand Lodges being formed on the same day, and Grand Officers of each assisting at the Installation of the other. The oldest lodge in North Dakota is Shiloh Lodge. It was originally No 105 under Minnesota, becoming No 8 under the Grand Lodge of Dakota, and finally No 1 under the Grand Lodge of North Dakota. The North Dakota Grand Lodge has the distinction of being the last Grand Lodge to be erected in the continental United States. In terms of America as a whole, its 'title' as youngest Grand Lodge was lost to Alaska in 1981.

Special Notes for Visitors
North Dakota is one of the smaller masonic jurisdictions in the United States, with a membership under 10,000. The State of North Dakota itself is largely rural, with no large cities from which to draw members. Nevertheless, the visitor will find it difficult to discover any town in the State without at least one lodge. North Dakota does not possess any masonic benevolent institutions, but nonetheless the Grand Lodge is involved in several substantial charity funds. The Grand Lodge building in Fargo possesses an excellent library and museum, which visitors will no doubt find of particular interest.

OHIO
The Grand Lodge of Free and Accepted Masons of Ohio
Founded: 1808.
Addresses: Grand Lodge Office: 634 High Street, Worthington 43085, Ohio. Postal Address: P.O. Box 629, Worthington. *Telephone:* (614) 885 5318.
Cincinnati: Masonic Temple, 317 East 5th Street, Cincinnati.
Cleveland: Masonic Temple, 3615 Euclid Avenue, Cleveland.
Dayton: Masonic Temple, 525 West Riverview Street, Dayton.
Masonic Temple, 4645 Heatherdowns Street, Toledo.
Lodges: 675. Permits Dual Membership outside Ohio only.
Membership: 220,336.
Descent: Massachusetts, Pennsylvania, Connecticut, and others. *Government:* Elective Grand Lodge.
Courtesy Degrees: Conferred on request. *Ritual:* Webb form.
Minimum Time Lapse between Degrees: One stated meeting until the next.
Major Publications: Constitution. Annual Proceedings.
Periodical: *The Ohio Mason.*

History

The first lodge established in Ohio was the American Union Lodge, which first met in Ohio at Marietta in 1790. This lodge is one of the most famous in the United States. It was originally a military lodge, warranted in 1776 by the Moderns' Provincial Grand Lodge of Massachusetts. At the close of the revolution, the then Master of the lodge, Jonathan Heart, moved to the Northwest Territory (now Ohio), where the lodge was re-opened. This lodge remains today as No 1 on the roll of lodges of Ohio.

The second lodge in Ohio was Nova Cesarea, chartered from the Grand Lodge of New Jersey. It had expired by 1805. Between 1803 and 1806, five lodges were chartered in Ohio, two with charters from Connecticut, with one each owing allegiance to Pennsylvania, Massachusetts and Kentucky. In 1808, these five lodges met together in convention with the American Union Lodge and agreed to form a Grand Lodge. It was erected the following year, but only four of the six lodges participated. The American Union Lodge decided to stand aloof, deciding that it could remain independent under its Massachusetts warrant. The new Grand Lodge of Ohio declared it to be clandestine, with the effect that in 1810 the lodge split. A number of its members petitioned the new Grand Lodge, to be chartered as American Union Lodge No 1. The recalcitrant members continued to work as a lodge, without legal charter, and it appears to have faded into oblivion about 1820. The original Nova Ceserea Lodge was re-chartered under Ohio in 1812 as Nova Cesarea Harmony Lodge No 2. It stills works happily at Cincinnati. The Grand Lodge of Ohio since its formation has developed into the largest Grand Lodge in North America, and one of the largest in the world.

Special Notes for Visitors

Ohio is a very populous American State, possessing several large cities. Of its 675 lodges, 26 are located in Cincinnati; 22 in Cleveland, 13 in Dayton; and 17 in Toledo. In being such a large jurisdiction, it uses an extensive District system. Ohio has a massive masonic home located at Springfield dating from 1890. It caters for both aged adults and children, and usually houses in excess of 500 residents. A substantial hospital is also located within its campus. Visitors to Ohio can readily gain assistance at the Grand Lodge office, or at the main temples in the large cities listed above.

OKLAHOMA

The Grand Lodge of Ancient, Free and Accepted Masons of the State of Oklahoma
Founded: 1874

Addresses: Grand Lodge Office: Masonic Temple, 117½ East Oklahoma Avenue, Guthrie. Postal Address: P.O. Box 1019, Guthrie 73044, Oklahoma. *Telephone:* (405) 282 3212.

Tulsa: Masonic Temple, 706½ South Boston Street, Tulsa.

Oklahoma City: Masonic Temple, 3415 North West 36th Street, Oklahoma City.

Lodges: 317. Permits Dual Membership.

Membership: 60,962.

Descent: Arkansas, Kansas. *Government:* Elective Grand Lodge.

Courtesy Degrees: Conferred on request.   *Ritual:* Webb form.
Minimum Time Lapse between Degrees: 28 days.
Major Publications: Annual Proceedings.   Constitution.   Periodical: *The Oklahoma Mason.*

History

The history of freemasonry in Oklahoma is the story of two Grand Lodges which united to form one. Originally, the area now covered by the State of Oklahoma consisted of two territories—the Indian Territory and the Oklahoma Territory. The Indian Territory in the east was inhabited by five tribes, and it was not until 1889 that it was opened up to white settlement. The first lodge in the Indian Territory was probably Cherokee Lodge, chartered from Arkansas in 1848. It had expired by 1868. The earliest surviving lodge was Muskogee Lodge No 93, gaining its charter from Arkanses in 1855. This lodge is now Eufaula Lodge No 1 on the roll of the Grand Lodge of Oklahoma. Eufaula Lodge, together with two other Arkansas-chartered lodges formed the Grand Lodge of the Indian Territory in 1874.

The Grand Lodge of the Oklahoma Territory, in the western part of present day Oklahoma, was formed by three lodges in 1892, but more lodges may have been present. The three lodges that definitely appear to have been present were Guthrie, Oklahoma City and Edmond Lodges. These lodges are now numbered 25, 36, and 37 respectively, on the roll of the Grand Lodge of Oklahoma. With the union of the two territories into modern Oklahoma, the two Grand Lodges subsequently decided to merge, and this was happily achieved in 1909, whereupon the Grand Lodge of the State of Oklahoma was created.

Special Notes for Visitors

While Oklahoma is largely a rural State, the cities of Tulsa and Oklahoma City are larger population centres, possessing eight and ten lodges, respectively. Oklahoma is a medium sized American jurisdiction, employing a District system under District Deputy Grand Masters. It is also one of those jurisdictions wherein lodges prescribe two stated meetings per month. Three aspects of particular interest concerning Oklahoma masonry are notable. The Masonic Home for the Aged at Guthrie caters for about 100 residents, and can be readily visited by travelling masons. The Grand Lodge possesses its own printing facility. The 'Print Shop' publishes all the Grand Lodge's publications, including the *Oklahoma Mason* which is issued monthly. It also derives considerable income for the Grand Lodge by printing commercially. The Oklahoma Indian Degree Team is very well known throughout America. It has performed extensively in many areas of the United States, with its members wearing traditional Indian Dress.

OREGON

The Grand Lodge of Ancient, Free and Accepted Masons of Oregon
Founded: 1851
Addresses: Grand Lodge Office: 3435 Pacific Avenue, Forest Grove. Postal Address: P.O. Box 96, Forest Grove 97116, Oregon. *Telephone:* (503) 357 3158.
Portland: Masonic Temple, 1119 South West Park Avenue, Portland.
Lodges: 174. Permits Dual and Plural Membership.
Membership: 28,443.
Descent: California and Missouri. *Government:* Elective Grand Lodge.
Courtesy Degrees: Conferred on request. *Ritual:* Webb form.
Minimum Time Lapse between Degrees: Four weeks.
Major Publications: Constitution. Annual Proceedings.

History

The first lodge established in the territory of Oregon was Multnomah Lodge No 84, chartered at Oregon City by the Grand Lodge of Missouri in 1846. Almost immediately after its erection, this lodge became dormant, doubtlessly as a result of losing most of its members to the Californian Gold Rush. However, it was revived in 1850, and today heads the Oregon Directory of Lodges. The second and third lodges erected in Oregon gained their charters from the Grand Lodge of California. These were Willamette Lodge No 11 (chartered 1850), and Lafayette Lodge, No 15 (chartered 1851). Today, they hold No 2 and No 3, respectively in the Oregon Directory. In September, 1851, these three lodges organised the Grand Lodge of Oregon.

Special Notes for Visitors

Oregon is a north western State, possessing one large city. This is Portland, which is currently the home of 29 lodges, including the Research Lodge of Oregon. Oregon possesses a large masonic home at Forest Grove, catering for about 60 aged residents. Its other charitable activities include an extensive Masonic Blood Bank programme.

PENNSYLVANIA

The Grand Lodge of Free and Accepted Masons of Pennsylvania
Founded: 1786
Address: Grand Lodge Office: Masonic Temple, One North Broad Street, Philadelphia 19107. *Telephone:* (215) 988 1900.
Pittsburgh: Masonic Temple, 4227 5th Avenue, Pittsburgh.
Lodges: 576. Permits single membership only.
Membership: 206,027.
Descent: England. *Government:* Elective Grand Lodge.
Courtesy Degrees: No Courtesy Degrees conferred, or requested. *Ritual:* Old 'Antients' form.
Minimum Time Lapse between Degrees: 28 days.
Major Publications: Constitution. Proceedings.
Periodical: *The Pennsylvania Freemason.*

History
The masonic history of Pennsylvania, in combination with that of Massachusetts and New York, virtually accounts for the introduction and establishment of the Craft in North America. The first records of masonry in Pennsylvania came in the form of an article in Benjamin Franklin's *Philadelphia Gazette* in 1730, wherein it was indicated that several lodges were working in the colony. Franklin joined the Tun Tavern Lodge in Philadelphia in 1731, which is the earliest known lodge for which records exist. This lodge appears to have expired about 1738. It was succeeded about this time by another lodge, known as the First Lodge. In 1750, Lord Byron, Grand Master of England, deputised one William Allen as Provincial Grand Master for Pennsylvania, and Franklin became his Deputy. By 1755, two more lodges were at work in the colony.

In 1758, the first Antients Warrant for America was issued for Lodge No 69 at Philadelphia, and by 1761, an Antients Provincial Grand Lodge was operating. The American Revolution brought some chaos to masonic organisation, and by its end all the Modern lodges had expired, with only Antient lodges surviving. It would appear that the Moderns Provincial Grand Lodge had disappeared by 1785 at the latest. In September, 1786, the Antients Provincial Grand Lodge declared independence from England, and thirteen lodges then met and erected the Grand Lodge of Pennsylvania.

Special Notes for Visitors
Pennsylvania is a heavily populated eastern State, possessing two very large cities, namely Philadelphia and Pittsburgh. The former contains 79 lodges, while the latter has 24. It is interesting to note that Pennsylvania had about ten lodges without names, but possessing numbers only. This harks back to Antient and Irish practices. Indeed, Pennsylvania retains many traditions which have largely lapsed elsewhere in America. Its Grand Lodge follows the English pattern of meeting in Quarterly Communications, and on 27 December each year (St John the Evangelist's Day) for its Grand Installation. Without doubt, the most interesting masonic edifice in the United States is to be found at Philadelphia. The Grand Lodge building rates with the Grand Temples in London and Stockholm as the most magnificent in the world. Its richly decorated temples, and huge library and museum, should not be missed by any visitor.

On the charitable front, the Grand Lodge is involved in a range of outstanding endeavours. The Masonic Home at Elizabethtown is one of the largest in the United States, catering for over 700 residents. On the same campus is a Masonic Children's Home. Guided tours are available through the homes complex. In addition, the Philadelphia Freemasons' Memorial Hospital carries out outstanding work. It is interesting to note that the Masonic Homes have a Farm Department. This runs a dairy, a poultry farm, an apiary, a piggery, and a cattle herd; all of which are substantial in size.

RHODE ISLAND

The Grand Lodge of Free and Accepted Masons of the State of Rhode Island and Providence Plantations
Founded: 1791
Address: Grand Lodge Office: Scottish Rite Cathedral, 2115 Broad Street, Cranston 02905. *Telephone:* (401) 467 2970.
Lodges: 45. Permits Dual and Plural Membership.
Membership: 11,230.
Descent: Massachusetts and New York. *Government:* Elective Grand Lodge.
Courtesy Degrees: Conferred on request. *Ritual:* Webb form.
Minimum Time Lapse between Degrees: None, candidates may advance when proficient.
Major Publications: Constitution. Annual Proceedings.
Periodical: *The Rhode Island Freemason.*

History
While there are undocumented references to masonic activity in Rhode Island as early as the 1650s, the first lodge established in the colony was warranted by the Provincial Grand Master of Boston, Massachusetts, in 1749. This lodge, meeting at Newport, was named simply 'The First Lodge', but later became called 'St John's'. In 1757, a second lodge was warranted at Providence, also from Massachusetts. These two lodges, both named St John's, met and formed the Grand Lodge of Rhode Island in 1791. Interestingly, they both emerged from the formation holding the number one. Both exist today, with St John's Lodge No 1 (Newport) apparently taking precedence over St John's Lodge No 1 (Providence). It is also interesting to note that Thomas Smith Webb, the 'founder' of American Craft ritual, was an early Grand Master of Rhode Island.

The anti-masonic fervour associated with the Morgan Affair had a grave effect in Rhode Island, and with the possible exceptions of New York and Vermont, was felt at its worse in that State. The campaign against Rhode Island freemasonry in the 1830s was most virulent, and even extended to six lodges having their charters 'revoked' by the State legislature. By 1840, the membership of Rhode Island masonry had faded to less than one thousand, a two-thirds drop in ten years. Nonetheless, the opposition soon waned, and sustained growth took place. The Grand Lodge reported a membership of 11,230 in 1983.

Special Notes for Visitors
Rhode Island is geographically the smallest continental American State. Its two main population centres are Cranston and Providence. The Grand Lodge is one of the many in the United States which employs a District system, under District Deputy Grand Masters. While basically an Elective Grand Lodge on the American model, Rhode island is one of the few American jurisdictions to designate Past Masters as members of the Grand Lodge in their own right. Rhode Island does not, as yet, possess a masonic home. However, it does have a fund for the establishment of such a home, which in 1982 stood close to two million dollars. Nonetheless, the Grand Lodge is involved in a wide range of charitable activities, including a Masonic Blood Bank.

SOUTH CAROLINA

The Grand Lodge of Ancient Freemasons of South Carolina
Founded: 1737
Address: Grand Lodge Office: 1401 Senate Street, Columbia 29201, South Carolina. *Telephone:* (803) 799 4377.
Lodges: 327. Permits Dual and Plural Membership.
Membership: 74,499.
Descent: England. *Government:* Elective Grand Lodge.
Courtesy Degrees: Conferred on Request. *Ritual:* Webb form.
Minimum Time Lapse between Degrees: 28 days.
Major Publications: Annual Proceedings. Constitution.
Periodical: *Masonic Light.*

History
The first lodge in South Carolina appears to have been warranted by the Grand Lodge of England in 1735, and a Provincial Grand Master appointed the following year. This was Solomon's Lodge, which appeared as No 251 on the English list of 1760. This lodge still works happily at Charleston, and heads the South Carolina roll of lodges, as No 1. Another six or seven lodges were granted English warrants up until about 1770. The Grand Lodge of South Carolina was organised during the American Revolution. While the exact date is somewhat obscure, it would appear it was formed about 1783. However, the Grand Lodge claims 1737 as its origin.

Of course, by this time the Antients had become well established as the rival masonic power in England, and moved into South Carolina, as well as other parts of eastern America. The Antients warranted three lodges in South Carolina in 1761, 1774, and 1786. The Provincial Grand Lodge of Pennsylvania (Antient) weighed in another three lodges between 1782 and 1786. In 1787, five of these lodges organised the Grand Lodge of Ancient York Masons of South Carolina. The result of this action led to about 30 years of bitter rivalry between the Moderns and the Antients in South Carolina. The story of this rivalry is too long to relay here, except to say that the matter finished up in the South Carolina Supreme Court! It was not until after the Union of Antients and Moderns in England in 1813 that the warring factions in South Carolina became convinced of the virtues of peace, although it was not until 1817 that a happy union was effected. The Grand Lodge has progressed steadily and harmoniously since that date.

Special Notes for Visitors
South Carolina is a large southern jurisdiction, with several population centres of some size, notably Charleston and Columbia. The Grand Lodge office is centrally located in the latter city. South Carolina has never opted to erect a masonic home, but instead assists the less fortunate and the aged in their own communities through various charitable funds.

SOUTH DAKOTA

The Grand Lodge of Ancient, Free and Accepted Masons of South Dakota
Founded: 1875
Address: Grand Lodge Office, 415 South Main Street, Souix Falls. Postal Address: P.O. Box 468, Sioux Falls 57101. *Telephone:* (605) 332 2051.
Lodges: 140. Permits Dual and Plural Membership.
Membership: 12,806.
Descent: Iowa. *Government:* Elective Grand Lodge.
Courtesy Degrees: Conferred on request. *Ritual:* Webb form.
Minimum Time Lapse between Degrees: Four weeks.
Major Publications: Constitutions and By-Laws. Annual Proceedings.
Periodicals: *Grand Lodge Newsletter*, and *Masonic Messenger*.

History

South Dakota and North Dakota were, until 1889, united as the Dakota Territory, and masonically it formed one jurisdiction until that date. The political separation of Dakota into two States prompted the Grand Lodge of Dakota to amicably divide into two jurisdictions. A fuller look at general Dakota masonic history is contained under the heading of North Dakota.

Special Notes for Visitors

South Dakota is another rural-based mid-western American State, which does not contain any large cities. Understandably, its regulations and forms are quite similar to those of North Dakota. South Dakota does not possess a masonic home or similar institution, although it does give support to one run by the Order of the Eastern Star. Nonetheless, the Grand Lodge has a number of substantial charity funds at its disposal, which it uses in supporting many benevolent activities. Of great interest to the visitor will be the Grand Lodge office and library building in Sioux Falls. It is a very large stone structure of particular beauty, both inside and out.

TENNESSEE

The Grand Lodge of Free and Accepted Masons of the State of Tennessee
Founded: 1813
Addresses: Grand Lodge Office: 100 Seventh Avenue North, Nashville, Tennessee. Postal Address: P.O. Box 24216, Nashville 37202. *Telephone:* (615) 255 2625.
Chattanooga: No Main Temple, check Telephone Directory.
Memphis: Scottish Rite Temple, 815 Union Avenue, Memphis.
Lodges: 381. Permits Dual Membership outside Tennessee only.
Membership: 95,824.
Descent: North Carolina. *Government:* Elective Grand Lodge.
Courtesy Degrees: Conferred on request. *Ritual:* Webb form.
Minimum Time Lapse between Degrees: 28 days.
Major Publications: Annual Proceedings. Constitution.

History
The State of Tennessee was originally part of North Carolina, being admitted into the United States in 1796. The first lodge established in Tennessee was St Tammany Lodge No 29, which was chartered in 1796 by the Grand Lodge of North Carolina. It had expired by 1813. It is interesting to note that out of respect for this lodge, no later Tennessee lodge ever came to use the number one. After Tennessee became a State, the Grand Lodge of North Carolina chartered a further six lodges up until 1811. In that year these lodges petitioned the Grand Lodge of North Carolina to form a Grand Lodge of Tennessee. The processes involved moved slowly, but in 1813, the so called *Great Charter* was drawn up by the Grand Lodge of North Carolina, in effect constituting the Grand Lodge of Tennessee. This was the first time such a procedure had ever been used in erecting a new Grand Lodge, and it created controversy at the time. However, the Grand Lodge of Tennessee did come into being as a result, and has since prospered as one the larger jurisdictions in the United States.

Special Notes for Visitors
Tennessee is a populous southern State possessing several larger cities, including Chattanooga with 16 lodges, Memphis with 20 lodges, and Nashville with 12 lodges. In the field of charity, the Grand Lodge is very active, supporting in particular its Widows and Orphans Home which it founded at Nashville in 1892. The Grand Lodge building in Nashville is a particularly fine structure and will be of particular interest to visitors.

TEXAS
The Grand Lodge of Texas, Ancient, Free and Accepted Masons
Founded: 1837
Addresses: Grand Lodge Office: Grand Lodge Memorial Temple, 724 Washington Street, Waco. Postal Address: P.O. Box 446, Waco 76703. *Telephone:* (817) 753 7395.
Dallas: Scottish Rite Temple, Corner of Harwood and Canton Streets, Dallas.
Forth Worth: Masonic Temple, 1100 Henderson Street, Fort Worth.
Houston: Masonic Temple, 4923 Rusk Street, Houston.
San Antonio: Masonic Temple, 125 West Maple Street, San Antonio.
Lodges: 969. Permits Dual Membership.
Membership: 206,881.
Descent: Louisiana. *Government:* Elective Grand Lodge.
Courtesy Degrees: Conferred on Request. *Ritual:* Webb form.
Minimum Time Lapse between Degrees: One month.
Major Publications: Constitution. Annual Proceedings.
Periodical: *The Texas Freemason.*

History
The earliest masonic history of Texas is somewhat obscure. It would appear that there was masonic activity in the area as early as 1828, when the York Grand Lodge of Mexico was petitioned for a charter. It would seem that this charter was never

issued. In 1835, the Grand Lodge of Louisiana issued a dispensation for a lodge at Brazoria. It moved to Houston during the Mexican-American War, and received a charter as Holland Lodge No 26 in 1837. Holland Lodge later became No 1 on the roll of lodges in Texas. At this time, Louisiana issued charters for two more lodges, and in December, 1837, these three lodges met at Houston and created the Grand Lodge of Texas.

Special Notes for Visitors

Texas is geographically the largest of the American States, and one of the biggest in terms of population. Not surprisingly, the Grand Lodge of Texas is one of the largest in America. Texas possesses several very big cities, including Dallas (with 30 lodges), Fort Worth (with 20 lodges), Houston (with 34 lodges), and San Antonio (with 21 lodges). Of the Urban lodges, quite a few have memberships in excess of 1000. Park Place Lodge No 1172, with a membership in 1981 of 2,632 is numerically the largest Lodge in Texas, and probably in the world. It meets at Houston. Not surprisingly, Texas uses a District system. It possesses well in excess of 100 Districts, each under a District Deputy Grand Master, with each District comprising an average of about ten lodges. Masonic charity is wide-spread in Texas. The Grand Lodge operates a Masonic Home and School at Fort Worth, catering for over 100 students. It also runs a home for aged masons at Arlington. It caters for in excess of 50 masonic widows. In addition, the Scottish Rite has a large hospital for crippled children at Fort Worth.

UTAH

The Grand Lodge of Free and Accepted Masons of Utah
Founded: 1872
Address: Grand Lodge Office: 650 East South Temple Street, Salt Lake City 84 102, Utah.   *Telephone:* (801) 363 2936.
Lodges: 31.   Permits Dual Membership.
Membership: 4,684.
Descent: Nevada, Montana, Kansas and Colorado.   *Government:* Elective Grand Lodge.
Courtesy Degrees: Conferred on request.   *Ritual:* Webb form.
Minimum Time Lapse between Degrees: Two weeks.
Major Publications: Constitution.   Annual Proceedings.

History

The first lodge in Utah was Rocky Mountain Lodge No 205, chartered as an army lodge in 1860 by the Grand Lodge of Missouri. However, it had expired by 1862. In 1866, Mt Moriah Lodge was established at Salt Lake City under a dispensation from the Grand Lodge of Nevada. It was stipulated that the lodge was not to admit Mormons, and after a protest from the lodge the dispensation was withdrawn. Montana granted a charter for Wasatch Lodge No 8 in 1867, also at Salt Lake City. Mt Moriah Lodge finally received a charter in 1868, from the Grand Lodge of Kansas. In 1871, the Grand Lodge of Colorado weighed in with a charter for Argenta Lodge No 21. These three lodges met in convention in 1872, and the Grand Lodge of Utah was opened.

Special Notes for Visitors
The Grand Lodge of Utah is one of the smallest Grand Lodges in the United States. This is largely accounted for by the fact that the large majority of the population of the State are members of the Mormon faith. There has long been hostility between the Mormon Church and masonry in Utah. Basically, the tenets and dogmas of the Mormon religion prevent masonic membership by any of its adherents. Indeed, no Mormon is permitted by his church to join freemasonry, and no Utah Lodge is permitted to initiate a Mormon. The Mormon Question has long plagued the Craft in Utah, and all the matters surrounding the situation are too long to enter into here. It is enough to say that for many years both sides have co-existed well enough, because neither group will have anything to do with the other. Salt Lake City is the only population centre in the State of Utah of any size, and it is the home of six of Utah's 31 lodges. Utah does not possess a masonic home, and it is doubtful if the jurisdiction would be large enough to support one. Nonetheless, some outstanding work in the area of benevolence is undertaken through various masonic charity funds.

VERMONT

The Grand Lodge of Free and Accepted Masons of the State of Vermont
Founded: 1794
Address: Grand Lodge Office: Masonic Temple, 143 Pearl Street, Burlington. Postal Address: P.O. Box 443, Burlington 05402, Vermont. *Telephone:* (802) 862 3975.
Lodges: 97. Permits Dual Membership in Vermont, and Plural Membership outside Vermont.
Membership: 12,500.
Descent: Massachusetts, Connecticut. *Government:* Elective Grand Lodge.
Courtesy Degrees: Conferred on request. *Ritual:* Webb form.
Minimum Time Lapse between Degrees: None, candidates may advance when proficient.
Major Publications: Constitution. Annual Proceedings. Periodical: *The Green Mountain Freemason.*

History
The first lodge in Vermont was Vermont Lodge No 17, which was warranted by the Massachusetts Grand Lodge in 1781, to meet at Springfield. However, it actually met in New Hampshire, before moving to Springfield in 1788. It was also instrumental in obtaining a Massachusetts charter for Faithful Lodge, erected at Charlestown in 1788. Faithful Lodge had a short history, and Vermont Lodge, while heading the roll of lodges at the formation of the Grand Lodge of Vermont, failed to survive the anti-masonry of the 1830s. Five lodges met in Convention in 1794, and formed the Grand Lodge of Vermont. In addition to Vermont Lodge, represented were North Star Lodge (chartered by Massachusetts in 1765), Dorchester Lodge (warranted from Ontario in 1791), Temple Lodge (warranted from Connecticut in 1793), and Union Lodge (warranted from Connecticut in 1794).

The anti-masonry of the 1830s following the Morgan Affair was severely felt in Vermont. By 1833, the Grand Lodge was virtually extinct. It re-organised finally in

1846, having been very badly depleted. Only Dorchester Lodge and Union Lodge, of the original five lodges, survived to 1846. These two lodges today occupy the first two places on the Vermont roll of lodges.

Special Notes for Visitors
Vermont is a small mountainous State located in the north-east of the United States. Its population is not overly large, and this is reflected in masonic membership. Nonetheless, Vermont is a very active jurisdiction. In the area of charity, it is not large enough to support a masonic home, but is involved in relief through a substantial charity fund. The majority of Vermont lodges advertise 7.30 pm as the starting time of their monthly stated meetings, although a small number commence at 8 pm. The vast majority hold their Annual Meetings in April.

VIRGINIA
The Grand Lodge of Ancient, Free and Accepted Masons of the Commonwealth of Virginia
Founded: 1778
Addresses: Grand Lodge Office: 4101 Nine Mile Road, Richmond. Postal Address: P.O. Box 27345, Richmond 23261. *Telephone:* (804) 222 3110.
Richmond: Masonic Temple, 4204 Hermitage Road, Richmond.
Norfolk: Masonic Temple, 7001 Granby Street, Norfolk.
Portsmouth: Masonic Temple, 463 Court Street, Portsmouth.
Lodges: 356. Permits Dual and Plural Membership. *Membership:* 66,000 (approx.).
Descent: England and Scotland. *Government:* Elective Grand Lodge.
Courtesy Degrees: Conferred on request. *Ritual:* Webb form.
Minimum Time Lapse between Degrees: None, candidates may advance when proficient.
Major Publications: Annual Proceedings. *Virginia Methodical Digest* (Constitution). Periodical: *Virginia Masonic Herald.*

History
The early history of masonry in Virginia is quite obscure. It is suspected that masonic activity was occurring as early as 1730, but evidence is scant. The first lodge in Virginia was Royal Exchange Lodge No 172, claimed to have been warranted by the Grand Lodge of England about 1733, but more probably erected about 1754. Other early warrants came from both England and Scotland. Nine lodges were invited to participate in the formation of the Grand Lodge of Virginia, and after long organisation, a convention met in October, 1778, and formed the new body with four lodges being represented. Norfolk Lodge No 1 (formerly Royal Exchange) heads the roll of lodges, with Atlantic Lodge as No 2, Blandford Lodge (warranted from Scotland in 1757) as No 3, and Fredericksburg Lodge (warranted from Scotland in 1758) as No 4. The Grand Lodge of Virginia is the oldest Grand Lodge in the United States in terms of continued existence.

Special Notes for Visitors
As a very old Grand Lodge, Virginia possesses several lodges of special interest. Fredericksburg Lodge No 4 was the mother lodge of George Washington, America's First President. It meets at the Masonic Temple, 803 Princess Anne Street, Fredericksburg, on the 2nd Friday monthly, at 8 pm. Another famous lodge is the Alexandria-Washington Lodge No 22. It was in this lodge that George Washington served as Master. It meets at the George Washington Masonic National Memorial in Alexandria (just outside of Washington DC), on the 2nd and 4th Thursdays monthly, at 7.30 pm. This lodge has over 700 members. Meeting details of other Virginia lodges can readily be obtained at the Grand Lodge office in Richmond. Virginia possesses a large masonic home located at Richmond catering for over 70 aged residents. The Grand Lodge also runs an extensive educational scholarship programme, and a statewide Masonic Blood Bank programme.

WASHINGTON

The Grand Lodge of Free and Accepted Masons of the State of Washington
Founded: 1858
Addresses: Grand Lodge Office: Masonic Temple, 47 St Helens Avenue, Tacoma 98402. *Telephone:* (206) 272 3263.
Seattle: Masonic Temple, corner Harvard Avenue and East Pine Street, Seattle.
Lodges: 261. Permits Dual Membership.
Membership: 43,476.
Descent: Oregon. *Government:* Elective Grand Lodge.
Courtesy Degrees: Conferred on request. *Ritual:* Webb form.
Minimum Time Lapse between Degrees: 14 days.
Major Publications: Annual Proceedings. Constitution.

History
The State of Washington was part of Oregon until it was severed from the latter by an act of the United States Congress in 1853. Quite obviously, all Craft masonry in Washington derived from the Grand Lodge of Oregon. The first lodge in Washington was Olympia Lodge, chartered in 1853. This was followed by Steilacoom Lodge in 1854, Grand Mound Lodge in 1857, and Washington Lodge in 1858. Delegates from these four lodges met in Convention in December, 1858 and formed the Grand Lodge of Washington. Of the four original lodges, all survive except Grand Mound Lodge. Olympia Lodge No 1, heads the Washington roster of lodges.

Special Notes for Visitors
The State of Washington is located in the north-west corner of the continental United States. It possesses two larger cities, namely Seattle (with 39 lodges), and Tacoma (with 15 lodges). The jurisdiction is divided into 33 Districts of about 10 lodges per District, each under a Deputy of the Grand Master. A large masonic home is located at Zenith, midway between Tacoma and Seattle. It originally cared for children, but today caters for about 140 aged residents, although it has a capacity of 200. Visitors are welcome to attend the homes. Washington also possesses a most substantial charity fund to assist those in need. It is interesting to note that Wash-

ington still controls seven lodges in southern Alaska subsequent to the erection of the Grand Lodge of Alaska. However, it is expected that these lodges will eventually exchange their Washington charters for those of the Alaskan jurisdiction.

WEST VIRGINIA

The Grand Lodge of Ancient, Free and Accepted Masons of West Virginia
Founded: 1865
Address: Grand Lodge Office: Masonic Building, 107 Hale Street, Charleston. Postal Address: P.O. Box 2346, Charleston 25301, West Virginia. *Telephone:* (304) 342 3543.
Lodges: 155. Permits Single Membership only.
Membership: 40,801.
Descent: Virginia, Pennsylvania. *Government:* Elective Grand Lodge.
Courtesy Degrees: Conferred on request. *Ritual:* Webb form.
Minimum Time Lapse between Degrees: None, candidates may advance when proficient.
Major Publications: Annual Proceedings. Constitution.

History
The State of West Virginia was part of Virginia until in became a separate State in 1863. Its first lodge was Greenbrier Lodge No 49, warranted by the Grand Lodge of Virginia in 1796. This was followed by Wellsburg Lodge No 78, warranted from Pennsylvania in 1799. This latter lodge is the oldest surviving in West Virginia, and currently holds No 2 on the West Virginia roll of lodges. However, it is preceded on the roll by Ohio Lodge, which was chartered from Virginia in 1815. This oddity of numbering is accounted for by the fact that Wellsburg Lodge was re-chartered by Virginia in 1817, and at the formation of the Grand Lodge it was therefore technically younger. Eight lodges met in Convention in 1864, and the Grand Lodge of West Virginia was formally constituted in the next year.

Special Notes for Visitors
West Virginia is a largely rural State, with no large population centres. However, virtually every town in the State has at least one lodge. The largest concentration of lodges is at Wheeling, which possesses four, including the premier lodge of the Jurisdiction, Ohio Lodge No 1. West Virginia has a substantial masonic home located at Parkersburg, which is supported by a large Grand Lodge Endowment Fund.

WISCONSIN

The Grand Lodge of Free and Accepted Masons of Wisconsin
Founded: 1843
Address: Grand Lodge Office: 1123 North Astor Street, Milwaukee 53202, Wisconsin. *Telephone:* (414) 273 3150.
Lodges: 266. Permits Dual and Plural Membership.
Membership: 38,084.
Descent: New York, Missouri, and Illinois. *Government:* Elective Grand Lodge.

Courtesy Degrees: Conferred on request.   *Ritual:* Webb form.
Minimum Time Lapse between Degrees: 20 days.
Major Publications: Constitution.   Annual Proceedings.   Periodical: *Wisconsin Masonic Journal.*

History

The first lodge erected in Wisconsin was Menominee Lodge No 374. It was chartered by the Grand Lodge of New York in 1824 for military personnel, but it subsequently expired. The second lodge in Wisconsin, and the oldest surviving, was Mineral Point Lodge No 49, chartered by the Grand Lodge of Missouri in 1842. It now heads the roll of lodges in Wisconsin. This was followed by Melody Lodge No 15, chartered from Missouri in 1843; and Milwaukee Lodge No 22 (later Kilbourn Lodge), chartered from Illinois in the same year. These three latter lodges met in Convention in December, 1843, and established the Grand Lodge of Wisconsin.

Special Notes for Visitors

Wisconsin is a large, mainly rural based State, possessing one substantial city. This is Milwaukee, which has 13 lodges working within it. Nonetheless, Wisconsin is far from a small jurisdiction, and there are few towns in the State not possessing at least one lodge. The Grand Lodge runs an excellent masonic home. It is located on a large site at Dousman, about 30 miles from Milwaukee.

WYOMING

The Grand Lodge of Ancient, Free and Accepted Masons of Wyoming
Founded: 1874
Addresses: Grand Lodge Office: 105 North Center Street, Casper. Postal Address: P.O. Box 459, Casper 82602, Wyoming. *Telephone:* (307) 234 2692.
Cheyenne: Masonic Temple: 1820 Capitol Avenue, Cheyenne.
Lodges: 52.   Permits Dual Membership only.
Membership: 10,463.
Descent: Colorado, Nebraska.   *Government:* Elective Grand Lodge.
Courtesy Degrees: Conferred on request.   *Ritual:* Webb form.
Minimum Time Lapse between Degrees: None, candidates may advance when proficient.
Major Publications: Annual Proceedings.   Constitution.
Periodical: *The Wyoming Mason.*

History

The first masonic meeting in Wyoming took place in 1862 at Independence Rock. This event is commemorated every ten years whereupon the Grand Lodge of Wyoming convenes a Special Communication at the site. The last such occasion occurred in 1980. The first lodge erected in Wyoming was Cheyenne Lodge No 16, chartered by the Grand Lodge of Colorado in 1868. This was followed by Wyoming Lodge No 28, chartered from Nebraska in 1870; Laramie Lodge No 18 chartered from Colorado in 1870; and Evanston Lodge No 24 chartered in 1874, also from Colorado. These four lodges, all of which still exist, met in Convention in December, 1874, and constituted the Grand Lodge of Wyoming.

Special Notes for Visitors
Wyoming is a large northern State. It is rural based, and possesses no large cities. The largest population centres are Casper and Cheyenne, each containing four lodges. Consequently, Wyoming is one of the smaller masonic jurisdictions in the United States. While it does not have a masonic home, it does possess a substantial charity fund. Of particular interest to the visitor will be the Grand Lodge library and museum, located in the Grand Lodge building at Casper.

Section IX

Visiting in Oceania

Australia

Australia possesses six Grand Lodges, one for each of the six Australian States. The lodges working in the Australian Capital Territory come under the jurisdiction of the United Grand Lodge of New South Wales, while those in the Northern Territory are governed by the Grand Lodge of South Australia.

The sources of Australian masonry are exclusively British, with all Australian Grand Lodges being formed by lodges originally under the Grand Lodges of England, Ireland and Scotland. The six Grand Lodges work together in perfect amity, with each having exclusive jurisdiction within its State.

NEW SOUTH WALES

The United Grand Lodge of New South Wales of Antient, Free and Accepted Masons
Founded: 1888
Address: The Masonic Centre of New South Wales, 279 Castlereagh Street, Sydney. Postal Address: P.O. Box A259, Sydney South 2000. Telephone: (02) 267 9133.
Lodges: 743. Permits Dual and Plural Membership.
Membership: 69,268.
Descent: England, Ireland, and Scotland. *Government:* Elective Grand Lodge.
Courtesy Degrees: Correspondence must be through Grand Lodges.
Minimum Time Lapse between Degrees: Four weeks. *Ritual:* English—type (with adaptations).
Main Publications: Book of Constitutions. Grand Lodge Proceedings. Almanac of Lodges. Periodical: *The NSW Freemason.*

History
There is evidence of a meeting of freemasons at Sydney in 1803 aboard a naval vessel, but it was not viewed kindly by the governor who ordered the temporary arrest of the participants. The first lodge to meet in Austrialia was a military one. This was the Lodge of Social and Military Virtues No 227, Irish Constitution, warranted in 1752. It was stationed in Sydney in 1813. This lodge was responsible for sponsoring the first stationary lodge at Sydney—the Australian Social Lodge No 260 IC, in 1820. This latter lodge now heads the NSW roll of lodges as Antiquity Lodge No 1. The first English lodge was the Lodge of Australia No 820, established in 1828. Scotland's premier lodge in NSW was Lodge St Andrew No 358, formed in 1851.

The Craft in NSW grew very rapidly, and an English Provincial (later District) Grand Lodge was established in 1839. Scotland approved a Provincial (later District) Grand Lodge in 1855, while an Irish Provincial Grand Lodge was formed in 1858. Upon the Colony of New South Wales receiving self-government, a groundswell of masonic sentiment arose for a local sovereign Grand Lodge. There were early differences of opinion in this regard, and these led to the separate erection of a Grand Lodge of New South Wales in 1877. It was composed initially of thirteen lodges, most of which were Irish. However, it failed to receive the recognition of the three 'home' Grand Lodges in Britain. It was not until 1888 that complete harmony was gained, and in that year the United Grand Lodge of New South Wales was formed. All lodges then operating in NSW regardless of allegience, came together to constitute this new regular Grand Body.

Since that time, the United Grand Lodge has prospered, and it has become numerically a large jurisdiction. In recent years, the Grand Lodge has erected a mammoth new Masonic Centre in central Sydney, and it is due to celebrate its centenary year in 1988.

Notes for Visitors to New South Wales

1. MEETING TIMES, AND DRESS

The vast majority of lodges in NSW meet at 7.30 pm for ordinary meetings, although a few meet up to half an hour earlier, or later. On nights of Installation, lodges generally meet an hour earlier, at about 6.30 pm.

Dress for all NSW lodges is a black dinner suit for evening meetings, white dress shirt, black bow tie, and black shoes and socks. In years gone by, full evening dress (black tails) was the normal dress, and while this is still permitted, most members attend in a dinner suit. However, Grand Lodge officers attending official masonic functions and Installations are still required to wear full evening dress. During the hot summer months, members may wear their dinner suit without its coat, although this practice is not permitted for lodge officers. If a lodge meets during the daytime, members can then wear a dark lounge suit. A visitor from outside New South Wales will certainly not be prevented from attending any lodge meeting if he is not carrying a dinner suit, and he will be made most welcome in a dark lounge suit.

2. LODGE AFTER-PROCEEDINGS

A festive board always follows a lodge meeting in New South Wales, and as with most other Australian States, it is commonly referred to as 'The South'. At ordinary meetings it consists of a fairly substantial supper, which is always accompanied by a Formal Toast List. The costs associated with the festive board are met equally by members as part of their lodge dues, although in some lodges a small charge is made on those attending to offset part of the costs of 'The South'. Nevertheless, visitors are rarely expected to contribute, but on attending an Installation banquet they may well feel inclined to do so.

On nights of Installation a banquet is normally held, and the toast list employed on such an occasion is often quite extensive. An example of such a toast list is as follows:
1. The Loyal Toast—The Queen.
2. The MW Grand Master of the United Grand Lodge of New South Wales.
3. The Installing Master.
4. The Worshipful Master.
5. The Visitors.
6. Absent Brethren.
7. The Junior Warden's Toast.

There is some variation to the toasts that might be proposed. The toast to absent brethren is not always given, depending on the lodge. On ordinary meeting nights, there is generally no toast to the Worshipful Master, nor to the Grand Master.

Other toasts employed on normal meeting nights are those to a candidate, or an affiliate. In NSW, it is usual that all candidates are toasted in the South, regardless of which degree they have received at that particular meeting. Similarly, many lodges will toast an affiliate on the night he joins it. It will be noted that the final toast in NSW is the Junior Warden's Toast, and not the Tyler's Toast used in all other Australian jurisdictions. The wording of this brief toast has an analogous import to the Tyler's Toast, and in any case forms the conclusion of the evenings proceedings.

Quite often, the Visitors' Toast will involve three responses—one from a visiting Master on behalf of all visiting Masters, one from a Past Master on behalf of all visiting Past Masters, and one from a Master Mason on behalf of all remaining brethren. Again, in some lodges there might only be one response, usually by a visiting Master. The toast to the Grand Master is proposed at Installation Meetings, but not at other meetings unless he is present, or when a District Grand Inspector of Workings pays an official visit to a lodge in his district. In New South Wales, it is fairly common for Master Masons to be involved in the proposition of toasts. A visitor will usually be asked in advance if it is desired for him to respond to the Visitors' Toast. While it is most rare for a charity collection to take place at a lodge meeting, the conducting of a raffle in 'The South' is very commonplace. Visitors are therefore well advised to carry a small amount of money with them when visiting a New South Wales Lodge. The vast majority of NSW lodges serve alcohol (generally beer) in 'The South', although there are a very small number of temperence lodges within the Constitution.

3. OF VISITING IN GENERAL

In New South Wales, visitors are often admitted according to masonic rank after the lodge has been opened. The first admission will normally be for visitors below the rank of Installed Master. Separate admissions will then usually be made for Past Masters, and for current Worshipful Masters. Lodges visiting on an official 'Fraternal', and officially visiting Grand Lodge officers, will be admitted after the Worshipful Masters.

Quite common practice in New South Wales is for one lodge to officially visit another. On such a visit, the Master, his Wardens, and members of the visiting lodge will be admitted as one group. These official visits are commonly known as Fraternals.

Lodges in New South Wales, for the most part, use a card system for admitting visitors. On arrival, each visitor fills out a card and hands it to the Tyler. On it he will have recorded his name, his masonic rank, his lodge, and the name of the lodge member vouching for him. These cards are then passed inside the lodge. They will be read out, and the vouching member will signify accordingly. No visitor will be admitted unless he has been properly vouched for. An unknown visitor will be examined by a Past Master of the lodge, who will then vouch for him inside. It is therefore most advisable for such a visitor to arrive early to enable these procedures to be undertaken.

4. ASPECTS OF MASONRY IN NEW SOUTH WALES

There are a number of lodges in New South Wales which annually hold a ladies night in association with a regular meeting, whereupon the ladies of members and visitors are invited to 'The South'. On such an occasion the lodge meeting will be short, with no degree ceremony being performed. The repast provided will normally be most expansive, and the only toasts that will be proposed are those to 'The Queen', and to 'The Ladies'. Ladies are also permitted, in New South Wales, to be present at an Installation Banquet, although only a few lodges avail themselves of this opportunity. There are special arrangements laid down when a lodge wishes to invite its ladies to its Installation Banquet. It must also be noted that quite a few lodges opt not to associate their ladies' nights with an actual lodge meeting, but rather hold them at some other convenient annual occasion—often in the festive season before Christmas.

The Craft in New South Wales involves itself in some quite outstanding charity work. The Grand Lodge itself has under its direct control a Masonic Hospital situated in Victoria Street, Ashfield (a Sydney suburb), and provides care for children who have suffered the loss of either or both parents, or in such cases of where one of the parents may be totally or permanently incapacitated. This care is in the form of Family Group Homes, or by way of financial assistance. In addition, there are three main Masonic Charities namely, The Royal Freemasons' Benevolent Institution of New South Wales, The Frank Whiddon Masonic Homes of New South Wales, and the New South Wales Masonic Youth Welfare Fund. The former two charities provide care for the aged in conjunction in many instances with local citizens' groups. The Royal Freemasons' Benevolent Institution administers Retirement Villages at Newcastle, Canberra, Tamworth, Cessnock, Dubbo, West Wyalong, and Ungarie. In addition, the Institution runs a surgical hospital at Shortland (a suburb of the city of Newcastle). The Frank Whiddon Masonic Homes operates Retirement Villages at Glenfield, Hornsby, Wingham, Temora, Kyogle, Maclean, Narrabri, Yamba, and Casino. The NSW Masonic Youth Welfare Fund provides for the care and welfare of youth, irrespective of whether or not they are the children of freemasons.

New South Wales possesses many lodges of instruction, basically on the English model. They either function under the charter of a lodge, or more commonly under special licence from the Grand Master. They exist to train lodge officers in ritual work, although they do replace the rehearsals which all New South Wales lodges hold on a regular basis. Visitors who are interested to attend a lodge of Instruction are welcome to make inquiries at the Grand Lodge office.

A candidate for a New South Wales lodge needs a proposer and a seconder, who must attend the meeting when the candidate's name is being submitted to the ballot. The usual procedures of Committee investigation, interview, and balloting apply in New South Wales. In addition to the quite usual reference to the Grand Secretary when a proposed candidate has been a bankrupt or been before a court of law; the Grand Lodge also requires that a candidate who has been involved in divorce proceedings be 'investigated' at Grand Lodge level, as well. Indeed, any lodge member involved in divorce proceedings is expected to have the relevant divorce documents examined by the Board of General Purposes.

The Masonic Centre of New South Wales is a massive, modern building located in central Sydney. It contains many lodge rooms, supper or function rooms, and ancillary facilities. The Grand Lodge office and Grand Lodge Library are located on the fourth floor. Guided tours of the complex are available. These are conducted every week day (except between Christmas and New Year, and on Public Holidays), at 10 am, 12 noon, and 2 pm. They are open to the general public.

New South Wales possesses one highly respected lodge of research—The Research Lodge of New South Wales No 971. It was formed in 1968, and a wide correspondence membership is attached to the lodge. All full and associate members receive its excellent *Transactions*. It meets at the Masonic Centre on the 1st Tuesday of March (Installation), May, July, September, and November.

Visitors to Sydney should not overlook the New South Wales Masonic Club, located close to the Masonic Centre at 169-173 Castlereagh Street (telephone: (02) 264 2281). The residential section of the club is available to masons and their wives. It possesses excellent motel-type twin-bedded rooms and single rooms, which are air-conditioned and have private facilities. Bookings for accommodation should be made as well in advance as possible, and masons from outside New South Wales are welcome.

Of interest to visitors will be the fact that, in addition to the jewels (medallions) applicable to Craft masonry, those appertaining to the degrees of Mark Master Mason, and the Holy Royal Arch, may also be worn in New South Wales Craft lodges. However, this does not extend to other additional masonic orders. In addition, masons holding civil or military decorations can wear them at NSW lodge meetings, as appropriate.

New South Wales possesses a number of lodges, in common with most other Australian jurisdictions, which meet during daylight hours, rather than in the evening. Some of these lodges meet on a Saturday, while some convene on weekdays. These lodges may well be of particular interest to a visitor with a tight travelling schedule, and details concerning them are readily obtainable at the Grand Lodge office.

Affiliating with a lodge in New South Wales involves fairly straightforward procedures. Basically, they are the same as for candidates, but lodges are required to make enquiries through the Grand Lodge office for masons seeking to affiliate who come from another recognised constitution.

5. MASONIC GOVERNMENT

The government of the United Grand Lodge is based very largely on British practices, particularly those of England. The Grand Lodge consists of all Grand Lodge officers, Past and Present; and the Masters, Wardens, and Past Masters of every constituent lodge. All Grand Lodge offices are nominally elective, with exceptions of Deputy Grand Master, Assistant Grand Master, Grand Secretary, and Assistant Grand Secretary. The Deputy Grand Master and Assistant Grand Master are appointed by the Grand Master, while the Grand Secretary and his assistant are appointed by the Grand Master on the recommendation of the Board of General Purposes. The two secretaries hold office at the pleasure of the Grand Lodge— usually until retirement.

The two main administrative organs of the United Grand Lodge are the Board of General Purposes and the Board of Benevolence. The former controls the functions of freemasonry in New South Wales between the meetings of the Grand Lodge, while the latter oversees the benevolent functions of the Grand Lodge. Both bodies consist of the senior ex-officio Grand Lodge officers, and a certain number of elected members.

The size of the NSW Craft has meant that forms of decentralised government have been seen as desirable. The Constitutions of the Grand Lodge provide for the appointment of Regional Grand Lodge officers, who are provided with fairly limited powers. New South Wales is currently divided into seventeen regions. In addition, and quite separately, New South Wales is also masonically divided into over one hundred Districts (with a number of lodges in each) each under the superintendence of a District Grand Inspector of Workings. They report to two Grand Inspectors of Workings who, in turn, report to the Board of General Purposes and the Grand Master. It is interesting to note that, although Grand Masters in New South Wales are subject to nominal re-election every year, they usually serve for a three year term.

6. LODGE WORKINGS, REGALIA, AND RITUAL

All lodges under the United Grand Lodge must work the ritual as prescribed by it. It is largely based on English-type ritual, but it does possess a few features—both in ,content and form—which are obviously the result of Scottish, and particularly Irish, influences. This is quite understandable in view of the masonic ancestry of New South Wales. The regalia worn in New South Wales is very similar to that of the United Grand Lodge of England, and to other Australian Grand Lodges. Of course, visitors are welcome to appear at a New South Wales lodge in their own regalia, whether it be different from local forms, or not. However, in common with most jurisdictions, NSW requires that masons actually joining one of its lodges from some other recognised Grand Lodge, wear NSW regalia upon obtaining membership.

List of Lodges

The jurisdiction of the United Grand Lodge of New South Wales extends throughout the State of New South Wales, and includes the Australian Capital Territory, which contains Canberra—Australia's Capital city. The very large number of New South Wales lodges precludes any attempt to list them here. However, such a list, with the full meeting details of each lodge, can be found in the *Almanac of Lodges* published annually by the Grand Lodge. In addition, many lodges (mainly in Sydney) publish their meeting details in the *NSW Freemason*. This magazine is published bi-monthly by the Grand Lodge, and is distributed to members in New South Wales. It is available on subscription.

As most visitors to New South Wales will arrive via Sydney, they should readily be able to visit the Masonic Centre and the Grand Lodge office therein contained. This is an appreciated courtesy. Of course, the many other reasons for visiting the Masonic Centre have already been mentioned. It is worthy of note that in excess of forty lodges meet there, and one will be found meeting on virtually every week-night. However, it must also be stressed that many NSW lodges do not meet just before or after Christmas, and some bring their meetings forward in December as a consequence. In addition, a number of lodges do not meet in the first week of January.

One particular lodge located in New South Wales merits special mention. This is the Coolangatta Lodge No 298, Queensland Constitution. This lodge meets at the Masonic Temple, Boyd Street, Tweed Heads, on the 2nd Thursday, monthly, at 7.30 pm (Installation: 2nd Saturday, September). It is the only Queensland lodge meeting in NSW, and indeed, it is the only Australian-warranted lodge meeting outside its own jurisdiction. Tweed Heads is a town located right on the New South

Wales/Queensland border, and the Masonic Temple where this lodge meets is scarcely more than one kilometre inside New South Wales.

While no expansive list of NSW lodges can be provided here, a list of the main temples in the major provincial population centres of New South Wales is provided below.

Albury:	Masonic Temple, 562 Kiewa Street, Albury.
Bathurst:	Masonic Hall, 9 Ilumba Way, Kelso.
Broken Hill:	Masonic Temple, corner Oxide Street, and Argent Lane, Broken Hill.
Canberra:	Masonic Hall, National Curcuit, Barton, Canberra, ACT.
Dubbo:	Masonic Temple, 33 Church Street, Dubbo.
Lismore:	Masonic Temple, Magellan Street, Lismore.
Newcastle:	Masonic Hall, 102 King Street (corner Wolfe Street), Newcastle.
Orange:	Masonic Hall, 35 Sale Street, Orange.
Tamworth:	Masonic Temple, 464 Peel Street, Tamworth.
Wollongong:	Masonic Hall, Gipps Street, Gwynneville, Wollongong.

THE NORTHERN TERRITORY

All lodges in the Northern Territory of Australia are governed by the Grand Lodge of South Australia, and so general details concerning lodge visiting within this jurisdiction can be found under the latter heading. Perhaps the only difference worth mentioning concerns the dress worn in Northern Territory lodges. The hot tropical climate of this area often stops the wearing of a full dinner suit, and coats are often absent in oppressive weather. As the lodges in the Northern Territory are somewhat geographically removed, a full list is given.

Lodges in the Northern Territory meet at five locations—Masonic Hall, Stokes Street, *Darwin*, denoted (a) below; Masonic Hall, Allchurch Street, *Alice Springs* denoted (b) below; Masonic Hall, Lindsay Street, *Katherine* denoted (c) below; Masonic Hall, Standley Street, *Tennant Creek* denoted (d) below; and the Arts Theatre, *Nhulunbuy*, Gove denoted (e) below.

Port Darwin Lodge No 41	Meets (a) 1st Friday at 7.30 pm. Inst: July.
Alice Springs Lodge No 156	Meets (b) 3rd Monday at 7.30 pm. Inst: July.
Darwin Lodge of Rememberance No 182	Meets (a) 3rd Friday at 7.30 pm. Inst: July.
Lodge Foelsche No 211	Meets (a) 4th Wednesday at 7.15 pm. Inst: July.
Katherine Lodge of Fidelity No 217	Meets (c) 3rd Saturday at 7.30 pm. Inst: July.
McDoull Stuart Lodge No 219	Meets (b) 1st Thursday at 7.30 pm. Inst: July.
Mica Lodge No 221	Meets (d) last Saturday at 7.30 pm. Inst: July.
Leichardt Lodge of Research No 225	Meets (a) 2nd Thursday at 7.30 pm. Inst: November.
Lodge Arafura No 223	Meets (e) 3rd Wednesday at 7.30 pm. Inst: July.

QUEENSLAND

The United Grand Lodge of Antient, Free and Accepted Masons of Queensland
Founded: 1921
Address: Masonic Memorial Temple, Ann Street, Brisbane.   *Telephone:* 2293533.
Lodges: 466.   Permits Dual and Plural Membership.
Membership: 29,160.
Descent: England, Ireland, Scotland.   *Government:* Elective Grand Lodge.
Courtesy Degrees: All correspondence must be through Grand Lodges.
Minimum Time Lapse between Degrees: Four weeks.   *Ritual:* English-type (with adaptations).
Main Publications: Constitutions.   Grand Lodge Proceedings.   Periodical: *The Ashlar.*

History
Queensland has possibly the most interesting masonic history of any of the Australian Jurisdictions. The first lodge in Queensland was the North Australian Lodge No 796 EC chartered at Brisbane in 1859. This lodge now heads the Queensland roll of lodges. A further three lodges quickly followed, all under England, and together they formed a Provincial (later District) Grand Lodge in 1862.
    Ireland's premier lodge in Queensland was St Patrick Lodge No 279, erected in 1863, and the first Scottish lodge—Lodge St Andrew No 435—was formed in the following year. More lodges under these two constitutions were subsequently warranted, and by 1866 they were formed into respective District Grand Lodges.
    Early efforts, were made in 1887 and 1897 to form a sovereign Grand Lodge, but without success. However, in 1904, a convention of delegates brought together twenty-five Irish lodges and fourteen Scottish lodges to establish the Grand Lodge of Queensland. Only about one-third of the Scottish lodges then working in Queensland joined this new Grand Body, while only one Irish lodge stood aloof. However, no English lodge could be persuaded to exchange its charter.
    By 1918, the need for masonic unity in Queensland had become obvious, and in 1920 the sixty-three English lodges then located in the State, and the remaining Scottish lodges, united to form the Queensland Grand Lodge. Later in the year 1920, delegates from lodges under both existing Grand Lodges met, and as a result the United Grand Lodge of Queensland was consecrated in 1921. However, a few English lodges stood out of the union, of which two still remain today. They are the Port Curtis Lodge No 2235, at Gladstone; and the Geraldton Lodge No 3544, at Innisfail. Both lodges are governed directly from London.
    At the formation of the United Grand Lodge, the State of Queensland was divided into three parts for the purposes of masonic administration. The large geographical size of Queensland made this necessary. All lodges between the cities of Townsville and Cairns come under the District Grand Lodge of North Queensland. Lodges from Cairns to far North come under the District Grand Lodge of Carpentaria, while lodges south of Townsville are under the direct control of the Grand Lodge. The District Grand Lodges are constructed in a similar manner to those of England.
    The Craft in Queensland has continued to expand since the Union. Its charitable and benevolent endeavours include the Sandgate Freemasons' Home in Brisbane, a

Masonic Aged Person's Home at Toowoomba, and a Masonic Educational Scholarship program.

Notes of Visiting in Queensland

1. MEETING TIMES, AND DRESS

The great majority of lodges in Queensland meet at 7.30 pm, although a few meet slightly earlier or later. Visitors are advised to arrive early, at least by 7 pm, in order that they may present their masonic credentials. On nights of Installation, lodges often open up to an hour earlier than usual. An Installation is followed by a banquet, or at least a full meal. Some lodges hold their installation meeting on a night different from their normal meeting nights, and intending visitors should make inquiries in this regard for obvious reasons.

Dress at Queensland lodge meetings is a black dinner suit, white shirt, black bow tie, black socks, and black shoes. In addition, it is usual for officers of a lodge to wear white gloves. During the summer months (December, January and February), Summer Dress is permitted. This consists of a white mess-jacket, white shirt, black trousers and shoes, and a black bow tie. Alternatively, permissible dress in summer is a dinner suit minus the coat, with a black cummerbund at the waist.

2. LODGE AFTERPROCEEDINGS

The lodge afterproceedings in Queensland consist of a festive board on the English model, comprising of supper and refreshments. Grace, spoken by the Chaplain of the lodge precedes the supper. The vast majority of lodges do not charge members or visitors for partaking of the supper, although a small number do require a contribution from members, but never from visitors. Generally, the costs of the festive board are covered by member's lodge dues.

Almost without exception, the festive board is conducted in a Hall on Masonic premises. Most lodges use a head table, at which are located the Master, Past Masters, and Visiting Masters. A structured toast list will follow the Supper, which is as follows:

1. The Queen and the Craft. This will be followed by the singing of *God Save the Queen*.
2. The Most Worshipful Grand Master. The Grand Master will respond, if present.
3. Distinguished Visitors. This will be proposed if a Grand Lodge Officer, or Officers, is specially present. The Grand Lodge Officer will respond.
4. The Candidate, or Lecturer. A response by the recipient of the Toast will follow.
5. Our Visitors. A visiting Master, forewarned, usually responds to this Toast.
6. Absent Brethren. The proposition of this Toast generally occurs at 10.30 pm.
7. The Tyler's Toast.

On nights of Installation, the toast list will be slightly longer, and will include a toast to the newly Installed Master. Similarly, the outgoing Master will receive a toast at the festive board following the last meeting at which he officiates. Most lodges serve alcohol at the festive board, although there are a small number of temperance lodges where no alcohol is served. As with New South Wales lodges, the festive board in Queensland is often referred to as 'The South'. Finally, it is not unusual for a charity collection to be taken up at the festive board. Doubtlessly, visitors will feel inclined to contribute.

3. OF VISITING IN GENERAL

In most Queensland Craft lodges, all members and visitors are seated in the lodge room for the opening of the lodge, as is usual English practice. However, the methods of examination and entry into the lodge vary somewhat throughout the jurisdiction. If arriving prior to the opening of the lodge, an unknown visitor will make himself known to the lodge Tyler, who will generally call upon two or three senior lodge members to attend. They will check the visitor's masonic credentials, and carry out an examination. He will then enter with his examiners, who will vouch for him inside the lodge.

If a visitor arrives after the lodge has been opened, he should approach the Tyler, who will pass his name to the Inner Guard, who in turn will see it is drawn to the attention of the Master. The Master will then ask if any member present can vouch for the visitor. If so, he will be permitted to enter when appropriate. If not, two or three senior members will retire to examine him. The visitor will then be admitted with his examiners, who will vouch for him. As can be readily appreciated this process is 'messy' and may cause a visitor embarrassment. Therefore, the 'golden rule' of visiting is most aptly applied here—be early.

Shortly before the opening of the lodge, the Master will ask every visitor to rise. Each visitor will then be vouched for either by a member present, or by his examiners.

In some lodges, it is not usual practice to have all visitors within the lodge room prior to the opening, but rather to admit them in groups. Where this procedure is used, the order of admission is as follows: Master Masons, Past Masters, Masters, Grand Lodge Officers. Masters and Grand Lodge officers are sometimes admitted individually, but are more usually admitted in groups on nights of Installation, or at ordinary meetings if their numbers are large. Past Masters, Masters, and Grand Lodge officers are all individually introduced to the Master, and are invited to sit in the East. Official visits by one lodge to another are not uncommon in Queensland, and where this occurs, the Master of the visiting lodge will be accompanied into the temple by his officers and lodge members present. Should the Grand Master, or his official representative, attend a lodge meeting (usually at Installations), he will enter last accompanied by a retinue of Grand Lodge officers.

4. NIGHTS OF INSTALLATION

All Queensland lodges install a new Master every year, at a set time. At the banquet which follows such a meeting, a charge may be levied in order to assist with its costs. However, it is unusual for a visitor to be asked to contribute. The festive board following an Installation is required to finish by 11.30 pm, as opposed to a finishing time of 11 pm at normal meetings.

Installations are always well supported by both members and visitors, and consequently detailed catering arrangements must be made by installing lodges. Therefore, it is highly desirable that a visitor planning to attend an installation informs the lodge concerned of his intended presence, so that accurate numbers can be determined. As visitors from outside Queensland are unlikely to have details of Installation meetings, they are well advised to seek assistance at the Grand Lodge office in Brisbane where they will readily obtain the necessary information.

It is usual for the Grand Master, or a District Grand Master where appropriate, or the nominee of either, to attend installation nights with a retinue of Grand officers and perform the ceremony. It is within the power of the Grand Master to attend and preside at any lodge meeting. This power also applies to a District Grand Master to lodges in his District.

5. INTERESTING ASPECTS OF MASONRY IN QUEENSLAND

Most Queensland lodges hold an annual ladies' night. Some ladies' nights are held separately from lodge meeting nights, while others are held in conjunction with a festive board. Many lodges hold their ladies' night in combination with a December meeting. Where a ladies' night is held in conjunction with a lodge meeting, no degree work is carried out, with only the opening, normal business, and the closing taking place. Such occasions are invariably accompanied by a dinner and entertainment. In most cases a lodge will pay for the costs of catering, but in others a levy will be charged on those attending.

Queensland abounds in interesting masonic structures. The Grand Lodge temple complex in Ann Street, Brisbane is classed as an example of architectural interest by the National Trust. It contains the Grand Lodge offices, several temples, and an excellent library. Several of the country temples are of attractive design, notably those at Mt Isa, Mt Morgan, and Warwick. Queensland's newest temple is at Stones Corner, in suburban Brisbane. Regarded as a showpiece, it follows modern concrete trends in its design.

Queensland possesses three research lodges, but only one of these is directly warranted. The warranted lodge is Barron Barnett Lodge No 146, meeting bi-monthly in Brisbane. Membership of this lodge is only open to Past Masters, but Master Masons are welcome to attend its meetings. It was originally an English lodge whose primary purpose was to demonstrate the *Emulation* ritual, but upon the foundation of the United Grand Lodge this function became redundant, whereupon it assumed its present activities.

The Toowoomba Lodge of Instruction, meeting monthly in that city, is Queensland's second research lodge. It operates under a charter from Fidelity Lodge No 357. The third research lodge in Queensland is the WHJ Mayers Lodge of Research, meeting at Cairns in Northern Queensland. It meets under a warrant from the Gregory Lodge No 50. It must be noted that Queensland has no lodges of instruction on the English model, as have some of the other Australian Grand Lodges. Instruction in ritual work is handled by the lodges themselves, or by teams under the Grand Superintendent of Workings. Dress for the Barron Barnett Lodge is a dinner suit, while a dark lounge suit is worn to meetings of the other two. Visitors are most welcome at any research lodge meeting.

Queensland possesses one lodge which meets during the day, rather than in the evening. This is the Thespian Lodge No 268, which meets on the 1st Thursday monthly (except January), at 12 noon, at the Masonic Temple, Stones Corner, Brisbane. Attendence at this lodge may well suit visitors on a tight travelling schedule. Dress is a lounge suit.

Queensland has developed a system for screening candidates and affiliates which varies somewhat from other Australian jurisdictions. A candidate for a Queensland lodge must be proposed and seconded by two masons. The proposer must be a member of the lodge to which admission is sought, although a recent constitutional amendment now allows the seconder to be a member of another lodge. It is from this point on that procedures in Queensland vary.

Upon being proposed and seconded, a candidate's application is handed to a committee of Inquiry of the lodge he seeks to join, which consists of the Master, Immediate Past Master, Secretary, and two Master Masons (the latter being elected annually by the lodge). This committee then satisfies itself as to the candidate and reports, not back to the lodge, but rather to Board of General Purposes of the Grand Lodge (or if under a District, to the District Grand Lodge Board of General Purposes). It is not until such a board's approval is granted that a candidate can further progress in his application. Upon approval being given, his name and details will then appear on the lodge summons, and he can be balloted for at the succeeding lodge meeting. Therefore, unlike other Australian jurisdictions, a candidate's name need only appear once on a lodge summons rather than three times, and his name does not have to be circulated to other lodges.

Members joining from one lodge to another within Queensland face the same procedure as a candidate, except that normally the matter is not referred to a Grand Lodge Board. However, in the case of a mason seeking to affiliate from outside Queensland, enquiries may be directed to his home Grand Lodge prior to approval being granted.

6. LODGE WORKINGS, REGALIA, AND RITUAL

Ritual practices in Queensland stem directly from its masonic history. As part of the settlement which created the United Grand Lodge, the oldest original lodges were permitted to retain their established workings and their distinctive regalia. Of course, lodges erected subsequent to 1921 were required to use the ritual of the Grand Lodge which it standardised at its inception. This ritual is similar to *Emulation*, but with some minor Scottish and Irish influences.

Nevertheless, many of the older lodges have come to adopt the *Queensland* ritual and standard regalia, which is composed of the usual pale blue English-style arons. Yet, there are still a few lodges that faithfully adhere to the English, Irish or Scottish practices used from their original consecration. A great difference exists between the regalia used by the old Scottish Lodges, which is mainly dark blue, and their rituals are certainly not uniform, especially in the third degree. The old English lodges largely prefer either the *Emulation* ritual, or the *Complete* Ritual; both of which are quite similar.

7. MASONIC GOVERNMENT

The United Grand Lodge of Queensland meets in Quarterly Communications on the 1st Wednesday in March, June, September and December; at the Masonic Memorial Temple, Ann Street, Brisbane; starting at 7.30 pm. The Installation of the Grand Master and the investiture of Grand Officers takes place at a special meeting of the Grand Lodge, held each year on the 1st Wednesday in July.

Visitors from outside Queensland may attend a meeting of the Grand Lodge, by invitation. Application can be made in person at the Grand Lodge office. Any written application, which must be made well in advance, must be directed through a visitor's own Grand Secretary. A banquet follows each meeting of the Grand Lodge for those attending, and visitors to the Grand Lodge are welcome to attend. While a charge is levied on Grand Lodge members for their meal, invited visitors are not required to contribute.

All Masters, Wardens, and Past Masters of any Queensland Constitution lodge are, by virtue of their office, members of the Grand Lodge. On nights of Grand Lodge meetings, each member attending fills out a card stating his name, lodge, and his masonic rank. No mason below the rank of a Master Mason can attend, and no member may be admitted once the Grand Master has entered.

The Constitutions of the Grand Lodge basically follow English masonic statutes, and are similar to other Australian jurisdictions, except that offices in the Grand Lodge are largely elective.

The Grand Master and all Grand Lodge officers, with the exceptions of the Pro Grand Master (if required), the Deputy Grand Master, the Assistant Grand Master, the Grand Secretary and the Assistant Grand Secretary; are elected at the December Communication of the Grand Lodge, having previously been nominated by the Board of General Purposes. The board nominates only one mason for each office to be filled. However, other members may be nominated for any elective office, and this occasionally occurs. Indeed, instances have occurred where a nominee of the board has failed to be elected, although this is not common. The Deputy Grand Master and the Assistant Grand Master are appointed by the Grand Master; while the Grand Secretary and the Assistant Grand Secretary are appointed by the Grand Master on the advise of the Board of General Purposes. The overall administration of the Grand Lodge is conducted by the Board of General Purposes, which consists of the Grand Master, senior Grand Lodge officers, and a number of elected members, half of whom must be members of metropolitan Brisbane lodges, and half members of country lodges. The Board of Benevolence is the other main Grand Lodge body, and its responsibilities devolve to governing the charitable institutions and functions of the Grand Lodge. Its membership is also largely elective, with its composition largely paralleling that of the Board of General Purposes.

List of Lodges

It is not possible to list all the Queensland lodges in these pages, although two special exceptions will be made. However, listed below are the main meeting places in the major population centres of the State. If at all possible, visitors should make themselves known at the Masonic Temple in Ann Street, Brisbane, where they will receive full assistance and details of any lodge meeting. The main meeting places are as follows:

Masonic Memorial Temple, Ann Street, *Brisbane.*
Masonic Temple, Cleveland Street, *Stones Corner, Brisbane.*
Masonic Temple, Vulture Street, *South Brisbane.*
Masonic Hall, Minnie Street, *Cairns.*
Masonic Hall, Kent Street, *Rockhampton.*
Masonic Temple, Neil Street, *Toowoomba.*
Robert Burns Masonic Temple, Anzac Avenue, Newtown, *Toowoomba.*

Queensland still possesses two English lodges, the survivors from those lodges which stood out at the Masonic Union in 1921. Their details are as follows:

Port Curtis Lodge No 2235 EC Meets at the Masonic Temple, Toolooa Street, *Gladstone*; each Wednesday on or before the full moon, Inst; May.

Geraldton Lodge No 3544 EC Meets at the Masonic Hall, The Esplanade, *Innisfail*; 4th Thursday in February, April, June, August, and September. Inst: June.

Both these lodges are governed directly from London, and both use the English *Emulation* ritual.

SOUTH AUSTRALIA

The Grand Lodge of Ancient, Free and Accepted Masons of South Australia
Founded: 1884
Address: Freemasons' Hall, North Terrace, Adelaide. 5000. *Telephone:* (08) 2231633.
Lodges: 208. Permits Dual and Plural Membership.
Membership: 16,284.
Descent: England, Ireland, Scotland. *Government:* Appointive Grand Lodge.
Courtesy Degrees: Correspondence must be through Grand Lodges.
Minimum Time Lapse between Degrees: One month. *Ritual:* English-type (with adaptations).
Main Publications: Constitutions. Annual Grand Lodge Proceedings. Periodical Magazine: *The South Australian Freemason.* The Masonic Year Book and Diary, published as a supplement to the magazine (February/March Edition).

History

Freemasonry in South Australia had a unique beginning, in that its first lodge was consecrated in London in 1834—two years before the Colony of South Australia was actually founded. This was the South Australian Lodge of Friendship No 613 EC; which now heads the South Australian roll of lodges as the Lodge of Friendship No 1. It met for the first time in Adelaide in 1838, having met previously several times in London. The next three lodges founded in the Colony were: Lodge Adelaide St John No 341 SC (now No 2, SAC); the Lodge of Harmony No 743 EC (now No 3, SAC); and the Duke of Leinster Lodge No 363 IC.

In 1848, an English Provincial (later District) Grand Lodge was formed, and this was followed in 1858 by an Irish Provincial Grand Lodge. A Provincial (later District) Grand Lodge for the Scottish lodges was erected in 1864. Construction of the first Freemasons' Hall in South Australia, built in Flinders Street, Adelaide; was begun in 1869. It remained the home of the South Australian Craft until 1925.

By 1883, the membership of the Craft in South Australia had grown enormously, and it became evident that unity was essential. At this time there were nineteen English, six Scottish, and six Irish lodges in the Colony. Union was harmoniously effected in April, 1884; with only one Irish lodge wishing to maintain its current allegience. This was the Duke of Leinster Lodge No 363 IC, which still works happily in Adelaide under the Irish Constitution to this day. The Grand Lodge of South Australia became the premier Grand Lodge in Australasia.

The Craft in South Australia has continued to flourish through the years. The many benevolent and charitable pursuits of South Australian masonry include the Masonic Memorial Village for the aged at Somerton Park, the Colonel Light Garden Homes, Masonic Educational Scholarships, and several Relief Funds.

Notes for Visiting in South Australia

1. MEETING TIMES, AND DRESS

South Australian lodges generally meet at 7.30 pm, although a very small number meet at 7.15 pm. Once again, visitors are advised to be early in order to present their masonic credentials and be examined as necessary. A letter of introduction produced by a visitor is sometimes endorsed by the signature of the Master,

Secretary or Examining Past Master of a visited lodge; together with the lodge name, number, and date of the visit. South Australia is one of few jurisdictions which follows this extra procedure, but it does afford the visitor an interesting record of his lodge visits.

On Nights of Installation, lodges open at an earlier time. In country lodges (ie: lodges located outside Adelaide), tyling is usually at 5 pm, and the meeting is often followed by a ball. In city lodges, the installation time is often 6.30 pm, although it may be earlier in the cases of the small number of Adelaide lodges which also hold a formal ball afterwards.

The dinner suit is the universal dress requirement for South Australian lodges, although often lodge officers will wear formal evening dress (tails). A visitor from outside South Australia will certainly not be prevented from attending if he is wearing a dark lounge suit. However, every visitor should bring his own masonic regalia, if possible.

The dress regulations of the Grand Lodge do allow for summer dress to be worn at lodge meetings between mid-October and mid-April. This consists of two alternatives, the latter of which is the most popular. Firstly, a mason may attend in a white mess-jacket, black trousers, socks and shoes, a white shirt and a black bow tie. The second alternative is a long sleeved white dress shirt, black bow tie, black trousers, shoes and socks, and a black cummerbund at the waist. Sports jackets and other forms of casual coats are not permitted. White gloves are considered essential parts of masonic dress by the Grand Lodge, but in practice they are often only worn by lodge officers. White gloves are not worn with summer dress.

2. LODGE AFTERPROCEEDINGS

A festive board follows every South Australian lodge meeting, and consists of a supper and refreshments. No charge is levied for attending as the costs involved are covered by members lodge dues, although a voluntary contribution is sometimes sought in some lodges. Visitors are most certainly not expected to contribute.

The festive board is invariably held in a hall within masonic premises. A head table is the norm, occupied by the Master, Past Masters, and Visiting Masters. The Director of Ceremonies of the lodge will normally regulate proceedings. A formal Toast list is always used, an example of which is as follows:

1. The Loyal Toast—'The Queen'. This is followed by the singing of the Australian National Anthem—*God Save the Queen*.

2. The Most Worshipful Grand Master, and Grand Lodge Officers. Interestingly, unlike most other Australian Jurisdictions, this Toast is proposed at every meeting, not just at an installation, or when the Grand Master or his representative is present. The toast will be responded to by a Grand Lodge officer, often the most senior present. After the proposition of this toast, the *Song of Australia* is sung by all present. This song, oddly enough, is not very well known outside South Australia, even in Masonic circles. Among Australian Grand Lodges, South Australia is the only one which uses it.

3. The Candidate. A toast is proposed to a candidate on the occasion of each of his degrees in South Australia, rather than just at the Festive Board following his 1st degree as is the practice in some Australian Jurisdictions. Often the proposer and seconder of the Candidate will take turns in the proposition of the toast, and the candidate will respond on each occasion.

4. The Visitors. This toast is generally proposed by the Junior Warden, and responded to by a visiting Master.
5. The Tyler's Toast.
The large majority of South Australian lodges serve alcohol at the festive board, although about ten percent of lodges are temperance lodges.

3. NIGHTS OF INSTALLATION

All South Australian lodges install a new Master annually, on a fixed night. No lodge installs in December and only one (Lodge Kilwinning No 220) in January. Similarly, only one lodge installs in February. No charge is made for attending an Installation festive board, which usually consists of an expansive meal. In the place of a festive board following an installation, many country lodges and a few city lodges hold a formal ball, which in itself includes a meal. A charge of $4–$6 can be expected for these occasions. Again, however, visitors are rarely asked to contribute.

The majority of South Australian lodges issue invitations to visitors for their Installation meeting. As the seating capacity of many temples in the State is often less than the number of masons wishing to attend an installation, the invitation system has developed. In addition, this practice greatly assists in catering arrangements. Visitors from outside South Australia are advised to express their wishes of attending an installation at the Grand Lodge office in Adelaide. Invariably, a complimentary invitation will be arranged for a suitable installation. If a formal ball is to be held in association with the selected installation, the visitor will also receive an invitation to attend that as well. Of course, ladies are in attendance at a ball, and a visitor's wife can naturally attend with her husband.

4. OF VISITING IN GENERAL

In South Australia, only lodge members are normally allowed to be present in the temple at the opening of their lodge. Visitors are not admitted until after the regular routine business of the lodge has been completed. At the opening of the lodge, it is usual for the Master and his principal officers to form a procession into the lodge room. A reverse procedure applies at the closing. It is possible for interested visitors to witness the actual opening of a lodge, having gained the permission of the Master. Such permission, of course, must be sought prior to the start of the evening, and it will normally be granted as a courtesy. After the private business of a lodge has been disposed of, visitors will then be admitted in groups, according to juniority. The South Australia Constitution is considered senior. The order of admission is:
1. Visitors from sister constitutions up to the Rank of Installed Master (if any be present).
2. Unattached Visitors (South Australian Masons not currently financial lodge members).
3. South Australian visitors up to the rank of Installed Master, and who are not accompanying the Master of their lodge. It must be noted that in many lodges, it is common for all Master Masons to be admitted together, if they are not accompanying their Master.
4. Masters of lodge of sister constitutions (if any be present).
5. Masters of South Australian lodges, visiting alone.
6. Masters of South Australian lodges accompanied by their Principal Officers, Past Masters, and other members.
7. A Grand Lodge officer on an official visit. A Grand Lodge officer not on an

official visit will enter as an unaccompanied visitor unless the Master of his own lodge is present, whereupon he would enter with him. The usual procedure is for Masters to enter singly. However, when it is considered desirable to expedite the reception of visitors, visiting Masters are received together. This often occurs. Indeed, the South Australian system is obviously quite flexible. It is possible to have only two admittances at a normal meeting—that of sitting Installed Masters, preceded by all other visitors. Regardless of the mode of admission, Masters enter in order of Juniority. Thus, the Master of the most senior lodge (the oldest lodge) enters last. He is also seated in the East closest to the Master. All Grand Lodge officers (who are officially visiting) and all visiting Masters are received with all present standing, and they are introduced individually to the Master in the East. If a Master, or other visitors, from one or more sister constitutions are present, they are received in order of juniority of constitution, as well as juniority of lodge and rank.

At the closure of the lodge, the Master asks three times, 'If any Brother has aught to propose for the good of freemasonry ...' In South Australia, the Master does so in a seated position, whereas in many other Australian jurisdictions, the Master rises. At the 'first time of asking', after Grand Lodge correspondence has been read, greetings can be conveyed on behalf of the Grand Master of South Australia by a Grand Lodge officer visiting officially. At the 'second time of asking', this can be done by representatives of other Grand Lodges in attendence. At the 'third asking', the Senior Warden offers greetings on behalf of the lodge, followed by visiting Masters on behalf of their lodges—firstly, the Masters of South Australian lodges, according to juniority; and secondly, those from other jurisdictions, similarly. The lodge is then closed. Visitors should be aware that it is extremely rare for them to be admitted in any other degree than the first, except as appropriate during an Installation ceremony, and certainly not after a ceremony has commenced. Punctuality is, therefore, strongly recommended.

5. ASPECTS OF MASONRY IN SOUTH AUSTRALIA

Many South Australian lodges hold an annual ladies' night, particularly in Adelaide. In country areas, in some cases, the Annual Installation Ball replaces the ladies' night. On normal ladies' nights, a lodge meeting is held, but it will be brief with no degree work being performed. Thereafter members and visitors retire to the festive board and join their ladies, who will have invariably been entertained by a speaker or entertainer while their partners were in the temple. The normal masonic toast list is followed, unusually for an Australian jurisdiction in this context, but without any masonic fires. Often the deep significance of the toasts, particularly the Tyler's toast, is explained to the ladies.

Unique to Australian masonry, and possibly to the regular masonic world, is the South Australian Grand Lodge's Masonic Education Course. The Course is done by correspondence, and runs for four years (one stage per year). Each stage consists of eight sections, posted monthly to students. It covers the usages, tenets, history, symbolism, government, and customs of masonry. While it is based on South Australian usages, it is certainly applicable and of interest elsewhere. Each topic covered by a student involves submitting a written assignment to a tutor for correction and comment. The logistical arrangements of the Grand Lodge allow for only a limited number of Master Masons (usually 100 maximum) to start the Course in any one year. Understandably, there is a waiting list. It is possible for members of sister jurisdictions to South Australia to seek admission to the Course. However, preference is given, naturally, to South Australian masons. Masons from outside South Australia should seek information about the course through their own Grand Secretary, and under no circumstances should they write directly to South Australia.

A visitor to South Australia will no doubt wish to visit Freemasons' Hall, in Adelaide. This magnificent old building is located in the heart of the city, and is currently in the process of restoration (to be completed for the Grand Lodge Centenary in 1984). It contains four floors, the Grand Lodge offices, three temples, a large hall, a library, and ancillary rooms.

South Australia, like many other Australian jurisdictions, possesses a licenced Masonic Club, which is currently located in association with The Commercial Travellers' Assocation of South Australia. It is probable that in the future it will be located in the basement of Freemasons' Hall. However, unlike its counterparts in Victoria and New South Wales, the South Australian Masonic Club has no residential facilities.

All candidates for freemasonry in South Australia must be at least twenty-one years of age (unless a Lewis), and be proposed and seconded by two members of the lodge they seek to join. A candidate's name must appear on a lodge summons, circulated to every lodge member, at least one month prior to, as well as on the summons for, the meeting at which a ballot for the candidate is to be held. A copy of the first summons containing the proposition must also be circulated to every other lodge in the area of the proposing lodge.

Each lodge annually elects three Past Masters, who together with the Master of the lodge for the time being, comprise a committee of inquiry. It is this committee's duty to inquire into the character of any candidate proposed to the lodge, and report back to it prior to any ballot.

Masons seeking to join from one South Australian lodge to another are required to undergo the procedures applicable to a candidate, except that their names need appear on only one summons prior to ballot, and the committee of inquiry need not necessarily undertake an examination unless the lodge considers this necessary. In the case of an affiliation by a mason from outside South Australia, the approval of the Grand Secretary must be obtained prior to ballot.

6. LODGE WORKINGS, REGALIA, AND RITUAL
With only two exceptions, all lodges in South Australia must work the ritual as promulgated and authorised by the Grand Lodge. This ritual is very similar to the English *Emulation*, but it does possess certain influences from Irish and Scottish practices. As with the other Australian Jurisdictions, South Australian lodges work the Chair Degree of Installed Master as part of an installation.

The two lodges which are permitted to work different rituals are Lodge Kilwinning No 220; and Lodge Concordia No 226. The former works a Scottish Ritual, while the latter works the *Schroeder* Ritual. Of course, mention has already been made of the Duke of Leinster Lodge No 363, which naturally works the Irish Ritual. The meeting details of these three lodges are set out below.

The regalia used in lodges working the *South Australian* ritual is prescribed by the Grand Lodge, and closely follows standard English-types. Visitors to Lodge

Kilwinning will notice some differences, and many members attend this lodge clothed in Scottish kilts and tartans.

7. MASONIC GOVERNMENT

The Grand Lodge of South Australia holds half yearly Communications in Adelaide on the third Wednesdays of April and October. The April meeting is the Annual Communication at which the Grand Master and Grand officers are installed and invested. Visitors from outside South Australia can attend Grand Lodge meetings, but an invitation is required. Interested visitors must make personal application at Freemasons' Hall. Any written application must be made well in advance through the intending visitor's own Grand Lodge office. An informal festive board generally follows a Grand Lodge Communication. Members are usually required to purchase a ticket at a small fee to contribute towards the repast. However, invited visitors are not asked to contribute.

The Constitutions of the Grand Lodge resemble those of England. The Grand Lodge is composed of the Grand Master, Grand Lodge officers, past Grand officers, Grand Stewards of the year; and the Masters, Past Masters and Wardens of all lodges on the roll of the Grand Lodge. All offices of the Grand Lodge are appointive, except those of Grand Master, Grand Sword Bearer, Pursuivant and Standard Bearer, which are annually elective. All Grand Lodge members must be Masters or Past Masters of a South Australian Lodge, except the Grand Director of Music and Grand Organist who may be a Master Mason. The Grand Tyler must be a Master Mason. All offices and titles follow the British model closely, except that no Grand Herald is appointed, and the Grand Librarian is a Grand Lodge officer, as such.

South Australia possesses a most interesting system for appointing Grand Stewards. Every South Australian Constitution lodge elects one of its Past Masters, every alternate year to be a Grand Steward—the even numbered lodges one year, the odd numbered lodges the following year. The Grand Stewards only hold Grand Lodge office for their year, and cease to be Grand officers at its expiry unless they are appointed to some other Grand office. On current calculations, the Grand Lodge of South Australia possesses one hundred and four Grand Stewards.

The two main administrative bodies of the Grand Lodge are the Board of General Purposes and the Board of Benevolence. Both consist of senior Grand Lodge officers and a certain number of elected members. Their functions closely parallel those of other Australian jurisdictions, and those of England.

List of Lodges

As with the other Australian jurisdictions, the large number of South Australian lodges prevents an extensive list being provided here. However, five lodges are detailed below because of their special interest. The first three in the list have already been discussed:

The Duke of Leinster Lodge No 363 *Irish Constitution*	Meets at Edwardstown Masonic Hall, Avenue Road, Clarence Gardens, Adelaide; 1st Tuesday monthly at 7.30 pm. Inst: June.
Lodge Kilwinning No 220 SAC	Meets at the Northern Masonic Hall, 565 Regency Road, Broadview, Adelaide; 4th Friday monthly at 7.15 pm. Inst: January.

Lodge Concordia No 226 SAC   Meets at the Masonic Temple, South Street,
                                            Henley Beach, Adelaide; 2nd Friday monthly at
                                            7.30 pm. Inst: May.

The fourth lodge to capture special attention is the Lodge of Research No 216. It meets at Payneham Masonic Hall, 393 Payneham Road, Marden, Adelaide; 3rd Friday, monthly at 7.30 pm. Installation: October. While the Lodge of Research does not publish transactions as such, it does have a correspondence circle whose members receive copies of research papers presented to the lodge. A second lodge of research, located at Darwin, also works under the South Australian Constitution. It has already been detailed under the heading of the Northern Territory. An interesting feature of both these research lodges is that, unlike their counterparts in other jurisdictions, they will perform degree ceremonial work (given the proposition of candidates), rather than merely present lectures at every meeting.

The fifth and final lodge is South Australia's first 'daylight lodge'. This is Lodge Meridian, No 227. It meets at the St Peters Masonic Hall, Payneham Road, St Peters, Adelaide; and was begun only in February, 1983. It convenes on the 3rd Thursday monthly at 10.30 am.

It must be noted that many South Australian lodges, although probably less than half, recess in December and January. Visitors planning to attend lodge meetings in these months should be sure to check details at the Grand Lodge office. A full list of South Australian lodges, with all meeting details, is published annually in the *Masonic Year Book and Diary*. This is contained as a supplement in the Grand Lodge magazine, *The South Australian Freemason*, usually in the February/March edition. The magazine is published six times per year, and is available on subscription. The 1983 rate was $A3.50, but this figure tends to rise with inflation.

TASMANIA

The Grand Lodge of Antient, Free and Accepted Masons of Tasmania
Founded: 1890
Address: Masonic Temple, 3 Sandy Bay Road, Hobart.   7000 (Grand Secretary)
   Telephone: 235814.
   Masonic Temple, 39 Brisbane Street, Launceston.   7250 (Assistant
   Grand Secretary)   *Telephone:* 315105.
Lodges: 80.   Permits Dual and Plural Membership.
Membership: 6819.
Descent: England, Ireland, Scotland.   *Government:* Elective Grand Lodge.
Courtesy Degrees: No specific rule.   Correspondence must be through Grand Lodges.
Minimum Time Lapse between Degrees: Four weeks.   *Ritual: Emulation* (a few adaptations).
Main Publications: Constitutions.   Grand Lodge Proceedings.   Periodical: *The Tasmanian Mason*.

History
Freemasonry was introduced into Tasmania by military lodges. A portion of the 48th British Regiment was stationed in Tasmania between 1817 and 1824, and had an Irish Military lodge attached to it. It was during the tenure of the 40th Regiment in

the Colony (1825-1830), with its attached military lodge, that the first stationary lodge in Tasmania was established. This was the Tasmanian Lodge No 313 IC, erected in 1828; and this was followed by the Union Lodge No 326 IC, in 1831. These two early lodges suffered a fluid infant nurture, being somewhat subject to the mercy of the changeover of stationed regiments in terms of membership.

However, out of these two early lodges came two permanent ones. These are the Tasmanian Operative Lodge No 345 IC (now No 1 on the Tasmanian roll); and the Tasmanian Union Lodge No 536 EC (now No 3 on the Tasmanian roll). The first Scottish lodge was formed in 1876, being St Andrew Lodge, No 591 SC (now No 6 TC). Further lodges under the three British Constitutions were formed, to the point where it became possible to establish Provincial Grand Lodges in the Colony. That of England was formed in 1856, later becoming extinct, and reforming in 1875. An Irish Provincial Grand Lodge was erected in 1884, and a Scottish District was established in 1885.

In 1890, there were nine Irish, eight English, and five Scottish lodges working in Tasmania. On 26 June of that year, representatives of all these lodges met in the Hobart Town Hall, and passed a resolution which formed the basis of the Grand Lodge of Tasmania. The Union was effected with harmony, and the Grand Lodge has continued to prosper.

The Craft in Tasmania is well known for its benevolence and charity. The Fred French Masonic Nursing Home was commenced in Launceston in 1961, and now has forty-eight beds. The Freemasons' Home of Southern Tasmania, located at Hobart, houses 120 aged residents. The other major masonic establishment is the Masonic Peace Memorial Haven (for the aged) of Northern Tasmania. These homes were built in 1947.

Notes for Visiting in Tasmania

1. MEETING TIMES, AND DRESS

Almost without exception, lodges in Tasmania meet at 7.30 pm, except on nights of Installation when they commence at 6.30 pm. A visitor is advised to arrive early, preferrably by 7 pm, as an unknown mason will be required to present his masonic credentials, and undergo an examination.

The dress for attendence at a Tasmanian lodge is a black dinner suit, white shirt, black bow tie, and black shoes and socks. Officers wear white gloves. In addition, it is not unusual for lodge officers to wear formal evening dress (tails), especially to installation meetings. However, a visitor from outside Tasmania is welcome to wear a dark lounge suit, if his travels make the carrying of a dinner suit difficult. A visitor is also welcome to wear his own regalia.

2. LODGE AFTER PROCEEDINGS

A festive board is always held after a lodge meeting in Tasmania, invariably in a hall forming part of masonic premises, and it largely follows the patterns of other Australian jurisdictions. It is conducted by the lodge Director of Ceremonies. The Master, Past Masters, and visiting Masters generally occupy a head table. A light supper is served, accompanied by refreshments. Alcoholic drinks are available at all but five Tasmanian lodge festive boards. No charge is made on visitors attending. However, a charge is often levied on members attending an Installation banquet; but it is unusual, nevertheless, for a visitor to be asked in contribute. The toast list is as follows: *The Loyal Toast (The Queen and the Craft) *The Candidate (if any) *The Visitors *The Tyler's Toast.

There are several variations to this pattern. On a Master's last night, a toast is directed to him. On Installation nights, the toast list is more extensive, and includes a toast to the new Master, and a toast to the Grand Master and Grand Lodge. As with several other Australian jurisdictions, the festive board in Tasmania is often referred to as 'The South'.

3. OF VISITING IN GENERAL

Only members of a lodge will normally be admitted to its opening, with visitors not entering until after the private business of the lodge has been completed. Nevertheless, a visitor may seek the permission of the Master to be present at the opening, if he is interested to witness it. Such permission will generally be granted.

After the lodge has conducted its business, visitors will be admitted in groups as follows: members (who are late) and visiting Master Masons, Past Masters, Visiting Masters, a lodge on an official visit (Master, Wardens, and members), and finally Grand Lodge officers on an official visit.

4. NIGHTS OF INSTALLATION

The annual Installation meeting of a Tasmanian lodge, generally commencing at 6.30 pm, is followed by a 'banquet' consisting of a full meal. Visitors are welcome to attend these meetings, but to assist with catering arrangements, prior notice is always appreciated. A visit to an Installation can be readily arranged at either of the Grand Lodge offices in Hobart or Launceston.

5. ASPECTS OF MASONRY IN TASMANIA

Visitors will find many of the masonic temples in Tasmania of historical interest, including those of Hobart and Launceston. The facade of the original Masonic Hall in Hobart, at 24 Murray Street, still stands and is classified by the National Trust for preservation.

Many Tasmanian lodges hold a ladies' night annually, at which the wives or partners of members and visitors are invited to attend. These functions are usually held on masonic premises, and include a short meeting. The ladies are suitably entertained in the lodge's festive board Hall until joined by their husbands. A full dinner is usually served, but the normal toast list is not used. Visitors wishing to attend such a meeting are welcome to make enquiries when visiting the Grand Lodge office, or the Launceston Temple. A few lodges have ladies present at the banquet following an Installation Meeting. In addition, balls and social dinner dances organised by lodges are quite common in Tasmania.

The procedures for examining proposed candidates in Tasmania are quite rigorous. In addition to common practices found in other Australian jurisdictions, a candidate for a Tasmanian lodge must have his name and particulars circulated to every other lodge in the jurisdiction prior to Ballot. The procedures for affiliating members are similar, except that the Grand Secretary must be informed prior to ballot. It is usual for the Grand Secretary to make enquiries with the proposed affiliate's home jurisdiction prior to his petition being accepted.

Tasmania possesses a few lodges of instruction based on the English model, whose purposes are to instruct lodge officers in ritual. These lodges are licensed by, or attached to, warranted Craft lodges. In addition, all Tasmanian lodges hold rehearsals in degree work.

Tasmania also has two research lodges under charter. The Hobart Lodge of Research No 62 meets on the 3rd Friday in even months, at the Masonic Temple, 3 Sandy Bay Road, Hobart. Installation: February. The Launceston Lodge of Research No 69 meets at the Masonic Temple, Brisbane Street, Launceston; on the 3rd Friday in February, May, July, August, and November. Installation: July.

In recent years, Tasmania has followed Victoria in erecting lodges that meet during the day. Two such lodges have so far been established. Launceston Daytime Lodge No 51 was the first to assume this function. It meets at the Brisbane Street Temple, Launceston, at 2.30 pm, 3rd Thursday monthly (except January). Hobart Meridan Lodge, erected in 1981, meets at the Masonic Temple, Sandy Bay Road, at 1 pm, 3rd Tuesday monthly (except January, June and July). It Installs on the Saturday following the 3rd Tuesday in August. Dress for both these lodges is a dark lounge suit.

6. LODGE WORKING, REGALIA, AND RITUAL

The ritual stipulated by the Grand Lodge is the English *Emulation* ritual. Only a few alterations to it have been adopted. A most interesting aspect of Tasmanian practice is to require candidates in each of the three degrees to recite their obligation before being elevated, in addition to answering the normal test questions. A Master Mason, subsequent to his raising, must also satisfactorily answer the test questions to that degree, and recite his third degree obligation. Tasmanian practice in this area largely stands it apart from the other Australian jurisdictions. Tasmanian regalia, however, closely resembles standard English types.

7. MASONIC GOVERNMENT

The Grand Lodge meets twice per year, in February (Annual Communication and Grand Installation), and in August. It is usual for the Annual Meeting to be held in Hobart and Launceston alternately. The other communication is held in various places in the State. Often a special (third) Grand Lodge meeting is held in the same year. Regular Grand Lodge meetings are generally held on a Saturday, commencing at 1 pm and concluding about 4 pm. As these meetings convene during the day, the dress required is a dark lounge suit, rather than a dinner suit. Only an informal afternoon tea is usually served in association with such a meeting, although a banquet is usual in the evening after an Annual Communication. Attendance at Grand Lodge Meetings by visitors is by invitation. Interested visitors should make personal inquiry when they visit the Grand Lodge office in Hobart, or the Assistant Grand Secretary's office in Launceston.

The structure of the Grand Lodge largely follows English norms. It is composed of all Masters, Wardens, and Past Masters of its constituent lodges. Its principal administrative bodies are a Board of General Purposes, and a Board of Benevolence. However, unlike England, Grand Lodge offices are largely elective. For the purposes of the election of Grand Lodge officers, Tasmania is divided into three geographical districts. Nominations for election to Grand Lodge offices must come from these districts on a rotation basis. This method of nomination and election does not apply to the most senior Grand Lodge positions, or to Grand Directors of Music, Grand Tylers, and Grand Stewards. The Grand Master is elected annually, and is eligible for re-election. All other Grand Lodge officers are elected annually, except the

Grand Secretary, Assistant Grand Secretary, Grand Chaplains, Grand Inspectors of Lodges, Grand Directors of Music, and Grand Tylers. These excepted offices are filled by Grand Master on the recommendation of the Board of General Purposes. The Deputy Grand Master is appointed by the Grand Master. Eighteen Grand Stewards are appointed annually by eighteen lodges on a rotation basis.

List of Lodges

There being eighty lodges on the Tasmanian roll of lodges, it is not practical to list them here. The majority of Tasmanian lodges meet in the two major population centres of the State—the capital city of Hobart, in the south; and the northern city of Launceston. However, most other towns in Tasmania possess at least one lodge. A full list of Tasmanian lodges, with meeting details, is found in the *Masonic Pocket Calendar and Directory*, published at regular intervals and obtainable from the Grand Lodge offices. Tasmania, as of very recent years, has published a newsletter on a bi-annual basis, called the *Tasmania Mason*, which is distributed to all subscribing masons in the jurisdiction.

VICTORIA

The United Grand Lodge of Antient, Free and Accepted Masons of Victoria
Founded: 1889
Address: The Masonic Centre of Victoria, 300 Albert Street, East Melbourne. 3002.   *Telephone:* (03) 419 2288.
Lodges: 774.   Permits Dual and Plural Membership.
Membership: 64,250.
Descent: England, Ireland, Scotland.   *Government:* Appointive Grand Lodge.
Courtesy Degrees: Correspondence must be through Grand Lodges.
Minimum Time Lapse between Degrees: One month.   *Ritual:* English-type (with adaptations).
Main Publications: Constitutions.   *Masonic Guide* (List of Lodges).   Grand Lodge Proceedings.

History

The first lodge to be warranted in Victoria was the Lodge of Australia Felix No 697 EC, in 1834. This lodge now heads the Victorian roll of lodges. The first Scottish lodge was Lodge Australian Kilwinning No 337, erected in 1843. The premier Irish lodge in the colony, the Australian Felix Lodge of Hiram No 349, was also established in 1843.

The gold rush of the 1850s brought with it a large number of new immigrants to the colony, some of whom were masons. Even so, the relations between the various lodges that were formed in these early days was not always harmonious, mainly as a result of inexperience in masonic administration. After two early unsuccessful attempts by a not insignificant number of masons unhappy with the prevailing lack of unity, a Grand Lodge of Victoria was established as a separate body in 1883. This new Grand Lodge had some success, commencing with six lodges and finishing with nineteen. The main effect of the formation of this fourth Constitution in the colony was that it hastened the formation of the United Grand Lodge of Victoria.

Subsequent to the erection of the Grand Lodge of Victoria, five years of disharmony followed between the four masonic allegiences in the colony. However, stability was found in the unique triple appointment of a prominent colonist, Sir William Clarke. He was made District Grand Master over the English lodges in Victoria, and was later appointed to the corresponding office over both the Irish and Scottish lodges. The United Grand Lodge of Victoria was consecrated in 1889, with Sir William Clarke as first Grand Master. The union was not created without problems, notably in administration, but these were eventually solved. However, after a slow start, united freemasonry in Victoria flourished. The United Grand Lodge now nearly over eight hundred lodges. One English Craft lodge, Combermere Lodge No 752 (dating from 1858) still works happily in Melbourne, the last reminder of the turbulent days of the four constitutions.

Notes for Visiting in Victoria

1. MEETING TIMES, AND DRESS

Lodges in Victoria generally meet at 7.30 pm, although a small minority meet at 7.15 pm. It is advisable to arrive early, in order that the visitor might provide sufficient proof of his masonic identity. On nights of Installation, the vast majority of lodges commence at 6.30 pm, in view of the longer ceremony.

Standard dress for all Victorian lodges is a black dinner suit. In some lodges, full evening dress (tails) is worn by lodge officers. However, the costs associated with purchasing evening dress, coupled with laundering costs, have led to a declining use of this form of attire. Nevertheless, the wearing of full evening dress remains mandatory for Grand Lodge officers when acting in an official capacity, either in attending a Grand Lodge meeting or assisting at a lodge Installation. A visitor who is not carrying a dinner suit can attend a lodge meeting in a dark lounge suit.

2. LODGE AFTERPROCEEDINGS

A festive board is always held after a lodge meeting in Victoria, and it is referred to in most lodges as 'The South'. This term probably arises from the position of the Junior Warden in the temple, and his responsibilities. The festive board is invariably held in a hall connected to each temple, and is under the sole control of the Master, although much of the proceedings are delegated to the Director of Ceremonies. The convention in Victoria is for the Master, Past Masters, and visiting Masters to occupy a head table, although in recent years buffet-style suppers have become more popular with the active encouragement of the Grand Lodge. A light supper is served, accompanied by refreshments. A common example of a toast list used in Victorian lodges is as follows:

1. The Loyal Masonic Toast (The Queen and the Craft). This is usually followed by the singing of the National Anthem—*God Save The Queen*.
2. The Candidate (1st Degree only). This is often proposed by the Initiate's proposer, or a Past Master of the Lodge. The Candidate will respond.
3. The Visitors. Usually, a visiting Master will respond to this Toast.
4. The Tyler's Toast.

The toast list on nights of Installation tends to be longer, with a toast to the Grand Master and Grand Lodge officers included after the Loyal Toast, and a toast proposed to the newly Installed Master. No charge is made for attending the festive board at any normal lodge meeting in Victoria. The costs associated with this are covered by members' lodge dues. There is a small minority of Victoria lodges that do not permit the availability of alcohol at the festive board. Many of these lodges tend to work in country areas. Almost without exception, a raffle for charity is conducted at Victorian festive boards, except on nights of Installation.

3. NIGHTS OF INSTALLATION

Whilst all visitors can readily attend normal lodge meetings, invitations are often required for nights of Installation. This especially applies to lodges located in metropolitan Melbourne, and in major provincial centres such as Geelong, Ballarat and Bendigo. However, in some of the rural lodges, invitations are not required. Invitations are usually issued by the lodge Secretary in the name of the Master, Master-Elect, or some other member. The reasons for this invitation system at Installations are twofold. Firstly, seating accommodation is often less than the numbers wishing to attend. Secondly, the high costs of providing catering at such meetings involve the obtaining of an accurate idea of numbers attending. In the past, it has been usual for the member inviting a visitor to pay the cost of his guest's meal. In recent years, some lodges have adopted a system whereby each person attending pays the cost of his own meal. Nevertheless, regardless of the method used in this regard, it is most unlikely that a visitor from outside Victoria will be asked to contribute. A visitor from outside the State is welcome to make inquiries at the Grand Secretary's office, whereupon a complimentary visit to an Installation meeting will be arranged.

4. OF VISITING IN GENERAL

Many Victorian lodges use a card system for admitting visitors, which is very similar to that used in New South Wales lodges, and previously explained under that heading. Only lodge members are generally permitted to be present at the opening of a lodge, and visitors are normally admitted after the regular business of the lodge has been completed, but prior to beginning of any degree ceremony or lecture. However, a visitor arriving prior to the opening is often invited to be present for the start. This is a matter for individual Masters, and such a visitor is welcome to ask the Master for his permission in this regard. Invariably, it will be granted. The order for the admission of visitors is as follows:

1. Members of the Lodge (who are late), and visitors (below the rank of Installed Master) who have been vouched for.
2. Visiting Past Masters.
3. Visiting Masters.
4. A Lodge on an Official Visit (The Master, his officers, and members will all enter together).
5. Grand Lodge Officers on an Official Visit. Grand Lodge Officers not visiting officially will enter as Past Masters.

5. INTERESTING ASPECTS OF MASONRY IN VICTORIA

The United Grand Lodge of Victoria has been the leader among the Australian jurisdictions in introducing daylight lodges. As at 1982, fifteen such lodges had been chartered, and there is no reason to believe that others will not follow in the future. These lodges meet mid-morning, usually at 10 am, and their festive board is composed of lunch. Daylight lodges have proved popular with elderly masons, and with those involved with shift-work or nighttime employment. Dress for these lodges is a dark lounge suit instead of a dinner suit, but otherwise they work in a manner identical to other Victorian lodges.

The vast majority of Victorian lodges hold an annual ladies' night in association with a regular lodge meeting. While their partners assemble in the temple for a short meeting, the ladies are entertained in an adjacent hall, generally by a speaker or entertainers. No degree work is performed by a lodge on such a night, and the temple meeting is often over in under an hour. The festive board which follows always involves a full meal, but masonic toasts are not used, with the exception of the Loyal Toast. However, a toast is proposed to The Ladies. Visitors are welcome to attend such a night with their wife or ladyfriend. There are a few lodges who do associate a ladies' night with a lodge meeting, but rather have a separate function of this nature, often with a dinner dance. Where this occurs, a charge is often made on all those attending.

It is also permissible for Victorian lodges to hold 'Male Friends in the South' nights, but these are held far less frequently then ladies' nights. The Grand Lodge lays down certain procedures for their conduct, and prior approval from the Grand Secretary is necessary before they can be held. The format of such an evening is very similar to that for ladies' nights. The main purpose of 'Male Friends' nights is to present information to non-masonic guests which will help clarify misconceptions in the public mind concerning freemasonry. As such, a Grand Lodge officer is always present at these gatherings, which he addresses.

Victoria possesses two lodges of research, namely the Lodge of Research No 218, meeting at the Masonic Centre in East Melbourne; and the Chisel Lodge (of Research) No 434, meeting at the country town of Kerang in northern Victoria. Meeting details are posted below.

Undoubtedly, masonic visitors to Victoria will avail themselves of the opportunity to visit the Masonic Centre of Victoria, located in East Melbourne. It is a very large structure, and was dedicated in 1969. It comprises many lodge rooms, rehearsal rooms, and supper rooms, and includes the Grand Lodge offices and a library. A particular feature of the centre is the magnificent Dallas Brooks Hall, which has a seating capacity of several thousand. As one of the largest venues in Melbourne, this hall is often hired out for concerts, recitals, and other cultural pursuits.

Victoria possesses more than twenty lodges of instruction, specially licensed by the Grand Master. They are generally sponsored by a regular Craft lodge, and their basic function is to train lodge officers. In recent years, new lodges of instruction have been formed with an expanded role to involve training in public speaking and a wide range of masonically associated skills. Lodges of instruction are run by a Lecture Master, and most meet bi-monthly, generally at 7.30 pm. Visitors are welcome to attend, and inquiries in this regard can readily be made at the Grand Lodge office.

6. LODGE WORKINGS, REGALIA, AND RITUAL

All Victoria Craft lodges work an identical degree ritual, as laid down by the Grand Lodge. The *Victorian* ritual is very similar to the English *Emulation* ritual. An Installation Ceremony in Victoria, as with England and the other Australian jurisdictions, includes an Inner Working, or Chair Degree of Installed Master, which only members of that rank may witness. The regalia worn in Victoria is largely identical to that prescribed for English lodges.

A custom pursued in Victoria is that of a Commemoration Ceremony, often called the Vacant Chair ceremony. This is performed to commemorate those who have fallen on the battlefields of war. A vacant chair draped with a flag, apron, and wreath is placed to the front of the Master's pedestal shortly before the closing of the lodge, but after any degree ceremony or lecture has taken place. The ceremony itself is quite short, and must be carried out in the form specified by the Grand Lodge.

The Vacant Chair Ceremony can be performed by any Victorian lodge, but in practice only lodges formed by, or of, ex-servicemen follow the practice. Again, visitors interested in attending a lodge which uses this ceremony can profitably make enquiries at the Grand Lodge office.

7. MASONIC GOVERNMENT

The United Grand Lodge of Victoria meets in Quarterly Communications, on the 3rd Wednesday of March, June, September and December, in each year. The latter three meetings commence at 8 pm, while the March meeting (Grand Installation) starts at 6 pm. A supper follows Grand Lodge meetings, for which tickets are required, and these are obtained by Victorian members at modest cost. It is possible for visitors to attend Grand Lodge meetings, including the Grand Installation. All Grand Lodge Communications are held in the very large Dallas Brooks Hall. Visitors wishing to attend an ordinary Communication can readily make personal arrangements at the Grand Lodge office prior to the date. However, as the Grand Installation in March is heavily attended in Victoria, visitors from outside Victoria must write to the Victorian Grand Secretary well in advance to secure an invitation to be present. Such a letter must be directed through the intending visitor's own Grand Lodge office.

The Victorian Grand Lodge is an appointive Grand Lodge, largely similar in structure to the United Grand Lodge of England, on which its constitutions are based. While the Grand Mastership is elective, the large majority of other Grand Lodge offices are held by appointment. A Board of General Purposes, and a Board of Benevolence are the main administrative organs of the Grand Lodge. The Grand Lodge is involved in many excellent charitable pursuits including a large Freemasons' Hospital in Melbourne, and the Royal Freemasons' Homes (for the aged), the latter of which has facilities in many parts of the State.

List of Lodges

It is not possible to list all the 774 lodges currently warranted in Victoria in this guide. A full list of all lodges working in Victoria, with all relevant details, is contained in the *Victorian Masonic Guide*. This book is published by the Grand Lodge twice yearly, in May and November. It is obtainable at the modest cost from the Grand Lodge office.

As the vast majority of visitors to Victoria will enter the State via Melbourne, it should be possible for them to attend readily the Grand Lodge office, where they will receive every assistance. However, there are several lodges in Victoria of special interest of which details are provided below. These include the daylight lodges, the surviving English lodge still working in Victoria, and Victoria's two research lodges. A visit to a daylight lodge may well suit the travelling schedule of a visitor. While daylight lodges meet less frequently as a rule, the majority of lodges meeting in the evening hold monthly meetings. However, most lodges either fail to meet in December or bring their meeting dates forward in that month. Similarly, most lodges do not meet in January. Visitors intending to visit in these two months are well advised to check with the Grand Lodge office before attempting to do so.

Daylight Lodges

Thespian Lodge No 232
Meets at the Masonic Hall, Liardet Street, Port Melbourne; 2nd Thursday monthly (except January), at 10 am. Inst: October.

The Orpheus Lodge No 394
Meets at the Masonic Centre, East Melbourne; 4th Tuesday monthly (except December and January) at 9.45 am; and 3rd Tuesday in December. Inst: October.

George Swinburne Lodge No 790
Meets at the Masonic Temple, Balmoral Avenue, Springvale, Melbourne; 3rd Monday monthly (except December and January), at 10 am; and 2nd Monday in December. Inst: April.

Allara Lodge No 855
Meets at the Dromana Masonic Temple, corner Reach and Gibson Streets, Dromana; 2nd Tuesday September to May (except January and February), at 10 am. Inst: April.

Blue Dandenongs Lodge No 859
Meets at the Arboreal Temple, Mount Dandenong Tourist Road, Olinda; 1st Wednesday September to May (except January); at 10 am. Inst: October.

Essendon Daylight Lodge No 861
Meets at the Masonic Temple, Mt Alexander Road, Essendon, Melbourne; 1st Monday even months; at 10 am. Inst: August.

Lodge Allunga No 862
Meets at the Masonic Temple, Bell Street, Coburg, Melbourne; 3rd Tuesday February to May, and August to November. Inst: October.

Warrawee Park Lodge No 863
Meets at the Masonic Temple, Drummond Street, Oakleigh, Melbourne; 3rd Wednesday monthly (except January), at 10 am. Inst: November.

Berwick Lodge of Light No 864
Meets at the Masonic Temple, High Street, Berwick; 1st Thursday monthly (except January and July), at 10 am. Inst: November.

Lodge Leawarra No 867
Meets at the Masonic Temple, Davey Street, Frankston; 2nd Wednesday even months, at 10 am. Inst: October.

Barwong Lodge No 868
Meets at the Masonic Temple, Learmonth Street, Queenscliff; 4th Tuesday September to May (except December and January), at 10 am. Inst: October.

Westgate Lodge No 869
Meets at the Masonic Temple, Willis Street, Yarraville, Melbourne; 2nd Tuesday in February, March, May, July, September, October and November; at 10 am. Inst: March.

Watsonia Daylight Lodge No 870	Meets at the Masonic Temple, Ester Street, Greensborough, Melbourne; 1st Tuesday monthly (except November), and 1st Wednesday after 1st Tuesday in November, at 10 am. Inst: May.
Ebden Lodge No 871	Meets at the Masonic Centre, Abbott Street, Sandringham, Melbourne; 3rd Wednesday, February to May, and August to November; at 10 am. Inst: August.
LaTrobe Valley Daylight Lodge No 872	Meets at the Masonic Temple, High Street, Moe; 2nd Monday monthly (except January); at 10 am. Inst: April.

Research Lodges

Lodge of Research No 218	Meets at the Masonic Centre, East Melbourne; 4th Friday; March to November, at 7.30 pm. Inst: October.
The Chisel (Research) Lodge No 434	Meets at the Masonic Temple, Victoria Street, Kerang; 3rd Thursday monthly (except December, January and August), at 8 pm. Inst: 1st Saturday, September.

English Lodge

Combermere Lodge No 752 EC	Meets at the Masonic Centre, East Melbourne; 3rd Thursday even months, at 7.30 pm. Inst: June.

WESTERN AUSTRALIA

The Grand Lodge of Ancient, Free and Accepted Masons of Western Australia
Founded: 1900
Address: Freemasons' Hall, 78 Terrace Road, Perth. 6000.   *Telephone:* 3253999.
Lodges: 286.   Permits Dual and Plural Membership.
Membership: 15,716.
Descent: England, Ireland and Scotland.   *Government:* Appointive Grand Lodge.
Courtesy Degrees: Correspondence must be through Grand Lodges.
Minimum Time Lapse between Degrees: Eight weeks.   *Ritual:* English-type (with adaptations).
Main Publications: Constitutions.   Grand Lodge Proceedings.   Periodical: *The Western Mason.*

History

The first lodge warranted in Western Australia was the Lodge of St John No 485 EC, in 1843 (now No 1 on the roll of the Grand Lodge of Western Australia). Ten years later, the Fremantle Lodge No 1033 EC was formed (now No 2 WAC), and this was followed by English lodges in outlying areas such as Geraldton, Albany and Bunbury. An English District Grand Lodge was established in 1887.

The premier Scottish lodge was Lodge St Andrew No 829, erected in 1896, at Perth. Other Scottish lodges followed in quick succession, until by 1900 there were thirty of that allegiance working in Western Australia. The Grand Lodge of Scotland formed the District Grand Lodge of Western Australia in 1897, to be followed by the District Grand Lodge of the Eastern Goldfields in 1906. Two lodges under Irish Charters were also formed in the State.

In 1894, and again in 1899, attempts were made to form a Grand Lodge of Western Australia, but it proved difficult to obtain consensus. Eventually, the Governor of Western Australia, Sir Gerard Smith, managed to get the English District Grand Lodge to take the initiative. A Convention was called, but total unanimity was not achieved. Nevertheless, the Grand Lodge of Western Australia was formed on 27 February 1900 with Sir Gerard Smith as first Grand Master. It consisted initially of twenty English, fifteen Scottish and two Irish lodges. Eight Scottish lodges still remain today under the District Grand Lodge of Western Australia, while seven range under the District Grand Lodge of the Eastern Goldfields. One English lodge, Plantagenet No 1454, remains under the United Grand Lodge of England. All surviving lodges which stood out at the Union work in complete harmony with the lodges under the Western Australian Grand Lodge. As is usual when a new Grand Lodge is formed, the UK 'home' Grand Lodges agreed not to warrant any new lodges in Western Australia.

Notes for Visitors to Western Australia

1. MEETING TIMES, AND DRESS
Western Australian lodges generally meet at 7.30 pm, although a small number meet slightly earlier or later. Unknown visitors will be called on for their masonic credentials and required to undergo avouchment procedures, so it is advisable to arrive early.

The dress for members is prescribed by the Grand Lodge, and consists of black dinner suit, white dress shirt, and black bow tie, socks and shoes. Full black evening dress (tails) is also permitted—indeed, it was once the norm. However, evening dress is still worn by lodge officers in some lodges, particularly at Installations, and remains mandatory for Grand Lodge officers engaged in official Grand Lodge functions. During the hot summer months, Summer Dress is optional. This consists of a black dinner suit without the coat, but replaced by a black cummerbund at the waist. Alternatively, a white mess jacket may be worn in summer. White gloves are required to be worn by all members, but may be removed at the discretion of the Master when conditions are oppressive.

In addition, lodges located north of 26th Parallel, which runs across the centre of Western Australia just south of Carnarvon, may wear tropical dress. This consists of a white shirt, white trousers, and black bow tie, with a white mess jacket being optional. Tropical dress in this area may be worn at any time of the year. As with all other Australian jurisdictions, the apron is worn outside the jacket. Regardless of the foregoing, a visitor from outside Western Australia is welcome to wear a dark lounge suit to a lodge meeting.

2. LODGE AFTERPROCEEDINGS
The festive board in Western Australia is sometimes referred to as 'The South', as is its common appellation in many other Australian jurisdictions. It is almost invariably held after a lodge meeting, usually on masonic premises, and it consists of a light repast and refreshments. The patterns and physical layout of the festive board largely follow those of other Australian jurisdictions. The toast list, preceded by grace and the supper, is as follows:

1. The Loyal Toast ('The Queen and the Craft'). This toast is usually followed by the singing of the first verse of the National Anthem (*God Save The Queen*).
2. The Most Worshipful Grand Master. This Toast is generally proposed by a Past Master, but will be responded to only if the Grand Master, or his official representative, is actually present.
3. The Initiate. This Toast is often proposed by a Past Master, and the Initiate will respond. In some lodges, the candidate of the evening, regardless which Degree he has taken, will be toasted.
4. The Visitors. Tradition in Western Australia gives this Toast to the Junior Warden, although the Grand Lodge has ruled that 'there is no reason why it should not be varied (the Proposer) with great advantage to all concerned'. Generally, a visiting Master will respond.
5. The Tyler's Toast.

Of course, there are variations to this pattern. On nights of Installation, the toast list is often extended to include the Installing Master and the newly installed Master. No charge is made on visitors attending the festive board. In some lodges, a charity collection or raffle is conducted. Visitors are welcome to contribute, and will doubtless feel so inclined. It needs to be noted that there are a small number of temperance lodges in Western Australia (about five percent) in which no alcohol is available at the festive board. Regardless, all lodges cater for the total abstainer.

3. NIGHTS OF INSTALLATION
Each lodge in Western Australia installs a new Master annually, at a fixed time. Nights of Installation generally commence an hour to an hour and a half earlier than for normal meetings. The festive board which follows such an occasion usually includes a full meal. As extensive catering is arranged for Installation meetings, it is always appreciated if a visitor communicates his intention to attend in advance. Nevertheless, a formal invitation is not required by either local members or visitors to attend any lodge meeting in Western Australia. Visitors from outside of Western Australia are advised to make arrangements at the Grand Lodge office prior to seeking to attend an Installation meeting, if at all possible.

4. OF VISITING IN GENERAL
Lodges under the Western Australian Constitution use a card system for admitting visitors, which tends to be even more extensive than similar systems employed in some other Australian jurisdictions. Every visitor arriving at a lodge will be given a card to complete. On it he will detail his name, lodge, and jurisdiction, and the name of the lodge member who will vouch for him inside the lodge. Unknown visitors will be required to present their masonic credentials and be masonically examined, whereupon his examiner (invariably a Past Master of the lodge) will endorse his card. The cards are all passed from the Tyler to the Inner Guard as appropriate, and each visitor will be vouched for inside the lodge prior to his admittance. Other provisions attached to the Western Australian card system involve all members and visitors retiring temporarily from the lodge (such as at an Installation meeting) being issued with a card necessary for re-admission.

Western Australian Constitution lodges do not normally admit visitors until after the opening and until normal routine lodge business has been completed. However a visitor, with the Master's permission, may witness the lodge opening. Visitors are admitted, using the card system, in the following groups:

1. Master Masons (unaccompanied) 2. Past Masters (unaccompanied) 3. Visiting lodges, when led by their Masters. The Masters will be accompanied by their officers, Past Masters and members. While Master Masons and Past Masters not accompanying their Lodge Master enter in groups, visiting lodges generally enter individually.

Visiting lodges enter in order of juniority—the youngest lodge entering first, and the oldest lodge last (judged by date of Warrant). Nevertheless, on occasions when the saving of time is desirable, such as at Installation meetings, visiting lodges will enter en bloc.

It is interesting to note that a group of visitors, subsequent to admission, do not salute and thereafter immediately take up seats, as is the practice is some other Australian jurisdictions. Instead, those entering stand surrounding the pavement, as opposed to them all standing in the West. After saluting they will then be seated. Past Masters and Masters will usually be escorted to the East to be greeted by the Master of the lodge.

Lodges often take up a charity collection inside the lodge, but this is usually done prior to the admission of visitors. Unlike some jurisdictions, it is not usual for visitors to convey fraternal greetings during lodge closing ceremonies under the Western Australian Constitution.

5. INTERESTING ASPECTS OF MASONRY IN WESTERN AUSTRALIA

As has already been mentioned, Western Australia possesses fifteen lodges, organised in two District Grand Lodges, under the Grand Lodge of Scotland. The comments and notes for visitors contained in this section apply largely to Western Australian Constitution lodges, and not to the Scottish lodges. The Scottish lodges, of course, follow practices aligned with their own allegiance.

The body of Western Australian masonry involves itself in excellent charitable works. Chief among these pursuits are Cottage Homes for the aged, a sixty-bed Hostel (for the aged), and a forty-five-bed Nursing Home.

It is usual for most Western Australian lodges to hold an annual ladies' night, although it is less usual for these to be held in association with a lodge meeting. In the latter situation, masonic toasts are not used. Ladies' nights often take the form of a dinner or dinner dance, and visitors are welcome to attend, subject to the purchase of a ticket. Of course, tickets are not required for ladies' nights held in conjunction with a lodge meeting, and visitors will not be asked to contribute to costs.

Western Australia does not possess any lodges of instruction on the English model, as found in some other Australian jurisdictions. However, it does possess one lodge of research. This is the Lodge of Research No 277, which meets at Freemasons' Hall, Perth. Interestingly, all lectures to be given in Western Australian lodges must first be submitted to the Grand Master for approval before they can be presented.

6. LODGE WORKINGS, REGALIA, AND RITUAL

All lodges under the Western Australian Constitution must use a standard ritual, as prescribed by the Grand Lodge. This ritual is largely similar to English *Emulation* ritual, but it does possess a few minor differences resulting from early Irish and Scottish influences, and small amendments promulgated, on occasions, by the Grand Lodge. Naturally, the Scottish lodges use Scottish rituals. The regalia used in Western Australian lodges largely follows that of England, while Scottish lodges use regalia forms inherited from their own Grand Lodge.

7. MASONIC GOVERNMENT

The Grand Lodge of Western Australia meets twice per year, in April and October. Both meetings are held in the evening, generally commencing at 7 pm, and are followed by a festive board. At the April meeting, this tends to be in the form of a supper, while a full meal often follows the October meeting (the Grand Installation). A small charge is levied on members attending. Visitors may only attend a Grand Lodge meeting with the express invitation of the Grand Master, and this is usually extended only to official delegations from sister Grand Lodges.

The Grand Lodge of Western Australia is structured as an appointive Grand Lodge, largely on the English model. It consists of all Grand Lodge officers, and the Masters, Past Masters and Wardens of its lodges. As with the other Australian jurisdictions, the two main administrative bodies of the Grand Lodge are a Board of General Purposes, and a Board of Benevolence. The two Scottish District Grand Lodges meet annually, and work under the forms dictated by the Grand Lodge of Scotland.

List of Lodges

As with the other Australian jurisdictions, the large number of lodges located in Western Australia prevents an extensive list being provided here. However, a full Directory of Western Australian lodges is contained each year in the March edition of the *Western Mason*. This magazine is published quarterly, and is available on subscription from the Grand Lodge at a rate (1983) of $A 3.50. Regardless, visitors in the first instance should as a matter of courtesy call at the Grand Lodge office in Freemasons' Hall, 78 Terrace Road, Perth. It contains two large lodge rooms, an excellent library, and accommodates thirty-four Craft lodges. Details of all lodges meeting in Western Australia, including Scottish lodges, and the State's sole English lodge can always be obtained at that address. As Western Australia's English lodge may be of special interest to visitors, its meeting details are as follows:

Plantagenet Lodge No 1454 EC   Meets at Freemasons' Hall, Albany; 2nd Tuesday, monthly, except March. Installation: Saturday following 2nd Tuesday in March.

Finally, it should be noted that many Western Australian lodges recess variously in the months of December, January and February. Visitors planning to attend in these months should be sure to check meeting details carefully.

NEW ZEALAND

New Zealand is an independent English-speaking country located in the Pacific Ocean to the south-east of Australia. It possesses a Grand Lodge dating from 1890. In addition, New Zealand still has a number of lodges warranted from England, Ireland, and Scotland.

The Grand Lodge of Ancient, Free and Accepted Masons of New Zealand
Founded: 1890
Address: Grand Lodge Office: 39–41 Ghuznee Street, Wellington 1. *Telephone:* 856622. *Postal Address:* P.O. Box 6439, Wellington 1, New Zealand.

Lodges: 428.   Permits Dual and Plural Membership.
Membership: 35,040.
Descent: England, Ireland, and Scotland.   *Government:* Appointive Grand Lodge.
Courtesy Degrees: Correspondence must be through Grand Lodges.
Minimum Time Lapse between Degrees: Four weeks.   *Ritual:* English-type (with adaptations).
Main Publications: Constitutions.   Grand Lodge Proceedings.   Periodical: *The New Zealand Freemason.*

History

The early development of freemasonry in New Zealand followed a similar path to that of the Australian colonies. As a British colony, the lodges formed in New Zealand from the outset owed their allegiance to either the English, Irish or Scottish Constitutions. However, oddly enough, the honour of holding the first recorded masonic meeting went to the French. This was held in 1837 at Port Levy, when a French whaling captain—a mason under the Grand Orient of France, gathered together all those masons on ships then in port and held a meeting.

The first lodge formed in New Zealand was the Auckland Social Lodge No 348 IC (now Ara Lodge, No 1, New Zealand Constitution), in 1843. This lodge was created by the Australian Social Lodge, No 260 IC meeting at Sydney, which granted a dispensation for the new lodge to meet. This type of practice was not totally unusual at the time. Communications in this era were often slow and irregular. A new lodge formed in this way would in due course receive its actual warrant from the home Grand Lodge concerned.

By the 1870s, New Zealand had a proliferation of lodges meeting within its shores under the three British Constitutions. Subsequently, each of the parent bodies set up a number of District and Provincial Grand Lodges. This devolution of administration was achieved rather haphazardly. Unlike other colonies where one local District Grand Lodge was generally deemed sufficient per constitution in each, many such Districts were formed in varying areas of New Zealand. It is quite likely that this overabundance of local masonic administrations had a detrimental effect on creating the unity of purpose necessary to enhance the creation of the Grand Lodge of New Zealand.

Nevertheless, by the late 1870s an infant movement for union was underway, and it quickly gathered momentum. Regrettably, freemasonry in New Zealand polarised into pro-union and anti-union forces. A series of meetings were held over several years, and the movement was often hampered by opposition from varying local administrative authorities. However, by 1889, the pro-union forces had enough strength to form a Union at a convention held in Wellington. Opposing arguments still raged after the convention, and often involved legal technicalities. The movement continued regardless, and the Grand Lodge of New Zealand was inaugurated on 29 April 1890. Sixty-five lodges (34 English, eight Irish, and 23 Scottish) formed the new Grand Lodge, and 45 others subsequently transferred their loyalty. Nonetheless, a significant number of lodges remained under their original Charters.

In 1983, England maintained two District Grand Lodges in New Zealand, viz. the District Grand Lodge of the North Island, New Zealand (with 23 lodges), and the District Grand Lodge of the South Island, New Zealand (with 17 lodges). Scotland also retains two District Grand Lodges, viz, the District Grand Lodge of New Zealand North (with four lodges), and the District Grand Lodge of New Zealand South (with seven lodges). A Provincial Grand Lodge of New Zealand (with four lodges) also works happily under the Grand Lodge of Ireland. It should be noted that as a result of a Concordat between the Grand Lodge of New Zealand and the three Home Grand Lodges, only the former may erect new lodges in the country. Of course, the disharmony of masonry in New Zealand at the time of the erection of the Grand Lodge has long since faded, and all constitutions working in New Zealand do so in amity.

Notes for Visitors to New Zealand
Unless otherwise specifically stated, the notes below refer only to the New Zealand Constitution and its lodges.

1. MEETING TIMES, AND DRESS
Lodges meeting in New Zealand, regardless of constitution, generally meet at a time between 7 pm and 8 pm, although some lodges meet as early as 6 pm. A visitor, particularly if he is unknown, should endeavour to arrive by at least 7 pm, as he will be required to undergo avouchment procedures.

The dress required for New Zealand Constitution lodges is full evening dress (tails), consisting of black or white waistcoat and white tie. However, a black dinner suit is also approved, and has become increasingly popular. A lodge may resolve (and some do) that in any, or either, of the months of December, January, February, or March, a dark lounge suit with white shirt, dark tie and black shoes, may be worn. At other times, a dark lounge suit may be worn provided the lodge meets regularly not later than 6.15 pm. White gloves are required regardless of attire. Masonic jewels are worn with a lounge suit. Members or visitors serving in Her Majesty's Armed Forces are also permitted to wear full dress or undress uniform on all masonic occasions. A visitor from overseas will certainly not be prevented at any time from attending a lodge meeting in a dark lounge suit.

2. LODGE AFTERPROCEEDINGS
The festive board, or refectory as it is often referred to in New Zealand, is invariably held after a lodge meeting. No charge is levied on a visitor attending under any circumstances. A visitor may be called upon to speak briefly in response to a visitors' toast, particularly if he comes from outside New Zealand. A light supper is served at a normal festive board, accompanied by refreshments. An example of a toast list employed is as follows:
1. The Loyal Toast ('The Queen and the Craft').
2. The Most Worshipful Grand Master.
3. The Provincial Grand Master, and officers of the Grand Lodge, past and present, if attending.
4. The Candidate.
5. The Visitors.
6. The Tyler's Toast.

All toasts, except the Loyal Toast and the Tyler's Toast, require a response if an appropriate recipient is present. Some Grand Lodge toasts might only be proposed if a recipient is actually present. Other toasts, such as that to a newly installed

Master at an Installation, may be added as necessary. It is not unusual for a visitor to be called upon to speak at the refectory.

3. NIGHTS OF INSTALLATION

As with all jurisdictions following British practices, lodges in New Zealand install a new Master annually, at a fixed time. Installation meetings generally commence about one hour earlier than ordinary meetings. They are almost invariably followed by an expansive festive board consisting of a full meal and a more extensive toast list. As installations in New Zealand are usually well attended, it is appreciated if intending visitors can provide some notice of attendance, as this will assist in catering arrangements. While some lodges in New Zealand do issue invitations to visitors to attend their nights of Installation, at no time does any visitor require a formal invitation to attend such a meeting. Arrangements can be made to attend a convenient Installation at the Grand Lodge office in Wellington.

4. OF VISITING IN GENERAL

Many lodges in New Zealand, in following practices inherited from England, form a procession into and out of the lodge room. These processions consist of the Master and his principal officers entering the lodge prior to opening. At the procession out of the lodge following a closing, Past Masters and visiting Installed Masters often join the egress. Under the New Zealand Constitution, lodges open in the presence of members only, with visitors not normally being admitted until after their usual routine business has been transacted. The order of admission, in groups, is Master Masons, Past Masters, visiting Masters, visiting lodges on an official visit (Master, officers, and members), and Grand Lodge officers visiting officially.

Upon arrival, an unknown visitor will be placed in the hands of the Past Master for the purposes of avouchment. It is usual for a visitor's examiner to enter the lodge with him and introduce him to the Master. In reference to avouchment procedures, New Zealand Constitution lodges have one peculiarity concerning visiting Installed Masters. It is usual for an Installed Master being examined to be asked for passgrip and password leading from the third degree to a Board of Installed Masters. This procedure is unknown in many jurisdictions, particularly in Australia. While this fact is well understood in New Zealand and a visiting Installed Master ignorant of these procedures will experience no problems in avouchment, it is useful for him to be aware of the fact. As New Zealand lodges do incorporate a Conclave of Installed Masters as part of an Installation ceremony, unknown visiting Installed Masters will be required to be examined as such before they can attend this section of the proceedings.

5. INTERESTING ASPECTS OF MASONRY IN NEW ZEALAND

In being a young country, New Zealand does not possess any structures of great antiquity. However, there are several masonic buildings and other points which a visitor may find of interest. One Masonic Hall of interest is that which used to house Lodge Kerikeri No 402 NZC. The building, called the Old Stone Store, was erected in sandstone in 1833 as part of a mission station. The lodge meets at Kerikeri, in the Northland of New Zealand, being named for the town.

The Masonic Hall at Clyde, in Central Otago (South Island), is a magnificent building. Built in 1869, it was originally the Town Hall, the foundation stone of which was laid by the Dunstan Lodge No 103 NZC. This lodge occupies it today.

Erected in local stone, it is fronted by four massive Corinthian pillars supporting the portico, with its windows and the main door in Egyptian design. Visitors interested in viewing these and other such edifices in New Zealand can readily receive assistance at the Grand Secretary's office.

Without doubt, the feature masonic tourist attraction in New Zealand is the famed Sign of the Takahe. This is a roadhouse near the top of one of the hills overlooking Christchurch, in the South Island. It was constructed in the 1930s by one brother Harry Ell, and it is in fact a large manor house in the English mould. Built with large blocks of local stone, its craftsmanship is superb, and one of its many features are two huge stained glass windows depicting the two great pillars of King Solomon's Temple.

New Zealand's Grand Lodge is involved in many outstanding charitable pursuits. Well worth visiting are the Roskill Masonic Village (for the aged) in Auckland, featuring the beautiful Edgar Faber Memorial Chapel; the Papakura Masonic Boys' Home in Auckland; and the new Wanganui Masonic Homes at Wanganui East.

As with most English-speaking Grand jurisdictions in the world, lodges in New Zealand usually hold a ladies' evening on at least an annual basis. In some cases, ladies will be invited to the festive board following a lodge meeting, but often these occasions are separately held and take the form of a dinner or dinner dance.

A fairly recent introduction into the body of New Zealand masonry has been the Grand Lodge of New Zealand deposit scheme. In 1977, the Grand Lodge arranged with the National Bank of New Zealand for investors to place modest sums of money into the scheme to attract high interest returns, yet have the capital invested available if required. The scheme is of particular value to elderly people, but it has also proved popular with all age groups. However, it must be noted that participation in the scheme is restricted to masons under the New Zealand Constitution, their immediate families, and lodges under that allegiance.

Undoubtedly, one of the most outstanding features of masonry in New Zealand is the large number of research lodges working in the country, all under the New Zealand Constitution. Ten such lodges currently range under its banner, and some of these have a world-wide reputation in the field, notably the United Masters Lodge No 167 (at Auckland), and the Masters' and Past Masters' Lodge No 130 (at Christchurch). These lodges largely restrict full membership to Installed Masters, but most offer associate membership to any Master Mason belonging to a Constitution in amity with the Grand Lodge. The majority of these research lodges regularly publish Transactions, which are available to members and associates. Interested Master Masons from outside New Zealand can make inquiries concerning associate membership with the Grand Lodge office, but any such correspondence must be directed through the inquirer's own Grand Lodge.

New Zealand also possesses a number of lodges of instruction on the English model. They meet at regular intervals, under licence from the Grand Master, and are restricted to Master Masons. Under the leadership of a preceptor, these lodges instruct lodge officers in proper masonic ceremonial, and related matters. Interested visitors are welcome to attend their meetings, and can make suitable enquiries at the Grand Lodge office.

6. LODGE WORKINGS, REGALIA, AND RITUAL
The ritual laid down for New Zealand Constitution lodges is standard and uniform,

and its content stems very largely from local masonic history. It needs to be recalled that the Grand Lodge of New Zealand was not formed in a sense of complete unanimity although, of course, these factors have long since passed into history. Nevertheless, at the creation of the Grand Lodge, many lodges under the three British Constitutions chose to maintain their current allegiances. The result of these factors has seen the evolution of the New Zealand Constitution ritual assume a form which takes into account the varying workings of the three original jurisdictions more so than in any other English-speaking country. The object of the 'new' New Zealand ritual when it was originally promulgated shortly after the forming of the Grand Lodge, was to recognise the strong hold the current rituals of the three British Constitutions had on their adherents. While the New Zealand ritual is based on English forms, it also possesses Scottish and Irish influences. Undoubtedly, the most interesting facet of the ritual is that a complete form of Scottish workings for the third degree is provided as an alternative to the English. Lodges are free to use either form.

The layout of the lodge room under the New Zealand Constitution can be more closely identified with Scottish practice, rather than the English. In addition, NZC lodges appointed a Deputy Master, Senior Steward, and Junior Steward—again attesting to non-English usages. Regardless of the existence and usage of the New Zealand ritual in NZC lodges, it must be noted that lodges which existed at the time of the Grand Lodge's formation are still permitted to use their original ritual, provided that it is consistently used. Lodges erected in New Zealand subsequent to 1890 must use the 'new' New Zealand ritual. Regalia for NZC lodges is very closely modelled on English types.

7. ENGLISH, IRISH AND SCOTTISH LODGES

As has already been noted, quite a number of lodges in New Zealand still work under the Grand Lodges of England, Ireland and Scotland. Intervisitation between members of all Constitutions represented in New Zealand is frequent and constant. While lodges under the three 'home' jurisdictions preserve their original rituals and practices as inherited, visitors will notice festive board practices adopted by lodges in New Zealand, regardless of warrant, are generally not dissimilar.

8. MASONIC GOVERNMENT

The Grand Lodge of New Zealand meets in Annual Communication in the month of November, when the Grand Master is elected and installed, together with his Grand Lodge officers, and the business of the Grand Lodge is transacted. The meeting generally opens at 9.30 pm. The Annual Communication is held in rotation between the major cities of the country, and is often accompanied by several social functions. An invitation is needed for a visitor to attend.

The Constitutions and Laws of the Grand Lodge follow British patterns, particularly those of England. It is composed of a Grand Master, a number of Provincial Grand Masters, other Grand Lodge officers past and present, and the Masters, Past Masters, and Wardens of its constituent lodges. In terms of masonic administration, New Zealand is divided into Provinces with a Provincial Grand Master and Provincial Grand Lodge officers. These bodies function in a manner similar to those of the British Constitutions.

Nevertheless, as we have seen in ritual matters, the forms of masonic government under the New Zealand Constitution exhibit traits readily attributable Scottish and Irish practices. The Grand Lodge is partly elective. Only the most senior Grand Lodge offices are appointive, while most are elective. A Board of General Purposes and a Board of Benevolence are the two main administrative bodies of the Grand Lodge.

List of Lodges

It is not logistically possible to list the lodges meeting in New Zealand here. However, a full list of all lodges meeting in New Zealand, with all meeting details, can be found in the *New Zealand Masonic Directory*. This publication is issued annually as a supplement to Grand Lodge periodical magazine—*The New Zealand Freemason*. This magazine is published quarterly, and is obtainable on subscription from the Grand Lodge, P.O. Box 6439, Wellington. Nonetheless, while a visitor possessing a current directory can readily plan his visits to lodges in New Zealand, it is always an appreciated courtesy for a visitor to make himself known at the Grand Lodge office in Wellington. It is necessary to note that the Grand Lodge office does not possess any masonic meeting facilities, but is purely an administrative centre. As New Zealand has a number of large cities, the major masonic meeting places in them are listed below:

Masonic Hall, Tinakori Road, *Wellington.*
Masonic Hall, Ormond Road, *Gisborne.*
Masonic Hall, Market Street, *Hastings.*
Masonic Hall, Nile Street, *Nelson.*
Masonic Hall, Hillside Road, *Dunedin.*
Masonic Hall, St Benedicts Street, *Auckland.*
Masonic Hall, Kennedy Road, *Napier.*
Masonic Hall, Darnell Street, *New Plymouth.*
Masonic Hall, Gloucester Street, *Christchurch.*
Masonic Hall, Forth Street, *Invercargill.*

Finally, it must be noted that very few lodges in New Zealand meet in the month of January, and some also fail to meet in February or December. Otherwise, except for some of the research lodges which meet less frequently, the vast majority of lodges in New Zealand meet monthly.

THE PACIFIC ISLANDS
FIJI

Fiji is located in the South Pacific Ocean to east of Australia and New Caledonia, and north of New Zealand. It consists of about three hundred islands grouped together, of which about one hundred are inhabited. The two largest islands, Viti Levu and Vanua Levu, comprise about 85% of the total land area of about 7,000 square miles. Ethnically, the country is comprised largely of roughly equal numbers of native Fijians and Indians, with a small white English-speaking population. Originally a British possession, Fiji gained political independence in 1970. Fiji contains one Scottish lodge, and four English lodges, the latter of which form part of the English Grand Inspectorate of the South West Pacific.

History

The first lodge in Fiji was Lodge Polynesia No 562 SC, founded in 1875. It remains the only Scottish lodge ever to be formed in the islands. The first English lodge, the Lodge of Fiji, No 1931, was warranted in 1881. This was followed by the Rewa Lodge of Viti No 2238 (in 1887), the Lodge of Lautoka No 3354 (in 1909), and the Ba Lodge of Fiji No 4883 (in 1926).

The Craft in Fiji has had a chequered history. The white population of Fiji has never been large, and a moving white population has been less than helpful to masonic development. Nevertheless, the body of masonry in Fiji has survived well, and continues on a stable path to this day.

Notes for Visitors to Fiji

The first thing a masonic visitor to Fiji is likely to notice is that membership is very largely white. The non-white communities of Fiji tend to view freemasonry as a European institution, and one reserved for people of that race. At the same time, the white population of Fiji is only about 5,000, placing an obvious limit on lodge memberships which are, as a result, relatively small. Indeed, approximately half of the membership of lodges in Fiji live outside Fiji! On first view, this would appear somewhat surprising. However, many of the whites (largely from Australia and New Zealand in recent times) reside in the country only on a fairly temporary basis in an occupational capacity. Upon the completion of their term of employment in the islands, they usually return to their home countries. This creates a fair degree of mobility in membership, and often deprives the lodges of experienced members.

Another major factor which affects the Craft in Fiji is local geographical isolation. Again, in view of the relative smallness of Fiji, this may surprise some. However, it must be remembered that Fiji is composed of a great many islands. Of the five lodges in the country, two work at the capital city of Suva on the main island of Viti Levu. Another works at Lautoka on the far side of the same island. Lodge Polynesia works on the small island of Ovalau, at its main town of Levuka. In years gone by communications were difficult, and the physical difficulty of travel made masonic visitation infrequent. In relatively recent years, the situation in this regard has greatly improved, but nevertheless a trip is not taken lightly. Regardless of these physical problems, it needs to be added that intervisitation has been, and remains, an important part of masonic life in Fiji.

Lodges in Fiji meet in the early evening, generally about 7.30 pm. Dress is a dark lounge suit, and visitors are welcome to wear their own regalia. Festive board practices resemble those of England, except that a full meal is usually held only following an Installation. Alcohol is available with all festive board repasts. A visitor will never be asked to contribute when attending any lodge afterproceedings in Fiji. However, should a visitor find himself in Fiji as a resident, he will almost invariably be invited to affiliate.

List of Lodges

The meeting details of the five lodges in Fiji are as follows:

Lodge Polynesia No 562 SC	Meets at the Masonic Temple, Levuka, Ovalau, Fiji; 3rd Saturday monthly.
The Lodge of Fiji No 1931 EC	Meets at the Masonic Temple, Gladstone Street, Suva, Viti Levu, Fiji; 3rd Monday monthly (except June). Inst: 3rd Saturday, June.

The Rewa Lodge of Viti No 2238 EC   Meets at the Masonic Temple, Gladstone Street, Suva, Viti Levu, Fiji; 2nd Wednesday monthly (except July). Inst: 3rd Saturday, July.

The Lodge of Lautoka No 3354 EC   Meets at the Masonic Rooms, Lautoka, Viti Levu, Fiji; 2nd Friday monthly (except May). Inst: 3rd Saturday, May.

The Ba Lodge of Fiji No 4883 EC   Meets at the Lodge Temple, Rarawai, Ba, Viti Levu, Fiji; 4th Saturday monthly (except December). Inst: September.

GUAM

The island of Guam is a possession of the United States of America. It is the largest and southermost of the Marianas Islands in the central Pacific Ocean. The site of large American naval and air force bases, it possesses three lodges chartered by the Grand Lodge of the Philippines. These are Charleston Lodge No 44; Milton C Marvin Lodge No 123; and Micronesia Lodge No 173. The Micronesia Lodge, until recent years, worked at Saipan in the Marianas Islands. All three lodges largely cater for American servicemen. Guam has become a major link in trans-pacific air and shipping routes, and as such has seen a steady growth of tourism. Masonic visitors are most welcome at any lodge meeting. Meeting details are as follows:

Charleston Lodge No 44   Meets at the Masonic Temple, Agana, Guam; 1st Monday monthly at 7.30 pm.

Milton C Marvin Lodge No 123   Meets at the Masonic Temple, Agana, Guam; 1st Wednesday monthly at 7.30 pm.

Micronesia Lodge No 173   Meets at the Scottish Rite Temple, Agana, Guam; 3rd Friday monthly at 7.30 pm.

MARSHALL ISLANDS

The Marshall Islands form part of the United Nations Trust Territory of the Pacific, administered by the United States. A large US military base is located on Kwajelein Island in the group, and it possesses a lodge chartered by the Grand Lodge of the Philippines. Its details are as follows:

Emon Lodge No 179   Meets at the Masonic Temple, Kwajelein, Marshall Islands; 3rd Monday monthly at 7.30 pm.

NEW CALEDONIA

New Caledonia is an elongated island located to the north-east of Australia. It is a French possession, and it has two lodges warranted by the irregular Grand Lodge of France. These two lodges have recently moved into a new temple at Noumea, the island's capital. No regular lodge yet exists in New Caledonia.

SAMOA

Samoa is an island group located in the South Pacific between Fiji and Tahiti. It consists of Western Samoa and American Samoa. Western Samoa was formerly administered by New Zealand, but it received its independence in 1962. American Samoa remains an unincorporated territory of the United States. Samoa possesses two lodges, both warranted by the Grand Lodge of New Zealand. Their meeting details are as follows:

Calliope Lodge No 252 — Meets at the Masonic Hall, Apia, Western Samoa; Thursday nearest the full moon monthly. Inst: August.

Benjamen Kneubuhl Lodge No 441 — Meets at the Masonic Hall, Tafuna, Tutuila, American Samoa; 1st Tuesday monthly (except January). Inst: September.

SOLOMON ISLANDS

The Solomon Islands is a former British possession situated to the west of Papua/New Guinea. It received its independence as a separate nation in 1978. Its capital, Honiara, located on the island of Guadalcanal, has had an English lodge since 1934. Its details are as follows:

Lodge Melanesia No 5516 — Meets at the Masonic Temple, Honiara, Solomon Islands; 2nd Friday monthly. Inst: September.

TAHITI

Tahiti is an exotic French possession in the western South Pacific, and has long been a popular tourist destination. The irregular Grand Orient of France had two lodges in the area in the 1850s, but neither survived. No regular lodge currently works in Tahiti.

VANUATU

Vanuatu is the new name for the New Hebrides Island group, which until recently was administered jointly by Britain and France. The New Hebrides recently achieved independence under its new designation. Vanuatu possesses one English lodge, dating from 1976. Its details are as follows:

The Lodge of Discovery No 8737 — Meets at Hong Kong and New Zealand House, Vila, Vanuatu; 2nd Tuesday monthly. Inst: February.

PAPUA/NEW GUINEA

Papua/New Guinea is an independent nation sharing half of the island of New Guinea, located to the north of Australia. It was formerly a British possession, later to be administered by Australia prior to its independence.

The first lodge established in New Guinea was Lodge Rabaul No 4468. This lodge appears to have been formed in 1919, but its warrant dates from 1922. It works at Rabaul, on the island of New Britain, and remains the only British lodge ever chartered in the area.

Subsequently, Papua/New Guinea has been accepted as forming part of the jurisdiction of the United Grand Lodge of Queensland. Queensland has warranted eight lodges in the country, commencing with New Guinea Lodge No 292 QC, at

Port Moresby in 1921. All lodges in the area were forced to close during the Second World War, but there were several Masonic Clubs formed during this period to service masons in the Armed Forces stationed in New Guinea.

Since the political independence of Papua/New Guinea, lodges in the country have lost some of their membership with a proportion of the white population moving back to Australia. However, no lodge currently appears to be in any real danger of becoming extinct, either through falling membership or as a result of outside pressures. As recently as 1981, the Grand Master of the United Grand Lodge of Queensland, whilst in New Guinea for the installation of Port Moresby Lodge, held discussions with government officials concerning the welfare of the Craft. This was seen as a good public relations exercise in view of the infancy of Papua/New Guinea as an independent country.

All lodges in Papua/New Guinea meet in the evening, usually about 7.30 pm. The Queensland lodges naturally follow the practices of that jurisdiction, although as New Guinea has a hot tropical climate, dress regulations are interpreted broadly.

List of Lodges

The meeting details of all lodges working in Papua/New Guinea are noted below:

Lodge Rabaul No 4468 EC	Meets at the Masonic Hall, Mango Avenue, Rabaul, New Britain; 4th Monday monthly (except April). Inst: 4th Saturday, April.
New Guinea Lodge No 292 QC	Meets at the Masonic Hall, Port Moresby; 4th Thursday monthly. Inst: October.
Morobe Lodge No 375 QC	Meets at the Masonic Hall, Bulolo; 4th Saturday monthly. Inst: July.
Madang Lodge No 380 QC	Meets at the Masonic Hall, Madang; 3rd Tuesday monthly. Inst: 3rd Saturday, October.
Lae Lodge No 419 QC	Meets at the Masonic Hall, Lae; 2nd Monday monthly. Inst: November.
Port Moresby Lodge No 445 QC	Meets at the Masonic Hall, Port Moresby; 1st Monday monthly. Inst: May.
Goroka Lodge No 456 QC	Meets at the Masonic Temple, Goroka; 2nd Thursday monthly; Inst: 4th Saturday, April.
Mount Hagen Lodge No 508 QC	Meets at the Masonic Temple, Mount Hagen; 3rd Thursday monthly. Inst: 2nd Saturday, July.
Bougainville Lodge No 514 QC	Meets at the Bougainville Copper Ltd. Offices, Loloho; last Thursday monthly. Inst: July.

Section X

Visiting in
Scandinavia

Scandinavia

An Overview

Scandinavia consists of the countries of Norway, Sweden, Denmark, Finland, and Iceland. Each of these beautiful, and often panoramic, northern countries have much to offer to the tourist and visiting freemason alike. All five of the Scandinavian countries possess regular Grand Lodges and, with the exception of Finland, all work the unique system of degrees known as the Swedish Rite. It is for this reason that, in terms of this guide, Scandinavia is treated separately to Europe. For the visitor to understand Scandinavian masonry, he must first appreciate the development of the Swedish Rite which, in turn, requires an insight into Swedish masonic history. Therefore, we must in this instance depart from our usual alphabetical approach and begin our discussion of Scandinavian masonry with Sweden.

SWEDEN

The Grand Lodge of Sweden
Founded: 1760
Addresses: The Grand Secretary, Nybrokajen 7, Stockholm 11148. *Telephone:* (08) 201608.
Masonic Temple: Baat Palace, Blasieholmgaten 6, Stockholm.
Lodges: 39 (Craft), 125 (total). Permits Dual and Plural Membership.
Membership: 24,000.
Descent: England, France. *Government:* Swedish form.
Courtesy Degrees: rarely conferred. *Ritual:* Swedish Rite.
Minimum Time Lapse between Degrees: 12 months.
Major Publications: Book of Constitutions. Proceedings. Book of Registration (List of Lodges). Periodical: *Frimuraren* (Freemason). All publications in Swedish.

Swedish Masonic History, and the Swedish Rite

It would appear that freemasonry came to Sweden originally from England, via France. The first lodge was founded at Stockholm in 1735, and was later named Den Nordiska Forsta—the First Northern Lodge. The early development of the Craft in Sweden is obscure, but almost from the first, the Swedish Craft has been controlled by the Swedish aristocracy. Den Nordiska Forsta (which still works in Stockholm) was erected by Count Axel Ericson Wrede-Sparre, who entered the Craft in Paris. Den Nordiska Forsta was a St John's Lodge, working the three Craft degrees. The first St Andrew's Lodge was erected in 1756, to work the 4th, 5th, and 6th degrees. It was called the Den Nordiska Cirkeln—the Northern Circle Lodge.

Thus, the Swedish (or Scandinavian) Rite would appear to date back to the early 1750s. It consists of ten degrees organised into three divisions, plus one Supreme degree, making eleven in all. The Rite was standardised in the 1770s by a Committee headed by Duke Charles of Sudermanland (afterwards King Charles XIII).

The first division consists of the three Craft degrees, conferred in what are known as St John's Lodges. Then follows the second division, also of three degrees, and usually referred to as the Scots Degrees. They are conferred in St Andrew's Lodges. The degrees are: Elect and Most Worshipful Scottish Apprentice (4th degree), Very Worthy Fellow of St Andrew (5th degree), and Illustrious Scottish Master of St Andrew (6th degree). The 4th and 5th degrees are usually conferred on the same evening, while the 6th is conferred separately.

A mason having achieved the 6th degree can then in due course proceed to the third division of degrees. There are four degrees in this division, and they are conferred in the Grand Lodge itself, or more normally in Provincial Grand Lodges (usually called Stewart Lodges, or Chapters). The degrees are: Stewart Brother (7th degree), Most Illustrious Confidant of Solomon (8th degree), Enlightened Confidant of St John (9th degree), and finally, Very Enlightened Confidant of St Andrew, or Knight of the Purple Ribbon (10th degree). The 7th degree (Stewart Brother) is basically only a short introductory degree to the Chapter.

Finally, at the pinnacle of the system is the Order of King Charles XIII. This forms the highest degree—the 11th degree—called Knights Commander of the Red Cross. This Order is totally unique in freemasonry, as not only is it a masonic rite, but it is also a Civil Order awarded by the King of Sweden (who is always either Grand Master, or Royal Protector of the Order), and its members are expected to wear its insignia in public. Only about thirty Swedish masons hold this degree, including all members of the Grand Master's Supreme Council.

There are quite a number of procedural differences between the Swedish Rite and those of other masonic systems. In the Swedish Rite, there is only one form of ritual for each of the degrees, and any deviations will not be tolerated. The Master of the lodge has, in each degree, an official manuscript before him (rituals, as such, cannot be printed), and he must personally check in every detail the work of himself and his officers. In order to further ensure the strict uniformity of the work, the Master of each lodge is a permanent appointment until his death or resignation. Before any mason can be considered for the Mastership of a St John's Lodge, he must hold the 10th degree. The other officers of Swedish lodges (including up to four Deputy Masters, and the two Wardens) are elected annually, but usually serve at least three year terms. Each lodge officer has several deputies, and these share the ritual work. This is a necessary precaution as up to the 6th degree lodges meet weekly (except when in recess). Lodge officers generally wear formal dress (as opposed to a dark suit for members); and the Master, Wardens, and Master of Ceremonies wear a top hat in addition. The Wardens, as in old operative practice, are both seated in the West.

Another unique feature of Scandinavian freemasonry is the Brodraforeninger (Brother Societies), or more literally—Fraternal Clubs, although they are quite formally structured. They are sometimes formed in population centres where St John's Lodges exist, but it is when they come to be erected in smaller towns that they serve a particularly valuable function. In these smaller population centres—too small to support a lodge—they serve as lodges of instruction. Of course, they form the same function in the larger centres where they exist. The Fraternals have a prescribed ritual, and elected officers. They hold lectures, and instruct in the workings of the Swedish Rite, but they do not normally have the function of actual degree conferment. Of course, members of Fraternals must be members of a St John's Lodge as well.

The Swedish Rite, as now outlined, is worked in Norway, Denmark, Iceland, and to some extent in Finland, as well as in Sweden itself. In all these masonic jurisdictions, save the difference of language, the workings and forms of the Rite are virtually identical. All the eleven degrees are worked in full, and progress from one degree to the next is slow, being far from automatic. Regular attendance, and a high proficiency are needed before any brother can advance. Indeed, many years are required before a mason under the Swedish Rite reaches the highest degrees.

Each 'division of degrees' under the Swedish Rite enjoys a certain amount of autonomy, but they are all nevertheless under the rule of the Grand Master and his Supreme Council. The current system appeared in Sweden in its final form about 1810, when the Chapter degrees were fixed in the system. In 1811, the 11th degree was added to complete the rite. As mentioned earlier, the conferment of the 11th degree in Sweden is the prerogative of the King; but in the other Swedish Rite Scandinavian jurisdictions, the Supreme Council decides upon preferment. It should be noted that in all Scandinavian countries, except in Finland under the Grand Lodge of Finland, freemasonry is completely Christian, and candidates must profess the Christian Faith to gain admission. In Sweden, there is a certain amount of truth in saying that the Craft is largely a 'subsidiary of the Swedish Crown'.

The Royal connection with the Swedish Craft began in 1770 when King Gustavus III, and his two brothers, Duke Charles (afterwards King Charles XIII), and Duke Frederick Adolphus, were initiated. The Grand Lodge of Sweden (Den Svenska Stora Landslogen) had been formed in 1760. Duke Charles soon appears to have become Grand Master, and in 1774 he formed a new St Andrew's Lodge, whereupon the Swedish Rite was basically formed into the system that is worked to this day. Duke Charles remained as Grand Master after he ascended the throne as King Charles XIII, and until recently, all successive Swedish Kings have been Grand Masters. The current Swedish King, Charles XVI Gustavus, is High Protector of the Order; while his uncle Prince Bertil, the Duke of Halland, is Grand Master.

Notes for Visitors to Sweden

Visitors wishing to attend a Swedish lodge should, in the first instance, call at the Masonic Temple in Stockholm. The giant Masonic Temple building in Stockholm is probably the most magnificent masonic structure in the world. It was built originally as a Palace, and was later given over to the Craft. Dating from 1660, it is a three-storey structure, with two wings, thus forming a 'U' shape. It houses administrative offices, the Grand Temple, various other Temples, a library and a museum. A wrought iron fence with iron gates extends from one wing to the other across its frontage. The inside is that of magnificent opulence, featuring great frescoes, black marble columns, and ornate decorations. A tour of the Baat Palace must form the highlight of any mason's visit to Stockholm, and this can be arranged at the Grand Lodge office.

As the Swedish Rite system is largely quite different to the forms of English-speaking masonry, intervisitation arrangements are unusual and must be discussed at some length. Obviously, there is no problem for a regular Craft mason visiting a St John's Lodge, which likewise works the three Craft degrees, albeit in a Continental-type form. However, as with Continental masonry generally, some small reversals in the ritual content of the Entered Apprentice and the Fellow Craft degrees restricts intervisitation, in terms of English-speaking masons, to those holding the Master Mason degree. In short, there is no problem in a regular Master Mason turning up unannounced at a Scandinavian St John's Lodge and seeking admission. Of course, the usual formalities as discussed near the beginning of this guide are applicable.

Upon moving into the area of a St Andrew's Lodge, the visitation situation becomes a little bit more complicated, but not much. It was agreed in the late 1950s in an informal concordant between England and Sweden that English Royal Arch masons could visit St Andrew's Lodges in Sweden and that Swedish masons holding the 6th degree could visit English Royal Arch Chapters. It must be added that the usual documentary evidence must be presented either way, as the ceremonies and modes of recognition are dissimilar in each system. As a further result, qualified masons visiting from either system to the other may be required to take an obligation of secrecy. In short, again, provided the forms just discussed are observed, a qualified mason (ie a holder of the Royal Arch Degree) will encounter no difficulty in visiting in Scandinavia up to the 6th degree.

However, when we enter the realms of the Chapter degrees of the Swedish Rite, the ground becomes less certain. There does exist a loose and tacit arrangement between the English Great Priory (Knights Templar), and the English Supreme Council (Ancient and Accepted Rite) with the Grand Lodge of Sweden concerning intervisitation with the Swedish Chapter degrees. While there are certain philosophical links between the 8th and 9th degrees of the Swedish Rite and the degrees of the Great Priory (Knight Templar and Knights of Malta), the forms of each 'side' are not close enough to allow intervisitation as a general rule. Similarly, there are problems associated with the Ancient and Accepted (Scottish) Rite. However, when the English Supreme Council considers admitting Swedish masons to its Rose Croix Chapters and those of its higher degrees, it is guided by the following comparisons. The 18th (Rose Croix) degree is seen as equivalent to the 8th degree of the Swedish Rite; the 30th degree as the equivalent of the 9th Swedish degree; the 32nd degree as equivalent to the 10th Swedish degree; and finally the 33rd degree as equivalent to the 11th Swedish degree.

It must be strongly emphasised that these comparisons are only a rough guide. Knights Templar and Rose Croix masons cannot simply arrive at the Grand Lodge of Sweden and expect admission as a visitor to its Chapters. Masons from either jurisdiction who are properly qualified, and who have a genuine interest in such a visit, must seek approval through their own Great Priory or Supreme Council *well in advance* of the intended visit. Permission must be obtained from both sides and it is certainly not automatic. Each individual case is treated on its merits. Qualified masons *must not under any circumstances* directly approach the Grand Lodge of Sweden concerning visiting Swedish Chapters, but must make all inquiries through their own appropriate Grand Body.

It can now be noted that the Supreme Councils (Scottish Rite) of Scotland, Ireland, Canada, and the United States (Southern and Northern Jurisdictions) exchange recognition with the Grand Lodge of Sweden. These are the only bodies of this nature outside Scandinavia with which the Swedish Grand Lodge deals. Therefore, qualified masons under these allegiances are probably in a position to visit Swedish Chapters, but doubtless on the same terms as just discussed concerning the English bodies. It is useful to add further that, as a rule, all the Scandinavian Grand Lodges working the Swedish Rite act in concert on matters of intervisitation, and so all the procedures just detailed are to be observed by qualified masons seeking to visit Chapters of the Swedish Rite in Norway, Denmark, or Iceland.

Sweden currently possesses 39 St John's Lodges (Craft), of which two work in Stockholm, and four in Finland (see under Finland). There are twenty St Andrew's Lodges, and eight Provincial Grand Lodges (Chapters) which have administrative, as well as Degree Conferment, functions. There are also about 60 Brodraforeninger (Brother Societies), the function of which has already been discussed. Many Swedish lodges have very large memberships, with one St John's Lodge in Stockholm having in excess of 500 members. The Swedish Grand Lodge, unusually for one that is widely recognised, is governed by a Supreme Council, consisting of the Grand Master and eighteen members. Doubtless, the unique character of the Swedish masonic system accounts for its governmental practices.

The dress for Swedish lodges is a dark or black suit, white shirt, black or grey tie, and black shoes. The vast majority of lodge meetings start at 6.30 pm punctually. A charity collection does take place during lodge meetings. Dinner always follows a lodge meeting, and a nominal charge is payable by all attending (and this will normally include visitors). There is not, however, any formal toast list, but informal speeches may be made under the direction of the Master of Ceremonies. Visitors may be called upon to speak. Those wishing to dine with a lodge after a meeting should give the Grand Lodge as much notice as possible.

Swedish regalia consists of a sash, variously inscribed, to denote the rank and degree held by its wearer. Regalia is available for loan to visitors, but visitors are most welcome to carry and wear their own. All lodges, of course, work in Swedish, but English is widely spoken or at least understood by a large number of Swedish freemasons. Language problems, therefore, will be slight.

DENMARK

The National Grand Lodge of Denmark
Founded: 1792

Address: Masonic Temple, Blegdamsvej 23, Copenhagen, Denmark. DK 2100.
Lodges: 56 St John's Lodges (Craft). Permits Dual and Plural Membership.
Membership: 20,000.
Descent: England and Germany.   *Government:* Swedish form.
Courtesy Degrees: rarely conferred.   *Ritual:* Swedish Rite.
Minimum Time Lapse between Degrees: 12 months.
Major Publications: Book of Constitutions. Annual Handbook (List of Lodges, etc.)

History

The first lodge in Denmark was St Martin Lodge, established by a German Baron at Copenhagen in 1743. In 1749, it was regularised with the granting of a warrant from England. Other lodges followed gaining warrants from England and Germany. About 1850, an English Provincial Grand Lodge was set up, but the State of the Danish Craft remained confused with lodges working under several different authorities.

This situation was stabilised in 1792, when freemasonry was recognised by the Danish Crown, provided that the ruling Prince of the country was its Grand Master. This promptly occurred and Prince Karl became head of the Danish Craft. This practice continued until 1950, with either the King, or a Royal Prince, as Grand

Master. Even today, the Danish King remains Protector of the Craft, in identical fashion to current Swedish practice.

There had for some time been an irregular Grand Lodge in Denmark, calling itself the Grand Orient of Denmark. Of very obscure origin, it worked under a Supreme Council 33rd Degree system. This body appears to have merged with the National Grand Lodge of Denmark in 1960, but a small section of it has evidently stood out until this day under an irregular Grand Body.

The accession of the Danish Royal Family to the progressive Grand Mastership of Denmark also brought with it the introduction of the Swedish Rite. The Swedish system was made mandatory for all Danish lodges in 1855, and the forms of Danish masonry today are very similar to those of Sweden and Norway.

Notes for Visitors to Denmark
The Grand Lodge building in Copenhagen is quite an imposing structure, containing both a library and a museum. Visitors to Denmark should, at least initially, make themselves known at the Grand Temple in Copenhagen. The details concerning lodge visitation in Denmark are similar to those of Sweden and Norway. Dress is a black or dark suit, and visitors are welcome to wear their own regalia. Lodges meet in the early evening, followed by a meal, at which visitors and members will be charged a small dining fee. A number of speeches are made, and visitors are sometimes called upon to speak.

It is interesting to note that, in common with most Scandinavian countries, members must profess the Christian faith. Masters of St John's Lodges in Denmark are elected for life, but rarely serve that long, as they usually gain promotion to office in the higher degrees, whereupon they must resign their St John's Mastership. New Masters are elected by the lodge from a list of three senior brethren recommended to the lodge by the Grand Master.

FINLAND

The Grand Lodge of Finland
Founded: 1924
Address: Masonic Temple, Kasarmikatu 16D, 00130 Helsinki 13.
Lodges: 93   Permits Dual Membership in special cases.
Membership: 4,100.
Descent: Sweden, and New York.   *Government:* Elective Grand Lodge.
Courtesy Degrees: Correspondence must be through Grand Lodges.
Ritual: Webb-form, Swedish.
Minimum Time Lapse between Degrees: One month.
Major Publications: Constitutions. Proceedings. Periodical: *Koilliskulma* (North East Corner).

History
In the early eighteenth century Finland was part of Sweden, so it is not surprising that the first masonic activity in the country stemmed from Sweden. The year 1756 saw the first Swedish lodge erected in Finland, and two others followed. The Russo-Swedish War of 1808-9 saw Finland fall under Russian control, whereupon free-masonry was progressively suppressed. In 1848, the Russian Czar decreed against

all secret organisations, and freemasonry ceased to exist in Finland until after independence in 1917.

In 1922, eight Finnish citizens who were masons in the United States of America returned to Helsinki and petitioned the Grand Lodge of New York for a Charter. This was duly granted, and Suomi Lodge No 1 was consecrated. Some of the earliest members of the masonic revival in Finland were men of high distinction in government and the Arts, and included the famous Finnish composer, Jean Sibelius. This new lodge grew in strength, and by 1923, two more lodges had been chartered. The Grand Lodge of Finland was then constituted by the Grand Lodge of New York in 1924. Thereafter, membership and the number of lodges expanded rapidly.

However, the Finnish Craft came under great pressure in the 1930s. In line with the tide of anti-masonic feelings flooding Germany, anti-masonry arose in Finland. It stemmed from various right-wing political groups, and also from the Lutheran Church. Fortunately, these oppositions did not find general currency amongst the Finns, and the Craft survived without too much trouble. The Second World War brought a renewal of pressure on the Craft, and the political situation became such that the work of the Craft was suspended by the Grand Lodge. From 1945 onwards, the Craft in Finland has grown with great rapidity. It now possesses 93 lodges, and over 4,000 members.

In recent years, the Royal Arch degree, the Mark Master Mason degree, and the Ancient and Accepted Rite have been introduced into Finland, all from England. There are now several lodges of each Order in Finland under Finnish Grand bodies, working the various Engish rituals in the Finnish language. The Finnish Grand Chapter was erected in 1961, and the Finnish Mark Grand Lodge in the 1970s. Naturally, these bodies maintain the warmest ties with the comparable British Grand bodies.

It now remains only to recount the development of Swedish masonry in Finland. One-tenth of the population of Finland is Swedish speaking, and naturally their affinities are Swedish in nature. So it is with their masonry. The Swedish lodges in Finland were basically erected beginning in 1923 with the St Augustin Lodge (a St John's Lodge), and several more were subsequently established under Swedish Warrant. The Swedish lodges suffered the same unsettled history until after the Second World War as did the Finnish lodges. In 1983, there was one Swedish Provincial Grand Lodge (Chapter), four St John's Lodges, and one St Andrew's Lodge operating in Finland under allegiance to Stockholm. Needless to say, the friendliest relations exist between the Swedish and Finnish Grand Lodges, and their respective constituent lodges in Finland.

Notes for Visitors to Finland

Of the 93 Finnish lodges, over 25 work in Helsinki, while every other Finnish population centre of any size possesses at least one lodge. The ritual used in the Craft lodges is basically that of the Grand Lodge of New York, translated into Finnish. Thus, the Grand Lodge of Finland tends to be fairly American in nature. As is normal with Webb ritual forms, Finnish lodges open in the 3rd degree, and only revert to the 1st or 2nd degrees when actually conferring them. Again, as with usual American practice, the Finnish jurisdiction is divided into Districts (currently eight), each with a District Deputy Grand Master.

The Grand Temple building at Kasarmikatu Street in Helsinki was purchased in

1965, as the previous building had become too small. The new building was renovated to include several temples and administrative areas in its three-storey structure. Finland also possesses a fine lodge of research (Research Lodge Minerva No 27) which meets in various parts of the country.

All Finnish lodges meet in the early evening, and dress is a dark suit, or a black suit. American-style regalia is used for the Craft degrees, but visitors are welcome to wear their own. In the first instance, visitors should attend the temple in Helsinki, where the Grand Lodge office will be only too happy to arrange a visit to a Finnish lodge.

ICELAND

The National Grand Lodge of Iceland
Founded: 1951
Address: Masonic Temple, Skulagata 55, Reykjavik, Iceland.
Lodges: 9 (Craft).   Permits Dual and Plural Membership.
Membership: 2,079.
Descent: Denmark.   *Government:* Swedish form.
Courtesy Degrees: rarely conferred.   *Ritual:* Swedish Rite.
Minimum Time Lapse between Degrees: 12 months.
Major Publications: Constitutions.

History
Icelandic masonic history is short. The first Craft lodge was erected in the country in 1919 under warrant from the National Grand Lodge of Denmark. Iceland gained political independence from Denmark in 1944; and in 1951, Denmark constituted the new Iceland Grand Lodge. The first Grand Master was the first President of Iceland, Brother Sveinn Bjornsson. At the time of the formation of the Grand Lodge there were two St John's Lodges, two St Andrew's Lodges, and one Chapter working in the country. Today, the number of St John's Lodges has expanded to nine, and one extra Chapter has been formed, although there still remain only the original two St Andrew's Lodges.

Notes for Visitors to Iceland
Of the nine St John's Lodges in Iceland, four work at Reykjavik, while the balance meet at other population centres. Reykjavik possesses one of Iceland's two St Andrew's Lodges, while Akureyri has the other. Similarly, these two centres share the two Chapters between them. Iceland adheres completely to the Swedish Rite system, and its forms and rituals are virtually identical to those of Denmark, Norway and Sweden; aside from the fact that its lodges work in Icelandic. Visiting freemasons will still find a number of English-speaking members when attending a lodge meeting, and so will have no trouble as a result of language.

As is usual with Scandinavian lodges, dress is a dark or black suit. Lodges meet in the early evening, followed by a dinner and informal toasts. Again, as is usual Scandinavian custom, visitors are not normally exempt from paying for their meal. Visitors to Iceland should make themselves known at the Masonic Temple in Reykjavik prior to visiting, whereupon they will receive every assistance. Iceland has evidently suffered several public attacks upon the Craft in years gone by, and the National Grand Lodge of Iceland tends to be somewhat more introspective than most others. While it is useful for the visitor to be aware of this, it will nonetheless not affect in any way the regular mason wishing to visit an Icelandic Craft lodge. As with the rest of Scandinavia, Icelandic lodges recess between May and August (inclusive), but during the months of September to April, St John's Lodges meet weekly.

NORWAY

The Grand Lodge of Norway
Founded: 1891
Address: Masonic Temple, Nedre Vollgate 19, Oslo 1, Norway.
Telephone: 336566
Lodges: 35 (Craft).   Permits Dual and Plural Membership.
Membership: 15,916
Descent: England, Sweden and Germany.   *Government:* Swedish form.
Courtesy Degrees: rarely conferred.   *Ritual:* Swedish Rite.
Minimum Time Lapse between Degrees: 12 months.
Major Publications: Book of Constitutions.   *Matrikkel* (List of Lodges, etc)

History
Norway was a possession of Denmark until 1814, when it was ceded to Sweden, which in turn granted it political independence in 1905. The first Norwegian lodge was erected in 1749, under an English warrant. The English warranted lodges existing in 1814 upon the Swedish takeover were united with the Grand Lodge of Sweden, which formed a new Provincial Grand Lodge in Norway working the Swedish Rite.

In 1882, a lodge was established in Norway by the Grand Lodge Zur Sonne, of Bayreuth, Germany; and several more lodges were subsequently established by the same authority. In 1891, the Grand Lodge of Norway was formed out of the current Swedish Provincial Grand Lodge. In 1920, the German warranted lodges formed their own Grand Lodge with four constituent lodges under it. The German body united with the Grand Lodge of Norway in 1947, and since that date only one Grand Lodge has existed in the country.

Notes for Visitors to Norway
Norwegian freemasonry is quite similar to its Swedish counterpart. In structure, the only real difference is that the King of Norway is not the hereditary Grand Master, although a Norwegian Grand Master is usually elected for life. Norway works the Swedish Rite of Eleven degrees, with St John's Lodges, St Andrew's Lodges, and Stewart Chapters for the highest degrees. The rituals, likewise, are very similar to the Swedish.

The Grand Temple in Oslo is probably second only to the one in Stockholm for its imposing beauty. It is one of Oslo's showpieces, bordering a large park in the centre of the city. Built originally in the early 1890s, the Temple was damaged and looted during the Nazi occupation, but it was completely restored after the War. It remains richly decorated, and contains an excellent library and a museum.

A visitor wishing to attend a Norwegian lodge should make himself known at the Grand Temple in Oslo, whereupon he will receive a warm welcome and full assistance. The details for visiting in Norway are similar to those for Sweden. Dress is a black or dark suit, and white gloves are also worn. A festive board is held after meetings. Meetings themselves start at about 6.30 pm to 7 pm. As with the rest of Scandinavia, except Finland, there is a charge for the meal which varies from 40 Kroner to 100 Kroner. Toasts are certainly part of the proceedings. The Master will toast all brethren, often degree by degree. Entered Apprentices will be welcomed with a short speech, often explaining some of the ritual experienced. This also often occurs when a brother is advanced to a higher degree. Speeches are replied to very briefly. Visitors, especially those from outside Norway, can expect to be toasted individually, and a short response is welcomed. Again, visitors must note that, as with all Scandinavian Grand Lodges, masonry goes into recess during May, June, July, and August. The Grand Temple works with a skeleton staff in this period, and is completely closed during July. Of course, during the active months, lodges meet weekly.

Oslo itself possesses seven St John's Lodges, and two St Andrew's Lodges. Lodges of instruction (currently about a dozen), with memberships as yet too small to charter a St John's Lodge, are found in some outlying areas. There are currently four St Andrew's lodges of instruction, formed on the same basis. In addition, there are also three Deputy Craft Lodges. These are branches of a regular St John's Lodge, attached to the Craft Lodge and operating in another place with special permission. The Norwegian practice in this regard is analogous to the American practice of creating lodges Under Dispensation.

Section XI

Visiting in
South America

South America

An Overview
It may surprise some to learn that not only does the Craft exist in South America, but that it is to be found in every country of the continent. As in Europe, the development of the Craft in Latin America has been greatly effected by political history. It has often faced repression, or at least opposition, but it has nevertheless survived and developed. Yet, this development has not been without discord, and the South American Craft remains somewhat discordant to this day. How this has occurred, and how it will affect the masonic visitor, will be examined shortly. In terms of an overview, the main point to note is that Latin masonry often tends to be more secretive than in most other places in the masonic world, although perhaps not quite as exclusive as that in Europe. Regardless, it will be readily seen that provided the correct approaches are undertaken, the travelling freemason will receive a most warm and hospitable welcome in his sojourn amongst his Latin brothers.

ARGENTINA

Argentina possesses one of the strongest indigenous Grand Lodges in South America, as well as English District Grand Lodge comprising twenty-two lodges.

The Grand Lodge of Free and Accepted Masons of Argentina
Founded: 1857
Address: Masonic Temple, Cangallo 1242, Buenos Aires, Argentina.
Telephone: 35 2585.
Lodges: 75   Permits Dual Membership.
Membership: 7,150.
Descent: Uruguay, England.   *Government:* Modified Grand Orient.
Courtesy Degrees: rarely conferred.   *Ritual:* large Scottish (Craft) Rite.
Minimum Time Lapse between Degrees: generally 12 months.
Main Publications: Constitutions. Annual Proceedings.

History
The first lodge in Argentina was formed in 1795, under the Grand Orient of France. The first English lodges were established in 1806, and Pennsylvania warranted a lodge in 1825. However, survival was short, with all lodges being suppressed by the Government in 1846.

By 1853, the United Grand Lodge of England had managed to charter Excelsior Lodge No 617; and several of the earlier Spanish-speaking lodges were revived about this time. In 1857, six lodges holding warrants from the Grand Lodge of Uruguay formed a sovereign Grand Lodge. At this stage a Supreme Council was erected, also sponsored from Uruguay. In 1935, another Scottish Rite Supreme Council was formed, called Federal Argentino. This body claimed control over the Craft degrees, and developed Craft lodges.

In 1860, the United Grand Lodge of England entered into a Treaty of Amity with the Grand Lodge of Argentina, similar to the one promulgated with the Grand

Orient of Brazil. In return for perpetual English recognition, Argentina gave England the right to warrant and maintain English-speaking lodges in its jurisdiction. In 1957, the Grand Lodge of Argentina merged with the Federal Argentino Supreme Council, thus forming one Sovereign Grand Lodge for the whole country.

Notes for Visitors to Argentina

Argentinian lodges appear to use a variety of rituals, with both Scottish and York Rite represented, although the former greatly dominates. While most Argentinian lodges work in Spanish, there are four that work in German, while a few work in Italian. Argentine lodges largely meet twice monthly, while English lodges meet once per month. English-speaking lodges generally convene about 7 pm to 7.30 pm, while Spanish-speaking lodges more commonly meet at about 8 pm. English lodges prefer to dine after a meeting. The practice of dining is less prevalent in Argentinian lodges. Dress for all lodges in Argentina is a dark lounge suit, and it is appreciated for visitors to carry their own regalia. As English-speaking visitors will probably be attracted to English-speaking lodges, at least for an initial visit, those working in Buenos Aires are listed below.

All English lodges in Argentina come under the District Grand Lodge of South America–Southern Division (English Constitution), and meet at its main Masonic Hall, located at Calle Cochabamba 223, Buenos Aires, unless otherwise stated.

Excelsior Lodge No 617	Meets 3rd Thursday April to November. Inst: June.
Lodge Star of the South No 1025	Meets 1st Monday April to November. Inst: June.
Victoria Lodge No 2393	Meets 2nd Thursday April to November. Inst: May.
Trevor Mold Lodge No 3293	Meets 3rd Friday in April, July and October. Inst: July.
Campana Lodge No 3364	Meets 1st Wednesday April to November. Inst: July.
Belgrano Lodge No 3466	Meets at the Smith Memorial Hall, 2224 Conesa Belgrano; 4th Tuesday March to November (except June). Inst: May.
Santa Rosa Lodge No 3579	Meets 4th Thursday April to November. Inst: August.
St George's Lodge No 3641	Meets 2nd Monday April to November. Inst: July.
St Andrew's Lodge No 3706	Meets 4th Wednesday March to October. Inst: April.
Victory Lodge No 3926	Meets at the Anglican Church Hall, Calle Lacar 4232, Villa Devoto: 1st Friday April to November. Inst: May.
St David's Lodge No 3952	Meets 2nd Wednesday April to November. Inst: June.
Pampa Lodge No 4075	Meets 4th Friday April to October (except May, then 3rd Friday). Inst: July.
St Patrick's Lodge No 4210	Meets 1st Thursday April to December. Inst: April.
Old Georgian Lodge No 5014	Meets 2nd Friday April to November. Isnt: September.

Eight other English lodges meet in Argentina outside Buenos Aires. Two meet in Acassuso, two in Lomas de Zamora, and one each in Mendoza, Quilmes, Rosario, and Sierras de Cordoba.

BOLIVIA

Unlike many Latin American countries, Bolivia does not possess lodges warranted by foreign Grand Lodges. However, it does possess an active regular Grand Lodge, with one of its constituent lodges working in the English language.

The Grand Lodge of Bolivia
Founded: 1929
Address: Masonic Hall, Calle Obispo Cardenas 1480, La Paz. *Telephone:* 29840.
   Postal Address: Casilla Postal 564, La Paz, Bolivia.
Lodges: 28   Permits Dual and Plural Membership.
Membership: Circa 1,500.
Descent: Chile. *Government:* Modified Grand Orient.
Courtesy Degrees: rarely conferred, or requested.
Ritual: Scottish (Craft) Rite, York Rite.
Minimum Time Lapse between Degrees: generally 12 months.
Main Publications: Constitution. Annual Proceedings.

History
Bolivia is named after Simon Bolivar, the Liberator of northern South America, and himself a noted freemason. While, traditionally, the Craft was supposed to have come to Bolivia in 1875, no positive proof of an extant lodge prior to 1928 appears to be available. Nonetheless, the Craft must have been established in some form prior to that date, as the Grand Lodge of Bolivia was sponsored by the Grand Lodge of Chile in late 1929, using seven Chilean lodges. The apparent lack of early masonic history can possibly be put down to the turbulent politics of the area well into this century.

Notes for Visitors to Bolivia
Of Bolivia's 28 lodges, eleven work in the Bolivian capital city of La Paz, while the remaining seventeen operate at provincial locations. All lodges work the Scottish Rite (Craft) ritual in Spanish, with the exception of three lodges which use the York Rite. In Bolivia's case the York Rite ritual used is the English *Emulation* working. Two of these three lodges work it in Spanish translation, while one lodge (Anglo-Bolivian Lodge No 7) uses the English language. Anglo-Bolivian lodge meets at the Masonic Hall in La Paz on the 2nd Monday, monthly, at 7 pm. All other Bolivian lodges appear to meet weekly, with starting times varying between 7 pm and 8.30 pm. Dress for all Bolivian lodges is a dark suit, and Bolivian regalia is not overly dissimilar to English regalia, although a sash is often added. Visitors are welcome to wear their own regalia.
   The Grand Lodge meets twice per year at the temple in La Paz, which has the distinction of possessing the highest masonic building in the world in terms of geographical elevation, at 11,600 feet above sea level. A new Masonic Hall is currently being built at the same site in La Paz, and it is scheduled for completion in 1984.
   The meeting places of the various Bolivian lodges are as follows:

La Paz:	Masonic Hall, Calle Obispo Cardenas 1480, La Paz.
Sucre:	Masonic Temple, Calle SanAlberto, Sucre.
Potosi:	Masonic Temple, Calle Matos 111, Potosi.
Santa Cruz:	Masonic Temple, Calle Ayacucho 431, Santa Cruz.
Cochabamba:	Masonic Temple, Calle Ayacucho 5924, Cochabamba.
Oruro:	Masonic Temple, Calle Ayacucho 754, Oruro.
Cobija:	Masonic Temple, Calle Racua, Cobija.
Tarija:	Masonic Temple, Calle 15 de Abril.

BRAZIL

The Craft in Brazil represents something of a problem. The oldest and largest Grand body in Brazil is the Grand Orient of Brazil. However, in addition, there are 22 Grand Lodges based on the boundaries of the Brazilian States. The State Grand Lodges are as follows:

Grand Lodge of Acre—founded in 1973, at Rio Branco, Acre.
Grand Lodge of Amazonas—founded in 1927, at Manaus, Amazonas.
Grand Lodge of Alagoas—founded in 1958, at Maceio, Alagoas.
Grande Loja Unita of Bahia—founded in 1927, at Salvador, Bahia.
Grand Lodge of Brasilia—founded in 1963, at Brasilia, Federal District.
Grand Lodge of Ceara—founded in 1928, at Fortaleza, Ceara.
Grand Lodge of Espirito Santo—founded in 1970, at Vitoria, Espirito Santo.
Grand Lodge of Goias—founded in 1951, at Goiania, Goias.
Grand Lodge of Guanabara—founded in 1927, at Rio de Janeiro, Guanabara.
Grand Lodge of Maranhao—founded in 1973, at Codo, Maranhao.
Grand Lodge of Mato Grosso do Sul—founded in 1962, at Campo Grande, Mato Grosso.
Grand Lodge of Minas Gerais—founded in 1927, at Belo Horizonte, Minas Gerais.
Grand Lodge of Para—founded in 1927, at Belem, Para.
Grand Lodge of Paraiba—founded in 1927, at Joao Pessoa, Paraiba.
Grand Lodge of Parana—founded in 1941, at Curitiba, Parana.
Grand Lodge of Pernambuco—founded in 1932, at Recife, Pernambuco.
Grand Lodge of Piaui—founded in 1948, at Teresina, Piaui.
Grand Lodge of Rio de Janeiro—founded in 1944, at Niteroi, Rio de Janeiro.
Grand Lodge of Rio Grande de Norte—founded in 1974, at Natal, Rio Grande do Norte.
Grand Lodge of Rio Grande do Sul—founded in 1928, at Port Alegre, Rio Grande do Sul.
Grand Lodge of Santa Catarina—founded in 1956, at Florianopolis, Santa Catarina.
Grand Lodge of the State of Sao Paulo—founded in 1927, at Sao Paulo, Sao Paulo State.

The problem is that the State Grand Lodges (which largely recognise each other) and the Grand Orient of Brazil are not in mutual accord. Outside of Brazil, the situation is that most of the United States and Canadian Grand Lodges tend to recognise an assortment of the State Grand Lodges but not the Grant Orient; whereas the English, Irish and Scottish Grand Lodges, together with most other Grand Lodges, recognise the Grand Orient but not the State Grand Lodges. Thus, it depends entirely upon which Grand Lodge a visitor comes from, as to what Brazilian lodges he may legally visit.

In addition to these complications, there are several lodges in Brazil holding warrants from the United Grand Lodge of England. As the parameters of this guide are set on the recognitions of the three British Grand Lodges; it is the Grand Orient of Brazil and the English-warranted lodges upon which discussion here must necessarily centre.

The Grand Orient of Brazil
Founded: 1822

Address: Masonic Hall, Rua do Lavradio 97, Rio de Janeiro. *Telephone:* 222 3102.

Postal Address: Caixa Postal 510, Rio de Janeiro, Brazil.

Lodges: 563   Permits Dual and Plural Membership.

Membership: Circa 64,000.

Descent: France.   *Government:* Modified Grand Oriennt.

Courtesy Degrees: rarely conferred.   *Ritual:* Scottish (Craft) Rite.

Minimum Time Lapse between Degrees: 12 months.

Main Publications. Annual Proceedings. Constitution.

The District Grand Lodge of South America-Northern District (English Constitution)
Founded: 1935

Address: Masonic Temple, Rua de Matriz 76, Rio de Janeiro.

Lodges: 11

History
While tradition has it that there were Brazilian lodges as early as 1797, the first recorded lodge was the Commerce and Arts Lodge, warranted by the Grand Orient of France in 1815. By 1822, three French lodges had formed the Grand Orient of Brazil under the patronage of Dom Pedro, the Brazilian Emperor. However, shortly afterwards the Emperor closed these Lodges because he considered them political. After the Emperor's abdication in 1831, the Grand Orient was revived, although a schism soon split it into discordant factions. At this time there were also masonic incursions from the Supreme Council of Belgium, which greatly aided the disunity of the Brazilian Craft. The schismatic nature of Brazilian masonry continued until 1883, whereupon Craft lodges largely united under the Grand Orient, following sustained attacks from the Roman Catholic Church.

The Brazilian Craft remained relatively united until the 1920s, whereupon a serious dispute arose within the Grand Orient concerning the control of the Craft degrees by the Grand Orient's Supreme Council. By 1927, many lodges had seceded from the Grand Orient to form the various State Grand Lodges. This breach has never been healed.

The United Grand Lodge of England maintains a District Grand Lodge in Brazil, with eleven constituent lodges. Ten of these lodges were originally warranted by the Grand Orient of Brazil, the earliest in 1891. The English Grand Lodge was the first to recognise the Grand Orient, and in 1935 these two Grand Bodies signed a Treaty of Fraternal Alliance, whereby England recognised the Grand Orient as the sole masonic power in Brazil. In return, England was given the right to maintain English lodges in the country. In practice, this treaty meant that the ten English-speaking lodges under the Grand Orient could transfer their allegience to London, which they did. Indeed, this is the only occasion that a group of lodges have transferred to the United Grand Lodge of England from another Grand body in this manner.

Notes for Visitors to Brazil

While the Grand Orient has lodges in many corners of Brazil, the largest concentration of lodges is in Rio de Janeiro and Sao Paulo, Brazil's two largest cities. The two relevant masonic buildings are: 97 Rua Lavradio, Rio de Janeiro; and 1120 Rua Lisboa, Sao Paulo.

Dress for all Brazilian lodges is a dark business suit, and visitors are welcome to wear their own regalia. Most lodges in Brazil tend to recess in at least the months of January, February and March. Grand Orient lodges mostly convene twice monthly, while the English lodges largely meet on a monthly basis. The early evening provides the commencement time for most lodges, with English lodges opening at around 7.30 pm, while some Grand Orient lodges start as late as 8.30 pm. Dinner is sometimes taken in association with meetings, but visitors are never expected to contribute. With few exceptions, Grand Orient lodges work in the Portuguese language. There are currently three that use the German language, namely Concordia et Humanitas No 1745, and Zur Eintracht No 551 (both at Rio de Janeiro), and Humanitas No 1419 (at Sao Paulo). The details of the eleven English lodges are as follows:

RIO DE JANEIRO

Eureka Lodge No 5557	Meets Masonic Temple, 76 Rua de Matriz; 2nd Thursday May to November. Inst: 2nd Saturday, April.
Duke of Clarence Lodge No 5558	Meets Masonic Temple, 76 Rua de Matriz; 2nd Thursday March; 3rd Thursday July; and 2nd Monday October. Inst: 3rd Saturday, June.
Friendship Lodge No 5563	Meets at 37 Rua Coronel Miranda, Santos; 3rd Thursday March, May, September, November. Inst: 3rd Saturday, July.
Royal Edward Lodge No 5566	Meets Masonic Temple, 76 Rua de Matriz; 1st Thursday March to November. Inst: 1st Saturday, August.
Lodge of Wanderers No 5562	Meets at 73 Rua 7 de Setembro, Santos; 2nd Wednesday April to November. Inst: 3rd Saturday, July.

SAO PAULO

Lodge of Unity No 5560	Meets Masonic Temple, 1120 Rua Lisboa; 3rd Monday February to November. Inst: 2nd Saturday, October.
St George Lodge No 5561	Meets Masonic Temple, 1120 Rua Lisboa; 2nd Thursday February to November. Inst: 1st Saturday, June.
Centenary Lodge No 5564	Meets Masonic Temple, 1120 Rua Lisboa; 1st Monday April to December. Inst: 2nd Saturday, September.

Campos Salles Lodge No 5565	Meets Masonic Temple, 1120 Rua Lisboa; 2nd Monday February to November. Inst: 1st Saturday, April.
Santo Amaro Lodge No 7250	Meets Masonic Temple, 1120 Rua Lisboa; 4th Monday February to November. Inst: 3rd Saturday, August.

BELO HORIZONTE

Morro Velho Lodge No 5559	Meets at Masonic Temple, 73 Rua Itambe; 1st Friday March to December (except May). Inst: 1st Saturday, May.

CHILE

Chile, a geographically elongated country, comprises a good portion of the coast of western South America. It possesses a strong Grand Lodge dating from 1862, plus three lodges holding charters from Massachusetts, one English lodge, and four Scottish lodges.

The Grand Lodge of Ancient, Free and Accepted Masons of Chile
Founded: 1862
Address: Masonic Temple, Marcoleta 659, Santiago de Chile.
  Postal Address: Casilla Postal 2867, Santiago de Chile.
  Telephone: 35 692.
Lodges: 151   Permits Dual Membership.
Membership: Circa 6,000.
Descent: France. *Government:* Modified Grand Orient.
Courtesy Degrees: rarely conferred. *Ritual:* mainly Scottish (Craft) Rite.
Minimum Time Lapse between Degrees: generally 12 months.
Main Publications: Annual Proceedings. Constitution.

History

The first lodge in Chile was warranted at Valparaiso in 1850, by the Grand Orient of France, and the first Massachusetts lodge followed four years later. In 1862, four French warranted lodges formed the Grand Lodge of Chile. Scotland weighed in with its first lodge in 1871. England granted a warrant for the Lodge of Harmony No 1411, in 1872; while the Grand Lodge of Hamburg chartered two lodges (Lessing—1877; and Three Rings—1894). At the closure of the Grand Lodge of Hamburg with the coming of the Second World War, these lodges transferred their allegiance to the Grand Lodge of Chile. Three more German-speaking lodges were subsequently chartered by the Grand Lodge of Chile after the War (Goethe—1948; Mozart—1949; and Humboldt—1963), bringing the total to five.

The Roman Catholic Church was, from the outset, rigorously opposed to the Craft in Chile, and resorted to all means to exterminate it, including, it is reputed, the burning of lodge buildings. The temples in both Santiago and Valparaiso have been burnt to the ground in the past (only to be rebuilt), but fortunately this religious opposition has largely abated since the Second World War. Nevertheless, these past persecutions have made masonry under the Grand Lodge of Chile fairly introverted in nature. Regardless, the visitor with a prudent understanding of Chilean masonic history can be assured of a warm and hospitable welcome.

Notes for Visitors to Chile

The lodges of the Grand Lodge of Chile largely work in Spanish, and as with general Continental-type practice these lodges meet weekly or fortnightly. Spanish-speaking lodges use a Scottish (Craft) Rite ritual, while German-speaking lodges use the *Schroeder* Ritual. The three Massachusetts lodges naturally use their home Webb-form ritual, the English lodge uses *Emulation*, while the Scottish lodges, not surprisingly, use Scottish rituals. Dress for all lodges is a dark business suit. The regalia worn in Chile varies between lodges according to their allegiances, and to cover all contingencies visitors are best advised to wear their own. Again, depending on individual custom, lodges dine either before or after meetings, or not at all. Chilean lodges occasionally dine prior to meeting, opening lodge at about 8 pm. The English and Scottish lodges largely arrange for sustenance after meetings, while the Massachusetts lodges often break for a repast in the middle of proceedings. The English-speaking lodges usually open at around 7.30 pm. Visitors to Chile can readily attend the Masonic Temples in Santiago or Valparaiso, whereupon they can be assured of every assistance:

The details of all English-speaking lodges working in Chile are as follows:

English Lodge

The Lodge of Harmony No 1411	Meets at 179 Calle Wagner, Valparaiso; 2nd Tuesday May to December. Inst: 2nd Saturday, April.

Scottish Lodges

Lodge Star and Thistle No 509	Meets at 179 Calle Wagner, Valparaiso; 1st Friday March to December.
Lodge Pioneer No 643	Meets at Freemasons' Hall, 2262 Calle Latorre, Antofagasta; 3rd Saturday March to December
Lodge Progress No 812	Meets at Freemasons' Hall, 2262 Calle Latorre, Antofagasta; 2nd Saturday March to December.
Lodge Britannia No 1033	Meets at the Masonic Temple, 659 Marcoleta, Santiago; 3rd Wednesday March to December.

Massachusetts Lodges

Bethesda Lodge	Meets at 179 Calle Wagner, Valparaiso; 2nd Wednesday monthly.
Huelen Lodge	Meets at the Masonic Temple, 659 Marcoleta, Santiago; 2nd Thursday monthly.
St John's Lodge	Meets at 560 Castellon, Concepcion; 2nd Monday monthly.

COLOMBIA

Colombia is an extremely mountainous country which possesses no fewer than seven Grand Lodges, three of which are regular and fairly widely recognised.

The National Grand Lodge of Colombia (*at Barranquilla*)
Founded: 1918
Address: Masonic Temple, Calle 39, No 41–56, Barranquilla.
Postal Address: Apartado Aereo 2378, Barranquilla.
Lodges: 6   Permits Dual Membership.
Membership: Circa 300.

Descent: Supreme Council-New Granada. *Government:* Modified Grand Orient.
Courtesy Degrees: No data. *Ritual:* Scottish (Craft) Rite.
Minimum Time Lapse between Degrees: 12 months.
Main Publications: Constitution.

The Grand Lodge of Colombia (*at Bogota*)
Founded: 1922

Address: Masonic Temple, 17-53 Carrera 5a, Bogota.
Postal Address: Apartado Aereo No. 6672, Bogota.
Lodges: 22   Permits Dual Membership.
Membership: Circa 2,000.
Descent: Supreme Council-New Granada. *Government:* Modified Grand Orient.
Courtesy Degrees: rarely conferred. *Ritual:* Scottish (Craft) Rite.
Minimum Time Lapse between Degrees: 12 months.
Main Publications: Constitution.

The National Serene Grand Lodge of Colombia (*at Cartegena*)
Founded: 1921

Address: Apartedo Aereo No 1969, Cartegena (Postal Address).
Lodges: 7   Permits Dual Membership.
Membership: Circa 400
Descent: Supreme Council-New Granada. *Government:* Modified Grand Orient.
Courtesy Degrees: No data. *Ritual:* Scottish (Craft) Rite.
Minimum Time Lapse between Degrees: 12 months.
Main Publications: No data.

History
Colombia probably possesses the most confused masonic history of any country. Grand Lodges, Grand Orients, and Supreme Councils have risen and fallen with great rapidity, at least up until the 1920s. The first lodge in Colombia appears to have been Concord Lodge No 792, warranted from England in 1824, followed by a Scottish lodge; both of which did not survive. The Grand Orient of New Granada, based at Cartagena, appeared on the scene about 1827, but its origins are obscure. It is thought to have been founded under a warrant from a Supreme Council at New York, but evidence is scant. The following sixty years saw the rise and fall of a succession of Grand Orients and Supreme Councils, with some merging, some splitting, and some simply fading away. By the 1920s, three Grand Lodges had more or less emerged in different parts of the country. All three managed to agree in terms of territorial jurisdiction, and to recognise each other. In turn, this has meant that each has been able to secure fairly wide recognition outside of Colombia.
    The other four Grand Lodges are not widely recognised outside of South America, and have not gained the recognition of England, Ireland and Scotland. The first of these is the Grand Lodge Occidental of Colombia, founded at Cali in 1935 by lodges under Supreme Council of New Granada. It reported twelve lodges in 1982. The second is the Grand Lodge Oriental of Colombia-Francisco de Paula Santander. This Grand Lodge was erected in 1945 by four lodges then under the Grand Lodge at Barranquilla. The third was the Grand Lodge of the Andes, founded by three lodges then under the Santander Grand Lodge, in 1972. It is centred on the city of Cucuta. The fourth, and newest, is the Grand Lodge Benjamin Herrera. It

was formed at Santa Marta in 1977 by lodges then chartered under the Grand Lodge at Barranquilla.

Notes for Visitors to Colombia

The first, and most important, point for the visitor to bear in mind is that there are great variations in Grand Lodge recognitions associated with the Colombian Grand Lodges. Indeed, while England recognises the Grand Lodges at Barranquilla, Bogota and Cartegena, the Grand Lodge of Ireland recognises only the one at Cartegena. Many other English-speaking Grand Lodges tend to recognise one or two of this group of three, but rarely all of them. On occasions, even the names of these Grand Lodges are confused—they all being similarly titled. Therefore, it is quite crucial that each visitor to Colombia is totally aware of just which Grand Lodge(s) is/are recognised as regular by his own.

A visitor arriving in Colombia will probably enter via Bogota, the capital city. Of the twenty-two lodges working under the Grand Lodge at Bogota, all but three work in Bogota itself. One of these lodges, Welcome Lodge No 6, works in English using a York Rite ritual. All other lodges in the country work in Spanish and use a Scottish (Craft) Rite ritual. Dress for lodges is a dark business suit. Lodges largely meet about 8 pm. Visitors are well advised, in the first instance, to call at the appropriate Grand Lodge Temple, where assistance will readily be attained.

ECUADOR

Ecuador is a relatively small Spanish-speaking country located in the north west of South America. It possesses a regular Grand Lodge which is widely recognised.

The Grand Lodge of Ecuador
Founded: 1921
Address: Masonic Temple, 222 P. Layaven Street, Guayaquil.
Postal Address: P.O. Box 932, Guayaquil. *Telephone:* 407063.
Lodges: 8.   Permits Dual Membership.
Membership: Circa 600.
Descent: Peru.   *Government:* Modified Grand Orient.
Courtesy Degrees: rarely conferred.   *Ritual:* Mainly Scottish (Craft) Rite.
Minimum Time Lapse between Degrees: generally 12 months.
Main Publications: Constitutions. Annual Proceedings.

History

The first lodge in Ecuador was probably formed at Quito in 1808 by the Supreme Council of New Granada (Colombia), but this is only scantily documented. By 1857, the Grand Lodge of Peru had established a lodge at Guayaquil, but the Catholic Church forced its closure. By the end of the nineteenth century the Government had closed all lodges that had sprung up, and arrested many masons. The revolution of 1895 in Ecuador brought a more liberal government, and by 1898 Peru was again warranting lodges in the country. In 1921, three Peruvian lodges formed the Grand Lodge of Ecuador. The Grand Lodge has developed slowly, and is centred on Guayaquil where most of its lodges meet.

Notes for Visitors to Ecuador
Of the eight Ecuador lodges, five meet at Guayaquil, two in Quito (the country's capital city), and one at Salinas. All work the Scottish Rite Craft degrees, save one lodge at Guayaquil which works a York Rite ritual. All lodges work in the Spanish language. Lodges meet in the evenings, usually around 7.30 pm, and dress is a dark business suit. English is understood and spoken by a number of members, so visitors should find no problems in the area of language. Visitors are also welcome to wear their own regalia. As a rule, lodges meet weekly, although a degree ceremony is often worked only once per month. The majority of lodges recess in December, January and February.

Ecuador also possesses a rather interesting masonic museum at its Guayaquil Temple, housing an exhibition of masonic relics of General Elroy Alfaro, a former President of Ecuador (indeed, one lodge at Guayaquil bears his name), and General Jose Villamil, a leader of the Ecuador Independence Movement in the 1820s. Visitors are most welcome to inspect the museum.

FRENCH GUIANA

French Guiana is an overseas department of Metropolitan France, situated between Brazil and Suriname on the north-east coast of South America. Until 1944, it was a penal colony, allowing for no masonic establishment to any marked extent. The first lodge warranted was from France in 1755, and others followed. The current situation is that both the irregular Grand Orient of France and the irregular Grand Lodge of France apparently have lodges working in the country. The regular Grande Loge Nationale Française (GLNF) reported no lodges in French Guiana in 1983.

GUYANA

Guyana, formerly the British Colony of British Guiana, possesses both an English and a Scottish District Grand Lodge.

The District Grand Lodge of Guyana (English Constitution)
Address: Freemasons' Hall, Company Path, Georgetown, Guyana. *Telephone:* 61872.
Postal Address: P.O. Box 10893, Georgetown.   *Lodges:* 11

The District Grand Lodge of Guyana (Scottish Constitution)
Address: Masonic Hall, 12 Wellington Street, Georgetown, Guyana.   *Lodges:* 5

History
The colony of Guiana changed hands several times during its colonial history, and this in turn led to several Grand Lodges warranting lodges within its shores. The first lodge was chartered from the Netherlands in 1771, followed closely by an Irish lodge, both of which expired soon after. The Grand Lodge of New York chartered a lodge in 1801, which later merged with Union Lodge No 247, warranted by England in 1813. Another ten English lodges followed, the latest receiving its warrant in 1976.

The first Scottish lodge in Guyana was formed in 1893. This was Lodge Unity No 767. Five Scottish lodges now work in the country, the fifth receiving its warrant in 1972.

Notes for Visitors to Guyana
Attending a lodge meeting in Guyana poses no problems for the masonic visitor. Both English and Scottish lodges meet in the early evening, usually about 7.30 pm, and follow with a repast. Dress is a dark business suit, and the visitor should carry his own regalia. The details of the English and Scottish lodges are as follows:

English Lodges
Nine English lodges work in Georgetown, meeting in Freemasons' Hall, Company Path.

Union Lodge No 247	Meets 3rd Tuesday monthly. Inst: February.
Mount Olive Lodge No 385	Meets 1st Thursday monthly. Inst: December.
Silent Temple Lodge No 3254	Meets 2nd Friday monthly. Inst: January.
Concord Lodge No 3508	Meets 2nd Wednesday monthly. Inst: March.
Roraima Lodge No 3902	Meets 3rd Friday monthly. Inst: May.
Mount Everest Lodge No 5868	Meets 4th Wednesday monthly. Inst: April.
Eureka Lodge No 8515	Meets 4th Tuesday in January, March, May, June, July, September and October. Inst: 4th Saturday, November.
Guyana Lodge of Research No 8525	Meets 4th Monday, in March, July and September. Inst: September.
Lotus Lodge No 8735	Meets 3rd Wednesday monthly except February, May, August, and November. Inst: October.

Two other English lodges meet in the towns of MacKenzie (Kara-Kara No 8349), and New Amsterdam (Ituni Lodge No 2642).

Scottish Lodges
All five Scottish lodges in Guyana meet at Georgetown in the Masonic Temple, 12 Wellington Street, except for Lodge Victory No 1203.

Lodge Union No 797	Meets 1st Wednesday monthly.
Lodge Harmony No 1110	Meets 1st Monday monthly.
Lodge Victory No 1203	Meets 1st Tuesday monthly; at the Masonic Hall, 86 Carmichael Street, Georgetown.
Lodge Alpha No 1594	Meets 1st Friday monthly.
Lodge Kyk-over-al No 1672	Meets 4th Friday monthly.

PERU

Peru contains a strong regular Grand Lodge dating from 1882, as well as three lodges holding warrants from Scotland.

The Grand Lodge of Ancient, Free and Accepted Masons of Peru
Founded: 1882

Address: Masonic Temple, corner Jose Galvez Barrenechea Avenue and Del Aire Avenue, Lima.

Postal Address: P.O. Box 587, Lima 100, Peru. *Telephone:* 234899, 245540, 324034.

Lodges: 138. Permits Dual and Plural Membership.

Membership: 5,004.

Descent: Colombia, Scotland. *Government:* Appointive Grand Lodge.

Courtesy Degrees: Correspondence must be through Grand Lodges.

Ritual: mainly Scottish (Craft) Rite.
Minimum Time Lapse between Degrees: generally 12 months.
Main Publications: Constitution. Annual Proceedings.

History
A number of lodges were soon to spring up in Peru after the country gained its political independence in 1820, chartered from Colombia. A Grand Lodge (later Grand Orient) was formed in 1831, but it expired within ten years. Several competing Grand Lodges appear to have sprung up in the 1850s, only to face a similar oblivion. In the 1860s and 1870s, the Grand Lodge of Scotland chartered twelve lodges. Of these five later joined the Grand Lodge of Peru, six subsequently expired, and one (Peace and Concord) remained under Scotland.

In 1882, five Peruvian lodges and five Scottish lodges formed the current Grand Lodge of Peru. In 1897, the then Grand Master ordered the Sacred Volume to be removed from lodges—a move which was unpopular in Peru and meant that several overseas Grand Lodges severed fraternal relations. This error was internally rectified within a year, but it did damage the prestige of the Grand Lodge in world masonic circles. Scotland warranted two more lodges in Peru in 1911 and 1912, bringing the total of Scottish lodges in Peru to three.

In 1945, the Grand Lodge split into two factions as the result of the outgoing Grand Master apparently 'rigging' the vote for his re-election. This schism lasted two years until a general assembly of masons met, leading to a re-unification. Peruvian masonic unity remained total until 1966 when four lodges working the Scottish Rite Craft degrees withdrew to form The Most Serene Grand Lodge of Peru under Supreme Council aegis.

Notes for Visitors to Peru
Peruvian lodges mostly work in the Spanish language, although one works in German using the *Schroeder* Ritual, while another works in Italian. The York Rite enjoys more popularity in Peru than elsewhere in South America largely as the result of Scottish influences, although plenty of lodges still work the Scottish Rite Craft degrees. Metropolitan Lima (which includes the port of Callao) contains 71 lodges working in seven Temples, with the balance operating in various provincial towns. The frequency of meetings varies between lodges depending on the ritual used, but all meet at least monthly, generally commencing between 7 pm and 8 pm. Dress is a dark suit, and the visitor is welcome to wear his own regalia. All three Scottish lodges meet in Lima—two at Callao, and one in central Lima. The locations of the Lima Temples are as follows:

Masonic Temple, 438 Santa Rosa Avenue, La Peria, Callao (1 lodge).
Masonic Temple, 240 Pedro Ruiz Street, Callao (5 lodges).
Masonic Temple, 672 Arenales Avenue, Lima (1 lodge).
Masonic Temple, 1066 Alfonso Ugarte Avenue, Lima (4 lodges).
Masonic Temple, 177 Mantes Street, Lima (5 lodges).
Masonic Temple, 1125 Washington Street, Lima (31 lodges).
Masonic Temple, Cnr. Jose Galvez Barrenechea Ave. and Del Aire Ave., San Isidro, Lima (24 lodges).

The three Scottish lodges in Peru work under a District Superintendent. Their meeting details are as follows:

Lodge Peace and Concord No 445	Meets at Callao (Santa Rosa Temple), 3rd Monday monthly.
Lodge Roof of the World No 1094	Meets at Callao (Santa Rosa Temple), 4th Wednesday in February, May, August, and November.
Lodge Unity No 1109	Meets at Lima (Washington Street Temple), 1st Saturday monthly, except July.

PARAGUAY

Paraguay is a small South American country, with an equally small Grand Lodge. It possesses no lodges warranted from outside the country. While recognised by England and Scotland (but not Ireland), the Grand Lodge of Paraguay does not enjoy widespread recognition outside of South America.

The Symbolic Grand Lodge of Paraguay
Founded: 1869
Address: Masonic Temple, 937 Palma Street, Asuncion, Paraguay.
Postal Address: P.O. Box 1178, Asuncion. *Telephone:* 92292.
Lodges: 8   Permits Dual Membership.
Membership: 750.
Descent: Brazil, Uruguay.   *Government:* Modified Grand Orient.
Courtesy Degrees: No data.   *Ritual:* Scottish (Craft) Rite.
Minimum Time Lapse between Degrees: 12 months.
Main Publications: Constitution. Proceedings.

History

The first lodge in Paraguay appears to have been warranted in 1881 by the Grand Orient of Brazil. By 1869, this lodge split itself into four and formed its own Grand Lodge. Subsequent history is somewhat confused, with the Grand Orient of Uruguay later setting up lodges and a Supreme Council. The original Grand Lodge (later called a Grand Orient) seems to have at some stage merged with Uruguayan lodges to form one Grand Body. In 1923, the current Grand Lodge of Paraguay became independent of the Supreme Council, and has remained so to date.

Notes for Visitors to Paraguay

The Grand Lodge of Paraguay has not progressed in leaps and bounds since its re-birth in 1923. The reasons for this appear to be that few Paraguayans are members, with many local masons being foreign nationals largely of British, Dutch, German and Argentinian origin. Nonetheless, good progress has been made in the last ten years in particular. Membership in 1973 stood at 450 (in 5 lodges), which had risen to 750 in 1983 (in 8 lodges), representing over a fifty per cent increase. Paraguayan lodges work in the Spanish language, using a Scottish Rite Craft ritual. Lodges largely meet about 8 pm, and dress is a dark business suit. Of its eight lodges, five operate in the Grand Lodge Temple in Asuncion. Visitors attending at this location will receive every assistance in visiting a lodge during their stay.

SURINAM

This small northern Latin American country was formerly known as Dutch Guiana prior to its political independence from the Netherlands. While it does not possess a Grand Lodge, it does have several lodges warranted from the home country. The first Dutch lodge formed was Concordia No 10, erected at Paramaribo in 1761, making it one of the oldest extant lodges in South America. Two further Dutch lodges were warranted at Paramaribo in 1964 (De Stanfaste No 238), and in 1968 (De Gouden Driehoek No 245). All three lodges meet at the Masonic Temple, Kwattaweg 85b, Paramaribo, generally on a weekly basis, commencing at 8 pm. Dress is a dark lounge suit. Naturally, the Dutch ritual and Dutch language are used.

URUGUAY

Uruguay possesses a Grand Orient of some age, which is widely viewed as irregular. Two English lodges also work in this country, attached to the English District Grand Lodge of South America (Southern Division).

History

There is a story that the Grand Orient of France established a lodge in Uruguay in 1827, but no proof of this remains. The first lodge for which records exist was warranted by the Grand Lodge of Pennsylvania in 1832, but it became extinct. In 1841, the French Grand Orient again warranted a lodge, and further lodges were formed from Brazil. By the mid 1850s the country appears to have possessed several Grand Orients and Supreme Councils. In the early 1980s, the Grand Orient of Uruguay had nearly fifty lodges working under it, and 2,000 members. Most of its lodges work in Spanish, while a few use the Italian language. The Grand Orient has long since been considered irregular, having abandoned the use of the Sacred Volume in its lodges in 1950. This action led to the withdrawal of recognition by most Grand Lodges, although those of South America have largely maintained their fraternal ties. As at September 1982, eleven American Grand Lodges maintained fraternal relations with Uruguay, evidently on the basis that Uruguay had corrected its past irregularities. However, most Grand Lodges appear to remain unconvinced on this point.

Uruguay's two English lodges are Acacia No 876, founded in 1861, and Silver City No 3389, formed in 1909. The former was originally warranted in Argentina, but later moved to Montevideo. After the Grand Orient of Uruguay sank into irregularity, the two English lodges decided to join the English District Grand Lodge of South America (Southern Division) based in Argentina.

Notes for Visitors to Uruguay

Both English lodges in Uruguay meet at the same temple, located at 1429 Canelones Street, Montevideo. Intending visitors should, if possible, make themselves known at the Temple prior to visiting. Meeting details for the two lodges are as follows:

Acacia Lodge No 876	Meets 3rd Monday March to November (except June). Inst: 24th June, annually.
Silver City Lodge No 3389	Meets 2nd Thursday March to November. Inst: November.

VENEZUELA

Venezuela has had a regular Grand Lodge since 1824. While English and Scottish lodges have been erected in the country in the past, none has survived.

The Grand Lodge of the Republic of Venezuela
Founded: 1824
Address: Masonic Temple, Este 3 No 5, Caracas.
Postal Address: Apartado 927, Caracas. *Telephone:* 819548 or 815776.
Lodges: 91   Permits Dual Membership.
Membership: Circa 4,500.
Descent: Obscure, possibly Spain.   *Government:* Modified Grand Orient.
Courtesy Degrees: rarely conferred.   *Ritual:* Scottish (Craft) Rite.
Minimum Time Lapse between Degrees: generally 12 months.
Main Publications: Annual Proceedings. Constitutions.

History

It has been claimed that the Craft came to Venezuela from Spain about 1808, and that lodges were warranted soon after from Vermont and Maryland, but extant proof appears to be lacking. England and Scotland did warrant lodges in 1824, but these expired along with virtually all other masonic activity in the country in 1827. In that year the Government issued an anti-secret society edict, with the ban remaining until 1838.

Subsequent to the lifting of the ban, the National Grand Lodge of Venezuela, and a Grand Orient, were erected. After several short lived schisms in both Grand Bodies, they united in 1865 to form a National Grand Orient. This latter body worked until 1916, when it voluntarily dissolved to allow the erection of an independent Grand Lodge, and a Supreme Council, both in amity with each other. Although there have been the occasional minor schisms since, the Grand Lodge of the Republic of Venezuela has developed steadily.

Notes for Visitors to Venezuela

All Venezuelan lodges work the Scottish Rite Craft ritual, except for three lodges which work a York Rite ritual in English, and one which works in German. The English-speaking lodges are George Washington Lodge No 100 at Caracas, Buena Vista Lodge No 116 at Maracaibo, and Lago de Maracaibo Lodge No 120 at Cabimas. The German-speaking lodge is Humboldt Lodge No 141, which meets twice monthly at Caracas, using the *Schroeder* ritual.

Virtually every population centre of any size in Venezuela has at least one lodge working within it. Twenty-one lodges meet in central Caracas (the capital city). Lodges recess in the months of December, January and February, but otherwise meet weekly or fortnightly, as is common Scottish Rite practice. Most lodges commence work between 7.30 pm and 8.30 pm, and a provision of a repast in association with a meeting is not uncommon. Dress is a dark business suit, and a visitor is welcome to wear his own regalia. Venezuela also possesses several masonic clubs which are locally known as Triangulos. Visitors can readily gain details of these Clubs and those of any lodge meeting, when attending the Masonic Temple in Caracas.

Section XII

Appendices

Appendix A

GRAND LODGE RECOGNITIONS

All the Grand Lodges detailed in the body of this guide, and for which addresses are given, are recognised as regular by either, or all of, the Grand Lodges of England, Ireland and Scotland. The recognitions of these three Grand Lodges, as of late 1982, are as follows:

The United Grand Lodge of England
Alabama, Alaska, Alberta, Argentina, Arizona, Arkansas, Austria, Belgium (Regular Grand Lodge), Bolivia, Brazil (Grand Orient), British Columbia, California, Colorado, Connecticut, Chile, Colombia (at Barranquilla), Colombia (at Bogota), Colombia (at Cartegena), Costa Rica, Cuba, Delaware, Denmark, District of Columbia, Dominican Republic, Ecuador, El Salvador (Cuscatlan), Finland, Florida, France (GLNF), Georgia, Germany (United Grand Lodges), Greece, Guatemala, Iceland, Idaho, Illinois, India, Indiana, Iowa, Ireland, Israel, Italy (Grand Orient), Kansas, Kentucky, Louisiana, Luxembourg, Maine, Manitoba, Maryland, Mexico (York), Massachusetts, Michigan, Minnesota, Mississippi, Missouri, Montana, Nebraska, Netherlands, Nevada, New Brunswick, New Hampshire, New Jersey, New Mexico, New South Wales, New York, New Zealand, North Carolina, North Dakota, Norway, Nova Scotia, Ohio, Oklahoma, Ontario (Canada in), Oregon, Panama, Paraguay, Pennsylvania, Peru, Philippines, Prince Edward Island, Puerto Rico, Quebec, Queensland, Rhode Island, Saskatchewan, Scotland, South Africa, South Australia, South Carolina, South Dakota, Sweden, Switzerland, Tasmania, Tennessee, Texas, Turkey, Utah, Venezuela, Vermont, Victoria, Virginia, Washington, West Virginia, Western Australia, Wisconsin, Wyoming.

The Grand Lodge of Ireland
The recognitions of the Grand Lodge of Ireland are the same as those of England, except that Ireland does not recognise Colombia (at Barranquilla), Colombia (at Bogota), El Salvador, and Paraguay.

The Grand Lodge of Scotland
The recognitions of the Grand Lodge of Scotland are identical to those of England, except that, in addition, Scotland also recognises the Grand Lodge of Japan.

The Inter-American Masonic Confederation (Confederacion Masonica Inter-Americana)
This body loosely unites most of the Grand Lodges of Central and South America, and as such can usefully be mentioned in the lists that follow. It was formed in 1947 to act as a liaison organisation between its member Grand Lodges. Its Secretariat is located at Caracas, Venezuela. The Organisation is divided into six zones, as follows: Zone I—Mexico (most of the State Grand Lodges, but not the York Grand Lodge of Mexico); Zone II—Cuba, Dominican Republic, Haiti, and Puerto Rico; Zone III—Costa Rica, El Salvador (Cuscatlan), Guatemala, Honduras,

Nicaragua, and Panama; Zone IV—Colombia (all its seven State Grand Lodges), Ecuador, and Venezuela; Zone V—Brazil (all the 22 State Grand Lodges of Brazil, but not the Grand Orient of Brazil); Zone VI—Argentina, Bolivia, Chile, Paraguay, Peru, and Uruguay. Oddly enough, not all members of the Confederation recognise each other, but most do. Nonetheless, membership of it seems to imply internal recognition as far as its members are concerned, even if in a few cases this recognition is not currently official.

Exceptions and Additions
It needs to be appreciated that many Grand Lodges recognised as regular by the Grand Lodges of England, Ireland, and Scotland recognise other Grand Lodges which are not recognised by the three British Grand Bodies. In the lists that follow, Grand Lodge Recognitions will be compared with those of England.

Where a Grand Lodge *does not recognise* another Grand Lodge which is recognised by England, this will be noted as an *exception*.

Where a Grand Lodge *does recognise* another Grand Lodge which is not recognised by England, this will be noted as an *addition*.

Alabama
Exceptions Bolivia, Brazil (Grand Orient), Colombia (Bogota), Cuba, Paraguay, Switzerland.
Additions All the State Grand Lodges of Brazil (except Alagoas, Bahia, Espirito Santo, Rio Grande do Norte), China (Taiwan), Colombia (Cali), Honduras, Japan, Mexico (Baja California, El Potosi, Nuevo Leon, Occidental Mexicans, Oriental Peninsular, Tamaulipas, Unida Mexicana, Valle de Mexico).

Alaska
Exceptions Argentina, Austria, Belgium (Regular), Bolivia, Brazil (Grand Orient), Colombia (at Barranquilla, Bogota, and Cartegena), Costa Rica, Cuba, Ecuador, El Salvador, Finland, Greece, Guatemala, Luxembourg, Paraguay.
Additions Brazil (Brazilia, Ceara, Parana, Rio Grande do Sul, Sao Paulo), China (Taiwan), Japan.

Alberta
Exceptions Bolivia, Brazil (Grand Orient), Colombia (Bogota and Cartegena), El Salvador, Paraguay.
Additions Brazil (Goias, Guanabara, Para, Paraiba, Pernambuco, Rio Grande do Sul, Santa Catarina, Sao Paulo), China, Honduras, Japan, Uruguay.

Argentina
Exceptions Alaska, Denmark, Iceland, South Africa, Sweden.
Additions China, Japan, and member Grand Lodges of the Inter-American Masonic Confederation not recognised by England.

Arizona

Exceptions Brazil (Grand Orient), Colombia (Certegena), Cuba, El Salvador, Paraguay.

Additions All Brazilian State Grand Lodges (except Acre, Alagoas, Amazonas, Espirito Santo, Minas Gerais, Pernambuco, Rio Grande do Norte), China (Taiwan), Honduras, Japan, Mexico (Baja California, Baja California Sur, Cosmos, Del Pacifico, El Potosi, Nuevo Leon, Occidental Mexicana, Valle de Mexico).

Arkansas

Exceptions Belgium (Regular), Bolivia, Brazil (Grand Orient), Cuba, Paraguay, South Africa, Switzerland.

Additions All Brazilian State Grand Lodges (except Acre, Alagoas, Amazonas, Ceara, Espirito Santo, Maranhao, Paraiba, Pernambuco, Rio de Janeiro, Rio Grande do Norte), China, Colombia (Cali), Honduras, Japan, Mexico (Nuevo Leon, Tamaulipas).

Austria

Exceptions Alaska, Colombia (Cartegena), El Salvador, Paraguay, Prince Edward Island, Tasmania, Saskatchewan.

Additions China, Japan.

Belgium (Regular G.L.)

Exceptions Alaska, Argentina, Arkansas, Bolivia, Chile, Colombia (Barranquilla and Cartegena), Colorado, Costa Rica, Cuba, Dominican Republic, El Salvador, Germany, Guatemala, Indiana, Luxembourg, Panama, Paraguay, Peru, Puerto Rico, Tasmania, Venezuela, Wyoming.

Additions China, Japan, and the Grand Lodge of Spain.

Bolivia

Exceptions Alabama, Alaska, Alberta, Arkansas, Belgium (Regular), Brazil (Grand Orient), British Columbia, Iceland, Illinois, Iowa, Maine, Manitoba, New Brunswick, New Mexico, North Dakota, Ontario, Quebec, Saskatchewan, South Africa, South Carolina, Tasmania, Utah, Virginia.

Additions Member Grand Lodges of the Inter-American Masonic Confederation not recognised by England.

Brazil (Grand Orient)

Exceptions The Grand Orient of Brazil does not exchange recognition with any United States Grand Lodge (except Rhode Isalnd), nor with any Canadian Grand Lodge (except British Columbia). Other exceptions are: Chile, Colombia (Barranquilla, Bogota, and Cartegena), Costa Rica, Cuba, Denmark, Dominican Republic, Ecuador, El Salvador, Finland, Guatemala, Iceland, Israel, Luxembourg, Norway, Philippines, Puerto Rico, Sweden, Venezuela.

Additions Mexico (Baja California, El Potosi, Unida Mexicana, Valle de Mexico), Nicaragua.

British Columbia
Exceptions Bolivia, Colombia (Barranquilla, Bogota, and Cartegena), Cuba, El Salvador, Guatemala, Panama, Paraguay.
Additions Brazil (Ceara, Goias, Guanabara), China, Honduras, Japan, Mexico (Benito Juarez).

California
Exceptions Brazil (Grand Orient).
Additions All the Brazilian State Grand Lodges (except Acre, Alagoas, Rio Grande do Norte), China, Colombia (Andes, Cali, Santander), Honduras, Japan, Mexico (Baja California, Baja California Sur, Cosmos, Del Pacifico, Nuevo Leon, Occidental Mexicana, Oriental Peninsular, Tamaulipas, Unida Mexicana, Valle de Mexico), Nicaragua.

Colorado
Exceptions Belgium (Regular), Brazil (Grand Orient), Paraguay.
Additions All the Brazilian State Grand Lodges (except Alagoas, Espirito Santo, Rio Grande do Norte), China, Honduras, Japan, Mexico (Baja California, Benito Juarez, Cosmos, Del Pacifico, El Potosi, Nuevo Leon, Occidental Mexicana, Oriental Peninsular, Tamaulipas, Valle de Mexico), Nicaragua.

Connecticut
Exceptions Brazil (Grand Orient), Paraguay.
Additions All the Brazilian State Grand Lodges (except Alagoas, Brazilia, Espirito Santo, Rio Grande do Norte), China, Colombia (Cali), Honduras, Japan, Mexico (Baja California, El Potosi, Nuevo Leon, Oriental Peninsular, Tamaulipas, Valle de Mexico), Nicaragua, Uruguay.

Chile
Exceptions Belgium (Regular), Brazil (Grand Orient), Denmark, Iceland, Luxembourg, Sweden.
Additions China, Japan, and member Grand Lodges of the Inter-American Masonic Confederation not recognised by England.

Colombia (Barranquilla)
Exceptions Alaska, Belgium (Regular), Brazil (Grand Orient), British Columbia, Denmark, Finland, Iceland, India, Ireland, Luxembourg, Maine, Manitoba, Mexico (York), Nevada, New Brunswick, Norway, Quebec, Queensland, Sweden, Tasmania, Virginia.
Additions Japan, and member Grand Lodges of the Inter-American Masonic Confederation not recognised by England.

Colombia (Bogota)
Exceptions Alabama, Alaska, Alberta, Brazil (Grand Orient), British Columbia, Denmark, Georgia, Iceland, Ireland, Luxembourg, Maine, Maryland, New Brunswick, Quebec, Saskatchewan, South Africa, Sweden, Vermont, Washington, West Virginia, Wyoming.

Additions   Japan, and member Grand Lodges of the Inter-American Masonic Confederation not recognised by England.

Colombia (Cartegena)
Exceptions   Alaska, Alberta, Arizona, Austria, Belgium (Regular), Brazil (Grand Orient), British Columbia, Delaware, Denmark, Finland, Iceland, Kansas, Luxembourg, Maine, Manitoba, Mississippi, Nebraska, New Brunswick, New Mexico, North Dakota, Norway, Oregon, Prince Edward Island, Quebec, Queensland, South Africa, South Carolina, South Dakota, Sweden, Tasmania, Tennessee, Vermont, Virginia, Washington, West Virginia, Western Australia.
Additions   Japan, and member Grand Lodges of the Inter-American Masonic Confederation not recognised by England.

Costa Rica
Exceptions   Alaska, Belgium (Regular), Brazil (Grand Orient), Denmark, Iceland, Philippines, Sweden.
Additions   China, Japan, and member Grand Lodges of the Inter-American Masonic Confederation not recognised by England.

Cuba
Exceptions   Alabama, Alaska, Arizona, Arkansas, Belgium (Regular), Brazil (Grand Orient) British Columbia, Denmark, Finland, Georgia, Germany, Iceland, Indiana, Luxembourg, Maine, Manitoba, Mexico (York), Nevada, New Brunswick, New Jersey, North Carolina, Philippines, Quebec, South Africa, South Carolina, Sweden, Tennessee, Virginia.
Additions   China, Japan, and member Grand Lodges of the Inter-American Masonic Confederation not recognised by England.

Delaware
Exceptions   Brazil (Grand Orient), Colombia (Cartegena), Paraguay.
Additions   All the Brazilian State Grand Lodges (except Alagoas, Espirito Santo, Maranhao, Mato Grosso, Pernambuco, Rio Grande do Sul), China, Colombia (Cali), Honduras, Japan, Mexico (El Potosi, Nuevo Leon, Tamaulipas).

Denmark
Exceptions   Argentina, Brazil (Grand Orient), Chile, Colombia (Barranquilla, Bogota, and Cartegena), Costa Rica, Cuba, Dominican Republic, Ecuador, El Salvador, Guatemala, Panama, Paraguay, Peru, Puerto Rico, Venezuela.
Additions   Nil.

District of Columbia
Exceptions   Brazil (Grand Orient).
Additions   All the Brazilian State Grand Lodges (except Alagoas, Espirito Santo, Rio Grande do Norte), Colombia (Cali, Santander), Honduras, China, Japan, Mexico (Neuvo Leon, Tamaulipas), Nicaragua.

Dominican Republic
Exceptions Brazil (Grand Orient), Belgium (Regular), Denmark, Iceland, Idaho, India, Maine, Mississippi, New Brunswick, North Dakota, Norway, Prince Edward Island, Quebec, Queensland, Sweden, Utah, West Virginia.
Additions China, Japan, and member Grand Lodges of the Inter-American Masonic Confederation not recognised by England.

Ecuador
Exceptions Alaska, Brazil (Grand Orient), Denmark, Iceland, Luxembourg, Maine, Mississippi, Quebec, Queensland, South Australia, Sweden.
Additions China, Japan, and member Grand Lodges of the Inter-American Masonic Confederation not recognised by England.

El Salvador
Exceptions Alaska, Alberta, Arizona, Austria, Brazil (Grand Orient), Belgium (Regular), Brazil (Grand Orient), British Columbia, Denmark, Iceland, Illinois, Ireland, Luxembourg, Maine, Manitoba, Maryland, Mississippi, Nebraska, Netherlands, Nevada, New Brunswick, New Jersey, New South Wales, Ohio, Ontario, Oregon, Pennsylvania, Prince Edward Island, Quebec, Queensland, Saskatchewan, Sweden, Tasmania, Tennessee, Utah, Vermont, Washington, West Virginia, Western Australia.
Additions Japan, and member Grand Lodges of the Inter-American Masonic Confederation not recognised by England.

Finland
Exceptions Alaska, Brazil (Grand Orient), Colombia (Barranquilla, and Cartegena), Cuba, Mississippi, Tasmania.
Additions Brazil (Bahia, Para, Rio Grande do Sul), Japan.

Florida
Exceptions Brazil (Grand Orient), Paraguay.
Additions All Brazilian State Grand Lodges (except Acre, Alagoas, Amazonas, Bahia, Para, Paraiba, Rio de Janeiro, Rio Grande do Norte), China, Colombia (Cali, Santander), Honduras, Japan, Mexico (Tamaulipas), Uruguay.

France (GLNF)
Exception Switzerland.
Addition Japan.

Georgia
Exceptions Brazil (Grand Orient), Colombia (Bogota), Cuba, Paraguay, Tasmania.
Additions All Brazilian State Grand Lodges (except Acre, Alagoas, Amazonas, Espirito Santo, Paraiba, Pernambuco, Rio Grande do Norte), China, Colombia (Cali), Honduras, Japan, Mexico (Tamaulipas).

Germany
(United Grand Lodges)
Exceptions   Belgium (Regular), Cuba, Tasmania.
Additions   Brazil (Rio Grande do Sul, Santa Catarina, Sao Paulo), China, Colombia (Cali), Honduras, Japan, Nicaragua.

Greece
Exceptions   Alaska, Tasmania.
Additions   China, Japan.

Guatemala
Exceptions   Alaska, Belgium (Regular), Brazil (Grand Orient), British Columbia, Denmark, Iceland, Luxembourg, Maine, Mississippi, Pennsylvania, Quebec, South Africa, Sweden, Utah, Virginia.
Additions   China, Japan, and member Grand Lodges of the Inter-American Masonic Confederation not recognised by England.

Iceland
Exceptions   Argentina, Bolivia, Brazil (Grand Orient), Chile, Colombia (Barranquilla, Bogota, and Cartegena), Costa Rica, Cuba, Dominican Republic, Ecuador, El Salvador, Guatemala, Maryland, Mexico (York), Panama, Paraguay, Peru, Philippines, Puerto Rico, South Africa, Venezuela.
Additions   Nil.

Idaho
Exceptions   Brazil (Grand Orient), Dominican Republic, Paraguay.
Additions   All Brazilian State Grand Lodges (except Acre, Alagoas, Amazonas, Bahia, Espirito Santo, Maranhao, Mato Grosso, Pernambuco, Rio Grande do Norte), China, Colombia (Cali), Honduras, Japan, Mexico (Baja California, Del Pacifico, El Potosi, Nuevo Leon, Tamaulipas, Unida Mexicana), Nicaragua.

Illinois
Exceptions   Bolivia, Brazil (Grand Orient), El Salvador, Paraguay.
Additions   All Brazilian State Grand Lodges (except Acre, Alagoas, Amazonas, Bahia, Minas Gerais, Paraiba, Rio Grande do Norte), China, Colombia (Andes), Honduras, Japan, Mexico (Nuevo Leon, Oriental Peninsular, Tamaulipas).

India
Exceptions   Brazil (Grand Orient), Colombia (Barranquilla), Dominican Republic.
Additions   Brazil (Rio Grande do Sul, Sao Paulo), China, Japan.

Indiana
Exceptions   Belgium (Regular), Brazil (Grand Orient), Cuba, Paraguay.

Additions All Brazilian State Grand Lodges (except Alagoas, Espirito Santo, Pernambuco, Rio de Janeiro, Rio Grande do Norte), China, Colombia (Cali, Santander), Honduras, Japan, Mexico (Baja California, Benito Juarez, Cosmos, El Potosi, Nuevo Leon, Occidental Mexicana, Oriental Peninsular, Tamaulipas, Valle de Mexico), Nicaragua, Uruguay.

Iowa
Exceptions Bolivia, Brazil (Grand Orient), Paraguay.
Additions All Brazilian State Grand Lodges (except Acre, Alagoas, Amazonas, Espirito Santo, Mato Grosso, Parana, Rio Grande do Norte), China, Colombia (Cali), Honduras, Japan, Mexico (Nuevo Leon, Tamaulipas), Nicaragua.

Israel
Exception Brazil (Grand Orient).
Additions All the Brazilian State Grand Lodges (except Acre, Alagoas, Amazonas, Bahia, Maranhao, Mato Grosso, Minas Gerais, Piaui, Goias, Santa Catarina, Rio Grande do Norte), Japan, Mexico (Baja California, Del Pacifico, Nuevo Leon, Occidental Mexicana, Valle de Mexico), Nicaragua.

Italy
(Grand Orient)
Exceptions Nil.
Additions All the Brazilian State Grand Lodges (except Maranhao), China, Colombia (Andes, Cali, Cucuta), Haiti, Honduras, Japan, Mexico (all Mexican State Grand Lodges, except El Potosi), Nicaragua.

Kansas
Exceptions Brazil (Grand Orient), Colombia (Cartegena), Paraguay.
Additions All the Brazilian State Grand Lodges (except Alagoas, Espirito Santo, Para, Rio de Janeiro, Rio Grande do Norte), China, Colombia (Santander), Honduras, Japan, Mexico (Baja California, Baja California Sur, Campeche, Cosmos, Del Pacifico, El Potosi, Nuevo Leon, Oriental Peninsular, Tamaulipas), Nicaragua.

Kentucky
Exception Brazil (Grand Orient).
Additions All the Brazilian State Grand Lodges (except Alagoas, Espirito Santo, Rio de Janeiro, Rio Grande do Norte), China, Colombia (Cali, Santander), Honduras, Japan, Mexico (all Mexican State Grand Lodges, except Baja California Sur, Oriental Peninsular, Queretaro, and Sur-Oeste), Nicaragua.

Louisiana
Exception Brazil (Grand Orient).
Additions All Brazilian State Grand Lodges (except Alagoas, Espirito Santo, Rio de Janeiro, Rio Grande do Norte), China, Colombia (Cali), Honduras, Japan, Mexico (all Mexican State Grand Lodges, except Baja California Sur, Sur-Oeste), Nicaragua.

Luxembourg

Exceptions Alaska, Belgium (Regular), Brazil (Grand Orient), Chile, Colombia (Barranquilla, Bogota, and Cartegena), Cuba, Ecuador, El Salvador, Guatemala, Maine, Manitoba, Mexico (York), Mississippi, New Brunswick, New Zealand, Norway, Nova Scotia, Panama, Paraguay, Philippines, Quebec, Queensland, Saskatchewan, South Africa, South Australia, Tasmania, Venezuela, Victoria, Western Australia.

Additions Brazil (Brazilia, Guanabara, Minas Gerais, Rio Grande do Sul, Sao Paulo), Japan.

Maine

Exceptions Bolivia, Brazil (Grand Orient), Colombia (Barranquilla, Bogota, and Cartegena), Cuba, Dominican Republic, Ecuador, El Salvador, Guatemala, Paraguay, Venezuela.

Additions Brazil (Espirito Santo, Goias), China, Japan.

Manitoba

Exceptions Bolivia, Brazil (Grand Orient), Colombia (Barranquilla, and Cartegena), Cuba, El Salvador, Luxembourg, Paraguay.

Additions Brazil (Guanabara, Para, Paraiba, Sao Paulo), China, Honduras, Japan.

Maryland

Exceptions Brazil (Grand Orient), Colombia (Bogota), El Salvador, Iceland, Norway, Paraguay, Switzerland, Tasmania.

Additions All the Brazilian State Grand Lodges (except Alagoas, Bahia, Ceara, Espirito Santo, Mato, Grosso, Paraiba, Pernambuco, Rio de Janeiro, Rio Grande do Norte), China, Honduras, Japan, Mexico (Chiapas, El Potosi, Nuevo Leon, Tamaulipas), Nicaragua.

Mexico

(York Grand Lodge)

Exceptions Colombia (Barranquilla), Cuba, Iceland, Luxembourg, Paraguay, Sweden.

Additions Brazil (Ceara, Goias, Guanabara, Paraiba, Rio Grande do Sul, Sao Paulo), China, Japan, Mexico (Nuevo Leon, Tamaulipas).

Massachusetts

Exceptions Brazil (Grand Orient), Paraguay.

Additions All Brazilian State Grand Lodges (except Acre, Alagoas, Amazonas, Paraiba, Rio Grande do Norte), China, Colombia (Cali), Honduras, Japan, Mexico (Baja California, Benito Juarez, Chiapas, El Potosi, Nuevo Leon, Occidental Mexicana, Oriental Peninsular, Tamaulipas, Unida Mexicana, Valle de Mexico), Nicaragua, Uruguay.

Michigan

Exception Brazil (Grand Orient).

Additions   All the Brazilian State Grand Lodges (except Espirito Santo, Pernambuco, Rio Grand de Norte), China, Colombia (Cali), Honduras, Japan, Mexico (all the Mexican State Grand Lodges, except Restauracion, Guadalope Victoria, Queretaro), Nicaragua, Uruguay.

Minnesota
Exception   Brazil (Grand Orient).
Additions   All the Brazilian State Grand Lodges (except Acre, Alagoas, Amazonas, Rio Grande do Norte), China, Colombia (Cali), Honduras, Japan, Mexico (Baja California, Nuevo Leon, Tamaulipas), Nicaragua, Uruguay.

Mississippi
Exceptions   Brazil (Grand Orient), Colombia (Cartegena), Dominican Republic, Ecuador, El Salvador, Finland, Guatemala, Luxembourg, Netherlands, Norway, Paraguay, Sweden, Switzerland, Venezuela.
Additions   Brazil (Goias, Paraiba, Santa Catarina), China, Japan, Mexico (Nuevo Leon, Tamaulipas).

Missouri
Exceptions   Bolivia, Brazil (Grand Orient), Paraguay.
Additions   All the Brazilian State Grand Lodges (except Alagoas, Brazilia, Espirito Santo, Parana, Rio de Janeiro, Rio Grande do Norte), China, Honduras, Mexico (all the Mexican State Grand Lodges, except Baja California Sur, and Sur-Oeste), Nicaragua, Uruguay.

Montana
Exceptions   Brazil (Grand Orient), Paraguay.
Additions   All the Brazilian State Grand Lodges (except Acre, Alagoas, Amazonas, Espirito Santo, Rio Grande do Norte), China, Colombia (Cali), Honduras, Japan, Mexico (Baja California, Benito Juarez, Cosmos, Del Pacifico, Hidalgo, Nuevo Leon, Occidental Mexicana, Oriental Peninsular, Tamaulipas, Unida Mexicana, Valle de Mexico), Nicaragua, Uruguay.

Nebraska
Exceptions   Brazil (Grand Orient), Colombia (Cartegena), El Salvador, Norway, Paraguay.
Additions   All the Brazilian State Grand Lodges (except Acre, Alagoas, Amazonas, Espirito Santo, Piaui, Rio de Janeiro, Rio Grande do Norte), China, Honduras, Japan, Mexico (Neuvo Leon, Tamaulipas), Nicaragua.

Netherlands
Exceptions   El Salvador, Mississippi.
Additions   Brazil (Brazilia, Goias, Guanabara, Para, Piaui, Rio Grande do Sul, Sao Paulo), China, Japan, Mexico (Valle de Mexico).

Nevada
Exceptions   Brazil (Grand Orient), Colombia (Barranquilla), Cuba, El Salvador, Paraguay.

Additions   All the Brazilian State Grand Lodges (except Alagoas, Rio de Janeiro, Rio Grande do Norte), China, Colombia (Andes), Honduras, Japan, Mexico (Baja California, Cosmos, Nuevo Leon, Occidental Mexicana, Oriental Peninsular, Tamaulipas, Valle de Mexico), Nicaragua.

New Brunswick
Exceptions   Bolivia, Brazil (Grand Orient), Colombia (Barranquilla, Bogota, Cartegena), Cuba, Dominican Republic, El Salvador, Luxembourg, Paraguay, Venezuela.
Additions   Brazil (Goias, Para, Rio Grande do Sul), China, Japan.

New Hampshire
Exceptions   Brazil (Grand Orient), Paraguay.
Additions   All the State Grand Lodges of Brazil (except Acre, Alagoas, Amazonas, Bahia, Espirito Santo, Minas Gerais, Rio de Janeiro, Rio Grande do Norte), China, Colombia (Cali, Santander), Honduras, Japan, Mexico (Baja California, Benito Juarez, Cosmos, El Potosi, Nuevo Leon, Occidental Mexicana, Tamulipas, Unida Mexicana, Valle de Mexico), Nicaragua.

New Jersey
Exceptions   Brazil (Grand Orient), Cuba, El Salvador, Paraguay.
Additions   All the Brazilian State Grand Lodges (except Acre, Alagoas, Amazonas, Espirito Santo, Maranhao, Mato Grosso, Parana, Pernambuco, Rio de Janeiro, Rio Grande do Norte), China, Honduras, Japan, Mexico (Nuevo Leon, Tamaulipas), Nicaragua.

New Mexico
Exceptions   Bolivia, Brazil (Grand Orient), Colombia (Cartegena), Paraguay.
Additions   All the Brazilian State Grand Lodges (except Acre, Alagoas, Amazonas, Minas, Gerais, Paraiba, Rio Grande do Norte), China, Colombia (Cali), Honduras, Japan, Mexico (Baja California, Baja California Sur, Benito Juarez, Cosmos, Del Pacifico, Nuevo Leon, Occidental Mexicana, Oriental Peninsular, Tamaulipas, Valle de Mexico).

New South Wales
Exceptions   El Salvador, Panama, Paraguay.
Addition   Japan.

New York
Exception   Brazil (Grand Orient).
Additions   All the Brazilian State Grand Lodges (except Alagoas, Espirito Santo, Mato Grosso, Minas Gerais, Paraiba, Piaui, Santa Catarina, Rio Grande do Norte), China, Japan, Mexico (Del Pacifico, Oriental Peninsular, Tamaulipas, Valle de Mexico), Nicaragua.

New Zealand
Exception   Luxembourg.
Addition   Japan.

North Carolina

Exceptions　Brazil (Grand Orient), Cuba.

Additions　All the Brazilian State Grand Lodges (except Alagoas, Espirito Santo, Mato Grosso, Parana, Pernambuco, Rio de Janeiro, Rio Grande do Norte, Santa Catarina), China, Colombia (Cali), Honduras, Japan, Mexico (Baja California, Benito Juarez, Chiapas, El Potosi, Nuevo Leon, Occidental Mexicana, Oriental Peninsular, Tamaulipas, Unida Mexicana, Valle de Mexico), Nicaragua.

North Dakota

Exceptions　Bolivia, Brazil (Grand Orient), Colombia (Cartegena), Dominican Republic, Paraguay.

Additions　All the Brazilian State Grand Lodges (except Alagoas, Bahia, Brazilia, Espirito Santo, Goias, Maranhao, Mato Grosso, Pernambuco, Piaui, Rio Grande do Norte, Santa Catarina), China, Honduras, Japan, Mexico (Baja California, Baja California Sur, Cosmos, Del Pacifico, El Potosi, Nuevo Leon, Occidental Mexicana, Oriental Peninsular, Tamaulipas, Valle de Mexico), Nicaragua, Uruguay.

Norway

Exceptions　Brazil (Grand Orient), Colombia (Barranquilla, Cartegena), Dominican Republic, Luxembourg, Maryland, Mississippi, Nebraska, Panama, Peru, South Africa, Tasmania, Venezuela, West Virginia.

Addition　Japan.

Nova Scotia

Exceptions　Brazil (Grand Orient), Luxembourg, Paraguay.

Additions　Brazil (Bahia, Brazilia, Goias, Guanabara, Mato Grosso, Para, Paraiba, Parana, Rio Grande do Sul, Sao Paulo, Santa Catarina), China, Honduras, Japan.

Ohio

Exceptions　Brazil (Grand Orient), El Salvador, Paraguay.

Additions　All the Brazilian State Grand Lodges (except Alagoas, Bahia, Espirito Santo, Maranhao, Rio de Janeiro), China, Colombia (Cali), Mexico (Nuevo Leon, Oriental Peninsular, Tamaulipas), Nicaragua.

Oklahoma

Exceptions　Brazil (Grand Orient), Paraguay.

Additions　All the State Grand Lodges of Brazil (except Alagoas, Espirito Santo, Rio Grande do Norte), China, Colombia (Cali), Honduras, Japan, Mexico (all the Mexican State Grand Lodges, except Campeche, Guadeloupe Victoria, Hidalgo, Oaxaca, Queretaro, Restauracion, Sur-Oeste), Nicaragua.

Ontario

Exceptions　Bolivia, Brazil (Grand Orient), El Salvador, Paraguay.

Additions   Brazil (Bahia, Ceara, Espirito Santo, Goias, Maranhao, Para, Paraiba, Parana, Pernambuco, Rio Grande do Norte), China, Honduras, Japan, Uruguay.

Oregon
Exceptions   Brazil (Grand Orient), Colombia (Cartegena), El Salvador, Paraguay.
Additions   All the Brazilian State Grand Lodges (except Acre, Alagoas, Amazonas, Bahia, Mato Grosso, Rio Grande do Norte, Santa Catarina), China, Honduras, Japan, Mexico (El Potosi, Nuevo Leon, Occidental Mexicana, Tamaulipas, Valle de Mexico), Nicaragua.

Panama
Exceptions   Belgium (Regular), British Columbia, Denmark, Iceland, Luxembourg, New South Wales, Norway, South Africa, Sweden, Tasmania, Western Australia.
Additions   Member Grand Lodges of the Inter-American Masonic Confederation not recognised by England.

Paraguay
Exceptions   All United States Grand Lodges (except California, District of Columbia, Kentucky, Louisiana, Michigan, Minnesota, New York, North Carolina, Tennessee, Texas, and Wisconsin), all Canadian Grand Lodges, and Austria, Belgium (Regular), Denmark, Iceland, Ireland, Luxembourg, Mexico (York), New South Wales, Queensland, South Africa, South Australia, Sweden, Tasmania, Western Australia.
Additions   Member Grand Lodges of the Inter-American Masonic Confederation not recognised by England.

Pennsylvania
Exceptions   Brazil (Grand Orient), El Salvador, Guatemala, Paraguay.
Additions   All Brazilian State Grand Lodges (except Acre, Alagoas, Amazonas, Bahia, Minas Gerais, Rio Grande do Norte), China, Colombia (Cali, Santander), Honduras, Japan, Mexico (Nuevo Leon, Occidental Mexicana, Oriental Peninsular, Tamaulipas, Unida Mexicana, Valle de Mexico), Nicaragua.

Peru
Exceptions   Belgium (Regular), Denmark, Iceland, Norway, Sweden.
Additions   China, Japan, and member Grand Lodges of the Inter-American Masonic Confederation not recognised by England.

Philippines
Exceptions   Brazil (Grand Orient), Costa Rica, Cuba, Iceland, Luxembourg, Sweden.
Additions   Brazil (Amazonas, Ceara, Guanabara, Minas Gerais, Paraiba, Rio Grande do Sul, Sao Paulo), China, Honduras, Japan, Mexico (Oriental Peninsular).

Prince Edward Island
Exceptions Austria, Brazil (Grand Orient), Colombia (Cartegena), Dominican Republic, El Salvador, Luxembourg, Switzerland, Paraguay.
Additions Brazil (Ceara, Goias, Guanabara, Mato Grosso, Rio Grande do Sul), China, Japan.

Puerto Rico
Exceptions Belgium (Regular), Brazil (Grand Orient), Denmark, Iceland, South Africa, Sweden.
Additions China, Japan, and member Grand Lodges of the Inter-American Masonic Confederation not recognised by England.

Quebec
Exceptions Bolivia, Brazil (Grand Orient), Colombia (Barranquilla, Bogota, Cartegena), Cuba, Dominican Republic, Ecuador, Guatemala, Luxembourg, Paraguay, Venezuela.
Additions China, Japan.

Queensland
Exceptions Colombia (Barranquilla, Cartegena), Dominican Republic, Ecuador, El Salvador, Luxembourg, Paraguay.
Addition Japan.

Rhode Island
Exception Paraguay.
Additions All Brazilian State Grand Lodges (except Alagoas, Espirito Santo, Mato Grosso, Pernambuco, Piaui, Rio de Janeiro, Rio Grande do Norte, Santa Catarina), China, Honduras, Japan, Mexico (El Potosi, Nuevo Leon, Occidental Mexicana, Oriental Peninsular, Tamaulipas, Unida Mexicana, Valle de Mexico), Nicaragua.

Saskatchewan
Exceptions Austria, Bolivia, Brazil (Grand Orient), Colombia (Bogota, Cartegena), El Salvador, Luxembourg, Paraguay, Tasmania, Venezuela.
Additions Brazilia (Brazilia, Ceara, Goias, Maranhao, Para, Paraiba, Parana, Pernambuco, Piaui, Rio de Janeiro, Rio Grande do Sul), China, Japan.

South Africa
Exceptions Argentina, Arkansas, Bolivia, Colombia (Bogota, Cartegena), Cuba, Dominican Republic, Guatemala, Iceland, Luxembourg, Norway, Panama, Paraguay, Puerto Rico, Sweden, Venezuela.
Additions China, Japan.

South Australia
Exceptions Ecuador, Luxembourg, Paraguay.
Addition Japan.

South Carolina
Exceptions Bolivia, Brazil (Grand Orient), Colombia (Cartegena), Cuba, Paraguay.
Additions All Brazilian State Grand Lodges (except Alagoas, Espirito Santo, Rio de Janeiro, Rio Grande do Norte), China, Colombia (Andes, Cali), Honduras, Japan, Mexico (El Potosi, Nuevo Leon, Occidental Mexicana, Oriental Peninsular, Tamaulipas), Nicaragua.

South Dakota
Exceptions Brazil (Grand Orient), Colombia (Cartegena), Paraguay.
Additions All Brazilian State Grand Lodges (except Acre, Alagoas, Amazonas, Bahia, Espirito Santo, Rio Grande do Norte), China, Japan, Mexico (Baja California, El Potosi, Nuevo Leon, Occidental Mexicana, Oriental Peninsular, Tamaulipas), Nicaragua.

Sweden
Exceptions Argentina, Brazil (Grand Orient), Chile, Colombia (Barranquilla, Bogota, Cartegena), Costa Rica, Cuba, Dominican Republic, Ecuador, El Salvador, Guatemala, Luxembourg, Mexico (York), Mississippi, Panama, Paraguay, Peru, Philippines, Puerto Rico, South Africa, Tasmania, Venezuela.
Addition Japan.

Switzerland
Exceptions Alabama, Arkansas, France (GLNF), Maryland, Mississippi, Prince Edward Island.
Additions All the Brazilian State Grand Lodges (except Acre, Alagoas, Espirito Santo, Rio Grande do Norte), Haiti, Japan, Mexico (El Potosi, Campeche, Nuevo Leon, Occidental Mexicana, Oriental Peninsular, Tamaulipas, Unida Mexicana, Valle de Mexico), Uruguay.

Tasmania
Exceptions Austria, Belgium (Regular), Bolivia, Colombia (Barranquilla, Cartegena), El Salvador, Finland, Georgia, Germany, Greece, Luxembourg, Maryland, Norway, Panama, Paraguay, Saskatchewan, Sweden, Venezuela.
Additions Japan, Mexico (Valle de Mexico).

Tennessee
Exceptions Brazil (Grand Orient), Colombia (Cartegena), Cuba, El Salvador.
Additions All Brazilian State Grand Lodges (except Acre, Alagoas, Amazonas, Paraiba, Rio Grande do Norte, Santa Catarina), China, Honduras, Japan, Mexico (Baja California Sur, Nuevo Leon, Occidental Mexicana, Oriental Peninsular, Tamaulipas, Valle de Mexico), Uruguay.

Texas
Exception Brazil (Grand Orient).

Additions All Brazilian State Grand Lodges (except Acre, Alagoas, Amazonas, Mato Grosso, Rio Grande do Norte), China, Colombia (Andes, Cali, Santander), Honduras, Japan, Mexico (Baja California, Baja California Sur, Benito Juarez, Chiapas, Cosmos, Del Pacifico, El Potosi, Nuevo Leon, Occidental Mexicana, Oriental Peninsular, Tamaulipas, Unida Mexicana, Valle de Mexico), Nicaragua, Uruguay.

Turkey
Exceptions Nil.
Addition Japan.

Utah
Exceptions Bolivia, Brazil (Grand Orient), Dominican Republic, El Salvador, Guatemala, Paraguay, Venezuela.
Additions All Brazilian State Grand Lodges (except Acre, Alagoas, Amazonas, Bahia, Brazilia, Paraiba, Parana, Rio de Janeiro, Rio Grande do Norte), China, Honduras, Japan, Mexico (El Potosi, Nuevo Leon, Tamaulipas, Valle de Mexico), Uruguay.

Venezuela
Exceptions Alaska, Belgium (Regular), Brazil (Grand Orient), Denmark, Iceland, Luxembourg, Maine, Mississippi, New Brunswick, Norway, Quebec, Saskatchewan, South Africa, Sweden, Tasmania, Utah.
Additions China, Japan, and member Grand Lodges of the Inter-American Masonic Confederation not recognised by England.

Vermont
Exceptions Brazil (Grand Orient), Colombia (Bogota, Cartegena), El Salvador, Paraguay.
Additions All Brazilian State Grand Lodges (except Acre, Alagoas, Amazonas, Espirito Santo, Rio Grande do Norte), China, Colombia (Cali), Honduras, Japan, Mexico (Baja California, El Potosi, Nuevo Leon, Occidental Mexicana, Oriental Peninsular, Tamaulipas, Unida Mexicana, Valle de Mexico), Nicaragua.

Victoria
Exception Luxembourg.
Addition Japan.

Virginia
Exceptions Bolivia, Brazil (Grand Orient), Colombia (Barranquilla, Cartegena), Cuba, Guatemala, Paraguay.
Additions All Brazilian State Grand Lodges (except Acre, Alagoas, Bahia, Espirito Santo, Minas Gerais, Paraiba, Pernambuco, Rio de Janeiro, Rio Grande do Norte), China, Honduras, Japan, Mexico (Neuvo Leon, Tamaulipas).

Washington
Exceptions Brazil (Grand Orient), Colombia (Bogota, Cartegena), El Salvador, Paraguay.

Additions All Brazilian State Grand Lodges (except Alagoas, Bahia, Mato Grosso, Pernambuco, Piaui, Rio Grande do Norte, Santa Catarina), China, Honduras, Japan, Mexico (Baja California, Baja California Sur, Nuevo Leon, Tamaulipas), Nicaragua.

West Virginia
Exceptions Brazil (Grand Orient), Colombia (Bogota, Cartegena), Dominican Republic, El Salvador, Guatemala, Norway, Paraguay, South Africa.
Additions All Brazilian State Grand Lodges (except Acre, Alagoas, Amazonas, Bahia, Brazilia, Espirito Santo, Goias, Maranhao, Paraiba, Parana, Rio de Janeiro, Rio Grande do Norte), China, Colombia (Cali), Japan, Mexico (El Potosi, Nuevo Leon, Tamaulipas).

Western Australia
Exceptions Colombia (Cartegena), El Salvador, Luxembourg, Panama, Paraguay.
Addition Japan.

Wisconsin
Exception Brazil (Grand Orient).
Additions All Brazilian State Grand Lodges (except Acre, Alagoas, Amazonas, Espirito Santo, Maranhao, Rio de Janeiro, Rio Grande do Norte), China, Honduras, Japan, Mexico (Baja California, Cosmos, El Potosi, Nuevo Leon, Tamaulipas, Valle de Mexico), Nicaragua, Uruguay.

Wyoming
Exceptions Brazil (Grand Orient), Colombia (Bogota), Paraguay.
Additions All Brazilian State Grand Lodges (except Alagoas, Bahia, Espirito Santo, Maranhao, Paraiba, Rio Grande do Norte), China, Colombia (Cali), Honduras, Japan, Mexico (Baja California, Cosmos, Del Pacifico, El Potosi, Nuevo Leon, Tamaulipas).

IMPORTANT NOTE

The recognitions of the various Grand Lodges are subject to change. Nonetheless, a deletion from a Grand Lodge's list of recognitions is a relatively rare event, although it can occur. Of course, the addition of a new recognition is more common. With reference to the above lists, it is likely that the two youngest Grand Lodges (the Regular Grand Lodge of Belgium, and the Grand Lodge of Alaska) will attract additional recognition subsequent to the date of the list provided here (late 1982).

In short, visitors are well advised to gain a current list of recognitions from their own Grand Lodge office prior to departure.

Appendix B

GRAND LODGE SENIORITY

The seniority of the Regular Grand Lodge of the world is denoted below in order of actual or accepted years of initial organisation. The dates in brackets, where they occur, indicate the claimed date of organisation by the Grand Lodge concerned.

1.	England	1717	34.	Venezuela	1824
2.	Ireland	1725	35.	Michigan	1826
3.	Scotland	1736	36.	Florida	1830
4.	Germany	1737	37.	Texas	1837
5.	Denmark	1745	38.	Arkansas	1838
6.	Netherlands	1756	39.	Illinois	1840
7.	Sweden	1760	40.	Wisconsin	1843
8.	Virginia	1778	41.	Iowa	1844
9.	South Carolina	1783	42.	Switzerland	1844
		(1737)	43.	California	1850
10.	Pennsylvania	1786	44.	Oregon	1851
11.	Georgia	1786	45.	Minnesota	1853
		(1735)	46.	Ontario	1855
12.	New Jersey	1786	47.	Kansas	1856
13.	Maryland	1786	48.	Argentina	1857
14.	New York	1787	49.	Nebraska	1857
		(1781)	50.	Dominican Republic	1858
15.	North Carolina	1787	51.	Washington	1858
16.	Connecticut	1789	52.	Cuba	1859
17.	New Hampshire	1790	53.	Colorado	1861
		(1788)	54.	Chile	1842
18.	Rhode Island	1791	55.	Mexico (York)	1862
19.	Massachusetts	1792	56.	Nevada	1865
		(1733)	57.	West Virginia	1865
20.	Vermont	1794	58.	Montana	1866
21.	Kentucky	1800	59.	Nova Scotia	1866
22.	Italy	1805	60.	New Brunswick	1867
23.	Delaware	1806	61.	Idaho	1867
24.	Ohio	1808	62.	Greece	1868
25.	Dist. of Columbia	1811			(1811)
26.	Louisiana	1812	63.	Luxembourg	1868
27.	Tennessee	1812	64.	Quebec	1869
28.	Indiana	1818	65.	Paraguay	1869
29.	Mississippi	1818	66.	British Columbia	1871
30.	Maine	1820	67.	Utah	1872
31.	Missouri	1821	68.	Oklahoma	1874
32.	Alabama	1821	69.	Wyoming	1875
33.	Brazil (Gr. Orient)	1822	70.	Manitoba	1875

71.	South Dakota	*1875*	91.	Philippines	*1912*
72.	Prince Edward Island	*1875*	92.	France (GLNF)	*1913*
73.	New Mexico	*1877*	93.	Panama	*1916*
74.	Arizona	*1882*	94.	Austria	*1919*
75.	Peru	*1882*	95.	Cartegena (Col.)	*1920*
76.	South Australia	*1884*	96.	Ecuador	*1921*
77.	Puerto Rico	*1885*	97.	Queensland	*1921*
78.	New South Wales	*1888*	98.	Barranquilla (Col.)	*1922*
79.	North Dakota	*1889*	99.	Bogota (Col.)	*1922*
80.	Victoria	*1889*	100.	Finland	*1924*
81.	New Zealand	*1890*	101.	Bolivia	*1929*
82.	Tasmania	*1890*	102.	Iceland	*1951*
83.	Norway	*1891*	103.	Israel	*1953*
84.	Costa Rica	*1899*			*(1932)*
85.	Western Australia	*1900*	104.	Japan	*1957*
86.	Guatemala	*1903*	105.	India	*1961*
87.	Alberta	*1905*	106.	South Africa	*1961*
88.	Saskatchewan	*1906*	107.	Belgium (Regular)	*1979*
89.	Turkey	*1909*	108.	Alaska	*1981*
90.	El Salvador	*1912*			

Appendix C

THE STRENGTHS OF THE REGULAR MASONIC JURISDICTIONS
The Ratio of Masons to Population (1982)

Ratios are determined by dividing Jurisdictional masonic membership into applicable populations. All figures are taken from Grand Lodge proceedings, or are estimates, for masonic membership. Population figures are sourced in the *Encyclopaedia Britannica*.

Scotland	1 : 18 –	North Carolina	1 : 80 +
Maine	1 : 29 –	Virginia	1 : 81 –
Kansas	1 : 34 –	Nova Scotia	1 : 81 –
Indiana	1 : 37 –	Rhode Island	1 : 81 –
Kentucky	1 : 38 –	Colorado	1 : 83 –
Vermont	1 : 40 –	Western Australia	1 : 86 –
South Carolina	1 : 41 –	Idaho	1 : 86 –
Wyoming	1 : 45 –	New Zealand	1 : 86 –
West Virginia	1 : 46 –	Ontario	1 : 87 –
Iowa	1 : 47 –	Minnesota	1 : 87 –
Ohio	1 : 47 –	New Brunswick	1 : 88 –
Tennessee	1 : 47 –	Saskatchewan	1 : 90 –
Nebraska	1 : 47 –	Prince Edward Island	1 : 91 +
Arkansas	1 : 49 –	Washington	1 : 92 –
Oklahoma	1 : 50 –	Ireland	1 : 95 –
South Dakota	1 : 52 –	Louisiana	1 : 96 –
Victoria	1 : 53 –	Manitoba	1 : 96 –
Mississippi	1 : 54 –	Oregon	1 : 97 –
Pennsylvania	1 : 56 –	Maryland	1 : 103 –
Alabama	1 : 59 –	Nevada	1 : 104 –
Tasmania	1 : 60 –	New Jersey	1 : 106 –
Georgia	1 : 60 –	New Mexico	1 : 106 –
Dist. of Columbia	1 : 61 –	Iceland	1 : 110 +
Massachusetts	1 : 63 –	New York	1 : 110 –
Arizona	1 : 66 –	British Columbia	1 : 116 –
Texas	1 : 67 –	Florida	1 : 117 –
Delaware	1 : 68 –	Wisconsin	1 : 120 –
New Hampshire	1 : 68 –	California	1 : 125 –
Queensland	1 : 71 –	Alberta	1 : 127 –
North Dakota	1 : 72 –	Alaska	1 : 208 –
New South Wales	1 : 73 –	Norway	1 : 253 +
Illinois	1 : 75 –	Denmark	1 : 254 +
South Australia	1 : 76 –	Utah	1 : 292 –
England	1 : 79 –	Sweden	1 : 344 +
Michigan	1 : 80 –	Cuba	1 : 493 –

Quebec	1 : 575 –	Panama	1 : 3542 –
Puerto Rico	1 : 726 –	Argentina	1 : 3756 –
Finland	1 : 1157 +	Paraguay	1 : 4125 +
Israel	1 : 1196 –	Austria	1 : 4179 +
Switzerland	1 : 1752 +	South Africa	1 : 6165 –
Chile	1 : 1775 +	Guatemala	1 : 6641 –
Luxembourg	1 : 1794 –	Colombia	1 : 6728 –
Netherlands	1 : 2039 –	Costa Rica	1 : 6870 +
Dominican Rep.	1 : 2489 –	France (GLNF)	1 : 8167 +
Greece	1 : 2627 +	Turkey	1 : 8167 +
Venezuela	1 : 2830 –	Salvador	1 : 12,150 –
Germany	1 : 2924 +	Ecuador	1 : 12,583 –
Philippines	1 : 2994 +	Japan	1 : 28,465 –
Bolivia	1 : 3192 –	India	1 : 44,307 +
Peru	1 : 3313 +	Mexico (York)	1 : 102,206 +
Italy	1 : 3418 +		

Notes:
(a) Falling membership denoted (–)
    Rising membership denoted (+)
(b) The masonic membership estimates for England, Ireland, and Scotland included overseas lodges. Ratios are therefore subject to varying marginal error.
(c) The masonic membership for Colombia is determined by the addition of its three regular Grand Lodges.
(d) Irregular masonic memberships are not included in any ratios.
(e) All figures are 1982 based.

Appendix D

COMMON MASONIC WORDS—IN TRANSLATION

Detailed below and cross-translated are a number of common masonic words, and several others, which will assist the travelling Freemason in making initial contacts.

English	French	German	Spanish	Portuguese
(Free)mason	Maçon	Freimaurer	Francmasón (Masones)	Maçom (maçon)
Lodge	Loge	Logen	Logia	Loja
Grand Lodge	Grande Loge	Grosslogen	Gran Logia	Grão Loja
Grand Master	Grande Maître	Grossmeister	Gran Maestro	Grão Mestre
Worshipful Master	Venerable Maître	Logenmeister	Venerable Maestro	Veneráble Mestre
Secretary	Secrétaire	Sekretär	Secretario	Secretário
Grand Secretary	Grande Secrétaire	Gross-sekrëtar	Gran Secretario	Grão Secretário
Masonic Temple	Temple Maçonnique	Logenhaus	Templo Masonico	Palacio Maconico
Entered Apprentice	Apprentis	Lehrling	Aprendice	Aprendiz
Fellow Craft	Compagnon	Geselleschafter	Compañero	Companheiro
Master Mason	Maître Maçon	Meister	Maestro Masone	Mestre Maçon
Brother	Frère	Bruder	Hermano	Irmão
Visitor	Visiteur	Besucher	Visitante	Visitante
Monday	Lundi	Montag	Lunes	Segunda-Feira
Tuesday	Mardi	Dienstag	Martes	Terça-Feira
Wednesday	Mercredi	Mittwoch	Miércoles	Quinta-Feira
Thursday	Jeudi	Donnerstag	Jueves	Quarta-Feira
Friday	Vendredi	Freitag	Viernes	Sexta-Feira
Saturday	Samedi	Samstag	Sábado	Sábado
Sunday	Dimanche	Sonntag	Domingo	Domingo

English	Italian	Dutch	Turkish
(Free)mason	Frammasone	Vrijmetselaar	Farmason (Masonluk)
Lodge	Loggia	Loge	Locasi (Masonlugun)
Grand Lodge	Gran Loggia	Groot Loge	Büyük Locasi
Grand Master	Gran Maestro	Groot Meester	Büyük Reisi
Worshipful Master	Venerabile Maestro	Edelachtbaar Meester	Muhterem Reisi
Secretary	Segretario	Secretaris	Kâtib
Grand Secretary	Gran Segretario	Groot Secretaris	Büyük Kâtib
Masonic Temple	Tempio Massonico	Maconniek Tempel	Masonik Mâbed
Entered Apprentice	Apprendista	Leerling	Curak
Fellow Craft	Compagno	Metgezel	Kalfa
Master Mason	Maestro Muratore	Meester Macon	Usta
Brother	Fratello	Broeder	Erkek Kardes
Visitor	Visatatore	Bezoeker	Misafir
Monday	Lunedì	Maandag	Pazartesi
Tuesday	Martedì	Dinsdag	Sali Günü
Wednesday	Mercoledì	Woensdag	Çarşamba
Thursday	Giovedì	Donderdag	Perşembe
Friday	Venerdì	Vrijdag	Cuma
Saturday	Sabato	Zaterdag	Cumartesi
Sunday	Domenica	Zondag	Pazar Günü